NEXT GENERATION OF
DATA-MINING
APPLICATIONS

NEXT GENERATION OF DATA-MINING APPLICATIONS

Edited by

MEHMED M. KANTARDZIC
J. B. Speed School of Engineering
University of Louisville

JOZEF ZURADA
Computer Information Systems
College of Business and Public Administration
University of Louisville

IEEE Computer Society, *Sponsor*

A JOHN WILEY & SONS, INC., PUBLICATION

Published by John Wiley & Sons, Inc., Hoboken, New Jersey.
Published simultaneously in Canada.

For general information on our other products and services please contact our Customer Care Department within the U.S. at 877-762-2974, outside the U.S. at 317-572-3993 or fax 317-572-4002.

Wiley also publishes its books in a variety of electronic formats. Some content that appears in print, however, may not be available in electronic format.

Library of Congress Cataloging-in-Publication Data is available.

ISBN 0-471-65605-4

Printed in the United States of America.

10 9 8 7 6 5 4 3 2 1

Next Generation of Data-Mining Applications

Despite all of their attractive bells and whistles, the tools alone will never provide the entire data-mining solution. There will always be the need for the practitioner to make important decisions regarding how the whole process will be designed, how and what techniques will be employed, and what characteristics and architecture of the application will be used. All requirements for modification and improvements of data-mining techniques and tools, even the ideas for new algorithms, are based on a practical experience of data-mining practitioners.

CONTENTS

CONTRIBUTORS

Ghaleb Abdulla, Center for Applied Scientific Computing, Lawrence Livermore National Laboratory, Livermore, California

Frank J. Accurso, University of Colorado Health Sciences Center, Denver, Colorado and The Children's Hospital, Denver, Colorado and Mike McMorris Cystic Fibrosis Center, Denver, Colorado

Richard Adderley, AE Solutions, Redditch, Worcestershire, England

Gedas Adomavicius, Information & Decision Sciences, Carlson School of Management, University of Minnesota, Minneapolis, Minnesota

Charu C. Aggarwal, IBM T.J. Watson Research Center, Yorktown Heights, New York

F. Alonso, Facultad de Informática, Universidad Politécnica de Madrid, Campus de Montegancedo, Madrid, Spain

Ali Al-Timimi, Center for Biomedical Genomics and Informatics, George Mason University, Fairfax, Virginia

Dirk Arndt, DaimlerChrysler AG, Research & Technology, Information Mining, Ulm, Germany

Kwei Aryeetey, Department of Computer Science, University of Regina, Regina, Saskatchewan, Canada

Chuck Baldwin, Center for Applied Scientific Computing, Lawrence Livermore National Laboratory, Livermore, California

Daniel Barbará, Information and Software Engineering Department, George Mason University, Fairfax, Virginia

Mark Brodie, IBM T. J. Watson Research Center, Hawthorne, New York

Erick Cantú-Paz, Center for Applied Scientific Computing, Lawrence Livermore National Laboratory, Livermore, California

Harsh Chaudhary, Information and Software Engineering Department, George Mason University, Fairfax, Virginia

Sen-ching S. Cheung, Center for Applied Scientific Computing, Lawrence Livermore National Laboratory, Livermore, California

Krzysztof J. Cios, Department of Computer Science and Engineering, University of Colorado at Denver, Denver, Colorado and Department of Computer Science, University of Colorado at Boulder, Boulder, Colorado and University of Colorado Health Sciences Center, Denver, Colorado and 4cData, Golden, Colorado

Terence Critchlow, Center for Applied Scientific Computing, Lawrence Livermore National Laboratory, Livermore, California

Ayhan Demiriz, Information Technology, Verizon Inc., Irving, Texas

Carlotta Domeniconi, Information and Software Engineering Department, George Mason University, Fairfax, Virginia

Guozhu Dong, Department of Computer Science & Engineering, Wright State University, Dayton, Ohio

Tina Eliassi-Rad, Center for Applied Scientific Computing, Lawrence Livermore National Laboratory, Livermore, California

Wei Fan, IBM T. J. Watson Research Center, Hawthorne, New York

Imola K. Fodor, Center for Applied Scientific Computing, Lawrence Livermore National Laboratory, Livermore, California

Patricia G. Foschi, Romberg Tiburon Center for Environmental Studies, San Francisco State University, Tiburon, California

David George, IBM T. J. Watson Research Center, Hawthorne, New York

Michael Gillette, The Broad Institute, Massachusetts Institute of Technology, Cambridge, Massachusetts

Petteri Hintsanen, Department of Computer Science and Helsinki Institute of Information Technology, University of Helsinki, Helsinki, Finland

Wynne Hsu, School of Computing, National University of Singapore, Singapore

Curtis Jamison, School of Computational Sciences, George Mason University, Fairfax, Virginia

Chandrika Kamath, Center for Applied Scientific Computing, Lawrence Livermore National Laboratory, Livermore, California

R. Kanapady, Department of Mechanical Engineering, University of Minnesota, Minneapolis, Minnesota

Mehmed Kantardzic, Department of Computer Engineering and Computer Science, University of Louisville, Louisville, Kentucky, email: mmkant01@louisville.edu

Steven Klooster, California State University, Monterey Bay, California and NASA Ames Research Center, Moffett Field, California

Jeffrey Kreulen, IBM Almaden Research Center, San Jose, California

Vipin Kumar, Department of Computer Science & Engineering, University of Minnesota, Minneapolis, Minnesota

Lukasz A. Kurgan, Department of Electrical and Computer Engineering, University of Alberta, Edmonton, Canada

A. Lazarevic, Department of Computer Science & Engineering, University of Minnesota, Minneapolis, Minnesota

Mong Li Lee, School of Computing, National University of Singapore, Singapore

Tachyang Lee, STMicroelectronics Pte Ltd., Singapore

Jinyan Li, Institute for Infocomm Research, Singapore

Huan Liu, Department of Computer Science and Engineering, Arizona State University, Tempe, Arizona

Sheng Ma, IBM T. J. Watson Research Center, Hawthorne, New York

Amit Mandvikar, Department of Computer Science and Engineering, Arizona State University, Tempe, Arizona

Sandeep Mane, Department of Computer Science, University of Minnesota, Minneapolis, Minnesota

D. R. Mani, The Broad Institute, Massachusetts Institute of Technology, Cambridge, Massachusetts

L. Martínez, Facultad de Informática, Universidad Politécnica de Madrid, Campus de Montegancedo, Madrid, Spain

Mark Mei, IBM T. J. Watson Research Center, Hawthorne, New York

C. Montes, Facultad de Informática, Universidad Politécnica de Madrid, Campus de Montegancedo, Madrid, Spain

Peter Neumann, Proctor & Gamble, Geneva, Switzerland

Päivi Onkamo, Department of Computer Science and Helsinki Institute of Information Technology, University of Helsinki, Helsinki, Finland

Witold Pedrycz, Department of Electrical & Computer Engineering, University of Alberta, Edmonton, Canada and Systems Research Institute, Polish Academy of Sciences, Warsaw, Poland

Christopher Potter, NASA Ames Research Center, Moffett Field, California

Kwei Quaye, Traffic Safety, Saskatchewan Government Insurance, Regina, Saskatchewan, Canada

Petteri Sevon, Department of Computer Science and Helsinki Institute of Information Technology, University of Helsinki, Helsinki, Finland

Shashi Shekhar, Department of Computer Science & Engineering, University of Minnesota, Minneapolis, Minnesota

Bernhard Sick, Chair, Institute of Computer Architectures, Passau, Germany

Jemmy Soenjaya, School of Computing, National University of Singapore, Singapore

Marci K. Sontag, University of Colorado Health Sciences Center, Denver, Colorado and The Children's Hospital, Denver, Colorado and Mike McMorris Cystic Fibrosis Center, Denver, Colorado

Elaine Parros Machado de Sousa, University of São Paulo—USP, São Carlos, Brazil

Scott Spangler, IBM Almaden Research Center, San Jose, California

Jaideep Srivastava, Department of Computer Science, University of Minnesota, Minneapolis, Minnesota

Michael Steinbach, Department of Computer Science & Engineering, University of Minnesota, Minneapolis, Minnesota

K. Tamma, Department of Mechanical Engineering, University of Minnesota, Minneapolis, Minnesota

Pang-Ning Tan, Department of Computer Science & Engineering, Michigan State University, East Lansing, Michigan

Nu Ai Tang, Center for Applied Scientific Computing, Lawrence Livermore National Laboratory, Livermore, California

Evimaria Terzi, Department of Computer Science and Helsinki Institute of Information Technology, University of Helsinki, Helsinki, Finland

Hannu Toivonen, Department of Computer Science and Helsinki Institute of Information Technology, University of Helsinki, Helsinki, Finland

Agma Juci Machado Traina, University of São Paulo—USP, São Carlos, Brazil

Caetano Traina Jr., University of São Paulo—USP, São Carlos, Brazil

J. P. Valente, Facultad de Informática, Universidad Politécnica de Madrid, Campus de Montegancedo, Madrid, Spain

Jamshid A. Vayghan, IBM Corporation, Rochester, Minnesota, Department of Computer Science, University of Minnesota, Minneapolis, Minnesota

Haixun Wang, IBM T. J. Watson Research Center, Hawthorne, New York

Limsoon Wong, Institute for Infocomm Research, Singapore

Li Yang, Department of Computer Science, Western Michigan University, Kalamazoo, Michigan

Philip S. Yu, IBM T. J. Watson Research Center, Hawthorne, New York

Mohammed J. Zaki, Computer Science Department, Rensselaer Polytechnic Institute, Troy, New York

Pusheng Zhang, Department of Computer Science & Engineering, University of Minnesota, Minneapolis, Minnesota

Wojciech Ziarko, Department of Computer Science, University of Regina, Regina, Saskatchewan, Canada

Jozef Zurada, Department of Computer Information Systems, College of Business and Public Administration, University of Louisville, Louisville, Kentucky

PREFACE

In our January 2003 call for papers we sought contributions to the book that would present new and unconventional applications in data mining. We sought contributions from a diverse body of authors, including the leading scientists and practitioners in the field, to stimulate a new wave of knowledge in the application area of data mining. The envisioned readers of the book are scientists and practitioners who perform research in this area and/or implement the discoveries.

After spending almost two years on the book's preparation, we are delighted to see it appearing on the market. We believe that this book will inspire academics, practitioners, and senior graduate students alike to engage in this new field that is so important to academia and business. We hope that this book may also be useful to a broader audience of readers who are not necessarily experts in data mining, but would like to learn about the current developments in the application field and gain some experience in the use of the data-mining tools.

This book contains a collection of 25 chapters written by a truly international team of 79 experts representing nine countries: Brazil, Canada, Finland, Germany, Poland, Singapore, Spain, Switzerland, and the United States. The authors are affiliated with universities, research, government, and health institutions, and scientific laboratories, as well as business firms offering data-mining solutions to their customers. Many of the authors who contributed to the book have worked and published extensively in the applications area of data mining.

We extend our gratitude to a group of about 100 anonymous reviewers whose work greatly enhanced each chapter in the book, and we also thank two IEEE reviewers whose comments improved the content and structure of the book. Finally, we also would like to express our sincere thanks to Kenneth Moore, Catherine Faduska, and Christine Kuhnen, IEEE Press/Wiley, for their help and enthusiastic encouragement throughout the entire project.

MEHMED M. KANTARDZIC
JOZEF ZURADA

Louisville, Kentucky
August 2004

TRENDS IN DATA-MINING APPLICATIONS: FROM RESEARCH LABS TO FORTUNE 500 COMPANIES

MEHMED KANTARDZIC AND JOZEF ZURADA

INTRODUCTION

Data is the basic form of information that needs to be collected, managed, mined, and interpreted to create knowledge. Discovering the patterns, trends, and anomalies in massive data is one of the grand challenges of the information age. Data mining solves a common paradox: The more data you have, the more difficult and time-consuming it is to effectively analyze and draw meaning from it. What should be a gold mine often lays unexplored due to a lack of personnel, time, expertise, or adequate technology. Data mining uses powerful analytic technologies to quickly and thoroughly explore mountains of data, isolating the valuable, usable information—the domain intelligence—that the user needs. Data mining is a multidisciplinary field drawing works from statistics, database technology, artificial intelligence, pattern recognition, machine learning, information theory, control theory, information retrieval, high-performance computing, and data visualization. The aim of data mining is to extract implicit, previously unknown, and potentially useful (or actionable) patterns and models from data. Advances in technology are making massive datasets common in many businesses and in scientific and engineering disciplines. To find useful information in these datasets, multidisciplinary teams are turning to an application system based on data-mining techniques. Progress in data mining is driven by applications, where the application is important feedback for improving strategies and performances of applied techniques.

Next Generation of Data-Mining Applications. Edited by Kantardzic and Zurada
ISBN 0-471-65605-4 © 2005 the Institute of Electrical and Electronics Engineers, Inc.

Data mining is primarily used by companies with a strong consumer focus such as retail industry, financial, communication, and marketing organizations. It enables these companies to determine relationships among "internal" factors such as price, product positioning, or staff skills and among "external" factors such as economic indicators, competition, and customer demographics. It also allows them to determine the impact on sales, customer satisfaction, and corporate profits. Finally, it enables companies to "drill down" into summary information to view detailed transactional or relational data and analyze the cause of events in a business environment. When business managers have a reliable guide to the future of their businesses or scientists have a reliable direction for their research, they have the power to make the right decisions today. Data mining empowers the users to direct the future of their activities by delivering accurate and useful information not available or not recognizable in raw data. Decisions in these situations are based on sound database intelligence, not on instinct or emotion reactions. Decisions that are the results of a data-mining application deliver consistent improvements that keep a company/organization/research institution ahead of the competition.

Over the past few years, the technology of data mining has moved from the research lab to Fortune 500 companies, requiring a significant change in focus. Instead of a process of working only with retrospective data applied off-line, the next generation of data-mining applications includes a much more complex framework. It is primarily distributed with real-time changing data. The sheer volume of data today poses the most serious problem for techniques deployed in data-mining applications and required computing resources. For example, many companies already have data warehouses in the terabyte range (e.g., FedEx, UPS, Wal-Mart, and Royal Dutch/Shell).* You might think that a giant conglomerate like the Royal Dutch/Shell Group has its data-mining and analytics problems all figured out, but like many companies, it still wrestles with the question of how to get the most out of its data.† The company—which operates a multicontinent oil, gas, and chemical business, from oil and gas exploration to running service stations—launched the current push for enhanced data mining and analytics back in 1997, when it realized it had to conquer the global challenge. Until the project was completed in February 2002, each country where Shell operates had its own data warehouse, each based on a different data-mining model. This made it nearly impossible to correlate product data and analyze global company decisions. To fix the problems, Shell first imposed some standards on how each country's operating units could define their data, so that the mining process would be consistent across the company. Then, to integrate the data, once a month the 125 local Shell offices, located throughout the world, upload their data to the central location. Reports for business analysts at both the corporate and local levels become available about three weeks later. Shell is now getting much more

*Zaki, M. J., and Pan, Y., Recent developments in parallel and distributed data mining, <u>Distributed and Parallel Databases</u> **11**, 123–127 (2002).
† Roberts-Witt, S. L., Data mining: what lies beneath?, <u>PC Magazine</u> November 19, 2002, pp. 87–95. http://www.pcmag.com/article2/0,1759,646153,00.asp

meaningful insight out of its data, which helps the company negotiate better contracts with its customers and identify product lines that are either doing well or declining globally. Shell's data-mining project is a success, but no such project is perfect—obviously, improvements are possible and modifications of current solutions are necessary.

In addition to business-oriented data-mining applications, this technology plays a significant role in knowledge discovery and refinement in engineering, scientific, and medical databases. The amount of data in these applications reaches gigantic proportions (for users such as NASA space missions or Human Genome Project) and requires both large memory and disk space and high-speed computing, but also new techniques.*

A wide variety of multimedia data (images, video, signal, text) available today in an electronic form, with temporal and spatial characteristics, shows the diversity of data types and structures that are the basic resources in the next generation of data-mining applications. The core data-mining algorithms now represent a small part of the overall application, being perhaps 10% of a larger integrated data-mining system. The Internet plays a major role as an infrastructure of these new data-mining applications, and it is changing the entire business and scientific landscape and revolutionizing the way many people are doing business or conducting research today. Besides changing the distinctions once made between functionality and information, the Web has changed our habits even as it has grown into a global connecting force. First, there is the Internet, which is merging the whole world into one community, and then there are Intranets and Extranets, which use the same technology to create communities within companies. Portals have become the new concept for integrating massive amounts of information and functionality, combining flexibility and structure to offer both aspects in one package tailored to the needs of employees. In this new Internet economy, a start-up company can quickly overtake even an established business. Given this environment, enterprises today are recognizing that they must develop and deploy innovative new strategies and find new Internet metrics that will help them succeed in e-Business. Given this environment, it is becoming increasingly critical for companies to get solid data analyses to help them make strategic decisions about their businesses.

Implementation of data-mining applications in high-performance parallel or Internet-based distributed computing environments is becoming crucial to ensure system scalability and interactivity as data continues to grow in size and complexity. The challenge is to develop methodologies that scale to thousands of attributes and millions of transactions. The techniques of interest span all major classes of data-mining methods such as association rules, sequences, classification, clustering, prediction, and deviation detection, as well as some new techniques previously not "recognized" by the data-mining community, including genetic algorithms, fuzzy and rough sets, and fractal dimensions. Various

---

*Zaki, M. J., and Pan, Y., Recent developments in parallel and distributed data mining, Distributed and Parallel Databases **11**, 123–127 (2002).

preprocessing and postprocessing operations like sampling, feature selection, data reduction and transformation, rule grouping and pruning, exploratory and interactive browsing, meta-level mining, and so on, are also enriched to support the next generation of data-mining applications.

CHARACTERISTICS OF THE NEXT GENERATION OF DATA-MINING APPLICATIONS

Data-mining applications have been shown to be highly effective in addressing many important business problems, research activities, and engineering solutions. We expect to see a continuing trend in the building and deployment of data-mining and knowledge discovery applications for crucial business and scientific decision support systems. Exemplary applications that employ data mining will require the technical community to continue making advances in techniques, methodologies, and infrastructure for model discovery and model understanding. The emphasis in model discovery will be on developing new mining techniques that are highly automated, scalable, dynamic and adaptable, and reliable. For domain understanding, the challenge is to continue developing more sophisticated techniques that can assist users in analyzing discovered knowledge easily and quickly.

Today, many companies are relying on Internet-based metrics such as site statistics, user demographics and audience measurement data. While valuable, such metrics are only part of the answer for real-time mining in distributed environments. Additionally, data mining coupled to linguistic techniques has produced the new field of text mining, and text mining coupled with image processing has produced a variety of on-line multimedia data-mining applications. These extensions opened new possibilities and a new quality in data-mining applications including building a bridge between businesses and engineering fields on the one hand, and businesses and social sciences on the other hand. We are expecting that the next generation of data-mining applications will be characterized by the following.

1. *Diversity of data-mining tasks*—such as summarization, characterization, association, classification, clustering, trend and deviation detection, pattern analyses, monitoring, and surveillance.

2. *Diversity of data organizations and data types*—such as relational and transactional databases, data warehouses and data marts, spatial, temporal and text databases, multimedia data and data streams, object-oriented data, web data, and so on.

3. *Diversity of infrastructures for data mining applications*—requiring solutions for problems like efficiency and scalability of the data-mining system, communication and integration of distributed data framework, on-line and real-time mining of data streams, and standards and data-mining services.

TABLE 1. Classes of Data-Mining Applications in 2003

Data-Mining Applications in 2003	Percentage
Banking	13
Bioinformatics/biotech	10
Direct marketing/fundraising	10
e-Commerce/web	5
Entertainment	1
Fraud detection	9
Insurance	8
Investment/stocks	3
Manufacturing	2
Medical/pharmaceuticals	6
Retail	6
Scientific data	9
Security	2
Supply chain analysis	2
Telecommunication	8
Travel	2
Other	4

Source: Kdnuggets, http://www.kdnuggets.com/

4. *Diversity of application domains*—Table 1 illustrates the diversity of problems and trends in application areas that can benefit from data mining. It shows that the next generation of data-mining applications covers a large number of different fields from traditional businesses to advanced scientific research. With new tools, methodologies, and infrastructure, this trend of diversification will continue each year.

5. *Emphasis on security and privacy aspects of data mining*—data mining is a powerful technology that, if abused, could have terrible consequences. Saying that it is "just a technology" does not contribute to ensuring that this promising technology is not abused. The media is already overloaded with news about the new lure of "intelligent" data-mining technologies and applications such as pattern matching for biometrics, profiling and information extraction about plane passengers, or advanced gene discoveries. Equally interesting, and probably more sensitive, is the application of real-time analytics to the confidentiality of distributed customer information within corporations.

A summary of these new characteristics for data-mining applications in business, science, and engineering, with the comparison to traditional approaches, is given in Table 2.

TABLE 2. Characteristics of the Next Generation of Data-Mining Applications

Dimension	From	Toward
Data	Numerical and alphanumerical data.	Multimedia data including text, images and video.
	Static, retrospective data.	Dynamic, time series and data streams.
Algorithms	Traditional decision trees, neural networks, association rules, regression methods.	Algorithms based on techniques previously not accepted by data-mining community such as genetic algorithms, fuzzy sets, rough sets, and fractal theory.
		Parallel and distributed implementations.
Infrastructure	Integrated software tools used in the professional lab environment.	Integrated environment based on web-based services and grid architectures.
	Off-line data mining.	Incremental, real-time, distributed, and mobile data mining.
Applications environ-ment	Business-oriented, supported by data warehouse.	Internet-based web mining and text mining, on-line images and video streams mining.
Security and privacy	No concerns about security and privacy in data-mining applications.	New standards, laws, and techniques to protect data, usually in a distributed environment.

With increased competition bearing down on all industries, the use of data mining to help in business, industrial, and scientific decision-making continues to grow. Tangible proof of this trend is the current wide adoption in a broad range of industries of advanced integrated tools, which use data mining for analysis and knowledge-supported decision-making. Different types of users expect fast, personalized data delivery from internal and external sources indicating that growing amounts of information are already straining the information supply chain. According to the research firm International Data Corp (IDC), the need for new and established companies to measure, predict, and optimize business performance has fueled demand for analytic application solutions where data mining is a significant part. It noted that worldwide revenue in this market space was expected to accelerate at an annual growth rate of 28%, from US$2 billion in 1999 to more than US$6 billion in 2004. IDC expects the data-mining market to pick up from few years' oscillations, reaching a 13% compound annual growth rate from 2001 through 2006.* As companies sharpen their focus on risk management, data monitoring, fraud detection, gene discovery, and web analyses,

*Perez, B., Data mining technology use growth, http://robotics.stanford.edu/users/ronnyk/kohaviInSCMP.pdf

data mining will see the revenues grow. Based only on income from licenses and maintenance for data-mining software, Figure 1 shows that the U.S. revenue of $536 million is projected for 2003.

The growth of data-mining applications could also be measured through other parameters. Almost two-thirds of the North American companies IDC interviewed are running some kind of data-mining system as represented in Figure 2. But data-mining technology is developing not only in the United States, but all over the world as well. Some analyses show that 40% researchers and application developers in data mining are from North America, 33% are from Europe, 15% from Asia, 6% from South America, 4% from Australia, and 2% from Africa.

There are plenty of "horror stories" about artificial intelligence, expert systems, and data warehousing projects of the 1980s and 1990s that were huge,

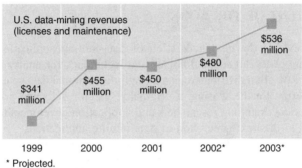

Figure 1. Growth of data-mining revenues. *Source*: Roberts-Witt, S. L., Data mining: what lies beneath?, PC Magazine November 19, 2002, pp. 87–95. http://www.pcmag.com/article2/0,1759,646153,00.asp.

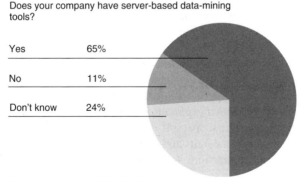

Figure 2. Data-mining software is available. *Source*: Roberts-Witt, S. L., Data mining: what lies beneath?, PC Magazine November 19, 2002, pp. 87–95. http://www.pcmag.com/article2/0,1759,646153,00.asp.

multi-million dollar efforts that never saw the light of day. They took too much time and money to develop, and the end product was often obsolete before it was deployed. Such experiences teach us that advances in new technologies have to go in tandem with real-world applications. Young data-mining researchers and practitioners, representing 81% of data-mining professionals, should and will understand these challenges.

Because of the rapid changes in data-mining technology and new trends in data-mining applications, we initiated this book to collect, systematize, and present information about the next generation of data-mining applications and to identify the requirements for an infrastructure, data, and tools. Our vision is based on the assumption that most of these applications will use new scalable techniques supported by high-performance computer systems.

THE CONTENT OF THE BOOK

This book reviews the next generation of data-mining applications. They are based on state-of-the-art methodologies and techniques for analyzing enormous quantities of raw often distributed data in high-dimensional data spaces. The book provides a forum for the sharing of original research results and practical development experiences among researchers and application developers from different areas related to the next generation of data-mining applications.

The origin of this book is our desire to have a single source, organized in a systematic way, in which we introduce the latest applications that are not only illustrative, but also educational for all professionals interested in computerized data analyses and knowledge discovery. Such readers include people from a wide variety of backgrounds and positions, who find themselves confronted by the need to make sense of large amount of raw data available at their workplace.

The book consists of eight parts covering promising classes of data-mining applications. The first seven parts are devoted to industrial, business, engineering and science, bioinformatics and biotechnology, medical and pharmaceutical, web and text mining, and security applications. The eighth part addresses new trends in data-mining technology. Each part includes several articles contributed by different authors, many of whom are well-known researchers in the data-mining field. The articles, represented as chapters in the book, are either of a *survey type*, presenting what has been done in a specific application sub-area including one's own experience, or *a detailed explanation of a selected data-mining application*. The chapters are designed to be self-contained so that an average reader can understand implementation details and appreciate their contribution. Each chapter also has the current connections to the rest of the literature, web sites, data repositories, and so on.

Industrial Applications

The first part contains three chapters on industrial applications of data mining. In Chapter 1, "Mining Wafer Fabrication: Framework and Challenges," Soenjaya et al. present a wafer fabrication as a complex process that generates gigabytes of data per day. They apply data-mining solutions to efficiently identify defective wafers automatically. The main advantage of the proposed approach lies in the significant time reduction to trace the cause of defects from a few weeks to merely a few hours. Chapter 2, "Damage Detection Employing Novel Data-Mining Techniques" by Lazarevic et al., explores a novel data-mining approach to address damage detection within the large-scale complex structure. In order to reduce the time complexity, the authors propose a hierarchical clustering-based approach for partitioning the structure into substructure and predicting the failure within these substructures. The methodology is applied on an electric transmission tower frame, and effectiveness of the approach is demonstrated. In the third chapter, "Data Projection Techniques and Their Applications in Sensor Array Data Processing," the author, Yang, argues that huge amount of sensor data and their real-time analyses require new data-mining techniques for data reduction. The chapter gives a survey of linear projection techniques, and it focuses on nonlinear projection techniques and their applications in data reduction obtained from odorant sensor arrays, known as electronic noses.

Business Applications

The second part of the book contains four chapters that cover an important class of business data-mining applications. In Chapter 4, entitled "An Application of Evolutionary and Neural Data-Mining Techniques to Customer Relationship Management," Neumann et al. deal with the challenging application in the area of analytical customer relationship management (CRM): the selection of promising addresses for an acquisition campaign. Using the methodology, which is based on integration of radial basis function (RBF) networks with an evolutionary algorithm, the authors show that the proposed approach gives significantly better results than traditional benchmark algorithms such as multilayer perceptrons and decision trees. Vayghan et al. describe an integrated solution that addresses a multistage, multimodel, cost-sensitive, and multiclass classification problem in sales analysis in Chapter 5, entitled "Sales Opportunity Miner: Data Mining for Automatic Evaluation of Sales Opportunity." The authors argue that for the best results it is necessary to build a classification model integrating different data-mining techniques, rather than applying a selected classification algorithm. Chapter 6, "A Fully Distributed Framework for Cost-Sensitive Data Mining" by Fan et al., explores tree-structured regression and variations of meta-learning to combine probabilities and benefits for fully and partially distributed cost-sensitive learning. The authors argue that these types of learning are as good as or even better than the global classifier trained on the all available data from every site (the centralized learning), and they exhibit zero communication and computation overhead. In Chapter 7, entitled "Application of Variable Precision Rough Set to Car Driver Assessment," Aryeetey et al. report on their experiences with the application of the variable precision rough set (VPRS) data-mining approach and the associated HDTL algorithm to modeling the complex interrelationships between drivers socioeconomic, demographic, traffic conviction and accident history, and other characteristics, and the future probability of being at fault in a car accident. The model developed enables for more accurate assessment of accident probabilities for different types of drivers, with different driving habits, thus leading to a more accurate and informed determination of insurance premiums.

Engineering and Science Applications

The third part of the book consists of four chapters related to science and engineering applications. Chapter 8, entitled "Discovering of Patterns in the Earth Science Data Using Data Mining" by Zhang et al., illustrates how preprocessing and data-mining techniques, such as clustering, extended association rules mining based on spatial information, correlation-based queries, outlier detection, collocation mining, and predictive modeling, can aid earth scientists to better understand both (a) global scale changes in biosphere processes and patterns and (b) the effects of widespread human activities. Liu et al. focus on the development of an iterative active learning approach to a real-world application—that is, an image mining problem of detecting *Egeria densa* (commonly called Brazilian waterweed) in digital imagery in Chapter 9, entitled "An Active Learning Approach to *Egeria densa* Detection in Digital Imagery." The authors propose to use the combined classifications of the ensemble of classifiers to reduce the number of uncertain instances in the image classification process and thus achieve reduced expert involvement in image labeling. In Chapter 10, entitled "Experiences in Mining Data from Computer Simulations," Kamath et al. survey the work being done in the mining of scientific simulation data, describe their experiences with the similarity-based object retrieval system in the analysis of data from a fluid mixing problem, and outline the challenges and opportunities in the mining of this relatively new form of data. Simulations of complex scientific phenomena generate large-scale data sets over the spatial–temporal space. Eliassi-Rad et al. present several systems that build "queriable" models to help scientists gather knowledge from their simulation data in Chapter 11, entitled "Statistical Modeling of Large-Scale Scientific Simulation Data." The authors perform two experiments on large-scale astrophysics simulation datasets to illustrate the value of Ad-hoc Queries for Simulation (AQSim) model generator, which reduces the data storage requirements and query access times.

Applications in Bioinformatics and Biotechnology

In recent years there has been an explosive growth in bioinformatics and biotechnology research such as the identification and study of human genome by discovering large-scale sequencing patterns and gene functions. Thus, this part contains four chapters dealing with DNA data analysis. Human beings have around 100,000 genes. A gene consists of individual nucleotides arranged in a particular order. There are very many ways in which the nucleotides can be ordered and sequenced to form distinct genes. It is extremely challenging to identify particular gene sequence patterns that play roles in various diseases and disabilities as well as in the discovery of new medicines and approaches for disease diagnosis, etiology, prevention, and treatment.

Toivonen and his research group describe and illustrate novel data-mining approaches such as association analysis, similarity analysis, and clustering to gene mapping using haplotypes contained within gene marker data in Chapter 12, entitled "Data Mining for Gene Mapping." The authors report on the successful use of the association-based gene mapping methodology that has been competitive with previous state-of-the-art methods. Chapter 13, "Data-Mining Techniques for Microarray Data Analysis" by Domeniconi et al., provides a survey of the advantages and limitations of data-mining techniques (based on supervised and unsupervised learning) currently used in microarray gene expression studies. The authors also present improved tools such as locally adaptive clustering for more accurate pattern discovery and assessment of biological significance. Dong et al. in Chapter 14, entitled "The Use of Emerging Patterns in the Analysis of Gene Expression Profiles for the Diagnosis and Understanding of Diseases," provide yet another survey of techniques for gene selection from microarray gene expression profiles. The authors demonstrate the use of an emerging pattern-based classification method called PCL for classifying disease states and subtypes, deriving treatment plans as well as understanding of gene interaction network from gene expression profiles. In Chapter 15, "Proteomic Data Analysis: Pattern Recognition for Medical Diagnosis and Biomarker Discovery," Mani and Gillette address the challenging issues regarding the collection and analysis of proteomic data. The analysis involves feature extraction and selection and pattern recognition directed toward distilling characteristic proteomic signatures of various disease-free and diseased states. These signatures provide the possibility of disease classification, early detection, and prognostication.

Medical and Pharmaceutical Applications

This part contains two chapters related to medical and pharmaceutical applications. The two applications deal with cystic fibrosis (a genetic disease affecting about 30,000 children and adults in the United States) and isokinetics.

In Chapter 16, entitled "Discovering Patterns and Reference Models in the Medical Domain of Isokinetics," Alonso et al. present a set of algorithms and methods for discovering patterns and reference models in a set of time series of a medical domain of isokinetics. The presented techniques are applied to a real isokinetic physiotherapy domain—that is, analyzing muscle strength curves to diagnose injuries in athletes and to indicate whether an individual matches a standard profile for a particular sport. The discovered knowledge was evaluated against the expertise of a physician specialized in isokinetic techniques. In Chapter 17, Mining the Cystic Fibrosis Data," Kurgan et al. discuss an application of a novel data-mining system based on a classical data-mining and knowledge discovery process model, called MetaSqueezer, that uses supervised inductive machine learning combined with a meta-learning concept to analyze clinical data describing patients with cystic fibrosis (CF). Despite the complexity of the data and high number of missing values, MetaSqueezer is able to generate new and clinically important knowledge such as discovering patterns that influence the pace of development of CF and factors that are related to particular kinds of CF.

Web and Text-Mining Applications

This part contains three chapters that deal with current topics of web crawling techniques, analyzing click streams, and text mining. The topics have been of considerable interest in recent years because of the rapid growth of the worldwide web and the Internet. As of today, there are more than a billion documents on the web, and more than a million of documents are added each day. Crawling techniques enable one to find documents belonging to specific topics. In addition, automatic text analysis techniques enhanced by a human allow one to better understand the details, including the semantic content, of text documents. By analyzing click streams, companies study browsing and purchasing patterns of customers on web stores. This way the companies can learn more about customer needs and likes, which can result in greater cross-selling of related products, one-to-one promotions, product affinities, and customer retention, to name a few.

In Chapter 18, "On Learning Strategies for Topic-Specific Web Crawling," Aggarwal discusses the collaborative crawler and intelligent crawler techniques, which are learning techniques for topical resource discovery. The author also presents some creative ways of combining different kinds of linkage- and user-centered methods in order to improve the effectiveness of the crawl. In Chapter 19, "On Analyzing Web Log Data: A Parallel Sequence Mining Algorithm," Demiriz proposes a stable and robust parallel sequence mining algorithm, webSPADE, which uses one full scan and several partial scans of the data, to analyze click streams found in site web logs. The author uses an innovative web-based front end for visualizing and querying the sequence mining results for value-added business analysis. In Chapter 20, "Interactive Methods for Taxonomy Editing and Validation," Spangler and Kreulen describe in detail a system with a unique combination of capabilities for the generation of practical quality taxonomies. The authors show that the combination of automated text mining with interactive human expert guidance integrated in an interactive platform provides a practical way to create natural taxonomies in a document collection.

Security Applications

Security applications of data-mining technology represent important trends in data mining, and two chapters illustrate how the technology helps in operational crime fighting and protection of computer networks from different types of attacks. In Chapter 21, "The Use of Data-Mining Techniques in Operational Crime Fighting," Adderley applies two types of neural networks: multilayer perceptron and self-organizing maps to recognize burglary offenses committed by a network of offenders. The results of applied data-mining techniques show that three months of undetected crimes were analyzed within minutes, increasing manual accuracy of 10% to 85%. In Chapter 22, "Using Data Mining for Intrusion Detection," Brodie et al. analyze network-based alert logs with different data-mining techniques including data enhancement, data visualization, event rate analysis, temporal association, and clustering. The results show significant reduction of the false alarms and detection of certain types of low-frequency attacks.

New Trends in Data-Mining Technology

The last part in the book represents a collection of three overview chapters describing some important classes of data-mining techniques (technologies). Mining frequent itemsets is a fundamental problem in many applications, and most of the proposed algorithms are variants of a priori. Special solutions are necessary for the long pattern mining problem where traditional algorithms are computationally inefficient. Zaki gives an overview of these techniques in Chapter 23, "Mining Closed and Maximal Frequent Itemsets," focusing analysis on the state-of-the-art Charm and GenMax algorithms. The performance of different algorithms depends on database characteristics, and the author shows under which condition a particular method is likely to perform well; very useful practical directions for selecting the technique for specific applications.

Traina et al. explain that keeping only relevant information of the large multidimensional datasets is a challenge that the next generation of data-mining techniques are pursuing in Chapter 24, entitled "Using Fractals in Data Mining." Knowing that in real-world applications datasets are often skewed, they exhibit intrinsic or fractal dimensionality that is much lower than their real, embedded dimensionality. While other data-mining methods for analysis of skewed data offer relatively high-computational complexity, the techniques Self-plots and Cross-plots presented in the chapter, which are based on fractal theory, provide algorithms with linear complexity especially useful for mining fast changing multidimensional data such as data streams. Finally, Chapter 25, "Genetic Search for Logic Structures in Data," presents the development of a coherent logic-based framework where the data can be fully described in the language of logic predicates using fuzzy logic formalisms and structure of neural networks. Pedrycz discusses the development of a heterogeneous structured network composed of logic neurons emphasizing interpretation mechanisms as the advantage of the proposed logically transparent architecture.

PART I

INDUSTRIAL APPLICATIONS

1

MINING WAFER FABRICATION: FRAMEWORK AND CHALLENGES

JEMMY SOENJAYA, WYNNE HSU, MONG LI LEE, AND TACHYANG LEE

1.1. INTRODUCTION

The increasing market expansion of electronic devices such as handphones, computers, and television sets has provided the impetus for development of high-tech industry. Wafer fabrication, or the process of producing an integrated circuit on semiconductor materials, plays an important role in manufacturing the fundamental components of electronic devices. Manufacturing is typically a controlled process, where the process flow is carefully and systematically designed. However, random events and subtle changes in environment might cause failures. As with many other manufacturing processes, wafer fabrication often faces fluctuation in products' quality.

In order to detect possible failures, various sensors monitor the process history and record intermediate quality measurements of the production process. The data collected aim to provide insight of the production process, to improve efficiency, and to identify the causes of problems that may during the manufacturing process. While the collection of large quantities of data has been facilitated by low-cost storage devices and automated data collection technologies, there has been relatively little effort made to automate the analysis of the accumulated data. Instead, human experts often analyze selected portions of the data only when problems occur during production or when it is required to optimize the production process. A lot of information regarding the production processes is left unexplored.

Knowledge discovery is described as "the non-trivial extraction of implicit, unknown, and potentially useful information from data" (Frawley et al., 1991).

Next Generation of Data-Mining Applications. Edited by Kantardzic and Zurada
ISBN 0-471-65605-4 © 2005 the Institute of Electrical and Electronics Engineers, Inc.

This consists of several steps, one of which is data mining, or automatic pattern extraction from data. Knowledge discovery aims to reduce a large amount of data into a manageable amount of useful knowledge, which can then be processed further by human experts for analysis purposes. Data mining can reduce the time needed to analyze these data as well as provide engineers with valuable insight extracted from the data, which is otherwise unknown.

Analyzing wafer fabrication data poses many challenges. The fabrication process is complex and error-prone. Many factors contribute to fluctuations in the yield obtained. This process utilizes machines with high precision, often measuring up to the nearest micrometer or even nanometer. The entire manufacturing process typically takes weeks or even months to complete, during which wafers go through hundreds of operations generating a huge amount of data to be collected from the various sensors each day. Engineers have to scan these data for relevant information to increase the yield.

Traditionally, engineers use an approach called "Design of Experiment" (Montgomery, 1991) to solve the low-yield problem. This approach consists of a series of experiments whereby several input factors are varied to see how they affect the output of the fabrication process. The key is to be able to formulate the hypothesis as quickly as possible in order to reduce the number of possible factors. This is because the number of experiments is exponential to the number of factors involved. To pinpoint the possible cause of low yield, engineers often have to dissect the faulty wafers to observe the layers of materials added, the patterns formed on its surface, and the graphical view of the faulty patterns. On average, engineers can take weeks or even months to formulate their hypothesis and perform experiments to verify their hypothesis. Furthermore, since a human can only handle a small number of factors at any one time, the large number of operations and thousands of possible factors are simply overwhelming.

In this chapter, we propose a framework that aims to integrate data-mining solutions into the wafer fabrication process to identify causes of failure and low yield. The framework is designed to support the efficient extraction of knowledge from wafer fabrication data, as well as to assist engineers in formulating their hypothesis within a shorter time period.

The rest of the chapter is organized as follows. Section 1.2 gives the background of the wafer fabrication process, and the types of data collected. We also discuss the various issues and challenges involved in mining from wafer fabrication data. Section 1.3 gives a survey of the related work done in mining wafer fabrication data, and the commonly used techniques in supervised and unsupervised learning. Section 1.4 describes the proposed framework, and the details of the preprocessing, defect detection and filtering steps. Section 1.5 shows the results of the experiments performed, and we conclude in Section 1.6.

1.2. BACKGROUND

Wafer fabrication is a process of producing integrated circuits using semiconductors. The basic material consists of a disk of silicon called a *wafer*. Each

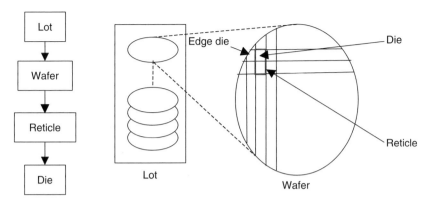

Figure 1.1. A production unit.

type of product has a *route*, which refers to a sequence of *operations* that has to be carried out on the raw wafer. Each *operation* in a *route* is identified by its *operation number*. Some of these operations include adding a layer to the wafer, drawing a pattern on the wafer, covering the pattern with a photo layer, and etching the pattern. Each *operation* is based on a specific *recipe*, which is the blueprint of what an *operation* entails. Examples of blueprints are the thickness of a layer to be added, or the pattern to be drawn on the wafer. An *operation* consists of several *scripts*, and each *script* consists of several *steps*. However, a *script* is seldom used to identify a particular operation. Instead, a unique identifier ⟨*route*, *operationno*, *step*⟩ is used for the process step. Some examples of process steps include "wafer enters a machine," "addition of a layer to a wafer," "wafer exits from a machine," and so on.

Figure 1.1 shows a unit of production. The largest unit is a *lot*, which is a stack of *wafers*. A *wafer* is a semiconductor disk, on which the integrated circuit is made. All the wafers in a *lot* go through the same route, and they undergo the same operations based on the same recipe. In general, a *lot* consists of 25 wafers. Note that in some situations a lot may consist of less than 25 wafers. This is because the engineers may take some wafers out for testing purposes so as to improve the *yield*, or to trace the cause of a *yield* drop. In this case the lot is split into several lots, and the resulting lots are called *child lots*.

A wafer disk is segmented into small rectangles, called *dies*, which are the smallest unit. A group of *dies* forms a functional unit called a *reticle*. A functional test structure is built at the boundary of each *reticle* for testing purposes. The size of a *die* and a *reticle* varies from product to product. Each product has its *standard die count*, which is the total number of dies a wafer should contain. The actual die count of a wafer is obtained during the final test.

1.2.1. Operational Data

Throughout the fabrication process, various types of data are collected, from process history, intermediate measurements, to final testing. Operational data are organized on a daily basis, recording all the operations that are carried out on that day together with the intermediate measurements, the machine's maintenance, the name of the operator performing the task, and other related data. There are two main operational data that we focus on: the process history, which is also called the *lot history*, and intermediate measurements, which is called *metrology*. Both *lot history* and *metrology* use *lots* as basic unit, since all the wafers in a lot undergo the same operations and stay together throughout fabrication process, unless a split is performed.

Lot history captures the operations executed on the lots in a particular day. Among other things, it records the date and time the operation was performed, the machine where the operation was performed, which has an event name and a process number, the lots' identification number (id), recipe, product name, and route used. In our analysis, all the wafers originate from the same product, and thus product name and route is inconsequential. The *lot history* uses the combined date and time as the main key for its relation table, and it uses event name and process number as the secondary key.

The second operational data is *metrology*. The metrology records intermediate measurements taken as part of process control. If a wafer's measurements differ from the specifications, then the wafer may lead to a lower yield. Some examples of these measurements are the thickness of added layer, the size of patterns drawn on the surface, and the depth of layer etched. Although process control is important in monitoring the state of the wafers throughout the fabrication process, it is also expensive in terms of required time and manpower. Too many measurements result in a slower fabrication process and a lower production throughput. Thus, measurements are done only after important steps as specified by the engineers. Furthermore, only some of the wafers in a lot are measured, on which randomly selected points are measured. The parameters of the measurements state how many wafers per lot and how many points per wafer should be measured. The lot id is not recorded in this table. The parameter also specifies the type of measurements—for example, the length of pattern in x dimension, or y dimension, or average length of both. The key of this relation is similar to *lot history*—that is, date and time as primary key, and event name and process number as secondary key.

1.2.2. Final Tests Data

In addition to operational data, there are also final tests data. The purpose of the final test is to ensure that all the dies/chips produced function as specified. There are two tests that are performed, a functional level test called the *parametric test*, and *die level test*. The parametric test evaluates the test structure of the reticle, which consists of hundreds of electrical characteristics tests. There are five sites (or reticles) tested for each wafer. The second test is performed at die level, where a probe wafer is used to label each die of the wafer. The labeling process is called *binning*. The bin number goes from 0 to a certain number as defined by engineers. Bin 1 denotes that the die is working properly. All other bin numbers denote some types of error/failure characteristic. At the end of this die level test, a wafermap is obtained, which is the graphical representation of the wafer with each die labeled by a bin number. The *yield* of the wafer is then defined as the number of dies that fall into bin 1 over standard die count. Both parametric and die level tests are performed on all wafers because it is important to package only the properly working chips.

1.2.3. Issues and Challenges

Some of the issues and challenges that affect the design and choice of algorithm in mining wafer fabrication data are as follows:

1. *Data Granularity.* Two different types of data are involved, namely, the operational data and the final tests data. Although these two types of data capture different aspects of the fabrication process, they are interrelated. However, there is a gap between these two types of data. The operational data are lot-based, while final test data are wafer-based. Thus, we need a way to bridge this difference in data granularity.

2. *High-Dimensional Data with Small Sample Size.* Operational data provide details on fabrication process. They contain various process parameters and intermediate measurements that can be used to trace the cause of the problem or to find ways to optimize fabrication output. These data contain long sequences and a small sample size. Mining high-dimensional data with very small sample size is inherently difficult. To overcome this problem, we need to reduce the dimensionality by eliminating parts of the sequence that are irrelevant.

3. *Large Number of Low-dimensional Data Points.* Final test data reveal the output of the fabrication process, from which we can assess the rate of success of the fabrication process by observing the yield obtained. This data are also the main source for identifying the existence of problems that arise in fabrication. The final test data have a huge number of points in relatively small dimensions. This requires us to design an algorithm that is efficient in terms of the number of points processed. Since the data are not labeled, the algorithm to extract pattern should be of the unsupervised class to group similar failure signature together.

4. *Skewed Data.* Both operational and final test data are highly skewed, since we can only obtain a small sample of problematic wafers or lots. The problem is usually short-lived; that is, once the problem is solved, we do not expect to see it reappearing again in the near future. Thus, an algorithm that is able to mine information from a small sample size is important. In addition, we also require the algorithm to be not only accurate, but also sensitive in detecting the problematic wafers. For example, if 80% of the wafers is normal, then an algorithm that outputs 100% of the wafers to be normal with a relatively high accuracy of 80% is not sensitive enough since it has failed to identify the existence of problematic wafers.

1.3. RELATED WORK

In this section, we discuss the existing methods to mine wafer fabrication data. The main approaches to supervised and unsupervised learning are also highlighted.

1.3.1. Mining Wafer Fabrication Data

Mining wafer fabrication data has generated a lot of interests because of its unique characteristics and the possible benefits gained. François and Ives (1999) advocated that data analysis can help discover causes of yield drop. They successfully identified the cause of a manufacturing problem using statistical techniques for data analysis such as ANOVA (Devore, 1995) and regression techniques. Coupled with the engineers' expertise, they demonstrated that data analysis can be a valuable tool in improving a wafer fabrication's yield.

Bertino et al. (1999) reported their work on wafer fabrication data. They applied two data mining tools, namely, Mineset (Brunk et al., 1997) and Q-Yield (Quadrillon, 2003). Based on their experience, they found that general data-mining approaches do not reveal much of the causes of failures. They highlighted the difficulties in using the association rule from Mineset—namely, that the minimum support and confidence used is inappropriate. In fact, it is necessary to set the minimum support to be very low because the number of problematic wafers is typically low. However, a low minimum support leads to an explosion in the number of frequent itemset candidates. To overcome this problem, they constructed an interest graph of factors that engineers are interested in. A general algorithm was designed to traverse this interest graph and to produce the hypothesis. While the interest graph also served as a filter to find the factors that may contribute to the low yield, the number of factors that needs to be checked remains exponential. Furthermore, the engineers are required to supply the interest graph, as well as to label each step of operational data to indicate if the process succeeded or failed.

Given that the semiconductor industry faces increasing product design complexity, and a decreasing window period to manufacture their products, it is becoming critical to identify factors that contribute to product defects. Tobin et al. (1999) presented techniques that can efficiently identify the spatial signature of problematic wafers. Wafers with similar spatial signature are grouped together. The cause of a defect can be deduced by examining the causes of previously stored wafers with similar problem signature. The signature can also be associated with one or more process steps to provide insight on the possible causes. For example, tightly clustered objects can be correlated with insufficient etching. Their results showed that wafer defects can be recognized based on their spatial signature. A technique that is able to reflect on past experiences for solving similar problems in future is also proposed.

Kittler and Wang (2000) explored several data-mining algorithms on wafer data, and they compared the results to the traditional statistical test approach.

In particular, they compared decision trees to statistical methods such as regression, ANOVA, and Kruskal–Wallis tests. They concluded that decision trees can perform as well as traditional statistical tests. However, the existence of large amounts of missing values may prevent useful analysis to be done. They also noted that the difference between statistical methods and data-mining techniques is that statistical methods typically assume a model; for example, ANOVA assumes that the underlying data has a normal distribution, and thus the result depends very much on whether the right model has been chosen. In contrast, most data-mining algorithms are nonparametric, that is, they do not make any assumptions about the data. However, one has to be careful in choosing the algorithm, because each algorithm has its own bias; for example, the association rule favors common items by having minimum support as one of its criteria.

Another data-mining case study on wafer manufacturing data is reported by Gardner and Bieker (2000). A total of three case studies were presented in the article. The techniques used are Self-Organizing Map/SOM (Kohonen, 1995)-based clustering and rule induction from clusters, embodied in a software tool named CorDex. Sets of data that have been handpicked by the engineers are presented to the system, which will cluster the data. The clusters are labeled according their yield, poor, medium, and high. Rule induction is used to extract discriminating rules that explain the cluster, which are then presented to the engineers. The system is able to find the clusters that represent the failure cases and extract relevant rules for all three case studies. However, the system also generates more clusters than is necessary, and it is unclear how a rule is selected from the list of rules presented. Another drawback of this approach is that the data must be first preprocessed by the engineers. As such, it does not provide for automatic integration to the manufacturing system. However, they have shown that data-mining techniques can be successfully applied to wafer manufacturing application.

Fountain et al. (2000) proposed a decision theoretic approach to construct efficient test procedures, thus reducing the number of dies that need to be tested at the die level test. However, since a mature wafer fabrication tends to have a more stable yield, an influence diagram and utility model can be developed to model the pattern of the output. This model can be used to predict the die pattern of the wafermap—that is, which die is likely to fail the test, how many dies need to be tested, and so on. The system gains by saving resources required by picking dies in a certain order to be tested, based on the model learnt from historical data, rather than testing all the dies. For a normal wafer, the number of dies tested will be small, and thus a high number of dies tested by this system indicates a possible failure. However, the system stops at identifying the existence of failure.

Kusiak (2000) explored yet another aspect of mining wafer fabrication data. He presented a way to decompose the huge amount of data into smaller relations, which can then be processed in parallel. Two possible ways to decompose the data are presented, namely, object-set-wise and feature-set-wise. A rule-based system was also deployed in an industrial case study. The benefits of this approach is that it reduces the time complexity of data-mining algorithms and selects only the relevant features for a particular segment/group.

All the previous works on wafer fabrication data addresses different aspects of applying data-mining techniques to analyze the data. There is a lack of framework that unifies these solutions into an automated data analysis that can be integrated into wafer fabrication.

1.3.2. Unsupervised Learning

A quick survey of data-mining algorithms reveals two big classes of algorithms: supervised and unsupervised. Supervised algorithms learn from labeled data, where each example has its class label, which is the output of the target function that we would like to find out. For example, in weather dataset, the class label can be sunny, cloudy, or raining. The task is then to find the structure of each of the class; in most cases, it aims to predict the label of future unlabeled examples. On the other hand, unsupervised algorithms learn from unlabeled data. The task is to find pattern, structure, or regularities that exist in the data, such as groups of similar examples.

Clustering is the most commonly used unsupervised algorithm. The aim of clustering is to discover clusters or groups of similar instances in the data. In general, the data are represented as points in multidimensional space. Each dimension corresponds to a feature of the data (columns in relational table). The task is then to group points that are *close/similar* to each other into a group, such that points that belong to a group are closer to each other compared to their *distance* to points that belong to another group. The definition of closeness or similarity (or distance and dissimilarity) often varies from one domain to another. Distance metrics such as Euclidean (squared difference) or Manhattan (absolute difference) is often used in geometrical applications, while Kullback–Leibler distance (Kullback and Leibler, 1951) and its variances are often used for color histogram and distributions of data.

Clustering techniques have been studied under various contexts and used in many disciplines. Jain et al. (1999) present an overview of clustering algorithms. There are two prominent classes: hierarchical and partitional algorithms. Hierarchical algorithms cluster n points in $n - 1$ steps, where at each step either two clusters are merged (bottom up, agglomerative) or one of the clusters is divided into two (top down, divisive). It produces a dendogram where the leaves represent the data points. Figure 1.2 shows an example of a dendogram.

The most popular partitional algorithm is the k-means (Lloyd, 1982; MacQueen, 1967; Linde et al., 1980). K-means divides the dataset into k distinct clusters, where k is supplied by the user. K-means works by first randomly selecting k representative points as the center of the cluster and then iteratively refining these points by moving the cluster's representative to the center of gravity of points that belong to that cluster—that is, points that are closer to this representative point as compared to the other $k - 1$ points. It can be proven that this algorithm will converge to local minima that minimize the sum of squared error between the points and their respective representative clusters. However, these local minima can be far from the global optimum. This algorithm is sensitive to

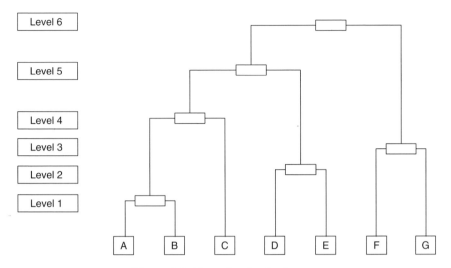

Figure 1.2. Example of a dendogram.

the starting k points chosen. Bradley et al. (1998a) present a way to choose a better set of k points by severely under-sampling the data.

Dubes and Jain (1988) study these two approaches of clustering and conclude that hierarchical clustering is superior to k-means in most cases. However, the cost of performing hierarchical agglomerative clustering (a bottom up hierarchical clustering) on n points of d-dimensional data is $O(dn^3)$ when a dissimilarity matrix is used and the fastest algorithm runs at $O(dn^2 \log n)$ by using a priority queue. K-means algorithm runs on $O(nktd)$, where k is the number of cluster desired and t is the number of iterations until the algorithm converges. Since k and t are much smaller than n, k-means runs linear in the number of data points. When n is large, the cost of performing hierarchical algorithm is too expensive. Bradley et al. (1998b) proposed a single-scan framework for clustering large databases.

Besides hierarchical clustering and k-means, clustering techniques such as density-based DBScan (Ester et al., 1996) and representatives-based CURE (Guha et al., 1998) make use of statistical properties of the database to generate clusters. Zhang et al. (1996) present a BIRCH that uses only one scan of the database to build the clusters under a small memory constraint.

There are also other works to discover regularities on temporal data. These techniques are used mainly in business applications, such as stock price, and in scientific experiments that measure changes over time, such as microarray data in bioinformatics. Regression-based methods such as auto-regression coupled with moving average are often used. Another alternative is a segmented line as used by Povinelli (1999).

For wafer fabrication data, we utilize a hybrid of k-means and hierarchical clustering techniques to achieve a tradeoff between speed and accuracy for a large number of points. We also employ segmented-line time-series analysis to filter out irrelevant features.

1.3.3. Supervised Learning and Feature Selection

Many methods have been proposed to learn from labeled examples, the majority of which are derived from the machine learning field. The objective is to learn a function that maps a set of features to a value. Techniques such as Bayesian Learning (Bayesian Belief Network or the simpler Naïve Bayesian), Neural Network, and Reinforcement Learning are discussed in Mitchell (1997).

Supervised learning algorithms aim to predict future unseen cases. This is referred to as *classification*. The classifier CBA (Liu et al., 1998) is based on association rules (Agrawal and Srikant, 1994), while C4.5 (Quinlan, 1992) is based on decision trees. When the number of features is large, some of these classifiers do not scale well. Furthermore, the robustness of the results is affected when the number of available data points is small.

This leads to the research on feature selection that addresses the problem of selecting relevant features for a particular problem. Various relevance definitions are defined by John et al. (1994), which labels the relevance of features based on the probability of output function. There are two types of feature selection algorithms: *wrappers*, which wrap around the classifier/learner, and *filters*, which are independent of the learner used. Tavalera (2000) presented a feature selection based on COBWEB's salience, which can be interpreted as how knowing the cluster label of this point can increase our belief that a feature of this point has a certain value. This is similar to the one that is defined by John et al. (1994). Dash and Liu (1997) presented various categories of feature selection algorithms.

Although there is a general consensus that a relevant feature must be somewhat correlated to the output that we would like to predict, the actual feature selection itself differs from one domain to another. The general guideline is correlation. In this work, we make use of domain knowledge coupled with correlation measures to design a filter for selecting the relevant features.

1.4. PROPOSED FRAMEWORK

In this section we propose a framework that serves as a glue to unify the various approaches to mining wafer manufacturing data. Figure 1.3 shows the overall framework. We separate the data into two parts—operational data and final test data—since they are used for different purposes. The operational data provide information required to identify the cause of the problem, while the final test data provide insight about observable problem signature.

Data preprocessing is an important step to convert the raw data collected from production process into a form suitable for mining. Different representations of the data can produce different results. Furthermore, data preprocessing also consolidates data that are scattered over several databases.

Defect detection plays an important role in discovering problem signature as it automatically labels the type of defect from final test. The simplest form of defect detection is thresholding, where "problematic" refers to those wafers whose yield is lower than a certain threshold. Here, we cluster the bin profiles to

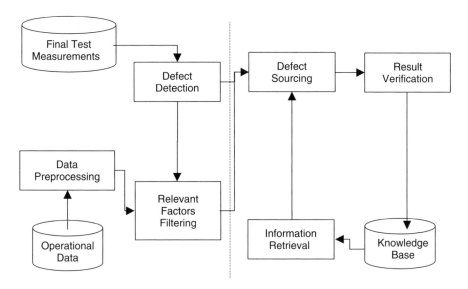

Figure 1.3. Schematic view of mining framework.

detect problem signature. It is reasonable to assume that if the problem signatures are similar, then it implies that the wafers share a similar problem cause.

Wafer manufacturing is a complex process that includes hundreds of steps. As such, a filtering step is required to eliminate irrelevant factors before proceeding to find the pattern from the data and determine the cause of the problem. Here, we utilize the domain knowledge and design a filter-type feature reduction technique. At the same time, we also use the feedback from defect detection to guide us in the removal of irrelevant features.

The right side of the framework in Figure 1.3 consists of a cycle of defect sourcing, verification, information retrieval, and knowledge base. In our framework, once the defect sourcing produces a hypothesis on the cause of the problem, the engineers can verify it by performing experiments and physical examinations of the wafers. A verified solution is subsequently added to the knowledge base for future reference. Details of each components of the framework are given below.

1.4.1. Data Preprocessing

There are three types of data in wafer fabrication: *lot history, metrology, and die level test results.* Lot history and metrology are operational data, while die level test results are the final test data.

Lot history and metrology data are stored daily in separate files. Each day, a list of operations performed, including intermediate measurements taken, are stored in the lot history. Each operation contains date and time, lot id, machine/equipment id, recipe, event name, process, step number, and so on. If the event is an intermediate measurement, then the results of the measurements are stored in metrology. The entries in metrology do not include the lot id of the wafers examined. Thus, we have to refer to the lot history to find the corresponding entry and fill in the lot id. In order to integrate the data in these two types of files, we use date and time as the primary key. Event name is used to resolve any entries with the same date and time. As the files are stored on a daily basis, we only search the entries of lot history from the same day as the one from metrology. Once we have combined the two files into a daily report, we group the subsequent processes and measurements into a single entry.

Next, we reformat the list into two types of sequences. The first sequence is based on the lots, where we the list of machines each lot went through and the measurements taken, if any. The second list is based on the machine and process number, which contains the lots that went through this machine, and intermediate measurements taken after this process, if any. Both lists are sorted based on date and time of the process performed.

The final test data that we obtained consist of wafermaps taken from die level tests. Instead of using spatial signature detection, we propose to use the *bin profile* as the problem signature. A bin profile is the distribution of dies that fall into the various bins as defined by the engineers. These bins represent different types of error/failure found during die level test. The exception is bin 1, which denotes that the die has passed the test. In order to obtain the bin profile from the wafermaps, we count the number of dies that falls into a particular bin.

Figure 1.4 shows an example of a wafer that contains 29 dies and four types of bins. The profile is normalized by total die count. For the product data that was given to us, the standard total die count is 2499. Sometimes the wafermap contains less than 2499 dies. This is mostly due to "zero yield," which is a condition whereby the yield of the wafer is so low that the test is only performed partially. To cater for this case, we add an additional special bin, which represents this set of untested dies. Note that Toblin et al. (1999) did not include the bin label of failed wafers; and, as such, our approach can act as a complement to their method.

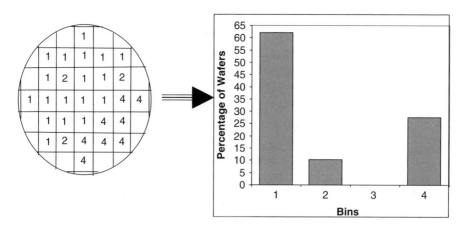

Figure 1.4. Conversion from wafermap to bin profile.

1.4.2. Defect Detection

Automatic defect detection is performed on the final test data. We obtained the production data for the first four months of year 2002 from STMicroelectronics. The die level test data consist of 6490 wafers organized into 286 lots. The bin profile has 15 dimensions, where all the bins other than bin 1 represent error types. We cluster these bin profiles to find wafers that have similar failure characteristics.

Although it has been shown that hierarchical clustering is superior to k-means (Dubes and Jain, 1988), its cost is much higher than that of k-means. Dash et al. (2001) address this high complexity and propose a method to segment the original space into p partitions with overlapping area δ between partitions. The parameter δ is taken from the observation that they refer to as 90–10 phenomenon. They observe that the lower portion of the dendogram mainly contain points that are close to each other. After a certain number of iterations, the intercluster distance will begin to increase rapidly. δ is then set to the this critical value when the distance starts to increase sharply. In effect, this method assumes that for the majority of the points, it is adequate to search the closest point locally within a certain area of neighborhood, and the overlapping δ area allows points from different parts to be combined. Dash et al. (2001) noted that in 90% of the steps, the intercluster distances are very small. When the distances are very small, it is not possible to differentiate small "inexactness" in the solution. This allows us to use a faster but less accurate method for these 90% of the points—that is, k-means.

However, it is well known that k-means might arrive at a local minimum that is far away from the global minimum. Matoušek (2000) presents an asymptotically efficient $O(n \log^k n)$ time algorithm that approximates the distortion of the result as close as $(1 + \varepsilon)$ times the optimal distortion. However, the run time is expensive when the number of dimensions, d, and the number of clusters needed, k, are large. There are many others that work on this problem. Among them, Bradley et al. (1998a) propose a way to select a good initial start point by subsampling the points, and then they cluster these samples to estimate the start point. These samples will reveal where the means are since the area near the means will have more points. This increases the likelihood that a sample will be picked from that area.

Based on these ideas, we propose to first sample the data and then use these samples as the starting cluster points for k-means. Once we have run the k-means, we perform a hierarchical clustering on the remaining k clusters by treating each cluster as a point. Note that uniform sampling does not apply in this situation. Instead, we propose a sampling method that takes into consideration the size of the bounding box of the group. Here, the number of points taken for the ith group is $\alpha n d_i / D$, where $0 < \alpha < 1$ is the fraction of points kept, d_i is the size of bounding box of the ith group, and $D = \sum_{i=1}^{i=Z} d_i$, where Z is number of groups.

Note that this sampling approach is area-sensitive, since it will include more points in a sparse area than in a denser area. Note that a dense area will have a smaller bounding box since the points are closer to each other. In this way, we can prevent points that are far away to be grouped by k-means.

Until now, we have assumed that there is a way to order the points and efficiently separate them into groups of equal sizes. Sorting and splicing can be easily carried out for one-dimensional data. However, for high-dimensional data, we have to assign weights to each dimension to reflect its importance. An alternative is to employ an algorithm such as BIRCH (Zhang et al., 1996) to provide the initial grouping. Here, we propose to use the Principal Component Analysis (PCA) proposed by Hotelling (1993) to map the original axis into principal components, which are orthogonal to each other, that is, there is no correlation between the principal components, which can be ranked based on the variance. Given the orthogonal property of the principal components, we can keep only the first few principal components that have large variances, and we transform our data into these selected components. Figure 1.5 shows an example of PCA where the dots represent the data points and the blue line represents the first principal components.

We observe that if we store the data using this new axis, we will lose the least amount of information. In the same manner, we can reduce the data that we are going to cluster to one-dimensional data by applying PCA and retaining only the first principal component. The data are then sorted, and they are divided into groups of equal size. While we cannot guarantee that we have performed the sorting on the right axis, we are assured that the reduced axis has the most variances. Thus, we can think of it as being the representative of the real distances between points.

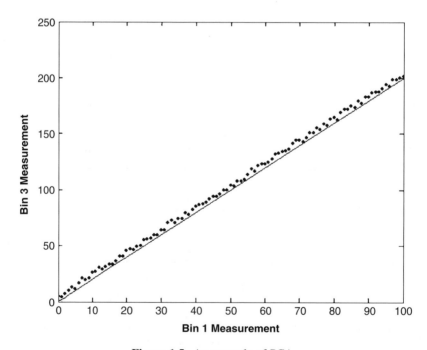

Figure 1.5. An example of PCA.

Another factor that affects cluster accuracy is that k should be some reasonably large number, such as 10% of the original number of points. This will allow more flexibility in selecting the initial start points, because each group can have more than one representative point.

1.4.3. Relevant Factors Filtering

Having clustered the bin profiles to identify problem signatures, we need to establish a link from the operational data to the problem signatures in order to derive possible causes of defects. However, when we examine the operational data, we realize that we have about 286 lots, each of which is a sequence of length 570 of unique machine id and measurements combinations. These are high-dimensional data, with very few data points.

To enable meaningful mining, we need to eliminate irrelevant features. In supervised learning, we can make use of the label to evaluate the fitness of a feature, such as to select minimum set of features that will result in good predictive performance. Dash (2002) propose the use of entropy to measure the regularity of a feature. Tavalera (2000) present a modified COBWEB's variable utility function to select feature that is more prominent in one cluster but not in other clusters.

Besides reducing the dimensionality of the data, we also need to bridge the granularity gap from wafer-based die level test to lot-based operational data. We do this by representing each lot as a series of n weights: $w_1, \ldots, w_n$ such that $w_i = l_i/z$, where l_i is the number of wafers that a lot belongs to in cluster i, z is the number of wafers in a lot, and n is the total number of clusters. The exception is in the clusters with high yield. Generally, there is only one good cluster. This is because the distance between the good wafers are small, and thus the good wafers will be naturally grouped together into a single cluster. This cluster is also the biggest cluster among all, because there are only a few wafers that experience a problem. As such, we require that a lot must have either 100% or 0% weight of a good cluster. If a lot has one wafer that belongs to a cluster which is not a good cluster, then the lot has 0% weight of good cluster. This is equivalent to saying that if a lot has one wafer that has problem, then the whole lot is labeled as problematic.

We employ two methods to help pinpoint the source of defects. The first method is to establish the expected behavior, any deviation from the expected behavior constitutes probable source of defects. We call this test the variability test. Suppose we have the measurements of wafers that went through a machine. If we transform them into time-series data, then the expected behavior of the machine is shown in Figure 1.6, where the performance of the machine is initially good, degrades over time, and then returns to its original state once maintenance is carried out. If we replace each point with the average of the value of previous x points, or the moving average, then we obtain the graph as shown on the right-hand side of Figure 1.6. We observe that there is little fluctuation in the expected behavior. In fact, once the graph is smoothed, most of the values will fluctuate slightly around a value and show a periodic pattern.

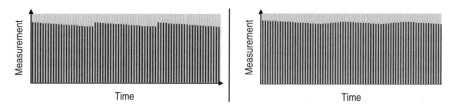

Figure 1.6. Ideal machine measurements: original and smoothened.

To find the deviation from the expected behavior, we first smooth the values of the measurements and find the change points, which are the local maxima and minima. We measure the number of local maxima and local minima and the amplitude difference in a sequence. Once we have found the local optima, we represent the sequence as segmented line. The squared error between the original value and the segmented line representation is calculated, along with the average fluctuations of the amplitude. Using this value, we rank the machines. The machines with a high squared error are likely to be the causes of the defects.

The second method to pinpoint the source of defects is to select the machines or measurements that are able to differentiate the bad lots from the good lots. Here we use the good cluster as the basis of comparison. The intermediate measurements of these high-yield lots are used as the ideal values. Based on this rationale, we collect the measurements for each cluster. The contribution of a lot is based on its weight of the cluster as mentioned above. We then test the difference between the distributions of a cluster and the high yield cluster. If there is a significant difference, then we mark this machine, along with the corresponding measurements and step number, as a probable cause. If there is no significant difference, then we can discard this machine because we cannot tell the difference in quality between low-yield clusters and high-yield clusters by observing the results of this machine. There are statistical tests available for testing the difference between two distributions, such as the T-test and the Wilcoxon Rank-Sum Test (Devore, 1995). The T-test assumes that both distributions are normal, while the Wilcoxon Rank-Sum Test is a nonparametric test that does not assume the underlying distribution of the data. Here, we adopt the Wilcoxon Rank-Sum Test. The degree of difference is taken from the difference of observed values obtained from the data and the critical value of Wilcoxon Rank-Sum Test. The higher the difference between the two values, the more likely the two distributions are actually two distinct distributions. The machines, along with the corresponding measurements and process number, are ranked based on the degree of difference that they exhibit.

1.5. EXPERIMENTAL STUDY

We develop a prototype of the wafer fabrication mining system for initial exploration. The algorithms are implemented in Java, while the data preprocessing is

TABLE 1.1. Number of Points and Their Corresponding Run Time

Number of Points	Run Time (seconds)
325 (5%)	2,395.44
649 (10%)	12,453.28
974 (15%)	24,922.63
1,298 (20%)	51,112.13
1,623 (25%)	N.A.[a]
1,947 (30%)	N.A.
2,272 (35%)	N.A.
2,596 (40%)	N.A.

[a]N.A., not available.

done by combination of perl and bash scripts. Our programming environment is a unix server Sunfire and linux based cluster connected via GigaEthernet as well as Myrinet. The principal component analysis is performed on a Windows-based machine using MATLAB.

We obtain 4 months of wafer fabrication data from STMicroelectronics that is known to contain problems. The engineers have already performed independent investigations on the cause of the problem in this data. Their findings, however, is not revealed to us until we obtain our results from our experiments.

The size of the raw data is approximately 70 GB, out of which approximately 2.5 GB of data are extracted after the preprocessing step. The data consist of 6490 wafers, spread across 286 lots. The die level test has 14 bins. Each machine has on average 172 lots going through it. The length of measurements and operations for each lot is approximately 570, and there are 1482 ⟨machine, measurements, process number⟩ combinations.

1.5.1. Defect Detection

Since the clustering algorithm uses k-means as part of the solution, we first perform experiments on the actual production run data to determine the number of points to be maintained for the hierarchical clustering. We execute our algorithm 10 times and obtain the average. Table 1.1 presents the average running time of our algorithm by varying the number of points reduced. We note that 10% is a reasonable value for number of points to be kept. Although we can gain better speed using only 5%, we use 10% to maintain the accuracy of the heirarchical clustering.

We also examine the effect of different distance metrics. We applied the Manhattan distance as well as the Kullback–Leibler distance (Kullback and Leibler, 1951) and its variants such as Jeffrey's divergence and Jessen's difference (Taneja, 1995), along with the resistor-average distance (Johnson and Sinanović, 2001). The results can be seen in Table 1.2. The stopping criteria used are the separateness of the clusters—that is, if the intercluster distance is at

TABLE 1.2. Distance Metrics

Distance Metric	Number of Clusters Obtained
Kullback–Leibler distance	2
Jeffrey's divergence	326
Resistor-average distance	261
Jesse's difference	256
Euclidean	6
Manhattan	3

least as large as the intracluster distance. As we can see, the Kullback–Leibler distance and its variants are not suitable for this application because they result in either too few or too many clusters. Manhattan and Euclidean distance performs similarly. The Euclidean distance is used for the rest of the experiments.

Due to the randomness in choosing the initial start points in our clustering algorithms, we execute our program a number of times and observe the trends of the clustering results. We find that, on average, there are five to six clusters produced, with three clusters having large enough members (>30 wafers), while the rest are most likely outliers, containing only one to two wafers per cluster. Therefore, we only use the three large clusters and omit the smaller clusters. The reason for this phenomenon can be best explained using Figure 1.7, where we plot the cumulative distribution of the wafer's yield. We observe that there are roughly three prominent areas: those above 0.8, those below 0.1, and those between 0.55 and 0.8. There is a concentration of points above 0.8 with a peak at around 0.92, which corresponds to those wafers with high yield. As for the defect clusters, there are two regions where the points are concentrated: those below 0.1, which are referred as zero yield wafers (wafers with very low yield and thus considered to have zero yield), and those wafers with 0.55 to 0.8 yield. This agrees with the three clusters that we found.

The bin distribution of clusters from one of our runs is shown in Figure 1.8. The first three bins are those with 1 or 2 members, while the last three are the larger clusters. Cluster 5 is the high-yield cluster, as can be seen from its high proportion of Bin 1.

We verify our results with the engineers. They point out that the problem they are interested in is represented by one of the cluster—in particular, the cluster with medium yield. This cluster contains three bins where the problem is prominent. They are Bins 3, 5, and 9. The zoomed-in version of these bins are shown in Figure 1.8. Bin 3 is most affected by the problem, and Cluster 6 has a significant portion of its die count fall into this bin. Cluster 3, which has only one member, has a profile similar to that of Cluster 6 on these bins. However, there is a big difference in Bin 4 that leads to it not being combined into Cluster 6. Cluster 4 represents the zero-yield wafers as can be seen from its distribution in Bin 15, which is also the special bin to cater for untested dies. Overall, our

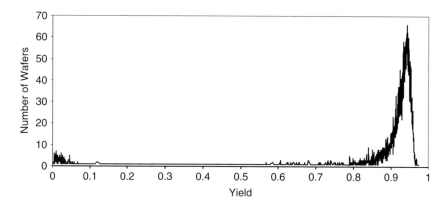

Figure 1.7. Yield plot of a wafer.

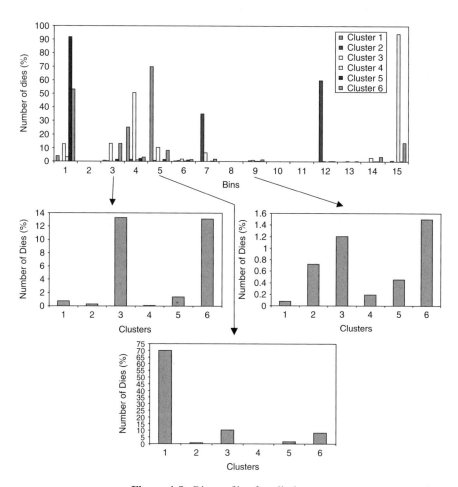

Figure 1.8. Bin profiles for all clusters.

defect identification has succeeded in identifying problematic wafers from their bin profiles as verified by the engineers.

In addition, we observe that it is important for the clustering algorithm to introduce the bias. Otherwise, the representatives will all come from the high-yield range, and we will miss the problem signature that the algorithm will consider as an outlier. This approach addresses the issue that we need to maintain sensitivity, yet at the same time efficiently zoom in to the right points.

1.5.2. Isolating Defect Source

Next, we focus our attention to determine the source of defects from the operational data. Since the problem has been found to be correlated to Cluster 6, we will describe our findings that are related to this cluster.

We use the filtering algorithm as discussed in Section 1.4.3, and we present the top 30% ⟨machine, process number⟩ list obtained for Cluster 6 to the engineers. We choose 30% since the list will include certain machines that are needed for several operations. The algorithm terminates when we have about 5 to 10 machines in the list.

An independent inspection that was carried out by the engineers confirmed that the source of the problem was due to an over-etching in the identified machine. In particular, one of the etch machines has a problem of over-etching the wafers throughout the end of February and March. Figure 1.9a shows the nitride residue

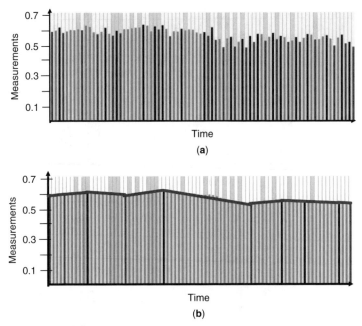

Figure 1.9. (a) Original thickness measure after etch process. (b) Smoothened thickness measure after etch process.

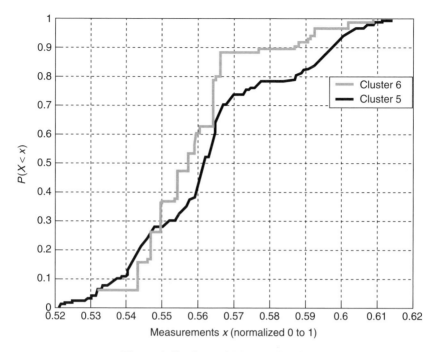

Figure 1.10. CDF of Clusters 5 and 6.

measurements of wafers, obtained after the etching process. The first half of the graph presents nitride measurements before the over-etching problem, and the second half of the graph presents nitride measurements after the over-etching problem occurred. The dark and light bars represent the change points detected. As we can see from Figure 1.9b, there is an obvious downward trend for the second half of the graph. This corresponds to thinner nitride residue observed after the etch process.

Figure 1.10 shows the difference in measurements of one of the listed machines for Cluster 5 (the good cluster) and Cluster 6 (the problematic cluster), respectively. It depicts the cumulative distribution function, cdf(x), which is the probability to observe a value less than x, that is, $P(X < x)$. We observe that for the same value of x (around 0.56 to 0.57), the cdf(x) for Cluster 6 is much higher than that of Cluster 5. This relates to the fact that Cluster 6 has a higher probability of having a value less than 0.57 than does Cluster 5. In other words, this machine is likely to be the source of the defects.

This study indicates that the filtering algorithm is able to (a) reduce the number of irrelevant features based on the variability of machine's measurements and (b) differentiate high-yield clusters from low-yield clusters. Furthermore, although we reduce the number of features used to 30% of the original number, we are able to identify the real cause of the defect. This filtering solution addresses the problem of small sample size. The weighting scheme bridges the data gap, and at the same it time considers as much data as possible to (a) maximize the number of data points that we can analyze and (b) derive a valid hypothesis.

1.6. CONCLUSION

In this chapter we have presented a framework to unify the various data-mining solutions for wafer manufacturing data. We have seen the complex wafer manufacturing process, and it is a challenge to mine wafer fabrication data: The small sample of operational data obtained from the fabrication process is high-dimensional, while the large amounts of final test data from the output of the fabrication process are low-dimensional.

We have designed a bin-profile-based defect detection method to discover problematic wafers. This method utilizes a two-phase clustering algorithm to efficiently group the defect wafers. This algorithm provides a speed-up over the traditional hierarchical agglomerative clustering at the cost of approximation for lower levels of the dendogram. We have also presented an area-sensitive sampling method to select initial starting points which introduces bias as to which local minima the k-means should reach in order to group points together. We have designed and implemented an efficient defect signature detection algorithm from the bin profile of the wafers.

We have also developed a domain-knowledge-aided feature filtering that is able to reduce 70% of the features, differentiate high-yield clusters from low-yield clusters, and yet retain the actual cause of problematic wafers. The experiment results indicate that data-mining techniques have the potential to help discover defective wafers as well as to identify the source of the problem. We have shown that the proposed approach is able to produce results much faster than the existing manual verification process.

Future works includes building the other components of the framework, as well as incorporating existing solutions such as combining bin profile defect detection with spatial signature of the wafers.

REFERENCES

Agrawal, R., and Srikant, R., Fast algorithms for mining association rules, in *Proceedings of the 20th VLDB Conference*, 1994.

Bertino, E., Catania, B., and Caglio, E., Applying data mining techniques to wafer manufacturing, *PKDD*, **1704** 41–50 (1999).

Bradley, P. S., Fayyad, U., and Reina, C., Initialization of iterative refinement clustering algorithms, in *Proceedings of ACM SIGKDD*, 1998a.

Bradley, P. S., Fayyad, U., and Reina, C., Scaling Clustering Algorithms to Large Databases, in *Proceedings of ACM SIGKDD*, 1998b.

Dash, M., Efficient Clustering for Knowledge Discovery in Large High-Dimensional Databases, Ph.D. Thesis, School of Computing, NUS, 2002.

Dash, M., and Liu, H., Feature selection for classification, *Intelligent Data Analysis* **1**, 1997.

Dash, M., Tan, K.-L., and Liu, H., Efficient yet accurate clustering, in *Proceedings of the 1st IEEE International Conference on Data Mining*, 2001.

Devore, J. L., *Probability and Statistics for Engineering and the Sciences*, 4th edition, Wadsworth, Belmont, CA, 1995.

Dubes, R. C., and Jain, A. K., *Algorithms for Clustering Data*, Prentice-Hall, Englewood Cliffs, NJ, 1988.

Ester, M., Kriegel, H-P., Sander, J., and Xu, X. A density based algorithm for discovering clusters in large spatial databases with noise, in *Proceedings of ACM SIGKDD*, pp. 226–231, 1996.

Fountain, T., Dietterich, T., and Sudyka, B., Mining IC test data to optimize VLSI testing, in *Proceedings of ACM SIGKDD*, 2000.

François, B., and Yves, C., Improving Yield in IC Manufacturing by Statistical Analysis of a Large Database, http://www.micromagazine.com/archive/99/03/bergeret.html, 1999.

Frawley, W. J., Piatetsky-Shapiro, G., and Matheus, C., Knowledge discovery in databases: An overview, in *Knowledge Discovery in Databases*, AAAI Press/MIT Press, Cambridge, MA, pp. 1–30, 1991.

Gardner, M., and Bieker, J., Data mining solves tough semiconductor manufacturing problems, in *Proceedings of ACM SIGKDD*, 2000.

Guha, S., Rastogi, R., and Shim, K., *CURE: An efficient clustering algorithm for large databases*, in *Proceedings of ACM SIGMOD*, 1998.

Hotelling, H. Analysis of complex statistical variables into principal components, *Journal of Educational Psychology* **24**, 417–441 (1993).

Jain, A. K., Murty, M. N., and Flynn, P. J., Data clustering: A review, *ACM Computing Surveys* **31**(3), 264–323 (1999).

John, G. H., Kohavi, R., and Pfleger, K., Irrelevant features and the subset selection problem, in *Proceedings of the Eleventh International Conference on Machine Learning*, 1994.

Johnson, D. H., and Sinanović, S., Symmetrizing the Kullback–Leibler distance, *IEEE Transactions on Information Theory*, 2001.

Kittler, R., and Wang, W., Data mining for yield improvements, in *International Conference on Modeling and Analysis of Semiconductor Manufacturing*, 2000.

Kohonen, K., *Self-Organizing Maps*, Springer-Verlag, Berlin, 1995.

Kullback, S., and Leibler, R. A., On information and sufficiency, *Annals of Math. Statistics* **22**, 79–86 (1951).

Kusiak, A., Decomposition in data mining: An industrial case study, *IEEE Transactions on Electronic Packaging Manufacturing* **23**(4), 238–283 (2000).

Linde, Y., Buzo, A., and Gray, R. M., An algorithm for vector quantizer design, *IEEE Transactions on Communications* **28**, 84–95 (1980).

Liu, B., Hsu, W., and Ma, Y., Integrating classification and association rule mining, in *Proceedings of ACM SIGKDD*, 1998.

Lloyd, S. P., Least squares quantization in PCM, *IEEE Transactions on Information Theory* **28**, 127–135 (1982).

MacQueen, J., Some methods for classification and analysis of multivariate observations, in *Proceedings of the 5th Berkeley Symposium on Mathematical Statistics and Probability*, 1967.

Matoušek, J., On approximate geometric k-clustering, *Discrete and Computational Geometry* **24**, 61–84 (2000).

Mitchell, T., *Machine Learning*, McGraw-Hill, New York, 1997.

Montgomery, D., *Introduction to Statistical Quality Control*, John Wiley & Sons, New York, 1991.

Povinelli, R. J., Time Series Data Mining: Identifying Temporal Patterns for Characterization and Prediction of Time Series Events, Ph.D. Dissertation, Marquette University, Milwaukee, WI, 1999.

Quadrillion Co., Semiconductor Yield Enhancement Software, http://www.quadrillion.com, 2003.

Quinlan, R., *c4.5: Program for Machine Learning*, Morgan Kaufmann, San Mateo, CA, 1992.

Taneja, I. J., New developments in generalized information measures, in *Advances in Imaging and Electron Physics*, Vol. 91, Academic Press, New York, 1995.

Tavalera, L., Dynamic feature selection in incremental hierarchical clustering, in *Proceedings of European Conference on Machine Learning*, 2000.

Tobin, K. W., Karnowski, T. P., Gleason, S. S., Jensen, D., and Lakhani, F., Using historical wafermap data for automated yield analysis, *Journal of Vacuum Science Technology* (1999).

Zhang, T., Ramakrishnan, R., and Livny, M., BIRCH: An efficient clustering algorithm for large databases, in *Proceedings of ACM SIGMOD*, 1996.

2

DAMAGE DETECTION EMPLOYING DATA-MINING TECHNIQUES

A. Lazarevic, R. Kanapady, C. Kamath, V. Kumar, and K. Tamma

2.1. INTRODUCTION

The phenomenon of damage in structures includes (a) localized softening or cracks in a certain neighborhood of a structural component due to high operational loads or (b) the presence of flaws due to manufacturing defects. Methods that detect damage in the structure are useful for nondestructive evaluations that are typically employed in agile manufacturing and rapid prototyping systems. In addition, with the increasing demand for safety and reliability of aerospace, mechanical, and civilian structures (see Figure 2.1), damage detection techniques will be critical to reliable prediction of damage to structural systems such as bridges, skyscrapers, aircraft structures, and various structures deployed in space. Structural damage results in (a) changes in structural responses such as static deformations and (b) dynamic characteristics such as natural frequency and the mode shapes. Although rigorous damage models exist, in this chapter we primarily focus on the aspect of structural damage that is assumed to be associated with structural stiffness as a reduction in Young's modulus or modulus of elasticity (E) (Szewczyk and Hajela, 1994). In these situations, there are three levels of damage identification: (1) recognition—qualitative indication that damage might be present in the structure; (2) localization—information about the probable position of the damage in the structure; and (3) assessment—estimate of the extent of severity of the damage in the structure.

A practical damage assessment methodology must be capable of predicting changes in the structural stiffness as a function of changes in structural response and dynamic characteristics (Wu et al., 1992). Standard analytical techniques

Next Generation of Data-Mining Applications. Edited by Kantardzic and Zurada
ISBN 0-471-65605-4 © 2005 the Institute of Electrical and Electronics Engineers, Inc.

Figure 2.1. Damage detection for aerospace, mechanical, or civilian structures.

employ mathematical models to approximate the relationships between specific damage conditions and changes in the structural response or dynamic properties. Such relationships can be computed by solving a class of so-called inverse problems (Chen and Bicanoc, 2000; Santos et al., 2000). Overall, the major drawbacks of the existing approaches are as follows: (i) A large amount of modal information such as eigenvalues and eigenvectors associated with the damaged structure has to be employed to identify the damage in the structure accurately; (ii) the more sophisticated methods involve computationally cumbersome system solvers that are typically solved by singular value decomposition techniques, nonnegative least-squares techniques, bounded variable least squares techniques, and so on; and (iii) all of these computationally intensive procedures need to be repeated for any newly available measured test data for a given structure. Hence there exists a need to explore alternative, more computationally efficient and accurate approaches for the damage identification problem. An immediate alternative is to design data-mining techniques whose data models enable the real-time prediction and identification of damage for newly available test data once a sufficiently accurate model is developed from the training data.

Recent work by a number of researchers (Szewczyk and Hajela, 1994; Xu et al., 1992; Zhao et al., 1998; Rix, 1994; Tsou and Shen, 1993) has shown that neural networks may provide a potential solution to this class of problems and predict damage using static displacements and dynamic characteristics. However, these studies are restricted to very small models with a small number of target variables (order of 10). The development of a predictive model that can correctly identify the location and severity of damage in practical large-scale complex structures using this direct approach can be a considerable challenge. Increased geometric complexity of the structure causes an increase in the number of target variables, thus resulting in a very large dataset that are high-dimensional and highly heterogeneous in nature. Since the number of prediction models that need to be built for each continuous target variable increases, the number of training data records required for effective training of artificial neural network (ANN) grows arbitrarily. This growth will increase not only the time required for training ANN but also the time required for data generation because each damage state (data record) requires an eigensolver to generate natural frequency and mode shapes of the structure. That is, if p is the number of target variables (number of finite elements) and each target variable has Z sampling points, the size of the whole dataset is Z^p requiring Z^p number of eigenanalysis. The earlier direct approach, employed by a number of researchers, required the prediction of the material property, namely, the Young's modulus considering all the elements in the domain individually or simultaneously. This approach does not scale to situations in which thousands of elements are present in the complex geometry of the structure or when multiple elements in the structure have been damaged simultaneously.

Therefore, some important considerations are of interest in this research to include addressing the issues pertaining to scalability of data-mining modeling when realistic and practical structural systems are involved. Therefore, we propose the notion of employing hierarchical substructures or domain decomposition to at least first enable the identification of the general subdomain encompassing the actual location and to subsequently facilitate the prediction of a more localized region within the subdomain. As a long-term goal, this also raises the question of scalability of the analysis as the problem size increases.

To address such situations, we propose the notion of hierarchically dividing the structure into substructures; and instead of predicting damage in every finite element, a model is built to first predict the presence of damage in identified substructure(s). Subsequently, it is of interest to zoom into a localized region within given substructure(s). This hierarchical approach termed here as substructuring also significantly reduces the number of target variables to foster achieving scalability of analysis. Furthermore, specific structural members or elements within the substructure(s), which have been damaged, can be subsequently identified. In effect, the substructuring approach zooms into the localized damaged zone instead of directly identifying the damaged elements in the structure in a single step. The substructuring approach is shown graphically in Figure 2.2. A numerical example analysis on an electric transmission tower frame is presented to demonstrate the effectiveness of the proposed method.

In this chapter we highlight the results due to existing data-mining techniques such as ANN for predicting the damage in the large-scale complex structures followed by our proposed data-mining approach to overcome the limitations and drawbacks. The proposed technique is based on a hierarchical clustering approach consisting of three phases that are applied recursively: partitioning, localization, and prediction. The effectiveness of the proposed approach is demonstrated

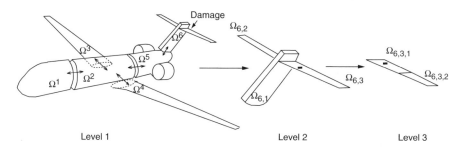

Figure 2.2. The substructuring approach by localizing to the damaged zone.

by applying it to the scientific simulation datasets (finite element analysis) that correspond to the damage prediction in complex structures as an illustration. Our experiments performed on the large-scale complex structures indicate that the proposed method is computationally more effective and more accurate than the straightforward approach of predicting each target variable individually using global prediction models.

2.2. PROBLEM DESCRIPTION

It is well known in mechanical engineering that each mechanical structure consists of several hundreds or even thousands of structure elements. The main goal of damage prediction models is to predict whether the damage exists, what structure elements are damaged, and what is the intensity of the damage. The simplest method is to construct a data-mining model that can predict the material property, namely, the Young's modulus of elasticity (E) for each structure element in a mechanical structure as a function of its natural frequencies. However, the direct method may be extremely time-consuming for complex structures with a very large number of structure elements. However, instead of predicting the Young's modulus of each finite element, the proposed approach first predicts the existence of the damage in the substructure of the mechanical structure and then identifies the intensity of the damage.

Predicting damages in mechanical structures using data-mining techniques requires the following steps for training data generation:

- *Feature Construction*:   To build the right data-mining model, it is important to construct a useful set of features that will successfully characterize the damage states, capture the physics of the problem at hand, and be independent of operational loads for a given structure. Since natural frequencies and mode shapes of the structure meet these criteria, they are selected as useful features. This selection is made due to the following considerations: (i) These quantities can be measured from the actual physical structures, (ii) the natural frequencies represent global behaviors of the structure, while the mode vectors represent the local characteristics of the structure, and (iii) the number of features can be limited to very few low natural frequencies and mode shapes compared to the number of degrees of freedom in the structure. In this study, however, the selection of features is limited to natural frequencies only.

- *Data Generation*:   The data for building prediction models are generated by using a typical finite element analysis code. The typical data layout is shown in Table 2.1, where dataset D contains data records $d_1, d_2, \ldots, d_N$, $i = 1, \ldots, N$. Each data record d_i is described with the pair $\{\mathbf{f}, \mathbf{E}\}$, where $\mathbf{f} = \{f_1, f_2, \ldots, f_m\}$ is the feature set that corresponds to the set of n natural frequencies, while $\mathbf{E} = \{E_1, E_2, \ldots, E_n\}$ is the set of target variables that represent the Youngs's modulus of elasticity for all n finite elements.

TABLE 2.1. A Typical Input to Data-Mining Model

Data Records	Features				Target Variables			
	f_1	f_2	...	f_m	E_1	E_2	...	E_n
1	72.833	151.67	...	213.45	$0.5E$	E	...	E
2	73.45	152.56	...	213.65	$0.6E$	E	...	E
...	...	...	...	...	...	...	...	...
N	74.01	153.01	...	214.21	E	E	...	E

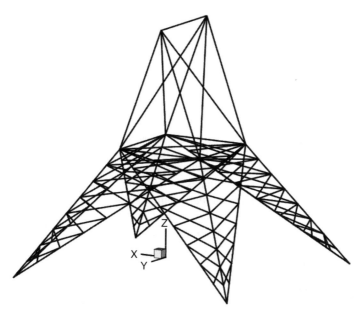

Figure 2.3. Three-dimensional model of electric transmission tower discretized using beam elements.

Each data record d_i in the dataset D pertains to a failure state, where the failure state is simulated by failing either one (single element failure) or more elements (multiple element failure) in the structure and performing the eigenanalysis of the finite element model. The elements are failed in steps (e.g., each element is failed by reducing **E** from the base value of E to E' in steps of ΔE, where Δ is a small fraction).

The electric transmission tower shown in Figure 2.3 and studied in Sandhu et al. (2001) was modified to investigate the substructuring approach. The modified electric transmission tower had 312 elements, which were then divided in five different substructures (four legs and the head of the transmission tower) for illustration (Figure 2.3). To study the effectiveness of our previous substructuring approach, four cases were considered:

- *Single Substructure—Single Element Failure*: Only a single element in the structure is failed.
- *Single Substructure—Multiple Element Failure*: Contiguous multiple elements of the same substructure are failed.
- *Multiple Substructure—Single Element Failure*: A more general case in which two elements belonging to different substructures are failed.
- *Multiple Substructure—Multiple Element Failure*: Most general case in which contiguous multiple elements belonging to different substructures are failed.

The substructuring approach has shown very good results for first three simpler cases. In this approach, the training data were used to train the first-level neural network classification model to predict the failure of logical substructures identified using background knowledge (Figure 2.3), instead of predicting the failure of individual elements. In addition, a hierarchical approach was also proposed to further zoom into the damaged area. This involved training yet another level of neural network classification model to predict the failure of subdivisions of the substructure(s) (Figure 2.3). Using this procedure, we attempted to converge to the elemental level of the structure, which is also the smallest substructure. However, manual partitioning of mechanical structures is not always straightforward since it requires exact coordinates of structure elements and the background knowledge. In addition, the manual partitioning sometimes does not give satisfactory results from second and higher levels of partitioning. In order to overcome these limitations, in addition to the limitations of a direct approach, in the case of single failure situations in the case of the second and higher levels of partitioning and for the case of multiple element failures in different locations in the structure, a hierarchical localized clustering-based approach for partitioning the structures and substructures at different levels is proposed, which is described next.

2.3. METHODOLOGY

In general, clustering algorithms divide data into meaningful or useful groups, called clusters. The goal of clustering is that the objects in a group be more similar (or related) to one another than to the objects in other groups. The greater the similarity (or homogeneity) within a group, and the greater the difference between groups, the "better" or more distinct the clustering is. In many applications, clusters are not well defined and not well separated from one another and typically depend on the user feedback. Nonetheless, most clustering algorithms search for nonoverlapping groups, although there are fuzzy clustering methods that allow objects to partially belong to several groups.

The proposed hierarchical localized clustering-based approach simplifies the prediction process of multiple elements that are failed within the complex mechanical structure. The simplification is performed by intelligent partitioning of the complex structure into several logical substructures using clustering algorithm and then by identifying the substructure (substructures) with the damaged elements using classification model. If multiple elements within multiple substructures are failed at the same moment, then it is possible that several substructures with the damage may be identified. This partitioning of the entire mechanical structure followed by identification of a damaged substructure (or substructures) corresponds to the first level of partitioning. The further localization of damaged elements is achieved by performing partitioning of all the identified substructures with the damage elements and by identifying smaller substructures with damaged elements. When the damaged substructure, identified at further levels of partitioning, is small enough (contains only a few structure elements), the direct approach can be applied only to the identified structure with the damage and used to predict the intensity of the damage for each element in the particular substructure. Therefore, instead of predicting intensity of the damage, typically for a few hundred or a few thousands structure elements from the complex structure, our approach needs to predict the intensity of the damage only for a few elements within the identified substructure with the damage.

Similar methodology has been shown to be successful in several data-mining applications. Recently, a mixture of experts' methods (Jacobs et al., 1991; Jordan and Jacobs, 1994) has gained a lot of attention for dealing with highly heterogeneous datasets. In mixture of experts, a function, which has to be learned, is divided into subspaces that are processed by different "expert" prediction models. Each expert's task is simpler and their generalization is expected to improve over a single model, since dividing up a function avoids undesirable talk between regions within it, irrespective of how representative a training sample is. A similar approach was also used in spatial domain, where the DBSCAN clustering algorithm (Sander et al., 1998) was used to partition the spatial fields into several similar regions and then to build localized regression models on each of them in order to predict the wheat yield (Lazarevic and Obradovic, 2002; Lazarevic et al., 2000). However, in all these methods, only one-level partitioning was employed in order to build more specialized models that will focus on specific regions of the entire spatial field.

Several clustering algorithms from the CLUTO clustering package (Zhao and Karypis, 2002) were employed to partition the mechanical structures into substructures. These clustering algorithms include k-way clustering algorithms with repeated bisections, direct k-way clustering, agglomerative clustering, and the graph partitioning clustering approach (Zhao and Karypis, 2002). In the k-way clustering with repeated bisections, clusters are obtained by performing a sequence of $k - 1$ repeated bisections. In this approach, the matrix is first clustered into two groups, then one of these groups is selected and bisected further. This process continues until the desired number of clusters is found. During each step, the cluster is bisected so that the resulting 2-way clustering solution optimizes a particular clustering criterion function. The direct k-way clustering algorithm simultaneously finds all k clusters. In general, computing a k-way clustering directly is slower than clustering via repeated bisections. In terms of quality, for reasonably small values of k (usually less than 10–20), the direct k-way clustering algorithm leads to better clusters than those obtained via repeated bisections. However, as k increases, the repeated-bisecting approach tends to be better than direct clustering. In agglomerative clustering approach, the desired clusters are computed using the agglomerative paradigm whose goal is to locally optimize (minimize or maximize) a particular clustering criterion function. The solution is obtained by stopping the agglomeration process when k clusters are left. Finally, in the graph partitioning method, the desired k-way clustering solution is computed by first modeling the objects using a nearest-neighbor graph (each object becomes a vertex, and each object is connected to its most similar other objects) and then splitting the graph into k-clusters using a min-cut graph-partitioning algorithm.

Once the substructures with the similar elements are identified, the next step involves the prediction of the existence of the damage within each of the discovered substructures. If there is at least one element within the substructure that has less than a 0.97 value of original value for E, which means that there is damage in the specific substructure, and then the corresponding data record is assigned a "damage class" label. Otherwise, the "nondamage" class label is assigned to a considered data record. For such created datasets with the labels, we perform classification of failure within a structure. As classification models, we have used multilayer (two-layered) feedforward neural network models with the number of output nodes equal to the number of classes, where the predicted class is from the output with the largest response. The number of hidden neurons was changed from 20 to 50 depending on the number of input attributes. The more input attributes, the more hidden neurons were used in the neural network model. We have used two learning algorithms: resilient propagation (Riedmiller and Braun, 1993) and Levenberg–Marquardt (Hagan and Menhaj, 1994). If there is damage within some particular substructure, further localizing of the damage within that substructure using partitioning. Finally, when the substructure contains the sufficiently small elements per substructure, the direct approach can be applied to predict the intensity of the damage for all the elements within the substructure.

2.4. EXPERIMENTAL RESULTS

Experiments were performed on the dataset that corresponds to the most general case of failure: multiple substructure with multiple elements failure. The training and testing dataset of 1030 records is generated by failing elements connected to two different nodes in different substructures by a random amount. In essence, elements in a specific area in two substructures are failed. Earlier experiments have shown that in this most general case, where the multiple elements in the structure are damaged, the direct approach totally breaks down and leads to an inaccurate model (Sandhu et al., 2001, 2002).

The results of applying the classification neural network models for predicting the existence of the damage within the substructures using a manual

TABLE 2.2. The Manual Substructuring Direct Approach Employing Neural Networks for Five Substructures by Partitioning Electric Transmission Tower Based on the Physical Consideration, Namely, Four Legs and a Head of the Structure

	Leg 1	Leg 2	Leg 3	Leg 4	Head
Accuracy	90.74	88.73	89.96	88.54	88.41
Recall for nondamage	98.27	25.56	93.19	94.35	93.15
Recall for damage	72.44	97.07	81.98	75.78	79.89

substructuring approach is given in Table 2.2. The prediction performance of neural network models is measured by computing the overall classification accuracy, as well as by computing the partial accuracies (recalls) for each class (damage class versus nondamage class). In order to alleviate the effect of neural network instability in our experiments, the prediction accuracy for each substructure is averaged over 20 trials of the neural network learning algorithm; that is, the neural network classification models are constructed 20 times, and accuracies achieved for all 20 trials are averaged.

From Table 2.2 it can be observed that by employing the manual substructuring approach, a model could be built to correctly predict which substructure had failed. Again the Young's modulus of the most badly failed element could not be accurately predicted using the above-mentioned number of records.

The experiments with the automated partitioning method were performed on the same datasets as for manual partitioning. The agglomerative approach within the CLUTO clustering algorithm (Zhao and Karypis, 2002) has discovered five well-balanced clusters C_i, $i = 1, \ldots, 5$. Figure 2.4 shows these five identified substructures S_i, whose sizes are 37, 174, 26, 35, and 40 structure elements. The results of applying the classification neural network models for predicting the existence of the damage within the substructures identified using our proposed automated substructuring approach is given in Table 2.3. The prediction performance of neural network models is measured by computing the overall classification accuracy, as well as by computing the partial accuracies (recalls) for each class (damage class versus nondamage class).

It is apparent from Table 2.3 that the proposed partitioning approach achieved similar prediction performance when identifying the existence of damage within discovered substructures. It can be observed that for two substructures the classification accuracies were better for automated than for the manual partitioning approach, while for the other three substructures the results for the automated partitioning approach were slightly worse than those for the manual partitioning approach.

It is interesting to note that both approaches failed when the direct approach was applied after the first level of partitioning. Namely, if it was predicted that there is damage within some specific substructure, predicting the real intensity of the damage for some of the structure elements from that substructure was

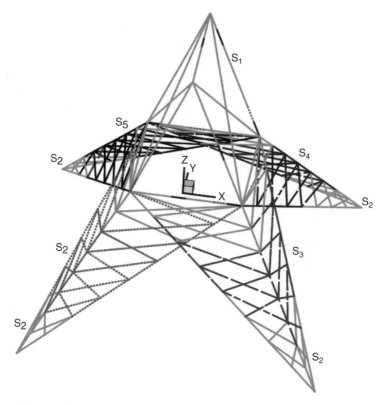

Figure 2.4. Illustrative five substructures at the first level of clustering.

TABLE 2.3. Results for the First Level of Partitioning Employing the Proposed Algorithm *Substructure*

	Sub-structure 1	Sub-structure 2	Sub-structure 3	Sub-structure 4	Sub-structure 5
Accuracy	87.72	89.51	89.06	92.17	87.57
Recall for nondamage	95.05	29.88	93.45	96.45	94.36
Recall for damage	70.22	97.08	79.27	82.49	76.17

not successful for either partitioning approach. However, the number of elements needed to be predicted was significantly smaller than using the original direct approach for all the structured elements from the entire structure.

In order to further reduce the number of structure elements that needs to be predicted, we performed an additional level of partitioning. Each of the clusters C_i identified at the first partitioning level was further partitioned into clusters

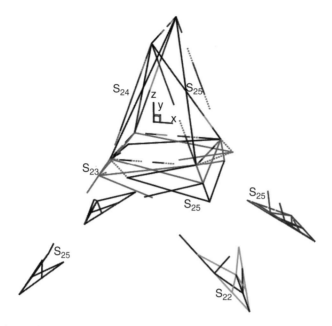

Figure 2.5. Substructures in the second substructure of the first level.

C_{ij}. The number of clusters at the second level varied, but in general it was kept to 5. Figure 2.5 shows the substructures of the biggest substructure identified at the first level of partitioning (substructure S_2). Table 2.4 reports the prediction performance for each of the substructures S_{ij} at the second partitioning level.

Our experimental results for classifying the damage within the substructures identified at the second level of partitioning using clustering have indicated that there is a slight decrease in overall classification accuracy. Our previous experimental results (Sandhu et al., 2002) for the manual partitioning approach have shown that the decrease in the prediction performance at the second level of partitioning was significant comparing to the drop observed for the automated partitioning approach.

Since most of the substructures identified at the second level of partitioning are still too large for direct approach, we performed the third level of partitioning. Since the number of substructures at the third level is extremely high, we do not report all classification accuracies for all the substructures, but we report their overall classification accuracy. Figure 2.6 illustrates the substructures identified at the third level by partitioning the biggest substructure identified at the second level of partitioning (substructure S_{25}). Our experimental results again confirmed that the overall classification accuracy is preserved even in the third level of substructuring. Due to the large number of possible substructures for which the classification accuracy may be computed, Table 2.5 reports the classification accuracy only for the worst case (the substructure with the worst classification accuracies from the second level of partitioning).

TABLE 2.4. Results for the Second Level of Partitioning Employing the Proposed Algorithm

Structure S_1	Sub-structure S_{11}	Sub-structure S_{12}	Sub-structure S_{13}	Sub-structure S_{14}	Sub-structure S_{15}
Accuracy	100	87.40	87.40	83.33	78.05
Recall for nondamage	100	89.47	88.88	81.48	77.48
Recall for damage	NA^a	82.67	76.67	84.78	78.52

Structure S_2	Sub-structure S_{21}	Sub-structure S_{22}	Sub-structure S_{23}	Sub-structure S_{24}	Sub-structure S_{25}
Accuracy	73.75	83.74	92.2	74.52	79.23
Recall for nondamage	80.26	89.03	94.97	81.37	28.5
Recall for damage	62.77	67.95	82.29	66.75	95.38

Structure S_3	Sub-structure S_{31}	Sub-structure S_{32}	Sub-structure S_{33}	Sub-structure S_{34}	Sub-structure S_{35}
Accuracy	88.41	82.25	77.29	91.78	79.23
Recall for nondamage	94.54	71.25	82.99	92.86	84.28
Recall for damage	41.67	86.59	65.00	90.12	62.5

Structure S_4	Sub-structure S_{41}	Sub-structure S_{42}	Sub-structure S_{43}	Sub-structure S_{44}	Sub-structure S_{45}
Accuracy	81.41	95.78	76.06	83.57	80.75
Recall for nondamage	72.91	98.53	82.35	90.16	80.62
Recall for damage	88	33.33	70.25	43.33	80.95

Structure S_5	Sub-structure S_{51}	Sub-structure S_{52}	Sub-structure S_{53}	Sub-structure S_{54}	Sub-structure S_{55}
Accuracy	100	71.11	87.78	80.0	90.0
Recall for nondamage	100	69.44	93.51	73.08	93.75
Recall for damage	NA	72.22	53.85	82.81	80.77

^{a}NA, not available.

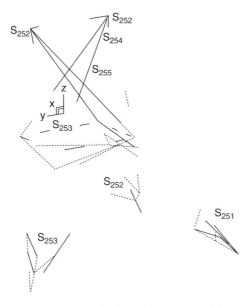

Figure 2.6. Substructures in the fifth substructure of the second level.

TABLE 2.5. Results of the Worst-Case Scenario for the Third Level of Partitioning Employing the Proposed Algorithm *Substructure*

	Sub-structure S_{251}	Sub-structure S_{252}	Sub-structure S_{253}	Sub-structure S_{254}	Sub-structure S_{255}
Accuracy	74.69	86.74	92.77	85.54	87.95
Recall for nondamage	87.69	93.33	94.81	86.84	96.88
Recall for damage	27.78	25.00	66.7	71.43	57.89

2.5. CONCLUSIONS

This chapter presented a general framework for the efficient prediction of multiple target variables from high-dimensional and heterogeneous datasets using the hierarchical clustering approach. This approach is effective where there is a natural relationship among target variables, which was effectively addressed by hierarchical partitioning approach using a different set of features. The effectiveness of the approach was demonstrated on the problem of damage detection in very large and complex mechanical structures. Performed experiments indicate that the proposed approach can be successfully used to predict the presence of damage within the structure, as well as the intensity of the damage in any of the several hundred structure elements that served as target variables. Furthermore, we have shown that the proposed approach is computationally more efficient and more accurate than (a) the direct approach that was earlier used for damage detection and (b) the manual partitioning approach.

This chapter makes several contributions that may be of particular interest for the data-mining community. First, to the best of our knowledge, this is one of the first successful attempts to deal with predicting very large number of target variables simultaneously. Second, the proposed algorithm achieves a reduction in both data records and the number of used features, which is of great importance for data mining, since learning a monolithic prediction model from very large datasets can be prohibitively slow. Finally, our proposed approach improves the prediction accuracy in the damage detection domain using a nondestructive paradigm, which is of great practical importance.

Although our experiments have provided evidence that the proposed method can be successful for prediction of multiple target variables, future work is needed to fully characterize this problem, especially in more complex scenarios involving, for example, multiple failures of elements within the structure. Special attention needs to be devoted to more accurate prediction of continuous target variables and improving the quality of our clustering algorithms. We also plan to investigate the applicability of the curds and whey algorithm (Breiman and Friedman, 1997), as well as other existing approaches in this area for damage detection problem. Finally, datasets with multiple target variables from different domains will be used to validate the effectiveness of the proposed hierarchical approach.

ACKNOWLEDGMENTS

The authors are pleased to acknowledge support in part by the Department of Energy LLNL B512340 and by the Army High-Performance Computing Research Center (AHPCRC) under the auspices of the Department of the Army, Army Research Laboratory (ARL) under contract number DAAD19-01-2-0014. The content does not necessarily reflect the position or the policy of the government, and no official endorsement should be inferred. Additional thanks are also due to S. S. Sandhu and M. Steinbach for related technical discussions. Access to computing facilities was provided by the AHPCRC and the Minnesota Supercomputing Institute (MSI).

REFERENCES

Breiman, L., and Friedman, J. H., Predicting multivariate responses in multiple linear regression, *Journal of the Royal Statistical Society, Series B* **59**, 3–54 (1997).

Chen, H., and Bicanoc, N., Assessment of damage in continuum structures based in incomplete modal information, *Computers and Structures* **74**, 559–570 (2000).

Hagan, M., and Menhaj, M., Training feedforward networks with the Marquardt algorithm, *IEEE Transactions on Neural Networks* **5**, 989–993 (1994).

Jacobs, R. A., Jordan, M. I., Nowlan, S. J., and Hinton, G. E., Adaptive mixtures of local experts, *Neural Computation* **3**(1), 79–87 (1991).

Jordan, M. I., and Jacobs, R. A., Hierarchical mixtures of experts and the EM algorithm, *Neural Computation* **6**(2), 181–214 (1994).

Lazarevic, A., and Obradovic, Z., Knowledge discovery in multiple spatial databases, *Journal of Neural Computing and Applications* **10**, 339–350 (2002).

Lazarevic, A., Pokrajac, D., and Obradovic, Z., Distributed clustering and local regression for knowledge discovery in multiple spatial databases, in *Proceedings 8th European Symposium on Artificial Neural Networks*, Bruges, Belgium, pp. 129–134, April 2000.

Riedmiller, M., and Braun, T., A direst adaptive method for faster backpropagation learning: The RPROP algorithm, in *Proceedings of the IEEE International Conference on Neural Networks*, San Francisco, 1993.

Rix, G. J., Interpretation of nondestructive integrity tests using artificial neural networks, in *Structure Congress 12*, ASCE, Reston VA, pp. 1246–1351, 1994.

Sander, J., Ester, M., Kriegel, H. P., and Xu, X., Density-based clustering in spatial databases: The algorithm GDBSCAN and its applications, *Data Mining and Knowledge Discovery* **2**(2), 169–194 (1998).

Sandhu, S. S., Kanapady, R., Tamma, K., Kamath, C., and Kumar, V., Damage prediction and estimation in structural mechanics based on data mining, in *Proceedings of the Seventh ACM SIGKDD International Conference on Knowledge Discovery and Data Mining/Fourth Workshop on Mining Scientific Datasets*, San Francisco, August 26–29, 2001.

Sandhu, S. S., Kanapady, R., Tamma, K. K., Kamath, C., and Kumar, V., A substructuring approach via data mining for damage prediction and estimation in complex structures, in *SIAM International Conference on Data Mining*, Arlington, VA, 2002.

Santos, J., Soares, C. M., Soares, C. A., and Pina, H., A damage identification numerical model based on the sensitivity of the orthogonality conditions and least squares estimators, *Computers and Structures* **78**, 283–291 (2000).

Szewczyk, Z. P., and Hajela, P., Damage detection in structures based on feature sensitive neural networks, *Journal of Computation in Civil Engineering, ASCE* **8**(2), 163–179 (1994).

Tsou, P., and Shen, M., Structural damage detection and identification using neural network, in *Proceedings 34th AIAA/ASME/ASCEAHS/ASC*, Structural Dynamics and Materials Conference, AIAA/ASME Adaptive Structure Forum, Pt. 5, 1993.

Wu, X., Ghaboussi, J., and Garrett, J. H., Use of neural networks in detection of structural damage, *Computers and Structures* **42**(4), 649–659 (1992).

Zhao, Y., and Karypis, G., *Criterion Functions for Document Clustering Experiments and Analysis*, Army High Performance Computing Research Center (AHPCRC) Technical Report #01-40, 2002.

Zhao, J., Ivan, J. N., and DeWolf, J., Structural damage detection using artificial neural network, *Journal of Infrastructure Systems* **4**(3), 93–101 (1998).

3

DATA PROJECTION TECHNIQUES AND THEIR APPLICATION IN SENSOR ARRAY DATA PROCESSING

LI YANG

3.1. INTRODUCTION

How to reduce the dimensionality of high-dimensional data is a key issue for data preprocessing in data-mining applications. It plays an important role in visual data exploration to understand data and to choose data-mining techniques for further processing. Dimensionality reduction has also important applications in other areas such as information classification, indexing, and information retrieval.

The application discussed in this chapter deals with the preprocessing and dimensionality reduction of data collected by odorant sensor arrays in electronic noses. To recognize odors of various chemicals, an electronic nose has to be trained by being exposed to many samples of chemicals. Data collected from each exposure is a vector of real numbers recording responses of all sensors to the sample. The objective of data mining in this application is to train a nose with samples of known chemicals so that, later on, the nose can recognize smells when it is presented to samples of unknown chemicals. This is a typical problem of clustering and classification in data mining.

Many clustering (Jain and Dubes, 1988; Jain et al., 1999; Kaufman and Rousseeuw, 1990) and classification algorithms (Weiss and Kulikowski, 1991; Michalski et al., 1998) could be used in this typical application. The clustering algorithms include the partition-based algorithms (McQueen, 1967; Ng and Han, 1994), agglomerative hierarchical algorithms (Kaufman and Rousseeuw, 1990; Zhang et al., 1996; Guha et al., 1998; Karypis et al., 1999), density-based algorithms (Ester et al., 1996; Ankerst et al., 1999), grid-based algorithms (Wang

Next Generation of Data-Mining Applications. Edited by Kantardzic and Zurada
ISBN 0-471-65605-4 © 2005 the Institute of Electrical and Electronics Engineers, Inc.

et al., 1997; Sheikholeslami et al., 1998; Agrawal et al., 1998), and various model-based algorithms (Shavlik and Dietterich, 1990; Kohonen, 1997). Classification algorithms that can be used include decision trees (Quinlan, 1993; Breiman et al., 1984), Bayesian classifiers (Duda and Hart, 1972; Weiss and Kulikowski, 1991), neural networks (Chauvin and Rumelhart, 1995), and those approaches (Lent et al., 1997; Liu et al., 1998) derived from association rule mining. Although there are so many choices of data-mining algorithms, no algorithm is superior over all others for all types of data and application domains. More importantly, many practitioners would agree that the final success of a data-mining project depends more on how the data are preprocessed rather than on which data-mining algorithm is used. From a practical point of view, data preprocessing is a determinant step for the success of a data-mining project.

One important task in data preprocessing is dimensionality reduction. In the application presented in this chapter, for example, it is reasonable to assume that different odorant sensors that are made of different polymers produce data that are correlated with each other. It is thus the task of dimensionality reduction to find these correlations and to extract independent features of data for further processing.

Many methods can be applied for dimensionality reduction. These methods can be roughly classified into two categories: linear methods and nonlinear methods. Many linear methods come from statistical analysis. Their application is often called feature extraction (Liu and Motoda, 1998) in data mining. It refers to the process to derive new dimensions based on transformations or combinations of the original dimensions. A simple case of feature extraction is feature selection that simply selects a subset of the original dimensions as the new dimensions. Data projection often has a broader meaning (Biswas et al., 1981) than does feature extraction, and it covers more techniques for the reduction of dimensionality. The problem of data projection is defined as follows: Given a set of high-dimensional points, project them to points in a low space so that the result configuration performs better than the original points in future processing such as clustering and classification.

Recently, research on nonlinear projection methods has become active. Nonlinear data projection not only reduces the cost of processing by reducing the number of dimensions, but in many cases it produces better representation of data than do linear methods. One way to understand this is to assume that, depending on the underlying mechanisms of how data are collected in many applications, data are usually located in low-dimensional nonlinear manifolds of the embedded high-dimensional space. Direct applications of linear methods may not produce the best results. Using the analogy of a scrunched paper on which data points are drawn, the paper needs to be straightened out before any meaningful results of the data could be obtained.

Data projection techniques contribute to data preprocessing in data mining in two effective and efficient ways: First, they give a revealing representation of data in low dimension, preparing a basis for further clustering and classification. We have found that, by projecting data to lower dimensions, applying clustering and classification algorithms to low-dimensional configurations often produce better results. Second, data projection techniques provide an efficient way to visualize data that enable human intervention into the data-mining process. In the case of clustering, for example, it has been shown (Siedlecki et al., 1988) that human analysts helped by mapping techniques significantly outperform automatic clustering methods. Data projection techniques help to visualize and understand the structure of data and, therefore, help to select appropriate data-mining algorithms and to set proper parameters of algorithms for further processing. Recently, data projection has also been found fundamental to human visual perception (Seung and Lee, 2000): An image can be thought as a point in high-dimensional space where each input dimension corresponds to the brightness of one pixel. Although the input dimensionality may be very high (e.g., 4096 for 64×64 small images), the perceptually meaningful structure of a set of such images has probably much fewer independent degrees of freedom. With a known number of degrees of freedom and the corresponding projection method, it is expected that we can "recover" the data to their simplest native form.

This chapter is organized as follows: Section 3.2 describes the application background by introducing electronic noses and odorant sensor arrays. The data-processing and data-mining procedures currently used in industry are summarized. Section 3.3 briefly introduces linear projection techniques. Section 3.4 discusses nonlinear projection techniques with an emphasis on features of each technique. Section 3.5 presents two mapping methods that we have developed. Section 3.6 discusses empirical comparisons of these projection techniques. Section 3.7 demonstrates the results of applying these techniques to the electronic nose data. Results of experiments show the usefulness of these techniques in finding low-dimensional structures of data. This chapter is concluded with a summary and discussion of future work.

3.2. ELECTRONIC NOSE AND SENSOR ARRAY

The senses of smell and taste play important roles in a lot of applications (Hurst, 1999) in industry, environmental monitoring, medicine, and national security. Examples include quality control, product matching, origin identification, spoilage detection, and flavor quantification that rely on the senses of expert sensory panels in food, beverage, and perfume industries. Unfortunately, the use of biological noses suffers from their high cost, long training time, easy fatigue, high degree of subjectivity, poor reproducibility, and the inapplicability to hazardous or extreme physical conditions. Electronic noses have been increasingly used in these applications to identify and characterize odors and mixtures of odors.

The two main components of an electronic nose are the sensing system and the data processing system. As with human nose, which has many olfactory receptors, the sensing system is usually an array of many different sensing elements (e.g., chemical sensors) where each sensor has only partial specificity to a wide range of odorant molecules. Each sensor in the array is made up of a particular type of polymer. When an electronic nose is exposed to an odor, the polymers absorb odorant molecules, change their electric resistances, and produce a data record of the exposure.

Raw data collected from the sensors often have a high noise level. The data-processing system does preliminary preprocessing of these raw data. The processing includes eliminating high-frequency noises by using a low-pass filter, reducing background bias by using baseline correction, and normalizing the data. The quality of the data collected can be easily affected by many physical parameters such as the speed of the flow that carries the odor to the sensor array and the ambient conditions such as pressure, temperature, and humidity. Multiple samples of each odor are often required to obtain reliable data.

Like humans, such a system needs training with an appropriately selected set of samples. After training, an electronic nose is designed to be able to identify unknown odors. Obviously, this gives a typical data-mining problem of clustering and classification of high-dimensional data.

The training techniques most commonly used in industry include principal component analysis and those in discriminant analysis, cluster analysis, and neural networks. Cross-validation is commonly used to identify and remove outliers in the training phase. Most applications of electronic noses allow resampling in the training phase. Once an outlier is identified, the same chemical is resampled and the outlier is replaced by the new data. This testing, resampling, and retesting process could continue until a satisfactory cross-validation is achieved for all samples. Training an electronic nose is a tedious process that may require considerable resampling.

Although data mining of electronic nose data is a new application (Bartlett et al., 1997), many standard statistical and data-mining methods have been applied. These include principal component analysis, discriminant analysis, factor analysis, and cluster analysis (Keller, 1999). Classification techniques such as K-nearest neighbors have been used for building identification models. The application of neural networks has also been reported (Keller, 1999; Hashem et al., 1995; Singh et al., 1996).

The application reported in this chapter uses data collected by using a Cyranose 320 electronic nose. The electronic nose contains an array of 32 polymer composite sensors. Each exposure of the nose to a chemical vapor generates a data record of 32 attributes. The electronic nose is a portable hand-held device that has the capability of on-board preprocessing such as noise filtering and normalization. The electronic nose uses PCA for dimensionality reduction, k-means for data clustering and detection of outliers, and two supervised algorithms for model building and prediction. The two supervised algorithms are K-nearest neighbors and canonical discriminant analysis. Data collected by the electronic nose can be uploaded to a computer where more sophisticated and customized processing can be done.

Dimensionality reduction is required in this application for two practical reasons: First, we need to reduce the dimensionality of data so as to visualize the data in 2D or 3D scatterplots. The visualization will be helpful to obtain a better understanding of data and thus to choose algorithms for data-mining and further processing. Second, dimensionality reduction helps to reduce the problem of "curse of dimensionality" in data mining. The problem causes very slow convergence of a classifier or estimator to the true value of high-dimensional data. In the application presented in this chapter, this means that we would need a large amount of samples to obtain a good result.

As we will show in Section 3.7, the PCA algorithm currently used in the electronic nose is not good enough for dimensionality reduction in this application. As a result, the resampling and cross-validation process detects too many outliers. After much testing and resampling of data records, the final training data would become highly biased. Consequently, the model built on the training data would have low recognition rate. One possible reason to explain this is that the PCA algorithm assumes that the data lie close to a hyperplane in high-dimensional space, which is often not the case in real-world applications. It is more reasonable to assume that data lie on a low-dimensional nonlinear manifold. That is why we think nonlinear data projection techniques should be applied for data preprocessing.

The test data we use in this chapter contain samples of odors of six chemicals: allyl caproate, a pineapple-like odor; methyl salicylate, a liniment odor; isoamyl acetate, a candy banana odor; myrcene, a mango-like odor; decanal, an orange peel odor; and diacetyl, a butter odor. Data were collected in a local flavor house where each chemical was put into five sample sets. We recorded 10 exposures of each sample set. This gives a total of 300 data records.

3.3. LINEAR DATA PROJECTION

Linear data projection techniques are among the most commonly used techniques for data preprocessing. To project a set of D-dimensional points to d-space ($d < D$), a linear projection is characterized by a $d \times D$ projection matrix T that orthogonally transforms the D-dimensional points to d-space. A linear projection can be expressed as $\mathbf{y}_i = T \cdot \mathbf{x}_i$, where $\mathbf{x}_i$ is a vector with D elements representing an original point in D space, $\mathbf{y}_i$ is a vector with d elements representing the projection of the point in d-space, and T is an $d \times D$ projection matrix.

The problem in linear projection is how to derive an "optimum" linear projection matrix T. It is well known that, in the sense of mean-square optimization, the rows of T should be the eigenvectors corresponding to the d largest eigenvalues of the $D \times D$ covariance matrix of data. This method is well known as Principal Component Analysis (PCA) (Chatfield and Collins, 1980), Karhunen–Loeve Transform, or eigenvector projection. Mathematically, let $\mathbf{m} = E(\mathbf{x}_i)$ represent the mean vector of the data, and let C represent the covariance matrix, $C = E(\mathbf{x}_i - \mathbf{m})(\mathbf{x}_i - \mathbf{m})^T$. Let $\lambda_1 > \lambda_2 > \cdots > \lambda_D$ represent the eigenvalues of C arranged in descending order, and let $\mathbf{e}_1, \mathbf{e}_2, \ldots, \mathbf{e}_D$ represent the corresponding eigenvectors. Then, the projection matrix T is assigned as $T = [\mathbf{e}_1, \ldots, \mathbf{e}_d]^T$. The remaining eigenvectors $\mathbf{e}_{d+1}, \ldots, \mathbf{e}_D$ corresponding to smaller eigenvalues are ignored.

Projecting data to low space will inevitably introduce distortion. A projection method would need an error measurement (often called stress) to measure the distortion. In PCA, the total squared error of the d-dimensional projection is $\sum_{i=d+1}^{D} \lambda_i$, where $\lambda_{d+1}, \ldots, \lambda_D$ are the eigenvalues ignored in the projection. If the data lie close to a d-dimensional linear manifold (hyperplane), we would expect to see d large eigenvalues and would expect the remaining eigenvalues to be zero or very small. Therefore, intrinsic dimensionality of data can be estimated by checking for a significant decrease of eigenvalues. PCA is a very popular method for dimensionality reduction.

Now we consider a problem in duality to PCA: Suppose that we know interpoint distances rather than individual data records; then we would want to find a low-dimensional configuration of these points so that the interpoint distances in the low-dimensional configuration match the given interpoint distances as much as possible. This optimization problem has an analytical solution: We can compute covariance of interpoint distances and find a configuration of points in d-space such that the distances between these points match as closely as possible the original interpoint distances. This procedure is in duality to PCA and is known as classical Multidimensional Scaling (MDS) (Cox and Cox, 2001). In fact, the coordinates of the result points in classical MDS are simply the components of the original points on the largest d eigenvectors of the covariance matrix of data. As an example, Figure 3.1 shows a 2D configuration of 60 major U.S. cities by applying classical MDS to a U.S. mileage chart of intercity driving distances.

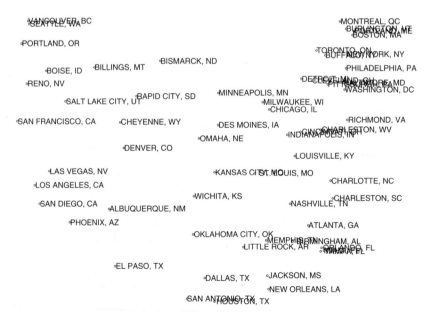

Figure 3.1. Classical MDS to representing 60 U.S. cities, given intercity driving distances.

Although we use driving distances instead of straight-line distances, we can see that the representation in Figure 3.1 is similar to where these cities are.

Besides the above "optimal" linear projections, there are a lot of other possibilities to linearly project high-dimensional data onto lower spaces. An interesting projection technique is projection pursuit (Friedman and Tukey, 1974). It allows the user to formulate an arbitrary index of interestingness of the projection. The algorithm then tries to maximize this index in its pursuit of an optimum projection over all possible ones. In this sense, principal component analysis is a special case of projection pursuit where the index of interestingness is the covariance of the dimensions of the projected data. Projection pursuit can be combined with the grand tour method (Asimov, 1985) to dynamically visualize data. The grand tour method moves a projection along geodesic paths through continuously changing the projection matrix. The entire process creates an illusion of continuous motion. Three-dimensional linear projection of using grand tour with volume rendering for the visual exploration of high-dimensional data was presented in Yang (2000, 2003).

3.4. NONLINEAR DATA PROJECTION

Depending on domain-specific mechanisms of how data are generated, data are often distributed on nonlinear manifolds in the embedded high-dimensional space. Nonlinear data projection is required to generate low-dimensional configurations in such a way that a swarm of data points on a nonlinear manifold are unfolded in low space. In fact, many existing techniques have this capability. For example, a neural network classifier might be able to approximate this low-dimensional subspace by its first layer and to perform the classification in this subspace by its output layer. There are also dedicated techniques for nonlinear data projection. These include earlier techniques such as Bennet's algorithm (Bennet, 1969), metric and nonmetric Multidimensional Scaling (MDS) (Kruskal, 1964), the well-known Self-Organizing Maps (SOM) (Kohonen, 1997), and Sammon's Nonlinear Mapping (NLM) (Sammon, 1969). Recently, new dedicated techniques have been developed for nonlinear projection of data. These techniques include Curvilinear Component Analysis (CCA) (Demartines and Herault, 1997), Curvilinear Distance Analysis (CDA) (Lee et al., 2000), Isomap (Tenenbaum et al., 2000), and Local Linear Embedding (LLE) (Roweis and Saul, 2000).

The nonlinear projection techniques discussed in this chapter are systematized in Figure 3.2. Each technique is first characterized by whether it is based on interpoint distances or not. If it is distance-based, it is further characterized by its strategy to determine the low-dimensional configuration—that is, whether it uses correlation matrix or an iterative optimization procedure. Those techniques using iterative optimization procedures are further classified by the error measurements they use. Finally, each distance-based technique is characterized by the type of distances it uses, Euclidean distances or geodesic distances. In addition to these

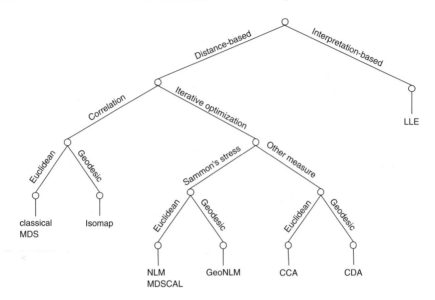

Figure 3.2. Systematization of nonlinear projection techniques.

distinguishing characteristics, each technique may employ specific data structures and routines for its own optimization.

MDS represents a large number of algorithms for producing low-dimensional configurations from distance matrix, among which the classical MDS is a linear projection technique. The well-known nonlinear metric MDS is Kruskal's MDSCAL (Kruskal, 1964). It uses an iterative deepest gradient algorithm that evaluates different configurations to minimize an error criterion until it arrives at a configuration whose interpoint distances best approximate those in the distance matrix. The error criterion to be minimized is defined as $E_{\text{MDSCAL}} = (\sum_{i<j} (d_{ij}^* - d_{ij})^2)/(\sum_{i<j} d_{ij}^{*2})$ where d_{ij}^* represents the interpoint distance between the point i and the point j in the original space, and d_{ij} represents the interpoint distance between them in the projected space. Nonmetric MDS extends metric MDS by further allowing that the distances between points are expressed on an ordinal scale. The projection then tries to keep the rank order of distances during projection. This is done by introducing a monotonic function that acts on the original distances and that always maps the distances to such values that best preserve the rank order.

MDS uses short distances and long distances equally in its definition of the error criterion. In practice, long distances usually dominate the error. That is why MDS can hardly unfold a data manifold. Sammon (1969) developed another popular nonlinear mapping (NLM) algorithm that prefers the preservation of short distances. The error criterion used in NLM is defined as $E_{\text{Sammon}} = (\sum_{i<j} (d_{ij}^* - d_{ij})^2/d_{ij}^*)/(\sum_{i<j} d_{ij}^*)$. The method starts with a random configuration of points in d-space. It calculates the steepest gradient descent of the error criterion to reconfigure the points in iteration. NLM follows MDSCAL closely.

The only difference between MDSCAL and NLM is that E_{MDSCAL} gives no preference to small distances. Rather, E_{Sammon} is normalized with the distances in the original space. Because of this difference, NLM emphasizes the preservation of short distances in its iterative optimization process and, therefore, has an effect of unfolding a data distribution. Kruskal (1971) has demonstrated how a configuration that is very similar to that of NLM could be generated from MDSCAL. Niemann and Weiss (1979) have proposed a more general criterion and a way to improve the convergence of NLM.

Apparently, both MDS and NLM require a lot of computation and memory space since $n(n-1)/2$ interpoint distances have to be calculated at each iteration. Several modifications have been proposed to reduce the computation by preserving only a small portion of interpoint distances. Chang and Lee (1973) proposed a heuristic relaxation approach called the frame method, where a user selects m of n points ($m < n$) to project first. The remaining $n - m$ points are projected one by one by adjusting distances only between that point and the initial frame of m points. Thus, the frame method results in considerable savings in computation time. A similar idea was used by Kruskal and Hart (1966) to study the intrinsic dimensionality of a large number of binary points. Shepard (1974) has summarized these early methods in psychometrics.

Curvilinear Component Analysis (CCA) (Demartines and Herault, 1997) was developed as a recent alternative for nonlinear data projection. The same as NLM, CCA favors local distances. However, CCA totally ignores distances longer than a threshold. Its error criterion is defined as $E_{CCA} = \sum_{i<j}(d_{ij}^* - d_{ij})^2 F(d_{ij}, \lambda)$, where F is a bounded decreasing function in order to favor local distance preservation. The F used in (Demartines and Herault, 1997) is defined simply as a binary function that totally ignores distances longer than λ—that is, $F(d_{ij}, \lambda) = 1$ when $d_{ij} \le \lambda$; and $F(d_{ij}, \lambda) = 0$ when $d_{ij} > \lambda$. By ignoring long distances, CCA performs better than NLM to unfold twisted data manifolds.

An important and fundamental improvement over the above distance-based techniques is the use of geodesic distances instead of Euclidean distances. The geodesic distance between two points on a manifold is the distance measured along the manifold. Because geodesic distance reflects more faithfully the underlying global geometry of a dataset, data projection based on geodesic distances is expected to give global solutions of highly folded, twisted, or curved nonlinear manifolds. In implementation, the geodesic distance between a pair of points can be estimated by the graph distance along the shortest path between them in the neighborhood graph of all points. The graph distance is calculated by using the following two steps:

1. The first step constructs a neighborhood graph by connecting neighbor points. There are two alternatives that can be used to define whether two points are neighbors: (1) if one is of the K nearest neighbors of the other (K-neighbor approach) or (2) they are closer than a user-defined threshold ε (ε-neighbor approach).

2. The second step computes graph distances between all pairs of points by calculating shortest paths using Floyd's algorithm or repeatedly using Dijkstra's shortest path algorithm.

Applying distance-based projection techniques to the matrix of geodesic distances is expected to produce better projection results. That is exactly what Isomap (Tenenbaum et al., 2000) and Curvilinear Distance Analysis (CDA) (Lee et al., 2000) did over MDS and CCA. Isomap applies classical MDS to geodesic distances. CDA applies CCA to geodesic distances. Each algorithm has two steps: The first step calculates the graph distance between any two points on the neighborhood graph. The second step applies the corresponding projection technique to the graph distances and finds a low-dimensional configuration that best approximates the graph distances.

The algorithms based on geodesic distances share some important characteristics: (1) Because graph distances approach intrinsic geodesic distances as the number of data points increases, these methods are guaranteed to converge asymptotically to the true intrinsic structure of data. (2) Each algorithm requires a parameter k, which is the number of neighbors, or a parameter ε, which is the fixed radius of neighborhood. (3) Because only the points within a range are considered as neighbors, these methods perform well when the data belong to a single well-sampled cluster. They fail to nicely project data when the data are spread among multiple clusters or the parameter k or ε is chosen too small. (4) If the parameter k or ε were chosen too large, on the other hand, the graph distances are not good estimates of geodesic distances and the so-called "short-circuit" problem (Balasubramanian et al., 2002) will occur.

LLE (Roweis and Saul, 2000) is another recently developed nonlinear projection technique. It assumes that each data point and its neighbors lie on a local linear patch. It tries to find an optimum reconstruction of each point from a linear composition of its neighbors and then applies the same reconstruction to generate the low-dimensional configuration.

3.5. GEONLM AND TETRAHEDRAL MAPPING

GeoNLM (Yang, 2004c) is a data projection method that we have developed to make the systematization in Figure 3.2 complete. It applies NLM to the matrix of graph-based geodesic distances. Its performance in unfolding data manifolds has been compared to the performance of NLM and the performance of Isomap. Experiments show that both GeoNLM and Isomap easily outperform NLM in unfolding data manifolds. However, GeoNLM usually finds better low-dimensional configurations than Isomap. The difference is significant especially when the short-circuit problem occurs due to the improper choice of a too-large neighborhood size in calculating the neighborhood graph.

As indicated by their error criteria, the above nonlinear mapping techniques have similar functionalities in the sense that they try to preserve many, if not all, distances and usually end with the case that no distance is exactly preserved. If our interest is on the overall distribution of data, they are usually adequate. On the other hand, if we are interested in knowing in detail local structures of data where the precise interpoint distances are important, they are usually inadequate.

We have developed a distance-preserving tetrahedral method (Yang, 2004a, b) based on the triangulation method (Lee et al., 1977). It works by projecting a point to d-space such that its distances to d previously mapped points are exactly preserved. We may visualize the situation by using the analogy of a physical structure in D-space in which the distances between nodes are maintained by rigid struts. Every node is a flexible joint allowing bending and rotation. To maintain all these distances means that the original D-dimensional structure has a strut between every pair of points. This structure is rigid and contains all distance information. The tetrahedral method considers only a d-simplex for each point to be mapped after the first d points. The method rotates the d-simplex so that all the result d-simplexes are within a single d-subspace. In this way, we project a structure of data points in D-space to d-space with the preservation of some interpoint distances that are on the edges of the simplexes.

For the purpose of unfolding a data manifold, local distances should be preserved first. Therefore, among the d points to which the distances from a point are preserved, one can be chosen as its nearest neighbor among the points already mapped. The other points can be chosen from the other already mapped near neighbors whose distances to the nearest neighbor have already been preserved. The sequence of mapping is based on maintaining the minimum spanning tree of the graph whose nodes are points and whose edges are interpoint distances. For each data point to be mapped, intuitively, the tetrahedral method chooses a d-simplex that uses its nearest neighbor among the already mapped points as a vertex, and then it grows another d-simplex along one facet of the d-simplex. The d-simplexes attach with each other along with the sequence of mapping. The resulting map is a crystal-like structure with points as vertexes and the preserved distances between points as edges. This method preserves local distances from a point to its nearest neighbor and to some of its other near neighbors. Therefore, in the case where data points are distributed on a manifold, the method can unfold the swarm of data points. This algorithm has no user-selectable parameters and works well when the data are organized into clusters. It is particularly useful in applications where the exact preservation of distances is important.

3.6. EXPERIMENTS AND EMPIRICAL COMPARISON

Figure 3.3 shows a Swiss-roll-like synthetic dataset and its 2D projections by using NLM, CCA, Isomap, LLE, and the tetrahedral method when d is set to 2. NLM fails to unfold the data. CCA splits the manifold into pieces. Isomap, LEE, and the tetrahedral method can unfold the manifold. The projection result of the tetrahedral method (Figure 3.3f) is roughly a rectangle with irregular patches

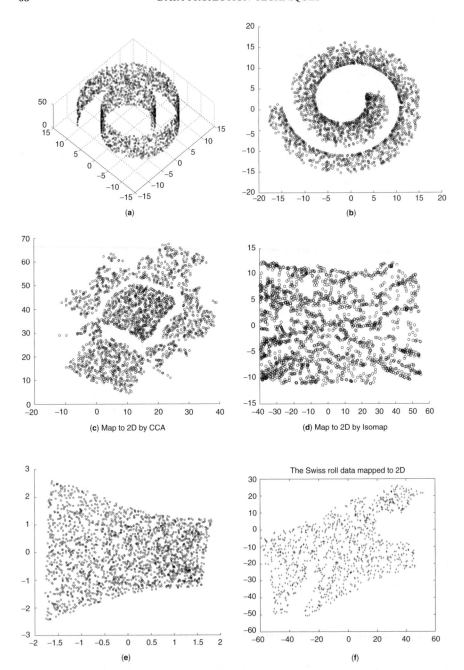

Figure 3.3. Nonlinear projections of **(a)** a 3D manifold: **(b)** by NLM, **(c)** by CCA, **(d)** by Isomap, **(e)** by LLE, and **(f)** by the tetrahedral method.

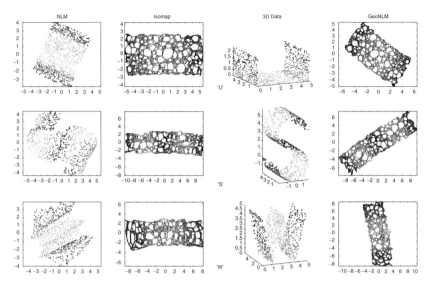

Figure 3.4. Experiment results of NLM, Isomap, and GeoNLM on synthetic data sets ($K = 7$).

rather than a perfect rectangle. This is because the tetrahedral method preserves exact local distances. Unlike Isomap or LLE, which can adjust interpoint distances and thus allows the elasticity of a data manifold, the tetrahedral method preserves exactly local distances and thus assumes rigid local patches of the data manifold. This is similar to what occurs when we peel an orange. Unless the orange skin were elastic, the resulting peel would break into pieces.

Figure 3.4 shows the results of applying GeoNLM, NLM, and Isomap to three 2D manifolds embedded in 3-space. Each test dataset contains 1000 points. The results of GeoNLM and Isomap are shown together with their neighborhood graphs. These results are produced when seven nearest neighbors of each point are used in constructing the neighborhood graph ($K = 7$).

From these results, we can see that both GeoNLM and Isomap have similar performance and both easily outperform NLM in unfolding manifolds. The difference between GeoNLM and Isomap is that GeoNLM uses NLM instead of classical MDS in the second step. Because NLM usually does better than classical MDS in finding low-dimensional configurations, a closer look shows that GeoNLM gives smaller stress values than Isomap. The difference becomes significant especially when the problem of the "short-circuit" edges occurs due to improper choice of a too-large neighborhood size in calculating the neighborhood graph.

Figure 3.5 gives two examples of using the tetrahedral method to unfold high-dimensional data. Figure 3.5a shows a two-dimensional projection of 698 records of human face images. Each record represents a human face rendered with different poses and lighting directions. The size of each image is 64×64. Therefore, the original dimensionality of these records is 4096. A sample of the original

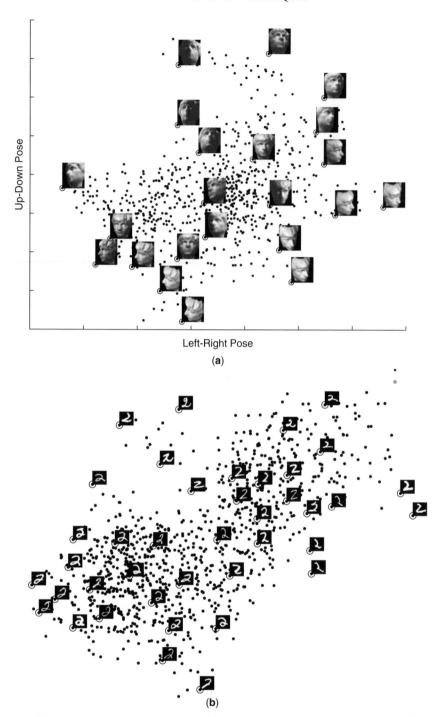

Figure 3.5. Two-dimensional configurations of **(a)** human face image data and **(b)** 1000 handwritten "2"s. Sample images are superimposed to interpret the projections. The circle at the bottom left corner of each image indicates the point representing the image.

images are superimposed in the figure. This projection extracts the data's underlying geometric structure. We can see that each axis of the 2D configuration correlates with one degree of freedom underlying the original data: The x-axis represents the left–right pose of the human face, and the y-axis represents the up–down pose of the human face. Figure 3.5b shows a two-dimensional projection of 1000 handwritten "2"s in the MNIST database (LeCun, 1998) of handwritten digits. Each digit is centered in a 28×28 image. The bottom left part of the projection represents the "2"s with big bottom loops, and the top right part represents the "2"s without bottom loop. Looking from the bottom left to the top right, we observe "2"s with smaller bottom loops. Using the tetrahedral method as a preprocessing tool, we envisage that data clustering of the projected data would give more meaningful results than data clustering of the original data.

3.7. NONLINEAR PROJECTIONS OF ELECTRONIC NOSE DATA

In this section we present the results of projecting the electronic nose data by using the nonlinear data projection techniques. These techniques give us powerful ways to visualize data and to understand data so as to choose right algorithms for further processing.

We start from finding the principal components of the electronic nose data. Figure 3.6a gives the result of 2D projection against two most significant components of the data by using PCA. We can see that the clusters for decanal and myrcene have some overlay, and both clusters distinguish from the rest points which are mixed together. A linear projection such as PCA does not perform well in this application.

Figure 3.6b shows a 2D projection of the data by using NLM. As we discussed, NLM uses an iterative optimization procedure trying to keep all interpoint distances with an emphasis on short ones. As a nonlinear data projection technique, it brings improvements over PCA. As we can see from Figure 3.6b, the cluster for decanal and the cluster for myrcene are separated from each other. But the remaining data points are still heavily mixed.

Figure 3.6c shows a 2D projection by using CCA. As we can see, not only the clusters for decanal and myrcene are separated from each other, but also the cluster for allyl caproate better separates from the rest clusters. CCA usually outperforms NLM in unfolding heavily curved or twisted manifolds because it uses an error criterion that totally ignores distances larger than a threshold.

The projection in Figure 3.6d makes further improvement to the result of CCA. It is obtained by running CCA with an initial configuration of NLM. We first run NLM on the data to get an initial configuration and, then, apply CCA to the data to optimize this configuration. Because NLM gives global optimized projection and CCA is able to unfold strongly nonlinear structure, an improvement we can see in Figure 3.6d is that the cluster for allyl caproate further separates from the other clusters.

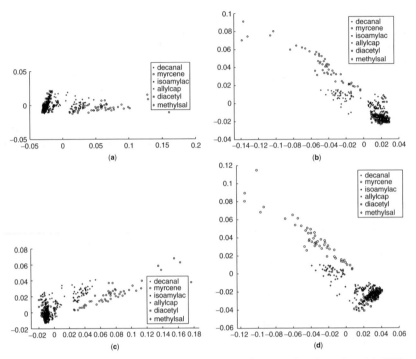

Figure 3.6. Two-dimensional projection of the electronic nose data by using **(a)** PCA, **(b)** NLM, **(c)** CCA, and **(d)** CCA with NLM initialization.

Figure 3.7a shows a projection of the electronic nose data by using LLE. Figure 3.7b shows a projection by using the tetrahedral method. Both methods use Euclidean distances and try to create low-dimensional configurations to best reflect the original Euclidean distances. Because some data points in a cluster have Euclidean neighbors in different clusters, the result projection often mixes boundaries of clusters.

Figure 3.7c shows a 2D projection by using Isomap when the number of neighbors of each point is set to 5 ($K = 5$) in searching for shortest paths. Because Isomap uses geodesic distances that goes hop-by-hop through points, the global data configuration in Figure 3.7c is quite different from the projections by using other techniques. Isomap tends to shrink data clusters. As what happens in this application, Isomap doesn't work well when data are distributed among several clusters.

GeoNLM replaces classical MDS in Isomap with NLM. Figure 3.7d shows a 2D projection of the data by applying NLM to the geodesic distances. It represents the best result that we have obtained so far on this dataset.

By this empirical comparison, we can see that all the above nonlinear techniques easily outperform PCA in projecting and unfolding data, among which the two promising results we have obtained are the projection by using CCA

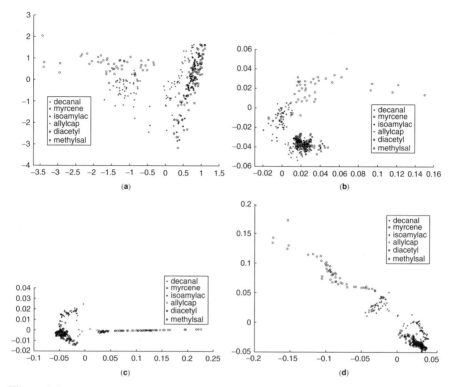

Figure 3.7. Two-dimensional projections of the electronic nose data by using **(a)** LLE, **(b)** the tetrahedral method, **(c)** Isomap, and **(d)** GeoNLM.

with NLM initialization (Figure 3.6d) and the projection by using GeoNLM (Figure 3.7d). The former takes advantage of CCA's ability to unfold heavily twisted manifolds. The latter takes advantage of using the global optimization of NLM with geodesic paths. GeoNLM has finally been used in this application to reduce the dimensionality of data.

3.8. CONCLUSION

This chapter has presented an application of nonlinear data projection techniques for dimensionality reduction in data preprocessing of electronic nose data. The data-processing techniques currently used in electronic noses have been summarized. This chapter gives a review of data projection techniques for the reduction of dimensionality. We have briefly introduced linear projection techniques and focused on nonlinear projection techniques with an emphasis of their features and applications. The usefulness of these techniques in unfolding manifolds of data is demonstrated through examples and their application in data mining of electronic nose data.

As we discussed, data projection techniques contribute to the preprocessing of data in two important ways: (1) Data-mining algorithms require the reduction of dimensionality, not only to reduce the complexity of computation but also to get better results; (2) data projection is needed for data visualization and better understanding of data. This enables human control to help in choosing mining algorithms and setting parameters in the process of data mining. We have observed experimentally that this human control gives "more revealing" results than the ones obtained by automatic data-mining methods, and it does so in a shorter period of time.

The role of data projection in data mining is not limited to data preprocessing. Data projection itself gives efficient techniques to extract meaningful features from data and to discover valuable, but often hidden, patterns from data. In fact, data projection is a fundamentally important research area with applications far beyond data mining. Studies have shown (Seung and Lee, 2000), for example, that data projection and manifold learning is closely related to human visual perception. Consequently, data projection has many important potential applications. Examples of these applications are the semantic indexing and searching of multimedia data for the purpose of content-based search and retrieval.

REFERENCES

Agrawal, R., Gehrke, J., Gunopulos, D., and Raghavan, P., Automatic subspace clustering of high dimensional data for data mining applications, in *Proceedings 1998 ACM-SIGMOD International Conference on Management of Data*, pp. 94–105, Seattle, June 1998.

Ankerst, M., Breunig, M., Kriegel, H.-P., and Sander, J., Optics: Ordering points to identify the clustering structure, in *Proceedings 1999 ACM SIGMOD International Conference on Management of Data*, pp. 49–60, Philadelphia, June 1999.

Asimov, D., The grand tour: A tool for viewing multidimensional data, *SIAM Journal of Scientific and Statistical Computing* **6**(1), 128–143 (1985).

Balasubramanian, M., Schwartz, E. L., Tenenbaum, J. B., de Silva, V., and Langford, J. C., The Isomap algorithm and topological stability: Technical comments, *Science* **295**, 7a, (2002).

Bartlett, P. N., Elliott, J. M., and Gardner, J. W., Electronic noses and their application in the food industry, *Food Technology* **51**(12), 44–28 (1997).

Bennet, R. S., The intrinsic dimensionality of signal collections, *IEEE Transactions on Information Theory*, **IT-15**(5), 517–525 (1969).

Biswas, G., Jain, A. K., and Dubes, R. C., Evaluation of projection algorithms, *IEEE Transactions on Pattern Analysis and Machine Intelligence* **PAMI-3**(6), 701–708 (1981).

Breiman, L., Friedman, J. H., Olshen, R. A., and Stone, C. J., *Classification and Regression Trees*, Chapman & Hall, New York, 1984.

Chang, C. L., and Lee, R. C. T., A heuristic relaxation method for nonlinear mapping in cluster analysis, *IEEE Transactions on Systems, Man, and Cybernetics* **SMC-3**(2), 197–200 (1973).

Chatfield, C., and Collins, A. J., *Introduction to Multivariate Analysis*, Chapman & Hall/CRC, London, 1980.

Chauvin, Y., and Rumelhart, D. E., *Backpropagation: Theory, Architectures, and Applications*, Erlbaum, Hillsdale, NJ, 1995.

Cox, T. F., and Cox, M. A. A., *Multidimensional Scaling*, 2nd edition, Chapman & Hall/CRC, London, 2001.

Demartines, P., and Herault, J., Curvilinear component analysis: A self-organizing neural network for nonlinear mapping of data sets, *IEEE Transactions on Neural Networks* **8**(1), 148–154 (1997).

Duda, R., and Hart, P., *Pattern Classification and Scene Analysis*, Wiley, New York, 1972.

Ester, M., Kriegel, H.-P., Sander, J., and Xu, X., A density-based algorithm for discovering clusters in large spatial databases with noise, in *Proceedings 2nd International Conference on Knowledge Discovery and Data Mining*, pp. 226–231, Portland, August 1996.

Friedman, J., and Tukey, J., A projection pursuit algorithm for exploratory data analysis, *IEEE Transactions on Computers* **C-23**(9), 881–890 (1974).

Guha, S., Rastogi, R., and Shim, K., CURE: An efficient clustering algorithm for large databases, in *Proceedings 1998 ACM SIGMOD International Conference on Management of Data*, pp. 73–84, Seattle, June 1998.

Hashem, S., Keller, P. E., Kouzes, R. T., and Kangas, L. J., Neural network based data analysis for chemical sensor arrays, *Proceedings of the SPIE* **2492**(5), 33–40, (1995).

Hurst, W. J., *Electronic Noses and Sensor Array Based Systems: Design and Applications*, CRC Press, 1999.

Sammon, J. J. W., A nonlinear mapping for data structure analysis, *IEEE Transactions on Computers* **C-18**(5), 401–409 (1969).

Jain, A. K., and Dubes, R. C., *Algorithms for Clustering Data*, Prentice-Hall, Englewood Cliffs, NJ, 1988.

Jain, A. K., Murty, M. N., and Flynn, P. J., Data clustering: A survey. *ACM Computing Surveys* **31**(3), 264–323 (1999).

Karypis, G., Han, E.-H., and Kumar, V., Chameleon: Hierarchical clustering using dynamic modeling, *Computer* **32**(8), 68–75 (1999).

Kaufman, L., and Rousseeuw, P. J., *Finding Groups in Data: An Introduction to Cluster Analysis*, John Wiley & Sons, New York, 1990.

Keller, P., Mimicking biology: Applications of cognitive systems to electronic noses, in *Intelligent Control/Intelligent Systems and Semiotics*, Cambridge, MA, pp. 447–451, 1999.

Kohonen, T., *Self-Organizing Maps*, 2nd edition, Springer, Berlin, 1997.

Kruskal, J., Multidimensional scaling by optimizing goodness-of-fit to a nonmetric hypothesis, *Psychometrika* **29**, 1–27 (1964).

Kruskal, J., Comments on a nonlinear mapping for data structure analysis, *IEEE Transactions on Computers* **C-20**(12), 1614 (1971).

Kruskal, J., and Hart, R. E., A geometric interpretation of diagnostic data from a digital machine, *Bell Systems Technical Journal* **45**, 1299–1338, (1966).

LeCun, Y., MNIST database, available at http://yann.lecun.com/exdb/mnist/, 1998.

Lee, J. A., Lendasse, A., Donckers, N., and Verleysen, M., A robust nonlinear projection method, in *Proceedings 8th European Symposium on Artificial Neural Networks (ESANN2000)*, Bruges, Belgium, 2000.

Lee, R. C. T., Slagle, J. R., and Blum, H., A triangulation method for the sequential mapping of points from N-space to two-space, *IEEE Transactions on Computers* **C-26**(3), 288–292 (1977).

Lent, B., Swami, A. N., and Widom, J., Clustering association rules, in *Proceedings 1997 International Conference on Data Engineering*, pp. 220–231, Birmingham, UK, April 1997.

Liu, B., Hsu, W., and Ma, Y., Integrating classification and association rule mining, in *Proceedings ACM International Conference Knowledge Discovery and Data Mining*, pages 80–86, New York, August 1998.

Liu, H., and Motoda, H., *Feature Extraction, Construction and Selection: A Data Mining Perspective*, Kluwer, Boston, 1998.

McQueen, J. B., Some methods of classification and analysis of multivariate observations, in *Proceedings 5th Berkeley Symposium in Mathematics, Statistics and Probability*, Vol. 1, pp. 281–296, 1967.

Michalski, R., Bratko, I., and Kubat, M., *Machine Learning and Data Mining: Methods and Applications*, Wiley, New York, 1998.

Ng, R. T., and Han, J., Efficient and effective clustering methods for spatial data mining, in *Proceedings 20th International Conference on Very Large Data Bases*, pp. 144–155, Santiago, Chile, September 1994.

Niemann, H., and Weiss, J., A fast converging algorithm for nonlinear mapping of high-dimensional data onto a plane, *IEEE Transactions on Computers* **C-28**(2), 142–147 (1979).

Quinlan, J. R., *C4.5: Programs for Machine Learning*, Morgan Kaufmann, San Mateo, CA, 1993.

Roweis, S. T., and Saul, L. K., Nonlinear dimensionality reduction by locally linear embedding, *Science* **290**, 2323–2326 (2000).

Seung, H. S., and Lee, D., The manifold ways of perception, *Science* **290**, 2268–2269 (2000).

Shavlik, J. W., and Dietterich, T. G., *Readings in Machine Learning*, Morgan Kaufmann, San Mateo, CA, 1990.

Sheikholeslami, G., Chatterjee, S., and Zhang, A., WaveCluster: A multi-resolution clustering approach for very large spatial databases, in *Proceedings 24th International Conference on Very Large Data Bases*, pp. 428–439, New York, August 1998.

Shepard, R. N., Representation of structure in similarity data—problems and prospects, *Psychometrika* **39**, 373–421 (1974).

Siedlecki, W., Siedlecka, K., and Sklansky, J., Experiments on mapping techniques for exploratory pattern analysis, *Pattern Recognition* **21**(5), 431–438 (1988).

Singh, S., Hines, E., and Gardner, J., Fuzzy neural computing of coffee and tainted-water data from an electronic nose, *Sensors and Actuators B* **30**, 185–190 (1996).

Tenenbaum, J. B., de Silva, V., and Langford, J. C., A global geometric framework for nonlinear dimensionality reduction, *Science* **290**, 2319–2323 (2000).

Wang, W., Yang, J., and Muntz, R. R., STING: A statistical information grid approach to spatial data mining, in *Proceedings 23rd International Conference on Very Large Data Bases*, pp. 186–195, Athens, Greece, August 1997.

Weiss, S. M., and Kulikowski, C. A., *Computer Systems that Learn*, Morgan Kaufmann, San Mateo, CA, 1991.

Yang, L., Interactive exploration of very large relational datasets through 3D dynamic projections, in *Proceedings 6th ACM KDD Conference on Knowledge Discovery and Data Mining*, pp. 236–243, Boston, August 2000.

Yang, L., Visual exploration of large relational data sets through 3D projections and footprint splatting, *IEEE Transactions on Knowledge and Data Engineering* **15**(6), 1460–1471 (2003).

Yang, L., Distance-preserving mapping of patterns to 3-space, *Pattern Recognition Letters*, **25**(1), 119–128, (2004a).

Yang, L., Distance-preserving projection of high dimensional data for nonlinear dimensionality reduction. *IEEE Transactions on Pattern Analysis and Machine Intelligence* **26**(9), 1243–1246 (2004b).

Yang, L., Sammon's nonlinear mapping using geodesic distances, in *Proceedings 17th International Conference on Pattern Recognition*, Vol. 2, pp. 303–306, Cambridge, UK, August, 2004c.

Zhang, T., Ramakrishnan, R., and Livny, M., BIRCH: An efficient data clustering method for very large databases, in *ACM SIGMOD International Conference on Management of Data*, pp. 103–114, Montreal, Canada, June 1996.

PART II

BUSINESS APPLICATIONS

4

AN APPLICATION OF EVOLUTIONARY AND NEURAL DATA-MINING TECHNIQUES TO CUSTOMER RELATIONSHIP MANAGEMENT

PETER NEUMANN, DIRK ARNDT, AND BERNHARD SICK

4.1. INTRODUCTION

As marketing and corporate strategy have moved away from product-centric marketing and shifted to a world of ever-more personalized, consumer-centric strategies and processes, customer relationship management (CRM) has become the key to gaining a competitive edge. Within CRM we distinguish between acquisition and loyalty programs. Acquisition aims mainly at establishing a dialogue with prospects belonging to predefined target groups and gradually converting them from prospects into customers. Loyalty clearly focuses on customer penetration and on keeping existing customers satisfied and loyal.

In order to complete these tasks, the CRM concept covers three groups of activities: (1) strategic CRM (sCRM), which comprises all the actions linked to long-term strategies in terms of customer interaction and the internal CRM infrastructure, (2) operational CRM (oCRM), which includes all the activities occupied with customer contact and related internal business processes, and (3) analytical CRM (aCRM), which provides all the components needed for customer data and information management (Arndt and Langbein, 2002).

The application at hand belongs to the acquisition program. The marketing challenge is to find promising addressees for a direct mailing conducted for the launch of the new Mercedes-Benz E-Class. A prerequisite was to avoid contacting

Next Generation of Data-Mining Applications. Edited by Kantardzic and Zurada
ISBN 0-471-65605-4 © 2005 the Institute of Electrical and Electronics Engineers, Inc.

existing customers. Either such addresses can be generated by organizing events for address-gathering such as on-line games, trade fares, contests, and so on, or they have to be purchased from outside. In fact, there are several data sources available for purchase of addresses. The most important external sources for customer acquisition in the automotive industry are lists, lifestyle data, micro-geographic data, and data bought from noncompetitive enterprises—for example, airlines or mail order companies. In order to choose the right data source(s) for a specific purpose, the data sources are weighted by certain criteria (Arndt and Gersten, 2001a). In our case the decision was made in favor of micro-geographic data; that is, the addressees are described using so-called micro-geographic features. Typical examples for micro-geographic information are the average degree of education and income of the inhabitants of a certain geographic unit, their average purchasing power, or the percentage of cars of a certain make owned. Given the kind of data to be used, the next step is to decide between several data providers. A process model for provider selection was introduced in Arndt and Gersten (2001b).

As soon as the provider has been selected, we continue by finding the most promising addressees within the provider's address pool. A common aCRM approach for completing this task is predictive modeling. Here, the goal is to predict a specific behavior of the individuals in order to identify those with a higher probability such that they will demonstrate the target behavior (i.e., buy a new E-Class), making them good prospects for acquisition. When generating a predictive model, classification between targets and nontargets often serves as an appropriate option (Gersten and Arndt, 2002). The micro-geographic features per micro-cell are utilized here to distinguish the two classes.

In the following we describe the business application in greater detail, discuss the current state of the art, and outline the two key contributions of our work. First, a new evolutionary technique for the optimization of radial basis function (RBF) network architectures (features and structure) was developed. Second, this approach yields best results for the application described compared to other techniques such as regression approaches, decision trees, or multilayer perceptrons (MLP).

4.2. APPLICATION DETAILS

The particular business application investigated came up in the CRM Department at DaimlerChrysler AG, where a direct mailing campaign targeting the launch of the new Mercedes-Benz E-Class was planned as part of the CRM acquisition program. The set of descriptive micro-geographic data was acquired from microm, a German data provider. The dataset that was available to build the prediction model consisted of approximately 18,000 records (samples) with 47 describing features. Some of these features are set out in Table 4.1.

From the algorithmic perspective, the objective is to set up a model that describes the nonlinear functional relationship between certain input features

TABLE 4.1. Examples for Micro-Geographic Features

Name	Range of Values	Number of Different Values	Explanation	Example
STATUS	1–9	9	Status (ref. to education and income)	8: Status far above-average
MOSGR	0–9	10	MOSAIC groups	7: Workers in small towns
MERC	1–9	9	Proportion of cars of the brand Mercedes	8: Above-average proportion of Mercedes cars
IND	14,03–354,25	6.725	Index of purchasing power calculated for total Germany	83,97
USAL	1–9	9	Balance of relocation in the micro-geographic unit	3: Negative balance of relocations (more persons moving out)

selected from the set of 47 possible input features (or constructed using these features) and a binary output variable. As mentioned, this binary output variable indicates whether a person bought a Mercedes-Benz passenger car after receiving a direct mail or not. Since this information is available for people who received a mailing during similar acquisition campaigns in past years, this means that patterns are available for a supervised training of a model. The trained model is then employed to assess all of the German micro-cells. That is, the model has to generalize on the basis of previously unseen input data. Even if the models are trained using data with binary outputs (buyer or nonbuyer), the actual output of the model receiving a new input vector is a real number. In the application at hand, such an output will be interpreted as an a posteriori probability (score). The evaluation of new, previously unseen data is, therefore, called "scoring." Only those people living in the micro-cells with the highest scores are selected for a mailing, because they appear to be best suited with respect to the target variable. Usually, the problem of selecting the input patterns with the highest correlation to one of the classes is called "subset selection." Patterns yielding lower scores are assumed to be more or less "irrelevant' for the marketing campaign.

The threshold for the higher percentile of scores is defined by the so-called cutoff point. Sometimes practitioners and scientists suggest calculating the cutoff point using the financial campaign profitability (Piatetsky-Shapiro and Masand, 1999; Elkan, 2001; Ratner, 1998). However, we view this approach as unsuited for most scoring applications. When attempting to estimate the most profitable cutoff point for a single campaign, we automatically make the same assumptions valid for calculating the break-even point. In Arndt and Gersten (2002) we reasoned that is not possible to calculate the cutoff point from the financial campaign profitability: We would only add new uncertainties to the complex modeling process. Instead we strongly recommended fixing it at the beginning of the project. Since we are generally confronted with restrictions in available resources (budget, people, hardware, etc.), we are able to determine the cutoff point for business reasons, and thus it can be included in the project goal at the outset (e.g., find within the customer database the 20,000 subjects with the highest probability of buying).

In Gersten et al. (2000) we described general requirements for, and approaches to, measuring the quality of scoring models. Here, one can differentiate between input-related and output-related measures (Arndt and Gersten, 2002). In the latter article we presented an experiment that yielded the lift factor (Piatetsky et al., 2000) as a key output-related measure (from other measures such as the error rate, precision, mean square error, F-measure, and lift index). We set out the application difficulties in a business environment and offered hints on how to overcome them. However, if setting the cutoff point from the outset is accepted for the business application at hand, the lift factor should be employed to assess the suitability of a model.

The lift factor is a direct function of the cutoff point. To evaluate the performance of a model, the hit rates of the selected model and another available model are compared with respect to the cutoff point in question. Here, the hit rate is the percentage of "buyers" amongst the recipients of the mails. A random selection model—for reasons of simplicity of calculation and interpretation—is used as a bias model. From the business perspective, this means that recipients are chosen randomly. That is, the response rate for a random selection reflects the percentage of "buyers" in the entire population. Thus, in our case, the lift factor is given by

$$\text{Lift (cut)} = \frac{\text{hit\_rate\_model (cut)}}{\text{hit\_rate\_random (cut)}} \tag{4.1}$$

where cut is the cutoff point in question and hit_rate_model(cut) and hit_rate_random (cut) are the hit rates of the two models at this cutoff point.

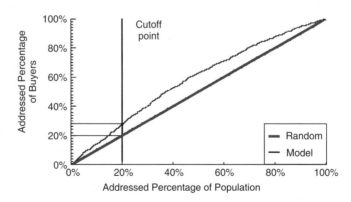

Figure 4.1. Graphical representation of the lift.

The graphical representation of the lift is the lift curve (see Figure 4.1). It shows the hit rates for different cutoff points. The gap between the two curves indicates the superiority of the model compared to the random selection.

4.3. STATE-OF-THE-ART: APPLICATION

4.3.1. Models for the Prediction of Customer Behavior

Previous work has shown that the single best data-mining technique that would be suitable for all datasets just does not exist (Gersten et al., 2000). For predictive modeling, we may, for example, choose between regression analysis, decision trees, neural networks, and rule sets. And for all of these data-mining paradigms, we can again choose from several algorithms. But the challenge does not merely lie in choosing from among the different paradigms and algorithms: The variety of parameters belonging to each algorithm needs to be considered, too. The general data-mining environment is summarized in Arndt and Langbein (2002).

Algorithms and the resulting models may be selected on the basis of time consumption, error handling, accuracy, stability, complexity, or comprehensibility. Since the results usually differ widely with regard to these characteristics, finding the perfect algorithm is unlikely. In most cases today, algorithm selection is a relatively pragmatic job. Organizations typically suffer from limited time and resources. And, sometimes only a single software tool is available, making utilization of the algorithms provided in the tool mandatory. Yet even when there is a choice of several tools, often a lack of the people with the necessary knowledge to use them hinders their application.

When performing the modeling for the original marketing campaign, DaimlerChrysler faced a tight deadline. For this reason, the decision was made to use the C4.5 algorithm (rule sets and decision trees) and the MLP networks provided by the commercially available software tool Clementine from SPSS, Inc. Several parameter settings for these algorithms were tested using mass modeling techniques (Gersten et al., 2000). Some of the results are set out in Table 4.3. Even when satisfactory results were returned, the belief remained that further improvements could be achieved by using other model paradigms such as RBF networks.

4.3.2. Selection of Appropriate Micro-geographic Input Features

So far, the only task would appear to be the selection of suitable model paradigms and algorithms for a given dataset. In practice, this job is more complicated. There is also a choice to be made between relevant features available in the prior-selected data source. It gets even more complicated because the whole process becomes more complex when taking into account that, even for fixed data-mining paradigms, algorithms, and a single data source with given features, there are several alternatives for data preparation that will have a significant impact on the final model quality.

In this chapter, we focus on the tasks of feature selection and data preparation. Currently, the data miner generally decides the features that are potentially useful. This is done either by judging general data characteristics or by applying data-mining algorithms. When diverse algorithms using different measures of relevance were tested (e.g., the Gini Index), we found that the more algorithms were applied, the larger the number of different lists of relevance. And this is primarily due to the fact that there is no universally accepted measure of relevance.

Two approaches have proven useful when searching the space of possible features: starting with an empty set and adding features step by step (forward selection) or starting with the full set and deleting one feature at a time (backward elimination) (Liu and Motoda, 1998). The same approach helps when deriving new features from the original dataset (feature construction). Since Daimler-Chrysler has gained extensive business experience with micro-geographic data over the years, this know-how was exploited to derive new features. In particular, common techniques such as recoding and scale transformation were employed. For the subset selection, regression analysis and CAID decision trees were applied in addition to the feature rankings provided by the modeling algorithms. However, as a result of this variety, a large number of different sets of features were constructed and it became difficult to decide between the wide range of options. In the end, the task was concluded using the subjective judgment of experts.

Ongoing research activities generally target either model selection or feature selection and preparation. But it is our view that these two issues go hand in hand. Although the techniques investigated showed a satisfactory performance, we upheld the belief that the results could be improved significantly by applying other feature selection techniques such as evolutionary algorithms.

4.4. ALGORITHM

If we assume that clusters in the input space (feature space) of the model (classifier) that is to be trained can be described by means of multivariate Gaussian distributions, radial basis function networks (RBF) can be utilized as classifiers. These neural networks employ a localized representation, which facilitates the interpretation of classification results. Clusters in the feature space are separated by means of smooth hyperspheres. For a detailed description of this network paradigm, see Bishop (1995) or Haykin (1994). Here, RBF networks are used to model the functional relationship between micro-geographic parameters (input features) and customer behavior (output feature). We work with networks with Gaussian basis functions in the hidden layer, a linear activation in the output layer, and shortcut connections between the input and the output layers (see Figure 4.2). The activation of a hidden neuron is high if the current input vector of the network is "similar" (depending on the value of the radius) to the center of its basis function. The center of a basis function can, therefore, be regarded as a prototype of a hyperspherical cluster in the input space of the network. The diameter of such a cluster is given by the radius of the basis function. The activation of an

ALGORITHM 87

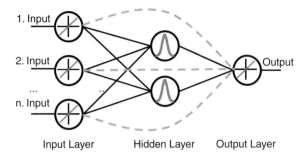

Figure 4.2. RBF network architecture.

output neuron is given by a linear combination of weights and activations of hidden, input, and bias neurons. Here, the networks are trained with a combination of k-means clustering, singular value decomposition, and backpropagation. First, centers and radii are initialized by means of the clustering algorithm. In a second step, weights of connections between the hidden and the output layer are determined, solving a linear least-squares problem. Finally, all parameters are adapted by means of a stochastic weight optimization method. Details of this approach can be found in Buchtala et al. (2003a) or Buchtala et al. (2003b). The combination of various techniques reduces the run time of the network training significantly.

An optimal classification or approximation result hinges not only on appropriate input features but also on an optimal network structure. Thus, we combine the two tasks of feature selection and structure optimization (also called model selection) within a single evolutionary approach [cf. Freitas (2002), Lacerda et al. (2001) and Kohavi and Sommerfield (1995)]. From an algorithmic perspective, evolution is a stochastic search strategy based on multiple solutions that can be used in solving a wide range of optimization tasks. Different classes of evolution techniques such as genetic algorithms, genetic programming, evolution strategies, or evolutionary programming evolved during the past (Baeck et al., 1997). Figure 4.3 provides an overview of the evolutionary algorithm employed here.

Individuals of the evolutionary algorithm are RBF networks. The representation of a network that is used by evolutionary operators for recombination and mutation is called a genotype, whereas the phenotype of an individual needed by selection mechanisms in order to evolve toward better solutions is the trained network.

4.4.1. Representation of Individuals

Here, we wish to select appropriate input features and to optimize the number of hidden neurons (prototypes of hyperspherical clusters). The set of possible features is represented by a vector of bits, with each bit representing the presence or absence of one of the features in the currently chosen subset. To represent the number of hidden neurons in the RBF network, a positive integer variable is appended to the binary string. This representation scheme may be

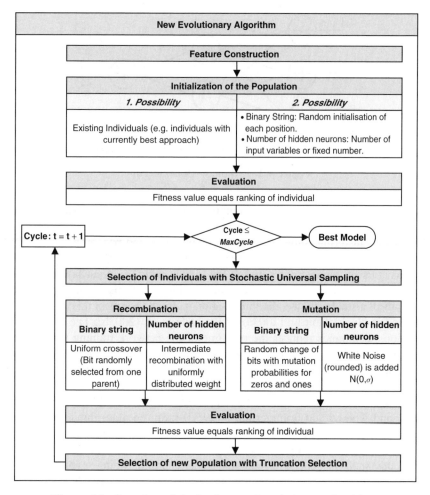

Figure 4.3. Overview of the implemented evolutionary algorithm.

viewed as a high-level specification scheme (weak encoding scheme) (Roberts and Turega, 1995).

4.4.2. Initialization of the Population

There are two main approaches to initialize the population that can also be applied in combination: random and nonrandom initialization. In a random initialization, the value in each position of the representation of an individual is determined by means of a random variable, taking into account the possible range of the values and the distribution of variables. Nonrandom initialization utilizes existing individuals or knowledge about successful values of individuals. These may result from prior optimizations, business knowledge, or other specific information concerning the application.

ALGORITHM   89

In the application at hand, a heuristic filter approach is employed to find appropriate input features in a prior optimization: The possible input features are ranked with respect to a class separability measure based on within-class scatter and between-class scatter, neglecting possible correlations of features (Theodoridis and Koutroumbas, 1998). The objective is to find features with a high discriminatory power. Based on this ranking, different feature subsets (with subset sizes of $1, 2, \ldots, x$) are selected. Next, these subsets are tested with different numbers of hidden neurons $(1, 2, \ldots, 2x)$. The best individuals from these experiments are taken for the initial population.

4.4.3. Fitness Evaluation

To eliminate stochastic influences and to arrive at a more realistic estimate of an individual's fitness, several instances of an individual (i.e., an RBF network with a specific architecture) are created and trained independently in accordance with a k-fold cross-validation technique (Bishop, 1995). The various instances are trained with respect to the least-squares error (LSE), whereas the fitness is determined using the lift factor computed for "unknown" data—that is, data not used for training purposes. A specific fitness value is assigned, corresponding to the rank of an individual in the current population. Hence, absolute differences between individuals are neglected.

4.4.4. Selection

The selection operator is responsible for modeling the principle of the "survival of the fittest." This principle can be realized in two different ways. While one way is to provide fitter individuals with a higher probability to build descendants, the other is to eliminate less suited individuals from the population. Thus, the selection mechanism is divided into two parts: (1) the selection of parents for creating descendants and (2) the selection for elimination from the population.

Typically, we find a number of different approaches for the selection of the parents—for example, roulette wheel, truncation, tournament, and stochastic universal sampling (Baeck, 1996). The advantages and disadvantages of the different approaches should be discussed in brief in order to explain our decision in favor of the implemented algorithm. Truncation is a deterministic approach. The best individuals are able to create offspring. In a stochastic search, every individual should receive a chance to inherit its genetic information to the offspring. But according to the principle of "survival of the fittest," the best individuals should receive a higher probability to survive and to create offspring. Therefore, truncation is a strong simplification and is only employed in huge populations to avoid calculations. Comparable conclusions can be made for the tournament selection. In tournament selection, the selection probability is better for individuals with a high fitness, but is not proportional to the fitness. The worst individual has no chance to create a descendant. Due to this disadvantage together with the low number of individuals in the population, tournament selection is not used for the implemented algorithm. Roulette wheel is the best-known approach because it is usually utilized for genetic algorithms. Yet it has some major drawbacks compared to stochastic universal sampling: The same individual can be chosen all the time. This is called large "spread." While stochastic universal sampling is also a fitness proportional method, it does not evidence spread. Today it is seen as the best approach for a fitness proportional selection, and it is used in the application to select the parents for recombination and mutation.

After recombination and mutation, the next generation of individuals must be established (next cycle). Again, different approaches can be drawn on to achieve this reduction of individuals (former parents and offspring). Here, the fittest individuals "survive"; that is, truncation selection is used. The benefits are that the best individual is preserved and that the former parents and offspring can be treated equally.

4.4.5. Pairing and Recombination

Recombination produces offspring from a set of parents by combining the genotype of the different parents. In the following, recombination is split into two steps. In the first step, pairs from a set of individuals that are to be combined are generated. In the second step, two descendants are produced from two parents using recombination operators.

There are various approaches for building pairs. Typical examples are exhaustive, random, rank-based, or distance-based pairing. Exhaustive pairing results in the maximum number of pairs. Therefore, in each cycle of the evolutionary algorithm, an enormous number of calculations are necessary. The disadvantage is that when a successful individual is generated, it still takes a long period of time until this individual can win recognition. Other approaches such as rank-based pairing are based on restrictive assumptions—for example, that the recombination of a very good individual with a bad individual can create a superior individual.

In the application, distance-based pairing is employed: The Euclidean distance reflecting the dissimilarity of two individuals is calculated for all possible pairs. For the chosen representation, the distance for two individuals is the sum of the input features being different added to the difference in the number of hidden neurons. Afterwards, the two individuals with the highest dissimilarity are paired and the pairing starts again for the remaining individuals. The assumption for the approach is that, by recombining different individuals, new regions in the search space can be achieved. Thus, in the application, this approach was chosen because the assumption intuitively applies to feature selection: The combination of relevant feature subsets (in this context, relevance is expressed by the fitness) may result in an even better subset.

After pairing, the recombination operator is used to create descendants. The recombination operator can be split into two parts: the recombination of the bit vector (input features) and the recombination of the integer value (number of hidden neurons). In the context of a string representation the recombination is called crossover. The commonly used crossover operators are single-point, multipoint, and uniform crossover (Baeck, 1996). The single-point and multipoint crossovers have a positional bias (dependency of the exchange probability on the position in the vector). This should be avoided in the feature selection application because the position of the feature in the vector is randomly chosen and does not exhibit any relation to the other variables. The uniform crossover independently swaps every bit with a given probability and leads to a binomially distributed number of exchanged bits.

For the integer variable (number of hidden neurons) a linear, intermediate recombination is employed. In order to take into account the fitness of the individuals, the values are weighted with their relative fitness.

4.4.6. Mutation

Mutation is a stochastic variation of the representation of individuals. Mutation operators are necessary to reach completely new regions in the search space and are, therefore, an essential part of evolution. In this subsection the mutation operator for the binary values is introduced with the method for the integer value 'number of hidden neurons' following.

For a binary encoding, mutation is the random change of a bit. The mutation operator employed in the algorithm is applied to every binary value and is controlled by the mutation probabilities. If the same mutation probabilities are applied to zeros and to ones, a drift toward the same number zeros and ones in the binary string is induced. To avoid this and to achieve that, on the average, the same numbers of zeros and ones are mutated, we work with two different probabilities for zeros and ones. In the application, the parameters are set in order to achieve that, on the average, one feature is taken out of the vector and one feature is added. Therefore, the mutation operator is better suited to search the local environment in the search space. However, with a low probability, the mutation operator is also able to yield access to completely new regions in the search space.

The integer value "number of hidden neurons" is mutated by adding a rounded white noise with a mean of zero and a certain standard deviation. This is derived from the typical approaches in evolutionary programming and evolution strategies (Baeck, 1996).

4.4.7. Stopping Criterion

The number of evolution cycles serves as a stopping criterion for reasons of its simplicity.

4.5. RESULTS

In the following, the evolutionary algorithm introduced in Section 4.4 is applied to the CRM problem set out in Section 4.2, and principal experimental results are presented. For the application, different runs using different initializations were tested. Instead of giving an overview of the results of these runs, the evolution process is explained in detail for one initialization. Results of the evaluation of some other experiments are cited in Neumann (2002) and Neumann et al. (2003).

4.5.1. Experimental Conditions

In this subsection the main experimental results are presented. The evaluation is performed by applying a fivefold cross-validation method to each network. Roughly 4000 samples were available for each training of the networks and an additional 8000 samples for each testing. The distribution of "buyers" to "nonbuyers" in the test sets reflects the real-world ratio, while a 50:50 ratio was selected for the training sets. The RBF networks are trained over 50 epochs (epoch learning). This number, which avoids an overfitting of the networks by early stopping, has been determined in prior experiments. The low number of epochs is largely the result of the RBF network training algorithm, combining k-means clustering, singular value decomposition, and backpropagation.

The initial population of the evolutionary algorithm is established using the heuristic filter approach described. The 10 best individuals from the filter approach are taken for the initial population. Hence, the initial population consists of networks with an average number of input features of 6.6 and an average number of hidden neurons of 11.7.

Table 4.2 provides an overview of the different parameters and their values.

The run time of the evolutionary algorithm is relatively high compared to other methods. For each evolution cycle, eight individuals have to be evaluated and, for each evaluation, five RBF networks are trained and tested. Therefore 4000 RBF networks have to be trained and tested for 100 evolution cycles. Assuming an average run time for each RBF network of about one minute (actually, the run time largely depends on the number of hidden neurons and the number of input features), the overall run time is about three days. For the application at

TABLE 4.2. Overview of Parameter Settings for the Evolutionary Algorithm

Setting	Test Run-Starting Heuristic Based on Discriminatory Power of Individual Features
Average subset size in initial population	6.6
Average number of hidden neurons in initial population	11.7
Maximal number of cycles	100
Population size	10
Number of mutations per evolution cycle	4
Number of recombinations per evolution cycle	4
Standard deviation for mutation	5
Number of epochs for training RBF networks	50

hand, a decision needs to be made as to whether this run time can be accepted by taking the advantage of the high lift factor or whether short run times are the more important criterion. The time required to apply the ultimately found model to some million input samples (scoring time) is also crucial in the context of the direct marketing application. Here, the time for evaluating a trained RBF network is comparable to other methods. In the end, the high overall training time can partly be compensated by the low effort for the scoring process. However, we remember that a parallel implementation of the evolutionary algorithm would be feasible.

4.5.2. Example Run of the Evolutionary Algorithm

When analyzing the evolutionary process, two aspects are of interest:

1. The development of the evaluation criteria chosen
2. The development of the RBF architectures

The lift factor and the mean sum-of-squares error (MSSE) of the networks (LSE divided by the number of patterns) are examined for test data. In addition, the development of the architecture parameters "number of input features" and "number of hidden neurons" is investigated.

Figure 4.4 depicts the development of the lift factor (measured at the beginning of each cycle). During the first cycles, the lift factor increases significantly even if it starts with the best network architectures selected by the initialization heuristic. The population converges toward a superior subset of features. Stagnation can be observed between the 11th and the 55th cycles. This is because all individuals in the population have the same input features from the 11th to the 55th evolution cycles. Improvements during these cycles result from a different number of hidden neurons. Finally, a new, appropriate input feature is selected in the 55th evolution cycle. However, an improvement in the lift factor is not

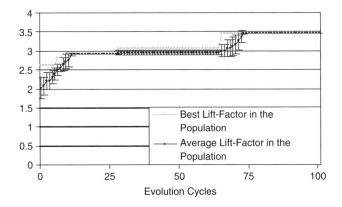

Figure 4.4. Evolution of the lift factor.

visible until the 65th cycle. Then, the process leaves the local optimum and converges to a lift factor of about 3.45. Hence, the model clearly outperforms the network architecture optimized by the initialization heuristic (and, of course, the random model).

Similar conclusions can be drawn for the MSSE. Figure 4.5 shows the development of the MSSE in the population. Initially, the improvement in the lift factor corresponds to an improvement (decrease) in the MSSE. This is not the case for the changes starting around the 55th cycle. The lift factor improves from 2.93 to 3.45, whereas the MSSE increases (i.e., worsens) from 0.172 to 0.195. This behavior shows that a low MSSE does not necessarily imply a high lift factor and that a higher MSSE even allows higher scores.

The evaluation of the network architecture during evolution is depicted in Figure 4.6.

Initially, the architecture evolves toward a small number of two-input features and a number of hidden neurons between 20 and 25. The development of the

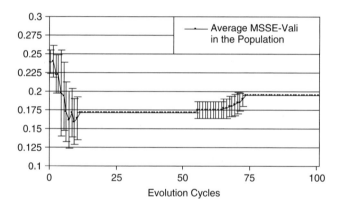

Figure 4.5. Development of the MSSE in the validation data.

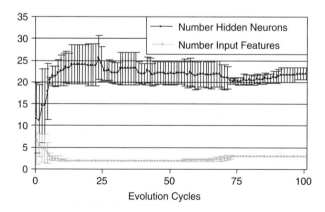

Figure 4.6. Evolution of the RBF network architecture.

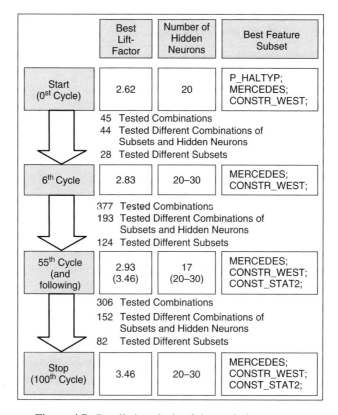

Figure 4.7. Detailed analysis of the evolution process.

architecture shows, together with the development of the lift factor, that key improvements are driven by feature selection. As long as the number of hidden neurons lies in a certain range around 23, no significant influence of the number of hidden neurons on the lift factor can be observed. Figure 4.7 provides a more detailed analysis of this evolution process.

Between cycles 0 and 6, for example, a total of 45 different individuals were tested before a new, optimal individual could be found. Of these 45 individuals, 44 were different in terms of their representations (genotypes). They used either different feature subsets or a different number of hidden neurons for the same subset. These 44 individuals included 28 individuals with different feature subsets.

4.6. SUMMARY AND OUTLOOK

4.6.1. Experience: Evaluation and Comparison to Other Paradigms

This chapter presented an evolutionary algorithm for feature selection and structure optimization of radial basis function networks. In order to measure the

**TABLE 4.3. Comparison of Results to
Other Modeling Paradigms**

Paradigm	Lift Factor
Random model	1
Decision tree	1.6
Multilayer perceptron	1.8
Radial basis function network (optimized with heuristic)	2.6
Radial basis function network (optimized with evolutionary algorithm)	3.4

success of the customized implementation, a short comparison to other standard paradigms should be given. The objective is to test (1) the impact of the RBF network paradigm and (2) the impact of the evolutionary optimization. In comparison to the decision tree and the multilayer perceptron, the RBF network achieved significantly higher results (see Table 4.3). The properties that are explained above clearly make this paradigm well-suited for the CRM application. But even these high results can be further improved by the evolutionary implementation. For a given dataset, the results obtained by manually optimized network architectures could be outperformed by about 32% (see Table 4.3).

The successful application of this algorithm to a business problem in the area of customer relationship management has been demonstrated. From a business perspective, the evolutionary algorithm turned out to be a breakthrough toward a more significant impact and higher efficiency of acquisition mailings. The economic yield points toward a higher number of products sold and, with it, an increase in profit. Specifically, there are three key reasons for the success:

1. *The Employment of RBF Networks with Their Specific Initialization Phase.* The comparison of results obtained for MLP and manually optimized RBF networks (for both, input features were selected using heuristics) indicates that the modeling approach on a basis of hyperspherical clusters in the feature space yields clear advantages for the application at hand.

2. *The Application of an Evolutionary Algorithm for Feature Selection and Network Optimization.* For the other models investigated, input features were selected either by means of business knowledge or by means of simple, manually executed heuristics. Hence, an automated approach was chosen here.

3. *The Optimization Toward the Business-Specific Measure "Lift Factor".* All other approaches are either only manually optimized or optimized toward the mean-sum-of-squares error (MSSE).

4.6.2. Suggestions: Applications and Algorithm Improvements

Application Point of View. However, we also mention the constraints we faced when deploying the evolutionary algorithm in the application at hand. An enormous effort in terms of human, computer, and financial resources was needed to adapt the algorithm. In practice, this effort may counterbalance the benefits of a more accurate target selection. The advantages of the evolutionary algorithm are largely contingent on the degree of improvement achieved. With soaring data and mailing costs, the benefit of identifying targets increases and, consequently, so does the potential of the evolutionary algorithm. This is also true for large scoring populations and repeated acquisition campaigns with the same or similar objectives. In today's buyer's markets the importance of individualized direct communication to prospects and customers is increasing rapidly. Therefore, the investment in customer relationship management and therewith the business potential of predictive modeling applications is growing as well.

When targeting these real-world applications of the evolutionary algorithm, a number of suggestions follow from our investigations:

- As the effort for setting up the evolutionary algorithm is not yet at a stage where the effort for marketing people to utilize it is acceptable, the evolutionary algorithm (and similar methods) should be integrated into easy-to-handle data-mining tools, and the parameters and their effects should be documented carefully.

- The superiority of the evolutionary algorithm compared to other feature selection and structure optimization methods should be investigated in greater detail.

In fact, the evolutionary algorithm described here may also be applied to comparable data mining and knowledge discovery problems. A combination with other network paradigms is feasible as well.

Algorithmic Point of View. A number of considerations regarding the development of evolutionary algorithms for architecture optimization of RBF networks follow from our investigations:

- The influence of recombination and mutation should be varied during evolution. Basically, the number of recombinations and mutations should be adapted to the progress of the evolution. The same also applies for the intensity of a single mutation (e.g., the number of bit switches). If a stagnation of the evolution is observed, completely new and different genotypes (individuals with a random initialization, for example) may be introduced.

- The influence of the distance-based pairing mechanism that opposes inbreeding should be investigated in greater detail.

- Another interesting notion is to change from a stochastic search to a deterministic search when the evolution process is assumed to be close to optimum. For example, all individuals having string representations with a Hamming distance lower than a given threshold can be evaluated.

- The clustering algorithm used for the initialization of centers and radii of the basis functions of the RBF networks could be improved by considering the membership of input patterns in one of the output classes.

- The extraction of rules from a trained RBF network should be investigated in detail.

To sum up, the automation of the feature selection and the structure optimization of a neural network is a valuable step ahead. However, it is well worth promoting future research into evolutionary algorithms for architecture optimization.

Our current algorithmic work deals with the application of the approach presented to comparable data-mining and knowledge discovery problems: Intrusions into computer networks are detected by means of statistical information extracted from TCP/IP header information (Hofmann and Sick, 2003), for instance. A second application example is the verification of handwritten signatures, where features from force sensors integrated in a biometric pen are utilized. In order to significantly improve both the run time and the performance of the evolutionary algorithms, we proposed a new training concept, introduced side conditions (e.g., small number of features or neurons) that influence the fitness of individuals, and built in a mechanism for an adaptive control of the evolutionary search with respect to the quality of the currently best solution (i.e., fittest individual). An overview of this new approach can be found in Klimek and Sick (2003).

REFERENCES

Arndt, D., and Gersten, W., Data management in analytical customer relationship management, in *Proceedings of the Workshop "Data Mining for Marketing Applications" at the ECML/PKDD 2001, ECML (European Conference on Machine Learning)/PKDD (Principles and Practices of Knowledge Discovery in Databases)*, Freiburg, pp. 25–38, 2001a.

Arndt, D., and Gersten, W., External data selection for data mining in direct marketing, in *Proceedings of the International Conference on Information Quality*, Boston, pp. 44–61, 2001b.

Arndt, D., and Gersten, W., Lift—A leading measure for predictive modeling, in *Proceedings of the International Conference on Machine Learning Applications (ICMLA'02)*, Las Vegas, pp. 249–255, 2002.

Arndt, D., and Langbein, N., Data quality in the context of customer segmentation, in *Proceedings of the International Conference on Information Quality*, Boston, pp. 47–60, 2002.

Baeck, T., *Evolutionary Algorithms in Theory and Practice: Evolution Strategies, Evolutionary Programming, Genetic Algorithms*, Oxford University Press, Oxford, 1996.

Baeck, T., Hammel, U., and Schwefel, H. P., *Evolutionary computation: comments on the history and current state*, reprinted from *IEEE Transactions on Evolutionary Computation* **1**(1), 1997; in *Evolutionary Computation: The Fossil Record*, Fogel, D. B. (ed.), IEEE Press, Piscataway, NJ, pp. 15–28, 1998.

Bishop, C. M., *Neural Networks for Pattern Recognition*, Oxford University Press, New York, 1995.

Buchtala, O., Hofmann, A., and Sick, B., *Fast and efficient training of RBF networks*, in *Artificial Neural Networks and Neural Information Processing—ICANN/ICONIP 2003 (Joint International Conference ICANN/ICONIP 2003)*, Lecture Notes in Computer Science 2714, Kaynak, O., Alpaydin, E., and Oja, E. (eds.), Springer, Berlin, pp. 43–51, 2003a.

Buchtala, O., Neumann, P., and Sick, B., *A strategy for an efficient training of radial basis function networks for classification applications*, in *Proceedings of the International Joint Conference on Neural Networks (IJCNN 2003), Portland*, Vol. 2, pp. 1025–1030, 2003b.

Elkan, C., *Magical Thinking in Data Mining: Lessons from CoIL Challenge 2000*, Department of Computer Science and Engineering, University of California, San Diego, 2001.

Fayyad, U., Piatetsky-Shapiro, G., and Smyth, P., Knowledge discovery and data mining: Towards a unifying framework, in *KDD-96 Proceedings: Second International Conference on Knowledge Discovery & Data Mining*, Simoudis, E., Han, J., and Fayyad, U. (ed.), American Association for Artificial Intelligence (AAAI) Press, Menlo Park, California, pp. 82–88, 1996.

Ferri, F. J., Kadirkamanathan, V., and Kittler, J., Feature subset search using genetic algorithms, in *Proceedings of the Second International Conference on Natural Algorithms in Signal Processing*, NASP '93, IEEE, Essex, pp. 23/1–23/7, 1993.

Freitas, A. A. (ed.), *Data Mining and Knowledge Discovery with Evolutionary Algorithms*, Springer Verlag, Berlin, 2002.

Gersten, W., and Arndt, D., Effective target variable derivation from multiple customer touchpoints, in *Proceedings of the workshop on Mining Across Multiple Customer Touchpoints for CRM at the Sixth Pacific-Asia Conference on Knowledge Discovery and Data Mining (PAKDD-02)*, Taipeh, pp. 1–13, 2002.

Gersten, W., Wirth, R., and Arndt, D., Predictive modeling in automotive direct marketing: Tools, experiences and Open Issues, in *Proceedings of the Sixth ACM SIGKDD International Conference on Knowledge Discovery and Data Mining, August 20–23, 2000, Boston, Massachusetts*, ACM Press, New York, pp. 398–406, 2000.

Haykin, S., *Neural Networks—A Comprehensive Foundation*, Macmillan, New York, 1994.

Hofmann, A., and Sick, B., Evolutionary optimization of radial basis function networks for intrusion detection, in *Proceedings of the International Joint Conference on Neural Networks (IJCNN 2003), Portland*, Vol. 1, pp. 415–420, 2003.

Klimek, M., and Sick, B., Architecture optimization of radial basis function networks with a combination of hard- and soft-computing techniques, in *2003 Proceedings of the IEEE International Conference on Systems, Man & Cybernetics, Washington, DC*, pp. 4664–4671, 2003.

Kohavi, R., and Sommerfield, D., Feature subset selection: Using the wrapper method: Overfitting and dynamic search space topology, in *KDD-95 Proceedings: First International Conference on Knowledge Discovery & Data Mining*, Fayyad, U., and Uthurusamy, R. (ed.), American Association for Artificial Intelligence (AAAI) Press, Menlo Park, CA, pp. 192–197, 1995.

Lacerda, E., de Carvalho, A., and Ludermir, T., *Evolutionary optimization of RBF networks*, in *Radial Basis Function Networks*, Vol. 1, Howlett, R. J., and Jain, L. C. (eds.), Physica Verlag, Heidelberg, 2001.

Liu, H., and Motoda, H., *Feature Selection for Knowledge Discovery and Data Mining*, Kluwer, Boston, 1998.

Mitchell, T. M., *Machine Learning*, WCB/McGraw-Hill, Boston, 1997.

Neumann, P., Soft-Computing Methods for the Identification of Relevant Features and the Prediction of Customer Behaviour in the Automotive Industry, Master's Thesis, Chair of Computer Architectures, University of Passau, Passau, 2002.

Neumann, P., Sick, B., Arndt, D., and Gersten, W., *Evolutionary Optimization of RBF Networks Architectures in a Direct Marketing Application*, in *Artificial Neural Networks and Neural Information Processing—ICANN/ICONIP 2003 (Joint International Conference ICANN/ICONIP 2003)*, Lecture Notes in Computer Science 2714, Kaynak, O, Alpaydin, E., and Oja, E. (eds.), Springer, Berlin, pp. 307–315, 2003.

Piatetsky-Shapiro, G., and Masand, B., Estimating campaign benefits and modeling Lift, in *Proceedings of the 5th International Conference on Knowledge Discovery & Data Mining* pp. 185–193, 1999.

Piatetsky-Shapiro, G., and Steingold, S., Measuring lift quality in database marketing, in *ACM SIGKDD-Explorations* (Association for Computing Machinery Special Interest Group on Knowledge Discovery and Data Mining), Vol. 2, Issue 2, pp. 76–80, 2000.

Ratner, B., *Assessment of Direct Marketing Response Models*, in *The New Direct Marketing: How to Implement a Profit-Driven Database Marketing Strategy*, 3rd edition, Shepard, D. (ed.), McGraw-Hill, New York pp. 340–344, 1998.

Roberts, S. G., and Turega, M., Evolving neural network structures: An evaluation of encoding techniques, in *Artificial Neural Nets and Genetic Algorithms*, Pearson, D. W., Steele, N. C., and Albrecht, R. F. (eds.), Springer Verlag, Vienna, 1995.

Theodoridis, S., and Koutroumbas, K., *Pattern Recognition*, Academic Press, San Diego, 1998.

5

SALES OPPORTUNITY MINER: DATA MINING FOR AUTOMATIC EVALUATION OF SALES OPPORTUNITY

JAMSHID A. VAYGHAN, JAIDEEP SRIVASTAVA, SANDEEP MANE, PHILIP S. YU, AND GEDAS ADOMAVICIUS

5.1. INTRODUCTION

In this competitive and unforgiving market, reliable financial and business forecasts have become more important than ever. An essential component of these forecasts is the awareness within an enterprise for the demand that exists for its offerings. A typical enterprise uses these forecasts to predict its future financial performance and to develop plans to support those predictions.

The demands for offerings of an enterprise are usually predicted by analyzing the size and quality of the sales opportunities and sales orders for those offerings. This analysis step is known as *pipeline analysis*. Figure 5.1 depicts major components of a sales management system that includes pipeline analysis.

The accuracy and reliability of pipeline analysis heavily depends on the quality of the sales opportunity data and techniques used to make predictions. For example, considering bad opportunities as good ones will make the predictions optimistic and unreal and will result in pursuing unprofitable opportunities. On the other hand, considering good opportunities as bad ones makes predictions pessimistic and results in losing profitable opportunities. Unreliable predictions might result in financial losses that may cause unrecoverable damages to the enterprise.

Next Generation of Data-Mining Applications. Edited by Kantardzic and Zurada
ISBN 0-471-65605-4 © 2005 the Institute of Electrical and Electronics Engineers, Inc.

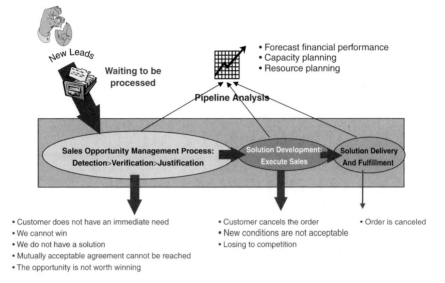

Figure 5.1. End-to-end sales management process.

Within a typical sales management system, the *Sales Opportunity Management Process (SOMP)* is responsible for the quality and reliability of sales opportunity data. A typical SOMP includes three stages that are executed in a sequential and iterative manner:

- *Opportunity Detection.* Evaluate sales leads to identify real sales opportunities for which there is a real customer who is seeking a solution.
- *Opportunity Verification.* Identify sales opportunities—identified in the previous stage—for which the enterprise can compete and possibly win.
- *Opportunity Justification.* Identify sales opportunities—verified in the previous stage—that are worthwhile to win and pursue.

Enterprises acquire sales leads through a number of channels. In a typical enterprise, human experts perform all evaluations without any significant assistance from decision aid tools. Each evaluation stage has its own unique criteria. Most enterprises continue to (a) look for ways to improve those evaluations and (b) find ways to provide better inputs to the pipeline analysis. They have following concerns with the current manual sales opportunity evaluation processes:

- *Shortage of Skilled Resources.* Manual evaluations of large number of sales leads and opportunities require a lot of skilled resources that may usually not be available. Therefore, many leads and sales opportunities may not get the necessary attention and may consequently be lost to the competition.
- *Human Error.* Human error is blamed for the loss of profitable opportunities or pursuit of worthless sales opportunities. Under both scenarios, resources

were needlessly spent and significant opportunities were lost due to the misallocation of time and effort on wrong endeavors. Furthermore, financial and business plans based on bad predictions might cause irreparable harm.

- *Execution Speed.* Slow execution speed can result in customer dissatisfaction, higher operational costs, and loss of opportunities to competition.

- *Opportunity Cost.* The above concerns increase the processing cost for sales opportunity data and reduce the capacity of an enterprise to process sales leads and opportunities efficiently.

Each identified sales opportunity is assigned to an owner. The owner is responsible for utilizing available resources to turn the sales opportunity into a deal that can produce revenue and profit for the enterprise. A wrong owner can lose a good sales opportunity, and a good owner can make a big win out of a mediocre sales opportunity.

The aforementioned concerns and challenges make *sales opportunity evaluation* an excellent domain for *data-mining* research. As shown later in this chapter, data-mining techniques can be utilized to develop the Sales Opportunity Miner that brings significant benefits to an enterprise. Some of these benefits are:

1. To improve the productivity and effectiveness of SOMP by *automating the* evaluation steps.

2. To extract actionable *knowledge* from the sales opportunity data. For example, SOM may predict that a given opportunity will fail to competitions for the reasons summarized by the feature values. That prediction can be used by sales agents and their managers to take proactive actions and prevent the loss of that opportunity to competition.

3. To use adaptive model (discussed later) to improve the performance of human experts responsible for opportunity evaluations.

The remainder of this chapter is organized as follows. Section 5.2 covers problem formulation. Section 5.3 includes a review of work on different areas of data mining that is relevant to automatic evaluation of sales opportunity data. Sections 5.3 and 5.4 cover development steps for Sales Opportunity Miner plus experimental results. Sections 5.5 and 5.6 include a conclusion and future work.

5.2. PROBLEM FORMULATION

The evaluation of sales opportunity data can be formulated as an iterative nonlinear multistage cost-sensitive classification system. The system is multistage because a number of different decisions are made in sequence. It is nonlinear because an optimal decision in one stage does not require optimal decisions in all previous stages. Also, differences in penalties for various misjudgments make

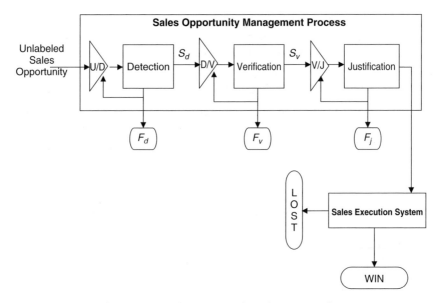

Figure 5.2. State transition diagram for sales opportunity process.

it a cost-sensitive problem. Figure 5.2 shows the state transition diagram for a typical enterprise sales opportunity system.

The process starts with a set of new and unlabeled sales leads. In the first stage, sales leads are evaluated to identify the ones for which there is a real customer need. Sales leads that fail to meet the "customer's need" criterion are archived as F_d. The sales leads that pass the test are usually known as *sales opportunities*, that is, S_d. In the next stage, sales opportunities are further evaluated to determine if the enterprise has capability, capacity, and resources to compete for and win the sale. The sales opportunities that fail this evaluation stage are archived as F_v, while the successful ones are classified as S_v. In the third stage of evaluation, they are verified against a set of criteria to determine if it is worthwhile (i.e., profitable now or in the future) to compete for them.

In a typical real-world situation, leads and sales opportunities that failed in one of the evaluation stages could be reevaluated again. Therefore, a sales opportunity instance labeled as F_v can be reevaluated and possibly be classified as S_v. This characteristic makes the process iterative.

Additionally, for a variety of reasons, a given opportunity may be broken into smaller opportunities at any stage. For example, a detected sales opportunity that contains customer needs for three different offerings may be broken into three separate opportunities before being passed to the verification stage. Each of the three new sales opportunities are verified and processed separately.

Conversely, for business reasons, justified opportunities going through the sales execution process may be combined. For example, the three opportunities from the previous example may be combined again when the sales execution team is negotiating a contract with the customer.

In a real situation, the state of each sales opportunity at a given stage depends on its present state and all of its previous states. From a computer science point of view, it would be difficult to model a state with many interdependencies. Even if such a model can be built, it would be complex and difficult to understand. One possible approach to manage the complexity is to construct each evaluation stage such that the state of any example in that stage only depends on its state in the most recent stage. This can be done if the entire process can be modeled as a *Markov decision process* (White, 1993). A brief description of a Markov decision process follows:

A sequence of random variables $S_1, S_2, \ldots$ taking values from a finite set X is said to have the Markov property provided that the conditional distribution of S_{i+1} given $S_1, \ldots, S_i$ is the same as the conditional distribution of S_{i+1} given only S_i. This is equivalent to the condition

$$P[S_{i+1} = s_{i+1} | S_1 = s_1, \ldots, S_i = s_i] = P[S_{i+1} = s_{i+1} | S_i = s_i]$$

A sequence of random variables $S_1, S_2 \ldots$ having the Markov property is called a Markov Decision Process.

To model the sales evaluation process as a Markov decision process, each evaluation stage is constructed in a way such that the state of an example in that stage only depends on its state in the most recent stage. Therefore, the evaluation of sales opportunity data can be considered as a *discrete-time Markov decision process* with a finite state space S and finite action space U. The dynamics within the process are defined by transition probabilities $P_{xy}(u)$, each representing the probability that the next state is $y \in S$ given that the present state is $x \in S$, and an action $u \in U$ is taken.

Let's use vector $\vec{X}$ to represent all features of a sales opportunity record and let's use y for its *class label*—that is, state of the opportunity. Using this notation, the sales opportunity data can be represented as $(\vec{X}, y)$. The evaluation performed in each stage can be represented as a function $f_i(x)$ that maps $\vec{X}$ to y_i for a sales opportunity example, with $i = 1, 2, 3$ referring to detection, verification, and justification stages, respectively:

$$f_i(\vec{X}) : \vec{X} \to y_i \quad i = 1, 2, 3$$

Historical sales opportunity data for an enterprise with a process like the one in Figure 5.2 includes evaluation results for all three stages of SOMP plus results from the sales execution process showing whether the sales opportunities that passed all the evaluation stages of SOMP ever resulted in any revenue or not. The final states are shown as *WIN* and *LOSS* in the Figure 5.2.

Supervised learning systems can be used to model $f(x)$ because historical data for sales opportunity includes class label. Decision trees and artificial neural networks are two of the most common techniques for building supervised learning systems. Prediction accuracy, understandability of classification models, and the way misclassification costs are accounted for are main criteria for selection of

TABLE 5.1. Confusion Matrix Definition

	Predicted Negative	Predicted Positive
Actual Negative	**True negative (TN)**	False positive (FP)
Actual Positive	False negative (FN)	**True positive (TP)**

a classification method. *Our experiments show that decision tree and artificial neural network classifiers have comparable predictability and accuracy for our dataset.* Therefore, the decision-tree classification method was selected since it builds a more understandable classification model.

Misclassification costs for a particular evaluation stage of a binary classification system are defined in this section. Possible final states for such a system with class labels of *Success* or *Failure* are shown in Table 5.1 and defined below:

- *True Positive (TP)*: Classifying an instance as success (i.e., positive) when it is *actually* a success.
- *False Positive (FP)*: Classifying an instance as positive when it is *actually* a failure (i.e., negative).
- *True Negative (TN)*: Classifying an instance as failure when it is *actually* a failure.
- *False Negative (FN)*: Classifying an instance as failure when it is *actually* a success.

Using the notation in Provost and Fawcett (2001), let the success and failure classes be denoted as $+$ and $-$, respectively. Let $\pi(+)$ and $\pi(-) = 1 - \pi(+)$ be the prior probabilities of a class. Let the cost of FP and FN be $C(+|-)$ and $C(-|+)$, respectively. Therefore, the expected misclassification cost for each classifier is $\pi(+)^*(1 - TP)^*C(-|+) + \pi(-)^*FP^*C(+|-)$.

The misclassification costs for TP and TN are assumed to be zero. In the above formula, TP and FP are the proportions of instances classified as true positive and false positive, respectively. It is easy to see that two classifiers have the same misclassification cost if

$$\frac{TP_2 - TP_1}{FP_2 - FP_1} = \frac{\pi(-)^*C(+|-)}{\pi(+)^*C(-|+)}$$

In a real enterprise, the false positive represents the bad sales opportunities that are perceived to be good ones. Pursuit of these worthless and unprofitable sales opportunities is one of the most costly activities for any enterprise, and it must be avoided when possible. On the other hand, the false negative represents the actual good sales opportunities that are perceived to be bad ones. Since these opportunities are never pursued, an enterprise may never know which of the rejected opportunities were indeed good opportunities. Consequently, it would be very difficult, if not impossible, to know, for certain, how many false negatives exist. Thus, reducing the proportion of false positive is usually more important to the business users.

The historical sales opportunity data that contain features and class labels can be used to build classifiers for each of the three evaluation stages. Since the class label indicates how a human expert classified an opportunity, the prediction accuracy of each classifier indicates how close the classifier's performance was in comparison to that of the human experts. These three classifiers form a multistage cost-sensitive classification system.

It is desirable to know if the above multistage classification system can be simplified if it is replaced by a single-stage classification system. A fourth classifier is built to investigate this hypothesis.

The real data show that many of the enterprise sales opportunities that successfully pass the three evaluation stages fail during the sales execution step. This is an indication that the performance of evaluations performed by the human experts for SOMP is not optimal. Therefore, there is a need to improve the performance of the above classifiers that match the human performance. One way to achieve this objective is to use the outcome of the sales evaluation step (i.e., WIN and LOSS) instead of the human judgments as the class label. Therefore, a fifth classifier will be built with a dataset that has WIN and LOSS as the class labels. This fifth classifier can be utilized to improve the performance of other classifiers while being an excellent training tool for human experts. Figure 5.2 shows the linkage between SOMP and the sales execution process.

To design the above classifiers, the sales opportunity evaluation process is modeled at three different levels of abstraction: white-box modeling, black-box modeling, and adaptive modeling.

5.2.1. White-Box Modeling

In this approach, all intermediate states within SOMP are taken into account and each wrong decision incurs a different penalty. Three separate sequential classifiers, one for each stage, are trained and tested. Each classifier is cost-sensitive and satisfies the Markov property and performs a different classification task—that is, opportunity Detection, Verification, and Justification.

Each of these classifiers uses different criteria to classify the sales opportunity data. Using different evaluation criteria implies the need for a different set of features and consequently a different dataset for each classifier. The class label for each of the three datasets indicates the human judgment. Therefore, the prediction accuracy of each classifier compares the classifier's performance with that of humans. In this approach, all intermediate states within SOMP are taken into account, and each wrong decision incurs a different penalty. Three separate sequential classifiers, one for each stage, are trained and tested. Each classifier satisfies the Markov property and will have its own unique dataset. Each dataset will have a different set of features.

5.2.2. Black-Box Modeling

To investigate the impact of ignoring the intermediate steps (i.e., using a single-stage classifier instead of a multistage classifier) within the white-box model, a fourth classifier is designed. In the black-box model, the intermediate success states within SOMP (i.e., S_d and S_v) are ignored. In this approach, the *success* class represents only those opportunities that pass all the evaluation stages of SOMP (i.e., S_j). The *failure* class includes all failed opportunities from SOMP (i.e., F_d, F_v, and F_j).

5.2.3. Adaptive Modeling

The class label for the training and test datasets used to train the classification models for the white-box and black-box approaches indicate how human experts evaluate a given sales opportunity. The prediction accuracy of these classification models is measured by how close they perform when compared to the human experts (i.e., class labels). However, many sales opportunities that successfully exit the SOMP are lost in the sales execution process and fail to generate any revenue. This phenomenon shows that the evaluation criteria used by human experts in the SOMP are not powerful enough to predict the final outcome of sales opportunities.

In addition, the dataset also contains the final outcomes (i.e., WIN or LOSS) of enterprise opportunities that successfully exited the SOMP. The historical data from the sales execution process is used to train a classification model (adaptive model) to predict the final outcome of enterprise sales opportunities for the sales execution process. The adaptive model can be used to predict the final outcome of opportunities that successfully exit the SOMP. The model is based on the features that are usually unknown to human experts responsible for sales opportunity evaluation within SOMP. The adaptive model can also be used to see how close human experts' evaluations within SOMP are to the final outcome within the sales execution process. In this approach, success reflects only opportunities that pass all the evaluation stages of SOMP plus the sales execution process (i.e., WIN). The *failure* class includes all failed opportunities from SOMP (i.e., F_d, F_v, F_j) plus any other opportunity that failed during the sales execution process (i.e., LOSS).

5.2.4. Rare and Infrequent Examples

A typical enterprise frequently encounters rare and one-of-a-kind sales opportunities that have not been seen in the past yet which may be indicative of new trends in the future. It is essential to capture these opportunities that have low probability but high misclassification costs and process them properly.

These rare opportunities may exist either in the training dataset or in the unlabeled dataset. When they are in the training dataset, the classifier can be trained to be more sensitive to those opportunities. This can be accomplished by using a cost matrix to make it more costly to misclassify rare opportunities as belonging to the dominant class.

When the rare opportunities are in the unlabeled dataset but not in the training dataset, they are separated from the dataset and processed separately. This is necessary to avoid losing them as outliers or having them misclassified as belonging to the dominant class. They can be separated from the unlabeled dataset using density-base outlier detection techniques.

5.3. RELATED WORK

Increasing demand for application of data-mining techniques to real-world business problems has introduced new and interesting challenges that have not been addressed before. Some of these challenges require integration and expansion of techniques that are already researched to some level and mostly with artificial data. To the best of our knowledge, no other work has been done in the application of data-mining techniques to the evaluation of sales opportunity data (Apte et al., 2002; Vayghan et al., 2003).

The automatic evaluation of sales opportunity data is unique in the sense that it requires integration and expansion of research work in a number of areas such as cost-sensitive classification, multiclass classification, multimodel classification, and nonlinear multistage classification. Using real-world data for this application makes the effort even more interesting and challenging. This section presents an overview of the current research work in the areas of cost-sensitive learning, sequential decision-making, and multiple-model estimation that are relevant to the automatic evaluation of sales opportunity data.

5.3.1. Cost-Sensitive Classification

Many researchers have worked on error-based or cost-insensitive learners (Zadrozny and Elkan, 2001a). The work in this area can be divided into two groups. The first group studies computational algorithms and how the cost matrix should be defined. The second group addresses issues in implementation strategy.

An interesting work in the first group is that of Elkan, which reviews the foundation of cost-sensitive learners (Elkan, 2001) and provides a discussion on how benefit can be used instead of cost as a way to define misclassification costs. However, he fails to address cost-sensitivity in multiclass classification systems and when costs are example specific. In another article, Zadrozny and Elkan (2001b) investigated cost-sensitive learners when misclassification costs are example-specific. They experimented with a number of estimation techniques like *smoothing*—that is, using techniques like the *Laplace correction method* to adjust estimates to be less extreme. However, this technique suffers from the problem of *sample selection bias*. Pednault et al. (2000) argue that high-cost and low-probability outcomes can have a disproportionate influence on the estimation error of the overall cost measure. They propose taking statistical estimation errors into account when constructing splits in decision trees. However, it is not always possible to have a good estimation for the error. Another research in this area is that of Fan et al. (2002), who define a generic framework for scalable cost-sensitive learning systems based on ensembles of classifiers. They propose an averaging method to combine probability and benefit outputs of cost-sensitive learners. They claim that their averaging method achieves a benefit level as good as or better than the respective single classifier trained from the same dataset as a whole.

There are two approaches to building cost-sensitive learners. One is to build a native cost-sensitive learner. The other is to make cost-insensitive learners become cost-sensitive. An example of the former approach is IBM ProbE (Probabilistic Estimation) (Pednault et al., 2000). ProbE explicitly uses statistical estimation errors when constructing splits in a decision tree. An example of the second approach is Domingos' proposal to develop a procedure to make existing error-based learners cost-sensitive. He proposed and evaluated MetaCost (Domingos, 1999), which provides a technique for wrapping a cost-sensitive procedure around cost-insensitive classifiers. Though MetaCost has been used by many groups, it may fail when there are a number of high-cost and low-probability examples in the training dataset—that is, rare and exceptional sales opportunities. Fan et al. (1999) propose AdaCost, a variant of the AdaBoost algorithm. Ada-Cost is a misclassification cost-sensitive boosting method that incorporates cost into the weight-updating rule of AdaBoost. It uses the cost of misclassifications to adjust the training data distribution on successive boosting iterations.

There are many other interesting articles on cost-sensitive learning. The majority of the published work deals with binary classifiers. We are not aware of any major work on multiclass cost-sensitive classifiers that SOMP deals with.

5.3.2. Multimodel Classification

A number of techniques have been proposed to build multimodel classification systems. The most common technique is to use the domain knowledge to segment the master dataset and build a classification model for each segment. This is a practical technique and can produce good results when data segmentation can be performed by domain experts or a simple decision tree. However, this technique is suboptimal because the predictive strength of the segment models is not considered when defining the segments. Apte et al. (2001) proposed a technique that performs segmentation and predictive modeling within each step simultaneously, thereby optimizing the segmentation so as to maximize overall predictive accuracy. However, their segmentation algorithm needs additional enhancements to allow the segment models to incorporate local covariate dependencies and feature selection.

The other technique is that of Ma and Cherkassky (2002). They propose a method for nonlinear classification using a collection of several simple linear classifiers. Their experiments show that their method yields similar or better prediction accuracy than standard nonlinear Support Vector Machine (SVM) classifiers. However, the majority of current techniques in the multimodel classification ignore the fact that there may be interdependencies across models and data segmentation. These interdependencies can have significant undesirable impacts on the performance of the final classification model.

5.3.3. Multistage Classification

Evaluation of the sales opportunity data is typically accomplished in a number of sequential stages. Each evaluation stage is supposed to answer a very specific question, for each sales opportunity, like "Is there a customer need?", "Can we win?", and "Is it worth winning?" Such a process can be formulated as a multistage classification system in which each stage has a particular classification task to perform. The multistage classification problem has not been well investigated by researchers yet.

The closest related work is the multistage classification of images that was done by Smith and Chang (1997). To control the complexity of each stage, they assume that there is a predefined template for each stage of classification. Therefore, their classification problem is reduced to a matching problem. However, the classification model for each stage of SOMP is not known in advance and is built from the training dataset. As was discussed before, the complexity of each stage of SOMP is reduced by modeling it as a Markov decision process. The Markov decision process is a mature area and has been applied to many applications (White, 1993).

5.3.4. Detection of Anomalies and Unexpected Patterns

Classification models are mostly trained to discover recurring and frequent patterns in a dataset. There is always the possibility of finding sales opportunity examples that have not been seen very often in the past but are important to the business. These rare opportunities might indicate future trends in the market that each enterprise wants to detect as early as possible. A typical inductive learning system is trained to classify examples based on patterns present in the training dataset. Therefore, rare and unexpected examples that are not present frequently enough in the past are usually misclassified as belonging to the dominant classes. Existing work on anomaly detection and discovery of unexpected patterns (Padmanabhan and Tuzhilin, 2002) may provide a few alternatives for detection of one-of-a-kind sales leads and opportunities.

5.3.5. Feature Subset Selection

The performance of data-mining applications that use real data depends a lot on the quality of data and performance of feature subset selection process. There has been significant research in this area. Dash and Liu (1997) surveyed many recent feature selection techniques and discovered that a common definition of feature selection does not exist. They propose the following definition:

Feature selection attempts to select the minimally sized subset of features according to the following criteria:

- *The classification accuracy does not significantly decrease.*
- *The resulting class distribution, given only the values for the selected features, is as close as possible to the original class distribution, given all features.*

5.3.6. Multiclass Classification

Multiclass classification is a central problem in machine learning, because the numbers of applications that require discrimination among several classes are increasing. There are two main approaches to building multiclass classifiers. The first approach is to combine several binary classifiers. This approach works fine when each class can be separated from the other classes. The other approach is to directly consider all the class labels at once. Implementation of the latter approach is computationally expensive when there are many class labels to consider. Hsu and Lin (2002) compare the performance of support vector machine-based multiclass classifiers built using both approaches. Their results show that the combination of binary classifiers is more practical and provides reasonable performance.

5.4. SALES OPPORTUNITY MINER

Figure 5.3 depicts the end-to-end process—steps 1 to 8—used to develop the Sales Opportunity Miner (SOM). It also shows how the final classification model—steps I to III—is used to classify unlabeled data. It includes data preparation, feature subset selection, training, and testing of the classification models. IBM Intelligent Miner for Data (referred hereafter as IM) was used to perform all of the data-mining functions.

The process of building the classification model starts with extraction of data from the master data source that is stored in IBM DB2. With the assistance of domain experts, four different datasets, one for the black-model and three for the white-box model, were generated. Candidate features for each dataset were selected after consultation with domain experts. Datasets were loaded into another instance of IBM DB2 that was configured to interact with IM. The next step was to select minimum feature subsets for each dataset that can be used together to predict class labels. The feature subset selection is an iterative process and is performed using feature correlation analysis.

After the feature subset selection step, each dataset is partitioned into training and testing dataset. To ensure the randomness of each dataset, the Bivariate statistics function of IM was used to generate mutually exclusive training and test datasets.

The next step is to use each training dataset and cost matrix to train and build the initial classification model. Each model is used to classify its corresponding

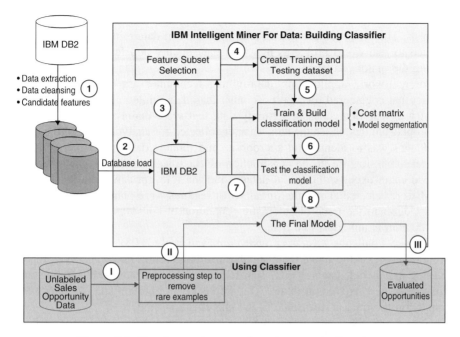

Figure 5.3. Development process for sales opportunity miner.

testing dataset. The confusion matrix for each testing dataset is used to analyze the performance of the classification model. The following subjective criteria are used as the *acceptance criteria* for each classification model:

1. Prediction accuracy: This is the percent of correct classifications for the entire testing dataset.
2. Benefit analysis: The false-positive and the false-negative distributions are used to evaluate the cost-sensitive part of the model.
3. Classification accuracy for the rare examples.

Depending on the analysis result, the feature subset and parameters of the classification builder (e.g., cost matrix, depth of tree, pruning level) at the training stage are adjusted and a new model is built. This step is repeated until the classification model meets the acceptance criteria. A model that satisfies the acceptance criteria is used to automatically evaluate the unlabeled sales opportunity data. The remainder of this section describes each step in further detail.

5.4.1. Data Source Identification

Data source identification is one of the important steps in development of any data-mining application that uses real-world data. One the other hand, applications that use artificial data are not usually concerned with this step because they assume that an adequate dataset is always available to them for use in their analysis. This is not an acceptable assumption when data-mining techniques are applied to real-world problems in which data quality and feature selection are among the major challenges.

For real-world applications, data-mining techniques are often applied to a dataset that is gathered for a purpose other than data mining. The data source for SOM was historical sales opportunity data that were mainly collected to track sales opportunities. Since the data was not collected for analytics, one of the early challenges was to identify an appropriate and reliable data subset that contains data elements for use in the construction of classification models. With support from domain experts, the initial dataset and the relevant candidate features for SOM were selected. Thus, the initial set of features were obtained from domain knowledge and the issue of automatic generation or construction of features for this domain is not addressed here.

The next challenge was *data preparation* (Tan et al., 2005). The initial datasets were preprocessed to make them suitable for data-mining functions. The preprocessing step included aggregation, transformation, discretization, binarization, and creation of new derived attributes. This step is very important and has significant impact on the final performance of the classification models.

Classification systems for the black-box model and three stages of the white-box model make different kind of predictions. Since classification criteria and class labels for each system are unique, each classifier requires its own dataset and features. However, features and class labels can exist in more than one dataset.

In addition to features, every opportunity data has a class label. The value of the class label indicates the state of an opportunity and why the opportunity is in that specific state. For example, an opportunity may be labeled as *lost to competition* in the Verification stage or being *successfully verified* and ready to move to the Justification stage.

5.4.2. IBM Intelligent Miner for Data

Data-mining experiments for SOM were performed using IBM Intelligent Miner for Data version 8.1 under MS Windows NT environment. The IM supports relational and nonrelational datasets. In addition to classification and clustering data-mining functions, it has a set of functions that can be used to preprocess and prepare data for mining. For example, it provides Bivariate statistics that could be used to analyze potential features and build random training and testing datasets.

For SOM, we used IM in a number of different ways. Its Bivariate statistics function was used to generate random training and testing datasets. Its k-means clustering function was used to build clusters in the feature subset selection step. Its decision-tree classification builder was used to construct classification models.

IM provides a number of ways to automatically build learning systems including tree-structured classifiers and feed-forward neural networks. Like other systems that build decision-tree-based classifiers, IM decision tree builder has a *tree growth phase* and *pruning phase*. IM uses the SPRINT algorithm (Shafer et al., 1996) to implement the tree growth phase. The pruning phase is based on the SLIQ algorithm (Mehta et al., 1996). Technical details of IM are described in *Using Oracle, SPSS and SAS as Sample Data Sources* (1998). IM also provides a number of ways to visualize the dataset and data-mining results.

5.4.3. Feature Subset Selection

The data source had many candidate features. The next challenge was to select the minimal subset of candidate features to build a classification model that could predict the class label. The feature subset selection process is an iterative process and has two main steps:

1. Using correlation analysis, the correlation between each candidate feature and class label is analyzed. Higher-order correlations of feature subsets with class label should also be analyzed. Due to high complexity for evaluating all such cases, here only features that show a strong correlation with a class label are selected for further analysis.

2. Features selected in the previous step are used together to train classification models. Classification models are analyzed by domain experts and data-mining experts to determine whether a feature should be selected or not.

To demonstrate the process, selection steps for candidate feature X5 are discussed. Using k-means clustering technique of IM, one of the datasets was partitioned into four clusters. Next, each cluster was analyzed to determine the correlation between X5 and the class label. Results are included in Table 5.2.

In the first cluster, which includes 44.14% of examples, the class label (i.e., Y) is predominantly Failure. In the second cluster, which includes 39.51% of examples, the class label is predominantly Success. IM also provides graphical representations of the clustering results that are not included in this section.

One possible outcome of the above analysis is that when X5 is used alone, there might be a strong correlation between X5 and the class label. In the next

TABLE 5.2. Correlation Analysis for Feature X5

Cluster Number	Size	Characteristics
1	44.14%	[Y] happens to be predominantly F and X5 is predominantly 25.
2	39.51%	[Y] happens to be predominantly S and X5 is predominantly 100.
3	9.87%	X5 is predominantly 50 and [Y] happens to be predominantly F.
4	6.48%	X5 is predominantly 75 and [Y] happens to be predominantly F.

TABLE 5.3. Confusion Matrix for X5, X6, and X9

	F (Predicted)	S (Predicted)	Total
F (Actual)	9,839 (55.16%)	548 (3.07%)	10,387 (58.24%)
S (Actual)	959 (5.38%)	6,490 (36.39%)	7,449 (41.76%)
Total	10,798 (60.54%)	7,038 (39.46%)	17,836 (100.00%)

TABLE 5.4. Confusion Matrix for X6 and X9 (X5 Is Removed)

	F (Predicted)	S (Predicted)	Total
F (Actual)	8,413 (47.17%)	1,974 (11.07%)	10,387 (58.24%)
S (Actual)	4,598 (25.78%)	2,851 (15.98%)	7,449 (41.76%)
Total	13,011 (72.95%)	4,825 (27.05%)	17,836 (100.00%)

step, features X5, X6, and X9 are used to build a decision tree classifier with the same training dataset. The trained model was run on a test dataset that included 16,329 examples. Table 5.3 is the confusion matrix for this step and shows a classification accuracy of 92% for the testing dataset.

Additional classifiers were built with X5. Analysis and examination of the classification models showed that every model that included X5 as a feature had a minimum accuracy of 92%. Follow up with the data management group responsible for the data uncovered that the value for X5 had been typically populated after the final state of an opportunity was known (i.e., success or failure). This new information explained why X5 was a dominant feature and had a bias and an unrealistic impact on the performance of classification systems. However, it is impossible to know the value of X5 for any unlabeled dataset because the final states are unknown. Therefore, X5 was removed from the feature set, and a new set of classifiers were built and tested. Table 5.4 is the confusion matrix for the new classifier.

5.4.4. Cost Matrix

Like many other real-world classification problems, the evaluation of sales opportunity data comes with a cost. For instance, there is the cost of failing to identify a winning sales opportunity and the cost associated with predicting an opportunity as a winner when it is actually a losing one. The optimal prediction of win or loss inherently depends on these costs. Thus the misclassification cost for sales opportunity data is nonuniform.

In the case of sales opportunity data, the misclassification cost is not just the monetary cost used to evaluate the opportunity. For example, misclassification of a good sales opportunity (i.e., false negative) causes the enterprise to lose all benefits from that opportunity plus any future benefits that may arise from that opportunity. On the other hand, misclassification of a bad opportunity as a good one (i.e., false positive) can tie up the scarce resources of an enterprise and prevent them from working on good opportunities. It is usually possible to estimate the penalties incurred for the false-positive examples. However, it would be much harder to estimate the penalties incurred for false-negative examples because a good estimate for their values and potential benefits may not be known at that stage of the process.

It is also important that estimates for misclassification costs be understandable and verifiable. Elkan (2001) suggested that in some real-world domains, using benefit instead of cost makes the cost-sensitive system more understandable. The estimated value of each opportunity (benefit to business) can be used to estimate the misclassification cost. When using cost, the objective of the classifier is to minimize the misclassification cost. When using benefit, the objective of the classifier would be to maximize the benefit.

IM provides capabilities to build cost-sensitive decision tree classifiers from data. By default, IM assumes that each misclassification has the same cost or weight. Using real-world sales opportunity data, the impact of cost function on the classification performance was evaluated.

5.4.5. Data Segmentation

A large enterprise typically has many offerings and uses a number of channels to sell them. This usually results in nonhomogenous datasets. The dataset used for SOM included sales opportunity data for many offerings. To create a more homogenous dataset, each dataset was partitioned into a number of smaller datasets using a k-means clustering function of IM. Classification trees were built for each new dataset.

5.4.6. Building Classification Model

As discussed earlier, SOM uses the decision tree classification model. To automatically induce the decision tree from the dataset, each dataset was partitioned into training and testing datasets. The training dataset was used to build the initial classification model. Then the model was evaluated using the testing dataset. When the testing results did not meet the acceptance criteria, decision tree parameters (e.g., pruning level, depth of tree, misclassification cost values) or features were adjusted. After adjustment, a new classification model was built. This iteration was continued until the constructed model satisfied the acceptance criteria. This final model was used for evaluation of unlabeled sales opportunity, as shown in Figure 5.3.

5.4.7. Detection of Rare and Infrequent Opportunities

A training dataset may include opportunity examples with very low frequency. Hence, a cost-insensitive classifier that mainly focuses on optimizing the prediction accuracy may misclassify them. Misclassification of these examples usually does not have a significant impact on the classification accuracy. However, from a practical point of view, a classifier that fails to find rare and infrequent examples may not be acceptable. To influence the classification model to be more sensitive to rare cases, we used the cost matrix concept to influence the classification model performance by making it more costly to misclassify rare examples.

For example, class label 5 from Table 5.5 has a population of less than 1%. To make the classifier more sensitive to 5, the cost of misclassifying 5 as 1 is defined to be higher than the cost of misclassifying 1 as 5. The following empirical formula is used to define the misclassification cost:

$$C(L_1|L_2) = \sqrt{m_1/m_2}$$

In this formula, $C(L_1|L_2)$ is the cost for misclassifying L_2 as L_1; m_2 and m_1 are the number of records for class 2 and class 1, respectively. Table 5.6 contains the cost matrix for the data in Table 5.5.

The unlabeled data might also have rare examples that were not present in the training dataset. To avoid misclassification of these rare examples, the unlabeled data was preprocessed (step I in Figure 5.3) to separate them. The rare examples in the unlabeled dataset were identified using outlier analysis. They will be processed by senior experts who are looking for new trends in the demand.

TABLE 5.5. Dataset with Rare Class

Label	Count
1	73722
2	1693
3	2801
4	783
5	191

TABLE 5.6. Cost Matrix for Dataset of Table 5.6

	1 (Actual)	2 (Actual)	3 (Actual)	4 (Actual)	5 (Actual)
1 (Predicted)	1	6.60	5.13	9.70	19.65
2 (Predicted)	0.15	1	0.78	1.47	2.98
3 (Predicted)	0.20	1.29	1	1.89	3.83
4 (Predicted)	0.10	0.68	0.53	1	2.02
5 (Predicted)	0.05	0.34	0.26	0.49	1

5.5. EXPERIMENTAL RESULTS AND MODEL EVALUATIONS

Four datasets were generated for SOM, and were used to build classification models for black-box model, and the Detection, Verification and Justification stages of the white-box model. With assistance from domain experts, candidate features for each dataset were selected. Each dataset went through the feature subset selection process to select the minimal subset of features that can build an acceptable classification model. Remaining part of this section include various results for each dataset.

5.5.1. Data Sensitivity Analysis

In any inductive learning system, it is important to reduce the system's sensitivity to minor data changes. Data sensitivity analysis methods estimate the rate of change in the output of a model that is caused by the changes of the model input. Sensitivity analysis has been applied in many fields including complex engineering systems, economics, physics, social sciences, medical diagnosis, and risk assessment (Yao, 2003). In the case of data mining, sensitivity analysis techniques can be used to measure the changes in the output of a model (i.e., its performance) when changes are made in model inputs (i.e., features and datasets).

   To measure the sensitivity of the classification models, three different datasets were created from the original datasets. Each of these datasets was used to train and test a model. Due to space limitations, confusion matrixes for those models are not included here. However, comparison of these matrixes shows very little variations in the prediction accuracy (i.e., model output) between the classification systems. The comparison results confirm the fact that the classification models developed for SOM are stable and insensitive to minor data changes.

5.5.2. Decision Tree Pruning

The recursive partitioning method of constructing decision trees subdivides the set of training examples until each subset in the partition contains examples of a single class, or until no test offers any improvement. This inductive process can create a very complex tree that overfits the data by inferring more structure than is justified by the training dataset. The extra structure that was added to the tree to overfit the model to the data usually lacks statistical validity and makes the tree structure less comprehensive (Mitchell, 1997).

   To determine the appropriate level of pruning and to avoid overfitting of the classification systems built for SOM, a number of experiments were conducted with both training and testing. Due to space limitations, results of these experiments are not included here.

5.5.3. Feature Subset Selection Results

The feature subset selection process described above was used for each dataset. The result for feature X6 of the black-box model is included in this section.

TABLE 5.7. Cluster Description for Feature X6

Cluster Number	Size	Characteristics
1	57.95%	X6 is predominantly 113 and [Y] happens to be predominantly F.
2	21.47%	X6 is predominantly 59 and [Y] happens to be predominantly F.
3	13.82%	X6 is predominantly 97 and [Y] happens to be predominantly S.
4	5.93%	X6 is predominantly 75 and [Y] happens to be predominantly F.
5	0.84%	X6 is predominantly 125 and [Y] happens to be predominantly S.

The master data source for the sales opportunity data contains data for active and closed sales opportunities. Data records for closed opportunities have a status field whose value indicates why an opportunity was closed. Possible reasons for closing an opportunity include *winning the opportunity, customer cancellation, losing to competition*, or *enterprise decision not to pursue*. To create training and testing datasets for the black-box inductive learner, only closed sales opportunity records were selected, that is, the value of status field was transformed to be either *"success"* or *"failure."*

The original opportunity record that is typically used for tracking and reporting purposes has more than 100 fields. From a data-mining point of view, some of these fields are redundant because they provide different views of the same information. For example, the estimated value of an opportunity may be reported in more than one currency. After consulting with domain experts, about half of these attributes were eliminated as irrelevant or redundant. Using feature subset selection process, 15 features were selected. To illustrate the process, analysis results for feature X6 is included. Table 5.7 contains clusters that were created for X6. It shows that there is a high degree of correlation between X6 and success or failure of an opportunity.

Further analysis showed that X6 is correlated to the class label when used with other features to build classification models. X6 was used to build the final classification model.

5.5.4. Classification Performance

As mentioned before, a number of classification systems were trained and tested for the white-box, black-box, and adaptive models. The performance of these classifiers is reported in this section using their confusion matrixes. All models are cost-sensitive. To make confusion matrix and model evaluations for white-box and adaptive models more comprehensible, results are reported at binary level. At the binary level, results for F1, F2, F3, and F4 are combined to form a single failure class (i.e., F).

Black-Box Model. In this approach, all intermediate stages within the white-box model are ignored. In other words, only one evaluation stage is used instead of the three defined for the white-box model. The results indicate that the trained model for the black-box model does not perform as well as the models developed for the white-box model when both are compared to the human experts.

The dataset used for the black-box model has 29,726 records, from which 12,627 (42.48%) are labeled S and 17,099 (57.52%) are labeled F. The dataset is divided into *training* and *testing* datasets. The training dataset includes 40% of the dataset (11,890 records). The testing dataset includes the remaining 60% of the dataset (17,836 records).

The confusion matrix for the testing phase of the classification model that includes all features except X5 is shown in Table 5.8. The model classified 13,809 records (77%) correctly. The low classification predictability can be used to conclude that the multistage classification system cannot be replaced by a single-stage classification system for the dataset used for this chapter.

White-Box Model. For this model, different classification systems were built for the Detection, Verification, and Justification phases. The overall performance of these classifiers was very close to the performance of the human experts. The predicted values (i.e., columns) in a confusion matrix reflect the prediction made by the trained model, while the actual values (i.e., rows) indicate the labels assigned by the human experts to these opportunities.

Detection Phase. The confusion matrix for the training and testing datasets for the Detection phase are given in Tables 5.9 and 5.10. In these tables, S_d represents

TABLE 5.8. Confusion Matrix for Black-Box Model

H				
U		Black-Box MODEL		
		F	S	**Total**
M	F	**9,884**	503	10,387
A	S	3,524	**3,925**	7,449
N	**Total**	13,408	4,428	**17,836**

TABLE 5.9. Confusion Matrix for Training Step of Detection Phase

H				
U		MODEL		
		F_d	S_d	**Total**
M	F_d	**2,800**	234	3,034
A	S_d	167	**40,379**	40,546
N	**Total**	2,967	40,613	43,580

TABLE 5.10. Confusion Matrix for Testing Step of Detection Phase

H   MODEL

U		F_d	S_d	Total
M	F_d	**2,035**	399	2,434
A	S_d	241	**32,935**	33,176
N	Total	2,276	33,334	35,610

TABLE 5.11. Confusion Matrix for Training Step of Verification Phase

H   MODEL

U		F_v	S_v	Total
M	F_v	**32,149**	1,600	33,749
A	S_v	55	**26,396**	26,451
N	Total	32,204	27,996	60,200

TABLE 5.12. Confusion Matrix for Testing Step of Verification Phase

H   MODEL

U		F_v	S_v	Total
M	F_v	**26,489**	966	27,455
A	S_v	1,184	**20,693**	21,877
N	Total	27,673	21,659	49,332

the *success* while F_d represents the *failure*. In the training step, 43,179 out of 43,580 records (99%) were classified correctly. In the testing step, 34,970 out of 35,610 records (98%) were classified correctly. At their best, the classification models trained by this dataset perform as well as the human experts who were not able to separate bad and good sales leads effectively.

Verification Phase. The confusion matrix for the training and testing datasets of the Verification phase are given in Tables 5.11 and 5.12. In these tables, S_v represents the *success* while F_v represents the *failure*. In the training step, 58,545 out of 60,200 records (97%) were classified correctly. In the testing step, 47,182 out of 49,322 records (95%) were classified correctly. At their best, the classification models trained by this dataset will perform as well as human experts.

TABLE 5.13. Confusion Matrix for Training Step of Justification Phase

H U M A N		MODEL		
		F_j	S_j	Total
	F_j	**49,456**	1,085	50,541
	S_j	281	**23,869**	24,150
	Total	49,737	24,954	74,691

TABLE 5.14. Confusion Matrix for Testing Step of Justification Phase

H U M A N		MODEL		
		F_j	S_j	Total
	F_j	**40,784**	739	41,523
	S_j	739	**18,859**	19,598
	Total	41,523	19,598	61,121

Justification Phase. The confusion matrix for the training and testing datasets of the Justification phase are presented in Tables 5.13 and 5.14. In these tables, S_j represents the *success* while F_j represents *failure*. In the training step, 73,325 out of 74,691 records (98%) were classified correctly. In the testing phase, 59,643 out of 61,121 records (97%) were classified correctly. At their best, the classification models trained by this dataset will perform as well as human experts.

Adaptive Model. The white-box and black-box approaches were used to develop classification models capable of evaluating sales opportunities as well as human experts. As discussed earlier, many sales opportunities that successfully exit the SOMP fail to generate any business (i.e., LOSS) in the sales execution step. These opportunities usually fail due to factors that are not known to the human experts responsible for sales opportunity evaluations within SOMP.

The dataset used for this chapter includes the historical data from the sales execution process. This dataset can be used to train an adaptive model that classify sales opportunities according to the final outcome—that is, *ground truth* instead of human evaluations that are done in SOMP. This historical dataset is used to train the adaptive classification model. Tables 5.15 and 5.16 give the confusion matrices for the training and testing steps of the adaptive model.

Human Experts Versus Adaptive Models. The testing dataset used for the Detection, Verification, and Justification phases of the white-box model are classified by the trained adaptive model. For the Detection phase, it showed that many examples classified by human experts as good opportunities are considered as

TABLE 5.15. Confusion Matrix for Training Step of Adaptive Model

ADAPTIVE MODEL

		F	S	Total
GROUND	F	**54,773**	207	54,980
TRUTH	S	465	**15,013**	15,478
	Total	55,238	15,220	70,458

TABLE 5.16. Confusion Matrix for Testing Step of Adaptive Model

ADAPTIVE MODEL

		F	S	Total
GROUND	F	**44,473**	423	44,896
TRUTH	S	1,185	**11,509**	12,694
	Total	45,658	11,932	57,590

bad ones by the adaptive model. This shows that human experts are not selective enough in the Detection phase and allow many bad opportunities to remain in the pipeline. For the Verification and Justification phases, it showed that many examples classified by human experts as bad opportunities are considered as good ones by the adaptive model. This shows that misjudgments by human experts may result in losing profitable opportunities. Due to space limitations, details are not included here.

5.6. CONCLUSIONS

Automatic evaluation of sales opportunity data is an interesting and challenging problem for data-mining research. Our theoretical and experimental results confirmed the fact that data-mining learning techniques, when accompanied with adequate data preparation steps and domain knowledge, can be applied to a dataset that was created and collected for a purpose other than analytics. This observation illustrates the power of data-mining techniques when accompanied with the right level of domain knowledge and good data.

Three classifiers created for the white-box model performed nearly as well as human experts. The classifier for the adaptive model uses the analytic results from the sales execution process to discover actionable knowledge that can be used to influence and improve the performance of sales opportunity evaluation steps in which human performance is not optimal. In other words, the adaptive model provides actionable knowledge that provides feedback from the sales execution process to SOMP. This additional feedback converts the end-to-end sales management process (Figure 5.1) into a *closed-loop adaptive system.*

Automatic evaluation of sales opportunity data introduces the challenge of creating an integrated solution to address a multistage, multimodel, cost-sensitive, and multiclass classification problem. Working with real-world data rather than artificial data puts the feature subset selection at the core of this effort. Creation of an understandable model that could automatically generate actionable knowledge was another objective for the development of SOM that was achieved.

Significant success was obtained in achieving the above objectives by:

- Applying the decision tree classification technique to classification problem. The Markov decision process was used to model the multistage sales evaluation process.

- Using experimental and theoretical results to show that in real-world applications like automatic evaluation of sales opportunity data, the optimal solution for one stage does not require optimal solution for all previous stages.

- Exploring application of multimodel estimation techniques to multiclass cost-sensitive classification algorithms.

- Developing a simple yet practical approach to discovering rare and less frequent patterns in a dataset.

- Showing that the performance of a classification system designed for real-world problems is mostly controlled by the quality of data and adequacy of features selected to build the classification model, rather than the classification algorithm.

5.6.1. Future Research

The real-world problem analyzed by this application has uncovered a number of interesting research problems like multistage classification and multiclass cost-sensitive classification that have not been fully investigated yet. Results of our work can be a good starting point for further research in some of these areas.

In a real business environment, an identified sales opportunity is assigned to an owner. The owner is responsible to utilize all available resources to win the sales opportunity. A wrong owner can lose a good sales opportunity, and a good owner can make a big win out of a mediocre sales opportunity. SOM can be extended to assign appropriate owners to the sales opportunities. The new assignment capability can be formulated as a content-based filtering problem.

REFERENCES

Apte, C., Bibelnieks, E., and Natarajan, R., Segmentation-based modeling for advanced targeted marketing, IBM Research Report RC-21982, in *Seventh ACM SIGKDD International Conference on Knowledge Discovery and Data Mining (SIGKDD)*, San Francisco, August 2001.

Apte, C., Liu, B., Pednault, E. P. D., and Smyth, P., Business applications of data mining, *Communications of the ACM* **45**(8), 49–53 (2002).

Dash, M., and Liu, H., Feature selection for classification, *Intelligent Data Analysis* **1**(3), 131–156 (1997).

Domingos, P., MetaCost: A general method for making classifiers cost-sensitive, in *Proceedings of Fifth International Conference on Knowledge Discovery and Data Mining (KDD-99)*, San Diego, California, 1999.

Elkan, C., The foundations of cost-sensitive learning, in *Proceedings of the Seventeenth International Joint Conference on Artificial Intelligence (IJCAI '01)*, pp. 973–978, 2001.

Fan, W., Stolfo, S. J., Zhang, J., and Chan, P. K., AdaCost: misclassification cost-sensitive boosting, in *Proceedings 16th International Conf. on Machine Learning*, Morgan Kaufmann, San Francisco, CA, pp. 97–105, 1999.

Fan, W., Wang, H., Yu, P. S., and Stolfo, S., A framework for scalable cost-sensitive learning based on combining probabilities and benefits, in *Second SIAM International Conference on Data Mining (SDM2002)*, April 2002.

Hsu, Chih-Wei, and Lin, Chih-Jen, A comparison of methods for multi-class support vector machines, *IEEE Transactions on Neural Networks*, **13**, 415–425 (2002).

Ma, Yunqian, and Cherkassky, Vladimir, Nonlinear classification using multiple model estimation approach, 2002.

Mehta, M., Agrawal, R., and Rissanen, J., SLIQ: A Fast Scalable Classifier for Data Mining, in *Proceedings of the Fifth International Conference on Extending Database Technology*, Avignon, France, March 1996.

Mitchell, T. M., *Machine Learning*, WCB/McGraw-Hill, New York, 1997.

Padmanabhan, B., and Tuzhilin, A., Finding unexpected patterns in data, in *Data Mining, Rough Sets and Garnular Computing*, Editors T. Y. Lin, Y. Y. Yao, L. A. Zadeh, Physica-Verlag, pp. 216–231, 2002.

Pednault, E. P. D., Rosen, B. K., and Apte, C., The Importance of Estimation Errors in Cost Sensitive Learning, IBM Research Report RC-21757, 2000.

Provost, F., and Fawcett, T., Robust classification for imprecise environment, *Machine Learning* **42**, 203–231 (2001).

Shafer, J., Agrawal, R., and Mehta, M., SPRINT: A scalable classifier for data mining, in *Proceedings of the 22nd VLDB Conference Mumbai (Bombay), India*, 1996.

Smith, J. R., and Chang, S. I., *Multi-stage classification of images from features and related text*, Fourth DELOS workshop, Pisa, Italy, August 1997.

Tan, P. N., Steinbach, M., and Kumar, V., *Fundamentals of Data Mining*, Addison Wesley, 2005.

Using Oracle, SPSS and SAS as Sample Data Sources, IBM Redbook SG24-5278-00, 1998.

Vayghan, J. A., Srivastava, J., and Yu, P. S., Automatic evaluation and assignment of business opportunities, in *Proceedings for International Workshop on Data Mining for Actionable Knowledge*. In conjunction with PAKDD03. Seoul, Korea., April 2003.

White, D. J., *Markov Decision Process*, John Wiley & Sons, Chichester, England, 1993.

Yao, J. T., Sensitivity Analysis for Data Mining, Department of Computer Science, University of Regina, Regina, Saskatchewan, Canada, 2003.

Zadrozny, B., and Elkan, C., Obtaining calibrated probability estimates from decision trees and naïve bayesian classifiers, in *Proceedings of Eighteenth International Conference on Machine Learning (ICML 2001)*, 2001a.

Zadrozny, B., and Elkan, C., Learning and making decisions when costs and probabilities are both unknown, in *Proceedings of the Seventh International Conference on Knowledge Discovery and Data Mining (KDD '01)*, pp. 204–213, 2001b.

6

A FULLY DISTRIBUTED FRAMEWORK FOR COST-SENSITIVE DATA MINING

Wei Fan, Haixun Wang, and Philip S. Yu

6.1. INTRODUCTION

During the last two decades, our ability to collect and store data has significantly outpaced our ability to analyze, summarize and extract "knowledge" from the continuous stream of input. A short list of business applications is probably enough to place the current situation into perspective:

- A typical credit card company processes millions of new transactions on a daily basis.
- NASA's Earth Observing System (EOS) of orbiting satellites and other space-borne instruments send one terabyte of data to receiving stations every day.
- A typical affiliate marketing company records nearly 1 billion click-through data on a normal business day.
- A large trading firm can have up to a few million trades per business line in a particular market on a weekly basis.

Traditional data analysis methods that require humans to process large datasets are completely inadequate; to quote John Naisbett, "We are drowning in information but starving for knowledge."

Data mining is the complex process of identifying valid, novel, potentially useful and ultimately understandable patterns in data. In a relational database context, a typical data-mining task is to explain and predict the value of some

Next Generation of Data-Mining Applications. Edited by Kantardzic and Zurada
ISBN 0-471-65605-4 © 2005 the Institute of Electrical and Electronics Engineers, Inc.

attribute given a collection of tuples with known attribute values. One means of performing such a task is to employ various machine learning algorithms. Given a set of training examples of the form $\mathcal{S} = \{(\mathbf{x}_1, y_1), \ldots, (\mathbf{x}_n, y_n)\}$, for some unknown function $y = f(\mathbf{x})$, the learning task is to compute a *classifier* that approximates the true function to correctly label any examples drawn from the same source as the training set. We denote classifiers by $C_1, \ldots, C_L$. The $\mathbf{x}_i$ values are feature vectors whose components are discrete or real values—for example, the amount of purchase, merchant category, location of the merchant, its distance from the billing address, payment history information, frequency of purchase, and so on. y_i is called the *class label*, and it is drawn from a finite set such as $\{fraud, nonfraud\}$.

One of the main challenges in machine learning and data mining is the development of inductive learning techniques that scale up to large and possibly physically distributed datasets. Many organizations seeking added values from their data are already dealing with overwhelming amounts of information. The number and size of their databases and data warehouses grows at phenomenal rates, faster than the corresponding improvements in machine resources and inductive learning techniques. Most of the current generation of learning algorithms are computationally complex and require all data to be resident in main memory, which is clearly untenable for many realistic problems and databases. Furthermore, in many cases, data may be inherently distributed and cannot be localized on any one machine (even by a trusted third party) for a variety of practical reasons including security and fault-tolerant distribution of data and services, competitive (business) reasons, statutory constraints imposed by law, and physically dispersed databases or mobile platforms like an armada of ships. In such a situation, it may not be possible, nor feasible, to inspect all of the data at one centralized processing site to compute one primary "global" classifier.

Lately, *cost-sensitive* learning has been an area of extensive research interests (Dietterich et al., 2000). In many areas of application where different examples carry different benefits, it is not enough to maximize the accuracy based on the simplified *cost-insensitive* assumption that each example has the same benefit, and there is no penalty for misclassification. For example, credit card fraud detection seeks to maximize the total transaction amount of correctly detected frauds minus the cost to investigate all (correctly and incorrectly) detected frauds. Undetected fraud causes a loss of the whole transaction amount; it is far more profitable to detect frauds with a high transaction amount than to detect those whose amount is not even higher than the cost to investigate. Charity donation seeks to maximize the total benefit made up of the sum of all donated charities minus any costs to send campaign letters to potential donors. Similarly, catalog mailing merchants maximize the total benefit comprised of the profit minus the cost of mailing catalogs to all potential buyers.

We are interested in studying accurate and efficient frameworks for distributed cost-sensitive learning. We develop a framework to perform distributed cost-sensitive learning using an *ensemble of classifiers* or multiple classifiers, and we maintain similar or even better benefit than the centralized system that trains a single "global" classifier by shipping all data from each site onto a single site. In the fully distributed framework, base classifiers are trained from each distributed data subset on each participating site. To classify an unknown instance, the outputs of multiple base classifiers are combined using various heuristics to produce the final prediction. It is important to point out that our methods require that the feature vector or schema of the data on different machines are the same and they describe the same model. When the schema is different, the data need to be transformed prior to learning,

We evaluate two types of distributed learning systems, *fully distributed* and *partially distributed*, using two different ways to combine the base models that are trained at participating sites. In the fully distributed approach, each distributed site computes its model locally without any interaction (neither model nor data exchange) with any other sites; therefore, the method has "zero" communication and computation overhead. To classify an unknown datum, the probabilistic prediction by multiple models are combined together using variations of *averaging*. Classifiers are much smaller than the training set and usually do not contain any private information. It is feasible to bring all the models into a single site or several sites for classification. We identify a few properties of both averaging and the cost-sensitive decision-making process. Due to these properties, a fully distributed averaging ensemble has good potential of higher benefit in addition to its obvious advantage of high scalability and zero communication and computation overhead. Our study has shown that the fully distributed averaging ensemble (of probabilities and benefits of base classifiers) is highly accurate while avoiding both computation and communication overhead.

In the partially distributed approach, learning among multiple sites are coordinated and synchronized. Both models and a limited amount of data are exchanged among participating sites. Tree-structured methods or *meta-learning* (Chan, 1996) have been demonstrated to be accurate to combine class labels (i.e., *fraud* and *nonfraud*) for *cost-insensitive* distributed learning, or each example has the same cost and there is no additional penalty for misclassification. Meta-learning learns the correlation of base models' predicted class labels to the true class label. The tree is built bottom up; it recursively combines a few models at a time until a tree is constructed. Both models and data are exchanged among multiple sites, and all participating sites have to be coordinated and synchronized. One form of tree-structured method has quadratic communication overhead. We propose partially distributed learning methods that use variations of meta-learning. Our studies have found that these more complicated methods yield neither higher benefit (or accuracy) nor less overhead than the simpler fully distributed averaging ensemble. *The conclusion of our study is that the fully distributed approaches based on averaging is an accurate framework for distributed and cost-sensitive data mining and it has neither communication nor computation overhead.*

The high accuracy and zero overhead of the fully distributed approach via averaging ensemble will solve a lot of practical problems. The intrinsic parallelism of multiple sites can be fully used. Since there is no communication overhead, the total training time is only bounded by the slowest site. For applications where reliable connection is impossible (such as military and mobile computing), participating parties cannot be interconnected due to security and statuary reasons (such as different banks), the fully distributed averaging ensemble is appropriate. Since the number of classifiers to coalesce is not predefined and can be changed at any time without any further computation, it provides both robustness and fault-tolerance. If one site is down or decides not to participate, the other sites won't be influenced and the fully distributed learning proceeds without interruption.

6.1.1. Organization

In Section 6.2, we discuss the optional decision-making policy and two of its important properties that are used to design the distributed learning algorithms. We also review the probability and benefit calculation methods. We discuss the details of the new methods in Section 6.3. We also analyze the overhead of these approaches in Section 6.3.2. The experimental design and results are presented in Section 6.4. In Section 6.5, we discuss some important issues of distributed cost-sensitive learning. Related work are reviewed in Section 6.6. This chapter ends with a concluding remark in Section 6.7.

6.2. BACKGROUND ON COST-SENSITIVE DECISION MAKING

We discuss some principles of cost-sensitive learning that are necessary to design an effective distributed cost-sensitive learning algorithm. We start with an example of cost-sensitive learning. Suppose that the cost to investigate a fraud for a credit card transaction $\mathbf{x}$ is \$90 and the amount of transaction for $\mathbf{x}$ is $Y(\mathbf{x})$. In this case, the *optimal decision-making policy* is to predict $\mathbf{x}$ being fraud if and only if $(R(\mathbf{x}) = P(fraud|\mathbf{x}) \cdot Y(\mathbf{x})) > 90$, where $P(fraud|\mathbf{x})$ is the estimated probability that $\mathbf{x}$ is a fraud. $R(\mathbf{x})$ is called the *risk* to solicit $\mathbf{x}$. This optimal decision policy is commonly used in risk management. It is optimal because $R(\mathbf{x})$ or $P(fraud|\mathbf{x}) \cdot Y(\mathbf{x})$ is the expected loss (or mathematical expectation in statistical sense) of a transaction due to possible fraud. Only when this expected loss is more than the overhead to investigate fraud, it is worthwhile for a business to detect and challenge a fraud.

This policy has a few interesting properties. For simplicity, we use $P(\mathbf{x})$ instead of $P(fraud|\mathbf{x})$ to denote estimated probabilities. First, the exact value of $P(\mathbf{x})$ is not important as long as it does not switch from above to below (or vice versa) a *decision threshold*. The decision threshold $T(\mathbf{x})$ is the threshold to predict $\mathbf{x}$ being *positive* or fraud in this example. For credit card fraud detection, $T(\mathbf{x}) = 90/Y(\mathbf{x})$. When we rewrite the optimal decision policy using decision threshold, if and only if $P(\mathbf{x}) > T(\mathbf{x})$, the optimal decision is to predict fraud; otherwise, the decision is nonfraud. It means that the exact value of $P(\mathbf{x})$ is not crucial; if $T(\mathbf{x})$ is 0.2, both $P(\mathbf{x}) = 0.4$ and 0.5 produce the same predictions. We call this property *error-tolerance*. It makes probability estimate resilient to small errors. The decision-making policy is biased toward predicting expensive examples (those with high $Y(\mathbf{x})$) to be positive. Since $T(\mathbf{x})$ is proportional to $1/Y(\mathbf{x})$, $T(\mathbf{x})$ is small for expensive instances. It is more likely for $P(\mathbf{x})$ of expensive examples to be higher than $T(\mathbf{x})$. We call this property *expensive example bias*. Both properties help us design effective combining mechanisms (Section 6.3.3).

Next we discuss several approaches to compute $P(\mathbf{x})$, and also $Y(\mathbf{x})$ if not given.

6.2.1. Computing Probabilities and Benefits

The calculation of $P(\ell|\mathbf{x})$ (for example, $P(fraud|\mathbf{x})$) is straightforward. For decision trees, such as C4.5, $\mathbf{x}$ is classified by a "decision path" starting from the root of the tree and ending at a leaf node. Suppose that n is the total number of examples and n_ℓ is the number of examples with class ℓ in the classifying leaf, then

$$P(\ell|\mathbf{x}) = \frac{n_\ell}{n} \tag{6.1}$$

For cost-sensitive problems, in order to avoid skewed probability estimate at the leaf of a tree, we compute *curtailed probabilities* or *curtailment* as proposed by Zadrozny and Elkan (2001)—we stop searching down the decision path if the non-leaf current node has fewer than v examples and compute the probabilities as in Eq (6.1).

For some problems, the benefit for each record $\mathbf{x}$ is given. For credit card fraud detection, the transaction amount of frauds is the benefit for correct prediction. For other problems, such as donation and merchandise purchase, the benefit (donation amount and purchase amount) is not known in advance. There are a few methods to estimate this benefit. In this chapter, we employ the multiple linear regression method. The dataset to train the benefit estimator uses feature sets that are different from the one to compute probabilities; otherwise, probability and benefit outputs would be highly correlated.

6.3. DISTRIBUTED LEARNING SYSTEMS

We first discuss fully distributed and partially distributed approaches, along with their communication overhead, and explain why they may work.

6.3.1. Methods

Assume that there are k participating distributed sites and the data subset at each site is denoted as S_i, and a classifier C_i is trained from S_i. The classifier outputs a class label such as *fraud* and *nonfraud* and its member probability $P_i(\mathbf{x})$ ($\in [0, 1]$) for each testing example $\mathbf{x}$. For problems for which the benefit of $\mathbf{x}$ is not known in advance (such as charitable donation), a separate dataset is used to compute a

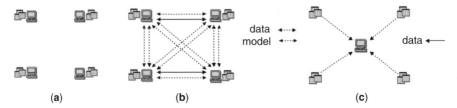

Figure 6.1. **(a)** Fully distributed. **(b)** Partially distributed. **(c)** Centralized.

model (such as linear regression) to estimate this benefit. Similarly, this dataset is partitioned, and a model $Y_i(\mathbf{x})$ is built from each partition. $R_i(\mathbf{x}) = P_i(\mathbf{x}) \cdot Y_i(\mathbf{x})$ is the individual risk of corresponding base models. In this section we propose several methods on how to combine the individual probabilities, risks, or class labels to compute a global or combined risk. We use $\overline{P}(\mathbf{x})$, $\overline{Y}(\mathbf{x})$, and $\overline{R}(\mathbf{x})$ to donate *combined probability*, *combined benefit estimate*, and *combined risk*, respectively.

Fully Distributed.   As shown in Figure 6.1a, each site computes its model locally without interaction with any other sites—that is, neither data nor model exchange. Consequently, it incurs neither communication nor computation overhead.

One straightforward approach is to simply average individual risks to compute combined risk,

$$\textit{Simple Averaging:} \quad \overline{R}(\mathbf{x}) = \frac{\sum R_i(\mathbf{x})}{k} = \frac{\sum P_i(\mathbf{x}) \cdot Y_i(\mathbf{x})}{k} \quad (6.2)$$

Alternatively, we can combine probabilities and estimates separately by averaging and then multiply them together. Using simple averages, averaged probabilities and averaged estimates are $\overline{P}_{avg}(\mathbf{x}) = \sum P_i(\mathbf{x})/k$ and $\overline{Y}_{avg}(\mathbf{x}) = \sum Y_i(\mathbf{x})/k$, respectively.

$$\textit{Multiplex Averaging:} \quad \overline{R}(\mathbf{x}) = \overline{P}_{avg}(\mathbf{x}) \cdot \overline{Y}_{avg}(\mathbf{x}) \quad (6.3)$$

We use *averaging* to refer to both *simple averaging* and *multiplex averaging* when the meaning is clear from the contexts. And we use *averaging ensemble* to refer to the ensemble combined using the averaging method. Multiplex averaging [Eq. formula (6.3)] is different from simple averaging [Eq. formula (6.2)] in that each $P_i(\mathbf{x})$ is multiplied with every $Y_j(\mathbf{x})$, then divided by k^2. The chance for the combined result being dominated by a big $P_i(\mathbf{x}) \cdot Y_i(\mathbf{x})$ is much lower than simple averaging.

Partially Distributed Learning.   In partially distributed learning as shown in Figure 6.1b, learning is distributed, coordinated, and synchronized among several sites. Both models and limited amount of data are exchanged among multiple sites. Typically, it proceeds in the following steps.

1. Each site computes its model locally.

2. Each site broadcasts its local model to all other sites.

3. Each site predicts with all models on a subset of its local data.

4. Subset of the predictions and true values are broadcast to either all or a few sites.

5. Either all or a few sites compute new models locally.

6. Iterate until a stopping condition is met.

The partially distributed algorithm usually incurs some amount of both communication and computation overhead. Previously, the tree-structured method or *meta-learning* (Chan, 1996) has been demonstrated to be effective to combine *class labels* (such as *fraud* and *nonfraud*) for *cost-insensitive* problems. Here, we borrow similar ideas for *cost-sensitive* problems. Meta-learning constructs a tree of classifiers "bottom-up." Let us use a binary tree as an example. In the first level of the tree, each base classifier will be randomly paired with another base classifier. For k distributed sites, there will be $k/2$ pairs in total. Each pair of base classifiers will be combined using some method, and a combining classifier will be computed to combine a pair of base classifiers. In order to produce the data to train each combining classifier, all base classifiers are exchanged among k sites, and a subset of predicted labels and true labels from all training data on all distributed sites is chosen and transferred to one single site.* The random selection of examples is to avoid a possibly un-uniform distribution of data among k sites. After generating the first level of combining classifiers, the resultant $k/2$ combining classifiers are combined in the same manner. This process proceeds recursively until a tree of combining classifiers with depth $\log_2(k)$ is constructed. A detailed description of meta-learning tree construction can be found in Chan (1996).

One of the most effective meta-learning methods is *combiner* or *stacking* (Wolpert, 1992). It learns the correlation of predicted labels (such as *fraud* and *nonfraud*) of base classifiers to the true class label of the same example. The training set to generate a combiner contains the predicted labels by two base classifiers and the true label of the same example $\mathbf{x}$, such as $((C_1(\mathbf{x}), C_2(\mathbf{x})), label(\mathbf{x}))$ or $((fraud, nonfraud), fraud)$ for one particular example $\mathbf{x}$. The original proposal of meta-learning outputs *class labels* (*fraud* and *nonfraud*) at the root of the tree. We manipulate the root of the combiner tree to output probabilities $\overline{P}_{combiner}(\mathbf{x})(\in [0, 1])$ using the method described in Section 6.2.1.

The second method is to use regression to directly combine probabilities instead of class labels. $P_i(\mathbf{x})$'s (the probability output of base classifiers) are interpreted as independent variables and true probabilities (1 for positives and 0 for negatives) of the same examples are used as dependent variables to compute a regression model, $\overline{P}_{reg}(\mathbf{x})$: $(P_1(\mathbf{x}), \ldots, P_{k'}(\mathbf{x})) \rightarrow \{0, 1\}$. The examples $\mathbf{x}$ are

---

*This is the most accurate and simplest way of meta-learning. In his thesis (Chan, 1996), Chan discusses more sophisticated methods.

chosen from the complete training set. Benefit estimates by base models can be combined similarly using regression, $\overline{Y}_{reg}(\mathbf{x}): (Y_1(\mathbf{x}), \dots, Y_{k'}(\mathbf{x})) \rightarrow y(\mathbf{x})$. When k' is big, training a regression model can be very inefficient. Instead, we generate a binary tree ($k' = 2$) of regression models that resembles a meta-learning tree as just described.

Depending on how the estimators are combined, we have

$$\textit{Combiner Averaging:} \quad \overline{R}(\mathbf{x}) = \overline{P}_{combiner}(\mathbf{x}) \cdot \overline{Y}_{avg}(\mathbf{x}) \tag{6.4}$$

$$\textit{Combiner Regression:} \quad \overline{R}(\mathbf{x}) = \overline{P}_{combiner}(\mathbf{x}) \cdot \overline{Y}_{reg}(\mathbf{x}) \tag{6.5}$$

$$\textit{Averaging Regression:} \quad \overline{R}(\mathbf{x}) = \overline{P}_{avg}(\mathbf{x}) \cdot \overline{Y}_{reg}(\mathbf{x}) \tag{6.6}$$

$$\textit{Regression Averaging:} \quad \overline{R}(\mathbf{x}) = \overline{P}_{reg}(\mathbf{x}) \cdot \overline{Y}_{avg}(\mathbf{x}) \tag{6.7}$$

$$\textit{Regression Regression:} \quad \overline{R}(\mathbf{x}) = \overline{P}_{reg}(\mathbf{x}) \cdot \overline{Y}_{reg}(\mathbf{x}) \tag{6.8}$$

If the benefit is given, we don't need to combine estimated benefits; thus there are three unique methods to combine probabilities, namely, *Averaging*: $\overline{P}_{avg}(\mathbf{x})$, *Regression*: $\overline{P}_{reg}(\mathbf{x})$, and *Combiner*: $\overline{P}_{combiner}(\mathbf{x})$.

Centralized Algorithm.   As a comparison, we also describe the centralized algorithm in Figure 6.1c. In centralized algorithm, the data from each participating sites are first sent to a single site. A global model is computed at that single site. Obviously, it suffers from heavy communication overhead to send all the data. In addition, most of the learning algorithms' complexity are worse than linear and request data to be resident in main memory. For example, the decision tree learner has a complexity of $O(n \cdot \log(n))$. If the data are too big or cannot fit into main memory in the worst case, the data will be swapped in and out, and training will be too slow.

6.3.2. Overhead Analysis

The total time to compute a model across a number of distributed sites consists of the training time of the slowest site, computation, and communication overhead.

$$\textit{Total Training Time} = \textit{slowest site} + \textit{communication overhead}$$

$$+ \textit{computation overhead} \tag{6.9}$$

We assume that there are k distributed sites, $k = 2^l$, and the total number of training examples from all k sites is n.

The fully distributed approach via averaging ensemble incurs neither computation nor communication costs. Since each site computes its model locally and independently, the intrinsic parallelism of multiple systems is taken full advantage of. The total training time is only bounded by the slowest site—that is, of

$c_2 \cdot O(g(n_{max}))$, where $O(g(N))$ is the complexity of the inductive learner and n_{max} is the size of the largest dataset. As shown in previous work (Fan et al., 2002b), averaging ensemble exhibits both linear speedup and scaled speedup when applied to scale up learning a very large dataset on a single site. Linear speedup and scaled speedup are the best possible.

On the contrary, both meta-learning and regression-based partially distributed methods incur communication and computation overhead. For simplicity, we assume that two models are combined at a time, and a random selection of n/k examples are used to train either the combiner or regressor (or combining model for short) in the tree. The tree has a total of l (or $\log_2(k)$) levels and $k-1$ combining models. At each level, all newly learned models are sent to every site to choose the random set of n/k examples. Totally, we transfer $\sum_1^l k \times ((k-1)+(\frac{k}{2}-1)+\cdots+1) \simeq 2k^2$ models for all l levels. To compute each combining model in the tree, $2n/k$ predictions and n/k true values are randomly chosen and sent to a single site. Considering all $k-1$ non-leaf combining models in the tree, there are $(k-1) \cdot 2n/k \simeq 2n$ predictions and $(k-1) \cdot n/k \simeq n$ true values, or $3n$ numbers or labels to be transferred. Besides transferring data and models, tree-structured approach consumes an additional computational overhead of $c_1 \cdot (k-1) \cdot O(f(n/k, 2))$ to compute $k-1$ combining models in serial or $c_1 \cdot l \cdot O(f(n/k, 2))$ in parallel. $O(f(N, K))$ is the complexity of the algorithm to train either the combiner or regressor, which depends on both the number of examples N and the number of feature k. To produce the training data for the combining models, all $2k-1$ (k base classifiers and $k-1$ combining models) predict on all n original training data, which brings an additional overhead of $c_3 \cdot (2k-1) \cdot n$.

As a comparison, the centralized system has to transfer all data to one single site for a total n original data points. The total training time on n data points is in the scale of $O(g(n))$, which is significantly slower than $O(g(n_{max}))$ when $n_{max} \ll n$, especially if n original training examples cannot fit into the main memory and memory swapping takes place.

As a summary, we list the overhead of all three methods in Table 6.1 as a comparison. The fully distributed averaging ensemble has obviously the lowest "zero" overhead, and the training time $O(g(n_{max}))$ is the quickest as well. It remains to be seen if its accuracy is as good as the other, more complicated tree-structured methods, and all distributed approaches will have accuracy similar to or better than the single "global" model of centralized learning.

It is important to point out that the overhead analysis is not comparing three different methods that will compute exact the same model. They actually compute very different kinds of models. It is not interesting and not useful to compute the same model since the ultimate purpose of data mining is to find a model with the highest accuracy. A truly effective and useful method is one that has the lowest overhead and highest accuracy. The simple motivation to compare different methods is to look for a method with highest accuracy and lowest overhead.

TABLE 6.1. Overhead Analysis

	Fully Distributed	Partially Distributed	Centralized
Communication overhead	0	$2k^2$ models $+ 3n$ numbers or labels	n original data points
Computation overhead	0	$c_1 \cdot l \cdot O(f(\frac{n}{2}, 2)) +$ $c_3 \cdot (2k - 1) \cdot n$	0
Slowest site	$c_2 \cdot O(g(n_{max}))$	$c_2 \cdot O(g(n_{max}))$	$c_2 \cdot O(g(n))$

k is the number of distributed site. $l = \log_2(k)$. n is the number of examples across all k sites. $O(f(N, K))$ is the complexity of the algorithm to train the combiner or regressor, which depends on both the number of examples and number of features. n_{max} is the size of the largest dataset at one of the k sites and $n_{max} \ll n$. $(2k - 1) \cdot n$ is the complexity to test all on n training examples using all $2k - 1 = k + k - 1$ models in the tree. $O(g(N))$ is the complexity of the learning algorithm to train on the training set. c_1, c_2, and c_3 are constants.

6.3.3. Statistical Explanation: How Money Is Saved

The total benefit or accuracy of the fully distributed averaging ensemble is also potentially higher as explained below.

The base models trained from disjoint data subsets make uncorrelated noisy errors to estimate probabilities. It is known and studied by Tumer and Ghosh (1996) that uncorrelated errors are reduced by averaging. The averaged probability may still be different from the global classifier of the centralized system, but the difference may not make a difference to final prediction due to the error tolerance property (Section 6.2).

The method that uses averaged probability for the fully distributed learning is very likely to have higher benefits than the "global" classifier because of its "even-ing effect" and stronger bias toward predicting expensive examples to be positive. To explain this effect, we use the *cost-sensitive decision plot*. For each data point $\mathbf{x}$, we plot its decision threshold $T(\mathbf{x})$ (Section 6.2) and probability estimate $P(\mathbf{x})$ in the same figure. The sequence of examples on the $\mathbf{x}$-axis is ordered increasingly by their $T(\mathbf{x})$ value. Figure 6.2 illustrates two exemplary plots. The left plot is conjectured for global classifier, while the right plot is conjectured for averaged probability of multiple classifiers. All data points above the $T(\mathbf{x})$ line (with $P(\mathbf{x}) > T(\mathbf{x})$) are predicted positive. Using this plot, we explain the *even-ing effect*. Since probability estimates by multiple classifiers are uncorrelated, it is very unlikely for all of them to be close to either 1 or 0 (the extremities) and their resultant average will likely spread more "evenly" between 1 and 0 (that's where "even-ing effect" comes from). This is visually illustrated in Figure 6.2 by comparing the right plot to the left plot. The even-ing effect favors more towards predicting expensive examples to be positive. $T(\mathbf{x})$ of expensive examples are low; these examples are in the left portion of the decision plots. If the estimated probability by global classifier $P(\mathbf{x})$ is close to 0, it is very

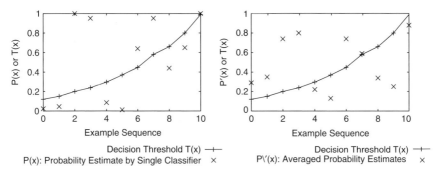

Figure 6.2. Cost-sensitive decision plots. The left plot is conjectured for a global classifier of the centralized system, while the right plot is conjectured for the averaged probability of multiple classifiers. Due to the *even-ing effect*, two expensive examples in the bottom left corner are predicted as positive by the multiple model.

likely for the averaged probability $P'(\mathbf{x})$ to be bigger than $P(\mathbf{x})$, and consequently bigger than $T(\mathbf{x})$ of expensive examples and predict them to be positive. The two expensive data points in the bottom left corner of the decision plots are predicted to be negative by the global classifier, but are predicted to be positive by the multiple model. Due to the even-ing effect, averaging of multiple probabilities biases more toward expensive examples than does the global classifier. This is a desirable property since expensive examples contribute greatly toward total benefit. Based on the above conjectured analysis, we think that averaging will actually increase total benefit.

6.4. EXPERIMENT

We have evaluated the distributed learning system for three types of cost-sensitive problems. They differ in how the profit of $\mathbf{x}$ is obtained and if there is any penalty for misclassification besides losing the profit. We discuss each dataset and different measurements in our experiments. This is followed by an analysis of the experimental results.

6.4.1. Business Application Datasets

We have obtained three actual datasets of cost-sensitive business applications of different levels of difficulty. In the first problem, neither the probability $P(\mathbf{x})$ nor the benefit $y(\mathbf{x})$ is known. Additionally, only positive example carries profit, and there is a penalty for false positives. We chose the famous donation dataset that first appeared in KDDCUP '98 competition. Suppose that the cost of requesting a charitable donation from an individual $\mathbf{x}$ is \$0.68, and the best estimate of the amount that $\mathbf{x}$ will donate is $Y(\mathbf{x})$. Its benefit matrix (converse of loss function) is

	predict *donate*	predict ¬ *donator*
actual *donate*	$Y(\mathbf{x}) - \$.0.68$	0
actual ¬ *donate*	$-\$0.68$	0

The accuracy is the total amount of received charity minus the cost of mailing. Assuming that $p(donate|\mathbf{x})$ is the estimated probability that $\mathbf{x}$ is a donor, we will solicit to $\mathbf{x}$ iff $p(donate|\mathbf{x}) \cdot Y(\mathbf{x}) > 0.68$. The data have already been divided into a training set and a test set. The training set consists of 95,412 records for which it is known whether or not the person made a donation and how much the donation was. The test set contains 96,367 records for which similar donation information was not published until after the KDD '98 competition. We used the standard training/test set splits to compare with previous results. The feature subsets (seven features in total) were based on the KDD '98 winning submission. To estimate the donation amount, we employed the multiple linear regression method. To avoid overestimation, we only used those contributions between $0 and $50.

In the second problem, the benefit is known and it is *per instance*. Only positives carry benefit, and there is also a penalty for false positives. We use a credit card fraud detection problem. Assuming that there is an overhead $v = \$90$ to dispute and investigate a fraud and $y(\mathbf{x})$ is the transaction amount, the following is the benefit matrix:

	predict *fraud*	predict ¬ *fraud*
actual *fraud*	$y(\mathbf{x}) - v$	0
actual ¬ *fraud*	$-v$	0

The accuracy is the sum of recovered frauds minus investigation costs. If $p(fraud|\mathbf{x})$ is the probability that $\mathbf{x}$ is a fraud, *fraud* is the optimal decision iff $p(fraud|\mathbf{x}) \cdot y(\mathbf{x}) > v$. The dataset was sampled from a one-year period and contains a total of .5M transaction records. The features (20 in total) record the time of the transaction, merchant type, merchant location, and past payment and transaction history summary. We use data of the last month as test data (40,038 examples) and use data of previous months as training data (406,009 examples).

In the third problem, the benefit is known and it is *per class* (as opposed to *per instance*). Unlike the first two problems, both positives and negatives carry benefits. Additionally, besides losing the benefit, there is no additional penalty for misclassification as opposed to the previous two cases. We use the "adult" dataset from UCI repository. We artificially associate a benefit of $1–$10 to class label **F** and a fixed benefit of $1 to class label **N**, as summarized below:

	predict **F**	predict **N**
actual **F**	$1–$10	0
actual **N**	0	$1

We use the natural split of training and test sets, so the results can be easily duplicated. The training set contains 32,561 entries, and the test set contains 16,281 records. The feature set contains 14 features that describe the education, gender, country of origin, martial status, and capital gain, among others.

6.4.2. Experimental Design

We use total benefit to compare different methods. It is the total profit obtained to solicit **x** being positive according to the optimal decision policy. For the donation dataset, this is the total donation amount minus the cost of campaign letters sent to both donors and nondonors. For the credit card fraud detection dataset, it is the total correctly detected fraudulent transaction amount minus the overhead of investigation of both true positives (*fraud* predicted as *fraud*) and false positives (*nonfraud* predicted as *fraud*). And for the adult dataset, this is the total profits of correct predictions.

Since we don't have truly distributed datasets, we simulate distributed learning by partitioning a single dataset into k subsets as if there were k distributed sites. Communication overhead records the total number of bytes to be transferred if these sites were indeed interconnected across a network. Computation overhead is the total extra training time to train the combiner or regressor. This is a widely adopted approach to evaluate distributed data-mining algorithms. One important aspect of our experiments is to test that the scalable methods' total benefit is independent of the number of sites k, or the total benefit of distributed learning across k sites is very close to the total benefit of the "global" single classifier of centralized learning system. We have chosen to use the following number of partitions, $k = 8, 16, 32, 64, 128$, and 256. To generate these data subsets, the original dataset is "sequentially" partitioned into smaller pieces.

We used the C4.5 decision tree learning algorithm (Quinlan, 1993) without pruning. We obtained the source code of release 8 and modified it to output probabilities. We measured the training time of C4.5 on each partition and the complete dataset to measure the empirical scalability of the ensemble.

6.4.3. Experimental Results

The total benefit serves as baseline to compare with the distributed approaches. We then find out how well the various distributed methods work and how the

TABLE 6.2. The Total Benefits Attained by Centralized Learning Method of the Global Classifier[a]

Dataset	Raw	Curtailment
Donation	12,489.6	13,292.7
Credit card fraud	552,400	733,980
Adult	16,255	16,443

[a]This is the baseline to evaluate distributed methods.

TABLE 6.3. Average Total Benefits of Ensemble Methods Over Different Numbers of Partitions[a]

	Donation		
Learning Methods		Raw	Curtailment
Fully distributed	Simple averaging	13,842.6	14,643.3
	Multiplex averaging	13,875.8	**14,702.9**
Partially distributed	Averaging regression	13,790.7	14,597.5
	Regression averaging	13,640.4	14,620.5
	Regression regression	13,545.4	14,512.2
	Combiner averaging	13,420.4	14,310.3
	Combiner regression	13,200.7	14,207.5

	Credit Card Fraud			Adult	
Learning Method		Raw	Curtailment	Raw	Curtailment
Fully distributed	Averaging	**808,438**	804,964	16,235	**16,435**
Partially distributed	Regression	729,384	784,310	15,910	16,021
	Combiner	738,294	789,845	15,845	15,945

[a]Results in bold font are the best result for that dataset for centralized, partially and fully distributed methods. Compared with the baseline results in Table 6.2. The results by distributed methods are all better.

benefits are influenced by the number of sites. Finally, we evaluate the training overhead of each approach.

Total Benefits. The results attained by centralized learning are shown in Table 6.2, and they serve as the baseline to evaluate distributed methods.

In order to compare distributed learning methods, we calculate the average of total benefits of each method over different numbers of sites k. The results are shown in Table 6.3. Since the benefit $y(\mathbf{x})$ is known for both credit card fraud and adult datasets, there is no need to estimate it, thus we only need to combine probabilities using *Averaging*, *Regression*, and *Combiner*.

First we have found that the different distributed methods all perform reasonably well, and they all have higher benefits than the baseline centralized learning method. The fully distributed learning via averaging ensemble consistently beats the more complicated partially distributed learning via combiner and regression tree across three datasets. This means that although it is remarkably simple, fully distributed learning (both simple and multiplex averaging) is a very accurate method, and using more complicated and expensive methods doesn't bring extra benefits.

In Table 6.4 and Figure 6.3, we plot changes of total benefits (using curtailment averaging*) with growing number of sites k using the fully distributed approach. We can clearly see that the total benefits are all higher than the baseline for all chosen k for both the donation and credit card fraud dataset. For the donation dataset, the results for $k = 32$ and $k = 64$, 15,141 and 15,004 respectively, are better than the winning entry of KDD '98 cup, which was 14,712. For the adult dataset, the ensemble method's total benefit is higher than that of the baseline with $k < 64$ and is slightly worse than but still close enough to the baseline when $k \geq 64$. When k increase, there is a very slow decrease in total benefits, but the tendency is very slow. At $k = 256$, the total benefit still remains higher than that of the single classifier for donation and credit card fraud datasets, and close enough to the baseline for adult (16,359 versus 16,443), but the training cost is much less. It is important to mention that the training set size of adults (32,561) is three times smaller than the donation dataset (95,412) and 13 times smaller than the credit card fraud dataset (406,009).

Communication and Computation Overhead. Both the communication and computation overhead are obviously 0 for the fully distributed approach. For the partially distributed approach, we use a credit card dataset with $k = 256$ as an example. The total number of extra models (combiner or regressor) are 255. Every regressor has three parameters ($y = a_0 + a_1 x_1 + a_2 x_2$), and each parameter is a real number stored as 8 bytes. The total number of bytes is 24 bytes per regressor, or $256 \times 511 \times 24$ bytes = 1Mbyte to transfer all the models.

TABLE 6.4. Changes in Total Benefits Relative to the Number of Sites k Using Curtailed Probabilities

	Baseline	$k = 8$	16	32	64	128	256
Donation	13,292.70	14,151.20	14,534.90	15,141.20	15,004.00	14,932.30	14,453.50
Credit Card Fraud	733,980	821,311	819,155	816,244	811,282	788,795	772,995
Adult	16,443	16,513	16,470	16,471	16,428	16,370	16,359

*The results for curtailment simple averaging and multiplex averaging are very close for the donation dataset; therefore, we choose to present the multiplex averaging result.

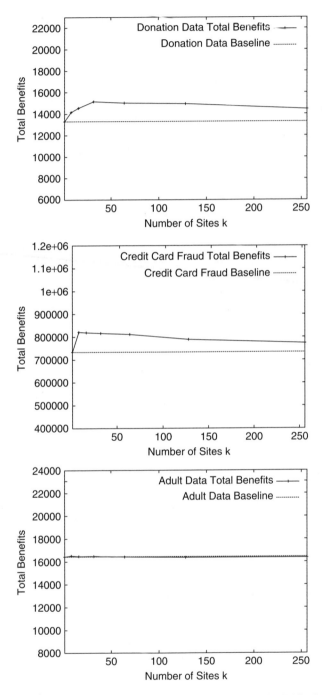

Figure 6.3. Plot of changes in total benefits as shown in Table 6.4.

The decision tree generated for each combiner is around 100 bytes, so the total bytes to transfer all combiners is approximately 4MBytes. The additional data (predictions and true values) transferred for both regressor and combiner tree is about 9MBytes $(406, 009 \times 3 \times 8)$. The extra time to train the regressors is around 40 minutes in serial training and 9 minutes in parallel; the extra time to train the combiners is about 15 minutes in serial and 5 minutes in parallel. Besides computing the combining models, both methods spend an additional 30 minutes to produce the training data to compute the combining model.

In our previous work (Fan et al., 2002b), we have shown that the total training time to compute the fully distributed averaging ensemble with $k = 256$ in parallel is about 5814 times faster than computing a single global classifier from all data (without counting the extra time to transfer all data to a single site).

6.4.4. Additional Experiment on Very Large Dataset and Different Learners

We have tested the fully distributed approach on a huge catalog mailing dataset on a completely different learning system. Due to agreement with the merchant, we cannot reveal more details about the dataset beyond what is discussed in this chapter. The dataset contains millions of records of ordering history of the merchant's customers. Each record is described by hundreds of features that profile the customer's geographic, demographic, lifestyle, and past ordering information. The merchant needs to choose the subset of customers to solicit a catalog (about $5 per copy) in order to maximize profits. The learning task is very challenging due to the large size of the dataset and the huge number of features and cost-sensitive nature of the problem. Due to proprietary reasons, the dataset has to be run on a designated learning system which uses variations of Naive Bayes and Linear Regression. We have randomly partitioned training set into five subsets. All five base classifiers were computed concurrently on the same computer where the centralized global model was trained (on the five subsets as a whole). The total profit by the global model for the centralized learning is $14,160.5 while the fully distributed averaging ensemble has achieved a profit of $15,009.5, which is an increase of 7% over the single model.

We have also tested the donation dataset on this learning system, which uses variations of Naive Bayes and Regression that are different from C4.5, and obtained higher profit and less training time with the fully distributed averaging ensemble approach.

6.4.5. How "Averaging" Saved Money for Business Applications

We explained the reason in Section 6.3.3 why averaging may have potentially higher benefits. The empirical results verified our conjecture. As an example, in Figure 6.4, we plot decision plots (as defined in Section 6.3.3) for the credit card fraud dataset. We choose raw probability estimates and $k = 256$ for the averaging ensemble.

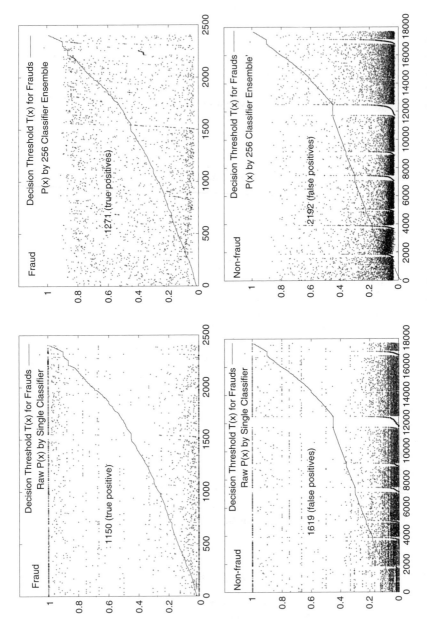

Figure 6.4. Decision threshold and probability output by a centralized single model and a 256-classifier fully distributed averaging ensemble for the credit card dataset.

The number on each plot shows the number of examples* where $P(x) > T(x)$ (predicted as frauds). The top two plots are fraudulent transactions, and those bottom plots are nonfraud. The overall effect of the averaging ensemble increases the number of true positives from 1150 to 1271 and increases the number of false positives from 1619 to 2192. However, the average transaction amount of the "extra number" of detected frauds by the ensemble $(121 = 1271 - 1150))$ is around \$2400, which greatly overcomes the cost of extra false alarm (\$90 per false alarm). For problems like credit card fraud, donation, and catalog mailing where positive examples have varied profits and negative examples have low or fixed cost, the ensemble methods tend to beat the single model.

6.5. DISCUSSION

Compared with both centralized and partially distributed systems, the fully distributed averaging ensemble has several advantages besides its zero communication and computation overhead. Since base models are computed independently on the local sites, it takes full advantage of the intrinsic parallelism of multiple systems. As shown in our previous work (Fan et al., 2002b), the fully distributed averaging ensemble has both linear speedup and scaled speedup. The method is simple and straightforward and doesn't require complicated control mechanism, if any. Since each site is computed individually without any communication, they do not have to be interconnected, and they can be completely detached in the extreme case. For applications where *security* is a major concern, an averaging ensemble provides a satisfactory solution; there is no information exchange during learning, and, consequently, there is little opportunity to leak and steal information. It also provides a natural solution for *heterogeneous systems, multiple schemas*, and *multiple learning algorithms*; each site can totally use its own code, own system, and data format (even legacy system) to compute its local models. As long as the format of the models are interchangeable, the local models can be shared and exchanged to form the averaging ensemble with ease. Since each learning procedure is totally independent, the failure of one site will not influence the other sites at all, which provide natural *fault-tolerance*. When more sites decide to participate in the ensemble, their models can be joined at any time; when some sites have new data available, their model can be upgraded at any time and replace the older model. This provide an easy solution for *incrementability*.

Unbalanced dataset size may be an important issue for some applications of distributed data mining; the size of the dataset at different site may be very different in size. A big dataset may dominate both training time and accuracy. Since the accuracy of an averaging ensemble doesn't depend on k, the number of sites, we can always make data size at different sites similar. Actually, when the dataset at one site is partitioned into data subsets, the learning on this site alone (sequential or parallel) also improves.

*To show these numbers clearly on the plot, we do not plot the surrounding data points around the text area.

6.6. RELATED WORK

In a separate work (Fan et al., 2002b), we have evaluated similar methods for scalable learning of a very large dataset on a single site. The focus of this chapter is on distributed cost-sensitive learning, where the data physically reside on different machines across the network. There are several distinctive concerns in distributed data mining; these include communication overhead, computation overhead, unbalanced dataset size, fault-tolerance, security, heterogeneous platforms, and incremental learning. One problem that faces all ensemble approaches is the low efficiency of model deployment since multiple models have to be used to predict an example. We have proposed a few pruning methods to reduce the number of models (Fan et al., 2002a). Our results have shown that with less than 10% of the original number of models, we can still achieve the same level of benefit as the original averaging ensemble with all the classifiers.

There has been extensive research on distributed data mining. However, they mostly focus on *cost-insensitive* problems where each example has the same price and there is no penalty for misclassification. Chan's meta-learning (Chan, 1996) builds up a tree of classifiers to combine *class labels* to scale up *cost-insensitive* learning. Neither probability nor benefit is combined or used in making a prediction. Meta-learning has been implemented as a Java-based Meta-learning System, or JAM (Prodromidis, 1999). Incremental learning, such as ID5 (Utgoff, 1994), assimilates one or a few examples at a time. The temporary model from a previous learned site can be transferred to other sites to complete learning; however, the intrinsic parallelism of multiple systems are not taken advantage of, and the modification to make each algorithm incremental is algorithm-specific. SPRINT (Shafer et al., 1996) utilizes data structure to scale up decision tree learning on a very large dataset, but it doesn't handle distributed learning among multiple sites. Some researchers parallelize a specific algorithm, such as a DRL rule-based algorithm for multiprocessor learning (Provost and Hennessy, 1996), to solve distributed learning problems. Like incremental learning, each parallel modification is algorithm-specific.

6.7. CONCLUSION

We have proposed and evaluated several ensemble approaches to combine probabilities and benefits for distributed cost-sensitive business applications, such as credit card fraud detection and catalog mailing campaign. We identify some properties of both averaging and optimal decision-making. Due to these properties, averaging offers higher benefit in addition to its obvious advantage of scalability. We propose two methods that use averages of probabilities and benefits for fully distributed learning. Since tree-structured combining methods have been shown previously to be effective to combine class labels, we explore tree-structured regression and variations of meta-learning to combine probabilities and benefits for partially distributed learning. We have chosen three different types of cost-sensitive problems for empirical study.

We have found that both fully and partially distributed methods achieve total benefit that is as good as or even better than the global classifier trained on the all available data from every site. The most accurate approaches are the two fully distributed averaging methods, whose total benefit is best among all the ensemble approaches and even consistently beat the centralized global classifier. They also exhibit zero communication and computation overhead. Our study has also shown that more complicated partially distributed tree-structured methods offer neither lower communication nor computation overhead.

Based on our extensive experimental and analytical study of many candidate combining methods, we find that the fully distributed averaging approaches are an effective framework for distributed cost-sensitive data-mining business applications.

REFERENCES

Chan, P., An Extensible Meta-learning Approach for Scalable and Accurate Inductive Learning, Ph.D. thesis, Columbia University, 1996.

Dietterich, T., Margineatu, D., Provost, F., and Turney, P. (ed.) *Cost-Sensitive Learning Workshop (ICML-00)*, 2000.

Fan, W., Chu, F., Wang, H., and Yu, P. S., Pruning and dynamic scheduling of cost-sensitive ensembles, in *Proceedings of Eighteenth National Conference on Artificial Intelligence (AAAI '02)*, AAAI Press, Menlo Park, CA, 2002a.

Fan, W., Wang, H., Yu, P. S., and Stolfo, S., A framework for scalable cost-sensitive learning based on combining probabilities and benefits, in *Second SIAM International Conference on Data Mining (SDM 2002)*, 2002b.

Prodromidis, A., Management of Intelligent Learning Agents in Distributed Data Mining Systems, Ph.D. thesis, Columbia University, 1999.

Provost, F., and Hennessy, D., Scaling up distributed machine learning via cooperation, in *Proceedings of Thirteenth National Conference on Artificial Intelligence (AAAI-96)*, 1996.

Quinlan, R., *C4.5: Programs for Machine Learning*, Morgan Kaufmann, San Francisco, 1993.

Shafer, J., Agrawl, R., and Mehta, M., SPRINT: A scalable parallel classifier for data mining, in *Proceedings of Twenty-second International Conference on Very Large Databases (VLDB-96)*, Morgan Kaufmann, San Francisco, pp. 544–555, 1996.

Tumer, K., and Ghosh, J., Error correlation and error reduction in ensemble classifiers, *Connection Science* **8**(3–4), 385–403 (1996).

Utgoff, P., An improved algorithm for incremental induction of decision, in *Proceedings of Eleventh International Conference on Machine Learning (ICML-94)*, pp. 318–325, 1994.

Wolpert, D., Stacked generalization, *Neural Networks* **5**, 241–259 (1992).

Zadrozny, B., and Elkan, C. Obtaining calibrated probability estimates from decision trees and naive bayesian classifiers, in *Proceedings of Eighteenth International Conference on Machine Learning (ICML '2001)*, 2001.

7

APPLICATION OF VARIABLE PRECISION ROUGH SET APPROACH TO CAR DRIVER ASSESSMENT

KWEI ARYEETEY, WOJCIECH ZIARKO, AND KWEI QUAYE

7.1. INTRODUCTION

In most jurisdictions in Canada and the United States, traffic violation and accident experience of drivers are closely monitored by jurisdictional licensing agencies (Quaye, 1997). In South Carolina (South Carolina Department of Insurance, 2003), among many other determining factors, accidents and traffic violations or a combination of both affect the cost of insurance sold to drivers. Automobile insurers apply an "objective standards test" to a driver before selling them insurance. Any driver who "fails" this test or does not qualify for the safe driver discount may be charged a higher rate for collision and comprehensive coverage.

These monitoring programs are known as Driver Improvement Programs (DIP). The goal of most DIP is to intervene in a way that will encourage an unsafe driver to be more careful, improve his/her driving attitude, and incur fewer violations and accidents in the future. The DIP is a quantitative point system guide that is used to determine when an intervention is necessary to address a driver's worsening driving record. One key problem with this scheme is that until this point system triggers an intervention, there is no way of determining the chances that a particular driver would be involved in a serious future traffic violation or accident until its too late. Accidents are costly, both socially and economically, to drivers and insurance companies.

In a study that used 4 years of accident violation records of over 2 million North Carolina drivers Stewart and Campbell (1972) investigated the performance

Next Generation of Data-Mining Applications. Edited by Kantardzic and Zurada
ISBN 0-471-65605-4 © 2005 the Institute of Electrical and Electronics Engineers, Inc.

of violations and accidents in predicting future violations and accidents. They found that the past accidents were better predictors of future accidents than were past violations. It is important to point out, however, that the quality of data greatly affects the determination of driver behavior from past records. Currently, driver behavior is determined from motor vehicle records (MVR). Sometimes these motor vehicle records are incomplete and inaccurate and therefore may not provide an accurate picture of a driver's behavior. According to a new study in 2002, conducted by the Insurance Research Council (2002) of court motor vehicle records in four states, 21% of convictions sampled in Florida were not found on the drivers' MVRs, 14% of traffic convictions were missing from a sample of MVRs in Ohio, and 10% of sampled convictions from the state of Washington were missing from MVRs.

The primary objective of this project is to investigate the feasibility of applying a novel rough set-based data modeling technique to past driving records to be able to identify potentially unsafe drivers and intervene through education, proper setting of insurance premiums, or other remedial actions. These measures could take the form of warnings, suspensions from driving for specific periods of time, or the imposition of high annual insurance premiums for these drivers. The approach presented is based on the Variable Precision Rough Set Model (VPRSM) [see, for instance, Ziarko (1993), Yao and Wong (1992), Ślęzak and Ziarko (2002), Aryeetey et al. (2001), Katzberg and Ziarko (1993), Grzymala-Busse and Ziarko (2003)]. It entails building a probabilistic model from the specified driver data elements to better assess drivers' driving behavior by identifying significant factors affecting the chances of them becoming involved in an at-fault accident. Additional information provided by this model can be used to calculate more accurate insurance premiums for drivers and hopefully lead to broader applications of the presented approach. It should be emphasized that the application discussed in this chapter could be approached with other methodologies such as decision trees and probabilistic or association rule mining. The comparison between approaches would definitely be of interest here, but this is out of the scope of this chapter and will be addressed in future research.

7.2. DRIVER HISTORY DATA

The data used in this case study consist of 292,127 driver records and make up about 50% of the entire driver population of interest. The records are described by five attributes that were selected with the help of a domain expert as presented in Table 7.1.

The attributes are divided into *condition attributes* and a *decision attribute*. The following condition attributes describe the driver's demographics and driving behavior: SEX, DOFB, CITYPOP, NUMOFCONV and NUMOFPASTACC. The decision attribute, which represents the analysis target, is HASACCIDENT. This indicates whether a driver has had an accident in this study's most recent year, which is 1999.

TABLE 7.1. Driver Attributes

	Attribute Name	Description
1	SEX	Sex of driver
2	DOFB	Date of birth of driver, used to calculate age
3	CITYPOP	Population size of city where a driver lives
4	NUMOFCONV	Number of convictions in 3 years (1997–1999)
5	NUMOFPASTACC	Number of past accidents in 2 years (1997–1998)
6	HASACCIDENT	Has driver had an accident in last year? (1999)

TABLE 7.2. Driver-Attribute Discretization Criteria

Attribute Code	Attribute	Domain Codes					
		0	1	2	3	4	5
C1	SEX		M	F			
C2	AGE (in years)		≥ 60	$\geq 20, \leq 59$	≤ 19		
C3	CITYPOP (in thousands)		$\geq 180K$	$\geq 30K$	$\geq 10K$	$\geq 5K$	$<5K$
C4	NUMOFCONV		<2	$\geq 2, \leq 5$	>5		
C5	NUMOFPASTACC		<2	$\geq 2, \leq 5$	>5		
D	HASACCIDENT	No	Yes				

Data preprocessing for this study involves data discretization. It is the process of mapping numeric values into meaningful discrete qualitative ranges. For example, the following ages of people—18, 25, 39, 50, 70, and 85—could be organized into three groups: **teenagers**, **adults**, and **senior drivers**, where the teenagers, adults, and senior groups correspond to age groups of up to 19 years, between 20 and 60 years, and above 60 years, respectively. After discretization, the resulting data ranges become more meaningful and data patterns become more pronounced. Too much detail, typically existing in the raw data, obscures patterns. A good and effective discretization process makes it possible to remove inconsistencies in the data and still retain the accuracy of the prediction. In this study, the data were discretized with the collaboration of the domain expert. Table 7.2 shows the criteria used in data discretization process. In this table, the attribute CITYPOP (C3) represents the population size of the city or town where a driver lives. All other attributes have the same meaning as defined in Table 7.1.

7.3. VARIABLE PRECISION ROUGH SET FRAMEWORK

In this section the basics of the variable precision rough set model (VPRSM), a generalization of Pawlak's original rough set approach (Pawlak, 1991), are briefly introduced. The VPRSM underlies the data-based modeling software that is used in our experiments. In particular, the Hierarchical Decision Tables HDTL algorithm (Ziarko, 2002) is summarized here.

7.3.1. Classification Table

The VPRSM is based on the prior knowledge of an equivalence relation called an *indiscernibility relation IND(C)*, where C is a set of *condition attributes* used to represent objects belonging to the domain of interest U. The indiscernibility relation represents preexisting classification knowledge about the universe of interest U. It is expressed in terms of identity of values of condition attributes C of objects. In the variable precision model, each equivalence class (also called an *elementary set*) E of the relation $IND(C)$ is associated with two measures:

- The probability $P(E)$ of the elementary set, which is normally estimated based on available data by $P(E) = card(E')/card(U')$, where *card* denotes set cardinality and $U' \subseteq U$, $E' \subseteq E$ are respective finite subsets of the domain corresponding to the available collection of sample data.
- The conditional probability $P(X|E)$ which represents the likelihood of an event such that an object belonging to the C-elementary set E would also belong to the set X. The conditional probability $P(X|E)$ is typically estimated by calculating the relative degree of overlap between sets X and E, based on available data, that is $P(X|E) = card(X' \cap E')/card(E')$, where $X' \subseteq X$, $E' \subseteq E$ are respective finite subsets of the domain corresponding to the available collection of sample data.

For example, Table 7.3 illustrates the classification of a domain U of driver records in terms of the condition attributes $C = \{C4, C5\}$ along with the specification of the conditional probabilities $P(X|E)$ with respect to the target subset X. The classification represented in the table has been obtained from the analysis of about 300,000 data records drawn from a very large domain. In general, to conduct rough set-based analysis of such a domain in the framework of variable precision model of rough sets, it is essential to:

TABLE 7.3. Classification Table

#Pos	#Neg	%Pos	%Neg	C4	C5	$P(X \mid E)$	$P(E)$
18949	240709	0.0730	0.9270	1	1	0.0730	0.8889
512	1742	0.2272	0.7728	2	2	0.2272	0.0077
3863	18858	0.1700	0.8300	2	1	0.1700	0.0778
839	4899	0.1462	0.8538	1	2	0.1462	0.0196
287	976	0.2272	0.7728	3	1	0.2272	0.0043
27	62	0.3034	0.6966	2	3	0.3034	0.0003
73	210	0.2580	0.7420	3	2	0.2580	0.0010
29	68	0.2990	0.7010	1	3	0.2990	0.0003
12	12	0.5000	0.5000	3	3	0.5000	0.0001

- Identify all, or most common, feasible combinations of attribute values occurring in the domain.
- For each elementary set E, compute close estimate of the probability $P(E)$.
- For the given target set X and for each elementary set E, compute close estimates of conditional probabilities $P(X|E)$.

The table summarizing all this information is referred to as a *classification table*, as shown in Table 7.3. Additional useful information contained in Table 7.3 includes, for each elementary set E, the following:

- The number of positive cases #Pos—that is, cases belonging to the set X
- The number of negative cases #Neg—that is, cases not belonging to the set X
- The percentages %Pos and %Neg of positive and negative cases, respectively

It should be noted that in the likely absence in the classification table of all feasible combinations of attributes occurring in the domain, all conclusions derived from the table will only apply to a subdomain of the domain. This subdomain equals to the union of all known elementary sets.

7.3.2. VPRSM Approximations

The information contained in the classification table can be used to construct generalized rough approximations of the subset $X \subseteq U$. The defining criteria are expressed here in terms of conditional probabilities and the *prior* probability $P(X)$ of the set X in the universe U. Two *precision control* or *probabilistic significance* criteria parameters are used.

The first parameter, referred to as the *lower limit l*, satisfying the constraint $0 \le l < P(X) < 1$, represents the highest acceptable degree of the conditional probability $P(X|E_i)$ to include the elementary set E_i in the negative region of the set X. In other words, the *l-negative region* of the set X, $NEG_l(X)$, is defined as

$$NEG_l(X) = \cup\{E_i : P(X|E_i) \le l\} \tag{7.1}$$

The *l*-negative region of the set X is a collection of objects for which the probability of membership in the set X is *significantly lower* than the prior probability $P(X)$—that is, the membership probability in the absence of any information about objects of the universe U.

The second parameter, referred to as the *upper limit u*, satisfying the constraint $0 < P(X) < u \le 1$, defines the *u-positive region* of the set X. The upper limit reflects the least acceptable degree of the conditional probability $P(X|E_i)$ to include the elementary set E_i in the positive region, or u-lower approximation of the set X. The u-positive region of the set X, $POS_u(X)$, is defined as

$$POS_u(X) = \cup \{E_i : P(X|E_i) \geq u\} \tag{7.2}$$

The l-negative region of the set X is a collection of objects for which the probability of membership in the set X is *significantly higher* than the prior probability $P(X)$.

The objects that are not classified as being in the u-positive region or in the l-negative region belong to the (l, u)-boundary region of the set X, denoted as

$$BNR_{l,u}(X) = \cup \{E_i : l < P(X|E_i) < u\} \tag{7.3}$$

The boundary is a specification of objects about which it is known that their associated probability of belonging, or not belonging, to the target set X is not significantly different from the prior probability $P(X)$, where the significance level is expressed in terms of the parameters l and u.

A classification table with determined allocation of each elementary set to exactly one of VPRSM approximation regions, as defined above, is referred to as a *probabilistic decision table*. The table with C set of condition attributes with respect to the target set X will be denoted here as $DT_{C,X}(U)$. In the probabilistic decision table, each elementary set is assigned a unique designation of its VPRSM approximation region based on preset values of the probabilistic significance parameters l and u. For example, a probabilistic decision table derived from the classification table given in Table 7.3 is shown in Table 7.10. In this table, as well as in similar tables, the abbreviations *POS, NEG,* and *BND* in the column *REG* (approximation region) denote positive, negative, and boundary regions, respectively.

7.3.3. Selection of Significance Parameters

The selection of the values of significance parameters l and u is an application problem and is application area-dependent. In problems where there is a measurable gain associated with correct predictions—such as, for instance, in casino game playing—the bounds for values of parameters can be precisely determined by using analytical formulas, which take into account the expected gains and costs of decision making (Ziarko, 1999). In problems where such information is not available, like in the case of drivers' data discussed here, the values of parameters are set according to preexisting knowledge about random misclassification rate due to measurement noise or other random factors. For example, if the observed random misclassification rate is 5%, then reasonable settings of significance parameters l and u would surround the prior probability of target X occurrence and also require that $l < 0.95 P(X)$ and $u > 1.05 P(X)$. In our study, the probabilistic decision tables shown in Tables 7.4 and 7.5 were derived based on the estimated prior probability of the target set X occurrence $P(X) = 0.0842$

with the assumed significance parameters $l = 0.08$ and $u = 0.13$. The parameters have been determined in consultation with the domain expert.

7.3.4. Linear Hierarchy of Decision Tables

The adopted method of model construction from data involves construction of a linear, as opposed to tree-structured, hierarchy of probabilistic decision tables (Ziarko, 1998, 2001a, 2002). It is based on the idea of treating the subdomain of the original domain corresponding to the whole boundary area as a new domain by itself. Such a subdomain can be identified by the vectors of attribute-value patterns describing elementary sets belonging to the boundary area. The subdomain would then be used to acquire a decision table for the subset of the target set, restricted to that subdomain. The attributes used in each layer would have to be different from those used in the original table (parent) layer to ensure that the new atomic sets are different from those defined in the parent layer. By applying the step indicated above recursively, layer after layer, a hierarchical linear structure of decision tables can be built. The expansion of the hierarchy would continue until a point when the last node would have no boundary or new attributes introduced at the node would not reduce the boundary area. The method is summarized in the algorithm **HDTL**, as presented below. The presented algorithm is a VPRSM generalization of the original **HDTL** method originally published in Ziarko (2002). In this algorithm, U' is the initial data set, C' is the initial set of discretized attributes, and D' is the decision attribute of the initial dataset. In addition, U, C, and D are variables representing current dataset, current condition attributes, and current decision attributes, respectively. We will assume that the values of precision control parameters l and u are fixed throughout the computation.

Initialization

    1. $U \longleftarrow U'$, $C \longleftarrow C'$, $D \longleftarrow D'$

    2. **Compute** $POS_u(X)$ and $NEG_l(X)$

Iteration

    3. **repeat**

      {

    4. **while** $(POS_u(X) = \emptyset$ and $NEG_l(X) = \emptyset)$

      {

    5. $C \longleftarrow$ **new** (C, U); *define new condition attributes*

    6. **Compute** $POS_u(X)$ and $NEG_l(X)$

      }

    7. **Output** $DT_{C,X}(U)$; *output decision table based on the union of the positive and negative regions*

    8. **If** $POS_u(X) \cup NEG_l(X) = U$ **Then exit.**

9. $U \longleftarrow U - (POS_u(X) \cup NEG_l(X))$

10. $C \longleftarrow$ **new** (C, U); *define new condition attributes*

11. $D \longleftarrow D|_U$; *restrict decision attributes to the current set of data U*

12. **Compute** $POS_u(X)$ and $NEG_l(X)$

    }

The algorithm HDTL produces a series of decision tables, creating after each pass a decision table obtained from the current universe corresponding to the prior level boundary region. The tables are subsequently linked into a hierarchical structure. The main advantage of HDTL is the elimination of the exponential explosion of the data structure size, which is common in tree-structured classifiers. Another advantage of this approach is that the overall reduction in the boundary area size does not require adding new attributes or increasing their precision at each parent level in the structure, thus bounding the growth of the root decision table. In the course of the experiments reported in this chapter, we constructed and analyzed HDTL's derived from the original data. For this, a Java-based data-analysis program was developed and used. It analyzes a given dataset in the following steps:

1. The program reads a user-supplied input file containing the attributes of the dataset to be analyzed.

2. The attributes are then discretized into a partial classification table using a set of user-defined discretization functions.

3. The program then calculates the conditional probabilities and local indicator measures, and it summarizes them into the HDTL hierarchy of probabilistic decision tables.

4. The final stage involves the analysis of the hierarchical decision tables and the subsequent calculations of global evaluative measures (Ziarko, 2001b).

7.4. SOME RESULTS AND INTERPRETATIONS

The VPRS model was applied to building probabilistic models that verified certain assertions regarding drivers' driving behavior. In verifying these assertions, new knowledge was also discovered. This new knowledge, in the form of combinations of driver characteristics that have significant influence on drivers likelihood of being involved in an accident, can be useful in decision-making regarding the management of drivers' driving behavior. The following are some of the interpretive assertions discovered about drivers' behavior, along with their verifications by the derived VPRS models.

1. **Assertion**: *Males are generally more likely to have at-fault accidents than females.*

TABLE 7.4. Probabilistic Decision Table Based on Driver's Location with $P(X) = 0.0842$ and $l = 0.08$, $u = 0.13$

#Pos	#Neg	%Pos	%Neg	C3	$P(X \mid E_i)$	$P(E_i)$	REG
11219	102820	0.0984	0.9016	**1**	**0.0984**	0.3904	**BND**
9545	117000	0.0754	0.9246	5	0.0754	0.4332	NEG
1372	17494	0.0727	0.9273	3	0.0727	0.0646	NEG
1734	20293	0.0787	0.9213	2	0.0787	0.0754	NEG
721	9929	0.0677	0.9323	4	0.0677	0.0365	NEG

Verification: Based on the analysis results, displayed in Table 7.7, the likelihood that a male (attribute C1 = 1) would become involved in an at-fault accident is higher than that of a female at 0.1045 even though this cannot be sufficiently determined by the sex attribute alone (i.e., classification for the male group falls in the boundary region). For females, it is significantly more likely than average that they will not become involved in an at-fault accident, with the accident probability of 0.0623.

2. **Assertion:** *Teenage drivers (attribute C2) drive more recklessly than adult and older drivers, and therefore have the highest probability of becoming involved in at-fault accidents.*

   Verification: According to Table 7.9, teenage drivers (attribute C2 = 3) are significantly more likely than average to become involved in an at-fault accident with the highest probability of 0.1850. Adults (attribute C2 = 2) are second, and likely not to become involved in at-fault accidents with the calculated probability of 0.0897. However, this figure is not much different from average probability of an accident (the prior probability 0.0842) and consequently considered not significant enough with our assumptions of the model parameters, which place it in the boundary area. On the other hand, seniors (attribute C2 = 1) have significantly the lowest probability of having accidents.

3. **Assertion:** *Drivers from smaller population centers tend to drive more carefully and less recklessly than others and therefore have significantly lower than average probability of becoming involved in at-fault accidents.*

   Verification: Based on the analysis results shown in Table 7.4, drivers from smaller cities (attribute C3 = 2 or 3 or 4 or 5), with population no more than 180,000 people, are placed in the negative region as a result of having low probability of getting in at-fault accidents. The results regarding drivers from larger cities are not conclusive since their frequency of being in at-fault accidents falls in the boundary area. A next HDTL layer with new attributes is required to arrive at more conclusive results within this category of drivers.

4. **Assertion:** *The single strongest predictive attribute of future accidents is past convictions (attribute C4).*

TABLE 7.5. Probabilistic Decision Table Based on Driver's Past Convictions with $P(X) = 0.0842$ and $l = 0.08$, $u = 0.13$

#Pos	#Neg	Region	%Pos	%Neg	C4	$P(X \mid E_i)$	$P(E_i)$	REG
19817	245676	0	0.0746	0.9254	1	**0.0746**	0.9088	**NEG**
4402	20662	2	0.1756	0.8244	2	**0.1756**	0.0858	**POS**
372	1198	2	0.2369	0.7631	3	**0.2369**	0.0054	**POS**

Verification: The predictive strength of the attribute is expressed by the percentage of all data objects belonging to either positive or negative approximation regions. The results presented in Table 7.5 demonstrate that drivers who belong to the worst 0.5% category (attribute C4 = 3) have the significantly higher than average (given by prior probability $P(X) = 0.0842$) likelihood of 0.2369 of becoming involved in at-fault accidents, which is placing them in the positive region. This is followed by those who belong to the worst 8.5% group (attribute C4 = 2), also in the positive region with the likelihood of 0.1756. Drivers who belong to the remaining 94% (attribute C4 = 1), have a significantly lower than average probability of 0.0746 of becoming involved in an at-fault accidents. This places them in the negative region. That is, the predictive strength of attribute C4 is expressed by the fact that 100% of all drivers fall into either positive or negative approximation regions based on the values of this attribute. In terms of driving habits, this supports the assertion that normal drivers who get reasonably small numbers of traffic convictions are unlikely to become involved in at-fault accidents. These results also show that with convictions, one can reasonably categorize drivers into **safe** versus **unsafe** categories, because number of convictions strongly affects the probability of who will and who will not become involved in at-fault accidents. This is consistent with the assertion that convictions is a strong predictor of the tendency to become involved or not involved in an at-fault accident and hence a driver's behavior.

5. **Assertion:** *High number of accidents indicates higher likelihood to become involved in at-fault accidents in the future.*

   Verification: From Table 7.6, we observe that drivers who belong to the worst 1% of all drivers (attribute C5 = 3) have the highest likelihood, 0.3238, of becoming involved in an at-fault accident followed by those who belong to the worst 5% (attribute C2 = 2) with a likelihood of 0.1721. However, it cannot be determined with significantly high or low probability that drivers who belong to the 94% percent of the population will become involved in an at-fault accident. In Table 7.7, this group has the least probability of 0.0814. That determination will require more than accidents alone to establish significant probabilistic separation. For example, one may need to combine this attribute with others. It is therefore evident from this analysis that convictions (attribute C4) is a much stronger predicting attribute

TABLE 7.6. Probabilistic Decision Table Based on the Number of Past Accidents with $P(X) = 0.0842$ and $l = 0.08$, $u = 0.13$

#Pos	#Neg	Region	%Pos	%Neg	C5	$P(X \mid E_i)$	$P(E_i)$	REG
23099	260543	1	0.0814	0.9186	1	**0.0814**	0.9710	**BND**
1424	6851	2	0.1721	0.8279	2	**0.1721**	0.0283	**POS**
68	142	2	0.3238	0.6762	3	**0.3238**	0.0007	**POS**

TABLE 7.7. First Layer Probabilistic Decision Table Based on Driver's Sex with $P(X) = 0.0842$ and $l = 0.08$, $u = 0.13$

#Pos	#Neg	Region	%Pos	%Neg	C1	$P(X \mid E_i)$	$P(E_i)$	REG
15827	135569	1	0.1045	0.8955	1	**0.1045**	0.5183	**BND**
8764	131967	0	0.0623	0.9377	2	**0.0623**	0.4817	**NEG**

TABLE 7.8. Second Layer HDTL Derived from Table 7.7 Using Driver's Age (C2) and Location (C3) with $P(X) = 0.1045$ and $l = 0.0993$, $u = 0.1493$

#Pos	#Neg	Region	%Pos	%Neg	C2	C3	$P(X \mid E_i)$	$P(E_i)$	REG
5770	40680	1	0.1242	0.8758	2	1	0.1242	0.3068	BND
1185	10141	1	0.1046	0.8954	1	1	0.1046	0.0748	BND
5030	43200	1	0.1043	0.8957	2	5	0.1043	0.3186	BND
640	6236	0	0.0931	0.9069	2	3	0.0931	0.0454	NEG
227	2593	0	0.0805	0.9195	1	2	0.0805	0.0186	NEG
1424	17747	0	0.0743	0.9257	1	5	0.0743	0.1266	NEG
376	3732	0	0.0915	0.9085	2	4	0.0915	0.0271	NEG
848	7423	1	0.1025	0.8975	2	2	0.1025	0.0546	BND
209	2414	0	0.0797	0.9203	1	3	0.0797	0.0173	NEG
88	1296	0	0.0636	0.9364	1	4	0.0636	0.0091	NEG
15	59	2	0.2027	0.7973	3	5	0.2027	0.0005	POS
10	24	2	0.2941	0.7059	**3**	**1**	**0.2941**	0.0002	**POS**
3	7	2	0.3000	0.7000	**3**	**4**	**0.3000**	0.0001	**POS**
1	5	2	0.1667	0.8333	3	2	0.1667	0.00003	POS
1	12	0	0.0769	0.9231	3	3	0.0769	0.00009	NEG

of becoming involved in at-fault accidents than accidents (attribute C5), for most normal drivers.

6. **Assertion:** *With reference to Assertion 1, Sex (attribute C1) alone cannot produce sufficient difference in accident probabilities to predict if male drivers will become involved in accidents.*

Verification: To deal with this case, the relationship between sex (attribute C1), age (attribute C2), and city (attribute C3) is explored. Based on the results displayed, in Tables 7.7 and 7.8, the interaction between male (attribute C1 = 1) and age (attribute C2) and city (attribute C3) is further explored. The results indicate that male teenagers from large cities (attribute C2 = 3, attribute C3 = 1) have significantly higher (almost triple) than average (given by prior probability of 0.1045) likelihood of becoming involved in at-fault accidents. The same is true for male teenagers from small cities (attribute C2 = 3, attribute C3 = 4), who are also significantly more likely than average to become involved in an at-fault accidents, with a probability of 0.2941. This indicates similar behavior patterns and supports the common assertion that male teenagers (i.e., from both large and small cities) drive recklessly, but those from larger cities seem to do so more, relatively, than those from smaller cities.

7. **Assertion:** *With reference to Assertion 2, to determine if adults (attribute C2 = 2) would become involved in an at-fault accident, with likelihood significantly higher or lower than average, one needs more information than just the age group.*

Verification: By exploring the interaction between convictions (attribute C4) and accidents (attribute C5) in Table 7.10, one finds that adults who have a low number of convictions (attribute C4 = 1) and a low number of accidents (attribute C5 = 1) are significantly less likely than average to become involved in at-fault accidents. In Tables 7.9 and 7.10, the interaction between adults (attribute C2 = 2) and convictions (attribute C4) and

TABLE 7.9. First Layer Probabilistic Decision Table Based on Driver's Age Group with $P(X) = 0.0842$ and $l = 0.08$, $u = 0.13$

#Pos	#Neg	%Pos	%Neg	C2	$P(X \mid E_i)$	$P(E_i)$	REG
20005	202956	0.0897	0.9103	2	**0.0897**	0.7632	**BND**
4539	64373	0.0659	0.9341	1	**0.0659**	0.2359	**NEG**
47	207	0.1850	0.8150	3	**0.1850**	0.0009	**POS**

TABLE 7.10. Single Layer Probabilistic Decision Table Based on Convictions (C4) and Accidents (C5) with $P(X) = 0.0897$ and $l = 0.0852$, $u = 0.1352$

#Pos	#Neg	%Pos	%Neg	C4	C5	$P(X \mid E)$	$P(E)$	REG
18949	240709	0.0730	0.9270	1	1	0.0730	0.8889	NEG
512	1742	0.2272	0.7728	2	2	0.2272	0.0077	POS
3863	18858	0.1700	0.8300	2	1	0.1700	0.0778	POS
839	4899	0.1462	0.8538	1	2	0.1462	0.0196	POS
287	976	0.2272	0.7728	3	1	0.2272	0.0043	POS
27	62	0.3034	0.6966	2	3	0.3034	0.0003	POS
73	210	0.2580	0.7420	3	2	0.2580	0.0010	POS
29	68	0.2990	0.7010	1	3	0.2990	0.0003	POS
12	12	0.5000	0.5000	3	3	0.5000	0.0001	POS

accidents (attribute C5) is further analyzed since age alone is insufficient to determine the likelihood of becoming involved in an at-fault accident (as seen in Table 7.9, the value of C2 = 2 is inconclusive with the corresponding elementary set located int the boundary region). This results in the finding (Table 7.9) that adults (attribute C2 = 2) who belong to the 94% of drivers' population would be involved in an at-fault accident significantly less likely than the average of 0.0897, with the likelihood of 0.0766, provided they have both low number of past convictions and accidents. In addition, we note the following:

- Drivers with less than 2 convictions and 2 accidents will be involved in an at-fault accident significantly less frequently—that is, with the probability of 0.0730—than average frequency of 0.0897 of being in an at-fault accident.

- Drivers with between 2 and 5 convictions and between 2 and 5 accidents will become involved in an at-fault accident with significantly higher than average probability of 0.2272.

- Drivers with more than 5 convictions and more than 5 accidents will become involved in an at-fault accident with particularly high probability of 0.5. This last observation, however, may not be representative with respect to a larger population because there are only 12 drivers in that category in our data.

- Most typical drivers who have less than two convictions and less than 2 accidents (attribute C4 = 1, attribute C5 = 1) (this group classification falls inside the negative region) are less likely to become involved in at-fault accidents, with a probability of 0.0730. This probability is significantly less than the average frequency of 0.0897, and it can be explained by the fact that most drivers get convicted for common and less serious traffic offenses and no accidents, which is not an indication that they are unsafe drivers.

8. **Assertion:** *With reference to Assertion 3, to determine with sufficient certainty if drivers from large cities (attribute C3) would become involved in at-fault accidents, one needs to know more than just the city size alone.*

Verification: By analyzing the interaction of city address (attribute C3) with sex (attribute C1) and age (attribute C2), one is able to identify significant increase in drivers' likelihood of becoming involved in at-fault accidents. According to Tables 7.11 and 7.12, the interaction between large city (attribute C3 = 1) and teenage males (attribute C1 = 1, attribute C2 = 3) and teenage females (attribute C2 = 2, attribute C2 = 3) indicate that it is significantly more likely than the average of 0.0984 that teenage males and females from large cities would become involved in at-fault accidents, with the probabilities 0.2941 and 0.2308, respectively. Male teenagers have slightly higher probability of getting in at-fault accidents

TABLE 7.11. First Layer Probabilistic Decision Table Based on Driver's Location with $P(X) = 0.0842$ and $l = 0.08$, $u = 0.13$

#Pos	#Neg	Region	%Pos	%Neg	C3	$P(X \mid E_i)$	$P(E_i)$	REG
11219	102820	1	0.0984	0.9016	**1**	**0.0984**	0.3904	**BND**
9545	117000	0	0.0754	0.9246	5	0.0754	0.4332	NEG
1372	17494	0	0.0727	0.9273	3	0.0727	0.0646	NEG
1734	20293	0	0.0787	0.9213	2	0.0787	0.0754	NEG
721	9929	0	0.0677	0.9323	4	0.0677	0.0365	NEG

TABLE 7.12. Second Layer HDTL Derived from Table 7.11 Using Driver's Sex (C1) and Age (C2) with $P(X) = 0.0984$ and $l = 0.0935$, $u = 0.1435$

#Pos	#Neg	Region	%Pos	%Neg	C1	C2	$P(X \mid E_i)$	$P(E_i)$	REG
5770	40680	1	0.1242	0.8758	1	2	0.1242	0.4073	BND
1185	10141	1	0.1046	0.8954	1	1	0.1046	0.0993	BND
610	9458	0	0.0606	0.9394	2	1	0.0606	0.0883	NEG
3638	42497	0	0.0789	0.9211	2	2	0.0789	0.4046	NEG
10	24	2	0.2941	0.7059	**1**	3	**0.2941**	0.0003	**POS**
6	20	2	0.2308	0.7692	**2**	3	**0.2308**	0.0002	**POS**

than female teenagers. This may suggest a social problem with teenage drivers in large cities.

7.5. CONCLUSIONS

The primary contribution of this chapter is the empirical investigation of the applicability of the VPRSM approach to a class of problems involving the analysis of a large collection of insurance data. The results obtained in this project indicate that the VPRS methodology and the associated HDTL algorithm provide an alternate way of analyzing attribute inter-relationships. The approach is not affected by the complex nature of the relationships that exist between the attributes under investigation, and one does not have to make any assumptions about the data being analyzed. The VPRSM approach derives its model directly from the data under investigation and quantifies the attribute relationships through probability estimates computed from the data. The driver records analysis application presented in this chapter demonstrates the workings of the methodology and provides some insights into the nature of interactions between various characteristics of drivers. The study also indicates that a broader category of insurance, medical, market, or similar data can be analyzed with the VPRSM methodology using the HDTL algorithm.

ACKNOWLEDGMENT

The research reported in this chapter was partially supported by a research grant awarded to the second author by the Natural Sciences and Engineering Research Council of Canada. The authors would like to thank anonymous referees for valuable detailed and insightful comments.

REFERENCES

Aryeetey, K., Ziarko, W., Tai, P., and Ago, C., Identification of rules for brain metastases and survival time prediction for small cell lung cancer patients, in *Proceedings of International Symposium "Intelligent Information Systems,"* Physica-Verlag, Zakopane, Poland, pp. 1–12, 2001.

Grzymala-Busse, J., and Ziarko. W., Data mining based on rough sets, in *Data Mining: Opportunities and Challenges*, IDEA Group Publishing, Hershey, PA, pp. 142–173, 2003.

Insurance Research Council: Motor vehicle records may not provide an accurate or complete account of driving histories, http://www.ircweb.org/news/NewsReleases/20020626.htm, 2002.

Katzberg, J., and Ziarko, W., Variable precision rough sets with asymmetric bounds, in *Proceedings of the International Workshop on Rough Sets and Knowledge Discovery (RSKD '93)*, pp. 163–191, 1993.

Pawlak, Z., *Rough Sets—Theoretical Aspects of Reasoning About Data*, Kluwer Academic Publishers, Dordrecht, 1991.

Quaye, K., Using Prior Convictions and Accidents to Identify Unsafe Drivers—An examination of Saskatchewan's Delinquent Driver Program, Saskatchewan Government Insurance, Regina, Saskatchewan, Canada, 1997.

Ślęzak, D., and Ziarko, W., Bayesian rough set model, in *Proceedings of FDM '2002*. December 9, Maebashi, Japan pp. 131–135, 2002.

South Carolina Department of Insurance: Factors Affecting Insurance Cost, http://www.doi.state.sc.us/Eng/Public/FormPub/CoatFactors.asp. 2003.

Stewart, J. R., and Campbell, B., *The Statistical Association Between Past and Future Accidents and Violations*, University of North Carolina, Chapel Hill, NC, 1972.

Yao, Y. Y., and Wong, S. K. M., A decision theoretic framework for approximating concepts, *International Journal of Man-Machine Studies* **37**, 793–809 (1992).

Ziarko, W., Variable precision rough sets model, *Journal of Computer and Systems Sciences* **46**(1), 39–59 (1993).

Ziarko, W., Approximation region-based decision tables, in *Rough Sets and Current Trends in Computing*, Polkowski, L., and Skowron, A. (eds.), Lecture Notes in AI 1424, Springer-Verlag, Berlin, pp. 178–185, 1998.

Ziarko, W., Decision making with probabilistic decision tables, in *Proceedings of the 7th International Workshop on Rough Sets, Fuzzy Sets, Data Mining and Granular Computing*, RSFDGrC '99, Yamaguchi, Japan, Lecture Notes in AI 1711, Springer-Verlag, Berlin, pp. 463–471, 1999.

Ziarko, W., Probabilistic decision tables in the variable precision rough set model, *Computational Intelligence: an International Journal* **17**(3), 593–603 (2001a).

Ziarko, W., Set approximation quality measures in the variable precision rough set model, Proceedings of the International Conference on Hybrid Intelligent Systems, in *Soft Computing Systems, Management and Applications*, IOS Press, Amsterdam, 442–452, 2001b.

Ziarko, W., Acquisition of hierarchy-structured probabilistic decision tables and rules from data, in *Proceedings of IEEE International Conference on Fuzzy Systems*, Honolulu, pp. 779–784, 2002.

PART III

SCIENCE AND ENGINEERING APPLICATIONS

8

DISCOVERY OF PATTERNS IN EARTH SCIENCE DATA USING DATA MINING

PUSHENG ZHANG, MICHAEL STEINBACH, VIPIN KUMAR,
SHASHI SHEKHAR, PANG-NING TAN, STEVEN KLOOSTER,
AND CHRISTOPHER POTTER

8.1. INTRODUCTION

NASA's Earth Observing System (EOS) consists of a series of satellites that generate global observations of the land surface, biosphere, solid Earth, atmosphere, and oceans. This remote sensing data, combined with historical climate records and predictions from ecosystem models, offers new opportunities for understanding how the earth is changing, for determining what factors cause these changes, and for predicting future changes. Data-mining techniques (Behnke et al., 1999) have the promise to aid this undertaking by discovering interesting patterns that capture complex interactions among ocean temperatures, land surface meteorology, and terrestrial carbon flux.

Collaboration between Earth Scientists and data-mining researchers has developed in two phases as illustrated in Figure 8.1. In the first phase, data-mining techniques are applied to discover some well-known patterns in Earth Science in order to build confidence in the use of data-mining techniques. As an example, consider the El Nino climate pattern and its well-known effects on temperature and precipitation (Taylor, 1998). The second phase includes the exploration of novel patterns found by data mining, but not well-known by Earth Scientists. This phase also includes the exploration of patterns that are well known to Earth Scientists, but are not discovered by existing data-mining techniques.

To explore Earth Science data, researchers have applied various data-mining techniques (Behnke et al., 1999), such as association rule mining for texture features in satellite images (Rushing et al., 2001), classification of land cover

Next Generation of Data-Mining Applications.   Edited by Kantardzic and Zurada
ISBN 0-471-65605-4   © 2005 the Institute of Electrical and Electronics Engineers, Inc.

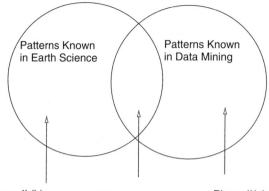

Phase II (b):   Phase I: Phase II(a):
New Challenges for Data Mining Confidence Building Candidates for Further Analysis
                                                 by Earth scientists
                                                 (Leap of Faith)

Figure 8.1. Using data mining to find Earth Science patterns.

TABLE 8.1. Connection of Data-Mining Techniques to Earth Science Questions

Earth Science Question	Examples of Data-Mining Techniques
How is the Earth changing?	Principal Component Analysis (PCA), Cluster Analysis, Anomaly Detection, ARIMA time series modeling, Trend Detection, Change Point Detection
What factors cause these changes?	Correlation, Canonical Correlation Analysis, Association Analysis, Causal Analysis
Can we predict future changes?	Regression, correlation

types (Kumar et al., 2002), and clustering of storm path trajectories (Gaffney and Smith, 1999). Table 8.1 shows some data-mining techniques that can be used to address basic Earth Science questions.

Although Earth Scientists have traditionally used statistical tools as their preferred method of data analysis, they are interested in using data-mining tools to complement statistical tools for the following reasons. First, the statistical method of manually analyzing a single dataset via the hypothesize-and-test paradigm is extremely labor-intensive due to the extremely large and growing families of interesting spatiotemporal hypotheses and patterns in Earth Science datasets. Second, statistical methods are not designed to scale to large Earth Science datasets. Third, Earth Science datasets have selection bias in terms of being convenience or opportunity samples rather than traditional idealized statistical random samples from independent and identical distributions (Duba et al., 2000; Fayyad et al., 1996; Grossman et al., 2001; Hand, 1998; Hand et al., 2001). Data mining allows Earth Scientists to spend more time choosing and exploring interesting families of hypotheses derived from the data. More specifically, by applying data-mining techniques, some of the steps of hypothesis generation and evaluation will be automated, facilitated, and improved, including steps involved in hypothesis generation, out-of-main-memory storage and manipulation of datasets, and the formation and evaluation of hypotheses from data with categorical attributes or data collected via opportunity sampling.

This chapter illustrates the application of data mining to the discovery of interesting and useful Earth Science patterns by describing some of the results (Kumar et al., 2001; Steinbach et al., 2001, 2002a, b, 2003; Tan et al., 2001; Zhang et al., 2003a–c) from our current project entitled *Discovery of Changes from the Global Carbon Cycle and Climate System Using Data Mining*. Section 8.2 describes the nature of the data, while Section 8.3 discusses data preprocessing techniques that are necessary before the data can be analyzed using data-mining techniques. Sections 8.4–8.7 describe the data-mining techniques used in Earth Science data, including clustering, association analysis, query processing, and other techniques. Section 8.8 concludes the chapter.

8.2. DATA DESCRIPTION AND DATA SOURCES

Earth Science data consist of a sequence of global snapshots of the earth taken at various points in time, as shown in Figure 8.2. Each snapshot consists of measurement values for a number of variables (e.g., temperature, pressure, and precipitation) collected globally. All attribute data within a global snapshot is represented using spatial frameworks. A spatial framework is a partitioning of the surface of Earth into a set of mutually disjoint regions that collectively cover the entire surface of Earth. Examples of spatial frameworks for land include the political boundaries of countries and latitude–longitude spherical grids at different

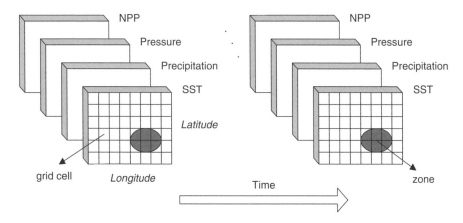

Figure 8.2. A simplified view of the problem domain.

resolutions—for example, $0.5° \times 0.5°$ or $1° \times 1°$. Variables derived from global satellite data—for example, net primary production (NPP)—are available at a resolution of $0.5° \times 0.5°$. (NPP is the net assimilation of atmospheric carbon dioxide into organic matter by plants.) Global snapshots—for example, values of variables for each location in a spatial framework—are available for periodic, discrete points in time that span a range of 20–100 years. These variable values can be either observations from different sensors [e.g., precipitation and sea surface temperature (SST)] or the result of model predictions (e.g., NPP from the NASA–CASA model).

The primary focus of our work has been the development of algorithms and tools to help Earth Scientists to discover changes in the global carbon cycle and climate system, and we have focused on the datasets that are most relevant to that task. In particular, Earth Scientists who work at the regional and global scale have identified NPP as a key variable for understanding the global carbon cycle and the ecological dynamics of the Earth. Terrestrial NPP is driven by solar radiation and can be constrained by precipitation and temperature. Keeping track of NPP is important because it includes the food source of humans and all other organisms and, thus, sudden changes in the NPP of a region can have a direct impact on the regional ecology. An ecosystem model for predicting NPP, known as NASA–CASA [the Carnegie Ames Stanford Approach (Potter et al., 1999)], has been used for over a decade to produce a detailed view of terrestrial productivity. This project has made use of the multiyear output of NASA–CASA, as well as long-term global sea surface temperature (SST) anomalies, to discover interesting patterns relating changes in NPP to land surface climatology and global climate. Predicting NPP based on sea surface temperature would be of great benefit given the near real-time availability of SST data and the ability of climate forecasting to anticipate SST El Nino/La Nina events.

8.3. DATA PREPROCESSING

Patterns derived from Earth Science data are often dominated by the presence of seasonal variations in the data. Although yearly patterns such as spring, summer, fall, winter, or rainy season/dry season are important, they are already well known. Earth Scientists are primarily interested in patterns that represent deviations from normal seasonal cycles. Examples of such patterns include anomalous climate events such as droughts, floods, heat waves, and so on. Such anomalous events become apparent only if the seasonal components of the climate time series are removed. In the following, we describe a technique known as the "monthly" Z-score transformation for removing these components.

This transformation takes the set of values for a given month (e.g., all Januarys), calculates the mean and standard deviation for that set of monthly values, and then standardizes each value by calculating its Z-score—that is, by subtracting off the mean and dividing by the standard deviation. Put another way, we express each data value in the time series in terms of its deviation from

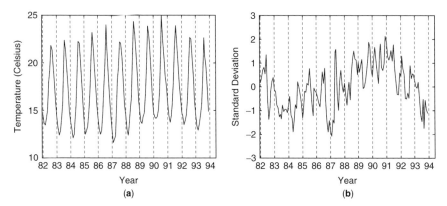

Figure 8.3. Monthly Z-score transformation applied to deseasonalize a sample SST time series. **(a)** Original SST Time-Series. **(b)** Transformed SST Time Series.

the mean value for its corresponding month, scaled by the volatility factor for that month. The month-by-month rescaling used in this transformation causes seasonal fluctuations to disappear. Figure 8.3 shows the result of applying the monthly Z-score to a sample SST time series.

Other data preprocessing issues include handling trends and spatial/temporal autocorrelations in the data. The trends are long-term upward or downward movements in the Earth Science time series data (Box et al., 1994). Spatial/temporal autocorrelation is the property by which measured values that are close in time and space tend to be highly correlated or similar (Cressie, 1993). Trends and spatial/temporal autocorrelations should be removed from data for two reasons. First, both have a direct impact on the statistical correlation computed between two time series. For example, temporal autocorrelation reduces the significance of a correlation by decreasing the degree of freedom in the time series. Second, removing trends and temporal autocorrelations makes the time series become stationary, a typical requirement of many statistical time series analysis techniques (e.g., ARIMA). For further details on these issues, we refer the reader to Tan et al. (2001).

8.4. CLUSTERING

It is well known that ocean, atmosphere, and land processes are highly coupled; that is, climate phenomena occurring in one location can affect the climate at a far away location. Indeed, understanding these climate teleconnections is critical for finding the answers to questions such as how the Earth's climate is changing and how ecosystems respond to global environmental change.

A common way to study such teleconnections is by using climate indices (http://www.cgd.ucar.edu/cas/catalog/climind/ and http://www.cdc.noaa.gov/USclimate/Correlation/help.html), which distill climate variability at a regional or global scale into a single time series. For example, the NINO 1+2 index, which is defined as the average sea surface temperature anomaly in a region off the coast of Peru, is a climate index associated with the El Niño phenomenon, the anomalous warming of the eastern tropical region of the Pacific. El Niño has been linked to climate anomalies in many parts of the world such as droughts in Australia and heavy rainfall along the eastern coast of South America (Taylor, 1998). Figure 8.4 shows the correlation between the NINO 1+2 index and land temperature anomalies, which are deviations from the mean. Observe that this index is highly correlated to the land temperature anomalies on the western coast of South America, which is not surprising given the proximity of this region to the ocean region defining the index. However, few outside the field of Earth Science would expect that NINO 1+2 is also highly correlated to land regions that

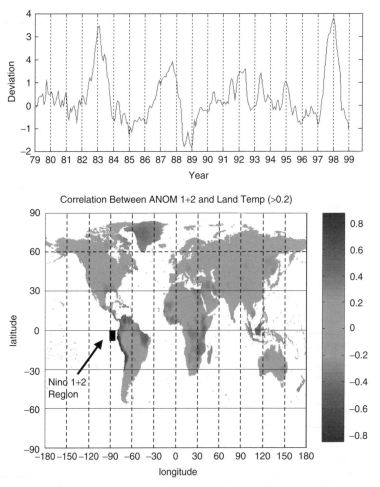

Figure 8.4. The NINO 1+2 climate index and its correlation to land temperature anomalies.

are far away from the eastern coast of South America (e.g., Africa and South-East Asia).

Most commonly used climate indices are based on sea level pressure (SLP) and sea surface temperature in ocean regions. These indices can ease the discovery of relationships of SST and SLP to land temperature and precipitation. These variables, in turn, impact plant growth and are therefore important for understanding the global carbon cycle and the ecological dynamics of the Earth.

As a result, Earth Scientists have devoted a considerable amount of time to developing/discovering climate indices, such as NINO 1+2 and the other indices described in Table 8.2. One of the approaches used to discover climate indices has been the direct observation of climate phenomenon. For instance, the El Niño phenomenon was first noticed by Peruvian fishermen centuries ago. The fishermen observed that in some years the warm southward current, which appeared around Christmas, would persist for an unusually long time, with a disastrous impact on fishing. In the early twentieth century, while studying the trade winds and Indian monsoon, scientists noticed large-scale changes in pressure in the equatorial Pacific region which they referred to as the "Southern Oscillation."

TABLE 8.2. Description of Well-Known Climate Indices

Index	Description
SOI	(Southern Oscillation Index) Measures the SLP anomalies between Darwin and Tahiti
NAO	(North Atlantic Oscillation) Normalized SLP differences between Ponta Delgada, Azores and Stykkisholmur, Iceland
AO	(Arctic Oscillation) Defined as the first principal component of SLP poleward of $20°N$
PDO	(Pacific Decadel Oscillation) Derived as the leading principal component of monthly SST anomalies in the North Pacific Ocean, poleward of $20°N$
QBO	(Quasi-Biennial Oscillation Index) Measures the regular variation of zonal (i.e., east–west) stratospheric winds above the equator
CTI	(Cold Tongue Index) Captures SST variations in the cold tongue region of the equatorial Pacific Ocean ($6°N$–$6°S$, $180°$–$90°W$)
WP	(Western Pacific) Represents a low-frequency temporal function of the "zonal dipole" SLP spatial pattern involving the Kamchatka Peninsula, southeastern Asia and far western tropical and subtropical North Pacific
NINO1+2	Sea surface temperature anomalies in the region bounded by $80°W$–$90°W$ and $0°$–$10°S$
NINO3	Sea surface temperature anomalies in the region bounded by $90°W$–$150°W$ and $5°S$–$5°N$
NINO3.4	Sea surface temperature anomalies in the region bounded by $120°W$–$170°W$ and $5°S$–$5°N$
NINO4	Sea surface temperature anomalies in the region bounded by $150°W$–$160°W$ and $5°S$–$5°N$

Scientists developed a climate index called the Southern Oscillation Index (SOI) to capture this pressure phenomenon. In the mid- and late 1960s, the Southern Oscillation was conclusively tied to El Niño, and the impact of both on global climate was recognized. Needless to say, finding climate indices in this fashion is a very slow and tedious process.

More recently, motivated by the massive amounts of new data being produced by satellite observations, Earth Scientists have been using eigenvalue analysis techniques, such as principal components analysis (PCA) and singular value decomposition (SVD), to discover climate indices (Storch and Zwiers, 1999). While eigenvalue techniques do provide a way to quickly and automatically detect patterns in large amounts of data, they also have the following limitations: (i) All discovered signals must be orthogonal to each other, making it difficult to attach a physical interpretation to them, and (ii) weaker signals may be masked by stronger signals.

We have developed an alternative clustering-based methodology for the discovery of climate indices that overcomes these limitations. The use of clustering (Dubes and Jain, 1988) is driven by the intuition that a climate phenomenon is expected to involve a significant region of the ocean or atmosphere, and we expect that such a phenomenon will be "stronger" if it involves a region where the behavior is relatively uniform over the entire area. *Shared nearest-neighbor* (SNN) clustering (Ertoz et al., 2001, 2002, 2003) has been shown to find such homogeneous clusters. Each of these clusters can be characterized by a centroid (i.e., the mean of all the time series describing the ocean points in the cluster); thus, these centroids represent potential climate indices. This approach offers a number of benefits: (i) Discovered signals do not need to be orthogonal to each other, (ii) signals are more easily interpreted, (iii) weaker signals are more readily detected, and (iv) an efficient way is proved to determine the influence of a large set of points (e.g., all ocean points) on another large set of points (e.g., all land points).

We applied SNN clustering on the SST data over the time period from 1958 to 1998. As shown in Figure 8.5, SNN found 107 clusters or candidate indices. Note that many grid points from the ocean do not belong to any clusters (these are the points belonging to the white background), because these points come from regions that are not relatively uniform and homogeneous.

Some of the cluster centroids (i.e., candidate indices) that we found are very highly correlated to known indices. Figure 8.6 shows clusters that reproduce some well-known climate indices. In particular, we were able to replicate the four El Niño SST-based indices: Cluster 94 corresponds to NINO 1+2, 67 to NINO 3, 78 to NINO 3.4, and 75 to NINO 4. The correlations of these clusters to their corresponding indices are higher than 0.9. In addition, cluster 67 is highly correlated to the CTI index, which is defined over a wider area in the same region. Clusters 58 and 59 are very similar to the other El Niño indices, and they correlate most strongly with NINO 3 and NINO 4, respectively, although their correlations to the El Niño indices are not as high as the other four clusters.

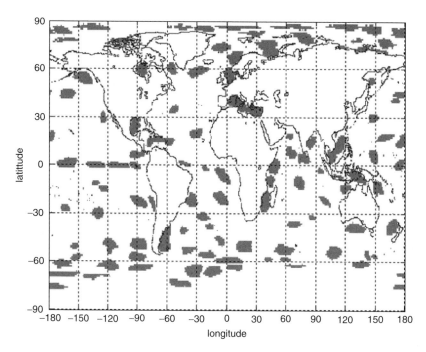

Figure 8.5. 107 SST clusters.

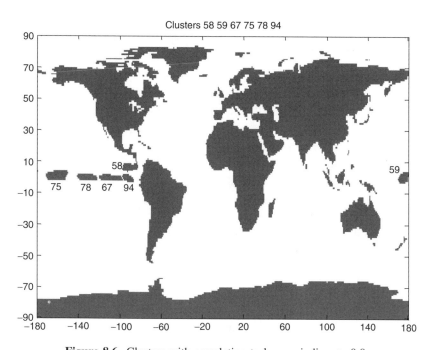

Figure 8.6. Clusters with correlation to known indices ≥ 0.8.

This rediscovery of well-known indices serves to validate our approach. In fact, we are able to rediscover most of the known major climate indices using our approach. In addition, some of the cluster centroids that have a high correlation to well-known indices may represent variants to well-known indices in that, while they may represent the same phenomena, they may be potentially better predictors of land behavior for some regions of the land. Finally, cluster centroids that have medium or low correlation with known indices may represent potentially new Earth Science phenomena. Further details on the application of clustering for discovering climate indices are available in Ertöz et al. (2001, 2002) and Steinbach et al. (2001, 2002a, b, 2003).

8.5. ASSOCIATION ANALYSIS

Association analysis can be used to derive spatiotemporal relationships hidden in Earth Science data. The goal of association analysis is to extract significant patterns, in the form of rules or sets of events, that will predict the occurrence of certain events based on the occurrence of other events. For example, the association rule $A \longrightarrow B$ suggests that event B is expected to occur whenever event A is observed.

Due to the spatiotemporal nature of Earth Science datasets, there are four types of association patterns that may be derived:

1. *Non-spatiotemporal Patterns.* This type of pattern captures events that occur simultaneously in the same location. An example of such a pattern is "low solar radiation events where there are low rainfall events."

2. *Spatial Patterns.* This type of pattern captures events that occur simultaneously at different locations. An example of such a pattern is "surface ocean heating affects climate at the nearby coastal areas."

3. *Temporal Patterns.* This type of pattern predicts events that are expected to occur in the future at the same location. An example of such a pattern is "low rainfall events eventually lead to an increase in wildfires."

4. *Spatiotemporal Patterns.* This type of pattern captures time-lagged teleconnections—that is, relationships among events that occur in geographically distant locations. An example of such a pattern is "surface ocean heating eventually affects regional wildfires and NPP."

Before applying association analysis, each time series is converted into a sequence of events. We define an event as an anomalously high or low value of the time series—specifically, if the value of the time series deviates by at least 1.5 standard deviations from its average. A standard association analysis algorithm, such as Apriori (Agrawal and Srikant, 1994), is then applied to extract rules from the transformed datasets. The rules extracted by the Apriori algorithm are evaluated using the well-known support and confidence measures

(Agrawal and Srikant, 1994). Rules with low support and low confidence tend to be statistically insignificant, and they are pruned automatically by the Apriori algorithm. For example, some of the non-spatiotemporal patterns extracted by Apriori include:

R1: {**FPAR-HI**} $\longrightarrow$ {**NPP-HI**} (support = 4.6%, confidence = 51%). Fraction of photosynthetically active radiation (FPAR) measures the proportion of available radiation in the photosynthetically active wavelengths (400–700 nm) that a plant canopy absorbs (Myneni et al., 1997). For rule R1, an anomalously high FPAR implies that the vegetation in the region has generated more "light-harvesting" photosynthetic capability than average, which leads to higher than normal NPP. There is a 51% probability that a high NPP event would occur at a land point where a high FPAR event is observed.

R2: {**PET-LO, FPAR-LO**} $\longrightarrow$ {**NPP-LO**} (support = 3.0%, confidence = 68%). The variable potential evapotranspiration (PET) measures the potential loss of water to the atmosphere by evaporation and transpiration through plants. Whenever both low PET and low FPAR events are observed at a land point, there is a 68% chance that a low NPP event also occurs at the same location.

The association rules found using this approach are consistent with the predictions made by the NASA–CASA model. In the NASA–CASA model, NPP is a direct product of five input factors: the cloud-corrected solar irradiance, FPAR, maximum light use efficiency, temperature, and moisture stress scalars. Both example rules (R1 and R2) confirm the relationship between NPP and the input variables of the NASA–CASA model. However, since each geographical region has its own climate and topographical features, the primary drivers for low or high NPP events may be different at different locations. Earth Scientists are interested in knowing the primary drivers for anomalous NPP events associated with each land cover feature, but such information is not directly available from the output of the NASA–CASA model.

To that end, we have incorporated land cover information into the association analysis. For example, Figure 8.7a shows the locations covered by the rule R1—that is, locations where both FPAR-HI and NPP-HI events are observed simultaneously. It is not surprising to find that the rule covers almost all the regions on Earth because (i) NPP is a derivative of FPAR and (ii) the association at a location could happen purely by chance. In the latter case, each Z-transformed time series of length 216 months (for a 17-year dataset) is expected to produce approximately $0.0668 \times 216 = 11$ HI and 11 LO events (where $P(|Z| \geq 1.5) = 0.0668$). If a pair of events, such as NPP-HI and FPAR-HI, are independent, then the probability of these events to co-occur together at least once is $1 - (1 - 0.0668^2)^{216} = 0.619$, which is better than random.

By increasing the support threshold at a location, the probability that these events co-occur together more than once will be significantly reduced. For

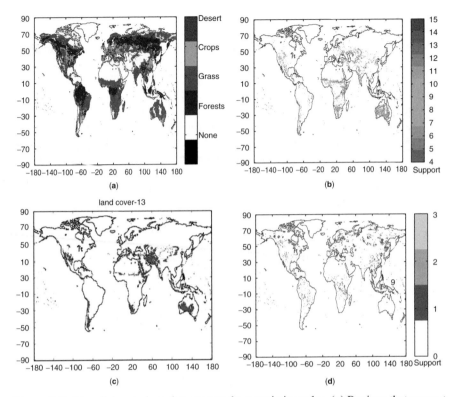

Figure 8.7. Visualizing regions that support the association rules. (a) Regions that support the association rule $\{FPAR - Hi\} \rightarrow \{NPP - Hi\}$. (b) Regions that have high support for the association rule $\{FPAR - Hi\} \rightarrow \{NPP - Hi\}$. (c) Grassland and Shrubland Areas. (d) Regions that support the association rule $\{FPAR - Lo, PET - Lo\} \rightarrow \{NPP - Lo\}$.

example, Figure 8.7b shows the locations covered by the rule R1, for which the events {FPAR-HI, NPP-HI} co-occur at least four times. More importantly, we observe that these locations coincide with grassland and shrubland regions, as shown in Figure 8.7c. In other words, even though NASA–CASA is a global model for predicting NPP, the support for a pattern such as R1 depends strongly on its geographical locations. Regions that show a prominent R1 pattern correspond mainly to grassland and shrubland areas, a type of vegetation that is able to more quickly take advantage of periodically high precipitation (and possibly solar radiation) than forests.

We observe that the R2 pattern occurs frequently in the regions of evergreen forests (Figure 8.7d). This leads us to believe that this pattern often appears in regions that are fire-prone (and, thus, that have temporarily lost their photosynthetic capability) or have suffered other major disruptive events, but this needs to be verified by consulting historical records, which are not easily accessible through conventional sources. For further details, we refer the reader to Tan et al. (2001).

8.6. QUERY PROCESSING

A spatial time series dataset (Zhang et al., 2003a) is a collection of time series (Box et al., 1994), each referencing a location in a common spatial framework (Worboys, 1995). NASA Earth observation systems currently generate a large sequence of global snapshots of the Earth, including various atmospheric, land, and ocean measurements such as sea surface temperature, pressure, and precipitation. These data are spatial time series data in nature. Queries that find highly correlated time series are frequently used to discover interesting relationships among observations in spatial time series data. For example, such queries are used to identify the land locations whose climate is severely affected by El Niño (Taylor, 1998). However, correlation queries are computationally expensive due to large spatiotemporal frameworks containing many locations and long time sequences. Therefore, the development of efficient query processing techniques is crucial for exploring these datasets.

Previous work on query processing for time series data has focused on dimensionality reduction (Agrawal, 1993; Chan and Fu, 1999; Faloutsos, 1996) followed by the use of low-dimensional indexing techniques (Guttman, 1984; Rigaux et al., 2001; Samet, 1990) in the transformed space. Unfortunately, the efficiency of these approaches deteriorates substantially when a small set of dimensions cannot represent enough information in the time series data. Many spatial time series datasets fall in this category. For example, finding anomalies is more desirable than finding well-known seasonal patterns. Therefore, the data used in anomaly detection is usually data whose seasonality has been removed. However, after transformations are applied to deseasonalize the data, the power spectrum spreads out over almost all dimensions. Furthermore, in most spatial time series datasets, the number of spatial locations is much greater than the length of the time series. This makes it possible to improve the performance of query processing of spatial time series data by exploiting spatial proximity in the design of access methods. We have proposed filter-and-refine query processing algorithms (Zhang et al., 2003a, b) to exploit spatial autocorrelation (Tobler, 1979) for facilitating correlation-based similarity queries on spatial time series data.

A normalized time series with m time measurements is a vector from the origin to the surface of an m-dimensional unit sphere (Zhang et al., 2003a). The correlation of two time series is directly related to the angle between the two normalized time series vectors in the multidimensional unit sphere. We have proposed the concept of a cone (Zhang et al., 2003a), a set of normalized time series in a multidimensional unit sphere. A cone is characterized by two parameters, the center and the span of the cone. The center of the cone is the mean of all the time series in the cone. The span of the cone is the maximal angle between any time series in the cone and the cone center. For simplicity, Figure 8.8 illustrates a cone in the two-dimensional case.

The proposed algorithms first divide the data into a collection of disjoint cells based on spatial proximity with a coarse resolution, where each cell corresponds to one cone in a multidimensional unit sphere. Each cell includes multiple time

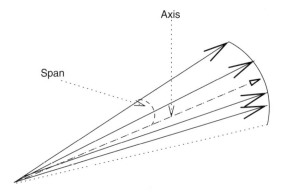

Figure 8.8. Illustration of a cone.

series, and the center and span are used to characterize each cone. Then each cell is divided recursively into quarters based on spatial autocorrelation to construct a cone-hierarchy search tree. The number of pairs of time series for correlation computations are substantially reduced by using a group-level join as a filtering step. Only the candidates that cannot be filtered are explored in the refinement step. The algorithms were proved to be correct and complete in Zhang et al. (2003b); that is, there were no false admissions or false dismissals.

We evaluated the performance of the proposed query processing algorithms using a NASA Earth Science dataset (Zhang et al., 2003b). Correlation-based range queries and join queries were carried out on the SST data in the eastern tropical region of the Pacific Ocean, and on the NPP data in the United States. The SST data contain 11,556 ocean cells of the Pacific Ocean, and the NPP data contain 2901 land cells of the United States. The records of SST and NPP were monthly data from 1982 to 1993. The experimental results showed that the proposed query processing algorithms often saved a large fraction of computational cost (Zhang et al., 2003b). For example, 10 NPP time series from the United States were chosen to carry out the correlation-based similarity range queries with the SST data from the eastern tropical region of the Pacific Ocean,

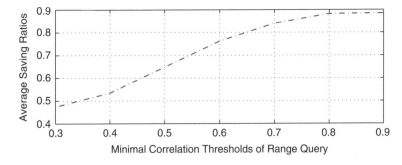

Figure 8.9. Savings for query processing.

respectively. The geographical locations of the 10 query time series were widely spread in the United States. Figure 8.9 shows that the average computational savings for the queries range from 48% to 89% as the minimal correlation threshold increased from 0.3 to 0.9. For further details, we refer the reader to Zhang et al. (2003a–c).

8.7. OTHER TECHNIQUES

8.7.1. Spatial and Temporal Outlier Detection

Outliers have been informally defined as observations that appear to be inconsistent with the remainder of the data (Barnett and Lewis, 1994) or that deviate so much from other observations so as to arouse suspicions that they were generated by a different mechanism (Hawkins, 1980). The identification of outliers can lead to the discovery of unexpected knowledge and has a number of practical applications in areas such as Earth Science, credit card fraud, voting irregularities, bankruptcy, weather prediction, and the performance analysis of athletes.

A spatial outlier is a spatially referenced object whose nonspatial attribute values are significantly different from those of other spatially referenced objects in its spatial neighborhood (Shekhar et al., 2001). Informally, a spatial outlier is a local instability (in values of nonspatial attributes) or a spatially referenced object whose nonspatial attributes are extreme relative to its neighbors, even though these attributes may not be significantly different from those of the entire population. For example, a new house in an old neighborhood of a growing metropolitan area is a spatial outlier based on the nonspatial attribute house age. A temporal outlier is an object in a snapshot whose attribute values are significantly different from those of neighboring snapshots in a time series. For example, 1987 was an abnormal year in terms of El Niño activity in the world, and the values of sea surface temperature in the eastern Pacific Ocean were very different from those of neighboring years when El Niño activity was not evident in the same locations. Outlier detection techniques are being applied to Earth Science data to identify abnormal and potentially useful spatiotemporal phenomenon.

8.7.2. Predictive Modeling

Classical data-mining algorithms often make assumptions (e.g., independent, identical distributions) that violate the first law of Geography, which says that everything is related to everything else but nearby things are more related than distant things. In other words, the values of attributes of nearby spatial objects tend to systematically affect each other. In spatial statistics, an area within statistics devoted to the analysis of spatial data is called *spatial autocorrelation*. Ignoring spatial autocorrelation may lead to residual errors that vary systematically over space exhibiting high spatial autocorrelation (Shekhar and Chawla, 2003;

Shekhar et al., 2002). The models derived may not only turn out to be biased and inconsistent, but may also be a poor fit to the dataset.

One way to model spatial dependencies is by adding a spatial autocorrelation term in the regression equation. This term contains a neighborhood relationship contiguity matrix. Such spatial statistical methods, however, are computationally expensive due to their reliance on contiguity matrices that can be larger than the spatial datasets being analyzed. We have developed an efficient algorithm, called PLUMS (Predicting Locations Using Map Similarity) (Grossman et al., 2001; Shekhar and Chawla, 2003), to search the parameter space of classification models utilizing spatial autocorrelation. We have used PLUMS for building models to predict bird nest locations on a wetland dataset. The preliminary results show that PLUMS outperforms classical regression models substantially on this dataset. We plan to apply PLUMS to Earth Science data and further refine the algorithm to better handle the more complex spatial context present in this domain.

8.7.3. Co-location Mining

The co-location pattern discovery process finds frequently co-located subsets of spatial event (Shekhar et al., 1999) types given a map of their locations (see Figure 8.10). For example, the analysis of the habitats of animals and plants may identify the co-location of predator–prey species, symbiotic species, and fire events with fuel, ignition sources, and so on. Readers may find it interesting

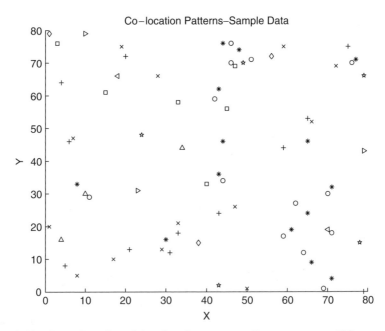

Figure 8.10. Illustration of spatial co-location patterns. Shapes represent different spatial feature types. Spatial features in sets {+, ×} and {○, *} tend to be located together.

to analyze the map in Figure 8.10 to find co-location patterns. In this example, finding a "+" implies a high chance of finding an "×" in its nearby region and vice versa. In fact, there are two co-location patterns of size 2 in this map.

The spatial co-location problem (Shekhar and Huang, 2001) looks similar to the association rule mining problem, but in fact is very different from it. Even though boolean spatial feature types (also called spatial events) may correspond to items in association rules over market-basket datasets, there is no natural notion of transactions. This makes it difficult to use traditional measures (e.g. support, confidence) and apply association rule mining algorithms that use support-based pruning. In market-basket datasets, transactions represent sets of item types bought together by customers. The purpose of mining association rules is to identify frequent item sets for planning store layouts or marketing campaigns. In many spatial application domains such as Earth Science, transactions are often not a natural concept. The transactions in market basket analysis are independent of each other. Transactions are disjoint in the sense of not sharing instances of item types. In contrast, the instances of boolean spatial features are embedded in a space and share a variety of spatial relationships (e.g., neighbor) with each other. We have developed one of the most natural formulations as well as one of first algorithms (Shekhar and Huang, 2001) for discovering co-location patterns from large spatial datasets and applying it to Earth Science data.

8.8. CONCLUSIONS

In this chapter we provided an overview of our preliminary efforts to apply data-mining techniques to the analysis of Earth Science data. We believe that our initial results are encouraging. For instance, we have been able to use clustering to find patterns that represent well-known climate indices. More importantly, we have also found new patterns that are not known to Earth Scientists—for example, candidate climate indices and association patterns that relate land covers to rules that connect climate variables and NPP. While more evaluation is necessary to assess the Earth Science significance of these results, one of the major goals of our work is to produce new patterns and hypotheses for Earth Scientists to investigate, and we feel that we have made progress towards that goal.

Nonetheless, there are many tasks remaining with respect to both data mining and the application of data-mining results. The main focus of the data-mining work has been clustering and association analysis, and we have only lightly explored outlier detection, co-location mining, predictive modeling, and other data-mining approaches. Also, while the Earth Science members of our team have evaluated and interpreted the data-mining results that we have produced so far, which has led to publications in Earth Science journals (Potter et al., 2003a–f), there is much more to do within the scope of our current project. Furthermore, in the long term, we are hopeful that data mining can play an important role in helping Earth Scientists understand both (a) global scale changes in biosphere processes and patterns and (b) the effects of widespread human activities. More broadly, improvements in data-mining techniques made during the investigation of Earth Science data may have potential applications in other domains, such as transportation, business logistics, public health, and public safety.

ACKNOWLEDGMENTS

We are particularly grateful to Professor George Karypis and other colleagues on the NASA project for their helpful comments and valuable discussions.

This work was partially supported by NASA grant # NCC 2 1231 and by the Army High Performance Computing Research Center under the auspices of the Department of the Army, Army Research Laboratory cooperative agreement number DAAD19-01-2-0014, the content of which does not necessarily reflect the position or policy of the government, and no official endorsement should be inferred. Access to computing facilities was provided by the AHPCRC and the Minnesota Supercomputing Institute.

REFERENCES

Agrawal, R., Faloutsos, C., and Swami, A., Efficient similarity search In sequence databases, in *Proceedings of the 4th International Conference of Foundations of Data Organization and Algorithms*, 1993.

Agrawal, R., and Srikant, R., Fast algorithms for mining association rules, in *Proceedings 20th International Conference on Very Large Data Bases, VLDB*, pages 487–499, 1994.

Barnett, V., and Lewis, T., *Outliers in Statistical Data*, 3rd edition, John Wiley & Sons, New York, 1994.

Behnke, J., Dobinson, E., Graves, S., Hinke, T., Nichols, D., and Stolorz, P., Final Report for NASA Workshop on Issues in the Application of Data Mining to Scientific Data, 1999.

Box, G., Jenkins, G., and Reinsel, G., *Time Series Analysis: Forecasting and Control*, Prentice-Hall, Englewood Cliffs, NJ, 1994.

Chan, K., and Fu, A. W., Efficient time series matching by wavelets, in *Proceedings of the 15th International Conference on Data Engineering*, 1999.

Cressie, N. A., *Statistics for Spatial Data*, revised edition, John Wiley & Sons, New York, 1993.

Duba, R., Hart, P., and Stork, D., *Pattern Classification*, 2nd edition, Wiley-Interscience, New York, 2000.

Dubes, R. C., and Jain, A. K., *Algorithms for Clustering Data*, Prentice-Hall, Englewood Cliffs, NJ, 1988.

Ertöz, L., Steinbach, M., and Kumar, V., Finding topics in collections of documents: A shared nearest neighbor approach, in *Proceedings of Text Mine'01, First SIAM International Conference on Data Mining*, Chicago, 2001.

Ertöz, L., Steinbach, M., and Kumar, V., A New Shared Nearest Neighbor Clustering Algorithm and Its Applications, in *Workshop on Clustering High Dimensional Data and Its Applications, SIAM Data Mining 2002, Arlington, VA*, 2002.

Ertöz, L., Steinbach, M., and Kumar, V., Finding clusters of different sizes, shapes, and densities in noisy, high dimensional data, in *Proceedings of 3rd SIAM International Conference on Data Mining, San Francisco*, May 2003.

Faloutsos, C., *Searching Multimedia Databases by Content*, Kluwer Academic Publishers, Hingham, MA, 1996.

Fayyad, U., Piatetsky-Shapiro, G., Smyth, P., and Uthurusamy, R., *Advances in Knowledge Discovery and Data Mining*, MIT Press, Cambridge, MA, 1996.

Gaffney, S., and Smyth, P., Trajectory Clustering with Mixtures of Regression Models, in *Proceedings of the Fifth ACM SIGKDD International Conference on Knowledge Discovery and Data Mining*, 1999.

Grossman, R., Kamath, C., Kegelmeyer, P., Kumar, V., and Namburu, R., *Data Mining for Scientific and Engineering Applications*, Kluwer Academic Publishers, Hingham, MA, 2001.

Guttman, A., R-Trees: A dynamic index structure for spatial searching, in *ACM SIGMOD*, 1984.

Hand, D., Data mining: Statistics and more, *The American Statistician* **52**, 112–118 (1998).

Hand, D., Mannila, H., and Smyth, P., *Principles of Data Mining*, MIT Press, Cambridge, MA, 2001.

Hawkins, D., *Identification of Outliers*, Chapman and Hall, New York, 1980.

http://www.cgd.ucar.edu/cas/catalog/climind/.

http://www.cdc.noaa.gov/USclimate/Correlation/ help.html.

Kumar, S., Ghosh, J., and Crawford, M., Hierarchical fusion of multiple classifiers for hyperspectral data analysis, *Pattern Analysis and Applications (Special Issue on Fusion of Multiple Classifiers)* **5**(2), 210–220 (2002).

Kumar, V., Steinbach, M., Tan, P. N., Potter, C., Klooster, S., and Torregrosa, A., Mining scientific data: Discovery of patterns in the global climate system, in *Joint Statistical Meeting*, 2001.

Myneni, R., Nemani, R., and Running, S., Algorithm for the estimation of global land cover, LAI and FPAR based on radiative transfer models, *IEEE Transactions on Geoscience and Remote Sensing* **35**, 1380–1393 (1997).

Potter, C., Klooster, S. A., and Brooks, V., Inter-annual variability in terrestrial net primary production: Exploration of trends and controls on regional to global scales, *Ecosystems* **2**(1), 36–48 (1999).

Potter, C., Klooster, S., Myneni, R., Genovese, V., Tan, P., and Kumar, V., Continental scale comparisons of terrestrial carbon sinks, *Global and Planetary Change*, **39**, 201–213 (2003a).

Potter, C., Klooster, S., Steinbach, M., Tan, P., Kumar, V., Shekhar, S., Nemani, R., and Myneni, R., Global teleconnections of ocean climate to terrestrial carbon flux, *Journal of Geophysical Research* **108**(D17), 1–12 (2003b).

Potter, C., Klooster, S., Tan, P., Steinbach, M., Kumar, V., and Genovese, V., Variability in Terrestrial Carbon Sinks over Two Decades. Part I: North America. *Earth Interactions* **7**(12), 1–26 (2003c).

Potter, C., Tan, P., Steinbach, M., Klooster, S., Kumar, V., Myneni, R., and Genovese, V., Major disturbance events in terrestrial ecosystems detected using global satellite data sets, *Global Change Biology*, **9**(7), 1005–1021 (2003d).

Potter, C., Klooster, S., Steinbach, M., Tan, P., Kumar, V., Shekhar, S., and Carvalho, C., Understanding global teleconnections of climate to regional model estimates of Amazon ecosystem carbon flux, *Global Change Biology*, **10**(5), 693–703 (2004).

Potter, C., Zhang, P., Klooster, S., Genovese, V., Shekhar, S., and Kumar, V., Land use—Understanding controls on historical river discharge in the world's largest drainage basins, *Earth Interactions*, **8**(2), 1–21 (2004).

Rigaux, P., Scholl, M., and Voisard, A., *Spatial Databases: With Application to GIS*, Morgan Kaufmann, San Francisco, 2001.

Rushing, J., Ranganath, H., Hinke, T., and Graves, S., Using association rules as texture features, *IEEE Transactions on Pattern Analysis and Machine Intelligence* **23**(8), 845–858 (2001).

Samet, H., *The Design and Analysis of Spatial Data Structures*, Addison-Wesley, Reading, MA, 1990.

Shekhar, S., and Chawla, S., *Spatial Databases: A Tour*, Prentice-Hall, Englewood Cliffs, NJ, 2003.

Shekhar, S., and Huang, Y., Discovering spatial co-location patterns: A summary of results, in *Proceedings of 7th International Symposium on Spatial and Temporal Databases*, 2001.

Shekhar, S., Chawla, S., Ravada, S., Fetterer, A., Liu, X., and Lu, C. T., Spatial databases: Accomplishments and research needs, *IEEE Transactions on Knowledge and Data Engineering* **11**(1), 45–55 (1999).

Shekhar, S., Lu, C. T., and Zhang, P., Detecting graph-based spatial outlier: Algorithms and applications (a summary of results), in *Proceedings of the Seventh ACM-SIGKDD International Conference on Knowledge Discovery and Data Mining*, August 2001.

Shekhar, S., Schrater, P., Vastsavai, R., Wu, W., and Chawla, S., Spatial contextual classification and prediction models for mining geospatial data, *IEEE Transactions on Multimedia (Special Issue on Multimedia Database)*, 2002.

Steinbach, M., Tan, P., Kumar, V., Klooster, S., and Potter, C., Discovery of climate indices using clustering, in *Proceedings of the 9th ACM SIGKDD International Conference on Knowledge Discovery and Data Mining*, August 2003.

Steinbach, M., Tan, P., Kumar, V., Potter, C., and Klooster, S., Data mining for the discovery of ocean climate indices, in *Proceedings of the Fifth Workshop on Scientific Data Mining*, 2002a.

Steinbach, M., Tan, P., Kumar, V., Potter, C., and Klooster, S., Temporal data mining for the discovery and analysis of ocean climate indices, in *Proceedings of the KDD Workshop on Temporal Data Mining*, 2002b.

Steinbach, M., Tan, P., Kumar, V., Potter, C., Klooster, S., and Torregrosa, A., Clustering Earth Science data: goals, issues and results, in *Proceedings of the Fourth KDD Workshop on Mining Scientific Datasets*, 2001.

Storch, H. V., and Zwiers, F. W., *Statistical Analysis in Climate Research*, Cambridge University Press, New York, 1999.

Tan, P., Steinbach, M., Kumar, V., Potter, C., Klooster, S., and Torregrosa, A., Finding spatio-temporal patterns in Earth Science data, In *Proceedings of KDD Workshop on Temporal Data Mining*, 2001.

Taylor, G. H., *Impacts of the El Niño/Southern Oscillation on the Pacific Northwest*, Technical Report, Oregon State University, Corvallis, Oregon, 1998.

Tobler, W. R., *Cellular Geography, Philosophy in Geography* (S. Gale and G. Olsson, eds.), Reidel, Dordrecht, 1979.

Worboys, M. F., *GIS—A Computing Perspective*, Taylor and Francis, London, 1995.

Zhang, P., Huang, Y., Shekhar, S., and Kumar, V., Correlation analysis of spatial time series datasets: A filter-and-refine approach, in *Proceedings of the 7th Pacific-Asia Conference on Knowledge Discovery and Data Mining*, 2003a.

Zhang, P., Huang, Y., Shekhar, S., and Kumar, V., Exploiting spatial autocorrelation to efficiently process correlation-based similarity queries, in *Proceedings of the 8th International Symposium on Spatial and Temporal Databases*, 2003b.

Zhang, P., Shekhar, S., Huang, Y., and Kumar, V., Spatial cone tree: An index structure for correlation-based similarity queries on spatial time series data, in *Proceedings of the International Workshop on Next Generation Geospatial Information*, 2003c.

9

AN ACTIVE LEARNING APPROACH TO *EGERIA DENSA* DETECTION IN DIGITAL IMAGERY

HUAN LIU, AMIT MANDVIKAR, AND PATRICIA G. FOSCHI

9.1. INTRODUCTION

Multimedia content is rapidly becoming a major research area of data mining. One task of mining information from digital imagery is to discover patterns and knowledge from images for the purpose of classification. The specific problem we address here is the detection of Brazilian waterweed (*Egeria densa*) in images. *Egeria densa* is an exotic submerged aquatic weed causing navigation and reservoir-pumping problems in the Sacramento–San Joaquin Delta of Northern California. As part of a control program to manage *Egeria*, it is necessary to map the areal extent of *Egeria* in scan-digitized aerial images. The detected *Egeria* regions are calculated and compared with previously detected regions. The analyzed results are then used to determine control strategies and form new solutions. The *Egeria* detection problem can be abstracted to one of classifying massive data without class labels. Relying on human experts to classify *Egeria*, or labeling each region with classes (*Egeria* or not), is not only time-consuming and costly, but also unreliable if the experts are overburdened with too many minute and routine tasks. Massive manual classification becomes impractical when images are complex with many different objects (e.g., water, land, *Egeria*) under varying picture-taking conditions (e.g., deep/shallow water, sun glint). The main objective of the work is twofold: (1) to learn to automatically detect *Egeria* and (2) to relieve experts from going through all the images and identify regions where *Egeria* exists in each image.

Next Generation of Data-Mining Applications. Edited by Kantardzic and Zurada
ISBN 0-471-65605-4 © 2005 the Institute of Electrical and Electronics Engineers, Inc.

The following desiderata for an image classification system present a unique challenge to data-mining research for novel solutions.

1. *Reduced Expert Involvement.* Classification algorithms that require less expert involvement are essential in real-world applications, because human involvement in decision making forms the most serious bottleneck for efficient processing.

2. *Fewer Labeled Training Images.* Labeled data are required to train automatic classifiers in a supervised fashion. The only source for such labeled data is to label data manually by experts, which is tedious, slow, and expensive. Consequently, it is sensible to reduce the number of images to be labeled. The reduced number of images, however, increases the difficulty for learning.

3. *Classification Performance.* An image classification system can produce *certain* and *uncertain* classifications—for example, based on its posterior estimates. Uncertain classifications require the intervention of human experts. Reducing the number of uncertain classifications translates directly to the reduction of expert involvement. In addition, classifications deemed certain should also be *correct*. Standard performance measures for detection problems such as accuracy, precision, recall, and F measure can be used in evaluation of correctness.

4. *Generalization.* To generalize, a classifier must perform well with unseen images. This is a central issue in pattern recognition and learning theory. A typical approach to avoid overfitting in training is to *regularize* the structure of the classifier. For example, regularization can help restrict a neural network to have smaller weights and forces the network response to be smooth, and hence the network is less likely to overfit (Tikhonov and Arsenin, 1977). Another approach is to combine the outputs of an ensemble of several, perhaps weak, classifiers (Breiman, 2001; Dietterich, 2000).

In this image mining application, we adopt an active learning approach to minimize the need for labeled data in training a classifier, propose the use of *class-specific ensembles* in implementing active learning, and demonstrate that active learning can be extended to *Egeria* detection in images unseen to the active learner. We will show that (1) by using active learning, we can significantly reduce expert involvement; (2) by having class-specific ensembles, we can conduct active learning effectively with a small number of labeled instances; and (3) by extending active learning to new images in an *iterative active learning* algorithm, we can rely on the learned results to further reduce expert involvement. Thus, we develop a novel data-mining approach to assist human experts in efficient *Egeria* detection.

The proposed class-specific ensembles stem from our observation that different types of classifiers are better suited to detecting different objects such as *Egeria*, land, and water. Since it is impractical to train one classifier (or ensemble) for each object (as experts need to provide training instances for all objects), we propose to learn class-specific ensembles for two classes: *Egeria* and non-*Egeria*. We will explain why the class-specific ensembles approach should outperform the conventional single ensemble approach. We also empirically show that this approach significantly reduces the number of uncertain image regions and is better than a single ensemble for the task of *Egeria* detection.

Being able to learn with limited labeled data during training does not solve the problem of generalization. We also need to show that active learning of class-specific ensembles can reduce expert involvement in classification of new images. This reduction is achieved by applying iterative active learning. With limited interaction with experts, our active learning scheme adapts the ensembles to new images. Because of the scarcity of training images, it is likely that images used in training only partially represent testing data (new images). Iterative active learning allows the ensembles to effectively work on new image data with limited expert involvement.

Section 9.2 introduces the problem domain of *Egeria* mining from digital images. Section 9.3 presents some conventional approaches for image mining and related work. Our approach is described in Section 9.4. The novel concept of class-specific ensembles and the algorithms to find optimal class-specific ensembles are introduced in Section 9.5. Section 9.6 provides empirical evaluation details. Section 9.7 concludes this work with some immediate extensions.

9.2. *EGERIA* DETECTION

Egeria, a submerged aquatic weed has grown uncontrolled in the Sacramento–San Joaquin Delta of Northern California for over 35 years and currently covers over 6000 acres of waterways. The presence of this exotic weed has disrupted navigation and recreational uses of waterways, clogged irrigation intake trenches, and caused reservoir-pumping problems (Foschi and Liu, 2002). The *Egeria* invasion has also displaced native flora and probably affected native fauna. In 1997, the California Department of Boating and Waterways started developing a control program to manage *Egeria*. At that time, researchers at the Romberg Tiburon Center for Environmental Studies (RTC) (2002) were commissioned to assess the effects of control protocols on fish and other fauna and to estimate the areal extent of *Egeria*. The RTC team has continued to monitor the areal extent of this weed every year since then, via visual/manual interpretation of color infrared (CIR) aerial photography. This imagery is flown at 1:24,000 scale and then scan-digitized to nominal 2-meter pixels.

Classifying *Egeria* in scan-digitized CIR imagery presents a challenging problem due to a number of variable and unfavorable conditions (Foschi and Liu, 2002). These include changes in imaging conditions (e.g., film exposure, vignetting, scanning anomalies), problems associated with water-related subjects (e.g., turbidity, sun glint, surface reflectance due to wind), and other environmental changes (e.g., exposure of *Egeria* at extremely low tide, shadows falling

Turbidity hiding *Egeria*   *Egeria* exposed at low tide   Dense submerged *Egeria*

Less dense
Egeria

Shadows
on land

Land vegetation   *Egeria* covered by algae   Shadows upon water

Figure 9.1. Scan-digitized CIR aerial photography showing spectral variations in *Egeria* and lack of spectral separation between *Egeria* and other extraneous classes.

upon the water, algal cover over *Egeria*). Figure 9.1, a scan-digitized CIR aerial photograph, illustrates the spectral variations in *Egeria* that may occur even within a short distance. The figure also exhibits some problems caused by lack of spectral separation between *Egeria* and other extraneous classes. For example, it shows that dense well-submerged *Egeria* appears black and is confused with shadows on land, while *Egeria* exposed during very low tide appears reddish and is confused with terrestrial vegetation. Digital analysis also indicates that subtle changes—for example, in *Egeria* canopy density, film vignetting, or water turbidity—produce overlapping spectral response patterns. Clearly, traditional computer-assisted multispectral classification methods face challenges under these conditions, and visual/manual image interpretation and analysis procedures are time-consuming and costly.

9.3. CONVENTIONAL APPROACHES

Conventional image classification methods focus on using single classification algorithms to detect the required patterns in images. Major categories of these classification algorithms are listed below. Details about these classification algorithms can be found, for instance, in Witten and Frank (2000) and Haykin (1999).

(a) Decision Tree-based algorithms, such as C4.5, Decision Stump, Id3, Alternating Decision Tree

(b) Rule/Discretization-based algorithms, like Decision Tree (PART), One Rule, PRISM, Hyper Pipes, Voting Feature Intervals

(c) Neural Networks-based algorithms, such as Voted Perceptrons, Kernel Density Estimators, Logistic

(d) Support Vector Machine (SVM)-based algorithms, like Sequential Minimal Optimization for SVMs

(e) Probability Estimators, such as Naive Bayesian Classifier, Naive Bayesian Classifier-simple

(f) Instance-Based algorithms, such as IB1, Decision Table

The choice of an appropriate learning algorithm usually depends on the domain. Commonly used algorithms for detecting patterns in images are probability estimators (Bayesian-based), neural networks, support vector machines, decision trees, and their variants. For example, Kitamoto (2001) developed a system using k-NN (k-Nearest Neighbors) for predicting the presence of typhoons from satellite images. In a different domain, Antonie et al. (2001) used neural networks along with association rule mining to detect breast cancer from medical images. Hermes et al. (1999) applied support vector machines (Burges, 1998; Joachims, 1998; Vapnik, 1995) to a remote sensing application of classifying satellite images into regions of forests, water bodies, grasslands, and so on. Salzberg et al. (1995) used CART (Breiman et al., 1984) and C4.5 (Quinlan, 1993) decision trees to detect cosmic ray hits from Hubble Space Telescope images.

In the above applications, the underlying function to be learned is uniform for all the different images in the task domain. As mentioned previously, *Egeria* detection presents its unique difficulty in *Egeria*'s spectral variations found in different images (as shown in Figure 9.1). Therefore, an ensemble approach with different types of classifiers may be better suited to detecting different objects such as *Egeria*, water, land, and so on. It is impractical to train separate classifiers for each different object. In order to do so, the experts would need to provide training data to separate each object from all the other objects. This could overburden the experts who are already overwhelmed with manual labeling. Giacinto and Roli (1997) documented that conventional methods do not perform well for such image mining applications. They proposed the use of ensembles of neural networks, wherein classification results from a multitude of neural networks are "merged" by using statistical combination methods. The authors concluded that this is a valid alternative for designing new, *more complex* classifiers. Active learning that is adopted to relieve the experts from tedious manual labeling can be implemented using an ensemble approach. The subsequent two sections will explain the concepts of *active learning* and *iterative active learning*, as well as the need for and the details of *class-specific ensembles* in *Egeria* detection.

9.4. AN ACTIVE LEARNING APPROACH

Many real-world applications generate massive unlabeled data as in the case of *Egeria*. Manually obtaining labels for massive unlabeled data is not only time-consuming but also unreliable. Experts can only process a small portion of the unlabeled images in a given period of time (Foschi and Liu, 2002). One goal of our work is to reduce human involvement in the labeling process by applying some learning methodology to automate this process of labeling for a large number of images.

Learning to detect *Egeria* requires an initial set of labeled training instances that differentiate *Egeria* and non-*Egeria*. In Section 9.2 we presented some difficult problems associated with *Egeria* detection, which indicates that a large number of training instances would be required in training an effective classifier. As mentioned earlier, obtaining labeled training data is very expensive, while gathering unlabeled data is often straightforward (McCallum and Nigam, 1998). Active learning is a supervised learning algorithm (Cohn et al., 1994; Roy and McCallum, 2001), in which the learner has the freedom to select the data points to be added to the training set. As in the case of labeling, we can rely on active learning to select those critical unlabeled instances for labeling. If we can design effective active learners that can learn from a smaller set of labeled data, we may be able to significantly reduce the number of critical unlabeled instances that need to be labeled. This means we can reduce expert involvement in labeling. The rest of this section discusses issues of active learning in *Egeria* detection. Section 9.5 is about designing an effective active learner.

9.4.1. Active Learning

Active learning (Schohn and Cohn, 2000) can help reduce the number of supervised training instances needed to achieve a given level of performance (Seung et al., 1992; Thompson et al., 1999). For example, an active learner can be trained with an initial set (S_0) of labeled data, and then it is applied to another set (S) of unlabeled data. If the active learner is confident (e.g., its posterior estimate is high) about its classification of an instance in S (the prediction of its class label), the prediction is *certain*; otherwise, it is *uncertain*. When manual labeling is time-consuming and labor-intensive, as is the case for *Egeria* detection, active learning may be able to help reduce the number of instances that need be labeled. An active learner may begin with a small set of labeled data and then predict class labels for unlabeled instances. The prediction can result in two sets of data: Their predictions are either certain or uncertain. The instances with uncertain predictions are presented to human experts to assign class labels. The active learner is then *retrained* with the newly labeled data to improve its prediction. In short, active learning is basically a supervised learning algorithm, and it requires an expert to resolve its uncertain classifications. If we can have an effective active learner, we can significantly reduce the number of instances with uncertain predictions. Thus, we will only ask human experts to resolve a small number of such instances.

Active learning has been used widely in classification applications on web documents. Some researchers (Liere and Tade Palli, 1997; Schohn and Cohn, 2000) have described applications of active learning that greatly enhance the generalization behavior of support vector machines (Burges, 1998; Joachims, 1998; Vapnik, 1995). Freund et al. (1997) suggested combining selective sampling with the Query-by-Committee algorithm (QBC) (Seung et al., 1992) for active learning. They used a committee of perceptrons to sample from a training dataset to reduce predictive error rates. Abe and Mamitsuka (1998) proposed two variants of the QBC algorithm, query-by-bagging and query-by-boosting. Both of them performed better than QBC, C4.5, and boosting with C4.5. McCallum and Nigam (1998) modified the QBC method to use the unlabeled pool of documents and to select the examples to be labeled by explicitly estimating the density of the documents. They further combined active learning with the Expectation–Maximization algorithm to obtain class labels for unlabeled instances. Active learning was also shown to be useful in improving query answering (Cohn et al., 1994). The authors demonstrated how selective sampling can be approximately implemented using neural networks.

Another line of recent research (Iyengar et al., 2000; Hakkani-Tur et al., 2002; Saar-Tsechensky and Provost, 2001, 2002) concentrates on developing algorithms to process data automatically so that much less expert involvement is needed. A variant of an active learning algorithm has been suggested in Iyengar et al. (2000) to learn from specific unlabeled instances via uncertainty sampling. Their goal is to reduce the number of queries that require attention from human experts. Hakkani-Tur et al. (2002) suggested a similar approach in the domain of automatic speech recognition (ASR). The difference between their approaches is in their distinct sampling methods that select the most informative examples for active learning.

Muslea et al. (2000) used selective sampling instead of uncertainty sampling to find the most informative unlabeled instances. The authors used two disjoint sets of feature-values *(views)* to learn separate classifiers and then proceeded to label the most informative unlabeled instances for which the two classifiers disagree, add them to the training data, and relearn the classifiers. They suggested that choosing the contention instances for which both classifiers are most confident provides maximal improvement. The authors continued their research (Muslea et al., 2002) and experimentally showed that their algorithm Co-Testing+Co-EM (Co-EMT) outperforms the algorithms EM (Nigam et al., 2000), Co-Training (Blum and Mitchell, 1998), and Co-EM (Nigam and Ghani, 2000) using artificial and real-world datasets.

Some researchers (Saar-Tsechensky and Provost, 2001, 2002) mentioned that most of the previous work on active learning focused on improving accuracy rather than reducing expert involvement. Instead, they concentrated on using class probability estimates to obtain the class probability rankings, which enable effective sampling from unlabeled instances. The authors proved that their sampling technique is better (in terms of size of the training data) than uncertainty sampling or bootstrapping.

The goal of applying active learning to *Egeria* detection is threefold: (1) to reduce the number of instances to be labeled by experts in digital imagery into *Egeria* and non-*Egeria* regions; (2) to learn an active learner from these labeled instances; and (3) to apply the active learner to the remaining unlabeled instances that are unseen in the training phase. Only when new instances cannot be handled confidently by the active learner will they be recommended to experts to resolve their labels. The number of recommended instances should be significantly smaller than the number of unlabeled instances. The reduction of these recommendations means reducing expert involvement. This interactive process can be repeated until almost all the unlabeled instances are confidently classified by the active learner. We now discuss performance measures that are used to evaluate active learning.

9.4.2. Performance Measures

Precision, recall, and accuracy are the common criteria used for performance comparison. These measures are defined in terms of the instances that are relevant and the instances that are correctly classified (or retrieved). The true positives (TP) and true negatives (TN) are the correctly classified instances. A false positive (FP) is when the outcome is incorrectly predicted as YES when it is in fact NO. A false negative (FN) is when the outcome is incorrectly classified as NO when in fact it is YES. Precision, recall, and accuracy are defined in terms of TP, TN, FN, and FP (Witten and Frank, 2000; Baeza-Yates and Ribeiro-Neto, 1999):

- *Precision* $= TP/(TP + FP)$: the fraction of the classified information which is relevant.
- *Recall* $= TP/(TP + FN)$: the fraction of the classified relevant information versus all relevant information.
- *Accuracy* $= (TP + TN)/(TP + FP + TN + FN)$: the overall success rate of the classifier.

Accuracy takes into account the true negatives (TN) in its numerator. If a particular image has a large number of class "negative" that are classified correctly, then the resultant accuracy rate may be misleadingly high, overshadowing the other components (TP, FN, FP). Particularly, in our application, we are mainly concerned with detecting *Egeria* (true positives). It has also been noted in Provost et al. (1998) that accuracy may not provide a good measure for classification. Since both precision and recall have only TP in their numerator, they are suitable for performance measuring. In addition, we consider *reduction in uncertain regions* (UC) as a third measure.

High precision or high recall alone is not a good performance measure because each describes only one aspect of classification. Combined as in the F measure (Makhoul et al., 1999; Van Rijsbergen, 1979), they provide a good measure.

- $F = 2 * P * R/(P + R)$: the harmonic mean of precision and recall.

If both precision and recall are 1, then F is 1, which means that all and only positive instances are classified as positive. When either precision or recall is 0, then the F measure is 0. Hence, the F measure is a good measure for both generality and accuracy. Having established the performance measures to be used, we next illustrate in detail how to apply iterative active learning to process unlabeled images.

9.4.3. Iterative Active Learning

Clearly, an active learner built using a small training dataset could have limitations. One key issue is whether the active learner can be successfully applied to instances of new images. It is possible that it might result in a large number of uncertain instances. Especially in the case of *Egeria* detection, as mentioned earlier, images were taken in varied conditions and had various noise elements, such as sun glint, turbidity, deep/shallow water, and so on. Many images may share some commonalities, but may also have unique characteristics of *Egeria*. In other words, *Egeria* in different images may not have uniform spectral distributions. This indicates that there may not be straightforward correlations between the instances of the training image(s) and those of the unseen images. When the correlations are strong, the active learner may produce fewer instances with uncertain predictions; in other cases, the number of such instances may be large. This observation necessitates the adaptation of the active learner to new images.

Instead of asking experts to resolve all these uncertain instances, we propose an iterative active learning approach. Considering both the function of active learning and the efficacy of an expert at labeling, we propose to ask an expert to resolve a small number of instances, say 25, and use this additional labeled dataset to adapt the original active learner to a new image. Iterative active learning allows the learner to efficiently work on new images with limited expert involvement. It is expected that this significant reduction should mitigate the task of labeling for a domain expert. The iterative active learning continues until no improvement can be made.

We present an iterative active learning algorithm (IALA) in Figure 9.2. It takes as input Tr, a new image Ts, the number of uncertain instances m to be labeled, and two classifiers (called dual ensembles, to be detailed in the next section). The value of m should be reasonably small so an expert can label m instances reliably. We set $m = 25$ in this work. The algorithm returns the adapted dual ensembles for Ts. The essence of the algorithm is to use a small amount of the expert's input to iteratively adapt the ensembles to a new image so that expert involvement can be further reduced while maintaining good performance. The oracle in the algorithm is the human expert. The iterative learning stops if the improvement of two performance measures (F_{gain} and UC_{gain} defined in the algorithm) is insignificant ($<5\%$ and $<10\%$, respectively) or if UC_{new} is smaller than m. UC is the number of uncertain regions that the active learner cannot classify with high confidence.

Now we encounter an issue of evaluating the performance of IALA when it iteratively relies on human experts to resolve the labels of some uncertain

input: Tr, Ts, $m = 25$, $E_{l=yes}$, $E_{l=no}$, $F' = 5\%$,
              $UC' = 10\%$;
output: $E'_{l=yes}$, $E'_{l=no}$: adapted ensemble pair,
              Tr: Updated training image;

01 $P_{old} \leftarrow 0$, $R_{old} \leftarrow 0$, $F_{old} \leftarrow 0$, $UC_{old} \leftarrow 0$;
02 Classify Ts with $E_{l=yes}$ and $E_{l=no}$;
03 Obtain Ts_{cer} and Ts_{uncer}, UC_{new} =#Ts_{uncer};
04 **if** $UC_{new} \geq m$
05   Calculate P_{new}, R_{new}, F_{new};
06   **do**
07        $Ts_{uncer} \leftarrow$ RandomSamples(Ts_{uncer},m);
08        $Ts_{cer} \leftarrow$ RandomSamples(Ts_{cer},m);
09        $Tr \leftarrow Tr + Ts_{cer}$;
10   **foreach** $x_i \in Ts_{uncer}$ **do**
11           $l \leftarrow$ class label(x_i) from an oracle;
12           $Tr \leftarrow Tr + \{x_i, l\}$;
13   Retrain $E_{l=yes}$ and $E_{l=no}$ with Tr; apply to Ts;
14   Obtain Ts_{cer} and Ts_{uncer};
15        $UC_{old} = UC_{new}$; $F_{old} = F_{new}$;
16   Recalculate P_{new}, R_{new} and F_{new};
17        $F_{gain} = \frac{F_{new} - F_{old}}{F_{old}}$;
18        $UC_{gain} = \frac{UC_{old} - UC_{new}}{UC_{old}}$;
19   **while** ($F_{gain} > F' \wedge UC_{gain} > UC') \vee UC_{new} > m$;
20   Return Tr, $E'_{l=yes}$ and $E'_{l=no}$;
21 **end**;

Figure 9.2. Iterative active learning algorithm.

instances. To recall, the performance measures are precision, recall, F, and number of uncertain regions. Under normal circumstances, one should always separate training data from testing data and estimate performance measures using testing data only. In the context of this work, let us denote Ts_{cer} and Ts_{uncer} as some testing image instances used for iterative training. We usually would estimate performance measures for the remaining testing data $Ts - (Ts_{cer} + Ts_{uncer})$. However, doing so in evaluating IALA would provide over-optimistic or false measures. This is because even when no iterative learning occurs, it would still provide improved performance because Ts is constantly shrinking as $Ts_{cer} + Ts_{uncer}$ are removed from Ts while Ts_{uncer} resolved by experts are still uncertain according to our active learner. Therefore, we adopt a more stringent way to evaluate performance of IALA: We always use the original Ts for performance measure estimation. It is more stringent because in the case where IALA does not work as expected, the performance can deteriorate, which reflects the fact that iterative learning may not help at all. Thus, we remove the superficial performance improvement. In other words, using Ts instead of $Ts - (Ts_{cer} + Ts_{uncer})$ in performance evaluation truly indicates our goal of evaluating IALA.

Another requirement specific to this project is that the classifiers employed in active learning should be effective. We therefore study ensemble methods below for active learning.

9.5. DUAL ENSEMBLES FOR ACTIVE LEARNING

Active learning is just a learning framework. In order to achieve highly accurate learning with a small set of labeled data (in order to reduce expert involvement), we need highly accurate base classifiers. The traditional approach of using a single classifier for detection in a complex domain becomes inadequate. Roli et al. (2001) documented that finding a single "appropriate" classifier for a particular classification task is very difficult, an appropriate classifier being the one with high predictive accuracy (i.e., generalizing well). Many recent approaches work with *ensembles* of classification algorithms and use a decision function to combine the classification outputs (Dietterich, 2000). The ensemble methods often produce accurate and robust classifiers. We therefore adopt ensembles as base classifiers for active learning.

One quandary arises for active learning using ensembles. In order for active learning to work, an ensemble of highly accurate classifiers is needed so that the classifiers will disagree with each other but not too often. However, highly accurate classifiers usually do not disagree with each other so the prediction of an ensemble is always certain; while highly inaccurate classifiers may disagree too much, leading to an unnecessarily high number of unlabeled instances being recommended. The challenge now is how we employ highly accurate and diverse classifiers to form good ensembles for active learning. Class-specific ensembles are an example. We show below the novel features of class-specific ensembles (in particular, dual ensembles) for active learning, and we elaborate on how to learn dual ensembles.

9.5.1. Single Versus Dual Ensembles

Assuming a domain of two classes, the two examples in Figure 9.3 illustrate the difference between a single ensemble and dual ensembles. A single ensemble contains a fixed number of classifiers, which learn the separation between the classes, *True* and *False*. A single ensemble can produce three outputs based on consensus: *True, False, Uncertain*, as shown in the left of Figure 9.3. The middle part is uncertain because the ensemble cannot reach consensus; its posterior probability is close neither to 1 nor to 0. The *True* and *False* parts do not overlap because in such an ensemble learning, the focus is on one class and the other class is determined by default. In a more general setting where the class distributions for *True* and *False* are not exactly reversed, being certain about *True* does not necessarily mean being certain about *False*. Such a scenario is depicted in the right of Figure 9.3. In a domain with variable class distributions, it can be observed that ensembles may not be highly certain about their predictions on

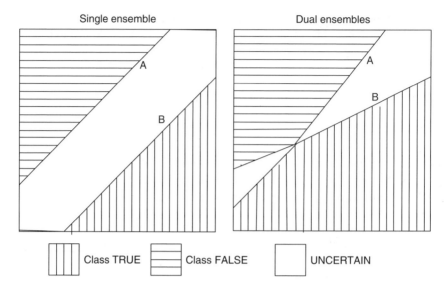

Figure 9.3. An illustrative example for two types of ensembles.

some instances of the unseen images. These instances, depicted by the regions between the lines A and B, are *don't know*s or uncertain. For a single ensemble, such uncertain predictions are observed when there is no obvious consensus among all the classifiers within the ensemble. A dual ensemble consists of two separate ensembles, one for each class. For a dual ensemble, one ensemble can predict the class of an unlabeled instance as either *True* or *Not True*, and the other ensemble can predict the class as either *False* or *Not False*. When the two ensembles do not agree in their classifications, the prediction is deemed *Uncertain*.

Using dual ensembles allows us to take advantage of the difference between two highly accurate classifiers. Each ensemble tries to predict its class with high accuracy and is expected to provide a better classification and a better separation between the certain and uncertain classifications. We not only can use a small number of training instances to effectively learn ensembles (each ensemble being tuned specifically for detecting one class), but also can ensure that high accuracy does not always produce false consensus. The subsequent problem to solve is how to identify relevant classifiers to form each of the dual ensembles.

9.5.2. In Search of Optimal Dual Ensembles

We may tend to use as many classifiers in an ensemble as possible for the following reasons.

- Each classification algorithm may have a different view of the training image. So different algorithms can capture varied aspects of the image because of their different biases and assumptions.

- No single classifier can completely cover a complex domain and generalize well. In other words, some algorithms may succeed in capturing some latent information about the domain, while others may capture different information.

However, problems can result from using too many classification algorithms. Some examples are as follows.

- Using more classification algorithms can result in longer overall training time, especially if some of the algorithms are time-consuming to train.
- Some classification algorithms may be prone to overfitting in the image domain. If these algorithms are included in the ensemble, there may be a high risk of allowing the ensemble to overfit the training image(s).

The above analysis suggests the necessity of searching for a relevant set of classifiers to form an ensemble. Exhaustive search for the best combination is impractical because the search space is exponential in the total number of classification algorithms for consideration. Thus we need a methodology to find the optimal combination of classifiers for the dual ensembles without resorting to exhaustive search. The optimality is defined in terms of performance measures as we discussed earlier. The search for optimal ensembles is to find a set of classifiers that forms an ensemble with best performance. An appropriate learning algorithm is needed that can optimize the performance measures in search of optimal ensembles.

Among many learning algorithms for classification, clustering, and association rules, we observe that association rule algorithms (Agrawal and Srikant, 1994) can search the attribute space to find the best combination of attribute-values associated with a class. An association rule $A \Rightarrow B$ satisfies the minimum support and minimum confidence. The support for a rule is the joint probability $P(A, B)$ and the confidence is the conditional probability $P(B|A)$, where A and B are itemsets of attribute values (e.g., $a_1 = v_1, a_2 = v_2, b_1 = c_1, b_2 = c_2$). In our case, B is a class value ($b = c$), and A is a combination of attribute values. Thus the confidence of a rule gives us the measure of accuracy of the rule, while the support gives us the measure of generality of the rule. Association rules with high support and confidence are both general and accurate. There are efficient algorithms to learn association rules from data (Han et al., 2000; Agrawal and Srikant, 1994).

Reviewing the definitions of precision and recall, we notice that precision and recall are parallel to confidence and support. Hence, we employ association rule algorithms to search for the optimal dual ensembles. This approach is different from feature selection (Blum and Langley, 1997; Dash and Liu, 1997; Kohavi and John, 1997), where the attribute space is searched to find the best combination of attributes rather than attribute values.

Now we need a dataset that links classifiers to the label of each image region in search of optimal ensembles. This new dataset can be obtained by applying all the classification algorithms to the training data so that each classifier is a feature (i.e., column) and its value is the prediction of the classifier. For each image region (one instance in the new dataset), there are predictions of all the classifiers and also the class label "*Egeria*" or "non-*Egeria*" given by experts. We are concerned only with those association rules that have the class label "*Egeria*" or "non-*Egeria*" on the right-hand side (consequent). We will restrict our search to such rules and obtain rules with the maximum number of features (classifiers) on the left-hand side (precedent) without a significant loss in support or confidence. The best rule for each class label indicates the best combination of classifiers for the ensemble. Thus the ensembles obtained from this procedure are optimal in terms of both support and confidence, and correspondingly recall and precision. Next we discuss in detail the algorithm that implements the idea described above.

9.5.3. Algorithm Searching for Optimal Dual Ensembles

The search algorithm is presented in Figure 9.4 and further illustrated in Figure 9.5. It takes as input the entire set of classification algorithms E and training data Tr with class labels l_{Tr}, and it produces as output the optimal ensembles for class label *yes* and class label *no*. The major steps are: (i) creating a new dataset D (steps 1–3) by training all the classifiers E with the training data; (ii) learning association rules from D for dual classes (step 4); and (iii) finding the best association rules for each class (steps 5–10). Rules with support-confidence product >90% of the maximum support-confidence for Tr are considered for selection. Each rule set is ranked according to *length*—the number of classification algorithms in the precedent. This is because such rules have the maximum number of tightly bound classifiers in predicting the class label. The longest rule from each set is selected to obtain the optimal ensemble for each class label.

The next task is to use the dual ensembles ($E_{l=yes}$ and $E_{l=no}$) to determine certain and uncertain instances. We need to decide the maximum number of

input:	Tr, E : Set of n classification algorithms
output:	$E_{l=yes}, E_{l=no}$

01   Train E with Tr to obtain n classifiers, cl_1 to cl_n;
02   Obtain class labels, l_{Tr}^1 to l_{Tr}^n for Tr using cl_1 to cl_n;
03   Form a data set, $D \leftarrow \{l_{Tr}^1, l_{Tr}^2, \ldots, l_{Tr}^n, l_{Tr}\}$;
04   Learn association rules, $Assoc$ from D;
05    $Assoc_1 \leftarrow$ Filter ($Assoc$ | consequent is $l_{Tr} = yes$);
06    $m_{l=yes} \leftarrow$ Max ($Assoc_1, supp * conf$);
07    $Assoc_1 \leftarrow$ Filter ($Assoc_1$ | supp*conf $\geq 0.9 * m_{l=yes}$);
08    $Assoc_1 \leftarrow$ Sort ($Assoc_1, length(precedent)$);
09    $E_{l=yes} \leftarrow$ Precedent(First($Assoc_1$));
10   Repeat steps 5 to 9 for $l_{Tr} = no$ to obtain $E_{l=no}$;

Figure 9.4. Algorithm for optimal ensemble selection.

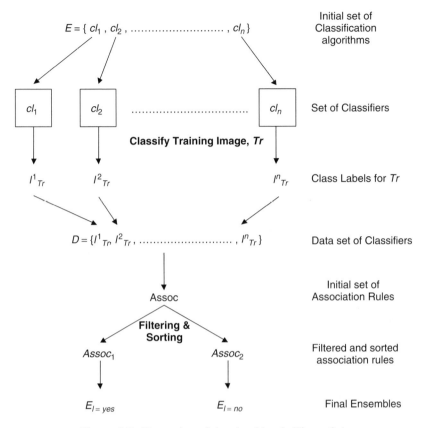

Figure 9.5. Illustration of the algorithm in Figure 9.4.

classifiers in an ensemble that should agree on a prediction to reach a decision of "certain" or "uncertain" for each ensemble. An ensemble with all classifiers being required to agree on a prediction would lead to high precision, but low recall; an ensemble with few classifiers being required to agree would lead to high recall and low precision. Thus, we need to find the maximum number of classifiers with which the ensemble gives the best estimated precision and recall, and hence the best F measure. The training data are used again for this task. $E_{l=yes}$ is certain only if all $n_{l=yes}$ classifiers agree on *yes*. The F measure (F_0) is recorded. If $(n_{l=yes} - 1)$ classifiers agree, then F_1 is checked. This process is repeated to find F_k for $(n_{l=yes} - k)$ classifiers by incrementing k until 1 classifier remains. The agreement threshold for $E_{l=yes}$ is then the maximum number of classifiers with highest F measure. The same procedure is repeated for ensemble $E_{l=no}$.

The dual ensembles $E_{l=yes}$ and $E_{l=no}$ work together to decide if an instance's prediction is certain or not as follows. In predicting an instance, if both $E_{l=yes}$ and $E_{l=no}$ are certain and agree with their predictions, the instance is considered certain and labeled with the prediction; if they are certain and disagree, the instance is considered uncertain; if one is certain and the other is uncertain, follow the certain one; and if both are uncertain, the instance is uncertain. We now turn to the experimental evaluation of the algorithms proposed above.

9.6. EMPIRICAL STUDY

We performed experiments with a set of digital images of size 300×300 pixels in TIF format (RGB). Working with domain experts, we extracted features from the training image that are different variants of color, texture, and edge features. There are 13 features in total:

- (1) luminance (Y)
- (2) chrominance (CB, CR)
- (1) edge (using Canny edge detection)
- (9) RGB components for three texture templates

The details of feature extraction were described in our earlier work (Foschi et al., 2002). The template for feature extraction is 8×8 pixels. With 50% overlap between neighboring regions, there are a total of 74×74 or 5476 regions (instances) per image. We designed four experiments to evaluate the following:

1. How dual ensembles fare against single ensembles
2. Whether we need to *learn* the dual ensembles
3. How the dual ensembles fare against classification rules determined by experts
4. Whether the dual ensembles learned from the training image are applicable to unseen images

With the principal goal of reducing the burden on experts, we used only one image for training and applied the learned results to another 16 testing images of different areas for *Egeria* detection. Among the classification algorithms available in the machine-learning package WEKA (Witten and Frank, 2000), we selected those that can be applied to the image domain to ensure the variety of classification algorithms. We applied the algorithm in Figure 9.4 with the complete set of classification algorithms as input. The optimal dual ensembles found by the algorithm are given below. The two ensembles are composed of different combinations of classifiers.

$E_{l=yes}$: C4.5, Alternating Decision Trees, Decision List Learners (PART), PRISM, Hyper Pipes, Kernel Density, Logistic, Decision Tables $\Rightarrow$ 'Class = **yes**'.

$E_{l=no}$: Id3, Alternating Decision Trees, Decision Trees (PART), PRISM, Kernel Density, Instance Based1, Decision Tables $\Rightarrow$ 'Class = **no**'.

Let F and the number of uncertain instances for the kth testing image from ensemble i be F_k^i and UC_k^i, and let the corresponding values from ensemble j be F_k^j and UC_k^j. We calculate the F measure gain and the uncertain instance increase averaged over n testing images as follows:

$$\text{Average } UC_{incr} = \frac{\sum_{k=1}^{n} UC_k^j - \sum_{k=1}^{n} UC_k^i}{\sum_{k=1}^{n} UC_k^i} \tag{9.1}$$

$$\text{Average } F_{gain} = \frac{\sum_{k=1}^{n} \frac{F_k^j - F_k^i}{F_k^i}}{n} \tag{9.2}$$

Table 9.1 summarizes experimental results in four columns (A, B, C, D). Image #1 is the training image. The last two rows show the average F_{gain} and average UC_{incr} with respect to the results in Column A.

Experiment 1. We compared single optimal ensembles (either $E_{l=yes}$ or $E_{l=no}$) with dual optimal ensembles ($E_{l=yes}$ and $E_{l=no}$). The results are shown in Column B. The average UC_{incr} is almost 53% and the average F_{gain} is -0.55%. It is evident that in general, dual ensembles are not only more accurate, but also separate certain and uncertain instances better than single ensembles, except for 2 cases (images #9 and #15).

Experiment 2. We compared 10 pairs of randomly selected dual ensembles with the optimal dual ensembles to check if the optimal dual ensembles could be found by chance. For each pair of random dual ensembles, each classifier was randomly chosen from one of the categories mentioned earlier and learned from the training image. So as there were six categories, each ensemble in the random dual ensemble pair had six classifiers. Although the average F_{gain} is only increased by 1.26%, the UC increases significantly by 846.6% as shown in Column C of Table 9.1. We conclude that it is necessary to search for optimal dual ensembles, as random dual ensembles work poorly in reducing UC.

Experiment 3. We compared the classification rules given by the domain experts with the optimal dual ensembles. The experts' rules outperform the optimal dual ensembles in terms of F_{gain} by 8.6%, but UC increases by 408.4% (in Column D of Table 9.1). The high F_{gain} and high UC for the expert classification rules is due to the fact that an expert can only directly work on the former (designing highly general and accurate rules), but not on the latter (finding low UC rules). Our active learning system is particularly designed to overcome this shortcoming.

Experiment 4. We explored if the optimal dual ensembles can be further improved via iterative active learning. This function would be very useful in dealing with new images for *Egeria* detection. We can observe in Table 9.1 that

TABLE 9.1. Experimental Results

#	Optimal Dual Ensembles (A)		Optimal Single Ensemble (B)		Random Dual Ensembles (C)		Domain Expert's Rules (D)	
	F^*	UC^*	F^*	UC^*	F^*	UC^*	F^*	UC^*
1	0.7557	0	0.7557	0.5	0.7561	23.6	0.8509	35
2	0.7851	0	0.7851	0	0.77011	523.2	0.8040	582
3	0.6609	7	0.6611	23	0.67101	305.3	0.7401	50
4	0.7101	8	0.7103	22.5	0.7053	161.5	0.7785	18
5	0.5920	9	0.5921	14	0.5989	290.6	0.7467	86
6	0.7711	20	0.7543	72	0.7428	230.2	0.7755	95
7	0.8169	5	0.8162	18.5	0.8091	224.3	0.7980	121
8	0.4540	159	0.4415	209.5	0.5139	349.9	0.7327	253
9	0.5069	29	0.5120	13.5	0.5121	252.3	0.4586	33
10	0.4950	44	0.4923	53.5	0.5425	152	0.4627	134
11	0.4403	66	0.4197	107	0.4122	241.1	0.5644	129
12	0.6806	8	0.6811	9.5	0.6677	85.5	0.6780	63
13	0.6002	16	0.6008	22	0.5962	121.9	0.5835	58
14	0.6736	24	0.6722	41.5	0.6954	396	0.7091	99
15	0.5850	14	0.5867	3	0.6044	268.4	0.6291	245
16	0.8024	12	0.8011	22	0.8039	85.4	0.8132	41
17	0.6957	7	0.6936	21.5	0.7254	340.3	0.7011	134
	Avg UC^*_{insts} 25.18		Avg UC^* 38.44		Avg UC^* 238.32		Avg UC^* 128	
			Avg UC^*_{incr} 52.7%		Avg UC^*_{incr} 846.6%		Avg UC^*_{incr} 408.4%	
	Comparative Results		Avg F_{gain} −0.55%		Avg F_{gain} 1.26%		Avg F_{gain} 8.60%	

TABLE 9.2. Experiment 4 Results

#	Before Iterative AL		After Iterative AL		F_{gain}	UC_{incr}	# Runs	# Queries
	F Measure	UC	F Measure	UC				
8	0.4540	159	0.5762	47	26.90%	−70.44%	3	75
9	0.5069	29	0.5069	29	0.0%	0.0%	1	25
10	0.4950	44	0.5385	11	8.77%	−75.0%	2	50
11	0.4403	66	0.5547	18	25.96%	−72.73%	3	75
	Average UC_{insts}	74.5	Average UC_{insts}	26.25	15.41%	−64.77%	2.25	56.25

some of the unseen testing images (e.g., #8) have a high number of uncertain instances. It is impractical to overwhelm the expert to resolve such a high number of uncertain instances. The algorithm in Figure 9.2 iteratively selects a small number of certain and uncertain instances (from such images) and adds them into the original training data after experts resolve the uncertain instances.

The results of iterative active learning are shown in Table 9.2. After a few more iterations of learning, three out of the four images with $UC > 25$ achieve F_{gain} (average 15.41%) and negative UC_{incr} (average −64.77%). These results suggest that it is practical to adapt the learned dual ensembles to new unseen images to achieve high performance in terms of F_{gain} and reduced uncertain instances.

9.7. SUMMARY AND CONCLUSION

We have introduced active learning to reduce expert involvement in data labeling, presented a novel approach of class-specific ensembles of classifiers, and proposed iterative active learning using the class-specific ensembles to adapt the active learner to new images. In particular, dual ensembles were implemented and tested, and one ensemble was trained for *each class*. The search of optimal ensembles was transformed into discovering association rules between classifiers and a class label. The learned ensembles were then adapted to new images via iterative active learning. Extensive experiments were conducted in the real-world domain of detecting "*Egeria*" in scan-digitized CIR aerial photography. The experiments compared the optimal dual ensembles with optimal single ensembles, with randomly selected dual ensembles, and with classification rules determined by domain experts. The class-specific ensembles outperformed other methods in terms of uncertain region reduction by 52.7%, 846.6%, and 408.4% respectively. Thus, active learning with dual ensembles can decrease expert involvement in instance labeling. The experimental results show that both components of the solution (class specific ensembles and iterative active learning) can significantly reduce expert involvement without compromising performance. The base classifiers used in ensembles are currently of different types. Future work will extend to explore other types of ensembles using one type of classifier (e.g., decision trees as in Random Forests). This may alleviate the problem of classifier selection, and pave the way to efficiently build class specific ensembles for more than two classes.

ACKNOWLEDGMENTS

The authors wish to thank Deepak Kolippakkam and Jigar Mody for their contributions to the *Egeria* Mining project.

REFERENCES

Abe, N., and Mamitsuka, H., Query learning using boosting and bagging, in *Proceedings of the 15th International Conference on Machine Learning*, pp. 1–10, 1998.

Agrawal, R., and Srikant, R., Fast algorithms for mining association rules, in *Proceedings of International Conference on Very Large Data Bases (VLDB)*, Santiago, Chile, pp. 487–499, September 1994.

Antonie, M., Zaiane, O., and Coman, A., Application of data mining techniques for medical image classification, in *Proceedings of Second International Workshop for Multimedia Data Mining (MDM/KDD '2001) in conjunction with ACM SIGKDD conference*, pp. 94–101, 2001.

Baeza-Yates, R., and Ribeiro-Neto, B., *Morden Information Retrieval*, Addison-Wesley and ACM Press, Reading, MA, 1999.

Blum, A., and Mitchell, T., Combining labeled and unlabeled data with co-training, in *Proceedings of the Workshop on Computational Learning Theory*, Morgan Kaufmann, San Francisco, 1998.

Blum, A. L., and Langley, P., Selection of relevant features and examples in machine learning, *Artificial Intelligence* **97**, 245–271 (1997).

Breiman, L., *Random Forests*, Technical Report, Statistics Department, University of California, Berkeley, 2001.

Breiman, L., Friedman, J. H., Olshen, R. A., and Stone, C. J., *Classification and Regression Trees*, Wadsworth & Brooks/Cole Advanced Books & Software, Belmont, CA, 1984.

Burges, C. J. C., A tutorial on support vector machines, *Journal of Data Mining and Knowledge Discovery* **2**, 000–000 (1998).

Cohn, D., Atlas, L., and Ladner, R., Improving generalization with active learning, *Machine Learning* **15**, 201–221 (1994).

Dash, M., and Liu, H., Feature selection methods for classifications, *Intelligent Data Analysis: An International Journal* **1**(3), 000–000 (1997).

Dietterich, T. G., Ensemble methods in machine learning, in *First International Workshop on Multiple Classifier Systems*, Springer-Verlag, Berlin, pp. 1–15, 2000.

Foschi, P., and Liu, H., Active learning for classifying a spectrally variable subject, in *2nd International Workshop on Pattern Recognition for Remote Sensing (PRRS 2002), Niagara Falls, Canada*, pp. 115–124, 2002.

Foschi, P., Kolippakkam, N., Liu, H., and Mandvikar, A., Feature extraction for image mining, in *International Workshop on Multimedia Information Systems (MIS 2002)*, pp. 103–109, October 2002.

Freund, Y., Seung, H., Shamir, E., and Tishby, N., Selective sampling using the query by committee algorithm, *Machine Learning* **28**, 133–168 (1997).

Giacinto, G., and Roli, F., Ensembles of neural networks for soft classification of remote sensing images, in *Proceedings of the European Symposium on Intelligent Techniques, Italy, 1997*, pp. 166–170, 1997.

Hakkani-Tur, D., Riccardi, G., and Gorin, A., Active learning for automatic speech recognition, in *International Conference on Acoustics Speech and Signal Processing 2002*, 2002.

Han, J., Pei, J., and Yin, Y., Mining frequent patterns without candidate generation, in *Proceedings of Special Interest Group on Management of Data, SIGMOD-2000*, pp. 1–12, 2000.

Haykin, S., *Neural Networks—A Comprehensive Foundation*, 2nd edition, Prentice-Hall, Englewood Cliffs, NJ, 1999.

Hermes, L., Frieauff, D., Puzicha, J., and Buhmann, J., Support vector machines for land usage classification in landsat tm imagery, in *Proceedings of International Geoscience and Remote Sensing Symposium (IGARSS '99)*, pp. 348–350, 1999.

Iyengar, V., Apte, C., and Zhang, T., Active learning using adaptive resampling, in *Proceedings of 6th ACM International Conference on Knowledge Discovery and Data Mining*, pp. 92–98, 2000.

Joachims, T., Text categorization with support vector machines: Learning with many relevant features, in *Proceedings of 10th European Conference on Machine Learning*, Nedellec, C., and Rouveirol, C., (eds.) pages 137–142, Springer, Chemnitz, Germany, 1998.

Kitamoto, A., Data mining for typhoon image collection, in *Proceedings of Second International Workshop for Multimedia Data Mining (MDM/KDD '2001) in conjunction with ACM SIGKDD Conference*, pp. 68–77, 2001.

Kohavi, R., and John, G. H., Wrappers for feature subset selection, *Artificial Intelligence* **97**(1–2), 273–324 (1997).

Liere, R., and Tadepalli, P., Active learning with committees for text categorization, in *Proceedings of the 14th National Conference on Artificial Intelligence and 9th Innovative Applications of Artificial Intelligence Conference (AAAI-97/IAAI-97)*, AAAI Press, Menlo Park, pp. 591–597, 1997.

Makhoul, J., Kubala, F., Schwartz, R., and Weischedel, R., Performance measures for information extraction, in *Proceedings of DARPA Broadcast News Workshop, 1999*, 1999.

McCallum, A., and Nigam, K., Employing EM in pool-based active learning for text classification, in *Proceedings of the Fifteenth International Conference on Machine Learning*, pp. 350–358, 1998.

Muslea, I., Minton, S., and Knoblock, C., Selective sampling with redundant views, in *Proceedings of the National Conference on Artificial Intelligence*, pp. 621–626, 2000.

Muslea, I., Minton, S., and Knoblock, C., Active + semi-supervised learning = robust multiview learning, in *Proceedings of the 19th International Conference on Machine Learning*, pp. 435–442, 2002.

Nigam, K., and Ghani, R., Analyzing the effectiveness and applicability of co-training, in *Proceedings of Conference on Information and Knowledge Management*, pp. 86–93, 2000.

Nigam, K., McCallum, A. K., Thrun, S., and Mitchell, T., Text classification from labeled and unlabeled documents using EM, *Machine Learning* **39**, 103–134 (2000).

Provost, F., Fawcett, T., and Kohavi, R., The case against accuracy estimation for comparing induction algorithms, in *Proceedings of the Fifteenth International Conference on Machine Learning*, Morgan Kaufmann, San Francisco, pp. 445–453, 1998.

Quinlan, J. R., *C4.5: Programs for Machine Learning*, Morgan Kaufmann, San Francisco, 1993.

Roli, F., Giacinto, G., and Vernazza, G., Methods for designing multiple classifier systems. In *Multiple Classifier Systems*, pp. 78–87, Springer-Verlag, Berlin, 2001.

Romberg Tiburon Center for Environmental Studies, *Egeria densa* project, 2002. http://romberg.sfsu.edu/egeria.

Roy, N., and McCallum, A., Toward optimal active learning through sampling estimation of error reduction, in *Proceedings of the Eighteenth International Conference on Machine Learning*, 2001.

Saar-Tsechensky, M., and Provost, F., Active learning for class probability estimation. In *Proceedings of International Joint Conference on AI*, pp. 911–920, 2001.

Saar-Tsechensky, M., and Provost, F., Active sampling for class probability estimation, in *Proceedings of Machine Learning*, 2002.

Salzberg, S., Chandar, R., Ford, H., Murthy, S., and White, R., Decision trees for automated identification of cosmic rays in hubble space telescope images, in *Proceedings of the Astronomical Society of the Pacific*, Vol. 107, pp. 279–288, 1995.

Schohn, G., and Cohn, D., Less is more: Active learning with support vector machines, in *Proceedings of the Seventeenth International Conference on Machine Learning*, pp. 839–846, 2000.

Seung, H. S., Opper, M., and Sompolinsky, H., Query by committee, in *Proceedings of the Fifth Annual Workshop on Computational Learning Theory*, ACM Press, New York, pp. 287–294, 1992.

Thompson, C. A., Califf, M. E., and Mooney, R. J., Active learning for natural language parsing and information extraction, in *Proceedings of the Sixteenth International Conference on Machine Learning*, Morgan Kaufmann, San Francisco, pp. 406–414, 1999.

Tikhonov, A. N., and Arsenin, V. Y., *Solutions of Ill-Posed Problems*, Halsted Press, Washington, 1977.

Van Rijsbergen, C., *Information Retrieval*, 2nd edition, Butterworth, Woburn, MA, 1979.

Vapnik, V. N., *The Nature of Statistical Learning Theory*, Springer-Verlag, New York, 1995.

Witten, I. H., and Frank, E., *Data Mining—Practical Machine Learning Tools and Techniques with JAVA Implementations*, Morgan Kaufmann, San Francisco, 2000.

10

EXPERIENCES IN MINING DATA FROM COMPUTER SIMULATIONS

Chandrika Kamath, Erick Cantú-Paz, Sen-ching S. Cheung, Imola K. Fodor, and Nu Ai Tang

10.1. INTRODUCTION

Computer simulations enable us to understand complex phenomena through the analysis of mathematical models on high-performance computers. By filling the gap between physical experiments and analytical approaches, computer simulations provide both qualitative and quantitative insights into physical phenomena. They are particularly useful when the phenomena is too complex to be analyzed analytically, such as the flow around an airplane, or too expensive, impractical, or dangerous to study experimentally. In the latter case, we include examples such as the effects of a volcano eruption on the Earth's surface temperature, the evolution of stars, car crash tests, the structural integrity of buildings and bridges under various wind conditions and loads, modeling of material behavior at macro- and microscales, the spread of diseases via entity-based simulations, and so on.

In this chapter we survey the work being done in the mining of simulation data, describe our experiences in the analysis of data from a fluid mixing problem, and outline the challenges and opportunities in the mining of this relatively new form of data. We first provide a brief introduction to simulation data in Section 10.2, followed by a survey of various applications in Section 10.3. Then, in Section 10.4 we discuss our work in similarity-based object retrieval and illustrate how it can be used in several problems of interest. Finally, in Section 10.5 we identify open problems in mining simulation data as well as potential solution approaches.

Next Generation of Data-Mining Applications. Edited by Kantardzic and Zurada
ISBN 0-471-65605-4 © 2005 the Institute of Electrical and Electronics Engineers, Inc.

10.2. A BRIEF INTRODUCTION TO SIMULATION DATA

To understand the role data mining can play in the analysis of data from simulations, we first need to understand the source of this data. Numerical simulations typically involve the solution of partial differential equations (PDEs). Using fundamental principles such as the conservation of mass, momentum, and energy, partial differential equations create a mathematical model of a physical phenomena. These models typically have several independent variables, such as space (i.e., x, y, z coordinates) and time, and several dependent variables (e.g., pressure, density, and velocity). The PDE describes how the dependent variables vary as a function of the independent variables. Since it is a continuous formulation, the PDE is solved numerically by discretizing it in space and time using mesh-based methods such as finite elements and finite differences, or through mesh-less methods. Then, as the PDE evolves over time, at each time step, determined by the discretization in time, we obtain the values of the dependent variables at each grid point—that is, the location in space identified by the spatial discretization.

The data from numerical simulations can be quite large, especially as complex phenomena are simulated in two and three spatial dimensions. For example, the simulation of a high-resolution 3-D shock tube was performed on a 2048 × 2048 × 1920 grid over 27,000 time steps, on 960 nodes of the IBM-SP Sustained Stewardship TeraOp system at Lawrence Livermore National Laboratory (Mirin et al., 1999). The simulation ran for just over a week, producing over 3 terabytes of graphics data (one byte per grid point), distributed over 300,000 files. In addition, much larger datasets were generated for the dynamical variables (e.g., density, pressure, velocity, material fraction) that were stored in 16-bit integer format. While this may be an extreme example, even moderate-sized computer simulations can produce datasets that require automated analysis techniques. As an example, consider the reanalysis data from the National Centers for Environmental Predictions (2003). The data are the result of a simulation in atmospheric sciences which outputs the mean temperature for each month. It is available over a 144 × 73 longitude-by-latitude grid, with 17 elevation levels, for 264 months. Even in these relatively smaller datasets, data mining can play an important role when it is used either in isolation or as a complement to the more traditional visualization approaches.

When mesh-based methods are used in computer simulations, the values of the variables are available at discrete mesh or grid points. Mesh data from simulations can be broadly categorized into structured and unstructured data. Structured data can be either regular in the form of a Cartesian mesh, (Figure 10.1a), or curvilinear as shown in Figure 10.1b. In the case of a regularly spaced Cartesian mesh, techniques from image processing can be applied to preprocess the mesh data. In the unstructured mesh data category—for example, Figure 10.1c—the data can be composed of either homogeneous elements (in this case triangles) or heterogeneous elements as in Figure 10.2. In addition to structured and unstructured meshes, there are also meshes that are the hybrid of the two; these include hierarchical meshes that are globally unstructured but locally structured (Figure 10.3),

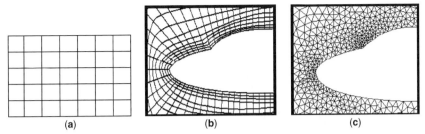

Figure 10.1. Examples of two-dimensional meshes: (**a**) An image of a regularly spaced Cartesian mesh, (**b**) two-dimensional structured mesh, and (**c**) unstructured mesh around the front of an aircraft. Panels b and c are from http://www.nas.nasa.gov/Pubs/Docs/FAST/chp_16.surferu.html.

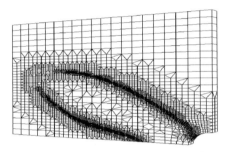

Figure 10.2. An example of a three-dimensional unstructured mesh with heterogeneous elements (http://cox.iwr.uni-heidelberg.de/ ug/Images/benchmark_grid.gif).

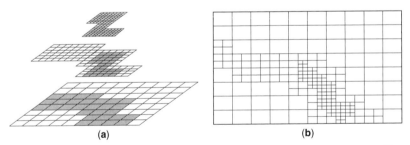

Figure 10.3. An example of a composite mesh made up of regular meshes illustrating (**a**) the hierarchy of regular meshes and (**b**) the composed "unstructured mesh" (http://www.llnl.gov/casc/samrai).

as well as meshes that are structured in one part of the problem domain and unstructured in another. In many problems, the meshes are not static: As the physical features in the simulation evolve, the mesh too must adaptively change to accurately model these features. There are also meshless methods used in simulations that result in irregularly spaced output data. In addition, as the simulation evolves in time, a series of two- or three-dimensional datasets are produced and output at each time step.

Thus the output from a simulation is essentially the values of the variables of interest (e.g., pressure or density) at discrete points in space and time. The spatial points can be regularly or irregularly spaced depending on the discretization.

10.3. ROLE OF DATA MINING IN COMPUTER SIMULATIONS

In this section we survey the role that data mining is beginning to play in the area of computer simulations. Simulation data are a relatively new source of massive data; as a result, there has been little work done in mining such data. Traditionally, data from simulations have been analyzed using classical visualization tools. With advances in scientific simulation technologies, the datasets resulting from these simulations are routinely approaching the terabyte and petabyte scale. Much of these data are not only never observed by scientists tasked with comprehending the data, but they are not even available to the scientist to help determine what subsets of the data warrant closer inspection (ASCI VIEWS Visualization Web page, 2003). The visualization community has made great strides in addressing these concerns through the use of advanced displays (e.g., power walls) for large volumes of data, novel data representations that allow out-of-core progressive visualization of data, high-accuracy volume rendering frameworks, and so on. However, analyses done through these traditional means have been mainly qualitative, and scientists are now interested in more quantitative analyses. In addition, they are also interested in ways in which they can directly focus on the areas of interest, instead of having to browse first through vast quantities of data. In Section 10.4, we discuss our approach to addressing these two problems through the use of data-mining techniques. But first, we survey existing work in the mining of simulation data.

10.3.1. Detection and Tracking of Coherent Structures

There are several examples of the use of data-mining techniques to identify and track coherent structures. For instance, (Ferre-Gine et al., 1996) use a fuzzy ARTMAP neural network to identify eddy motions in a turbulent wake flow, using data from a wind tunnel. Frames of 3×3 adjacent velocity vectors are considered, and patterns are represented by normalized velocity vectors. From these data, the training patterns are selected by manually identifying patterns that represent clockwise and counterclockwise structures. The neural network is applied multiple times varying a "vigilance" parameter. Those patterns labeled as eddies by all the neural networks are reported as the final results. The results agree with previous work that used template matching to find the eddies.

In other applications, there is an interest to identify and track coherent structures over multiple time steps. Traditionally, tracking is done by a human or by computationally expensive heuristics that track objects through all intermediate time steps. Banerjee et al. (1995) propose an alternative tracking method based on machine learning techniques and describe an application to track vortices. Vortices change shape, split, merge, appear, and cease to exist unexpectedly.

Their method begins by constructing a training dataset composed of vectors that describe related and unrelated vortices after a time gap. The training set is used to create a decision tree, which is then applied to identify related vortices in different time steps. As expected, the accuracy degrades as the time gap increases. The decision tree performs worse than the tracking approach for small time gaps, but over intermediate and long time gaps the decision tree performs better than a traditional tracking program.

Another technique that has been extensively used for the analysis of coherent structures is wavelets (Farge et al., 1996). As wavelets operate on different scales, the information they extract from the data are ideal for identifying structures at different scales in problems such as turbulent flow. For example, Farge and Schneider (2002) describe a nonlinear procedure to filter wavelet coefficients to separate the coherent vortices from the background flow. Their work shows that very few of the wavelet modes contain most of the enstrophy (the variable of interest), and selecting the top modes (2% or 3%) is sufficient to select the coherent structures. In a similar manner, Siegel and Weiss (1997) use wavelet packet technology, again in the context of fluid flow, to separate signals into coherent and noncoherent parts. They are particularly interested in a quantitative analysis of vortex behavior to complement the qualitative analysis obtained through visualization technology. Their experience shows that by keeping only a small subset of the wavelet coefficients, they are able to extract individual coherent structures in turbulent flow. A slightly different approach is taken by Hangan et al. (2001), who combine wavelets with the more traditional template matching approach from pattern recognition to match patterns at different scales.

10.3.2. Understanding Simulations

Data-mining methods can also be used to interpret results from simulations. For example, Mladenić et al. (1994) describe the use of regression trees and a rule inducer to interpret results from simulations of a supermarket and a pub. The simulators take user-defined parameters as input (number of cashiers, arrival rates, etc.) and produce summary statistics (cashier utilization, length of customer's queues, etc.). The goal is to examine which input parameters affect the output of the simulators. The simulators are executed multiple times with different parameters, and their outputs are recorded. Each execution produces a training example that is used as input to the tree or rule inducers. Both the regression tree algorithm and the rule inducer created accurate models that could be interpreted by humans.

In a similar way, Mladenić et al. (1995) applied decision trees to a simulation of a steel production plant with the goal of identifying the reasons for excessive waste. Decision trees have also been used to analyze the massive datasets from simulations in (Bowyer et al., 2000).

10.3.3. Dimension Reduction

Principal component analysis (PCA) is an important analysis tool used in many fields. In simulation data, it can be used to analyze the spatial or temporal variability of physical fields. The technique has been used extensively under the name of Empirical Orthogonal Functions (EOFs) in atmospheric sciences (Preisendorfer and Mobley, 1988) and as Proper Orthogonal Decomposition (POD) in turbulence (Lumley, 1967). In particular, it has been used to build low-dimensional models by Lumley and Blossey (1998), who exploit the fact that in certain problems, some parts of the domain are dominated by large-scale coherent structures. These can be resolved by a low-dimensional model of the region, while parameterizing the smaller-scale effects. This low-dimensional model is generated by keeping a few eigenfunctions obtained from the POD.

Nonlinear extensions to Principal Components Analysis, based on auto-associative neural networks, have been studied by Sengupta and Boyle (1995; PCMDI Web page, 2003). They found that the nonlinear method effected some-what greater data reduction and that the leading nonlinear mode captured the seasonal cycle of precipitation more clearly than the leading linear mode. They concluded that nonlinear techniques should be considered especially when lin-ear PCA fails to uncover physically meaningful patterns in climatological data analysis.

A different application of dimension reduction technique has been used in the Sapphire project to separate signals in climate data (Sapphire Web page, 2003). Since simulation data contain the effects of many different sources, such as El Niño and volcano signals, they must be removed in order to make meaningful comparisons between different climate models. This separation is made compli-cated by the fact that recent volcano eruptions coincided with El Niño events. Our experiences showed that by combining the traditional Principal Component Anal-ysis with the newer Independent Component Analysis (Hyvärinen et al., 2001), we obtained better separation than by just using PCA alone (Fodor and Kamath, 2003).

10.3.4. Information Retrieval in Simulation Data

Finding objects of interest in simulation data is a task that is essential to analyzing the data. The traditional solution to this problem has been the use of visualization techniques for "feature" extraction and tracking. In contrast to data mining, where the term "feature" is a descriptor of an object in the data, the visualization community uses the term to refer to the object itself. For example, Machiraju et al. (2001) describe the detection of swirl, which is a scalar quantity used to identify features such as vortices, which are characterized by swirling flow. The swirl is a well-defined mathematical quantity derived from the velocity and velocity gradients at each grid point. However, since simulation data are often stored in a compressed form using wavelets, it is important to be able to calculate the swirl feature directly from the compressed data. Machiraju et al. (2001) illustrate how the velocity and velocity gradients can be approximated using data only in the compressed wavelet domain. They borrow ideas from multi-grid algorithms and finite-difference approximations to incorporate correction terms that account for the different spacing between the grid points at different levels in the wavelet representation of the compressed data.

A more recent development in the analysis of simulation data is the use of techniques from the Content-Based Image Retrieval (CBIR) and related communities. In CBIR, the task is to find images in a database that are similar to a query image. Since simulation data that have been processed for visualization, and mapped to a rectangular display, can be considered to be an image, CBIR techniques can be applied to these processed data.

CBIR systems extract various features or descriptors from the images and model similarity through the use of mathematical distance functions between the feature vectors. Extensive research has been performed to derive compact, representative features and distance functions to model visual cues such as color, texture, and shapes. Excellent reviews of different CBIR systems can be found in Castelli and Bergman (2002), Djeraba et al. (2002), Veltkamp et al. (2001), Yeung et al. (2001), Perry et al. (1999), Forsyth et al. (1997), Faloutsos (1996), Picard et al. (1996). All of these systems focus on photographic imagery, remotely sensed images, medical images, or geological images. However, simulation data are different from such image data. First, unless the underlying grid is a simple Cartesian mesh, simulation data are not available at regular points in a rectangular domain. So, many of the image processing algorithms cannot be directly applied. One solution is to sample the data at regular intervals, similar to the approach used when the data are converted to a regular rectangular grid for display in visualization. Second, there are often several physical quantities associated with each grid point, unlike an image, which is just a single quantity. Third, the "objects" in a simulation rarely correspond to physical objects such as a car or a person. In addition, the "objects" in an image often change shape as the simulation evolves, and they may even appear or disappear with time. Finally, we observe that much of the CBIR work focuses on extracting features for, and retrieves, the entire image, while in simulation data we are interested in parts of an image. This implies that the image must be segmented to identify these parts prior to the extraction of features.

Despite these differences, a couple of efforts have begun to use CBIR techniques in the context of simulation data. The Feature Extraction and Evaluation for Massive ASCI Data Sets (FEEMADS) project (FEEMADS Web page, 2003) is extracting features using the data from a hydrodynamics simulation. The grid used is from an adaptive mesh refinement scheme (similar to Figure 10.3). The authors consider two scenarios: one, where the adaptive mesh data are resampled on a uniform grid so image processing techniques can be directly applied, and the other, where the data are directly obtained from the oct-tree data structure used to store the unstructured mesh. In the latter scenario, they exploit the fact that in the areas of interest, the mesh is refined, and the level of refinement can be used to limit the search. An approach more closely resembling the traditional CBIR systems is taken in the Sapphire project (SBOR Web page, 2003). This work is described in more detail in Section 10.4.

10.3.5. Code Validation

Another area where data-mining techniques are being applied in simulation data is the area of code verification and validation. In particular, for code validation, high-quality experiments are now becoming available, enabling effective comparisons of simulations to experiments. While such comparisons are in the preliminary stages (Rider et al., 2002; Zoldi, 2002; Fishbine, 2002), it is clear that techniques from data mining have a greater role to play in this area.

10.4. SIMILARITY-BASED OBJECT RETRIEVAL

Similarity-based object retrieval (SBOR) is a system being developed as part of the Sapphire project at Lawrence Livermore National Laboratory (SBOR Web page, 2003). The original motivation for the system was to support searches in simulation data that are similar to those in CBIR systems. Instead of having a scientist visually browse through vast amounts of simulation output looking for regions of interest, we wanted to provide a semi-automated system where the scientist would give an example of a region of interest and the system would retrieve similar regions from either the same simulation or a series of simulations.

However, there are several ways in which the SBOR system is different from most CBIR systems. Unlike many of the CBIR systems that focus on the entire image, we are interested in retrieving subimages, or objects, in the data. In addition, we use the term "object" in a somewhat abstract sense. It does not imply a physical object, such as a car or a house, but instead refers to structures seen in the simulations such as vortices or mushroom-shaped structures that result from the mixing of two fluids as in Figure 10.4. Furthermore, in simulation data, if the data are in the form of a Cartesian mesh as in Figure 10.1a, it can be considered as an image, albeit one where the pixel values are floating point numbers instead of 8-bit data. If the data are on an unstructured grid, then it is not as straightforward to treat the data as images; we discuss possible ways of addressing this issue later on.

We have also applied this system to other image data such as remote-sensing imagery, and we have found other uses of the modules that form such a system. As an example, consider the code validation problem in Figure 10.4, where we need to determine how close a simulation is to an experiment. The current solution to this problem is a side-by-side visual comparison of the experimental and simulation images, an approach that not only lacks a quantitative aspect, but also is one that is not scalable to a large number of comparisons. This is an area where data-mining techniques can play an important role. One approach to this would be to consider each of the mushroom-shaped objects in the simulation and measure its similarity to the corresponding object in the experiment. This would require techniques similar to those used in CBIR. Having measured the similarity of these objects taken in isolation, we could then combine these measures with additional information such as the number and locations of the mushrooms to quantitatively compare the experimental image with the ones from the simulation.

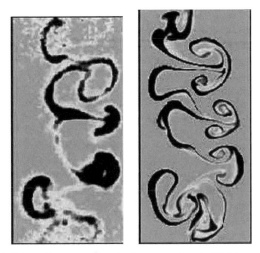

Figure 10.4. The left-hand image shows the flow pattern of a Richtmyer–Meshkov experiment performed at Los Alamos National Laboratory. The same experiment is simulated by high-resolution numerical methods, and the result is shown in the right-hand image (Rider et al., 2002).

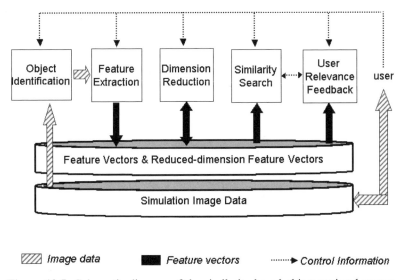

Figure 10.5. Schematic diagram of the similarity-based object retrieval system.

The SBOR system consists of five major functional modules: object identification, feature extraction, dimension reduction, similarity search, and relevance feedback. Figure 10.5 shows the flow of data in the SBOR system. We assume that the user has identified an object of interest in a query image and that he or she is interested in finding other similar objects in the image database. Here, we use the term "database" in the context of a data store, rather than a true database.

We also use the term "object" in a generic sense. The image database contains simulation data in the form of images; The query image is also part of this database. First, the images in the database are input to the object identification module. This module is responsible for extracting objects of interest within the images for subsequent analysis. These objects are not used directly, because a pixel-to-pixel comparison of objects is very sensitive to small changes in geometry and intensity. Instead, for each object in the image, we extract higher-level features that are invariant under various conditions such as rotation, translation, and scaling. The feature extraction module supports several different features, enabling the user to extract the subset that best meets the goals of the similarity search. After the feature vectors are generated for each region in an image, we identify the most important subset using dimension reduction techniques. This can lead to a significant speedup in the similarity search, with little effect on the retrieval performance. Once we have the features (in the reduced dimension) for the query object and for all the objects in the image database, we use the similarity search module to find those objects that are "close-to" the query object. Different distance measures and search methods can be used to capture the notion of similarity. Further refinement is also possible through relevance feedback, where user feedback is used to improve the retrieval results.

It is important to realize that not all modules are used in every situation. During the initial stages of data exploration, users may want to experiment with a large number of different features. Sophisticated object identification techniques and dimension reduction may be unnecessary at this stage. Once the set of features is determined, the user can invoke more complex object identification schemes to capture objects of different scales and can apply dimension reduction to speed up the similarity search. We next describe each module of the SBOR system in further detail.

10.4.1. Object Identification

In the SBOR system, given a query object of interest in a simulation image, we are interested in finding similar objects in other images. Thus far, we have used the term "object" in a generic sense. In its simplest form, an object could be a tile—that is, a rectangular region in the image. Or, it could be more complex, and correspond to an object with a complex shape that clearly stands out from the background, such as the mushroom-shaped objects in Figure 10.4. We next compare and contrast the various options we have considered for the object identification module.

Tile-Based Versus Object-Based.   In the tile-based approach, an image is covered by tiles of a given size. The tiles can be overlapping or non-overlapping, and they can be square or rectangular (assuming two-dimensional simulation data). Overlapping tiles would require more storage because there are more of them covering each image. However, they are more likely to include objects that might be split among tiles. Since a tile is very easy to define—it just needs the coordinates of opposite corners—the task of object identification is relatively simple. But, there are several drawbacks to the tile approach. First, some of the tiles may not have any interesting information—for example, a tile with all pixels with approximately the same value. In this case, it may not make sense to process such tiles any further. Second, a tile may be much smaller than the object of interest; therefore, a tile-based approach would completely miss the object. However, a multi-resolution approach, as described later in this section, can be very useful in identifying such objects. Third, a tile may contain more than one object, with only one of the objects satisfying the similarity criterion. Since the tile is treated as a whole, this object may be missed in the retrieval. An obvious solution to these problems is the object-based approach, where we have processed each image in the database to extract the objects in the image. Such a system might be more efficient than the tile-based approach because it only stores and computes feature vectors for individual objects. However, it requires segmentation of images, which is known to be a very difficult problem (Forsyth and Ponce, 2003, Chapter 14). For simulation data such as the images shown in Figure 10.4, such a segmentation may not even exist because there is no precise definition of an object. In addition, even if we successfully segmented an object from an image, the retrieval results may be poor if the query object was part of an object rather than the whole.

In the SBOR system, we support both the tile-based and the object-based approaches. Object segmentation is done using a simple thresholding scheme; more sophisticated techniques will be added in the future.

Fixed-Size Versus Variable-Size Tiles. In the case of fixed-sized tiles, the same tile size is used for all tiles in an image. This works well when the feature extracted describes a characteristic of the entire tile, such as texture. However, when we are interested in objects of a size larger, or smaller, than the tile size, the retrieval results may be poor. An object-based approach could provide a solution to this problem. Another alternative is to use variable-sized tiles. The SBOR system allows the user to select different tile sizes through multi-resolution. A dyadic wavelet transform is first applied to each image in the dataset to create multiple images at different resolutions. A constant-sized tile is then applied to each resolution, effectively creating tiles of variable sizes. Due to the reduction in image dimension, this approach is computationally more efficient than using large tiles on the original image. In addition, multi-resolution can also be applied to the query object, or a smaller tile used, enabling us to retrieve objects smaller than the query object.

Query-Dependent Versus Query-Independent Tile Size. The tile size can be fixed prior to the use of the SBOR system, or determined when the query is made. If the tile size is dependent on the query, then the features must be extracted on-line, after the query has been made. Because a quick response is often needed, this limits the number of images that can be queried. On the other hand, a query-independent tile size allows the features to be precomputed, resulting in a faster turnaround.

Shape of the Tile. In addition to a rectangular or square-shaped tile, a circular shape can also be used to ensure that the resulting tiles are rotational invariant. However, care must be taken to ensure that the entire image is adequately covered by such tiles.

We note that these options can be used in combination. For example, a circular tile may be query-dependent or query-independent. Or, we can use the object-based approach in conjunction with the tile approach by initially segmenting the image and then considering the (complete or partial) objects that fall within each tile. Our experiences indicate that this might help in the identification of partial objects. Also, the multi-resolution approach can be applied to both the tiles and the objects.

10.4.2. Feature Extraction

This section describes the features provided in the SBOR system. We focus primarily on features that are scale, rotation, and translation invariant. The features selected for use in any application are based on the characteristics of the objects to be retrieved. If shape or texture are important in characterizing the object of interest, then the corresponding features should be selected. In our experience, we found that some experimentation is necessary to determine the best combination of features for an application.

Simple Features. This set of features consists of the mean, the standard deviation, the maximum, and the minimum of all pixel values in a tile image.

Histogram. This is a 16-bin histogram of pixel values in a tile image. The bins are uniform across the dynamic range.

Simple Geometry. The simple geometry feature contains the parameters of the ellipse that best represents the spatial distribution of the pixel values. It consists of five numbers: the location of the centroid, the lengths of the major and minor axes, and the angle between the major and the x axes.

ART. The angular radial transform (ART) belongs to a broad class of shape analysis tools based on moments (Mukundan and Ramakrishnan, 1988). Our implementation of ART is based on the region-shape descriptor defined in MPEG-7 (Manjunath et al., 2002, Chapter 15). ART projects a two-dimensional signal within the unit circle onto a set of complex orthonormal basis functions. The ART basis function of angular order m and radial order n in polar coordinates is given by

$$V_{nm}(\rho, \theta) = \begin{cases} \exp(jm\theta)/2, & n = 0 \\ \exp(jm\theta)\cos(\pi n\rho), & n \neq 0 \end{cases}$$

The ART coefficient F_{mn} of a two-dimensional signal $f(\rho, \theta)$ is defined by

$$F_{mn} = \frac{1}{\pi} \int_0^{2\pi} \int_0^1 V_{nm}^*(\rho, \theta) f(\rho, \theta) \rho \, d\rho \, d\theta \qquad (10.1)$$

The ART feature is implemented by discretizing Eq. (10.1). The origin of the functions is set at the centroid of the tile image. In order to cover the entire tile image, each basis function has a square-shaped support with each dimension equal to twice the longer side of the tile image. Rotational invariance is achieved by using only the magnitude of F_{mn}, and scale invariance is achieved by normalizing all F_{mn} by the area of the image, that is, F_{00}. Following the MPEG-7 standard, 12 angular bases and three radial bases are used. This results in a 35-dimensional feature vector as the normalized F_{00} is always one and thus dropped from the representation. Unlike MPEG-7, we do not quantize the coefficients and retain the full floating-point precision for similarity search.

Binary Simple Geometry. This feature is just the simple geometry feature applied to a tile in which the objects have been extracted by segmentation using simple thresholding. All object pixels are set equal to 255, and the background to 0.

Binary ART. The binary ART feature is just the ART feature applied to the tile in which the objects have been extracted by segmentation using simple thresholding.

Texture Features. These features, applied at the tile level, capture the texture of the tile. The wavelet-based texture features are obtained by calculating the mean and standard deviation of the pixel values in each band at different levels of the wavelet decomposition (Manjunath and Ma, 1996). The power spectrum features are statistical measures such as the average magnitude and variance of magnitude derived from the Fourier spectrum of the image (Augusteijn et al., 1995).

10.4.3. Dimension Reduction

The large number of features extracted from the simulation data can pose problems during the retrieval. First, not all features may be relevant to the query of interest. Second, extracting, storing, and using the irrelevant features will take additional computational resources and slow down the retrieval time. Third, many of the efficient data structures that support fast retrieval are designed for 10–15 features. And, finally, if the number of features is very large, we encounter the "curse of dimensionality" problem associated with high-dimensional spaces. To address this problem, we include dimension reduction techniques such as principal component analysis and independent component analysis in the SBOR system. Additional techniques, borrowed from the information retrieval community, will be added in the future.

10.4.4. Similarity Search

The similarity search module identifies the feature vectors in the database that are close to the query feature vector. We define similarity between two feature vectors by a distance function, where the similarity between two objects decreases as the distance between their feature vectors increases. We support some of the more commonly used distance measures as defined in Table 10.1. Each feature can also be normalized by subtracting the mean and dividing by the standard deviation to ensure that the dynamic range of each feature is the same.

We currently support two types of search functions: ϵ-search and k-nearest-neighbor (k-NN) search. In the k-NN search, the k feature vectors in the database closest to the query feature vector are returned. A small k in a k-NN search allows a user to quickly examine the small set of returned results. In an ϵ-search, the module returns all feature vectors in the database whose distance from the query feature is within a positive threshold ϵ. ϵ-search is intended for experienced users who can correlate distance values with the level of similarity.

10.4.5. Relevance Feedback

The SBOR system also includes options for relevance feedback. Relevance feedback is the process by which user input is included in the retrieval by having the user provide feedback on the relevance or irrelevance of the current retrieval results. The simplest form of relevance feedback either changes the weights on the features being used or modifies the query itself to be closer to the user input of relevant results and farther from the irrelevant results. An alternative method to incorporate the user's feedback is to use machine learning techniques. To apply these techniques, the user creates a training set with positive and negative examples by labeling the results of the similarity search. The training set is used to train a classifier, which is applied to the entire database of feature vectors. The classifier assigns positive and negative labels to each feature vector in the

TABLE 10.1. Table of Different Types of Distance Measures

Distance Measures	Definitions
Manhattan or l_1	$\sum |x_i - y_i|$
Euclidean or l_2	$\sum (x_i - y_i)^2$
Chebychev or l_∞	$\max |x_i - y_i|$
Cosine	$\arccos\left[\dfrac{\sum(x_i-\bar{x}_i)(y_i-\bar{x}_i)}{\sqrt{l_2(x,\bar{x})\cdot l_2(y,\bar{x})}}\right]$
Kullback–Leibler divergence	$\sum x_i \log(x_i/y_i)$
Chi-square	$\sum \dfrac{x_i^2 - y_i^2}{y_i}$

$X = (x_1, \ldots, x_n)$ and $Y = (y_1, \ldots, y_n)$ are the two feature vectors. $\bar{X} = (\bar{x}_1, \ldots, \bar{x}_n)$ denotes the average of all feature vectors in the database. The range of summation or maximum is always from 1 to n.

database, and the positive examples are returned to the user. If necessary, the user can relabel the results and iterate the feedback process.

10.4.6. Sample Results

In this section we illustrate the use of the SBOR system using the data from a high-resolution simulation of a three-dimensional shock tube. Initially, two fluids of different densities are separated by a membrane in the tube; then the membrane is pushed against a wire mesh. The simulation uses a regular three-dimensional grid (described in Section 10.2) to model the resulting mixing of the two fluids (Mirin et al., 1999). The data generated for visualization consist of the entropy variable at each grid point. Working with 256×256-sized slices of these data, we demonstrate how we can use the SBOR system to find mushroom-shaped objects in the data. As an illustration, we use a tile-based method for object identification, with the tile size determined by the query size. The image database is generated using the three images shown in Figure 10.6.

The user interacts with the SBOR system through a graphical menu-driven system. The user first brings up the image of interest and identifies the area that forms the query object as in Figure 10.7a. When the user clicks the search button, it brings up the window that enables the choice of files to search on, the overlapping factor for the tiles, and the directory to be used for saving the results, as shown in Figure 10.7b. Next, in Figure 10.8a, the user selects the

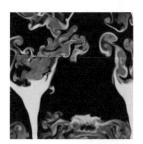
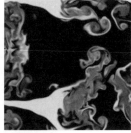

Figure 10.6. Three sample images used to illustrate the SBOR system. These are 256×256-sized slices through a three-dimensional data. They are taken at slightly different times from different locations in the grid. They may appear similar, though they are different in pixel intensities. Each has a mushroom-shaped "object" at different orientations.

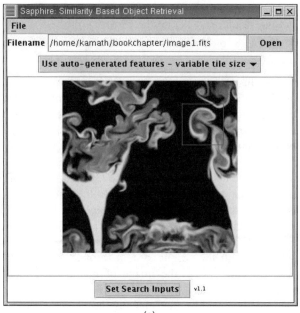

(a)

(b)

Figure 10.7. (**a**) Query selection on an image of interest. (**b**) Options for the tile-based approach.

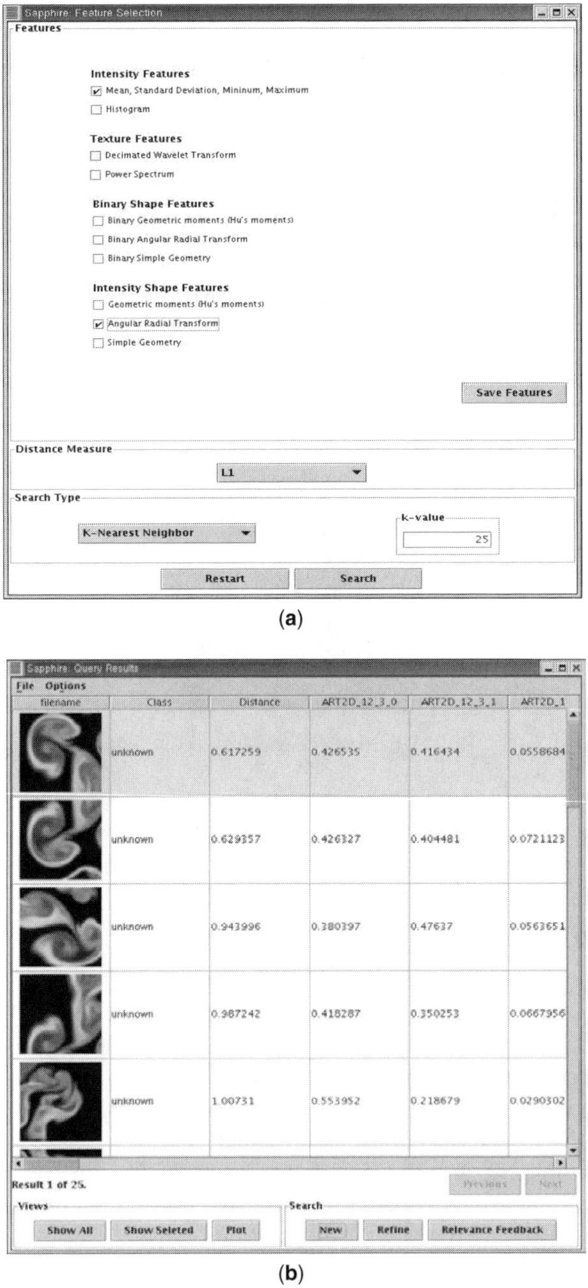

Sapphire: Feature Selection

Features

Intensity Features
☑ Mean, Standard Deviation, Mininum, Maximum
☐ Histogram

Texture Features
☐ Decimated Wavelet Transform
☐ Power Spectrum

Binary Shape Features
☐ Binary Geometric moments (Hu's moments)
☐ Binary Angular Radial Transform
☐ Binary Simple Geometry

Intensity Shape Features
☐ Geometric moments (Hu's moments)
☑ Angular Radial Transform
☐ Simple Geometry

[Save Features]

Distance Measure
[L1 ▼]

Search Type
[K–Nearest Neighbor ▼]   k–value [25]

[Restart]   [Search]

(a)

Sapphire: Query Results

File Options

filename	Class	Distance	ART2D_12_3_0	ART2D_12_3_1	ART2D_1
	unknown	0.617259	0.426535	0.416434	0.0558684
	unknown	0.629357	0.426327	0.404481	0.0721123
	unknown	0.943996	0.380397	0.47637	0.0563651
	unknown	0.987242	0.418287	0.350253	0.0667956
	unknown	1.00731	0.553952	0.218679	0.0290302

Result 1 of 25.   [Previous] [Next]

Views
[Show All] [Show Selected] [Plot]

Search
[New] [Refine] [Relevance Feedback]

(b)

Figure 10.8. (a) Choosing the features of interest and options for the search. (b) Results returned in decreasing order of similarity.

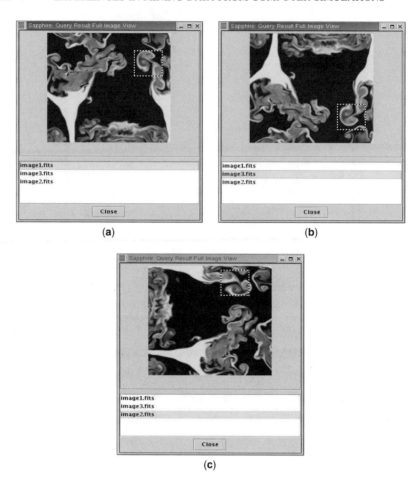

Figure 10.9. The three results returned are outlined on the respective images.

features to use in the similarity search, the distance metric, and the type of search, which results in the output shown in Figure 10.8b. Using the histogram and ART features, with the l_1 norm, we see that all the three mushroom-shaped objects are returned as being very similar to the query object. Figure 10.9 shows the top three results on the corresponding images.

In this example, we use the histogram feature because it captures the distribution of pixel intensities within a tile, and we use the ART feature because it represents shape—for example, the "mushroom-shaped" object in the query tile. A tile overlap of 50% allowed sufficient coverage of all objects in the image without a substantial increase in processing time. For this dataset, we found that the use of the L_1 norm in the similarity search usually gave good results. Our experiences have shown that, to keep response times low, it is preferable to first experiment with a smaller sample of the dataset, determine the best choice of options, and then gradually increase the size of the dataset. However, for very large datasets, with thousands or more images, it may make sense to run the system in a batch mode or use pregenerated features that have been obtained off-line.

10.5. CHALLENGES AND OPPORTUNITIES IN MINING SIMULATION DATA

The application of data mining to scientific simulation data is a relatively new field. As a result, there are several challenges and opportunities that await a data-mining practitioner analyzing such data. Much of our work thus far has been with data on a regularly spaced grid. While these data are similar to an image, it is not possible to directly use image processing software because simulation data are mainly in floating point format, while image data are often in integer or byte format. Thus, we found it necessary to rewrite the image processing techniques for floating point data. In addition, in computer simulations, several different variables are generated at each mesh point. A straightforward approach to this might be to apply techniques from the data fusion community, where data from different sensors are combined to exploit the complementary information from each sensor.

A different problem arises when the data are available on an unstructured mesh, where we cannot directly apply the techniques from traditional image processing. As mentioned earlier, we could sample the data at regular points and treat them as data on a regular grid. Alternatively, we could locally use variable-sized tiles to process a mesh such as the one in Figure 10.3. Also, we could use ideas from the PDE-based image processing community to directly extract the features of interest. The issue gets more complex when the data are available in the compressed form, and the size of the data is such that it is preferable to operate on it without uncompressing it. In Section 10.3 we have reviewed some approaches being used to process the data in the compressed form.

In our experiences, we found that simulation data share some problems common to other scientific datasets, such as the need to work with spatiotemporal data, massive sizes of the data, the lack of sufficient training examples, the need to mine data as they are being generated, and the need for real-time turnaround. In addition, as in the case of image data, we found that the initial preprocessing of the data is very time-consuming and difficult.

10.6. SUMMARY

In this chapter we summarized our experiences on mining a relatively new type of data—that is, data from computer simulations. We surveyed the work done in this field, and we discussed our experiences with the similarity-based object retrieval system that is being used to mine such data. Finally, we briefly discussed the issues that are specific to simulation data, and we presented potential solutions that are being considered in the solution of these problems.

ACKNOWLEDGMENTS

We would like to thank the reviewer of this chapter whose questions helped us enhance the motivation for the use of data mining in simulation data.

UCRL-BOOK-200043: This work was performed under the auspices of the U.S. Department of Energy by University of California Lawrence Livermore National Laboratory under contract No. W-7405-Eng-48.

REFERENCES

ASCI VIEWS Visualization Web page, 2003. http://www.llnl.gov/icc/sdd/img/viz.shtml.

Augusteijn, M. F., Clemens, L. E., and Shaw, K. A., Performance evaluation of texture measures for ground cover identification in satellite images by means of a neural network classifier, *IEEE Transactions on Geoscience and Remote Sensing* **33**(3), 616–626 (1995).

Banerjee, A., Hirsh, H., and Ellman, T., Inductive learning of feature tracking rules for scientific visualization, in *Proceedings of the IJCAI-95 Workshop on Machine Learning in Engineering*, 1995.

Bowyer, K., Hall, L., Chawla, N., Moore, T., and Kegelmeyer, W., A parallel decision tree builder for mining very large visualization datasets, in *IEEE International Conference on Systems, Man, and Cybernetics*, IEEE, 2000.

Castelli, V., and Bergman, D., eds., *Image Databases: Search and Retrieval of Digital Imagery*, John Wiley & Sons, New York, 2002.

Djeraba, C., et al. Special issue on content-based multimedia indexing and retrieval, *IEEE Multimedia Magazine* **9**(2), 18–60 (2002).

Faloutsos, C., *Searching Multimedia Databases by Content*, Kluwer Academic Publishers, Hingham, MA, 1996.

Farge, M., Kevlahan, N., Perrier, V., and Goirand, E., Wavelet and turbulence, *Proceedings of the IEEE* **84**(4), 639–669 (1996).

Farge, M., and Schneider, K., Analyzing and compressing turbulent fields with wavelets. Technical report, Institute Pierre Simon de Laplace, June 2002. http://monteverdi.ens.fr/.

FEEMADS Web page: Feature Extraction and Evaluation for Massive ASCI Data Sets, 2003. http://www.c3.lanl.gov/feemads/.

Ferre-Gine, J., Rallo, R., Arenas, A., and Giralt, F., Identification of coherent structures in turbulent shear flows with a fuzzy artmap neural network, *International Journal of Neural Systems* **7**(5), 559–568 (1996).

Fishbine, B., Code validation experiments. Technical Report Fall 2002, Los Alamos National Laboratory, 2002. http://www.lanl.gov/quarterly/q_fall02/.

Fodor, I. K., and Kamath, C., Using independent component analysis to separate signals in climate data, in *Proceedings, Independent Component Analyses, Wavelets, and Neural Networks, number 5102 in SPIE Proceedings*, SPIE, pp. 25–36, 2003.

Forsyth, D., Malik, J., and Wilensky, R., Searching for digital pictures, *Scientific American* **June** 88–93 (1997).

Forsyth, D. A., and Ponce, J., *Computer Vision A Modern Approach*, Prentice-Hall, Englewood Cliffs, NJ, 2003.

Hangan, H., Kopp, G. A., Vernet, A., and Martinuzzi, R., A wavelet pattern recognition technique for identifying flow structures in cylinder generated wakes, *Journal of Wind Engineering and Industrial Aerodynamics* **89**, 1001–1015 (2001).

Hyvärinen, A., Karhunen, J., and Oja, E., *Independent Component Analysis*, Series on Adaptive and Learning Systems for Signal Processing, Communications, and Control, John Wiley & Sons, New York, 2001.

Lumley, J., and Blossey, P., Control of turbulence, *Annual Review of Fluid Mechanics* **30**, 311–327 (1998).

Lumley, J. L., The structure of inhomogeneous turbulent flows, in *Atmospheric Turbulence and Radio Propagation*, Yaglom, A. M., and Tatarski, V. I., eds., pp. 166–178, Nauka, Moscow, 1967.

Machiraju, R., Fowler, J. E., Thompson, D., Soni, B., and Schroeder, W., EVITA—efficient visualization and interrogation of tera-scale data, in *Data Mining for Scientific and Engineering Applications*, Grossman, R. L., Kamath, C., Kegelmeyer, P., Kumar, V., and Namburu, R. R., eds., Kluwer Academic pp. 257–279, Publishers, Hingham, MA, 2001.

Manjunath, B. S., and Ma, W. Y., Texture features for browsing and retrieval of image data, *IEEE Transactions on Pattern Analysis and Machine Intelligence* **18**(8), 837–842 (1996).

Manjunath, B. S., Salembier, P., and Sikora, T., eds., *Introduction to MPEG-7: Multimedia Content Description Interface*, John Wiley & Sons, New York, 2002.

Mirin, A., et al., Very high resolution simulation of compressible turbulence on the IBM-SP system, Technical Report UCRL-JC-134237, Lawrence Livermore National Laboratory, 1999.

Mladenić, D., Bratko, I., Paul, R. J., and Grobelnik, M., Using machine learning techniques to interpret results from discrete event simulation, in *Proceedings of the Sixth European Conference on Machine Learning ECML94*, Springer-Verlag, Berlin, 1994.

Mladenic, D., Grobelnik, M., Bratko, I., and Paul, R. J., Classification tree chaining in data analysis, in *IJCAI Workshop on Data Engineering for Inductive Learning*, Montreal, 1995.

Mukundan, R., and Ramakrishnan, K. R., *Moment Functions in Image Analysis: Theory and Applications*, World Scientific, Singapore, 1988.

National Centers for Environmental Predictions Web page, 2003, http://www.ncep.noaa.gov/.

PCMDI Web page: Principal-Component Statistical Studies, 2003, http://wwwpcmdi.llnl.gov/pcmdi/statistics.html.

Perry, B., et al., *Content-Based Access to Multimedia Information—from Technology Trends to State of the Art*, Kluwer, Boston, Chapter 4.3, 1999.

Picard, R. W., and Pentland, A. P., et al., Special issue on digital libraries, *IEEE Transactions on Pattern Analysis and Machine Intelligence*, **18**(8), 769 (1996).

Preisendorfer R. W., and Mobley, C. D., *Principal Component Analysis in Meteorology and Oceanography*, Elsevier Science, New York, 1988.

Rider, W., et al., Using Richtmyer–Meshkov driven mixing experiments to impact the development of numerical methods for compressible hydrodynamics, in *Proceedings of the Ninth International Conference on Hyperbolic Problems Theory, Numerics, Applications*, pp. 84–88, 2002, http://www.acm.caltech.edu/hyp2002/program.html.

Sapphire Web page: Separation of climate signals, 2003, http://www.llnl.gov/casc/sapphire/sep_climate/index.html.

SBOR Web page: Similarity-Based Object Retrieval, 2003, http://www.llnl.gov/casc/sapphire/sbor.html.

Sengupta, S. K., and Boyle, J. S., Nonlinear principal component analysis of climate data. Technical Report PCMDI Report No. 29, Program for Climate Model Diagnosis and Intercomparison (PCMDI), 1995.

Siegel, A., and Weiss, J. B., A wavelet-packet census algorithm for calculating vortex statistics, *Phys. Fluids* **9**(7), 1988–1999 (1997).

Veltkamp, R. C., Burkhardt, H., and Kriegel, H.-P., eds., *State-of-the-Art in Content-Based Image and Video Retrieval*, Kluwer Academic Publishers, Hingham, MA, 2001.

Yeung, M., et al., Special section on storage, processing, and retrieval of digital media, *Journal of Electronic Imaging* **10**(4), 833–834 (2001).

Zoldi, C. A., A Numerical and Experimental Study of a Shock-Accelerated Heavy Gas Cylinder, Ph.D. thesis, State University of New York at Stony Brook, 2002.

11

STATISTICAL MODELING OF LARGE-SCALE SCIENTIFIC SIMULATION DATA

TINA ELIASSI-RAD, CHUCK BALDWIN, GHALEB ABDULLA, AND TERENCE CRITCHLOW

11.1. INTRODUCTION

By utilizing massively parallel computer systems, scientists are able to simulate complex phenomena such as explosions of stars. Specifically, scientists encode complex equations into computer programs (known as *simulation codes*). These computer programs produce tera-scale datasets, which contain millions of distinct spatial elements, thousands of discrete time steps, and hundreds of physical variables (such as temperature and pressure) at each point in the spatial–temporal dimensions.*

To gain new insight into the simulated scientific phenomena, scientists require computer applications that can rapidly analyze and display such massive datasets. However, the shear sizes of these datasets make even the best analysis and visualization tools inadequate (see Figure 11.1). Consequently, the need to efficiently and effectively explore such huge datasets has led to a surge of interest in scalable analysis and visualization techniques (Abdulla et al., 2001; Acharya et al., 1999; Agrawal et al., 1998; Chakrabarti et al., 2000; Eliassi-Rad et al., 2002; Freitag and Loy, 1999; Ng and Han, 1994; Wang et al., 1997). This chapter examines the statistical approaches that are utilized for rapid exploration of large-scale scientific simulation data.

The most commonly utilized techniques in building statistical models for huge datasets are sampling, histograms, and/or assumptions about the *a priori* distribution on the data. Unfortunately, such techniques are not desirable for scientific

---

*The spatial–temporal dimensions are defined to be x, y, z, and *time*.

Next Generation of Data-Mining Applications. Edited by Kantardzic and Zurada
ISBN 0-471-65605-4 © 2005 the Institute of Electrical and Electronics Engineers, Inc.

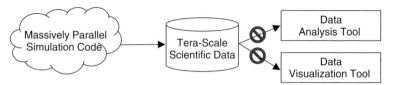

Figure 11.1. Currently available analysis and visualization tools cannot efficiently process tera-scale scientific data.

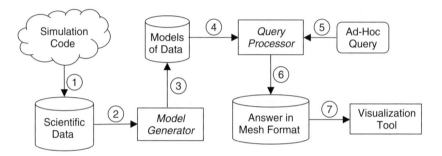

Figure 11.2. AQSim's architecture.

simulation datasets since they tend to be computationally expensive for high-dimensional data and can miss outliers.* Despite these drawbacks, systems that do not rely on such techniques are rare. In particular, our *Ad-hoc Queries for Simulation (AQSim)* infrastructure constructs *queriable statistical models* without the use of the aforementioned techniques. We define queriable statistical models to be descriptive statistics that (i) summarize and describe the data within a user-defined modeling error, and (ii) are able to answer complex range-based queries over the spatiotemporal dimensions.†

AQSim has two processors: (i) *model generator* and (ii) *query processor*. Figure 11.2 illustrates an overview of AQSim's architecture. AQSim's two pro-cessors enable reduction of both the data storage requirements and the query access times. The model generator builds and stores statistical queriable models of the data at multiple resolutions. Since models take less storage space than the original dataset,‡ AQSim is able to reduce the data storage requirements. AQSim's query processor takes as input the generated models, a user's query, and the amount of time that the user is willing to wait for an answer. Then, while its running time is less than the user-defined time limit, the query proces-sor searches the generated models and returns those models that satisfy the given query. AQSim's query processor decreases the query response time since models of the data are queried (instead of the entire dataset). This chapter focuses on

---

*Outliers are very important in scientific simulation data since the insights gained from them are commonly higher than from trends.
†Queriable models are very useful to scientists since such models can answer specific user's queries.
‡The original dataset typically resides on tertiary storage.

AQSim's model generator.* In particular, Section 11.3 describes three simple but effective statistical modeling techniques: (i) *mean modeler*, (ii) *goodness-of-fit modeler*, and (iii) *multivariate clusterer*.

AQSim's mean modeler is univariate and captures the true mean of systematic spatial–temporal partitions of the data. It has two major advantages. First, it makes no assumptions about the distribution of the data. Second, it calculates its model parameters through one sweep of the data. The error on the mean modeler is a variant of the *root mean square error* (RMSE).

AQSim's goodness-of-fit modeler is also univariate and captures the normality of systematic spatial–temporal partitions of the data by utilizing the *Anderson–Darling* goodness-of-fit test (D'Agostino and Stephens, 1986). Similar to the mean modeler, the goodness-of-fit modeler is able to calculate its model parameters through one sweep of the data. However, this modeler assumes that since the data describe a physical phenomenon, they probably fit a normal distribution. The error on this model is the *Type I error* associated with the goodness-of-fit test.

AQSim's multivariate clusterer captures the interrelationships between a dataset's *physical variables* by finding "similar" behavior among them. Physical variables are all variables except the spatial (i.e., x, y, z) and temporal (i.e., *time*) variables. For example, *temperature, pressure*, and *density* are considered physical variables. The exclusion of the spatial dimensions from the clustering process is important since "similar" characteristics could be far from each other in the spatial region. For example, the temperature of the outer shell of a star is more homogeneous than its inner shell even though the outer shell spans a spatial area several times larger than that of the inner shell.

AQSim's multivariate clusterer defines "similar" behavior by utilizing a variant of the *cosine similarity measure*, which has been used in information retrieval applications (Van Rijsbergen, 1979). We chose the cosine similarity measure instead of other metrics (such as the Euclidean distance metric) since our clusters will be used for query retrieval (Wang et al., 1999).

To scale AQSim's multivariate clusterer for large-scale datasets, we take advantage of the geometrical properties of the cosine similarity measure. Specifically, we utilize the user-defined clustering threshold to place a tighter upper-bound on the similarity of items within a cluster. This allows us to reduce the clustering time from $O(n^2)$ to $O(n \times g(f(u)))$, where n is the number of data points, $f(u)$ is a function of the user-defined clustering threshold, and $g(f(u))$ is the number of data points satisfying the new threshold $f(u)$. Eliassi-Rad and Critchlow (2003) empirically showed that, on average, $g(f(u))$ is much less than n.

Even though spatial variables do not play a role in building AQSim's clusters, it is desirable to associate each cluster with its correct spatial region. In particular, it is important for AQSim's clustering model to frame the answers to scientists' queries in the spatial region of the original data. While this information is trivially

---

*For more information on AQSim's query processor, see Baldwin et al. (2003a), Eliassi-Rad et al. (2002), and Lee et al. (2003).

contained in AQSim's univariate models, an additional step must be performed to map clusters to their appropriate spatial representations. To accomplish this, we use a *linking* algorithm for connecting each cluster to the appropriate nodes of the dataset's *topology tree*. Such a topology tree captures and stores the spatial connectivity of the dataset by utilizing the intrinsic topology given in the original scientific problem (Baldwin et al., 2003b). AQSim's linking technique is embedded into its clustering algorithm. That is, connections between a cluster and the correct nodes of the topology tree are made as the cluster is being constructed. In this way, AQSim avoids traversing the clusters after they are made, which in turn reduces its execution time. The main challenge for AQSim's linking algorithm is to find the best m nodes in the topology tree for a particular cluster, c, where m is much less then the number of items in c.

This chapter is organized as follows. We define the format of our scientific simulation data in Section 11.2. In Section 11.3, we present AQSim's model generator and other notable statistical model generators. Section 11.4 describes future directions. Finally, Section 11.5 summarizes the material in this chapter.

11.2. SCIENTIFIC SIMULATION DATA IN MESH FORMAT

Most scientific simulation programs generate data in *mesh* format. Mesh datasets commonly contain the following information:

1. *Zones*, which are distinct spatial elements. Interconnected grids on the x, y, and z axes in the Euclidean space generate zones. The shapes of the zones can be regular (e.g., rectilinear) or irregular (e.g., arbitrary polygons). Each zone is identified by its x, y, and z coordinates. For example, a cubic zone contains eight $\langle x, y, z \rangle$ triples, which identify its corners.

2. *Time steps*, which are discrete steps in the temporal space. Since data changes over time, it is stored at different time steps.

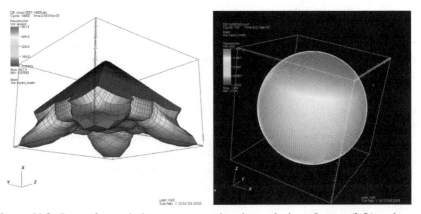

Figure 11.3. Parts of a mesh dataset representing the explosion of a star (**left**) and a star in its mid-life (**right**).

3. *Physical variables*, which denote nonspatial and nontemporal information. For each step in time, physical variables can be assigned values at a zone's corners or its center.

Figure 11.3 depicts two mesh datasets produced by astrophysics simulations. The first simulation represents the explosion of a star. The second simulation depicts the interactions of the various components of a star at its mid-life. AQSim operates on scientific simulation data in mesh format.

The three major factors determining the size of a mesh dataset are its number of zones, time steps, and physical variables (Abdulla et al., 2003). Musick and Critchlow (1999) provide a nice introduction to scientific mesh data.

11.3. STATISTICAL MODEL GENERATORS FOR SCIENTIFIC DATA

This section presents three different approaches used in AQSim's model generator and briefly describes several other notable statistical model generators.

11.3.1. AQSim's Model Generator

AQSim's model generator builds statistical summaries of mesh data for description. To achieve this, the original dataset is systematically partitioned (by utilizing a top-down approach) or agglomerated (by utilizing a bottom-up approach). The partitions/agglomerations divide the data in the spatiotemporal region. Then, statistical models of the data are either built on top of the partitions/agglomerations or independently constructed and subsequently associated with each agglomeration. This subsection describes three of AQSim's model generation strategies: (i) top-down partitioning with univariate modelers, (ii) bottom-up agglomeration with a univariate modeler, and (iii) bottom-up agglomeration with a multivariate modeler.

Top-Down Partitioning with Univariate Modelers. AQSim's top-down partitioning algorithm employs a four-way octree-like partitioning on the spatiotemporal space (see Figure 11.4). In particular, a four-way bisection on the x, y, z, and *time* dimensions repeatedly subpartitions the data. The major advantage of this algorithm is the generation of a global decomposition of the data. However, this global partitioning comes with several drawbacks. First, it is computationally too expensive to scale to terabyte datasets. This is largely due to its need to convert a mesh data file from its original simulation-specific format into a consistent vector-based representation. Second, it is not able to capture a mesh dataset's topology, which stores the connectivity relationships between the zones. Third, this approach is closely coupled with the models chosen to represent the data in each partition. In particular, this algorithm repeatedly divides the data until the *a priori*-defined model error for a partition falls below a user-specified threshold (Eliassi-Rad et al., 2002). Thus, the bisection procedure works best

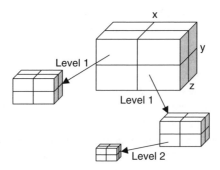

Figure 11.4. Top-down partitioning of data at a particular time step.

when there is a uniform density throughout the whole problem domain. Despite these shortcomings, our empirical evaluations illustrate the value of this simple partitioning when combined with either the mean modeler or the goodness-of-fit modeler.

Mean Modeler.   Each top-down partition of the data has a set of variables associated with it. For each variable v_i, the mean modeler is μ_i, where μ_i is the mean of the data points associated with v_i in partition p_k.

For the mean modeler, partitioning of the data stops when either one of the following two conditions is true:

1. $\forall v \in NonPartitioningVariables$ in node η, $\sigma_v = 0$.
2. $\forall v \in NonPartitioningVariables$ in node η, $(\mu_v - (c \times \sigma_v) \leq min_v)$ & $(max_v \leq \mu_v + (c \times \sigma_v))$.

The first stopping criterion represents the simple case of partitions with either 1 data point or a set of data points with standard deviation of zero. In the second stopping criterion, the partition threshold, c, is a real number greater than or equal to zero. This user-defined threshold is a scaling factor for the standard deviation of variable v. For example, $c = 1$ means that the minimum and maximum values for each nonpartitioning variable must be within 1 standard deviation of the mean of the data points in the node.

Since the *true mean* (which is an unbiased estimator) is used as the model, standard deviation is the same as *RMSE* (root mean square error) (Devore, 1991). We use each variable's RMSE to represent the error associated with the variable's model. Consequently, c can be thought of as regulating the relative error allowed in each variable's model. The advantage of the above stopping criteria is that they do not assume any distribution on the data points.

Goodness-of-Fit Modeler.   For each variable v_i in partition p_k, the goodness-of-modeler is $N(\mu_i, \sigma_i)$. That is, the model for v_i is a normal distribution with mean, μ_i, and standard deviation, σ_i.

For the goodness-of-fit modeler, partitioning stops when the hypothesis test for normality is not rejected. For our goodness-of-fit test, we use the *Anderson–Darling test for normality*, which is considered to be the most powerful goodness-of-fit test for normality (D'Agostino and Stephens, 1986).

The Anderson–Darling test involves calculating the A^2 *metric* for variable $v_i \sim N(\mu_i, \sigma_i)$, which is defined to be

$$A^2 = -\frac{1}{n}\left(\sum_{j=1}^{n}(2j-1)(\ln(z_j) + \ln(1 - z_{n+1-j}))\right) - n$$

where n = number of data points for v_i and $z_j = \Phi(\frac{x_j - \mu_i}{\sigma_i})$. $\Phi(\cdot)$ is the standard normal distribution function. We reject H_0 if $A^2\left(1 + \frac{0.75}{n} + \frac{2.25}{n^2}\right)$ exceeds the *critical value* associated with the user-specified error threshold (D'Agostino and Stephens, 1986). Otherwise, we accept H_0.

For each variable v_i, the error on this model is defined to be $Pr(reject\ H_0 | H_0\ is\ true)$, where H_0 is the null hypothesis and states that the distribution of the variable v_i is normal. In other words, the model error is equal to the Type I error (Devore, 1991).

Experiments with AQSim's Univariate Modelers. AQSim's univariate modelers were used to build statistical models of a star in its mid-life. The dataset, called *Djehuty-5*, has 18 variables, 16 time steps, and 1,625,000 zones. The variables associated with this dataset are: time, x axis, y axis, z axis, distance, grid vertex values, grid movement along the x and y axes, d(energy)/d(temperature), density, electron temperature, temperature due to radiation, pressure, artificial viscosity, material temperature, and material velocity along the x, y, and z axes. Figure 11.5a depicts this dataset in its first time step when all the 1,625,000 zones are plotted.

Table 11.1 lists the compression results on Djehuty-5 for the mean modeler. Recall that the partition threshold for this modeler restricts the difference between

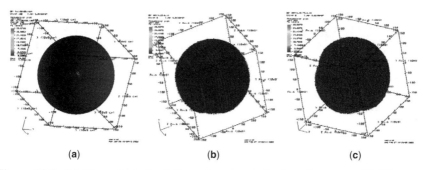

(a)   (b)   (c)

Figure 11.5. (a) The actual simulation of a star at its first time step. (b) The mean modeler's representation of the first time step with partition threshold of 3.00. (c) The goodness-of-fit modeler's representation of the first time step with partition threshold of 99.99%.

TABLE 11.1. Mean Modelers' Compression Results on the Djehuty-5

Partition Threshold	% of Compression	Total Number of Partitions	% of Nonleaf Partitions	% of Leaf Partitions	Average Number Data Point in a Partition
1.75	67.4	728,081	17.9	82.1	2.9
2.00	70.1	511,395	17.8	82.2	4.1
2.25	79.7	347,471	17.7	82.3	6.0
2.50	85.8	242,840	18.7	81.3	8.7
2.75	89.6	177,448	19.0	81.0	11.9
3.00	92.1	135,548	17.8	82.2	15.3

TABLE 11.2. Goodness-of-Fit Modeler's Compression Results on Djehuty-5

% Partition Threshold	% Compression	Total Number of Partitions	% of Nonleaf Partitions	% Leaf Partitions	Average Number of Data Point in a Partition
80.0	66.7	564,718	16.8	83.2	3.6
85.0	71.2	492,029	16.7	83.3	4.2
90.0	76.4	404,136	16.9	83.1	5.1
95.0	82.8	293,585	16.8	83.2	7.0
99.99	94.3	97,819	13.3	86.7	20.2

the minimum and maximum values of a variable and its mean value with respect to RMSE.

For AQSim's mean modeler experiments, Figure 11.5b shows Djehuty-5 at its first time step when the query *time > 0* is posed with no constraint on execution time and with partition threshold of 3.00. As expected, we get better compression as the partition threshold for the mean modeler increases since we are allowing the range of values for a variable to also increase. However, as you see in Figure 11.5b, even with 92.1% compression, we are able to return a highly precise answer.

Table 11.2 lists the compression results on Djehuty-5 for the goodness-of-fit modeler. Recall that the partition threshold in this table represents the confidence region of our normality test, which is equal to $100 \times (1 - $ Type I error$)$.

For our goodness-of-fit modeler experiments, Figure 11.5c shows Djehuty-5 at its first time step when the query *time > 0* is posed with no constraint on execution time and with partition threshold of 99.99%. Again not surprisingly, we get better compression as the partition threshold for the goodness-of-fit modeler increases since the confidence region shrinks. However, as you see in Figure 11.5c, even with 94.3% compression, we are able to return a highly precise answer.

Our experimental results illustrate the value of using simple statistical modeling techniques on scientific simulation datasets. Both of our approaches require only one sweep of the data and generate models that compress the data up to 94%.

The goodness-of-fit modeler performed better than the mean modeler on Djehuty-5. This is not surprising since Djehuty-5 describes a physical phenomenon and the goodness-of-fit modeler is biased toward such normally distributed datasets. In general, we prefer the mean modeler since it makes no assumptions on the dataset.

Bottom-Up Agglomeration with a Univariate Modeler. AQSim's bottom-up partitioning algorithm overcomes the aforementioned shortcomings of the top-down approach by utilizing the intrinsic topology of the data given in the original scientific problem. The topology of a mesh data is the (true physical) connectivity information of its zones. For AQSim's bottom-up algorithm, we remove the time dimension from the partitioning space and redefine our partitions on the three-dimensional spatial structure of the data. This new partition space allows us to produce agglomerations that can easily be parallelized for data access.

AQSim's bottom-up algorithm starts at the mesh data's initial grid configuration (i.e., at the zones). From this fine level collection of grid cells, it iteratively produces *coarse* level collections of cells (see Figure 11.6). In particular, it uses a two-pass approach. In the first pass, each coarse cell is assigned the "best" neighborhood configuration (with respect to its rectilinear cell shape). This operation is a local search on the 2^N possible neighborhood configurations of a coarse cell, where N is the number of dimensions. For instance, in two dimensions, the gray boxes in Figure 11.7 denote the four possible locations for a given cell within a coarse agglomeration.

Figure 11.8 illustrates the first step in the agglomeration of a collection of fine cells. The first pass of the bottom-up algorithm starts at fine cell [#]1 and agglomerates the fine cells 1, 2, 5, and 6 into coarse cell *C1*. Then, it investigates the neighborhood configuration around fine cell 3 (which is the next unassigned fine cell) and builds coarse cell *C2* from fine cells 3, 4, 7, and 8. Finally, it

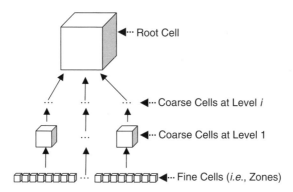

Figure 11.6. AQSim's bottom-up algorithm generates a *topology tree*.

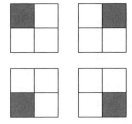

Figure 11.7. Four possible locations for a cell within a coarse agglomeration in two dimensions.

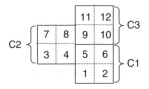

Figure 11.8. A non-quad tree coarse cell arrangement.

explores the neighborhood configuration around fine cell [#]9 and groups fine cells 9, 10, 11, and 12 into coarse cell $C3$.

The first pass of the bottom-up algorithm is a local operation on cells. That is, when creating coarse cells from fine cells, no information about the past and/or future agglomerations in other regions are taken into consideration. For this reason, some coarse agglomerations can result in trees that are non-binary, non-quad, or non-octree. For instance, it is easy to be in a situation where the coarse cells are arranged as shown in Figure 11.8 after the first pass.

The coarse cells ($C1$, $C2$, and $C3$ given by solid lines) have been arranged in such a way that indeterminate behavior for neighbors exists for the coarse cells. For example, $C2$ has two neighbors to its right. A second pass corrects such structural problems associated with indeterminate behavior for neighbors of coarse cells. In particular, the second pass has N-dimensional subphases. Each subphase, s, uses information from all the previous subphases to correctly place the $(N - s)$-dimensional structures, planes, lines, and points. Conceptually, this corresponds to sliding the coarse cells so they line up nicely. It is important to note that the second pass only adjusts each coarse cell's neighbor relations (if needed). For example, in two dimensions, the problem illustrated in Figure 11.8 can be fixed by (i) adjusting the face neighbors so that cell $C2$ "slides" down half of a coarse grid cell and (ii) making sure the neighbors for all local coarse cells reflect this slide (see Figure 11.9). The $C1$, $C2$, and $C3$ cells can then be combined at the next level in the agglomeration to form the coarse cell $C4$ (which in this case is also the root of the topology tree).

A heuristically complex procedure is used to compute the corrections in the bottom-up algorithm's second pass. Our correction procedure utilizes the information about the (faces, edges, and corners of) neighbors of the coarse

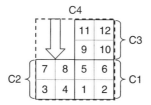

Figure 11.9. A fix for a non-quad tree coarse cell arrangements.

cells' descendants to establish neighbors at the coarse level. For instance, to find the neighbors for $C2$ (shown in Figure 11.8), we utilize the information for neighbors of fine cells 1, 2, 5, 6, 9, 10, 11, and 12.

After the topology tree is constructed, the statistical information associated with the mean modeler is propagated upwards through each level of the tree. The information about the number of data points (n), minimum (min), and maximum (max) values of the data points are calculated as follows:

$$n = \sum_i n_i, \qquad min = \min_i(min_i), \qquad max = \max_i(max_i)$$

When calculating the mean and standard deviation values, we do not use the number of data points, instead we rely on the volume of the coarse cell and its associated fine cells. The volume of a cell is the amount of nonempty space that it occupies in the three-dimensional Euclidean space. By making this switch, we are able to avoid any assumptions about the distribution of the data in the fine cells. Therefore, the probability (or weight) of each fine cell's mean and standard deviation measure is based on vol_i/vol, where $vol = \sum_i vol_i$. Thus, the mean (μ) and standard deviation (σ) of a coarse cell are calculated by using the following equations:

$$\mu = \frac{\sum_i(\mu_i \times vol_i)}{vol}, \qquad \sigma = \sqrt{\frac{\sum_i((\sigma_i^2 + \mu_i^2) \times vol_i)}{vol} - \mu^2}$$

Note that by using the sum of the volumes of the fine cells, we do not inflate the coarse cell's volume artificially in cases where the coarse cell is not "full" (e.g., $C4$ in Figure 11.9).

Bottom-Up Agglomeration with a Multivariate Modeler. In this section we continue utilizing the bottom-up agglomeration algorithm of the previous section but switch from a univariate modeler to a multivariate one. Our motivation for using a multivariate modeling algorithm is to capture the interrelationships among a mesh dataset's physical variables in one metric.* In this way, we are able to collectively measure the similarity between zones.

---

*Recall that physical variables are all variables except the spatial (i.e., x, y, z) and temporal (i.e., *time*) variables.

TABLE 11.3. AQSim's Multivariate Clustering Algorithm

Inputs

- List of zones
- User-defined clustering threshold $u \in [0, 1]$, where 0 and 1 indicate complete dissimilarity and similarity, respectively.

Output

- A list of clusters

Assumptions

- A zone is either **GREEN** (i.e., available for clustering) or **RED** (i.e., already included in a cluster).
- Initially, the colors of all zones are **GREEN**.

Algorithm

For each zone, z, do
  If ($z.color \equiv$ **GREEN**) then

    (a) $C = $ new Cluster();

    (b) Add z to C;

    (c) $C.stats = z.stats$; /*$z.stats$ contains z's $\vec{\mu}, \vec{\sigma}, \overrightarrow{max}$, and $\overrightarrow{min}$. */

    (d) $z.color = $ **RED**;

    (e) For each zone, z', do
        If ($z'.color \equiv$ **GREEN**) and ($CosSim(z, z') \geq f(u)$) then

        1. Add z' to C;

        2. Update $C.stats$;

        3. $z'.color = $ **RED**;

    (f) Add C to the list of clusters;

Table 11.3 describes AQSim's multivariate clustering algorithm. The inputs to our algorithm are (i) the list of zones in the mesh dataset and (ii) a user-defined clustering threshold in [0,1]. A clustering threshold of 0 indicates complete dissimilarity between zones. On the other hand, a clustering threshold of 1 shows total similarity among zones. The output of our algorithm is a list of clusters, where each cluster is represented by its (zonal) population, N, and the following four vectors:

$$\vec{\mu} = \begin{pmatrix} \mu_1 \\ \mu_2 \\ \ldots \\ \mu_m \end{pmatrix}, \quad \vec{\sigma} = \begin{pmatrix} \sigma_1 \\ \sigma_2 \\ \ldots \\ \sigma_m \end{pmatrix}, \quad \overrightarrow{max} = \begin{pmatrix} max_1 \\ max_2 \\ \ldots \\ max_m \end{pmatrix}, \quad \overrightarrow{min} = \begin{pmatrix} min_1 \\ min_2 \\ \ldots \\ min_m \end{pmatrix}$$

$\vec{\mu}, \vec{\sigma}, \overrightarrow{max}$, and $\overrightarrow{min}$ are the mean, standard deviation, maximum, and minimum values of the zones represented in a cluster. The variable m is the number of physical variables in the mesh dataset.

Initially, we assume that all zones are available for clustering (i.e., they are assigned the color **GREEN**). Then, as each zone is placed in an appropriate cluster, it becomes unavailable (i.e., its color changes from **GREEN** to **RED**). Our clustering algorithm iterates over all **GREEN** zones. At each iteration, a variant of the cosine similarity measure (Van Rijsbergen, 1979; Hilderman and Hamilton, 2001) is used to find an appropriate cluster for each **GREEN** zone.

The standard cosine similarity measure is a function of two vectors $\vec{\alpha}$ and $\vec{\beta}$ of equal length. In particular, it is defined as follows:

$$CosSim(\vec{\alpha}, \vec{\beta}) = \begin{cases} \cos(\vec{\alpha}, \vec{\beta}) = \dfrac{\vec{\alpha} \cdot \vec{\beta}}{\|\vec{\alpha}\|_2 \times \|\vec{\beta}\|_2}, & \text{if } \vec{\alpha} \neq 0 \text{ and } \vec{\beta} \neq 0 \\ 1, & \text{if } \vec{\alpha} = \vec{\beta} \\ 0, & \text{if } (\vec{\alpha} = 0 \ \& \ \vec{\beta} \neq 0) \text{ or } (\vec{\alpha} \neq 0 \ \& \ \vec{\beta} = 0) \end{cases}$$

AQSim utilizes the aforementioned *CosSim* metric by representing a zone's physical data points as a vector. In particular, such a vector contains the mean values of a zone's physical variables. For example, if a mesh dataset contains only two physical variables (say *temperature* and *pressure*), then each zone is represented by a vector of two elements (namely, one value for temperature and another for pressure). AQSim's *CosSim* normalizes the elements of its vectors such that all the values of physical variables are between 0 and 1. This normalization step is important since the ranges of values for our physical variables differ considerably.

Suppose, the vectors $\vec{\alpha}$, $\vec{\beta}$, and $\vec{\gamma}$ represent normalized mean values of physical variables for three zones in a mesh dataset. Traditionally, when $CosSim(\vec{\alpha}, \vec{\beta})$ is greater than or equal to the user-defined similarity threshold, $\vec{\alpha}$ and $\vec{\beta}$ are placed into one cluster. Then, a new vector, $\vec{\gamma}$, is placed in the same cluster as $\vec{\alpha}$ and $\vec{\beta}$ only if both of the following inequalities are true:

$$CosSim(\vec{\alpha}, \vec{\gamma}) \geq user\_threshold \text{ and } CosSim(\vec{\gamma}, \vec{\beta}) \geq user\_threshold$$

Since we have a huge number of zones to process, calculations of all pairwise *CosSim* measures can be quite burdensome. Furthermore, sampling from the mesh data is not an option since scientists are interested in outliers and do not tolerate results from sampled data. However, by increasing the similarity threshold, we are able to eliminate the need to compute all the pairwise comparisons—that is, if we increase the user-defined similarity threshold by using the following function:

$$f(u) = \cos\left(\frac{\cos^{-1}((2 \times u) - 1)}{2}\right)$$

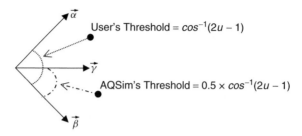

Figure 11.10. User-defined threshold and AQSim's threshold.

where u is the user-defined similarity threshold.* The function $f(u)$ returns the *cosine* of an angle that is equal to half the angle of the user-defined similarity threshold. Based on the geometrical properties of the *cosine* function, we obtain the following inequality: $((2 \times u) - 1) < f(u)$.† Thus, if we encounter a zone with vector $\vec{\beta}$ and $f(u) \leq CosSim(\vec{\alpha}, \vec{\beta})$ for any $\vec{\alpha}$ in a cluster C, then it must be the case that $CosSim(\vec{\alpha}, \vec{\beta}) \geq f(u)$ for all $\vec{\alpha}$ in cluster C. In other words, we are guaranteed that any new zone added to a cluster, C, satisfies the user-defined similarity measure. Figure 11.10 pictorially illustrates this fact. Based on the user's threshold, any two vectors $\vec{\alpha}$ and $\vec{\beta}$ are considered similar if and only if the cosine of the angle between $\vec{\alpha}$ and $\vec{\beta}$ is greater than or equal to $f(u)$. In our clustering algorithm, if there exists some cluster C with a vector $\vec{\gamma}$ and the angle between $\vec{\gamma}$ and any vector $\vec{\beta}$ is half the size of the angle between $\vec{\alpha}$ and $\vec{\beta}$, then $\vec{\beta}$ is safely added to the cluster C (without any additional pairwise comparisons). In other words, for each cluster C, we only need to compute the *CosSim* metric for an unassigned (**GREEN**) zone and the first zone added to C.

Increasing the user-defined similarity threshold helps us in two ways. First, we do not spend time on pairwise comparisons. Second, we do not need to shuffle zones between clusters since our bound, $f(u)$, eliminates zones that are on the cluster boundaries. In the best case, our clustering algorithm runs in $O(n)$ time, where n is the number of zones in the mesh datasets. In the worst case, our algorithm runs in $O(n^2)$ time. However, on average, our algorithm runs in $O(n \times g(f(u)))$ times, where $g(f(u))$ is the number of zones that satisfy the $f(u)$ bound. Eliassi-Rad and Critchlow (2003) empirically showed that on average $g(f(u))$ is much less than n.

Even though spatial variables do not play a role in building clusters in AQSim's multivariate clusterer, it is desirable to associate each cluster with its correct spatial region. In particular, it is important for the multivariate clusterer to return answers to scientists' queries in the spatial region of the original mesh. Since our mesh datasets have millions of zones, it would be very inefficient (and at times impossible) to link each cluster with all of its zones. Therefore, we present a linking algorithm for connecting each cluster to a small set (e.g., 512) of nodes

---

*The original user-defined threshold is mapped from [0,1] to [−1, 1] by the equation $((2 \times u) - 1)$.
†The *cosine* of any angle g is always less than the *cosine* of the angle $g/2$.

in the dataset's *topology tree* (constructed using the algorithm in the previous subsection, entitled "Bottom-Up Agglomeration with a Univariate Modeler"). Recall that a topology tree stores the spatial information of a dataset by utilizing the intrinsic topology of the data given in the original scientific problem (see Figure 11.6).

Figure 11.11 shows sample links between the list of clusters and the topology tree. Our linking technique is embedded into the multivariate clustering algorithm. That is, connections between a cluster and the correct nodes of the topology tree are made as the cluster is being constructed. In this way, we are able to avoid traversing the clusters after they are made, which in turn reduces our execution times. The main challenge for our linking algorithm is to find the "best" k nodes in the topology tree for a particular cluster, C, where k (e.g., 512) is much less than the number of zones in C (which typically range in the thousands).

Table 11.4 describes the multivariate clusterer's linking algorithm. When the list of links for a cluster is full, we traverse the topology and the list of links to find the lowest-level topology node with the most number of descendants in the list of links. Each link between a cluster and a tree node has a metric, called *percentage_intersection*, which measures the percentage intersection between the zones in the clusters and the descendants of a node. For example, if a zone, z, is in cluster C and the list of links for C has a link connected to z, then that link's *percentage_intersection* is 100. This *percentage_intersection* metric measures the "quality" of a link. A threshold can be placed on the *percentage_intersection* metric so that the trade-off between execution time and links to the best-fitting nodes can be exploited. As we will show in the next section, our linking algorithm

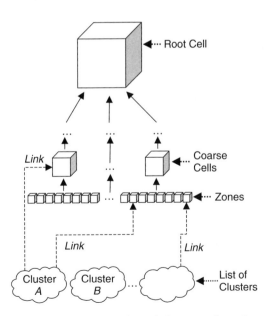

Figure 11.11. Links among lists of clusters and topology tree.

TABLE 11.4. AQSim's Linking Algorithm

Input

- *links* = list of links for cluster, *C*
- *z* = zone being added to *C*

Output

- An updated *links* list

Algorithm

If (*links* is not full) then

- *z*.*percentage_intersection* = 100;
- Add *z* to *links*;
- Return *links*;

Else

- For *l* = 0 (leaf level) to *r* (root level), do
  /* *z.ancestor*[*l*] is *z*'s ancestor at *l*. */ If (*z.ancestor*[*l*] is in *links*) then
    (a) Update *z.ancestor*[*l*]. *percentage_intersection*;
    (b) Return *links*;

- *new_link* = NULL;
- For each link, *j*, in *links*, do
  /* *best_ancestor*[*j*] is *j*'s ancestor with the most number of descendents in *links*. */
  If (*best_ancestor*[*j*].*num_descendants* ≡ MAX_NUM_DESCENDANTS), then
    (a) *new_link* = *best_ancestor*[*j*];
    (b) break;

- If (*new_link* ≡ NULL) then *new_link* = argmax$_{j \in links}$ *best_ancestor*[*j*];
- Clear all descendants of *new_link* from *links*;
- Set *new_link.percentage_intersection*;
- Add *new_link* to *links*;
- *z*.*percentage_intersection* = 100;
- Add *z* to *links*;
- Return *links*;

---

performs quite well. This is mainly due to the very small number of levels in a topology tree (usually less than 20).

Experiments with AQSim's Multivariate Modeler.   Table 11.5 describes the two mesh datasets used in the experiments on AQSim's multivariate modeler. Both datasets are a simulation of a star at a certain stage of its life and represent readings in point locations of a continuous medium. The datasets use cubic zones (with eight vertices each). Values of variables are associated either with each vertex or with the center of each zone. The White Dwarf dataset (see Figure 11.12a)

TABLE 11.5. Characteristics of Our Two Astrophysics Datasets

Dataset	Size (in GB)	Number of Zones	Number of Variables	Number of Time Steps
White Dwarf	3	557,375	20	22
Djehuty-5	5	1,625,000	18	16

is a simulation of a star exploding. The Djehuty-5 dataset (see Figure 11.12b) is a simulation of a star at its mid-life.

Our experiments describe the performance of AQSim's multivariate clusterer with and without the linking algorithm on the aforementioned two simulation datasets. We also compare these performances to the bottom-up agglomeration algorithm, where the statistical information of the physical variables is propagated upwards in the tree (see earlier subsection entitled "Bottom-Up Agglomeration with a Univariate Modeler").

Figure 11.13 shows the number of clusters constructed *per time step* for White Dwarf. The user-defined clustering threshold for the blue and pink lines are 0.95 (in [0,1]) and 0.99 (in [0,1]), respectively. An intuitive way of thinking about the user-defined clustering threshold is to state that the user requires all zones in a cluster to be ($user\_threshold \times 100$) percent similar. So, when $user\_threshold$ is 0.95, the required similarity between zones in a cluster is 95%. AQSim's threshold tightens the 95% and 99% similarities among the zones in a cluster to 98.5% and 99.75% similarities, respectively.

Notice the small number of clusters that we are able to build from hundreds of thousands of zones. There is a dramatic increase in the number of cluster made for the White Dwarf dataset from time step = 0 to time step = 1 (due to the start of explosion in the star). Tables 11.6 and 11.7 summarize the minimum, average, and maximum number of clusters and execution times for White Dwarf with the given clustering thresholds, respectively. As expected, the execution times are also longer with the bound of 99.75% similarity as opposed to a bound of 98.5% similarity.

Figure 11.14 shows the number of clusters constructed per time step for Djehuty-5. Similar to experiments on White Dwarf, the user-defined clustering threshold for the blue and pink lines are 95% and 99%, respectively. Again, AQSim's threshold tightens the 95% and 99% similarities among the zones in a cluster to 98.5% and 99.75% similarities, respectively.

Notice again the small number of clusters that we are able to build from more than 1.6 million zones. Tables 11.8 and 11.9 summarize the minimum, average, and maximum number of clusters and execution times for Djehuty-5 with the given clustering thresholds, respectively. Again, as expected, the execution times are also longer with the bound of 99.75% similarity as opposed to a bound of 98.5% similarity.

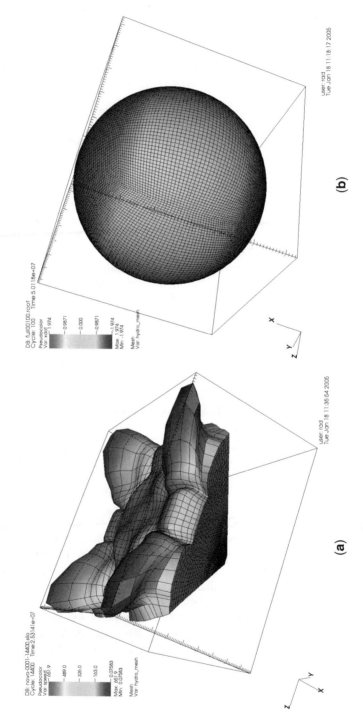

Figure 11.12. (a) White-Dwarf dataset and (b) Djehuty-5 dataset.

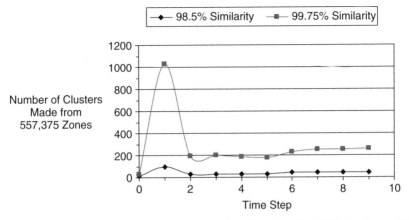

Figure 11.13. Number of clusters made for White Dwarf with AQSim's threshold of 98.5% and 99.75%.

TABLE 11.6. Clustering on White Dwarf
(*user_threshold* = 95% and $f(u)$ = 98.5%)

	Min	Avg	Max
Number of clusters Made from 557,375 zones	13	39.14	98
Execution time without linking in seconds	78.48	138.94	204.79

TABLE 11.7. Clustering on White Dwarf
(*user_threshold* = 99% and $f(u)$ = 99.75%)

	Min	Avg	Max
Number of clusters made from 557,375 zones	28	281.3	1029
Execution time without linking in seconds	94.10	1568.62	4727.93

Tables 11.10 and 11.11 show the execution times of multivariate clusterer with and without linking on the first six time steps of White Dwarf and Djehuty-5, respectively. In addition, they list the best and worst quality of links made between clusters and the topology tree. As expected, it takes longer to build clusters <u>and</u> connect them to the topology tree. However, the most increase is by

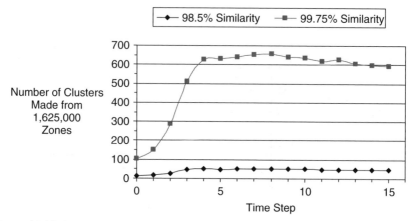

Figure 11.14. Number of clusters made for Djehuty-5 with AQSim's threshold of 98.5% and 99.75%.

TABLE 11.8. Clustering on Djehuty-5
(*user_threshold* = 95% and $f(u) = 98.5\%$)

	Min	Avg	Max
Number of clusters made from 1,625,000 zones	14	43.56	53
Execution time without linking in seconds	519.78	579.40	800.39

TABLE 11.9. Clustering on Djehuty-5 (*user_threshold* = 99% and $f(u) = 99.75\%$)

	Min	Avg	Max
Number of clusters made from 1,625,000 Zones	101	536.20	657
Execution time without linking in seconds	939.44	4787.21	11,319.7

a factor of 5.6 (see time step = 0 in Table 11.10). Both the White Dwarf and the Djehuty-5 topology trees have a maximum of 11 levels. The highest level in the tree reached for a connection between a cluster and a node is 4 and 5 for White Dwarf and Djehuty-5, respectively. This is quite good since a link accessing a high level in the tree usually has a worse fit (i.e., *percentage_intersection*) as

TABLE 11.10. Clustering on White Dwarf (*user_threshold* = 99% and *f(u)* = 99.75%)

Time Step	Execution Time Without Linking in Seconds	Execution Time With Linking in Seconds
0	94.10	867.24
1	1259.80	1489.42
2	622.99	763.51
3	361.91	712.41
4	323.89	672.48
5	384.50	753.06
Max Level Reached in Topology Tree	Max Level Reached with Linking	Min and Max % intersection at Max Level
11	4	Min = 25% and Max = 100%

TABLE 11.11. Clustering on Djehuty-5 (*user_threshold* = 99% and *f(u)* = 99.75%)

Time Step	Execution Time Without Linking in Seconds	Execution Time With Linking in Seconds
0	939.44	2467.04
1	1148.61	2569.44
2	1650.27	2926.92
3	2288.11	3524.46
4	3382.61	4828.16
5	4047.15	5597.04
Max Level in Topology Tree	Max Level Reached with Linking	Min and Max % intersection at Max Level
11	5	Min = 12.5% and Max = 100%

compared to a link connecting to a lower level in the tree. Even so, in both datasets, the maximum *percentage_intersection* at the highest level is 100% for both datasets. That is, for the Djehuty-5 dataset, there are nodes at level 5 which contain all the zones in a cluster. The minimum *percentage_intersection* at the highest level is 25% and 12.5% for White Dwarf and Djehuty-5, respectively. This minimum *percentage_intersection* value shows the quality of the worst links. For example, in the Djehuty-5 dataset, there are nodes at level 5 which contain only 12.5% of the zones in a cluster.

TABLE 11.12. Execution Times for Our Multivariate Clustering Algorithm (without Linking) and Average Value for $g(f(u))$

Dataset	User Threshold	Avg $O(n)$ in Seconds	Avg $O(n \times g(f(u)))$ in Seconds	Avg $g(f(u))$
White Dwarf	95%	232.32	732.09	3.15
White Dwarf	99%	281.33	2179.6	7.75
Djehuty-5	95%	351.22	1249.6	3.56
Djehuty-5	99%	763.91	1587.1	2.08

TABLE 11.13. Average Distortion Within Clusters

Dataset	User Threshold	Average d in $(\vec{\mu}_c - d \times \vec{\sigma}_c) = \overrightarrow{min}_c$ and $\overrightarrow{max}_c = (\vec{\mu}_c + d \times \vec{\sigma}_c)$
White Dwarf	95%	2.96
White Dwarf	99%	2.39
Djehuty-5	95%	2.79
Djehuty-5	99%	2.48

Table 11.12 illustrates the execution times of AQSim's multivariate clusterer (without linking). As was expected, the average value of $g(f(u))$, which is the number of zones satisfying our threshold $f(u)$, is much less than n (the total number of zones). In fact, the average $g(f(u))$ is in single digits while the average n is in hundreds of thousands.

Table 11.13 depicts average distortion within the clusters that were made for White Dwarf and Djehuty-5. This average distortion measures the diversity within the clusters. For each cluster c with mean $\vec{\mu}_c$, standard deviation $\vec{\sigma}_c$, maximum $\overrightarrow{max}_c$, and minimum $\overrightarrow{min}_c$, the distortion within clusters is computed by finding the value for d in these two equations: $(\vec{\mu}_c - d \times \vec{\sigma}_c) = \overrightarrow{min}_c$ and $\overrightarrow{max}_c = (\vec{\mu}_c + d \times \vec{\sigma}_c)$. The average distortion is then computed by taking the average of the d values for all physical variables in the mesh data. When an average d is equal to 3.0, it implies that on average the minimum and maximum values within a cluster are three standard of deviations away from its mean. As we showed in an earlier subsection entitled "Experiments with AQSim's Univariate Modelers," AQSim is able to produce excellent results within this range. As expected, the distortion within clusters decreases as the similarity threshold increases.

Tables 11.14 and 11.15 compare the multivariate clusterer with linking to the bottom-up agglomeration algorithm with the mean modeler. The number of nodes made by the bottom-up agglomeration algorithm (in one level) is much larger than the number of clusters made by our clustering algorithm. This is mostly due to the design of the bottom-up agglomeration algorithm, which combines no more than eight zones at a time. This strategy of agglomerating only a small number

TABLE 11.14. White Dwarf Dataset: Comparison of Multivariate Clusterer (with Linking) Versus the Bottom-Up Agglomeration (with Mean Modeler)

Data Set = White Dwarf Time Step = 0 User Threshold = 99%	Execution Time in Seconds	Number of Agglomerations Made from 557,375 Zones
Bottom-up agglomeration algorithm with mean modeler	753.44	73924
Multivariate clusterer with linking	867.24	28

TABLE 11.15. Djehuty-5 Dataset: Comparison of Multivariate Clusterer (with Linking) Versus the Bottom-Up Agglomeration (with Mean Modeler)

Data Set = Djehuty-5 Time Step = 0 User Threshold = 99%	Execution Time in Seconds	Number of Agglomerations Made from 1,625,000 Zones
Bottom-up agglomeration with mean modeler	946.57	203,125
Multivariate clusterer with linking	2467.04	101

of zones based solely on their topology also makes the bottom-up agglomeration algorithm run faster than our clustering algorithm.

11.3.2. Other Model Generators

AQUA (Acharya et al., 1999) is an approximate query answering system. It uses cached statistical summary of the data in *on-line analytical processing* (a.k.a. OLAP) applications. Unfortunately, AQUA uses sampling and histogram techniques to compute summaries of the data. Such techniques are not desirable for scientific datasets because by sampling you might miss outliers (which are important in scientific simulation datasets).[*] Moreover, histograms are computationally expensive on high-dimensional data.

STING (Wang et al., 1997) is also similar to AQSim in that it builds a grid cell hierarchy and then propagates the data upwards in the hierarchy. However, STING assumes that the underlying distribution of the data is known. In most scientific phenomena, this assumption does not hold. In addition, STING has only been tested on small datasets containing only tens of thousands of data points.

Freitag and Loy (1999) describe an approach similar to AQSim for visualization of large scientific data sets. Their system builds distributed octrees from large scientific datasets. Unlike AQSim, they reduce the data points by constraining the physical data values to their spatial locations. In addition, they do not

---

[*] AQSim's statistical modelers capture outliers by not sampling and allowing users to specify error bounds on the models' descriptive statistics.

allow the user to query the octree; instead, the user can view the tree at different resolutions.

DuMouchel et al. (1999) present a method for compressing flat files. However, they use binning techniques to "squash" files, which impose an *a priori* distribution on the data. For large-scale scientific datasets, it is not desirable to use binning techniques since *a priori* distribution on the data is unknown. Also, most simulation data are not stored in flat files, and their conversion can be computationally burdensome (see earlier section entitled "Top-Down Partioning with Univariate Modelers").

Clustering algorithm such as BIRCH (Zhang et al., 1996), CHAMELEON (Karypis et al., 1999), CLARANS [16], CLIQUE (Agrawal et al., 1998), CURE (Guha et al., 1998), and DBSCAN (Ester et al., 1996) cannot be used or scaled to large-scale simulation datasets for one or more of the following reasons:

1. They employ sampling techniques. Scientists already sample the data produced by their simulation programs. They do not accept models that sample the sampled data, particularly since they are mostly interested in outliers.

2. They initially divide the data in subspaces and then build clusters locally on those subspaces. Such strategies are not desirable for clusters, which are supposed to capture the global properties of the simulation data.

3. They utilize some kind of binning or histogram techniques, which can be computationally expensive on high-dimensional data sets. In addition, it is unrealistic to assume an *a priori* distribution on large-scale simulation datasets.

As for partitioning and agglomeration techniques, spatial data structures have been utilized in the database and visualization communities (Adelson-Velskii and Landis, 1962; Cormen et al., 1989; Friedman et al., 1977). The database community uses these structures to build efficient indexing algorithms for query processing. The visualization community uses them for adaptive mesh refinement and fast graphics display.

Samet (1989a, 1995) describes a method for using quad-trees and octrees to index objects in two- and three-dimensional spaces. His approach involves (i) laying an artificial grid on top of the data, (ii) splitting the background grid with a top-down methodology, and (iii) establishing spatial relations between the objects. Unlike AQSim, Samet's algorithms are not able to capture topological problems (such as singular edges) or construct trees that are independent of the data's distribution over the initial grid (Samet, 1989b).

The visualization community provides subdivision methods for surfaces and objects. Arden (2001) approximates surfaces by choosing subsets of the original points that make up a surface and "fitting" the newly constructed surface through them. This work does not address topological problems. The multigrid community has also examined issues related to grid coarsening (McCormick, 1989). However, they do not deal with topological problems as well.

11.4. FUTURE DIRECTIONS

The most desirable modelers for large-scale scientific simulation data (i) require only one sweep of data, (ii) are good at finding outliers, (iii) can be easily parallelized, and (iv) can efficiently answer complex queries.

Separating the modeling process for the spatiotemporal variables and the physical variables is an interesting approach. In particular, if the clustering algorithm is able to capture similar behavior across time steps, then a cluster hierarchy can be constructed from each time step. Subsequently, such hierarchies can speed up response times for queries on both the physical variables and the spatiotemporal variables since the cluster hierarchy will be shallower than the topology hierarchy. The success of this approach will rely on scalable algorithms that find a manageable and representative number of links from the cluster hierarchy to the topology hierarchy.

Allowing the user to specify his/her desired similarity behavior for clusters is an important step in building nongeneric clusters. In addition, tools that track particular zones as they change clusters across time steps will provide valuable insight into the scientific simulation and the similarity metric.

Scaling more intelligent partitioning algorithms such as K-d and AVL trees to massive datasets is another area for future research. In addition, efficient techniques are needed to capture the topology of mesh datasets with zones of arbitrary polygonal shapes (Bowers and Wilson, 1991).* Finally, algorithms that construct topology hierarchies with "non-octree-like" structures need further investigations.

11.5. CONCLUSIONS

Massively parallel computer programs (which simulate complex scientific phenomena) generate large-scale datasets over the spatiotemporal space. Modeling such massive datasets is an essential step in helping scientists discover new information from these computer simulations. We present several systems that build queriable statistical models. Such models help scientists gather knowledge from their large-scale simulation data. In particular, we discuss AQSim, which consists of two components: (i) the model generator and (ii) the query processor. The model generator reduces the data storage requirements by creating and storing queriable statistical models of the data at multiple resolutions. The query processor decreases the query access times by evaluating queries on the models of the data instead of on the original dataset. We describe three simple but effective statistical modeling techniques for simulation data. AQSim's univariate mean modeler computes the unbiased mean of systematic spatiotemporal partitions of the data. It makes no assumptions about the distribution of the data and uses a variant of the root mean square error to evaluate a model. AQSim's univariate

---

* Such adaptive meshes ensure that the grid better conforms to the complex shapes such as tetrahedrons.

goodness-of-fit modeler utilizes the Andersen–Darling goodness-of-fit method on systematic spatiotemporal partitions of the data. This modeler evaluates a model by how well it passes the normality test on the data. AQSim's multivariate clusterer utilizes the cosine similarity measure to cluster the physical variables in a dataset. The exclusion of the spatial location is important since "similar" characteristics could be located (spatially) far from each other. To scale AQSim's multivariate clustering algorithm for large-scale datasets, we take advantage of the geometrical properties of the cosine similarity measure. This allows AQSim to reduce the modeling time from $O(n^2)$ to $O(n \times g(f(u)))$, where n is the number of data points, $f(u)$ is a function of the user-defined clustering threshold, and $g(f(u))$ is the number of data points satisfying the threshold $f(u)$. We show that, on average, $g(f(u))$ is much less than n. Finally, even though spatial variables do not play a role in building a cluster, it is desirable to associate each cluster with its correct spatial location. To achieve this, we present a linking algorithm for connecting each cluster to the appropriate nodes in the dataset's topology tree. Our experimental analyses on two large-scale astrophysics simulation datasets illustrate the value of AQSim's model generator.

ACKNOWLEDGMENTS

This work was performed under the auspices of the U.S. Department of Energy by the University of California Lawrence Livermore National Laboratory under contract No. W-7405-ENG-48.1. UCRL-BOOK-200014. We thank Bill Arrighi, Kevin Durrenberger, Susan Hazlett, Roy Kamimura, Nu Ai Tang, and Megan Thomas for their assistance.

REFERENCES

Abdulla, G., Baldwin, C., Critchlow, T., Kamimura, R., Lozares, I., Musick, R., Tang, N. A., Lee, B., and Snapp, R., Approximate ad-hoc query engine for simulation data, in *Proceedings of the 1st ACM + IEEE Joint Conference on Digital Libraries (JCDL)*, ACM Press, New York, pp. 255–256, 2001.

Abdulla, G., Critchlow, T., and Arrighi, W., Simulation Data as Data Streams, Lawrence Livermore National Laboratory (LLNL) Technical Report, UCRL-JC-152697, 2003.

Adelson-Velskii, G. M., and Landis, E. M., An algorithm for the organization of information, *Soviet Mathematics Doklady* **3**, 1259–1262, 1962.

Acharya, S., Gibbsons, P. B., Poosala, V., and Ramaswamy, S., The Aqua approximate query answering system, in *Proceedings of the 1999 ACM SIGMOD Conference*, ACM Press, New York, pp. 574–576, 1999.

Agrawal, R., Gehrke, J., Gunopulos, D., Raghavan, P., Automatic subspace clustering of high dimensional data for data mining applications, in *Proceedings of the 1998 ACM SIGMOD Conference*, ACM Press, New York, pp. 94–105, 1998.

Arden, G., Approximation Properties of Subdivision Surfaces, Ph.D. thesis, University of Washington, Seattle, 2001.

Baldwin, C., Abdulla, G., and Critchlow, T., Multi-resolution modeling of large scale scientific simulation data, in *Proceedings of the 12th International Conference on Information and Knowledge Management*, ACM Press, New York, pp. 40–48, 2003a.

Baldwin, C., Eliassi-Rad, T., Adbulla, G., and Critchlow, T., The evolution of a hicrarchical partitioning algorithm for large-scale scientific data: Three steps of increasing complexity, in *Proceedings of the 15th International Conference on Scientific and Statistical Database Management*, IEEE Computer Society, pp. 225–228, Cambridge, MA, USA, 2003b.

Bowers, R. L., and Wilson, J. R., *Numerical Modeling in Applied Physics and Astrophysics*, Jones & Bartlett Publishers, Boston, 1991.

Chakrabarti, K., Garofalakis, M., Rastogi, R., and Shim, K., Approximate query processing using wavelets, in *Proceedings of the 26th International Conference on Very Large Data Bases*, Morgan Kaufmann, San Francisco, pp. 111–122, 2000.

Cormen, T. H., Leiserson, C. E., and Rivest, R. L., *Introduction to Algorithms*, McGraw-Hill, New York, 1989.

D'Agostino, R. B., and Stephens, M. A., *Goodness-of-Fit Techniques*, Marcel Dekker, New York, 1986.

Devore, J. L., *Probability and Statistics for Engineering and the Sciences*, 3rd edition, Brooks/Cole, Pacific Grove, CA, 1991.

DuMouchel, W., Volinsky, C., Johnson, T., Cortes, C., and Pregibon, D., Squashing flat files flatter, In *Proceedings of the 5th ACM SIGKDD International Conference on Knowledge Discovery and Data Mining*, ACM Press, New York, pp. 6–15, 1999.

Eliassi-Rad, T., and Critchlow, T., Multivariate Clustering of Large-Scale Scientific Simulation Data, Lawrence Livermore National Laboratory (LLNL) Technical Report, UCRL-JC-151860-REV-1, 2003.

Eliassi-Rad, T., Critchlow, T., and Abdulla, G., Statistical modeling of large-scale simulation data, in *Proceedings of the 8th ACM SIGKDD International Conference on Knowledge Discovery and Data Mining*, ACM Press, New York, pp. 488–494, 2002.

Ester, M., Kriegel, H.-P., Sander, J., and Xu, X., A density-based algorithm for discovering clusters in large spatial databases with noise, in *Proceedings of the 2nd International Conference on Knowledge Discovery and Data Mining*, AAAI Press, Menlo Park, CA, pp. 226–231, 1996.

Freitag, L. A., and Loy, R. M., Adaptive, multiresolution visualization of large data sets using a distributed memory octree, in *Proceedings of the 1999 Supercomputing Conference*, ACM Press, New York, Article 60, 1999.

Friedman, J. H., Bentley, J. L., and Finkel, R. A., An algorithm for finding best matches in logarithmic expected time, *ACM Transactions on Mathematical Software*, Vol 3, ACM Press, New York, pp. 209–226, 1977.

Guha, S., Rastogi, R., and Shim, K., Cure: An efficient clustering algorithm for large databases, in *Proceedings of the 1998 ACM SIGMOD Conference*, ACM Press, New York, pp. 73–84, 1998.

Hilderman, R. J., and Hamilton, H. J., *Knowledge Discovery and Measures of Interest*, Kluwer Academic Publishers, Boston, 2001.

Karypis, G., Han, E.-H., and Kumar, V., Chameleon: Hierarchical clustering using dynamic modeling, *IEEE Computer* **32**(8), 68–75, 1999.

Lee, B., Critchlow, T., Abdulla, G., Baldwin, C., Kamimura, R., Musick, R., Snapp, R., and Tang, N. A., The framework for approximate queries on simulation data, *International Journal of Information Sciences*, **157**(1–4), 3–20, 2003.

McCormick, S., Multilevel adaptive methods for partial differential equations, in *Frontiers in Applied Mathematics*, Vol. 6, Society for Industrial and Applied Mathematics, 1989.

Musick, R., and Critchlow, T., Practical lessons in supporting large-scale computational science, in *Proceedings of the 1999 SIGMOD Record*, Vol. 28, No. 4, ACM Press, New York, pp. 49–57, 1999.

Ng, R. T., and Han, J., Efficient and effective clustering methods for spatial data mining, in *Proceedings of the 20th International Conference on Very Large Data Bases*, Morgan Kaufmann, San Francisco, pp. 144–155, 1994.

Samet, H., *The Design and Analysis of Spatial Data Structures*, Addison-Wesley, Reading, MA, 1989a.

Samet, H., Applications of spatial data structures: Computer graphics, in *Image Processing and GIS*, Addison-Wesley, Reading, MA, 1989b.

Samet, H., Spatial data structures, in Kim, W., ed., *Modern Database Systems: The Object Model, Interoperability, and Beyond*, Addison-Wesley/ACM Press, Reading, MA, pp. 361–385, 1995.

Todorovski, L., and Dzeroski, S., Using domain knowledge on population dynamics modeling for equation discovery, in *Proceedings of the 12th European Conference on Machine Learning*, Springer, Berlin, pp. 478–490, 2001.

Van Rijsbergen, C. J., *Information Retrieval*, 2nd edition, Butterworths, London, 1979.

Wang, W., Yang, J., and Muntz, R., STING: A statistical information grid approach to spatial data mining, in *Proceedings of the 23rd International Conference on Very Large Data Bases*, Morgan Kaufmann, San Francisco, pp. 186–195, 1997.

Wang, J., Wang, X., Lin, K.-I., Shasha, D., Shapiro, B. A., and Zhang, K., Evaluating a class of distance-mapping algorithms for data mining and clustering, in *Proceedings of the 5th ACM SIGKDD International Conference on Knowledge Discovery and Data Mining*, ACM Press, New York, pp. 307–311, 1999.

Zhang, T., Ramakrishnan, R., and Livny, M., BIRCH: An efficient data clustering method for very large databases, in *Proceedings of the 1996 ACM SIGMOD Conference*, ACM Press, New York, pp. 103–114, 1996.

PART IV

BIOINFORMATICS AND BIOTECHNOLOGY APPLICATIONS

12

DATA MINING FOR GENE MAPPING

HANNU TOIVONEN, PÄIVI ONKAMO, PETTERI HINTSANEN, EVIMARIA
TERZI, AND PETTERI SEVON

12.1. INTRODUCTION

Modern biomedical research is uncovering the pathology of diseases once considered to be hopelessly complex and incurable. A great deal of this progress
can be attributed to gene mapping—that is, localization of disease susceptibility
genes to certain areas in the human genome by a combination of state-of-the-art
laboratory and computational methods.

Gene mapping is often based on analyzing genetic sequences called *haplotypes*. (We will review basic concepts of genetics in more detail in the next
section; here we aim to give a brief introduction to the topic of this chapter.) A
haplotype is a sparse representation of DNA in (some part of) one chromosome:
Only the contents of some selected polymorphic locations of the chromosome
are included as symbols in the haplotype. In any particular study, haplotypes
are strings of a fixed length. When inherited from generation to generation,
haplotypes are recombined by crossovers. This adds variance to the observed
haplotypes, and the variance reflects the history of each haplotype: two haplotypes that have a common ancestor potentially share a segment in common from
that ancestor. In so-called association mapping, geneticists search for segments
that are overrepresented in patients of a given disease. The locations of those
segments are likely sites of genes that affect the disease, because the segments
are potentially inherited from a common ancestor together with the gene.

In this chapter we study data mining of haplotypes. A central goal is gene
mapping, but we also consider haplotype similarity and clustering as tools to analyze haplotypes and find some structure in their relationships. All the methods we

Next Generation of Data-Mining Applications. Edited by Kantardzic and Zurada
ISBN 0-471-65605-4 © 2005 the Institute of Electrical and Electronics Engineers, Inc.

propose are based on discovering regularities or similarities in haplotypes; in the case of gene mapping, this is done in relationship to the disease/healthy status of individuals in the study. A big challenge is the large amount of stochasticity in the data: the recombination process that has led to the observed haplotypes is stochastic, and the disease status typically correlates only weakly with any single gene.

Association mapping has several alternative formulations as a data-mining problem (Section 12.3). The first is an extension of *association rule mining*: The task is to find sets or sequences of polymorphic locations and their variants ("attribute-value pairs") that are associated with the disease status with a high confidence. A straightforward application of association rules does not work, however. Three issues need to be addressed: specification of the pattern language, prediction of gene position based on discovered patterns, and removing the effect of random associations. An alternative formulation is *classification*: Use a machine learning method to classify individuals to cases and controls, and predict a gene to be close to the polymorphic locations used by the classifier.

Association mapping is based on the assumption that several carriers of the gene have inherited it from a common ancestor and therefore they share haplotype fragments. *Similarity measures* for individuals are a useful tool for assessing how closely related patients are and for finding structure in the haplotypes (Section 12.4). *Clustering*, based on similarity measures or directly on genetically motivated concepts, such as haplotype sharing, can be used to locate groups of individuals that are likely to share the same genetic etiology (Section 12.5).

The methods we provide are intended to be used as exploratory tools by geneticists. Like in any real data-mining task, the user's expertize and insight are in a key role. They are needed in choosing the methods and parameter values, they are crucial in interpreting the results and in designing better ways of mining the data. We hope that these tools will help the geneticist to make useful discoveries.

In Sections 12.3–12.5 we will describe how different data-mining approaches can be applied on gene mapping and closely related problems, and we will illustrate the methods using both synthetic and real data. Section 12.6 concludes with a discussion.

12.2. GENETIC CONCEPTS

The human genome is organized into 23 different *chromosomes*,* each present in every cell as two homologous copies (Figure 12.1A), one from mother and another from father. A chromosome is a single, giant DNA molecule, consisting of millions of consecutive pairs of nitrogenous *bases*, A-T (adenine and thymine), and C-G (cytosine and guanine), which form the well-known double-helix structure with a four-letter alphabet. Most of the DNA has no known functional relevance; only minority of DNA is estimated to be *genes* or their regulatory factors (Figure 12.1B).

---

*All genetic concepts that are printed in italics when mentioned for the first time can be found in the glossary in Table 12.1.

TABLE 12.1. Genetics Glossary

Allele:	An alternative form of a gene or a marker.
Base pair (bp):	A pair of complementary nitrogenous bases (adenine and thymine or guanine and cytosine) in a DNA molecule. Also, the length unit for DNA sequences (e.g., 200 bp).
Chromosome:	A single DNA molecule containing genes (and markers) in linear order. In humans, 23 pairs of chromosomes, each pair containing one chromosome from each parent, carry the entire genetic code.
Crossing over:	The interchange of sections between pairing homologous chromosomes during meiosis.
Disease model:	Number of genes, environmental factors, and interactions that affect the disease susceptibility for a certain disease. Disease with genetic contribution may be monogenic (Mendelian one-gene disease), oligogenic, where just a few genes are involved, or polygenic with several genes with weak effects each, for example.
Gene:	Basic element of heredity that determines traits, coding for proteins.
Genetic association:	Correlation of presence of a disease or a trait with presence of certain marker allele(s) (or alleles at genes), observed at the population level
Genotype:	The particular alleles at specified locus present in an individual.
Haplotype:	A string of alleles from genes or markers that are located closely together on the same chromosome and that tend to be inherited together.
Identity by descent (IBD):	Where two copies of an identical allele have been inherited from a common ancestor (see IBS).
Identity by state (IBS):	Any two copies of an allele which are chemically identical. Need not to be inherited from same source (see IBD).
Linkage:	The tendency of genes in proximity of each other to be inherited together. The closer the loci, the greater the probability that they will be inherited together.
Linkage disequilibrium (LD):	Alleles of separate loci occur together at population level more often than can be accounted for by chance. Usually indicates that the loci are physically close to each other on the chromosome.
Locus (plural loci):	The specific site of a particular gene or marker on its chromosome.
Marker:	A gene or a stretch of noncoding DNA sequence, the alternative forms (alleles) of which can be reliably detected by genotyping technologies.
Marker map:	The positions of a set of marker genes chosen for some particular mapping study.
Meiosis:	Cell division that produces reproductive cells in sexually reproducing organisms; the nucleus divides into four nuclei each containing half the chromosome number (leading to gametes in animals and spores in plants).
Morgan, centiMorgan (cM):	A unit of genetic distance between two loci, defined as the expected number of crossovers occurring between them in a single generation. cM is 1/100 of Morgan. In human beings, 1 centimorgan is equivalent, on average, to 1 million base pairs of DNA.
Pedigree:	A family tree diagram which shows the genetic history of a particular (often multigenerational) family.
Phase:	Parental origin of a haplotype or chromosome.
Phenotype:	The observable and measurable characteristics of an organism (e.g., presence of a disease), which may or may not be genetic.
Population:	A group of organisms of the same species relatively isolated from other groups of the same species.
Recombination:	The process by which offspring derive a combination of genes (or markers) different from that of either parent. Occurs by crossing over.
SNP:	Single nucleotide polymorphism differing in a single base pair.
Trio, triplet:	An offspring and the parents (family trio).

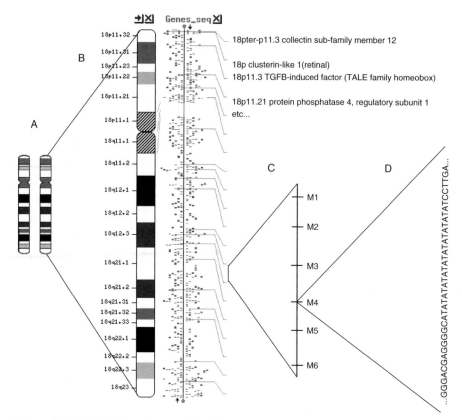

Figure 12.1. **(A)** A homologous pair of human chromosome 18. **(B)** Enlargement of a chromosome view from NCBI GenBank: the annotated human chromosome 18. Cytogenetic locations are given on the left, and the right side contains the known and predicted genes, shown with shaded dots along the vertical line. In the upper right corner there are examples of names of the genes as they appear in NCBI site. **(C)** Zoom-in on a small section of chromosome showing some marker loci (denoted by M1–M6). The alleles at M1–M6 constitute a *haplotype*. **(D)** Enlargement from part C, a stretch of DNA sequence including an 11-repeat allele of locus M4, flanked by unique DNA sequence.

The order of the bases and genes is the same from individual to individual, with only minimal variation: One of the most recent estimates, by Lon Cardon (in his presentation in the Annual Meeting of The American Society of Human Genetics, 2003), is that there are individual differences in 1 out of 330 base pairs. This variation inside the genome is utilized as genetic *markers* (Figure 12.1C): The alternative forms of the markers, *alleles*, can readily be distinguished from each other using standard laboratory methods (genotyping), and therefore they can be used in comparing individuals or *populations* and in estimating co-occurrence of a disease with certain combination of marker alleles. A *haplotype* is a string of alleles in an individual's chromosome. Haplotypes can be considered sparse, economic representations of chromosomes, whose focus and density is set by the

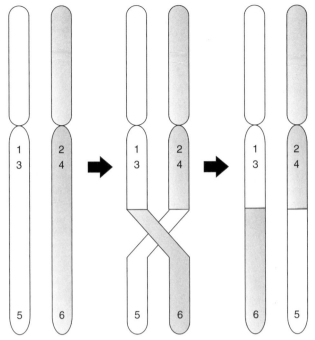

Figure 12.2. Crossing over and recombination. Two homologous chromosomes have been duplicated in the process of *meiosis*. (Here, only two of the four are shown for the sake of simplicity.) Crossing over and recombination occurs between a pair, chromosomal arms are exchanged **(middle)**, and the resulting daughter chromosomes are transmitted to different gametes **(right)**.

location and the density of the *marker map* used in the study. For genome scans the marker map covers the whole genome or a full chromosome, whereas for fine mapping studies the markers are more densely located in a candidate area for a disease susceptibility gene.

A very basic phenomenon in genetics is that of *recombination*: A pair of homologous chromosomes (represented by haplotypes for a gene mapping study) exchanges genetic material in the process of gamete production (Figure 12.2). As a result, a chromosome transmitted from a parent to an offspring is not an exact copy of either parental chromosomes, but a mosaic of them. Consequently, recombination ensures that between-individual variation is maintained in each generation. (On a large scale, such as those typically used in gene mapping, the probability of recombination is approximately constant along the chromosome, and the number of recombinations correlates well with the physical distance in the chromosome.) Recombination is the key factor for gene mapping: Since it fragments haplotypes, the genealogies of different loci in the genome are different, and this helps to localize genes.

In *association mapping*, correlation between the disease or trait (*phenotype*) and markers is sought in a sample of affected and healthy individuals from a

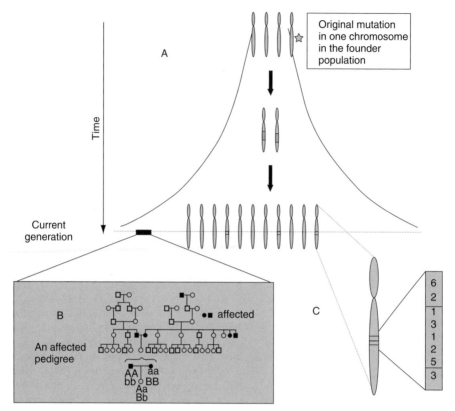

Figure 12.3. Gene mapping strategies. **(A)** Association analysis. The disease mutation has originated in a common ancestor, and it has spread in the population. In the course of generations, consecutive recombinations narrow down the area of conserved haplotype around the disease mutation. In the current generation, only a short stretch of original ancestral haplotype is remaining; now, genotyping a dense map of markers along the chromosome in affected and unaffected individuals and comparing the haplotypes would reveal the area of increased sharing in the disease-associated chromosomes. **(B)** Linkage approach. Co-segregation of the phenotype and genetic markers is tracked in pedigrees of closely related individuals. If several related, affected individuals seem to have inherited the same chromosomal area from a common ancestor more often than based on bare chance, it is deduced that the disease gene is somewhere inside that area. Linkage is often utilized in the first stage of gene mapping project, and when approximate areas of interest have been detected, fine-scale mapping is carried out with association-based methods. **(C)** Enlargement of a disease-mutation-carrying chromosome.

given population (Figure 12.3A). It is assumed that disease mutations derive from one ancestral chromosome (thus, they are *identical by descent*, IBD), where a single mutation occurred a long time ago. (In contrast, alleles that are chemically identical but cannot be traced to common ancestor are *identical by state*, IBS.) As the generations have passed, the disease mutation has been transmitted onward, while recurrent recombinations have narrowed down the stretch of the ancestral haplotype around the mutation. Therefore, in the present generation, one observes a haplotype segment overrepresented in the affected individuals compared to the unaffected (Figure 12.3C). There is then *linkage disequilibrium* (LD) between the actual disease gene and the surrounding markers. The longer the time that has passed since the original ancestral mutation, the shorter the ancestral segment that contains the mutation.

Association methods are utilized when (1) prior candidate genes exist or (2) initial linkage to a genetic region has been observed. Compared to association mapping, *linkage* analysis, the search of co-segregation of marker alleles and disease in carefully chosen *pedigrees*, is the means to get an initial clue of a position of disease genes (Figure 12.3B). Even though linkage analysis is not very accurate, as only few recombinations can be expected to happen in a chromosome during a couple of generations, it has proven very useful in locating areas where fine-mapping efforts should be concentrated. Ultimately, both linkage analysis and association methods search for shared genetic factors between affected individuals, the difference lying in the size of the "pedigree" concerned (Figure 12.3). In this article, we will only consider association mapping.

We will describe novel data-mining approaches to association mapping (and the term "gene mapping" in the rest of this chapter refers to association mapping, not linkage mapping). Due to historical reasons, the vast majority of gene mapping methodology is based on statistical modeling, in a field that is referred to as "genetic epidemiology." The idea of applying data-mining methods to the mapping problem is quite unique, and we are not aware of any similar publications. We will illustrate our methods with two different datasets.

1. A simulated but realistic dataset. The simulated population is an isolate whose age is 20 generations; the marker map is relatively sparse and covers a small chromosome. The final sample consists of 200 cases and 200 controls. The simulation procedure is described in more detail in Appendix A.

2. A dataset for SLE (systemic lupus erythematosus), where a founder mutation haplotype has been found very recently (Koskenmies et al., 2004a,b). SLE is a rare autoimmune disorder. Its pathogenesis is polygenic with potential environmental effects. Genes are not yet very well known, though some candidates have been found by genome scans. We concentrate on a linkage peak area in chromosome 14 (Koskenmies et al., 2004a,b). Both the linkage peak and an association peak were shown to reside at the same position, in close vicinity of marker D14S1055 at 50.30 cM, which for the present knowledge is, or is very near to, the actual position of the susceptibility gene. The proportion of affected individuals actually carrying the particular founder mutation in chr 14 is on the order of 20%, which is typical for multifactorial diseases.

12.3. GENE MAPPING

12.3.1. The Problem

The goal in gene mapping is to locate disease-predisposing genes. A usual setting consists of cases and controls: Cases are persons that have the disease that is being studied, and controls are healthy individuals. The existence and importance of a genetic component in the etiology of the disease has usually already been identified, so the question now is about where the disease susceptibility (DS) gene or genes are located. Given the haplotypes of cases and controls, the basic idea in association mapping is to search for genetic patterns that are more common within cases than controls. Sometimes the trait to be analyzed is quantitative (e.g., blood pressure), rather than dichotomous case versus control. In this chapter we consider case–control settings and will only briefly outline how to extend the methods for quantitative traits and covariates.

In the following we assume that the gene has been initially mapped to an area on a chromosome. The area has been saturated with markers and genotyped in a number of individuals. Each individual in our sample contributes a chromosome pair (one maternal and one paternal chromosome), so the number of chromosomes in the data is twice the number of individuals. For simplicity, we consider the input data as consisting of a set of disease-associated haplotypes (from the cases) and a set of control haplotypes (from the controls). It is typical that many or most of the disease-associated haplotypes do not carry the actual predisposing mutation, and many control haplotypes do carry it.

The Association-Based Gene Mapping Problem. The input consists of a marker map $M = (1, \ldots, m)$, a set $A = \{A_1, \ldots, A_p\}$ of disease-associated haplotypes A_i over map M, and a set $C = \{C_1, \ldots, C_q\}$ of control haplotypes C_j over map M. A haplotype H over map M is a vector $H = (a_1, \ldots, a_m)$ of alleles, where $a_i \in A_i$ and A_i is the set of alleles at marker i. The task is to predict the location of a disease susceptibility gene on the map M.

12.3.2. Standard Data-Mining Formulations of the Gene Mapping Problem

The problem formulation is vague: It does not say anything about how to predict the gene location. We next briefly review possible straightforward data-mining formulations of the problem.

From a data-mining or machine learning viewpoint, gene mapping can be seen as a classification problem. This seems obvious, since the input data are readily classified into cases and controls. The strategy for gene mapping as a classification task is as follows. First, learn to predict whether a haplotype is a case or a control. Then, by looking at the prediction model, identify the area of the chromosome that is most important for the classification. The gene is potentially in this area.

While the classification approach may seem tempting, due to the existence of a large variety of effective and well-known classification methods, there are severe problems in any straightforward application of machine learning methods to this problem. First, the search space is usually huge with respect to the number of training instances. The number of haplotypes is typically on the order of tens or hundreds, while the number of markers can be of the same order or much larger. Machine learning methods would often find over-fit classifiers that perform perfectly with the available training data, but whose predictions are based on totally irrelevant markers. Furthermore, the data are extremely noisy. Both cases and controls contain both mutation carrying and noncarrying haplotypes (class noise), and haplotypes have errors and missing data (attribute noise). Finally, depending on the classifier, it can be difficult to tell which markers are the most important for classification.

Another possible approach is to use association rules of the form $X \rightarrow C$, where X is a set of (marker, allele) pairs and C is the case–control status. This is similar to looking for conjunctive classification patterns, and this approach shares the problems of the classification approach. Although the pattern language is quite restricted and therefore the danger of over-fitting is smaller, association rules still typically consist of markers that are not related to the mutation. Still another possibility from machine learning and data mining would be to use feature selection methods to rank or choose the markers that are most important and thus potentially close to the gene. Again, in most cases, irrelevant markers would be identified as most important ones.

12.3.3. Haplotype Pattern Mining

Like practically any application of data mining or machine learning, the gene mapping problem requires careful engineering of the types of patterns to be used—that is, feature construction. The following three issues need to be addressed:

1. Definition of a pattern language that expresses meaningful concepts of the problem at hand
2. Prediction of gene locus based on discovered patterns
3. Removing the effect of random associations

We next describe Haplotype Pattern Mining (HPM), a method that has been successfully applied on gene mapping, and explain how it solves these three issues.

HPM is based on the simple observation that linkage disequilibrium with the DS gene is likely to be strongest around it and, consequently, the gene locus is likely to be where most of the strongest associations are. The method looks for haplotype patterns, and it predicts the DS locus to be where strongly disease-associated haplotype patterns are. We give a declarative specification of the HPM method after Toivonen et al. (2000a); implementation details can be found elsewhere (Toivonen et al., 2000a,b).

Haplotype Patterns and Disease Association. We examine linkage disequilibrium by looking for haplotype patterns that consist of a set of nearby markers, not necessarily consecutive ones. Given a marker map $M = (1, \ldots, m)$, a *haplotype pattern* P on M is a vector $(p_1, \ldots, p_m)$, where $p_i \in \mathcal{A}_i \cup \{*\}$ for all $i, 1 \leq i \leq m$, where $\mathcal{A}_i$ is the set of alleles at marker i, and $*$ is the "don't care" symbol. A haplotype pattern P *occurs* in a given haplotype vector (chromosome) $H = (h_1, \ldots, h_m)$ if either $p_i = h_i$ or $p_i = *$ for all $i, 1 \leq i \leq m$.

Example 1. Consider a marker map of 10 markers. The vector

$$P_1 = (*, 2, 5, *, 3, *, *, *, *, *)$$

where $1, 2, 3, \ldots$ are marker alleles, is an example of a haplotype pattern. This pattern occurs, for instance, in a chromosome with haplotype $(4, 2, 5, 1, 3, 2, 6, 4, 5, 3)$. ∎

HPM is based on recognizing disease-associated haplotype patterns that are potentially identical by descent—that is, derived from a common ancestor. Gaps are allowed in the patterns to better accommodate for mutations, errors, missing data, and recombinations.

Example 2. Assume that a continuous chromosomal region including markers 2–5 is inherited from a common founder by a number of individuals and that a marker mutation early in the coalescence history of the disease chromosome has changed the allele in marker 4 for a large fraction of current chromosomes. The haplotype shared by these individuals can be expressed as a haplotype pattern of the form of P_1 in Example 1. ∎

Example 3. Assume that a continuous chromosomal region including markers 2–5 is inherited from a common diseased founder by a number of individuals. Errors in genotyping marker 4 may lead to a situation where a continuous haplotype pattern is not as significantly associated to the disease status as the one with a gap.

Errors of another type can be introduced in the construction of marker maps, by inferring a wrong order of markers. Assuming the physical order of markers 4 and 5 is actually the reverse, situations may occur where pattern P_1 is observed for continuous shared regions. ∎

Gaps caused by marker mutations and errors are short, whereas missing information can span several consecutive markers, depending on how the data have been collected. Long gaps could be introduced by double recombinations, but they are rare on the genetically short distances where patterns can be observed in the first place. Since long patterns are not likely to exist, at least not in significant amounts, it can be useful for performance reasons to restrict the length of the patterns that are used in gene localization.

Assume a haplotype pattern $P = (p_1, \ldots, p_m)$. The *(genetic) length* of P is the maximum genetic distance (in *Morgans*) between any two markers i, j with $p_i \neq * \neq p_j$. Gaps are maximal subsequences of "don't care" symbols, excluding the tails of the pattern: A *gap* in P is a contiguous sequence $p_u, \ldots, p_v$ of alleles, where

1. $p_i = *$ for all $i, u \leq i \leq v$ (the gap consists of "don't care" symbols),

2. $u > 1$ and $v < m$ (the gap is not at either end of the pattern), and

3. $p_{u-1} \neq *$ and $p_{v+1} \neq *$ (the gap is bounded by alleles, rather than "don't care" symbols). The length of the gap is $v - u + 1$.

The HPM algorithm takes as parameters the maximum number and maximum length of gaps, as well as the maximum length of patterns to be considered.

We use the signed χ^2 statistic, denoted $\pm\chi^2$, to measure the marker–disease association. A signed version of the measure is used in order to discriminate disease association from control association—that is, from protective haplotypes. The *signed χ^2 measure* $\pm\chi^2(P)$ of a haplotype pattern P is the standard χ^2 measure where the sign is positive if the relative frequency of P is higher in cases than in controls, and negative otherwise. Given a positive *association threshold* x, we say that P is *strongly associated* with the disease if $\pm\chi^2(P) \geq x$. Given the data—markers M, a set A of disease-associated haplotypes, and a set C of control haplotypes on M—and an association threshold x, we denote the collection of all strongly disease-associated patterns by $\mathcal{P}$, that is, $\mathcal{P} = \{P \text{ is a haplotype pattern on } M \mid \pm\chi^2(P) \geq x\}$.

If pattern parameters are specified—a maximum genetic length, a maximum number of gaps, or a maximum length for gaps—the set $\mathcal{P}$ is refined by requiring that these additional restrictions are also fulfilled by the patterns in $\mathcal{P}$. Fisher's exact test could also be used instead of χ^2, especially if any of the values used in the computation of χ^2 are small. Since we do not use χ^2 for exact p value computations, the selection of the test is not critical.

Prediction of Gene Locus. Haplotype patterns close to the DS locus are likely to have stronger association than haplotypes further away; consequently the locus is likely to be where most of the strongest associations are. The *marker frequency* $f(i)$ of marker i (with respect to M, A, C, x as above) is the number of strongly disease-associated patterns that contain marker i, possibly in a gap:

$$f(i) = |\{P = (p_1, \ldots, p_m) \in \mathcal{P} \mid \text{there exist } t \leq i$$
$$\text{and } u \geq i \text{ such that } p_t \neq * \neq p_u\}|$$

The idea is that each haplotype pattern roughly corresponds to a continuous chromosomal region, potentially identical by descent, where gaps allow for corruption of marker data. While markers within gaps are not used in measuring the disease association of the pattern, the whole chromosomal region of the pattern is relevant under the assumption of the region being identical by descent.

The marker frequency gives a score for each marker. On the condition that we assume a DS gene to be present (e.g., based on linkage analysis), we would predict the gene to be somewhere close to the markers with largest frequencies. As a point prediction we can simply give the locus of the most frequent marker: The HPM *point prediction* of DS gene locus is the location of the marker i that has maximal frequency $f(i)$.

This prediction method does not, of course, imply that we assume the DS locus to really overlap with the marker; we simply predict at the granularity of marker density. Consequently, the optimal point predictions of our method are within one-half of the inter-marker distance from the true loci.

Removing the Effect of Random Associations.   The frequency-based approach has some potentially severe problems: Uneven marker spacing, different allele distributions of markers, unevenly distributed missing and erroneous data, and background linkage disequilibrium all can change the observed marker frequencies from what they would be in an ideal situation. This can lead to a situation where, for instance, a large number of patterns are observed in a certain region due to larger heterogeneity in and weaker LD between the markers. Some of these patterns can seem significant just by random. To avoid these problems, we estimate the statistical significance of marker frequencies. Given a marker i, $p(i)$ is the statistical significance of the frequency $f(i)$ of i under the null hypothesis that "chromosomes are drawn from the same distribution"—that is, that there is no gene effect.

Marker significance can be estimated by standard permutation tests. Under the null hypothesis, case and control haplotypes come from the same distribution; by randomly permuting the statuses of haplotypes, we obtain samples from the null distribution. We generate, for instance, 10,000 such random permutations and compute the marker frequencies in each of those. The p value $p(i)$ is then estimated as the fraction of permutations that achieved frequency of at least $f(i)$.

The HPM *significance-based point prediction* is the location of the marker i that has minimal (i.e., highest) significance $p(i)$. The use of marker significances can be illustrated as follows. Consider the frequency of a fixed marker as the test statistic. If it is very unlikely that at least that large a frequency occurs by chance, then it is likely that the DS locus is genetically close to that marker. The significance-based approach predicts the DS gene to be in the vicinity of the marker with the smallest p value. Consecutive markers are dependent, and thus a large number of mutually dependent p values are produced. This is not a problem, however, since we do not use the p values for hypothesis testing, but only for ranking markers.

Outline of the HPM algorithm

Input: Marker map, set of disease-associated haplotypes, set of control haplotypes, association threshold.

Output: (Marker, significance) pairs in decreasing order of likelihood of DS gene association.

Method:
1. Compute a lower bound lb for the frequency of strong patterns
2. Find all patterns that are frequent with respect to lb
3. Evaluate the strength of the frequent patterns
4. For each marker i, compute the marker frequency $f(i)$ in the strong patterns
5. For $j = 1, \ldots, K$:
6.   Randomly permute the status fields of haplotypes
7.   Evaluate the strength of the frequent patterns
8.   For each marker i, compute the marker frequency $f_j(i)$ in the strong patterns
9. For each marker i compute $p(i) = |\{j \mid f_j(i) \geq f(i)\}|/K$
10. Output pairs $(i, p(i))$ sorted by decreasing $p(i)$

Figure 12.4. The HPM algorithm.

12.3.4. HPM Algorithm

In a nutshell, the HPM algorithm is as follows (Figure 12.4). First, given an association threshold for the χ^2 statistic, a lower bound can be derived for the frequency of strongly disease-associated haplotype patterns (Step 1). Second, given such a frequency threshold, all patterns exceeding the threshold can be enumerated efficiently with a fairly straightforward depth-first search method [Step 2; see Toivonen et al. (2000a,b) for more information about these first two steps].

The strengths of the patterns are then computed, and the strong ones are used to compute the marker frequencies $f(i)$ (Steps 3–4). The permutation testing is carried out next (Steps 5–9). The same set of frequent patterns is reused in every iteration, but the strengths are recomputed based on the randomized status fields. The final output is a sorted list of markers and their significances. The first markers in the output have the highest likelihood of being close to the DS gene.

12.3.5. Extensions of HPM

It is relatively easy to modify HPM to accommodate different kinds of input data. QHPM (Sevon et al., 2001; Onkamo et al., 2002) is an extension of HPM which can handle quantitative traits and covariates, such as body mass index, smoking habits, and so on. The pattern–trait association is measured via a linear model having the trait as the response variable and the covariates and also having an indicator variable for the occurrence of the pattern as explanatory variables. The significance of the pattern as an explanatory variable can be tested by comparing the best-fit model to the best-fit model where the coefficient corresponding to the pattern is zero. We also replaced marker frequencies with a score function measuring the skew of the p values of the overlapping patterns.

F-HPM by Zhang and Zhao (2002) uses family data instead of independent haplotypes. A family-based association test proposed by the same authors is used for measuring the pattern–trait association.

12.3.6. Examples

Figure 12.5 gives graphical representations of the output of HPM on the simulated data set (Appendix A). The parameters for HPM were set as follows: χ^2 threshold was 9, maximum pattern length was 7 markers, maximum number of gaps was 1, and maximum length of gap was 1 marker. Permutation tests were carried out with 100,000 iterations. Negated logarithms of p values are used to illustrate the significance-based predictions, because they are more intuitive than plain p values: Higher values mean stronger association and differences between small

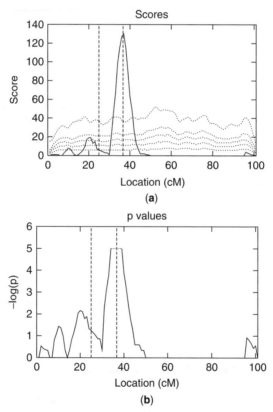

Figure 12.5. An example of the output of HPM on a simulated dataset. **(A)** Observed scores (solid curve) and critical scores for p values 0.001, 0.005, 0.01, 0.02, and 0.05 obtained by permutation tests (dotted curves). **(B)** Negated logarithms (base 10) of the p values. The finite number of permutations causes a cutoff at $y = 5$. The dashed vertical lines denote the true gene loci.

p values are more easily observed. The signal is very strong for the locus on the right, and the number of permutations was not sufficient to differentiate the markers around the locus. With real data one usually does not expect to find such a strong signal. The locus on the left is more difficult to detect, and the peak is off the correct location by 5 cM.

Next, we demonstrate HPM on real Type 1 diabetes data (Bain et al., 1990; Toivonen et al. 2000a) and the SLE dataset described in Section 12.2. The original diabetes data consisted of 385 affected sib-pair families. There were 25 markers spanning over a 14-Mb region. There are two known genes affecting risk for diabetes, very close to each other. The genes lie inside the HLA complex, a region of very high LD, making the mapping task more difficult. We down-sampled the data to 200 disease-associated and 200 control haplotypes. The same parameters were used as with the simulated dataset above. The result in Figure 12.6A indicates that HPM is capable of localizing genes even in the presence of very strong background LD.

The SLE dataset consisted of 104 disease-associated and 100 control haplotypes. There were 32 markers spread over a 25-cM region. The results (Figure 12.6B) show suggestive association at 45–50 cM, coinciding with earlier linkage results (Koskenmies et al., 2004a,b). Some of the patterns strongly associated with SLE are listed in Table 12.2.

HPM has been found to be a valuable tool for narrowing down the region resulting from an initial linkage analysis. It has been utilized in several disease projects—for instance, asthma and high IgE (Kauppi et al., 2001; Polvi et al., 2002), SLE (Koskenmies et al., 2001, 2004a,b), glioma (Paunu et al., 2002), asthma (Laitinen et al., 2004), and dyslexia (unpublished).

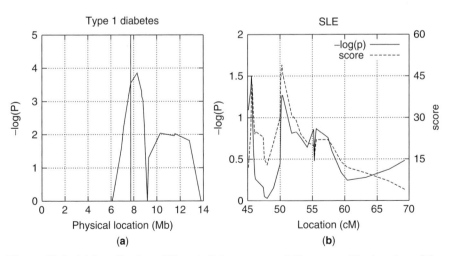

Figure 12.6. (a) Localization of Type 1 diabetes susceptibility genes. The location of the known susceptibility gene is denoted by the solid vertical line. (b) Results for the SLE dataset. The susceptibility gene is located at 50,3 cM.

TABLE 12.2. Haplotype Patterns Over Markers 1–10 Strongly Associated with SLE

	Markers/Alleles									
χ^2	1	2	3	4	5	6	7	8	9	10
8.6095	*	1	*	5	*	*	*	*	*	*
7.1138	*	*	5	*	6	*	*	*	*	*
6.2421	*	*	*	*	6	*	1	1	1	*
5.8522	*	*	*	*	6	*	2	1	*	*
5.8163	*	*	*	*	*	3	2	*	2	*
5.3402	*	1	1	*	6	2	*	*	*	*
5.3402	*	1	1	*	6	*	*	*	*	*
5.2571	*	*	1	*	6	*	*	*	*	*
5.0892	*	*	*	*	6	*	1	1	*	*

12.4. HAPLOTYPE SIMILARITY

Gene mapping, as described above, is indirectly based on finding similar haplotypes among the affected individuals. In this section we consider explicit similarity measures for haplotypes. Formally, given a set G containing n haplotypes with m markers, we want to define a *similarity function sim* $: G \times G \to [0, 1]$, where 0 means total dissimilarity and 1 total similarity. This function allows us to quantitatively measure a (genetic) similarity between any pair of haplotypes taken from the set G. The idea is that the similarity is greater if the haplotypes are closely related and share more of the genome IBD (identical by descent). Depending on the genealogical properties of the haplotypes G and the exact formulation of *sim*, this function can be used, for example, to distinguish between different disease gene mutation carriers or to measure a relationship between haplotypes or individuals.

12.4.1. Similarity Measures

Given a haplotype pair $H_1, H_2 \in G$, we compare the alleles at the same locus (marker) within the haplotypes. By performing this pairwise comparison at every marker, we obtain a *similarity vector* $\vec{s}_{H_1, H_2} = (s_1, \ldots, s_m)$, where each element s_i, $1 \le i \le m$, is a result of an allele comparison at the ith marker: $s_i = 1$ if the alleles at ith marker match and $s_i = 0$ otherwise. The similarity vector $\vec{s}_{H_1, H_2}$ is the base for all our similarity functions.

To begin with, we could simply count the number of 1s in the vector and divide by m, which yields a similarity function $sim(H_1, H_2) = (\sum_{i=1}^{m} s_i)/m$. Observe that $1 - sim(H_1, H_2)$ is a (normalized) Hamming distance between H_1 and H_2. The Hamming distance gives an equal weight to every match and completely ignores LD (linkage disequilibrium). Therefore it weakly distinguishes IBD sharing from IBS sharing: It is possible that most of the matching markers are identical by state and do not reflect true genetic relatedness. (Obviously, the probability that two alleles are identical by state is higher when the number of different alleles in the corresponding marker is low. SNP markers only have two alleles, so the probability of IBS sharing is considerably high.) Longer sequences of matching markers are more likely to be identical by descent due to the LD between adjacent markers. We consider two simple methods that give more weight for probable IBD sharing, along with a bit more elaborate method.

Elementary Measures. First we consider a sliding window technique. Fix a window width $w \in \mathbb{N}$. For each marker k in $\vec{s}_{H_1,H_2}$, we count the amount a_k of matching markers covered by the window starting at the marker: $a_k = \sum_{i=k}^{k+w-1} s_i$, where $s_i = 0$ for $i \notin \{1, \ldots, m\}$ (we allow the window to slide "over the edges" of $\vec{s}_{H_1,H_2}$). The windowing technique is not sensitive to mismatches in the middle of the sequence of matches in $\vec{s}_{H_1,H_2}$. This property makes it robust against genotyping errors, missing data, and point mutations, and it gives a smooth weighting for consecutive or near-consecutive matches.

Now, compute the similarity as $a = \sum_{k=(-w+2)}^{m} a_k^{\alpha}$ for some constant $\alpha \geq 1$. The exponent α gives the desired weight for the possible observed LD: Larger values of α put more emphasis on longer matches. Finally we normalize a by dividing it by the maximum possible score $C = (m - w + 1)w^{\alpha} + 2\sum_{k=1}^{w-1} k^{\alpha}$ and let $sim(H_1, H_2) = a/C$ be the normalized value.

In the second method, we consider each sequence of consecutive matches separately. Let $s_i, \ldots, s_k$, for $1 \leq i < k \leq m$, be a substring of $\vec{s}_{H_1,H_2}$ such that $s_j = 1$ for all $i \leq j \leq k$ and $s_{i-1} = s_{k+1} = 0$. Denote by S the set of all such sequences. Let $a = \sum_{s \in S} |s|^{\alpha}$ for some $\alpha \geq 1$, where $|s|$ is the length of the sequence s. Finally we normalize a so that $sim(H_1, H_2) = a/m^{\alpha}$.

As with the sliding window, constant α gives the desired weight for the possible observed LD. However, unlike the sliding window, this method does not allow any gaps in sequences of consecutive matches.

Second-Order Similarity. In the *second-order similarity* [similar in spirit to *external similarity* (Das et al., 1998)] we do not compare a pair of haplotypes directly to each other, but instead consider their relations with other haplotypes. The general idea can be described as follows: If two persons share a lot of (close) relatives, then they probably are (close) relatives, too. We use the above-described elementary similarity measures to estimate which other haplotypes are related and to which degree with the two haplotypes at hand.

This second-order similarity is useful since the elementary similarity has a large variance due to the stochasticity of the recombination process and random sharing of alleles. The second-order similarity helps us see more systematic relations between haplotypes. As an extreme example, suppose that two haplotypes A and B share a DS gene. Assume further that there have been recombinations very close to the gene in the genealogies of both A and B, but on different sides of the gene. The haplotypes thus share only few alleles, if any, around the gene locus. The elementary measures obviously would not consider these haplotypes similar (unless A and B share a significant amount of alleles somewhere else by chance). If there are other haplotypes carrying the same mutation, they can help us see A and B as similar. Consider such a mutation carrier C with its own history of recombinations, all further away from the gene. Then C shares a haplotype fragment with A (on one side of the gene), shares another fragment with B (on the other side of the gene), and has high elementary similarity with *both* A and B. With several other such haplotypes, we say that A and B are similar in the second order since they share many closely related haplotypes.

We use the observed correlation of elementary similarities to measure the second-order similarity. First we construct a similarity matrix SM, where $\text{SM}_{H_1,H_2} = sim(H_1, H_2)$ for $H_1, H_2 \in G$ (here we use the haplotype set G also as an index set), by applying either of the elementary methods described in the previous section. Denote by sm_{H_1} and sm_{H_2} the H_1th and H_2th row in the matrix SM with the H_1th and H_2th columns removed (in other words, we drop H_1 and H_2 from inspection). We define the second-order similarity between two haplotypes $H_1, H_2 \in G$ as the correlation coefficient between these rows:

$$\text{SM}^2_{H_1,H_2} = \frac{\text{Cov}(\text{sm}_{H_1}, \text{sm}_{H_2})}{\sqrt{\text{Var}(\text{sm}_{H_1}) \cdot \text{Var}(\text{sm}_{H_2})}}$$

where SM^2 is the second-order similarity matrix and $\text{SM}^2_{H_1,H_2} \in [-1, 1]$.

Comments on the Similarity Measures. Although the similarity methods discussed above are rather simple, they seem to perform quite well in practice. The simplicity has also advantages: We can easily convert a similarity function into distance function by applying some strictly decreasing transformation. For example, consider a mapping $d : G \times G \to [0, 1]$, $d(H_1, H_2) = 1 - sim(H_1, H_2)$, where $sim(H_1, H_2)$ is one of the elementary methods described above. It can be proved that d satisfies metric properties, which is important in some applications. Both methods can be trivially implemented into algorithms with $\Theta(m)$ time complexity.

However, defining the constants w and α is not straightforward. They should be large enough to adequately distinguish between probable IBD sharing and random sharing. Some proposed models [see, e.g., McPeek and Strahs (1999)] for estimating the expected length of an IBD-shared segment, given an estimate of the age of the population, could be helpful here. On the other hand, the parameters should not be too large: This can lead to a situation where similarity values are negligible and, hence, the methods separate haplotypes inadequately. To be on a safe side, we suggest to start the exploration with relatively small constants ($w \leq 5$, $\alpha \leq 2$), especially with long marker maps.

12.4.2. Identification of Most Likely Mutation Carriers

To illustrate how the proposed similarity measures can be applied, we consider the problem of identifying most likely mutation carrying chromosomes. The task is far from trivial. First, each individual contributes two chromosomes and carries the mutation potentially in one of them, both, or none. Second, a typical study setting in disease gene mapping is one with a so-called complex disease, where several genes and environmental factors contribute to the disease susceptibility, and potentially only a small proportion of the chromosomes carry any particular disease mutation. A single haplotype can carry several mutations, although we restrict our attention to only single mutation per haplotype for simplicity.

Since carriers sharing a common mutation potentially share several markers IBD around the mutation locus (depending on the time since the last common ancestor and the density of the marker map), they are likely to be similar to each other. In addition, any two persons in the dataset could be related via a common ancestor, so mutation sharing is not the only source of similarity. Finally, haplotypes can be similar just by chance. We show how the proposed similarity measures can be applied to distinguish between carrier and noncarrier haplotypes.

Separating Noncarriers from Carriers.   Noncarrier haplotypes are not likely to share substantial amounts of markers with many other haplotypes, since there should be no systematic relationship between them. Therefore we can expect that the noncarrier haplotypes do not have many close neighbors. Formally, we classify haplotype $H \in G$ as noncarrier if $q(H) < t$ for some *qualifying function* $q : G \rightarrow \mathbb{R}$ and threshold constant $t \in \mathbb{R}$. Otherwise we classify H as carrier. For the qualifying function q we set $q(H) = |\overline{B}(H, \varepsilon)|$, where $\overline{B}(H, \varepsilon) = \{H_2 \in G : sim(H, H_2) \geq \varepsilon, H \neq H_2\}$ denotes the (closed) ε-neighborhood of the haplotype H. Parameter ε is the amount of similarity we require for a given pair of haplotypes to be considered as close neighbors. By adjusting the threshold parameter t, we can control the number of remaining haplotypes. This model introduces two new parameters with which the geneticist can experiment in exploratory haplotype analysis. Usually we would begin with larger values and gradually descend down if the amount of noncarriers seems to be implausible.

The model for separating carriers and noncarriers is simple and guarantees only that the predicted carrier haplotypes have a certain number of close neighbors. It does not require any relation between the carriers. If we are very unlucky, we just get a set of predicted carriers that are dissimilar to each other. We could try to construct the carrier set $S \subset G$ more elaborately, though. We want the set S to contain dense subsets $S_1 \subset S, \ldots, S_k \subset S$, such that the haplotypes in a certain subset S_i consist of similar haplotypes. This, obviously, is a clustering problem. We will return to clustering in the next section.

We construct a set $S \subseteq G$ of most likely mutation carriers by iteratively removing least related (noncarrier) haplotypes from the haplotype set G with the qualifying function q defined in the previous section. First we compute similarities between all haplotype pairs in the set G. Then we discard all haplotypes $H \in G$ for which $q(H) < t$ with some fairly large threshold and neighborhood "radius" (for example, $t = 10$ and $\varepsilon = 0.3$ using second-order similarity). If all of the haplotypes get discarded, we drop the threshold t by one and prune again.

If the threshold drops to one (or some other lower bound we set for the density), we have to adjust ε and try again. We emphasize the exploratory nature of the process, as well as the use of genetic insight in the interpretation of the results.

Every haplotype in the set S has a certain number of close neighbors. However, these haplotypes do not need to be close to each other. Therefore we repeat the pruning described above for the set S without adjusting the parameters t and ε. This removes possible "distant" haplotypes from the set S. Denote the resulting set of this iteration by S'. If $|S| = |S'|$, we are done (now the set S contains only haplotypes which form group or groups). Otherwise we set $S = S'$ and repeat the pruning again. Since $|S|$ decreases monotonically, iterating will stop. The subset S might end up empty, in which case we have to relax threshold parameters.

12.4.3. Examples

In our first set of examples we use the simulated dataset with 400 haplotypes from affected individuals with 101 microsatellite markers (Appendix A). There are three different mutations (labeled M2, M1, and M11) in the sample represented by 58, 56, and 42 carriers. (Two other mutations still present in the final population are ignored, because they have only one carrier haplotype each.) Thus, we have four classes, one for each mutation and one for noncarriers.

Similarity Between Classes. First we verify that carriers of a particular mutation are indeed similar to each other. This is done by calculating the median similarity with respect to all classes for each haplotype. We can do this since we know whether a certain haplotype in the simulated dataset is a carrier or not and, if it is, which mutation the haplotype carries (that is, we know the correct class for each haplotype). More precisely, for each haplotype $H \in G$ and class i we calculate

$$S_{H_i} = \operatorname*{median}_{\substack{H_2 \in C_i \\ H_2 \neq H}} sim(H, H_2), \qquad 1 \leq i \leq 4$$

where $C_1, \ldots, C_4$ are the known classes.

Figure 12.7 shows the distributions of S_{H_i}. Most of the carrier haplotypes have, as expected, greater median similarity within their own classes. Observe that most of the noncarrier haplotypes do not appear to be significantly similar to any group. This is a crucial property when predicting the carrier haplotypes.

Identification of Mutation Carriers. We next apply the approximation heuristic to the prediction of mutation carriers. For the threshold parameters we set $\varepsilon = 0.35$ and $t = 5$ and use the second-order similarity with the sliding window method for measuring pairwise similarities between haplotypes (with parameters $w = 5$ and $\alpha = 2$). Our results are summarized in Table 12.3.

From the table we observe that all classes are present in the set of predicted carriers. Figure 12.8 illustrates the trade-off in selectivity. In the figure, two

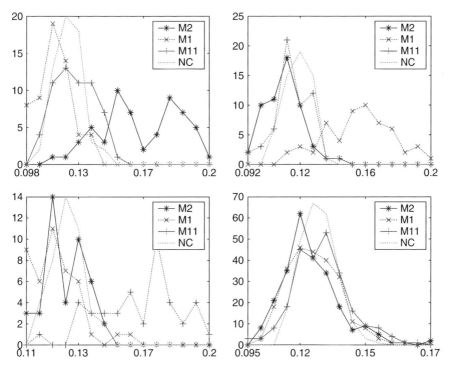

Figure 12.7. Distributions (histograms) of S_{H_i} values in the simulated data. **Upper left:** Plot showing the distribution of median similarities of mutation M2 carriers to each of the classes (M1, M2, M11, noncarriers). Other plots contain similar distributions for members of class M1 **(top right)**, M11 **(bottom left)**, and noncarriers **(bottom right)**.

**TABLE 12.3. Number of Predicted Mutation
Carriers (Approximative Method)**

Class	Haplotypes in Total	Predicted Mutation Carriers
M2 carriers	58 (14.5%)	32 (35.2%)
M1 carriers	56 (14.0%)	32 (35.2%)
M11 carriers	42 (10.5%)	19 (20.9%)
Noncarriers	244 (61.0%)	8 (8.7%)
Total	400	91

different parameter combinations have been used and the resulting sets are plotted onto the plane after multidimensional scaling. Although the heuristic discards a substantial amount of carriers during the process, the remaining haplotypes are the most likely carriers, and they are likely to show the most distinctive haplotype patterns of carrier haplotypes. They can be useful, for instance, for developing gene tests before the actual gene is recognized and can be tested directly.

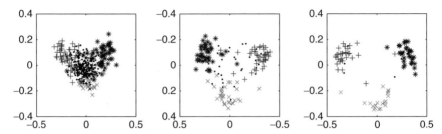

Figure 12.8. Predicted mutation carriers from the approximative method, with gradually more restricting parameters. Symbols +, *, and × denote carriers of different mutations; noncarriers are denoted by dots. The plot on the left contains the whole dataset. In the middle plot ($\varepsilon = 0.3$, $t = 5$) most of the carriers are present, but there is visible overlap. In the rightmost plot ($\varepsilon = 0.35$, $t = 5$) the three groups are clearly separate (except for few outliers) from each other and the amount of noncarriers is minimal.

Structure Discovery from Real Data. In our last example we look for similarities in the real SLE dataset described in Section 12.2. There are 204 haplotypes with 32 microsatellite markers. Approximately 8.5% of the alleles are missing. When comparing two alleles, the result is conservatively considered to be a mismatch if either one of the alleles is missing.

We calculate the pairwise similarities with the second-order similarity using the sliding window method with parameters $w = 5$ and $\alpha = 2$. Figure 12.9a shows the whole dataset plotted onto a plane with Sammon's mapping. There are roughly two clusters, which do not seem to be in direct relation with the disease status or mutation.

To better distinguish the two clusters, we apply the approximation heuristic with parameters $\varepsilon = 0.375$ and $t = 10$. This removes exactly half of

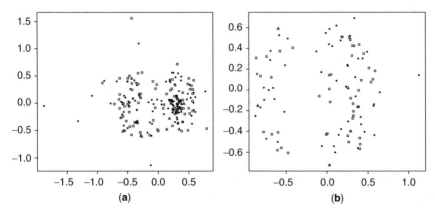

Figure 12.9. Experiments with the SLE dataset. Triangles, boxes, and dots denote mutation carriers, affected, and controls, respectively. **(a)** The whole dataset shows roughly two clusters. **(b)** After applying the approximation heuristic, these two clusters become more obvious.

the haplotypes. We calculate the pairwise similarities for the remaining haplotypes with the second-order similarity using the same parameters as before (Figure 12.9b). The two clusters are now more clearly visible. Again, the disease status or gene does not seem to have any significance in the separation of the two clusters. The two clusters suggest, however, that there is some clear structure in the data besides the disease status.

12.5. HAPLOTYPE CLUSTERING

12.5.1. The Clustering Problem

By haplotype clustering we aim to identify groups of related haplotypes. In some gene mapping studies, such groups could correspond to different disease gene mutations. Assume a population isolate created by a relatively small number of founders, constituting the initial generation. Furthermore, assume that disease susceptibility mutations for the disease of interest have been introduced by few of the founders. Can the corresponding groups of carriers of different mutations be identified in the current population? This can be seen as a clustering problem: The goal is to group together individuals of the present population that have inherited specific regions of their haplotypes from specific individual founders. Solving this problem can be a rather difficult task, particularly when the number of generations between the initial and the final population is large, due to the large number of recombinations and mutations that might have occurred at multiple points.

The problem is closely related to gene mapping, as described in Section 12.3. The main difference is that here we are not (directly) concerned with the disease status of the individuals and the goal is not to separate the control haplotypes from cases but to find groups of haplotypes that have inherited the mutation from the same ancestral haplotype.

Clustering is the process of grouping together items that have something in common. Several clustering algorithms exist, most of them requiring a measure of similarity between the items. [An extensive review of these clustering methods is provided, for instance, by Jain et al. (1999).] As discussed in previous sections, a consequence of the recombination process is that haplotypes that have inherited the mutation from the same ancestor are expected to share some more genetic material around the mutation locus, and haplotypes that share alleles in consecutive markers should be considered similar to each other.

This notion of similarity implies that conventional similarity measures are not very useful for haplotype clustering. Consider, for example, the three haplotypes shown in Table 12.4. The table shows the alleles of three haplotypes for markers 1–9. By observation the substring *3 4 3* shared by H_1 and H_2 seems to be genetically significant, since it may correspond to a part of their common ancestral haplotype. However, using Hamming or Euclidean distance, haplotype H_1 is closer to H_2: *Hamming_Distance*$(H_1, H_2) = 6$, *Hamming_Distance*$(H_1, H_3) = 4$, and *Euclidean_Distance*$(H_1, H_2) = 36$, *Euclidean_Distance*$(H_1, H_3) = 5$.

TABLE 12.4. Example of Three Haplotypes and Their Similarities

	Markers/Alleles								
	1	2	3	4	5	6	7	8	9
Haplotype H_1	1	4	1	2	1	2	3	4	3
Haplotype H_2	3	1	4	4	4	4	3	4	3
Haplotype H_3	1	3	1	1	1	3	3	3	3

Since our goal is to identify groups of haplotypes that share a mutation from a common ancestor, the clustering method should be based on some groupwise similarity measure rather than any pairwise similarity.

12.5.2. Conceptual Clustering

Conceptual clustering builds on the idea that the clustering algorithm should produce clusters that can be described in a given language $\mathcal{L}$, which has been designed to express meaningful concepts of the domain. [For a discussion of the properties of certain conceptual clustering models, see Pitt and Reinke (1987).] In the sequel we describe the concept language as well as the haplotype clustering algorithms that have been employed for automating the concept formulation.

The Concept Language.   Given that the haplotypes of each cluster are expected to be genetically related by sharing a gene inherited from a common ancestor, the concept language should consist of expressions that describe shared haplotype segments. Due to recombinations, however, it is possible that there is no single haplotype segment that would both match most haplotypes in the (desired) cluster as well as separate them from other haplotypes. Therefore, the clusters are described by disjunctions of partially overlapping haplotype segments; the goal is that they are likely to be parts of ancestral haplotypes shared by subgroups. Disjunctions allow flexibility that is necessary due to different recombination histories of different haplotypes, while the overlap potentially contains the disease susceptibility gene and also makes it more likely that the haplotypes within a cluster are related.

Example 4. An example of a disjunctive concept is shown in Table 12.5. Marker 88 is probably inherited from a common ancestor, while the different haplotype segments to the left and to the right are the results of different recombinations. ∎

Formally, the *haplotype cluster description language* $\mathcal{L}$ consists of disjunctions of overlapping haplotype segments of the form

$$i : a_i, a_{i+1}, \ldots, a_{i+L_i} \text{ or } j : a_j, a_{j+1}, \ldots, a_{j+L_j} \text{ or } \cdots k : a_k, a_{k+1}, \ldots, a_{k+L_k}$$

TABLE 12.5. Example of a Disjunctive Concept

	Markers/Alleles						
	85	86	87	88	89	90	91
85:	4	3	1	3	—	—	—
88:	—	—	—	3	4	2	3
85:	3	3	2	3	—	—	—
88:	—	—	—	3	2	1	4

where $i, j, \ldots, k$ are markers, a_i is an allele at marker i, $L_i, L_j, \ldots, L_k$ are the lengths of the disjuncts, and there is at least one shared marker h such that $i \leq h \leq i + L_i, j \leq h \leq j + L_j, \ldots, k \leq h \leq k + L_k$.

The Clustering Algorithm. As potential disjuncts in the concepts, we consider all haplotype segments shared by more than a certain number of haplotypes. For finding them efficiently we use a slight modification of the Apriori algorithm (Agrawal et al., 1996). We then focus on each marker in turn and construct the subsegment containment lattice of overlapping segments that contain this marker. An abstract description of the haplotype clustering algorithm is given in Figure 12.10, while some details of the method are discussed in the sequel.

At each marker i we construct the containment lattice $LATT_i$ of the frequent haplotype segments that contain i (Steps 1 and 2). In the first level of $LATT_i$ we consider the alleles that are frequent in this marker and use them as the roots of the lattice. In the next level, segments of length two that contain the marker-allele pairs already considered in the previous level are considered, and so on.

The use of the lattice structure is biologically motivated. Assuming that a locus is identical by descent in the given haplotypes, the genealogy of the locus is tree-shaped. Under the assumption of no marker mutations, this tree is contained in the haplotype segment lattice build at that locus. These assumptions are not

Outline of the haplotype clustering algorithm
Input: Set of haplotypes, threshold p of the number of disjunctions per cluster.
Output: Set of clusters, the disjunctive concepts for each cluster.
Method:
1. For each marker i
2. form the haplotype segment containment lattice $LATT_i$ of frequent segments containing i
3. Select the lattices that have the largest number of nodes and store them in $S\_LATT \subseteq LATT = \{LATT_1, LATT_2, \ldots, LATT_m\}$
4. For each $\overline{LATT}_i \in S\_LATT$
5. select the p highest scoring nodes of $LATT_i$
6. output the disjunction of the haplotype segments in the selected nodes

Figure 12.10. The haplotype clustering algorithm.

fully realistic: First, only an unknown subset of haplotypes shares a mutation of interest IBD; second, marker mutations, errors, and missing data can violate the second assumption. Since we do not know the loci of interest, we build a lattice at every marker locus to obtain a representative collection of lattices that potentially contain an interesting genealogy. Unlike the unknown trees, the lattices are unique and efficient to construct.

We next select the most promising lattices, based on the number of nodes in each lattice. Close to the mutation locus, where several haplotypes have segments identical by descend, the lattices are expected to have more internal nodes when compared to the number of internal nodes in the lattices for loci where sharing is by state only.

Finally we select the most descriptive nodes of each lattice and output their disjunction as a cluster description (Steps 4–6). We assign a score for each node (haplotype segment) of the lattice, based on the heuristic that a haplotype segment constitutes a good description if it is long and frequent. These two requirements of a good description are combined in the following heuristic, recursive definition of the score of a node n:

$$
\text{score}(n) = \begin{cases} n \cdot \text{length} + n \cdot \text{frequency}, & \text{if } n \text{ is a leaf} \\ \sum_{u \in \text{children\_of}(n)} \dfrac{u \cdot \text{frequency}}{n \cdot \text{frequency}} \times \text{score}(u) & \text{if } n \text{ is not a leaf} \end{cases}
$$

For each lattice $LATT_j \in S\_LATT$ the score of the nodes in the lattice is evaluated and the nodes are sorted in decreasing order. A disjunction of the p highest scoring haplotype segments is used as the cluster description. There can be logically redundant disjuncts in a cluster description; we have decided to keep them since they may be informative to the user, even if they do not affect cluster memberships.

12.5.3. Examples

Figure 12.11 shows the distributions of different mutations (founder/locus pair) in clusters discovered in the simulated dataset. Most original mutations have disappeared in the course of the history of the population, and only three are left in the final sample (1, 2, 11). Label NC in the graphs corresponds to noncarriers. Mutation 1 is best picked out by clusters 8–10, mutation 2 by cluster 7, mutation 11 by clusters 4 and 5, and noncarriers by none of the clusters, as expected. For our goal, the best clusters have one dominant mutation. Clusters 4 and 7, which are among the best in this respect, are also those that correspond to the marker positions closest to the mutation loci. There is considerable noise in the results—that is, clusters do not match to mutations one-to-one—but this is inherent due to the stochasticity of the data.

The real SLE dataset (Section 12.2) has been used for clustering experiments as well. We carried out two experiments, where the goal was to test if we can rediscover some already known structure from these real data. In the first experiment we only considered affected individuals of the population (Table 12.6).

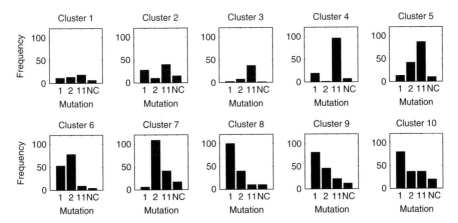

Figure 12.11. Distributions of carriers of different mutations within different clusters.

TABLE 12.6. Cluster Descriptions for the Affected Individuals in the SLE Data

Cluster 1	C	NC	Cluster 5	C	NC	Cluster 9	C	NC
15:[1]	10	34	9:[1]	7	52	6:[2]	5	33
15:[1, 3]	6	10	9:[1, 2]	1	14	6:[2, 2]	1	10
15:[1, 1]	3	16	9:[1, 11]	2	2	6:[2, 1]	2	17
15:[1, 3, 3]	1	5	9:[1, 5]	2	10	6:[2, 2, 5]	0	5
14:[3, 1, 1]	3	1	8:[5, 1, 1]	0	3	5:[6, 2, 2, 5]	0	3
Cluster 2	C	NC	Cluster 6	C	NC	Cluster 10	C	NC
19:[1]	8	44	11:[1]	7	52	30:[1]	5	56
19:[1, 1]	1	12	11:[1, 1]	0	12	29:[11, 1]	0	6
19:[1, 3]	3	7	10:[2, 1, 1]	0	5	30:[1, 2, 3]	1	6
18:[1, 1, 3]	1	5	11:[1, 1, 4]	0	9	29:[7, 1, 1]	0	4
18:[1, 1, 3, 2]	1	4	10:[2, 1, 1, 4]	0	5	29:[7, 1, 1, 3]	0	4
Cluster 3	C	NC	Cluster 7	C	NC	Cluster 11	C	NC
21:[2]	8	68	17:[3]	6	50	13:[4]	1	44
21:[2, 1]	0	13	17:[3, 1]	1	26	13:[4, 2]	0	21
21:[2, 8]	5	15	16:[3, 3, 1]	0	12	13:[4, 1]	0	15
20:[3, 2, 8]	2	5	16:[4, 3, 1]	0	4	12:[1, 4, 1]	0	5
19:[1, 3, 2, 8]	2	3	17:[3, 1, 1, 3]	1	4	12:[4, 4, 2]	0	3
Cluster 4	C	NC	Cluster 8	C	NC			
2:[1]	7	56	27:[1]	6	43			
1:[4, 1]	1	10	27:[1, 1]	1	7			
2:[1, 1]	2	11	26:[3, 1, 1]	0	4			
2:[1, 1, 3]	2	6	25:[3, 3, 1, 1]	0	3			
2:[1, 1, 3, 6]	2	4	25:[3, 3, 1, 1, 7]	0	3			

In all cases, the first line in the description is the only logically nonredundant disjunct, but others are listed for their potential information to the user. The distributions of carriers (C) and noncarriers (NC) of the mutation are also shown for each disjunct.

There are 104 affected haplotypes, and 11 of them are actual mutation carriers. In the clusterings, done without information about who is a carrier and who is not, 10 out of 11 mutation carriers are in cluster 6, together with 34 noncarriers. In general, the two classes are not separated well. An obvious reason is that the discovered cluster descriptions are so short that they will match a large number of haplotypes. However, it is interesting to note that the topmost clusters contain more than half of the 11 carriers; that is, the clusters tend to have been created around them rather than around the dominating set of 93 predicted noncarriers.

In the second experiment we considered the whole population. In this case the dataset consists of the 104 affected individuals, 11 of which carry the mutation, and 100 control haplotypes, and all information about these classes was held back in the clustering process. The resulting clusters (not shown) typically contain the same amount of cases and controls and contain zero or one mutation carrier. It seems that in this case the signal from 11 carriers is too weak, and the clusters reflect haplotype patterns of the general population.

12.6. DISCUSSION

Analysis of haplotypes is important for human health care. Gene mapping helps to locate disease susceptibility genes; similarity and clustering analysis, in turn, can be used to find different subtypes of the mutations or to develop diagnostic tests: A new patient probably carries a disease mutation if the haplotype is similar to many carrier haplotypes or falls into one of the carrier clusters.

In this chapter we described novel data-mining approaches to haplotype analysis tasks. Practically none of the previous research on gene mapping has originated from computer science community, as the problem has been approached mostly with statistical perspectives. Data mining and machine learning can contribute to the field with their concepts and algorithms, as we have illustrated with associations and classification, similarity, and clustering. The association-based gene mapping methodology, HPM, has been applied successfully to real gene mapping studies and has been competitive with previous state-of-the-art methods (Toivonen et al., 2000a; Kauppi et al., 2001; Onkamo et al., 2002; Paunu et al., 2002; Koskenmies et al., 2004b; Laitinen et al., 2004). The similarity and clustering research is more recent and has yet to demonstrate its value in practical gene mapping.

The presented methods are mostly meant to be used as tools for exploratory data analysis. For instance, choosing parameter values for similarity computation is not straightforward. Suitable values depend on the dataset and application, and need to be tuned manually. Tests with simulated data sets are also one possible approach to finding roughly suitable values.

This chapter has two major lessons for data miners. First, gene mapping has a number of important problems where data mining can have interesting applications. Second, it is often crucial to tailor data mining methods to the problem at hand. Even though the data mining techniques in this chapter are quite simple, they are successful because they have been tuned for these particular problems: the similarity measures are novel, haplotypes are clustered using a suitable concept language, and an appropriate pattern language is also needed for finding associations that are useful for gene mapping.

Several interesting gene mapping related data analysis problems have not been covered here. First, most interesting hereditary diseases are affected by several genes, there are interactions between genes, and between genes and the environment. The signal to detect only one gene at a time might be weak, and models for multiple genes and interactions could be more powerful for gene mapping. Second, there are a number of recent directions for research on haplotypes. It has been observed that haplotypes are made up of blocks, within which recombinations are unlikely [see, e.g., Daly et al. (2001) and Gabriel et al. (2002)]. Haplotype blocks thus tend to be inherited as whole from generation to generation. Identification and utilization of such blocks is now a popular topic. A closely related topic is marker selection [see, e.g., Avi-Itzhak et al. (2003)]: Given that haplotyping is expensive and not all markers can be used in a particular study, which markers are the most informative? Finally, haplotypes are not obtained directly from the wet lab. Instead, they need to be inferred from genotype data where for each marker there is a pair of alleles from the two chromosomes of the individual, without information about which allele belongs to the chromosome (haplotype) inherited from the mother, and which to the one from the father. Haplotyping is an interesting combinatorial problem [see, e.g., Gusfield (2001) and Eronen et al. (2004)]. An alternative approach would be to try to map genes directly from the genotype data instead of using haplotypes.

REFERENCES

Agrawal, R., Mannila, H., Srikant, R., Toivonen, H., and Verkamo, I., Fast discovery of association rules, in *Advances in Knowledge Discovery and Data Mining*, pp. 307–328, AAAI Press, Menlo Park, CA, 1996.

Jain, A., Murty, M., and Flynn, P., Data clustering: A review. *ACM Computer Surveys* **31**, 264–323 (1999).

Avi-Itzhak, H., Su, X., and De La Vega, F., Selection of minimum subsets of single nucleotide polymorphisms to capture haplotype block diversity, in *Pacific Symposium on Biocomputing*, pp. 466–477, 2003.

Bain, S., Todd, J., and Barnett, A., The British Diabetic Association—Warren repository, *Autoimmunity* **7**, 83–85 (1990).

Daly, M., Rioux, J., Schaffner, S., Hudson, T., and Lander, E., High-resolution haplotype structure in the human genome, *Nature Genetics* **29**, 229–232 (2001).

Das, G., Mannila, H., and Ronkainen, P., Similarity of attributes by external probes, in *Proceedings of the Fourth International Conference on Knowledge Discovery and Data Mining*, pp. 23–29, 1998.

Eronen, L., Geerts, F., and Toivonen, H., A Markov chain approach to reconstruction of long haplotypes, in *Pacific Symposium on Biocomputing 2004*, pp. 104–115, 2004.

Gabriel, S., Schaffner, S., Nguyen, H., Moore, J., Roy, J., Blumenstiel, B., Higgins, J., DeFelice, M., Lochner, A., Faggart, M., Liu-Cordero, S., Rotimi, C., Adeyemo, A., Cooper, R., Ward, R., Lander, E., Daly, M., and Altshuler, D., The structure of haplotype blocks in the human genome. *Science* **296**, 2225–2229 (2002).

Gusfield, D., Inference of haplotypes from samples of diploid populations: Complexity and algorithms, *Computational Biology* **8**, 305–324 (2001).

Kauppi, P., Lindblad-Toh, K., Sevon, P., Toivonen, H., Rioux, J., Villapakka, A., Laitinen, L., Hudson, T., Kere, J., and Laitinen, T., A second-generation association study of the 5q31 cytokine gene cluster and interleukin-4 receptor in asthma, *Genomics* **77**, 35–42 (2001).

Koskenmies, S., Lahermo, P., Julkunen, H., Ollikainen, V., Kere, J., and Widén, E., Linkage mapping of systemic lupus erythematosus (SLE) in Finnish multiplex families, *Journal of Medical Genetics* **41**, e2–e5 (2004a).

Koskenmies, S., Widén, E., Kere, J., and Julkunen, H., Familial systemic lupus erythematosus in Finland, *Journal of Rheumatology* **28**(4), 758–760 (2001).

Koskenmies, S., Widén, E., Onkamo, P., Zucchelli, M., Sevon, P., Julkunen, H., and Kere, J., Haplotype associations define target regions for susceptibility loci in SLE, *European Journal of Human Genetics* **12**, 489–494 (2004b).

Laitinen, T., Polvi, A., Rydman, P., Vendelin, J., Pulkkinen, V., Salmikangas, P., Mäkelä, S., Rehn, M., Pirskanen, A., Rautanen, A., Zucchelli, M., Gullstén, H., Leino, M., Alenius, H., Petäys, T., Haahtela, T., Laitinen, A., Laprise, C., Hudson, T.J., Laitinen, L.A., and Kere, J., Characterization of a common susceptibility locus for asthma-related traits, *Science* **304**, 300–304 (2004).

McPeek, M., and Strahs, A., Assessment of linkage disequilibrium by the decay of haplotype sharing, with application to fine-scale genetic mapping, *American Journal of Human Genetics* **65**, 858–875 (1999).

Ollikainen, V., Simulation Techniques for Disease Gene Localization in Isolated Populations, Ph.D. thesis, University of Helsinki, Department of Computer Science, 2002.

Onkamo, P., Ollikainen, V., Sevon, P., Toivonen, H., Mannila, H., and Kere, J., Association analysis for quantitative traits by data mining: QHPM, *The Annals of Human Genetics* **66**, 419–429 (2002).

Paunu, N., Lahermo, P., Onkamo, P., Ollikainen, V., Helen, P., Rantala, I., Simola, K., Kere, J., and Haapasalo, H., A novel low-penetrance susceptibility locus for familial glioma at 15q23-q26.3, *Cancer Research* **62**, 3798–3802 (2002).

Pitt, L., and Reinke, R., Polynomial-Time Solvability of Clustering and Conceptual Clustering Problems: The Agglomerative-Hierarchical Algorithm, Technical Report UIUCDCS-R-87-1371, University of Illinois, Department of Computer Science, 1987.

Polvi, A., Polvi, T., Sevon, P., Petäys, T., Haahtela, T., Laitinen, L. A., Kere, J., and Laitinen, T., Physical map of asthma susceptibility locus in 7p15-p14 and an association study of TCRG. *European Journal of Human Genetics* **10**, 658–665 (2002).

Sevon, P., Ollikainen, V., Onkamo, P., Toivonen, H., Mannila, H., and Kere, J., Mining associations between genetic markers, phenotypes, and covariates, *Genetic Epidemiology* **21**(Suppl. 1), S588–S593 (2001).

Toivonen, H., Onkamo, P., Vasko, K., Ollikainen, V., Sevon, P., Mannila, H., Herr, M., and Kere, J., Data mining applied to linkage disequilibrium mapping. *American Journal of Human Genetics* **67**(1), 133–145 (2000a).

Toivonen, H., Onkamo, P., Vasko, K., Ollikainen, V., Sevon, P., Mannila, H., and Kere, J., Gene mapping by haplotype pattern mining, in *IEEE International Symposium on Bio-Informatics & Biomedical Engineering*, pp. 99–108, IEEE Computer Society, Los Alamitos, 2000b.

Zhang, S., and Zhao, H., On a family-based haplotype pattern mining method for linkage disequilibrium mapping, in *Proceedings of Pacific Symposium on Biocomputing*, pp. 100–111, World Scientific, Singapore, 2002.

APPENDIX A: SIMULATION OF DATA

A simulated dataset is used for examples in the chapter. The simulation was carried out using the Populus-package by Ollikainen (2002).

The simulated population expands from the initial 100 individuals to 80,000 over 20 generations. Random mating and meioses were simulated at each generation. A single 100-cM chromosome is considered with 101 evenly spaced microsatellite markers. In the initial population there are four alleles at each marker: a single allele with frequency 0.4, and three alleles with frequency 0.2. Marker mutations were not simulated.

There are two genes in the simulated chromosome with identical effect on the disease risk. The locations of the genes were randomly selected. At both loci, a mutated allele was inserted to six randomly chosen founder chromosomes. Some founder mutations may have disappeared during the course of the generations.

The disease model is based on liability: a person is affected with probability

$$p = \frac{e^L}{1 + e^L}$$

Liability L is defined by

$$L = 5x_{g1} + 5x_{g2} + x_r\sqrt{3} + C$$

where x_{g1} and x_{g2} are indicator variables for the presence of the mutated allele at the two loci, and x_r is a normal random variable. C is a constant, whose value is adjusted to obtain prevalence of 4%.

From the final population of 80,000 individuals, 200 affected individuals were randomly selected to form the dataset. (The parents were used in the inference of their haplotypes.)

13

DATA-MINING TECHNIQUES FOR MICROARRAY DATA ANALYSIS

Carlotta Domeniconi, Daniel Barbará, Harsh Chaudhary,
Ali Al-Timimi, and Curtis Jamison

13.1. INTRODUCTION

Gene expression profiling studies via DNA microarrays offer unprecedented opportunities for advancing fundamental biological research and clinical practice (Schena et al., 1995; Debouck and Goodfellow, 1999; Aitman, 2001). Microarray technology allows researchers to simultaneously measure the expression level of tens of thousands of genes, creating a comprehensive overview of exactly what genes are being expressed in a specific tissue under various conditions. However, these studies produce a massive amount of data which need to be treated using informatics and algorithms that are sensitive to the biological context to produce meaningful results.

Microarray technology is based upon the ability of single-stranded nucleic acids to uniquely hybridize with a complementary nucleic acid to form a double-stranded complex. Single-stranded DNA probes derived from genomic sequences are affixed to a solid substrate, usually a glass microscope slide. Messenger RNA (mRNA) is extracted from experimentally treated cells or tissues and labeled with a fluorescent dye. The labeled mRNA is then applied to the microarray, and the mRNA binds to the complementary probes. A laser is then used to excite the chromofluor, and the level of emitted light is measured (Schena et al., 1995).

The affixed DNA probes are referred to as features. Typically, each feature is derived from a single gene, either as an actual cDNA clone or as a specially engineered oligonucleotide calculated to be unique to a specific gene. A microarray can contain upwards of 20,000 features, each of which recognizes mRNA from a single gene.

Next Generation of Data-Mining Applications. Edited by Kantardzic and Zurada
ISBN 0-471-65605-4 © 2005 the Institute of Electrical and Electronics Engineers, Inc.

The raw data output from the scanner is an image of the microarray. The image is then analyzed to identify features. Feature intensity is calculated by identifying the outline of the feature (usually a spot) and then subtracting the local background. Since the background levels are typically heterogeneous across the microarray, a normalization algorithm is often applied to ensure the measured intensities are comparable between features.

In general, the goal of these studies is to compare the gene expression of cells under experimental or disease conditions to that of cells under normal conditions. Thus gene expression measurements are often expressed as the differential between the experimental and the normal gene expression level. Often one of the experimental conditions is time, so a series of gene expression measurements is taken, allowing the researcher to follow the expression profile of a feature across a time interval.

From the initial adoption of microarray technology as a basic research tool, it became apparent that to exploit the full potential it was necessary to overcome the informatics burden created by the scale and complexity of microarray data (Eisen et al., 1998; Basset et al., 1999). Specifically, pattern recognition algorithms can be used to impart ordering upon the data. In theory, genes with similar expression profiles should have similar control mechanisms, and possibly be involved in related cellular processes. Thus by examining genes with similar profiles a biologist may be able to identify genes with similar functions that can further elucidate the biology of the cell.

This chapter provides a survey of techniques currently used in microarray gene expression studies. Most of these approaches utilize a fixed distance measure, thus failing to capture correlations among the data that may be local in nature. For example, to compute gene similarity, different conditions may have different importance for a given gene, and the relevance of one condition may vary from gene to gene. Moreover, existing tools are based solely upon the numerical properties of the microarray data, ignoring the volumes of biological knowledge already in existence. In an effort to overcome these limitations, this chapter also introduces novel clustering techniques, together with a system of biological knowledge agents.

The chapter is organized as follows. Section 13.2 is a survey of techniques currently used for microarray data analysis. Both classification and clustering approaches are discussed. Section 13.3 presents novel clustering techniques for discovering knowledge in microarray data, and for incorporating existing external knowledge. In particular, Section 13.3.1 introduces a subspace clustering method (LAC) that is able to learn local correlations of data, without requiring critical parameters in input, and without making assumptions on data distributions. (The subspace clustering problem is extensively discussed in the subsection of Section 13.2.2 entitled "Subspace Clustering", which also emphasizes the limitations of existing techniques.) Experimental results using breast cancer data are presented. Section 13.3.2 introduces the problems of measurement errors and of spurious correlations in microarray data. The idea of incorporating external knowledge in the form of additional categorical features is discussed, with the intent of suppressing correlations caused by artifacts in microarrays. A clustering algorithm (COOLCAT) able to handle such additional dimensions is then introduced. Section 13.3.3 emphasizes the fact that clustering analysis is insufficient to identify possible networks of interactions between genes. In an effort to capture such interactions among co-regulated genes, loglinear models are discussed, and experimental results using yeast data are presented. Section 13.3.4 describes a system of software agents for assessment of biological significance of clustering results. The biological data mart is validated using breast cancer data, and the annotation of a set of biological processes clustered together by the LAC algorithm is discussed. Finally, Section 13.4 summarizes the topics discussed, and it provides a vision for future work.

13.2. EXISTING TOOLS

Approaches to the computational analysis of gene expression data attempt to learn functionally significant groups of genes, either in an *unsupervised* or in a *supervised* fashion. Cluster analysis belongs to the unsupervised learning paradigm. As of today, it is the most widely used technique for gene expression data analysis. Cluster analysis of gene expression data begins with a definition of similarity (or a measure of distance) between expression patterns, with no prior knowledge on the true functional classes of the genes. Genes are then grouped according to their similarity, as given by the measure in use. Examples of clustering algorithms widely used with gene expression data are hierarchical clustering (Eisen et al., 1998; Spellman et al., 1998) and self-organizing maps (Tamayo et al., 1999). Classification, instead, belongs to the supervised learning setting. Supervised learning techniques, as applied to gene expression data, begin with a collection of genes for which the functional classes are known. (They are opposite to cluster analysis in this respect.) They learn the characteristics that make a given gene to be part of a certain functional group, and then exploit such characteristics to make decisions about the group of unknown genes. Examples of classification algorithms are support vector machines and decision trees.

In the following we describe in more details classification and clustering tools used and developed for microarray data analysis.

13.2.1. Classification Tools

Classification tools are a set of mathematical, statistical, and computing techniques that are generally used to sort objects into two or more identifiable classes or groups. This genre of data analysis emphasizes on deriving mechanisms for assigning new objects to the already identified classes. Objects are represented as vectors of feature measurements $\mathbf{x} = (x_1, \ldots, x_n)^T \in \Re^n$. A set of objects (*training set*) for which the corresponding classes are known is given: $\{(\mathbf{x}_i, y_i)\}_{i=1}^l$. In this set each object $\mathbf{x}$ is coupled with the corresponding class label y, with $y = 1, \ldots, J$ (where J is the number of identified classes). The problem is then to predict the class label of a new object $\mathbf{q} \in \Re^n$, based on its measurement values. It is assumed that there exists an unknown probability distribution $P(\mathbf{x}, y)$ from which data are drawn. Thus, to predict the class label of a given query $\mathbf{q}$, one needs to estimate the class posterior probabilities $\{P(j|\mathbf{q})\}_{j=1}^{J}$.

Support Vector Machines. Support vector machines (SVMs) (Cristianini and Taylor, 2000) have been successfully used as a classification tool in a variety of areas, and the maximum margin boundary they provide has been proved to be optimal in a structural risk minimization sense. The solid theoretical foundations that have inspired SVMs convey desirable computational and theoretic properties to the SVM's learning algorithm. Specifically, SVMs have many features that make them attractive for gene expression analysis, including flexibility in choosing a similarity function, sparseness of solution when dealing with large data sets, ability to handle large dimensional spaces, and ability to identify outliers.

Each vector in the gene expression matrix may be thought as a point in an n-dimensional space. A simple way to build a binary classifier is to construct a hyperplane in this space that separates class members from non-class members. In the simple case of two linearly separable classes, a support vector machine selects, among the infinite number of linear classifiers that separate the data, the classifier that minimizes an upper bound on the generalization error. The SVM achieves this goal by computing the classifier that satisfies the maximum margin property—that is, the classifier whose decision boundary has the maximum minimum distance from the closest training point.

Unfortunately, most real-world problems involve data for which a hyperplane that successfully separates class members from non-class members does not exist. If this case, the SVM looks for the hyperplane that maximizes the margin and that, at the same time, minimizes an upper bound of the error. The trade-off between margin and upper bound of the misclassification error is driven by a positive constant C that has to be chosen beforehand. The corresponding decision function is then obtained by considering the $sign(f(\mathbf{x}))$, where $f(\mathbf{x}) = \sum_i \alpha_i y_i \mathbf{x}_i^T \mathbf{x} - b$, and the coefficients α_i are the solution (Lagrange multipliers) of a convex quadratic problem, defined over the hypercube $[0, C]^l$. The parameter b is also computed from the data. (Here we assume the following: class labels $y_i \in \{-1, 1\}$.) In general, the solution will have a number of coefficients α_i equal to zero, and since there is a coefficient α_i associated to each data point, only the data points corresponding to nonzero α_i will influence the solution. These points are the support vectors. Intuitively, the support vectors are the data points that lie at the border between the two classes, and a small number of support vectors indicates that the two classes can be well separated.

This technique can be extended to allow for nonlinear decision surfaces. This is done by mapping the input vectors into a higher-dimensional feature space, $\phi \colon \Re^n \to \Re^N$, and by formulating the linear classification problem in the feature space. Therefore, $f(\mathbf{x})$ can be expressed as $f(\mathbf{x}) = \sum_i \alpha_i y_i \phi^T(\mathbf{x}_i)\phi(\mathbf{x}) - b$.

If one were given a function $K(\mathbf{x}, \mathbf{y}) = \phi^T(\mathbf{x})\phi(\mathbf{y})$, one could learn and use the maximum margin hyperplane in feature space without having to compute explicitly the image of points in $\Re^N$. It has been proved (Mercer's Theorem) that for each continuous positive definite function $K(\mathbf{x}, \mathbf{y})$ there exists a mapping ϕ such that $K(\mathbf{x}, \mathbf{y}) = \phi^T(\mathbf{x})\phi(\mathbf{y})$, $\forall \mathbf{x}, \mathbf{y} \in \Re^n$. By making use of such function K (*kernel function*), the equation for $f(\mathbf{x})$ can be rewritten as

$$f(\mathbf{x}) = \sum_i \alpha_i y_i K(\mathbf{x}_i, \mathbf{x}) - b \qquad (13.1)$$

Brown et al. (2000) describe a successful use of SVMs to classifying unseen genes. In Furey et al. (2000), SVMs are used to classify tissue samples (ovarian cancer tissues) and to explore the data for mislabeled or questionable tissue results. In Brown et al. (2000), a total of 2467 genes of the budding yeast *S. cerevisiae* are represented as 79 dimensional gene expression vectors and are classified according to six functional classes (Eisen et al., 1998). In most cases the number of positives is less than 20, and this, combined with the presence of noise, makes the learning task particularly hard. A trivial solution in which all training data are classified as negative can be easily found, but it is clearly uninformative. To overcome this problem, Brown et al. (2000) modify the matrix of kernel values during SVM optimization. [The kernel matrix $\mathbf{K}$ is the matrix defined by the kernel function on the training set: $\mathbf{K}_{ij} = K(\mathbf{x}_i, \mathbf{x}_j)$.] In order to separately control the number of misclassified points in the two classes, a constant, whose magnitude depends upon the class of the training example, is added to the diagonal of the kernel matrix. This was designed to produce smaller Lagrange multipliers in the dominant negative class and produce larger multipliers in the small positive class. This technique ensures that the positive points are not regarded as noisy labels. The resulting SVM outperformed the other methods used for comparison (i.e., Parzen windows, Fisher's linear discriminant, and the decision tree algorithm C4.5).

Decision Trees. Decision trees constitute a local learning paradigm that employs local averaging to estimate the class posterior probabilities (Breiman et al., 1984; Quinlan, 1986, 1993). The regions over which the averaging takes place are constructed in a highly adaptive manner by using a top-down recursive splitting strategy, from which the alternative name of *recursive partitioning* (RP) is derived. RP begins with a single region R_0 containing all the training data. At each step every existing region is split into two subregions, thereby increasing the number of regions. This recursive splitting procedure is continued until a region meets a local terminal criterion; that is, it contains training observations of the same class and is not further split. When all regions have met the terminal criterion, they provide the final input space partition for local estimation of class probabilities.

The shape of the terminal regions is governed by the splitting procedure. One defines a splitting function $g(\mathbf{x}, \mathbf{a})$ of the input variables $\mathbf{x}$, characterized by a set of parameters $\mathbf{a}$, and a real-valued split point s. The form of the split function is usually taken to be linear: $g(\mathbf{x}, \mathbf{a}) = \mathbf{a}^t\mathbf{x}$ (CART) (Breiman et al., 1984), often with the restriction of being parallel to the coordinate input axes (CART,

C4.5) (Breiman et al., 1984; Quinlan, 1993), that is, $\mathbf{a} \in \{\mathbf{e}_1, \ldots, \mathbf{e}_n\}$. Here $\mathbf{e}_j$ is the basis unit vector for the jth input coordinate. The particular variable j and location s used to define the split are those that jointly minimize a given criterion. In general, such a criterion is related to the average misclassification risk associated with using the resulting subregions to classify all training observations that respectively lie within them. In other words, the variable j and location s that best separate the data in the current region are chosen.

After the splitting is completed, a "pruning" procedure is usually applied that recursively recombines adjacent regions in a bottom-up manner using cross-validated misclassification risk to determine when to stop the pruning. Other approaches are also possible. For example, all available data can be used for training, and a statistical test (e.g., chi-square) is then applied to estimate whether pruning a particular node is likely to produce an improvement beyond the training set. Techniques that stop growing the tree earlier, before it reaches the point where it perfectly classifies the training data, are also in use (Mitchell, 1997).

The resulting set of regions represents a disjoint partition of the input measurement space. The region used for estimating the class probabilities and making the class assignment for any prediction point $\mathbf{q}$ is the resulting region in which the point lies. Thus, a gene expression vector is matched against a constructed decision tree to determine its functional class (Schoch et al., 2002).

A drawback of RP methods is their high instability with respect to minor perturbations of the training data. This leads to high variance predictions, induced by sampling fluctuations of the mechanism that produces the training data. Minor changes in an early split can have a major impact on later splits producing very different terminal regions. Several approaches have been proposed to mitigate the instability of RP methods. Among them are the *bagging* and *boosting* procedures (Breiman, 1996; Quinlan, 1996). Both algorithms have been used for classifying gene expression data (Dudoit et al., 2000; Fridlyand and Dudoit, 2000).

13.2.2. Clustering Tools

Hierarchical Clustering.   Hierarchical clustering (Johnson and Wichern, 1988) has been one of the most popular approach for grouping gene expression data (Eisen et al., 1998; Spellman et al., 1998). It is a bottom-up technique that starts with each data point in its own cluster. It proceeds by merging the closest pair of clusters in an iterative fashion, until all the data points are in a single cluster. The distance between clusters is usually computed in one of three different ways: *Single linkage* is the minimum distance between a point in one cluster and a point in the other cluster; *average linkage* is the average of the distances between points in one cluster and points in the other cluster; *complete linkage* is the largest distance between a point in one cluster and a point in the other cluster.

To compute distance between points, the Euclidean distance has traditionally been the most commonly used one (the main reason being that it is easy to compute). For gene expression data the Pearson correlation coefficient has been more effective and popular (Eisen et al., 1998). The sequence of clustering results is represented by a hierarchical tree, called a *dendogram*, which can be cut at any level to yield a specific number of clusters.

Eisen et al. (1998) developed a software package that implements a hierarchical clustering algorithm based on the average linkage distance. The software is called *Cluster*, and it is equipped with a visualization program called *TreeView*. Both programs are available at http://rana.Stanford.edu/software/. A form of correlation coefficient is used to measure similarity between genes. The algorithm iteratively merges genes whose similarity is the highest. The output of the software is a dendogram and an ordered fingerprint matrix. The rows of the matrix are permuted based on the dendogram, so that groups of genes with similar expression patterns are adjacent. Colors are used to graphically represent cells according to their content.

K-Means. K-means (Johnson and Wichern, 1988) is another classical algorithm that has been applied to clustering gene expression data (Tavazoie et al., 1999). This approach assumes that the number of clusters k is known *a priori*, and it starts by selecting k cluster centers (called *centroids*) (either randomly or by using some prior knowledge). A partition of the data is then computed by assigning points to the closest centroid. Euclidean distance is the most commonly used distance measure. Data points within each cluster are averaged to compute the coordinates of a new centroid. Thus, a new partition is computed, and the process is iterated until no changes in the coordinates of centroids are observed. The algorithm converges to a local minimum of the total within cluster variance.

A variation of the K-means algorithm was developed by Herwig et al. (1999) to cluster cDNA oligo-fingerprints. This approach does not require a prespecified number of clusters. It uses, instead, two parameters corresponding to (a) the maximal possible similarity between two distinct clusters and (b) the maximal possible similarity between a point and a cluster different from its own cluster. (The similarity to a cluster is defined as the similarity to its centroid.) Points are handled one at the time, added to sufficiently close clusters, or otherwise assigned to a new cluster. If centroids become too close (beyond the maximal similarity), they are merged. Unlike in the K-means algorithm, a point may be temporarily assigned to multiple clusters, and thus influence the location of more than one centroid to which it is sufficiently close.

Self-Organizing Maps.   Self-organizing map (SOM) (Kohonen, 1982, 1989) is a technique similar to K-means, with the additional constraint that centroids are restricted to lie in a two-dimensional grid. SOMs have a number of characteristics that make them well suited for clustering of gene expression data (Tamayo et al., 1999). They allow one to incorporate partial structure in the clusters, as opposed to the rigid structure of hierarchical clustering, and the absence of structure in K-means. SOM is easy to implement, reasonably fast, and scalable to large datasets. In addition, it can facilitate visualization and interpretation.

The SOM is a neural network with two layers: an input layer and an output layer (also called *topological map* layer) of radial units. The units of the output layer are laid out in space, typically in two dimensions. A SOM performs a nonlinear projection of n-dimensional input vectors onto a two-dimensional array of nodes.

Suppose we want to cluster n-dimensional gene expression vectors $\mathbf{x} \in \Re^n$. Each output node i of the SOM is connected to an n-dimensional weight vector $\mathbf{c}_i \in \Re^n$. Such weight vectors represent the centroids. An iterative learning algorithm allows the setting of the weight values. The $\mathbf{c}_i$ vectors are initialized to random values or to samples drawn from the dataset. During training, the algorithm gradually adjusts the weight values to reflect the clustering of the data. At each step t, an input vector $\mathbf{x}$ is chosen, and the closest weight vector $\mathbf{c}_{i*}$ to $\mathbf{x}$ is computed. (Euclidean distance is usually used.) The output node connected to $\mathbf{c}_{i*}$ is defined to be the *winner*, and the weight vectors of the SOM are updated according to the learning rule:

$$\mathbf{c}_i^{t+1} = \mathbf{c}_i^t + \mu^t \Lambda^t(i, i^*)(\mathbf{x}^t - \mathbf{c}_i^t) \qquad (13.2)$$

for all weight vectors $\mathbf{c}_i$ in the map. $\Lambda^t(i, i^*)$ is the neighborhood kernel function centered around the winner node i^* at time t. The neighborhood kernel is a nonincreasing function of time and of the distance of node i from the winner i^*. [A typical choice of $\Lambda(i, i^*)$ is the Gaussian kernel.] It defines the region of influence that the input vector has on the SOM. μ^t is the learning rate, which is a decreasing function of time. A typical choice for μ^t is $t^{-\alpha}$, where $0 < \alpha \le 1$. Initially, μ^t and the width of the kernel function $\Lambda^t(i, i^*)$ are set to relatively large values. During training they are gradually decreased. This corresponds to first tuning the SOM to approximately the same space as the input data and then fine-tuning the map. The learning process stops when $\mu^t = 0$.

Tamayo et al. (1999) developed a gene expression clustering software, *GeneCluster*, which implements the SOM algorithm. The program accepts in input a file of expression level vectors, together with a two-dimensional grid geometry for the output nodes. The number of grid nodes is the prescribed number of clusters. The resulting clusters are visualized by plotting for each cluster its average expression pattern with error bars. Clusters are presented according to their grid order, because clusters of close nodes tend to be similar.

Subspace Clustering.   The definition and use of proper similarity metrics are fundamental for the achievement of accurate clustering results. The problem is made particularly difficult by the curse of dimensionality (Bellman, 1961) that affects clustering (as well as any pattern classification tasks) in high-dimensional spaces. For microarray data the number of dimensions can be on the order of hundreds, if the axes are associated with different conditions, or on the order of thousands, if the axes are associated with the genes. In such high-dimensional spaces, it is highly likely that, for any given pair of points within the same cluster, there exist a considerable number of dimensions along which the points are far apart from each other. As a consequence, similarity functions that use all input features with equal relevance may not be effective.

Furthermore, clusters may exist in different subspaces, comprised of different combinations of features. In many real-world problems, some data are correlated with some dimensions, while others are correlated with different ones. Each dimension could be relevant to at least one of the clusters. For example, to compute gene similarity, different conditions may have different importance for a given gene, and the relevance of one condition may vary from gene to gene.

The problem of high dimensionality could be addressed by requiring the user to specify a subspace (i.e., subset of dimensions) for clustering analysis. However, the identification of subspaces by the user is an error-prone process. More importantly, the user may not know which dimensions are important to capture clustering information. Indeed, we desire feature relevance to be part of the findings of the clustering process itself.

An alternative solution to high-dimensional settings consists of reducing the dimensionality of the input space. Traditional feature selection algorithms select certain dimensions in advance. Methods such as Principal Component Analysis (PCA) (Duda et al., 2001; Fukunaga, 1990) transform the original input space into a lower-dimensional space by constructing dimensions that are linear combinations of the given features and that are ordered by decreasing variance. While PCA may succeed in reducing dimensionality, it has several major drawbacks. The new dimensions can be difficult to interpret, making it hard to understand clusters in relation to the original space. Furthermore, all global dimensionality reduction techniques (like PCA) are not effective in identifying clusters that may exist in different subspaces. In this situation, in fact, since data across clusters manifest different correlations with features, it may not always be feasible to prune off too many dimensions without incurring a loss of crucial information. This is because each dimension could be relevant to at least one of the clusters.

These limitations of global dimensionality reduction techniques suggest that, to capture the local correlations of data, a proper feature selection procedure should operate locally in the input space.

Local dimensionality reduction approaches for the purpose of efficiently indexing high-dimensional spaces have been recently discussed in the database literature (Keogh et al., 2001; Chakrabarti and Mehrotra, 2000; Thomasian et al., 1998). Applying global dimensionality reduction techniques when data are not globally correlated can cause significant loss of distance information, resulting in a large number of false positives and hence a high query cost. The general approach adopted by the authors is to find local correlations in the data and to perform dimensionality reduction on the locally correlated clusters individually. For example, Chakrabarti and Mehrotra (2000) first construct spacial clusters in the original input space using a simple technique that resembles K-means. Principal component analysis is then performed on each spatial cluster individually to obtain the principal components.

In general, the efficacy of these methods depends on how the clustering problem is addressed in the first place in the original feature space. A potential serious problem with such techniques is the lack of data to locally perform PCA on each cluster to derive the principal components. Moreover, for clustering purposes, the new dimensions may be difficult to interpret, making it hard to understand clusters in relation to the original space.

The problem of finding different clusters in different subspaces of the original input space has been addressed in Agrawal et al. (1998). The authors use a density-based approach to identify clusters. The algorithm (CLIQUE) proceeds from lower- to higher-dimensionality subspaces and discovers dense regions in each subspace. To approximate the density of the points, the input space is partitioned into cells by dividing each dimension into the same number ξ of equal length intervals. For a given set of dimensions, the cross product of the corresponding intervals (one for each dimension in the set) is called a *unit* in the respective subspace. A unit is dense if the number of points it contains is above a given threshold τ. Both ξ and τ are parameters defined by the user. The algorithm finds all dense units in each k-dimensional subspace by building from the dense units of $(k-1)$-dimensional subspaces, and then it connects them to describe the clusters as union of maximal rectangles.

Recently (Procopiuc et al., 2002), another density-based projective clustering algorithm (DOC/FastDOC) has been proposed. This approach requires the maximum distance between attribute values (i.e., maximum width of the bounding hypercubes) as parameter in input, and it pursues an optimality criterion defined in terms of density of each cluster in its corresponding subspace. A Monte Carlo procedure is then developed to approximate with high probability an optimal projective cluster. In practice, it may be difficult to properly set the parameters of DOC, because each relevant attribute can have a different local variance value.

The problem of finding different clusters in different subspaces is also addressed in Aggarwal et al. (1999). The proposed algorithm (PROjected CLUStering) seeks subsets of dimensions such that the points are closely clustered in the corresponding spanned subspaces. Both the number of clusters and the average number of dimensions per cluster are user-defined parameters. PROCLUS starts with choosing a random set of medoids, and then it progressively improves the quality of medoids by performing an iterative hill-climbing procedure that discards the 'bad' medoids from the current set. In order to find the set of dimensions that matter the most for each cluster, the algorithm selects the dimensions along which the points have the smallest average distance from the current medoid. The PROCLUS algorithm may be prone to loss of information if the number of dimensions is not properly chosen. ORCLUS (Aggarwal and Yu, 2000) modifies the PROCLUS algorithm by adding a mechanism to merge clusters and by selecting for each cluster principal components instead of attributes.

Generative approaches have also been developed for local dimensionality reduction and clustering. The approach in Ghahramani and Hinton (1996) makes use of maximum likelihood factor analysis to model local correlations between features. The resulting generative model obeys the distribution of a mixture of factor analyzers. An expectation-maximization algorithm is presented for fitting the parameters of the mixture of factor analyzers. The choice of the number of factor analyzers, as well as the number of factors in each analyzer (that drives the dimensionality reduction), remains an important open issue for the approach in Ghahramani and Hinton (1996).

Tipping and Bishop (1999) extend the single PCA model to a mixture of local linear submodels to capture nonlinear structure in the data. A mixture of principal component analyzer models is derived as a solution to a maximum-likelihood problem. An EM algorithm is formulated to estimate the parameters.

We observe that, while mixture of Gaussians models, with arbitrary covariance matrices, could in principle capture local correlations along any directions, lack of data to locally estimate full covariance matrices in high-dimensional spaces is a serious problem in practice.

13.3. IMPROVED TOOLS

This section describes novel approaches for more accurate pattern discovery in microarray data. It contains four major contributions: the LAC algorithm, the COOLCAT algorithm, loglinear models, and a system of software agents. In Section 13.4 we sketch our view of a system that integrates the four components to discover clusters in microarray data utilizing external knowledge.

13.3.1. Locally Adaptive Clustering

In order to capture the local correlations of data, a proper feature selection procedure should operate locally in the input space. Local feature selection allows different distance measures to be embedded in different regions of the input space. Most of the algorithms discussed in an earlier subsection, entitled "Subspace Clustering," requires a critical input parameter that guides the selection of features and, thus, the discovery of clusters in the data. In general, results are highly sensitive to the values used in input (Yip et al., 2003), and, unfortunately, the correct values are rarely available in real applications. Therefore, it is highly desirable to avoid introducing such critical parameters.

In the following, we discuss in depth a *soft* feature selection procedure (LAC) (Domeniconi et al., 2004; Papadopoulos et al., 2003) that addresses the subspace clustering problem without requiring critical parameters in input and without assuming any data distribution model.

The technique assigns (local) weights to features according to the local correlations of data along each dimension. Dimensions along which data are loosely correlated receive a small weight, which has the effect of elongating distances along that dimension. Features that correlate strongly with data receive a large weight, which has the effect of constricting distances along that dimension. Figure 13.1 gives a simple example. The top plot depicts two clusters of data, one elongated along the x dimension, and the other along the y dimension. The bottom plot shows the same clusters, where within-cluster distances between points are computed using the respective local weights generated by the Locally Adaptive Clustering (LAC) algorithm (Domeniconi et al., 2004; Papadopoulos et al.,

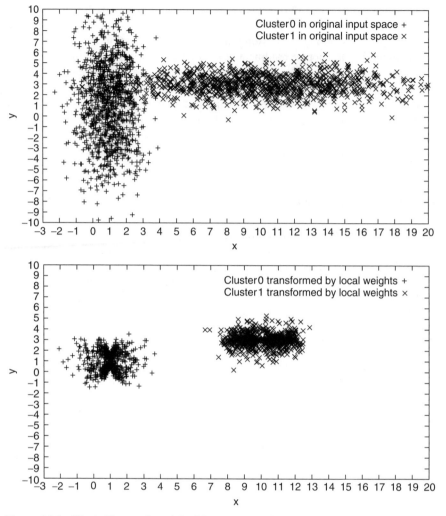

Figure 13.1. (**Top**) Clusters in original input space. (**Bottom**) Clusters transformed by local weights.

2003). The weight values reflect local correlations of data, and reshape each cluster as a dense spherical cloud. This directional local reshaping of neighborhoods better separates clusters, thereby discovering patterns in different subspaces of the original input space.

In the following we formalize the problem of finding different clusters in different subspaces within the paradigm of the LAC algorithm.

Problem Statement. Consider a set of points in some space of dimensionality n. A *weighted cluster* C is a subset of data points, together with a vector of weights $\mathbf{w} = (w_1, \ldots, w_n)$, such that the points in C are closely clustered according to the L_2 norm distance weighted using $\mathbf{w}$. The component w_j measures the degree of correlation of points in C along feature j. The problem becomes now how to estimate the weight vector $\mathbf{w}$ for each cluster in the data set.

In this setting, the concept of *cluster* is not based only on points, but also involves a weighted distance metric; that is, clusters are discovered in spaces transformed by $\mathbf{w}$. Each cluster is associated with its own $\mathbf{w}$, which reflects the correlation of points in the cluster itself. The effect of $\mathbf{w}$ is to transform distances so that the associated cluster is reshaped into a dense hypersphere of points separated from other data.

In traditional clustering, the partition of a set of points is induced by a set of *representative* vectors, also called *centroids* or *centers*. The partition induced by discovering weighted clusters is formally defined as follows.

Definition. Given a set S of D points $\mathbf{x}$ in the n-dimensional Euclidean space, a set of k centers $\{\mathbf{c}_1, \ldots, \mathbf{c}_k\}$, $\mathbf{c}_j \in \mathfrak{R}^n$, $j = 1, \ldots, k$, coupled with a set of corresponding weight vectors $\{\mathbf{w}_1, \ldots, \mathbf{w}_k\}$, $\mathbf{w}_j \in \mathfrak{R}^n$, $j = 1, \ldots, k$, partition S into k sets $\{S_1, \ldots, S_k\}$:

$$
S_j = \left\{ \mathbf{x} \mid \left(\sum_{i=1}^{n} w_{ji}(x_i - c_{ji})^2 \right)^{1/2} < \left(\sum_{i=1}^{n} w_{li}(x_i - c_{li})^2 \right)^{1/2}, \forall l \neq j \right\}
$$

(13.3)

where w_{ji} and c_{ji} represent the ith components of vectors $\mathbf{w}_j$ and $\mathbf{c}_j$ respectively (ties are broken randomly).

The set of centers and weights is *optimal* with respect to the Euclidean norm, if they minimize the error measure:

$$
E_1(C, W) = \sum_{j=1}^{k} \sum_{i=1}^{n} w_{ji} e^{-X_{ji}}
$$

(13.4)

subject to the constraints $\sum_{i=1}^{n} w_{ji}^2 = 1 \; \forall j$. C and W are $(n \times k)$ matrices whose column vectors are $\mathbf{c}_j$ and $\mathbf{w}_j$, respectively; that is, $C = [\mathbf{c}_1 \ldots \mathbf{c}_k]$ and $W = [\mathbf{w}_1 \ldots \mathbf{w}_k]$. X_{ji} represents the average distance from the centroid $\mathbf{c}_j$ of points in cluster j along dimension i and is defined as follows:

$$
X_{ji} = \frac{1}{|S_j|} \sum_{\mathbf{x} \in S_j} (c_{ji} - x_i)^2
$$

The exponential function in Eq. (13.4) has the effect of making the weights w_{ji} more sensitive to changes in X_{ji} and, therefore, to changes in local feature relevance. This allows larger error improvements as we adapt the values of weights and centers, and therefore a faster computation to achieve spherically shaped clusters (separated from each other) in the space transformed by optimal weights (see Figure 13.1). The following section presents an algorithm that finds a solution (set of centers and weights) that is a local minimum of the error function [Eq. (13.4)].

Locally Adaptive Clustering Algorithm. This section describes a feature relevance estimation procedure that assigns local weights to features according to the local correlation of data along each dimension. The technique progressively improves the quality of initial centroids and weights, by investigating the space near the centers to estimate the dimensions that matter the most—that is, the dimensions along which local data are mostly correlated.

The technique starts with *well-scattered* points in D as the k centroids: The first centroid is chosen at random, and the others are selected so that they are far from one another and from the first chosen center. Initially the values of weights are set to 1. Given the initial centroids c_j, for $j = 1, \ldots, k$, the corresponding sets S_j are computed as defined in Eq. (13.3), where $w_{ji} = 1 \; \forall j$ and $\forall i$. Then, the average distance along each dimension from the points in S_j to c_j is computed. Let X_{ji} denote this average distance along dimension i. The smaller the value of X_{ji}, the larger the correlation of points along dimension i. The value X_{ji} is used in an exponential weighting scheme to credit weights to features (and to clusters):

$$w_{ji} = \exp(-h \times X_{ji}) \bigg/ \left(\sum_{l=1}^{n} (\exp(-h \times 2 \times X_{jl})) \right)^{1/2} \tag{13.5}$$

where h is a parameter that can be chosen to maximize (minimize) the influence of X_{ji} on w_{ji}. When $h = 0$ we have $w_{ji} = 1/n$, thereby ignoring any difference between the X_{ji}. On the other hand, when h is large, a change in X_{ji} will be exponentially reflected in w_{ji}. The value of h can be empirically determined through cross-validation. The exponential weighting is more sensitive to changes in local feature relevance (Bottou and Vapnik, 1992) and gives rise to better performance improvement. In fact, it is more stable because it prevents distances from extending infinitely in any direction (i.e., zero weight). This, however, can occur when either linear or quadratic weighting is used.

The weights w_{ji} enable us to elongate distances along less important dimensions—that is, dimensions along which points are loosely correlated—and, at the same time, to constrict distances along the most influential ones—that is, features along which points are strongly correlated. Note that the technique is centroid-based because weightings depend on the centroid.

The computed weights are used to update the sets S_j and, therefore, the centroids' coordinates. The procedure is iterated until convergence is reached; that is, no change in centers' coordinates is observed. The resulting algorithm, LAC (Locally Adaptive Clustering), is summarized in the following.

Input: Set D of points $\mathbf{x} \in R^n$, and the number of clusters k.

1. Start with k initial centroids $c_1, c_2, \ldots, c_k$;

2. Set $w_{ji} = 1$, for each centroid $\mathbf{c}_j$, $j = 1, \ldots, k$ and each feature $i = 1, \ldots, n$;

3. For each centroid $\mathbf{c}_j$, $j = 1, \ldots, k$, and for each data point $\mathbf{x}$:

   - Set $S_j = \{\mathbf{x} | j = arg \min_l WDist(\mathbf{c}_l, \mathbf{x})\}$,

     where $WDist(\mathbf{c}_l, \mathbf{x}) = \left(\sum_{i=1}^{n} w_{li}(c_{li} - x_i)^2\right)^{1/2}$;

4. **Compute new weights**. For each centroid $\mathbf{c}_j$, $j = 1, \ldots, k$, and for each feature i:

   - Set $X_{ji} = \sum_{\mathbf{x} \in S_j}(c_{ji} - x_i)^2 / |S_j|$, where $|S_j|$ is the cardinality of set S_j (X_{ji} represents the average distance of points in S_j from $\mathbf{c}_j$ along feature i);

   - Set $w_{ji} = exp(-h \times X_{ji}) / \left(\sum_{l=1}^{n}(exp(-h \times 2 \times X_{jl}))\right)^{1/2}$;

5. For each centroid $\mathbf{c}_j$, $j = 1, \ldots, k$, and for each data point $\mathbf{x}$:

   - Recompute $S_j = \{\mathbf{x} | j = arg \min_l WDist(\mathbf{c}_l, \mathbf{x})\}$;

6. **Compute new centroids**. Set $\mathbf{c}_j = \frac{\sum_{\mathbf{x}} \mathbf{x} 1_{S_j}(\mathbf{x})}{\sum_{\mathbf{x}} 1_{S_j}(\mathbf{x})}$, for each $j = 1, \ldots, k$, where $1_S(.)$ is the indicator function of set S;

7. Iterate 3,4,5,6 until convergence (i.e., no change in centroids' coordinates)

The sequential structure of the LAC algorithm is analogous to the mathematics of the *EM* algorithm (Dempster et al., 1977). The hidden variables are the assignments of the points to the centroids. Step 3 constitutes the E step of the *EM* algorithm: It finds the values of the hidden variables S_j given the previous values of the parameters w_{ji} and c_{ji}. The following step (M step) consists in finding new matrices of weights and centroids that minimize the error function with respect to the current estimation of hidden variables. It can be shown that the LAC algorithm converges to a local minimum of the error function [Eq. (13.4)] (Domeniconi, 2002).

Empirical Results with Gene Expression Data. Gene expression data are often represented as matrices of expression levels of genes (rows) under different conditions (columns). One of the usual goals in expression data analysis is to cluster genes according to their expression levels under different conditions, or to cluster conditions (e.g., patients) based on the expression of a number of genes. Usually, all conditions are given equal weights in the investigation of gene similarity, and vice versa. In practice, though, different conditions may have different levels of relevance when measuring similarities among genes. Moreover, the same condition may have a different relevance within different groups of genes. Similarly for genes, when seeking groups among conditions.

The LAC algorithm is well suited to perform simultaneous clustering of both genes and conditions in a microarray data matrix, as well as to exploit the different degrees of relevance of conditions and genes. The feasibility of the LAC algorithm for finding set of genes showing similar up-regulation and down-regulation under a set of conditions has been tested. The task is to seek subsets of genes and conditions with a *high similarity score*.

A particular score that applies to expression data is the *mean-squared residue score* (Cheng and Church, 2000). Let I and J be subsets of genes and experiments, respectively. The pair (I, J) specifies a submatrix A_{IJ} with a mean-squared residue score defined as follows:

$$H(I, J) = \frac{1}{|I||J|} \sum_{i \in I, j \in J} (a_{ij} - a_{iJ} - a_{Ji} + a_{IJ})^2 \qquad (13.6)$$

where $a_{iJ} = \frac{1}{|J|} \sum_{j \in J} a_{ij}$, $a_{Ij} = \frac{1}{|I|} \sum_{i \in I} a_{ij}$, and $a_{IJ} = \frac{1}{|I||J|} \sum_{i \in I, j \in J} a_{ij}$. They represent the row and column means and the mean of the submatrix, respectively. The lowest score $H(I, J) = 0$ indicates that the gene expression levels fluctuate in unison. The aim is then to find clusters with low mean-squared residue score (below a certain threshold). The mean-squared residue score is minimized when subsets of genes and experiments (or dimensions) are chosen so that the gene vectors (i.e., rows of the resulting cluster) are close to each other with respect to the Euclidean distance. As a result, the LAC algorithm is well suited to perform simultaneous clustering of both genes and conditions in a microarray data matrix.

The LAC algorithm has been tested with a DNA microarray of gene expression profiles in hereditary breast cancer, available at research.nhgri.nih.gov/microarray/ NEJM_Supplement/ (Hedenfalk et al., 2001). The microarray contains expression levels of 3226 genes under 22 conditions. The dataset is presented as a matrix: Each row corresponds to a gene, and each column represents a condition under which the gene is developed.

The mean-squared residue score as defined in Eq. (13.6) has been utilized to assess the quality of the clusters detected by LAC and PROCLUS (Aggarwal et al., 1999) algorithms. The lowest score value 0 indicates that the gene expression levels fluctuate in unison. The aim is to find clusters with low mean-squared residue score (in general, below a certain threshold).

The LAC and PROCLUS algorithms are tested using the microarray data and small values of k ($k = 3$ and $k = 4$). Among the subspace clustering techniques available in the literature, PROCLUS was chosen since, as the LAC algorithm, it computes a partition of the data. On the contrary, the CLIQUE technique (Agrawal et al., 1998) allows overlapping between clusters, and thus its results are not directly comparable with those of LAC. [The DOC algorithm (Procopiuc et al., 2002) was also used in these experiments, but it failed to find any clusters. It has been observed (Yip et al., 2003) that the DOC algorithm has a tendency of discarding too many points as outliers. In high-dimensional spaces, this may be the cause of failure in finding clusters.] Tables 13.1 and 13.2 show sizes, scores, and dimensions of the clusters detected by the two algorithms. For LAC the dimensions with the largest weights have been selected.

TABLE 13.1. Size, Score, and Dimensions of the Clusters Detected by LAC and PROCLUS Algorithms on the Microarray Data ($k = 3$)

$k = 3$	LAC	PROCLUS
C0 (size, score)	1220×5, **11.98**	1635×4, **9.41**
dimensions	9,13,14,19,22	7,8,9,13
C1 (size, score)	1052×5, **1.07**	1399×6, **48.18**
dimensions	7,8,9,13,18	7,8,9,13,19,22
C2 (size, score)	954×4, **5.32**	192×5, **2.33**
dimensions	12,13,16,18	2,7,10,19,22

TABLE 13.2. Size, Score, and Dimensions of the Clusters Detected by LAC and PROCLUS Algorithms on the Microarray Data ($k = 4$)

$k = 4$	LAC	PROCLUS
C0 (size, score)	1701×5, **4.52**	1249×5, **3.90**
dimensions	7,8,9,19,22	7,8,9,13,22
C1 (size, score)	1255×5, **3.75**	1229×6, **42.74**
dimensions	7,8,9,13,22	7,8,9,13,19,22
C2 (size, score)	162 outliers	730×4, **15.94**
dimensions	—	7,8,9,13
C3 (size, score)	108 outliers	18×5, **3.97**
dimensions	—	6,11,14,16,21

For $k = 3$, within each cluster four or five conditions received significant larger weight than the remaining ones. Hence, those dimensions were selected. By taking into consideration this result, the value of the input parameter of the PROCLUS algorithm (i.e., average number of dimensions per cluster) was set to five. For $k = 4$, within two clusters five conditions receive again considerably larger weight than the others. The remaining two clusters contain fewer genes, and all conditions receive equal weights. Since no correlation was found among the conditions in these two cases, the corresponding tuples were "labeled" as outliers.

Different combinations of conditions are selected for different biclusters, as also expected from a biological perspective. Some conditions are often selected, by both LAC and PROCLUS (e.g., conditions 7, 8, and 9). The mean-squared residue scores of the biclusters produced by LAC are consistently low, as desired. On the contrary, PROCLUS provides some clusters with higher scores (C1 in both Tables 13.1 and 13.2). Evidence of biological significance for the clustering results of LAC is further discussed in Section 13.3.4.

In general, the weighting of dimensions provides a convenient scheme to properly tune the results. That is, by ranking the dimensions according to their weight, we can keep adding to a cluster the dimension that minimizes the increase in score. Thus, given an upper bound on the score, we can obtain the largest set of dimensions that satisfies the given bound.

13.3.2. Categorical Clustering of External Features

It is well known that microarray data contains a significant component of measurement errors that can significantly impact the conclusions scientists make about the data collected. Particularly troubling is the presence of artifacts such as the strong interactions between neighboring spots on the array. For instance, Qian et al. (unpublished observations) show that the closer two genes are situated on the chip, the higher their correlation is, meaning that the major reason these two genes are detected as coexpressed is that they are collocated in the array. Any clustering algorithm will likely put these two genes together in the same cluster, leading to erroneous conclusions. Notice that this effect will not change even if the experiments are replicated (as long as the genes remain in the same array position).

Other sources of correlations have been found. Yu et al. (unpublished data) report correlations between genes due to large-scale chromosomal superstructure. Biology and artifact correlations are intermingled in nontrivial ways, making the removal of the artifacts a very difficult problem. A popular method of "local normalization" (Colantuoni et al., 2002) reportedly fails to remove the effects of the artifact completely. In Qian et al. (unpublished observations), signal convolution methods are used, and even though they are proven effective, there is no biological interpretation of why they work, thus leaving open the possibility of their wide applicability.

We believe that an effective method to suppress correlations promoted by artifacts in microarray data is to subject the clusterings obtained using the expression data to further scrutiny using external features readily available to the scientific community. A large body of experiments and literature pre-dates microarray technology, and even today other types of experiments contribute to enrich our knowledge about genes. We believe that more sound conclusions can be obtained by bringing this body of knowledge to play a role in the analysis of microarray data.

We can capture this external knowledge in the form of extra attributes or features that enrich both the rows (genes) and the columns (observations) of the matrix coming from the microarray expression data. External data can come from a variety of sources, such as patience's information (e.g., age, sex, environmental factors) or previous studies about gene's characteristics (e.g., gene functions, pathways). It is important to notice that most of this data are categorical—that is, data whose attribute values cannot be sorted in a natural way (sex or color are examples of this type of data; there is no natural way to sort "female" and "male" or to sort "blue" and "red"). It is also important to notice that some of these data might be incomplete or incompletely specified (e.g., we may not know yet what the function of a gene is; or we may know that there is a set of functions that the gene carries out in different scenarios, but we are not sure which one is applicable in the current microarray experiment).

Clustering categorical data requires a different approach from the methods used for numerical data. We have developed an efficient approach to clustering of categorical data that is based on information theoretical concepts. Our approach is to minimize the expected entropy of the clusters formed. Our algorithm, COOL-CAT, achieves high-accuracy clustering while being extremely efficient in terms of space utilized and running time. Moreover, COOLCAT can cluster new information in an incremental way, without having to re-visit the already processed dataset. In what follows we describe our technique for clustering categorical data.

Information Theory and Clustering.   Entropy is the measure of information and uncertainty of a random variable (Shannon, 1948). Formally, if X is a random variable, $S(X)$ the set of values that X can take, and $\Pr(x)$ the probability function of X, the entropy $H(X)$ is defined as shown in Eq. 13.7:

$$H(X) = - \sum_{x \in S(X)} \Pr(x) \log(\Pr(x)) \tag{13.7}$$

The entropy of a multivariate vector $\hat{X} = X_1, \dots, X_n$ can be computed as shown in Eq. (13.8), where $\Pr(\hat{X}) = \Pr(X_1, \dots, X_n)$ is the multivariate probability distribution:

$$H(\hat{X}) = - \sum_{X_1 \in S_1} \cdots \sum_{X_n \in S_n} Pr(\hat{X}) \log \Pr(\hat{X}) \tag{13.8}$$

The problem we are trying to solve can be formulated as follows. Given a dataset D of N points, where each point is a multidimensional vector of d categorical attributes (i.e., $\hat{P}_j = p_{j_1}, \dots, p_{j_d}$), and given an integer k, we would like to separate the points into k groups $C_1, \dots, C_k$, or clusters, in such a way that we minimize the entropy of the whole arrangement. Unfortunately, this problem is NP-complete and, moreover, difficult to approximate (Garey and Johnson, 1979). In fact, the problem is NP-complete for any distance function $d(x, y)$, defined over pairs of points x, y, such that the function maps pairs of points to real numbers (hence, our entropy function qualifies); therefore we need to resort to heuristics to solve it. We aim to minimize the expected entropy, whose expression is shown in Eq. 13.9, where $H(C_1), \dots, H(C_k)$ represent the entropies of each cluster, and C_i denotes the points assigned to cluster i, $C_i \subseteq D$, with the properties that $C_i \neq \emptyset$, $C_i \cap C_j = \emptyset$ $i, j = 1, \dots, k$, $i \neq j$, and $\cup C_i = D$. The symbol $\check{C} = C_1, \dots, C_k$ represents the clustering.

$$H(\check{C}) = \sum_j \frac{|C_j|}{|C|} H(C_j) \tag{13.9}$$

COOLCAT.   We describe here a categorical clustering algorithm, COOLCAT (Barbará et al., 2002), based on information theory concepts that we have developed and used successfully for this task. The algorithm consists of two steps: initialization and an incremental step.

Initialization.   The initialization step "bootstraps" the algorithm, finding a suitable set of clusters out of a sample S, taken from the dataset $|S| \ll N$, where N is the size of the entire dataset. We first find the k most "dissimilar" records from the sample set by maximizing the minimum pairwise entropy of the chosen points. We start by finding the two points p_{s_1}, p_{s_2} that maximize $H(p_{s_1}, p_{s_2})$ and placing them in two separate clusters C_1, C_2. From there, we proceed incrementally; that is, to find the record we will put in the jth cluster, and we choose an unmarked point p_{s_j} that maximizes $\min_i H(p_{s_i}, p_{s_j})$. However, if we just select the most "dissimilar" records from the sample, we run the risk of selecting an "outlier" as the seed of a cluster. To avoid this we exclude any point whose average pairwise entropy with respect to all the other points in the sample is bigger than the mean of the pairwise entropies in the sample plus two times the standard deviation of the distribution of pairwise entropies. In formal terms, if $\bar{H} = \text{ave}(H(p_i, p_j))$ is the average entropy of all the pairwise entropies in the sample, and δ is the standard deviation of the distribution of pairwise entropies, and $\bar{H}_i = \frac{1}{|S-1|} \sum_{i \neq j} H(p_{s_i}, p_{s_j})$ is the average pairwise entropy for point s_i in the sample, we do not consider as the initial point any point whose $\hat{H}_i > 2\delta + \hat{H}$.

Incremental Step.   After the initialization, we process the remaining records of the dataset (the rest of the sample and points outside the sample) incrementally, finding a suitable cluster for each record. This is done by computing the expected entropy that results of placing the point in each of the clusters and selecting the cluster for which that expected entropy is the minimum. We proceed in the incremental step by bringing a buffer of points to main memory and clustering them one by one.

The experimental evaluation of COOLCAT shows that it is an efficient algorithm, whose solutions are stable and robust, and that it is scalable for large datasets (since it incrementally adds points to the initial clusters). In our comparisons with other algorithms, COOLCAT always shows advantage in terms of the quality measures, with a significant improvement in running time.

13.3.3. Gene Interaction Analysis Using Loglinear Models

Clustering algorithms have been quite successful in the molecular profiling of human cancers; however, they might be insufficient to identify molecular networks. The goal of most clustering methods is to define each gene as being part of a self-contained cluster. Hence, each gene is assigned to only one cluster. However, a gene can usually be characterized in more than one way (e.g., the p53 protein belongs to more than one physiological pathway). Furthermore, it is impossible to determine the interactions that can exist between different genes from just looking at the cluster composition.

Association rules are defined as follows. Let $I = i_1, i_2, \ldots, i_m$ be a set of items and let D be a set of transactions T, where $T \subseteq I$. An association rule is an implication of the form $A \Rightarrow B$, where $A \subseteq I$, $B \subseteq I$, and $A \cap B = \emptyset$. This rule holds in D with *support* s equal to the fraction of transactions in D that contain both A and B, and with *confidence* c, equal to the fraction of those transactions in D containing A that also contain B. It has been proven that support is not a measure of correlation between A and B (in fact, the occurrence of A does not necessarily imply B). Alternative definitions for interesting relationships have been proposed in the literature.

Association rules, used widely in the area of market basket analysis, can be applied to the analysis of expression data. Association rules are defined by the support of the set of overexpressed or underexpressed genes that are involved in the rule (number of samples in the data set that contain the gene) and by their confidence (number of times that the right-hand side appears in records where the left-hand side gene set appears). For example, the kind of rule that can be discovered is of the following form: "When gene a and gene b are overexpressed within a sample, then often gene c is overexpressed too." The user simply defines thresholds for frequency (support) and validity (confidence) levels. An association rule mining algorithm then identifies every rule that is frequent and valid according to their user-defined thresholds. The well-known Apriori approach applies anti-monotonicity of the minimal frequency (i.e., an itemset cannot be frequent if one of its subsets is not frequent) as a constraint. Thus, by sequentially identifying singletons, pairs, gene sets of size 3, and so on, it is possible to prune most of the search space. One might infer that genes involved in association rules participate in some type of gene network based on frequent itemsets. Creighton and Hanash (2003) first applied association rules (Agrawal et al., 1993) to investigate how the expression of one gene may be associated with the expression of a set of genes.

However, the association rule method can only capture gene coexpression, but not interactions. For example, it cannot discover the following rule: "A gene is over- or underexpressed only if several genes are jointly over- or underexpressed, but not if at least one of them is not over- or underexpressed." In other words, the association rule is unable to discover the interactions between different genes.

Real interactions can be discovered by building all k-way interaction loglinear models and examining their parameters and residuals using microarray data (Wu et al., 2003). The method involves first finding large gene sets by using the Apriori algorithm, building all k-way interaction models iteratively, and screening large gene sets based on the estimates from k-way interaction model. The method can be sketched as follows:

- Step 1. Transform gene expression raw data to build a Boolean matrix.
- Step 2. Apply the *A priori* method to find all large gene sets.

- Step 3. For $k = 1$ to K and for each large gene set:

    1. Fit a k-way interaction model.

    2. If the *residual* is larger than τ, include the set into the result set.

The key to finding interactions worthy of examining is to compute the residual, which is the difference between the actual support of the set and the estimated value given by a k-way interaction model. When the residual is large, it means that the support of the set cannot be explained by the k-way interactions; thus, higher-order interactions are at play.

Loglinear Models.   Loglinear modeling is a methodology for approximating discrete multidimensional probability distributions. The multiway table of joint probabilities is approximated by a product of lower-order tables. Here we should note that loglinear models use only categorical attributes and continuous attributes must be converted to discrete values first.

For a value $y_{i_1,i_2,\ldots,i_n}$ at position i_r of the rth dimension $d_r (1 \le r \le n)$, we define the log of anticipated value $y_{i_1,i_2,\ldots,i_n}$ as a linear additive function of contributions from various higher-level group-bys as shown in Eq. 13.10.

$$\log \hat{y}_{i_1,i_2,\ldots,i_n} = \sum_{G \subseteq d_1,d_2,\ldots,d_n} \gamma^G (i_r | d_r \in G) \qquad (13.10)$$

We will refer to the γ terms as the coefficients of the model. The coefficients corresponding to any group-by G are obtained by subtracting from the average value at group-by G all the coefficients from higher level group-by-s. For instance, in a four-dimensional table with dimensions A, B, C, D, we use i, j, k, l, y_{ijkl} to denote the cell in a four-dimensional space, where $i = 0, \ldots, I - 1, j = 0, \ldots, J - 1, k = 0, \ldots, K - 1, l = 0, \ldots, L - 1$. Equation 13.11 shows the saturated loglinear model that contains all the possible k-factor effects, all the possible $k - 1$-factor effects, and so on down to the 1-factor effects and the mean γ. For example, γ_i^A is a one-factor effect and γ_{ij}^{AB} is a two-factor effect that shows the dependency within the distributions of the associated attributes A, B. The singly subscripted terms are analogous to main effects, and the doubly subscripted terms are analogous to two-factor interactions.

$$\log \hat{y}_{ijkl} = \gamma + \gamma_i^A + \gamma_j^B + \gamma_k^C + \gamma_l^D$$
$$\gamma_{ij}^{AB} + \gamma_{ik}^{AC} + \gamma_{il}^{AD} + \gamma_{jk}^{BC} + \gamma_{jl}^{BD} + \gamma_{kl}^{CD}$$
$$+ \gamma_{ijk}^{ABC} + \gamma_{ijl}^{ABD} + \gamma_{jkl}^{BCD} \qquad (13.11)$$

Equation 13.12 shows the linear constraints among coefficients, where a dot "." means that the parameter has been summed over the index. (For example, $\gamma_{i.}^{AB} =$

$\sum_{j=0}^{J} \gamma_{ij}^{AB}$.) In short, the constraints specify that the loglinear parameters sum to 0 over all indices.

$$\gamma_{.}^{A} = \gamma_{.}^{B} = \gamma_{.}^{C} = \gamma_{.}^{D} = 0$$

$$\gamma_{i.}^{AB} = \gamma_{.j}^{AB} + \gamma_{i.}^{AC} + \gamma_{.k}^{AC} = \cdots = \gamma_{kl}^{CD} = 0$$

$$\gamma_{ijk.}^{ABCD} = \gamma_{ij.l}^{ABCD} = \gamma_{i.kl}^{ABCD} = \gamma_{.jkl}^{ABCD} = 0 \qquad (13.12)$$

Equation 13.13 shows how to compute the coefficients in a four-dimensional table, where l represents the average of a group-by.

$$\gamma = l_{....}$$

$$\gamma_i^A = l_{i...} - \gamma$$

$$\cdots$$

$$\gamma_{ij}^{AB} = l_{ij..} - \gamma_i^A - \gamma_j^B - \gamma$$

$$\gamma_{ijk}^{ABC} = l_{ijk.} - \gamma_{ij}^{AB} - \gamma_{ik}^{AC} - \gamma_{jk}^{BC} - \gamma_i^A - \gamma_j^B - \gamma_k^C - \gamma$$

$$\cdots \qquad (13.13)$$

In Sarawagi et al. (1998) a fast computation technique called the UpDown method that makes this approach feasible for large sets is described.

Experimental Results of Loglinear Modeling in Yeast Data. These results, which appeared in Wu et al. (2003), were obtained by using the compendium from Hughes et al. (2000) of expression profiles for 6316 transcripts corresponding to 300 diverse mutations and chemical treatments in yeast. In Creighton and Hanash (2003), this dataset is transformed by binning an expression value greater than 0.2 for the log base 10 of the fold change as being up; a value less than −0.2 as being down; and a value between −0.2 and 0.2 as being neither up nor down.

In the yeast dataset, the application found tens of thousands of frequent itemsets of size seven or greater. However, the number of itemsets whose residual exceeds a threshold is much smaller. As an indication, Table 13.3 shows the frequencies and estimates from the all k-way interaction model for large 4-gene sets. Table 13.4 gives a description for each of the ORFs (open reading frame) included in Table 13.3. The information of each ORF was retrieved from the *Saccharomyces* Genome Database (http://genome-www.stanford.edu/Saccharomyces/).

YMR096W (SNZ1) and YMR095C (SNO1) are present in 8/8 groups in Table 13.3 while YMR096W (SNZ1)/YMR095C (SNO1)/YMR094W (CTF13) is present in 6/8 groups in Table 13.3. SNZ1 belongs to three-membered gene families SNZ1-3. Each of these three genes is found adjacent to another conserved gene family named SNO1-3 (Snz-proximal open reading frame). The

TABLE 13.3. The Frequencies and Estimates from All k-Way Interaction Model for Large 4-Gene Sets.

Gene Set	Frequency	1-Way	2-Way	3-Way
YHR029C, YMR094W, YMR096W, YMR095C	56	0	15	26
YJR109C, YGL117W, YMR096W, YMR095C	54	0	15	23
YJR109C, YMR094W, YMR096W, YMR095C	56	0	17	32
YGL117W, YER175C, YMR096W, YMR095C	54	0	24	28
YGL117W, YMR094W, YMR096W, YMR095C	56	0	21	27
YHR071W, YMR094W, YMR096W, YMR095C	54	0	22	33
YBR047W, YMR094W, YMR096W, YMR095C	59	0	14	18
YER175C, YMR094W, YMR096W, YMR095C	61	0	20	24

[a] All of the genes listed in each set represent the gene being up in the sample.

DNA sequences and relative positions of SNZ and SNO genes have been phylogenetically conserved. SNZ–SNO gene pairs are coregulated under various conditions (Padilla et al., 1998). Snz1p and Sno1p are initially identified as a protein whose synthesis increases dramatically as yeast cells enter stationary phase (Fuge et al., 1994). Recent studies indicated that SNZ1 and SNO1 are involved in cellular responses to nutrient limitation. Both of them are required for yeast to grow in pyridoxine (vitamin B_6) lacking media, indicating that they are involved in pyridoxine metabolism (Rodriguez-Navarro et al., 2002). CTF13 (centromere transmission fidelity, CTF) is an essential protein in the Cbf3 kinetochore protein complex, which binds to the centromeres during mitosis. ctf13 mutants missegregate chromosomes at permissive temperature and transiently arrest at nonpermissive temperature as large-budded cells with a G2 DNA content and a short spindle (Doheny et al., 1993). CTF13, SNO1, and SNZ1, located adjacent to each other, are situated proximal to the centromere on the right arm of chromosome XIII. We conjecture that the co-regulation of these three genes might be caused by the conformational changes of chromosomal structure during transcription activation even though the possibility that they are involved in the same biological process is not excluded.

In addition, Table 13.3 indicated that other genes that may have interaction with SNZ1/SNO1/CTF13 include ORFs YER175C (TMT1), YHR071W (PCL5), YJR109C (CPA2), YBR047W, YHR029C, and YGL117W. YER175C encodes the *trans*-aconitate methyltransferase (Tmt1p) of *Saccharomyces cerevisiae*, which is localized in the cytosol and increases markedly as cells undergo

TABLE 13.4. Selected Genes Involved Large Gene Sets that Cannot Be Explained by the All 3-Way Interaction Model

ORF	Gene	Biological Process	Molecular Function	Cellular Component
YBR047W	Unknown	Unknown	Unknown	Unknown
YER175C	TMT1	Unknown	*trans*-Aconitate 3-methyltransferase	Activity cytosol
YGL117W	Unknown	Unknown	Unknown	Unknown
YHR029C	Unknown	Unknown	Unknown	Unknown
YHR071W	PCL5	Cell cycle	Cyclin-dependent protein kinase regulator activity	Cyclin-dependent protein kinase holoenzyme complex
YJR109C	CPA2	Arginine biosynthesis	Carbamoyl-phosphate synthase (glutamine-hydrolyzing) activity	Cytosol
YMR094W	CTF13	Centromere kinetochore complex maturation	DNA bending activity	Condensed nuclear chro-mosomekineto-chore
YMR095C	SNO1	Pyridoxine metabolism	Imidazoleglycerol phosphate synthase activity	Unknown
YMR096W	SNZ1	Pyridoxine metabolism	Unknown	Unknown

the metabolic transition at the diauxic shift (Cai et al., 2001). It may explain the co-regulation with SNO1 and SNZ1 which are involved in cellular responses to nutrient limitation. YHR071W (PCL5) encodes a protein that interacts with Pho85, a cyclin-dependent kinase (Cdk) involved in the entry into the mitotic cell cycle (Start) in budding yeast (Measday et al., 1997). The co-regulation of PGL5 with SNO1 and SNZ1 leads us to conjecture that protein encoded by PGL5 may inhibit the function of Pho85, thereby delaying the entry into mitosis and maintaining growth arrest when nutrients are limited. YJR109C (CPA2) encodes one of the two subunits of carbamoylphosphate synthase in the arginine synthesis pathway. The expression of CPA2 is increased when arginine is limited (Kinney and Lusty, 1989). The overexpression of CPA2 indicated that certain conditions in Hughes experiments may somehow limit arginine, which leads to increased expression of CPA2. The co-regulation of CPA2 and SNO1/SNZ1 implies that they might be involved in the same biological process. The ORFs YBR047W, YHR029C, and YGL117W have not been characterized.

13.3.4. Biological Knowledge Agents

The application of unsupervised and supervised learning algorithms to gene expression data produces lists of genes of potential interest based upon numerical relationships. The task of discovering and interpreting the underlying biological relationships that underlie the clustering is left to the user. Since these genes clusters may include large numbers of genes, it is well beyond the ability of even domain experts to detect and organize these data along the multiple lines of conceptual similarity by inspection alone (Masys et al., 2001).

The data needed to interpret gene expression clustering data lies in the scientific literature (Masys, 2001; Zhou et al., 2002). A great deal of the data has been extracted from the literature into biological databases, where it can be searched and extracted. Unfortunately, there is no standardization between these databases, and a great deal of work as well as an intimate understanding of the various schemas and information content is required to extract relevant data (Gribskov, 2003). Automated data-mining technologies are the answer to this issue.

We have created a biological data mart that employs an agent framework to maintain the currency of the data. The architecture consists of a data mart generated in MySQL, a Java agent framework and user interface, and a JDBC communication layer that resides between the data mart, the agent framework, and the user interface. The architecture is shown in Figure 13.2.

The data mart consists of a number of separate MySQL databases containing the source data from various external databases. The data sources include the Gene Ontology (Ashburner et al., 2000), a controlled vocabulary for describing the roles of genes and gene products; LocusLink (Pruitt and Maglott, 2001), which provides a locus-centric view of genomic information from the human and other genomes; CGAP (Strausberg et al., 2000), which contains information about gene expression profiles of normal, precancerous, and cancerous cells; UniGene (Wheeler et al., 2000), which creates similarity-based clustering of expressed sequence tags (ESTs) that are often used as gene expression targets, relating these to known genes; and GeneCards (Safran et al., 2002), which contains information about known genes implicated in disease processes. In addition, a database of predicted transcription factor binding sites created from TFD motifs (Ghosh, 1992, 2000) and the complete set of predicted genes is used to investigate if genes with common expression profiles have common transcription factor binding sites in their promoters.

Based upon the gene targets in the experiment, the data sources are aggregated into seven knowledge stores. These knowledge stores represent subject-oriented views of the primary data, and they are used by the cluster interpretation agents to annotate the clustering results (see below). As more data sources are added, the data are incorporated into existing data stores.

Four classes of agents have been developed: data manipulation agents, knowledge generation agents, cluster interpretation agents, and reporting agents. The data manipulation agents perform relational operations for creating and populating the data mart, while the knowledge generation agents link the data from the

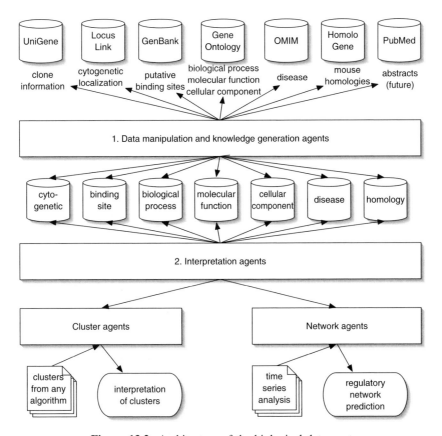

Figure 13.2. Architecture of the biological data mart.

sources and generate the knowledge stores. Cluster interpretation agents attempt to discover the underlying biological themes in the clusters formed by the partitioning algorithms, and reporting agents turn the results of the interpretation into executive summaries for presentation to the user.

The cluster interpretation agents take as input a list of genes and their cluster or group membership, allowing the annotation of clusters from any algorithm. In order to discover any bias in the cluster (Muller and Alcalay, 2002) the biological relationships posited by the interpretation agents are scored using a standard z-score, dividing the difference between observed and expected genes by the standard deviation of the observed genes.

To validate the knowledge agents, we used a published dataset of breast cancer mutations (Hedenfalk et al., 2001). The researchers identified 176 discriminatory genes from a microarray containing 6512 feature representing 5361 genes that were differentially expressed between tumors with BRCA1-positive and tumors with BRCRA2-positive mutations. We applied our agents to this list to determine if there were any biological themes in this gene list.

With any microarray classification prediction method, we may expect that there will exist more than one set of genes that permit classification of the samples. This is primarily due to the asymmetric nature of microarray data, whereas there are typically 102–104 more covariates (genes) than samples in a microarray data matrix. Optimally we seek a set of genes that will successfully classify the samples and, in turn, be biologically informative. Thus, if we are to imagine two or more lists of statistically close classifiers, we would prefer the list that is more biologically informative because we can assume that this list best captures the varying processes that bring about the differing molecular phenotypes. Our agents can be used to help us discern the most biologically informative list.

From data sources containing over six and one-half million records, the agents assembled knowledge stores totaling 216,303 records. Because biological annotations are sparser in some domain areas than others, there was a distribution of records among the knowledge stores, ranging from 1735 in the pathology knowledge store to 110,168 in the transcription factor knowledge store, the latter being relatively complete. The complete distribution is shown in Table 13.5.

The application of the chromosomal position agent shows us a number of hot spots where there are more genes in our list than one would expect by mere chance. Many of these localizations have been identified in the literature as areas related to breast carcinoma in one fashion or the other.

For example, a number of genes in the list are found at the 1p36 locus. p73, a tumor suppressor gene, was isolated and mapped to 1p36. Studies have shown that this region is commonly associated with loss of heterozygosity in human breast carcinomas (Schwartz et al., 1999). Another area known for high rates of loss of heterozygosity in human breast carcinomas is 19p13 (Oesterreich et al., 2001). Again, we found genes at this locus in our list.

We also found genes at the 5q31 locus. To this locus the SPARC gene has been mapped. This gene is known to affect various bone matrix proteins, which have been shown to play a role in human breast carcinoma (Bellahcene and Castronovo, 1997). As a final illustration, genes on our list were found on the

TABLE 13.5. Distribution of Records Used to Annotate 176 Genes

Knowledge Store	Number of Records
Positional	18,431
Pathology	1,735
Homology	45,567
Binding factors	110,168
Biological process	13,320
Cell components	10,264
Molecular functions	16,818
Total	**216,303**

22q13 locus. The PARVG gene, a candidate tumor suppressor, has been mapped to this locus (Castellvi-Bel et al., 2003).

Other agents, especially the functional agents, make little sense in application to discriminatory gene lists. This is because the genes that discriminate between two conditions might be altered by either of the conditions, resulting in a gene list that must be assuredly heterogeneous in nature. The functional agents, and specifically the biological process agent from the GO ontology, were therefore applied only to clusters generated from the discriminatory list by the LAC algorithm. From the clustered list, we would expect genes with similar expression profiles to be controlled by either the same or similar mechanisms, and perhaps form a functional unit such as a regulatory pathway.

The LAC algorithm generated eight clusters, and we immediately notice themes in some of these clusters, as shown in Table 13.6. For example, in one cluster there exists a number of cell cycle genes. The terms for cell cycle regulation all score high. As with all cancers, BRCA1- and BRCA2-related tumors involve the loss

TABLE 13.6. Biological Processes Annotated in One Cluster Generated by the LAC Algorithm

Biological Process	z-Score
DNA damage checkpoint	7.4
Nucleocytoplasmic transport	7.4
Meiotic recombination	7.4
Asymmetric cytokinesis	7.4
Purine base biosynthesis	7.4
GMP biosynthesis	5.1
rRNA processing	5.1
Glutamine metabolism	5.1
Establishment and/or maintenance of cell polarity	5.1
Gametogenesis	5.1
DNA replication	4.6
Cell cycle arrest	4.4
Central nervous system development	4.4
Purine nucleotide biosynthesis	4.1
mRNA splicing	4.1
Cell cycle	3.5
Negative regulation of cell proliferation	3.4
Induction of apoptosis by intracellular signals	2.8
Oncogenesis	2.6
G1/S transition of mitotic cell cycle	2.5
Protein kinase cascade	2.5
Glycogen metabolism	2.3
Regulation of cell cycle	2.1

of control over cell growth and proliferation; thus the presence of strong cell-cycle components in the clustering is expected. Other measures using the GO ontology are not as informative. This is due to the sparseness of the biological information available with some criteria. For example, the cellular component agent only produced two labels for the first cluster: nucleus and nucleosome. When looking at the biological process agent, we see terms like G1/S transition of mitotic cell cycle, nucleosome assembly, and RNA processing. These results might indicate the existence of a theme of translation control within the cluster, however, the data are too sparse to draw definite conclusions.

The complete annotation of the 176 genes in the list would take several days and would be prone to errors if done by hand. The agent framework allows annotations to be gathered from many sources and assembled in a few hours of compute time. The analysis of the results still requires a domain expert to assess the meaning of the annotations, but the more complete annotation of the clusters increases the accuracy of that assessment and can bring to light unsuspected correlations.

13.4. CONCLUSIONS

Approaches to the computational analysis of gene expression data attempt to learn functionally significant groups of genes, in either an unsupervised or supervised fashion. In this chapter, we have discussed data-mining techniques of both learning paradigms, which have been used and developed for microarray data analysis. We have emphasized the importance of capturing local correlations of data, in order to discover different patterns that may exist in different groups, and provided an effective tool to achieve this goal.

The use of external knowledge (i.e., scientific literature) is necessary to isolate the inevitable artifacts present in microarray data, as well as to interpret the results of cluster analysis. We have described a clustering technique that can handle categorical attributes, and thus is well suited to work with external features to complement the microarray data. In addition, in an effort to capture networks of interactions among co-regulated genes, we have discussed loglinear models and have shown experimental results using yeast data. Finally, we have presented a system of software agents that can assist the annotation of clustering results for assessment of biological significance.

In our future work we envision a system that integrates the four components, to discover clusters in microarray data utilizing the scientific literature. External knowledge can be analyzed via the COOLCAT algorithm and can be formalized as constraints among the genes. The dynamic of the LAC procedure can then be modified to guarantee convergence to a configuration that satisfies such constraints, and it incorporates the results of loglinear modeling as well. The process can be carried out in an iterative fashion until the changes to the clustering are minimal. Our future research efforts will pursue the realization of such a system.

REFERENCES

Aggarwal, C., Procopiuc, C., Wolf, J. L., Yu, P. S., and Park, J. S. Fast algorithms for projected clustering, in *Proceedings of the ACM SIGMOD International Conference on Management of Data*, 1999.

Aggarwal, C., and Yu, P. S., Finding generalized projected clusters in high dimensional spaces, in *ACM SIGMOD International Conference on Management of Data*, 2000.

Agrawal, R., Imielinski, T., and Swami, A. Mining association rules between sets of items in large databases, in *ACM SIGMOD International Conference on Management of Data*, 1993.

Agrawal, R., Gehrke, J., Gunopulos, D., and Raghavan, P., Automatic subspace clustering of high dimensional data for data mining applications, in *Proceedings of the ACM SIGMOD International Conference on Management of Data*, 1998.

Aitman, T. J., DNA microarrays in medical practice, *BMJ* **323**, 611–615 (2001).

Ashburner, M., Ball, C. A., Blake, J. A., Botstein, D., Butler, H., Cherry, J. M., Davis, A. P., Dolinski, K., Dwight, S. S., Eppig, J. T., Harris, M. A., Hill, D. P., Issel-Tarver, L., Kasarskis, A., Lewis, S., Matese, J. C., Richardson, J. E., Ringwald, M., Rubin, G. M., and Sherlock, G. Gene ontology: Tool for the unification of biology. The Gene Ontology Consortium, *Nature Genetics* **25**, 25–29 (2000).

Barbará, D., Couto, J., and Li, Y. COOLCAT: An entropy-based algorithm for categorical clustering, in *Eleventh International Conference on Information and Knowledge Management (CIKM '02)*, 2002.

Basset, D. E., Eisen, M. B, and Boguski, M. S., Gene expression informatics—it's all in your mine, *Nature Genetics* **21**, 51–55 (1999).

Bellahcene, A., and Castronovo, V., Expression of bone matrix proteins in human breast cancer: Potential roles in microcalcification formation and in the genesis of bone metastases, *Bulletin du Cancer* **84**(1), 17–24 (1997).

Bellman, R. E., *Adaptive Control Processes*, Princeton University Press, Princeton, NJ, 1961.

Bottou, L., and Vapnik, V., Local learning algorithms, *Neural Computation* **4**(6), 888–900 (1992).

Breiman, L., Bagging predictors, *Machine Learning* **24**, 123–140 (1996).

Breiman, L., Friedman, J. H., Olshen, R. A., and Stone, C. J., *Classification and Regression Trees*, Wadsworth, Belmont, CA, 1984.

Brown, M., Grundy, W., Lin, D., Cristianini, N., Sugnet, C., Furey, T., Ares, M., and Haussler, D., Knowledge-based analysis of microarray gene expressions data by using support vector machines, *National Academy of Sciences* **97**(1), 262–267 (2000).

Cai, H., Dumlao, D., Katz, J., and Clarke S., Identification of the gene and characterization of the activity of the *trans*-aconitate methyltransferase from *Saccharomyces cerevisiae*, *Biochemistry* **40**, 13699–13709 (2001).

Castellvi-Bel, S., Castells, A., Johnstone, C.N., Pinol, V., Pellise, M., Elizalde, J. I., Romo, N., Rustgi, A. K., and Pique, J. M., Evaluation of PARVG located on 22q13 as a candidate tumor suppressor gene for colorectal and breast cancer, *Cancer Genetics and Cytogenetics* **144**, 80–82 (2003).

Chakrabarti, K., and Mehrotra, S., Local dimensionality reduction: A new approach to indexing high dimensional spaces, in *Proceedings of VLDB*, 2000.

Cheng, Y., and Church, G. M., Biclustering of expression data, in *Proceedings of the Eighth International Conference on Intelligent Systems for Molecular Biology*, 2000.

Colantuoni, C., Henry, G., Zeger, S., and Pevsner J., Local mean normalization of microarray element signal intensities across an array surface: Quality control and correction of spatially systematic artifacts, *Biotechniques* **32**, 1316–1320 (2002).

Creighton, C., and Hanash, S., Mining gene expression databases for association rules, *Bioinformatics* **19**(1), 79–86 (2003).

Cristianini, N., and Taylor, J. S., *An Introduction to Support Vector Machines and Other Kernel-Based Learning Methods*, Cambridge University Press, New York, 2000.

Debouck, C., and Goodfellow, P. N., DNA microarrays in drug discovery and development, *Nature Genetics* **21**, 48–50 (1999).

Dempster, A. P., Laird, N. M., and Rubin, D. B., Maximum likelihood from incomplete data via the EM algorithm, *Journal of the Royal Statistical Society* **39**(1), 1–38 (1977).

Doheny, K., Sorger, P., Hyman, A., Tugendreich, S., Spencer, F., and Hieter, P., Identification of essential components of thes. cerevisiae kinetochore, *Cell* **73**, 761–764 (1993).

Domeniconi, C., Locally Adaptive Techniques for Pattern Classification, Ph.D. thesis, University of California, Riverside, 2002.

Domeniconi, C., Papadopoulos, D., Gunopulos, D., and Ma, S., Subspace clustering of high dimensional data, *SIAM International Conference on Data Mining*, 2004.

Duda, R. O., Hart, P. E., and Stork, D. G., *Pattern Classification*, Wiley-Interscience, New York, 2001.

Dudoit, S., Fridlyand, J., and Speed, T., Comparison of Discriminant Methods for the Classification of Tumors Using Gene Expression Data, Technical Report 576, University of California, Berkeley, 2000.

Eisen, M. B., Spellman, P. T., Brown, P. O., and Botstein, D., Cluster analysis and display of genome-wide expression patterns, *Proceedings of the National Academy of Sciences USA* **95**, 14863–14868 (1998).

Fridlyand, J. and Dudoit, S., Comparison of supervised learning methods for the classification of tumors using gene expression data, in *Workshop on Quantitative Challenges in the Post Genomic Sequence Era*, 2000.

Fuge, E., Braun, E., and Werner-Washburne, M., Protein synthesis in long-term stationary phase cultures of *Saccharomyces cerevisiae*, *Journal of Bacteriology* **176**, 5802–5813 (1994).

Fukunaga, K., *Introduction to Statistical Pattern Recognition*, Academic Press, New York, 1990.

Furey, T. S., Cristianini, N., Duffy, N., Bednarski, D. W., Schummer, M., and Haussler, D., Support vector machine classification and validation of cancer tissue samples using microarray expression data, *Bioinformatics* **16**(10), 906–914 (2000).

Garey, M., and Johnson, D., *Computers and Intractability: A Guide to the Theory of NP-Completeness*, W.H. Freeman, San Francisco, 1979.

Ghahramani, Z., and Hinton, G. E., The EM Algorithm for Mixtures of Factor Analyzers, *Technical Report CRG-TR-96-1, Department of Computer Science, University of Toronto*, 1996.

Ghosh, D., TFD: The transcription factors database, *Nucleic Acids Research* **20** (Suppl), 2091–2093 (1992).

Ghosh D., Object-oriented transcription factors database (ooTFD), *Nucleic Acids Research* **28**, 308–310 (2000).

Gribskov, M., Challenges in data management for functional genomics, *OMICS* **7**, 3–5 (2003).

Hedenfalk, I., Duggan, D., Chen, Y., Radmacher, M., Bittner, M., Simon, R., Meltzer, P., Gusterson, B., Esteller, M., Kallioniemi, O. P., Wilfond, B., Borg, A., and Trent, J., Gene expression profiles in hereditary breast cancer, *New England Journal of Medicine* **344**, 539–548 (2001).

Herwig, R., Poustka, A. J., Muller, C., Bull, C., Lehrach, H., and O'Brien, J. Large-scale clustering of cDNA-fingerprinting data, *Genome Research* **9**, 1093–1105 (1999).

Hughes, T., Marton, M., Jones, A., Roberts, C., Stoughton, R., Armour, C., Benett, H., Coffey, E., Dai, H., He, Y., Kidd, M., and King, A. M., Functional discovery via a compendium of expression profiles, *Cell* **102**, 109–126 (2000).

Johnson, R. A., and Wichern, D. W., *Applied Multivariate Statistical Analysis*, Prentice-Hall, Englewood Cliffs, NJ, 1988.

Keogh, E., Chakrabarti, K., Mehrotra, S., and Pazzani, M., Locally adaptive dimensionality reduction for indexing large time series databases, in *Proceedings of the ACM SIGMOD Conference on Management of Data*, 2001.

Kinney, D., and Lusty, C., Arginine restriction induced by delta-n-(phosphonacetyl)-l-ornithine signals increased expression of his3, trp5, cpa1, and cpa2 in *Saccharomyces cerevisiae*, *Molecular and Cellular Biology* **9**, 4882–4888 (1989).

Kohonen, T., Self-organized formation of topologically correct feature maps, *Biological Cybernetics* **43**, 59–69 (1982).

Kohonen, T., *Self-Organization and Associative Memory*, Springer-Verlag, Berlin, 1989.

Masys, D. R., Linking microarray data to the literature, *Nature Genetics* **28**, 9–10 (2001).

Masys, D. R., Welsh, J. B., Lynn-Fink, J., Gribskov, M., Klacansky, I., and Corbeil, J., Use of keyword hierarchies to interpret gene expression patterns, *Bioinformatics* **17**, 319–326 (2001).

Measday, V., Moore, L., Retnakaran, R., Lee, J., Donoviel, M., Neiman, A., and Andrews, B., A family of cyclin-like proteins that interact with the pho85 cycli-dependent kinase, *Molecular and Cellular Biology* **17**, 1212–1223 (1997).

Mitchell, T. M., *Machine Learning*, McGraw-Hill, New York, 1997.

Muller, H., and Alcalay, M., Tumor cell lines: Identification of statistically robust gene expression patterns in model cell lines and their use in functional expression data mining, in *Microarrays and Cancer Research*, Warrington, J. A., Todd C. R., and Wong, D. (eds.), Eaton Publishing, Westboro, MA, 45–60 (2002).

Oesterreich, S., Allredl, D. C., Mohsin, S. K., Zhang, Q., Wong, H., Lee, A. V., Osborne, C. K., and O'Connell, P., High rates of loss of heterozygosity on chromosome 19p13 in human breast cancer, *Br J Cancer* **84**, 493–498 (2001).

Padilla, P. A., Fuge, E. K., Crawford, M. E., Errett, A., and Werner-Washburne, M., The highly conserved, corregulated sno and snz gene families in *Saccharomyces cerevisiae* respond to nutrient limitation, *Journal of Bacteriology* **180**, 5718–5726 (1998).

Papadopoulos, D., Domeniconi, C., Gunopulos, D., and Ma, S., Clustering gene expression data in SQL using locally adaptive metrics, in *Proceedings of the 8th ACM SIGMOD Workshop on Research Issues in Data Mining and Knowledge Discovery*, 2003.

Procopiuc, C. M., Jones, M., Agarwal, P. K., and Murali, T. M., A Monte Carlo algorithm for fast projective clustering, in *Proceedings of the ACM SIGMOD Conference on Management of Data*, 2002.

Pruitt, K. D., and Maglott, D. R., RefSeq and LocusLink: NCBI gene-centered resources, *Nucleic Acids Research* **29**, 137–140 (2001).

Qian, J., Kluger, Y., Yu, H., and Gerstein, M. B., Spatial artifacts in microarray data: Spurious correlations and techniques to remove them. Unpublished observations. http://bioinfo.mbb.yale.edu/

Quinlan, J. R., Induction of decision trees, *Machine Learning* **1**, 81–106 (1986).

Quinlan, J. R., *C4.5: Programs for Machine Learning*, Morgan Kaufmann, San Francisco, 1993.

Quinlan, J. R., Bagging, boosting and C4.5, in *Fourteenth National Conference on Artificial Intelligence*, 1996.

Rodriguez-Navarro, S., Llorente, B., Rodriguez-Manzaneque, M., Ramme, A. Uber, G., Marchesan, D., Dujon, B., Herrero, E., Sunnerhagen, P., and Perez-Ortin, J., Functional analysis of yeast gene families involved in metabolism of vitamins B1 and B6, *Yeast* **19**, 1261–1276 (2002).

Safran, M., Solomon, I., Shmueli, O., Lapidot, M., Shen-Orr, S., Adato, A., Ben-Dor, U., Esterman, N., Rosen, N., Peter, I., Olender, T., Chalifa-Caspi, V., and Lancet, D. GeneCards 2002: Towards a complete, object-oriented, human gene compendium, *Bioinformatics* **18**, 1542–1543 (2002).

Sarawagi, S., Agrawal, R., and Meggido, N., Discovery-driven exploration of OLAP data cubes, *International Conference on Extending Data Base Technology*, 1998.

Schena, M., Shalon, D., Davis, R.W., and Brown, P. O., Quantitative monitoring of gene expression patterns with a complementary DNA microarray, *Science* **270**, 467–470 (1995).

Schoch, C., Kohlmann, A., Schnittger, S., Brors, B., Dugas, M., Mergenthaler, S., Kern, W., Hiddemann, W., Eils, R., and Haferlach, T., Acute myeloid leukemias with reciprocal rearrangements can be distinguished by specific gene expression profiles, *Proceedings of the National Academy of Sciences of the USA* **99**(15), 10008–10013 (2002).

Schwartz, D. I., Lindor, N. M., Walsh-Vockley, C., Roche, P. C., Mai, M., Smith, D. I., Liu, W., and Couch, F.J., p73 mutations are not detected in sporadic and hereditary breast cancer, *Breast Cancer Research Treatment* **58** 25–29 (1999).

Shannon, C. E., A mathematical theory of communication, *Bell System Technical Journal* **27**, 379–423, (1948).

Spellman, P. T., Sherlock, G., Zhang, M. Q., Iyer, V. R., Anders, K., Eisen, M. B., Brown, P. O., Botstein, D., and Futcher, B., Comprehensive identification of cell cycle-regulated genes of the yeast *Saccharomyces cerevisiae* by microarray hybridization, *Molecular Biology of the Cell* **9**, 3273–3297 (1998).

Strausberg, R. L., Beutow, K. H., Emmert-Buck, M. R., and Klausner, R. D., The Cancer Genome Anatomy Project: Building an annotated gene index, *Trends in Genetics* **16**, 103–106 (2000).

Tamayo, P., Slonim, D., Mesirov, J., Zhu, Q., Kitareewan, S., Dmitrovsky, E., Lander, E., and Golub, T., Interpreting patterns of gene expression with self-organizing maps, *Proceedings of the National Academy of Sciences* **96**, 2907–2912 (1999).

Tavazoie, S., Hughes, J. D., Campbell, M. J., Cho, R. J., and Church, G. M., Systematic determination of genetic network architecture, *Nature Genetics* **22**, 281–285 (1999).

Thomasian, A., Castelli, V., and Li, C. S., Clustering and singular value decomposition for approximate indexing in high dimensional spaces, in *Proceedings of CIKM*, 1998.

Tipping, M. E., and Bishop, C. M., Mixtures of principal component analyzers, *Neural Computation* **1**(2), 443–482 (1999).

Wheeler, D. L., Chappey, C., Lash, A. E., Leipe, D. D., Madden, T. L., Schuler, G. D., Tatusova, T. A., and Rapp, B. A., Database resources of the National Center for Biotechnology Information, *Nucleic Acids Research* **28**, 10–14 (2000).

Wu, X., Barbará, D., and Ye, Y., Screening and interpreting multi-item association based on log-linear modeling, in *ACM SIGKDD International Conference on Knowledge Discovery and Data Mining*, 2003.

Wu, X., Barbará, D., Zhang, L., and Ye, Y., Gene Interaction analysis Using k-way interaction loglinear model: A case study on yeast data, in *ICML Workshop on Machine Learning in Bioinformatics*, 2003.

Yip, K. Y., Cheung, D. W., and Ng, M. K., A highly-usable projected clustering algorithm for gene expression profiles, in *3rd ACM SIGKDD Workshop on Data Mining in Bioinformatics*, 2003.

Yu, H., Kluger, Y., Qian, J., and Gerstein, M. B., The effect of chromosome structure on gene expression. Unpublished observations. http://bioinfo.mbb.yale.edu/

Zhou, X., Kao, M. C., and Wong, W. H., Transitive functional annotation by shortest-path analysis of gene expression data, *Proceedings of the National Academy of Sciences of the USA* **99**, 12783–12788 (2002).

14

THE USE OF EMERGING PATTERNS IN THE ANALYSIS OF GENE EXPRESSION PROFILES FOR THE DIAGNOSIS AND UNDERSTANDING OF DISEASES

GUOZHU DONG, JINYAN LI, AND LIMSOON WONG

14.1. INTRODUCTION

Microarrays are surfaces bearing arrays of DNA fragments at discrete locations. These DNA fragments on the microarray are hybridized to chemically labeled DNA or RNA samples. After a washing and staining process, the locations at which hybridization has taken place can be determined and the expression level of the corresponding genes can be derived. Today, a single microarray can contain tens of thousands of DNA fragments. Thus, microarrays are a technology for simultaneously profiling the expression levels of tens of thousands of genes in a patient sample. A detailed description of the production and characteristics of the different types of microarray is outside of the scope of this chapter; however, interested readers can consult Figure 14.1 for a little more background information on microarrays.

It is hoped that better diagnosis methods and better understanding of disease mechanisms can be derived from a careful analysis of microarray measurements of gene expression profiles. This chapter discusses several types of analysis of such gene expression profiles using a form of supervised learning based on the idea of emerging patterns. The types of analysis discussed are (a) diagnosis of disease state or subtype, (b) derivation of disease treatment plan, and (c) understanding of gene interaction networks.

Next Generation of Data-Mining Applications. Edited by Kantardzic and Zurada
ISBN 0-471-65605-4 © 2005 the Institute of Electrical and Electronics Engineers, Inc.

RNA fragments with fluorescent tags from sample to be tested

(a)

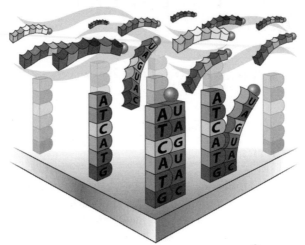

RNA fragment hybridizes with DNA on GeneChip®array

(b)

Figure 14.1. (a) A microarray produced by Affymetrix called the GeneChip® microarray. On such a microarray, specific DNA fragments are positioned at specific locations. (b) A cartoon depicting hybridization of tagged probes to Affymetrix GeneChip microarray. According to the well-known Crick–Watson rule for hybridization of DNA strands—namely, A pairs with T (equivalently, U for RNA), C pairs with G, and vice versa—a tagged RNA fragment can only hybridize to its complement on the microarray. Thus, after a microarray experiment as depicted in the cartoon, only those locations on the microarray where hybridizations have taken place would be fluorescent. Since the specific DNA fragments on these locations are known by design, the RNA fragments that hybridize to them are known too. In this way, the expression level of a gene can be "read off" by determining the amount of its RNA fragments that are hybridized to the microarray. Interested readers are encouraged to consult Fodor et al. (1991) and Shalon et al. (1996) for a deeper understanding of the two main types of microarray technology platform. *Both images courtesy of Affymetrix.*

The first type of analysis mentioned above reasonably postulates that the expression levels of various genes in a patient are dependent on his/her disease state and/or subtype. Therefore, by a careful analysis of gene expression profiles, it is hoped that we can determine the signature pattern of gene expression profiles associated with specific disease states and/or subtypes that are useful for diagnosis purposes. The second type of analysis mentioned above suggests the converse—that is, that the state of a disease can be affected by the expression levels of certain genes. That is, the improper expression of these genes is the cause of the disease. Hence, by a careful analysis of gene expression profiles, one might be able to infer such "causal" genes and to plan a course of treatment to modulate these genes. The third type of analysis is motivated by the two major causes of treatment failure by drug substances: side effects and compensation effects. Side effects arise because genes other than the intended ones are also modulated by the drug substances in unexpected ways. Compensation effects arise due to the existence of parallel pathways that can perform similar functions of the genes targeted by the drug substances, and these parallel pathways are not affected by those drug substances. This third type of analysis is useful both for identifying causal genes and for suggesting how best to target them.

This chapter is organized as follows. Section 14.2 discusses a method of classification/prediction, called PCL, that uses collective likelihood based on emerging patterns. Section 14.3 deals with the selection of relevant genes. Section 14.4 considers the diagnosis of disease states or subtypes using PCL. Section 14.5 presents an approach to deriving treatment plans based on emerging patterns. Section 14.6 discusses approaches to understanding molecular circuits. Section 14.7 provides closing remarks.

14.2. PREDICTION BY COLLECTIVE LIKELIHOOD BASED ON EMERGING PATTERNS

In the field of machine learning, there are many good prediction methods including k-nearest neighbors (k-NN) (Cover and Hart, 1967), C4.5 (Quinlan, 1993), support vector machines (SVM) (Burges, 1998), Naive Bayes (NB) (Langley et al., 1992), and so on. C4.5 is a widely used learning algorithm that induces from training data rules that are easy to comprehend. However, it may not have good performance if real decision boundary underlying the data is not linear. The NB model uses Bayesian rules to estimate probabilistic score for each class. When given a test sample, NB uses the probabilistic scores to rank the classes, and it assigns the sample to the highest scoring class. An important assumption used in NB is that the underlying features are statistically independent. However, this is not appropriate for gene expression data analysis because genes involved in an expression profile are often closely related and appear not to be independent. The k-nearest-neighbor method assigns a test sample the class of its nearest training sample in terms of some distance functions. Even though the k-NN is intuitive and has good performance, it is not helpful for understanding complex cases in depth. The support vector machines construct complicated mappings between samples and their class labels. SVM has good performance, but it functions as a black box. Similarly, traditional data-mining methods that look for high-frequency patterns are often not useful on gene expression data in terms of diagnostic accuracy. We are therefore motivated to seek a classification method that enjoys the advantages of both high accuracy and high comprehensibility. In this section we describe the method of Prediction by Collective Likelihood based on emerging patterns (PCL).

PCL (Li and Wong, 2002a; Li et al., 2003) is a classification method that we have been developing during the last couple of years. This method focuses on (a) fast techniques for identifying patterns whose frequencies in two classes differ by a large ratio (Dong and Li, 1999), which are the so-called "emerging patterns", and (b) combining these patterns to make decisions. A pattern is a set of expression conditions of the form $c_{i1} \leq G_i < c_{i2}$ if feature G_i is numerical, and of the form $G_i = c_i$ if feature G_i is discretized. Often we discretize numerical features first. Example emerging patterns are given in Section 14.4. For the purpose of PCL, we use only emerging patterns that are the most general and have infinite ratio. That is, we use only emerging patterns that occur in one class of data but not the other class and that do not contain any subsets which are also infinite-ratio emerging patterns. From now on, by emerging patterns we mean infinite-ratio most-general emerging patterns.

Basically, the PCL classifier has two phases. Given two training datasets D^A and D^B (instances of classes $\mathcal{A}$ and $\mathcal{B}$, respectively), PCL first discovers two groups of most general emerging patterns from D^A and D^B. Denote the most general emerging patterns of D^A as $EP_1^A, EP_2^A, \ldots, EP_i^A$, in descending order of frequency. Similarly, denote the most general emerging patterns of D^B as $EP_1^B, EP_2^B, \ldots, EP_j^B$. Let T be a test sample. Suppose T contains the following most general emerging patterns of D^A: $EP_{i_1}^A, EP_{i_2}^A, \ldots, EP_{i_x}^A, i_1 < i_2 < \cdots < i_x \leq i$, and the following most general emerging patterns of D^B: $EP_{j_1}^B, EP_{j_2}^B, \ldots, EP_{j_y}^B, j_1 < j_2 < \cdots < j_y \leq j$. Next, PCL calculates two scores for predicting the class label of T. Suppose we use k ($k \ll i$ and $k \ll j$) top-ranked most general emerging patterns of D^A and D^B. Then we define the score of T in the D^A class as

$$\text{score}(T, D^A) = \sum_{m=1}^{k} \frac{\text{frequency } (EP_{i_m}^A)}{\text{frequency } (EP_m^A)}$$

and the score in the D^B class is similarly defined in terms of $EP_{j_m}^B$ and EP_m^B. The use of summation allows us to combine signals captured by different emerging patterns, and the use of ratio allows us to somehow normalize the scores for situations where one class has many strong (high-frequency) emerging patterns but another class has very few or even no strong emerging patterns. If $\text{score}(T, D^A) > \text{score}(T, D^B)$, then T's predicted class is D^A. Otherwise its predicted class is D^B. We use the size of D^A and D^B to break a tie. The PCL classifier has proved to be a good tool for analyzing gene expression data and proteomic data (Li et al., 2002, 2003; Yeoh et al., 2002; Li and Wong, 2002a,b, 2003).

Dong and Li (1999), Li et al. (2000), and Zhang et al. (2000) give fairly efficient methods to mine the most general emerging patterns, using novel border-based algorithms and constraint-based algorithms. Wang et al. (2003) give results showing that emerging pattern mining is hard theoretically. In the remainder of this chapter, we discuss the use of emerging patterns and PCL in the analysis of microarray gene expression profiles.

14.3. SELECTION OF RELEVANT GENES

A single microarray experiment can measure the expression level of tens of thousands of genes simultaneously (Lockhart et al., 1996; Ramsay, 1998). In other words, the microarray experiment record of a patient sample—see Table 14.1 for an example—is a record having tens of thousands of features or dimensions. This extremely high dimensionality causes many problems with regard to existing data-mining and machine learning methods. One such problem is that of efficiency because most data-mining and machine learning methods have time complexity that are high with respect to the number of dimensions (Han and Kamber, 2000). Another such problem is that of noise because most data-mining and machine learning methods suffer from the "curse of dimensionality"—these methods typically require an exponential increase in the number of training samples with respect to an increase in the dimensionality of the samples in order to uncover and learn the relationship of the various dimensions to the nature of the samples (Hastie et al., 2001).

Let us assume that we have two classes A and B of microarray gene expression profiles of patient samples. For example, A could be gene expression profiles of colon tumor cells and B could be gene expression profiles of normal (matching) cells. Then a feature—in this case, a gene—is relevant if it contributes to separating samples in A from those in B. Conversely, a feature may be irrelevant if it does not contribute much to separating samples in A from those in B. In order to alleviate the impact of the problems caused by high dimensionality mentioned above, it is desirable to first discard as many features that are irrelevant as possible. In this section, we present several techniques for deciding whether a feature is relevant, namely, t-statistics, signal-to-noise, and entropy measures.

One concept to capture significant difference among feature values in multiple classes is to use the difference between mean values μ_f^A and μ_f^B of a feature in the different classes A and B. However, we caution that the mean difference itself is not good enough for selecting relevant features. Indeed, if the values of a feature f varies greatly within the same class of samples, even if μ_f^A differs greatly from μ_f^B, the feature f is still not a reliable one. The deficiency of the mean difference concept leads us to a second concept to capture significant difference among feature values in multiple classes: the standard deviation σ_f^A

TABLE 14.1. A Partial Example of a Processed Microarray Measurement Record of a Patient Sample Using the Affymetrix U95A Gene Chip[a]

Probe	Positive	Negative	Pairs in Average	Average Difference	Presence/ Absence/ Margin Call	Description
...	...	...	...	...	...	...
106_at	4	1	15	1527.6	A	Z35278 Human PEBP2aC1 ...
107_at	4	4	15	3723.3	A	Z95624 Human DNA from ...
108_g_at	5	2	15	1392.4	A	Z95624 Human DNA ...
109_at	6	2	16	2274.7	M	Z97074 Human mRNA for ...
...	...	...	...	...	...	...

[a]Each row represents a probe. Typically, each probe represents a gene. The U95A Gene Chip contains more than 12,000 probes. The fifth column contains the gene expression measured by the corresponding probe. The second, third, fourth, and sixth columns are quality control data. The first and last columns are the probe identifier and a description of the corresponding gene.

of f in $\mathcal{A}$ and the standard deviation $\sigma_f^{\mathcal{B}}$ of f in $\mathcal{B}$. We also use the variance $(\sigma_f^{\mathcal{A}})^2$ and $(\sigma_f^{\mathcal{B}})^2$ that can be derived from the standard deviation.

One way to combine these two concepts is the signal-to-noise measure, proposed in the first article (Golub et al., 1999) that applied gene expression profiling for disease diagnosis,

$$s(f, \mathcal{A}, \mathcal{B}) = \frac{|\mu_f^{\mathcal{A}} - \mu_f^{\mathcal{B}}|}{\sigma_f^{\mathcal{A}} + \sigma_f^{\mathcal{B}}}$$

However, the statistical property of $s(f, \mathcal{A}, \mathcal{B})$ is not fully understood. Subsequently, a second and older way—the t-test—to combine these two concepts was rediscovered. The classical t-test statistical measure (Baldi and Long, 2001; Caria, 2000) is known to follow a Student distribution with $(h(\mathcal{A}) + h(\mathcal{B}))^2/((h(\mathcal{A})^2/(n^{\mathcal{A}} - 1)) + (h(\mathcal{B})^2/(n^{\mathcal{B}} - 1)))$ degrees of freedom, where $h(\mathcal{C}) = (\sigma_f^{\mathcal{C}})^2/n^{\mathcal{C}}$ and $n^{\mathcal{A}}$ and $n^{\mathcal{B}}$ are, respectively, the number of samples in $\mathcal{A}$ and $\mathcal{B}$. The t-test statistical measure is given by

$$t(f, \mathcal{A}, \mathcal{B}) = \frac{|\mu_f^{\mathcal{A}} - \mu_f^{\mathcal{B}}|}{\sqrt{(\sigma_f^{\mathcal{A}})^2/n^{\mathcal{A}} + (\sigma_f^{\mathcal{B}})^2/n^{\mathcal{B}}}}$$

Both of these measures are easy to compute and thus are straightforward to use. However, these measures have three significant deficiencies in the context of gene expression profiles. First, in gene expression profile experiments, the population sizes $n^{\mathcal{A}}$ and $n^{\mathcal{B}}$ are often as small as 2 or 3. These small population sizes can lead to significant underestimates of the standard deviations and variances. Second, due to some technological limitations of microarrays, there is no guarantee that two measurements of gene expression values taken from the same sample will agree with each other. That is, the value of a gene f may be different in these two microarray measurements taken from the same sample. However, if the ranges of f in $\mathcal{A}$ and $\mathcal{B}$ do not overlap, then the variances with respect to $\mathcal{A}$ and $\mathcal{B}$ should not matter all that much. Unfortunately, both $t(f, \mathcal{A}, \mathcal{B})$ and $s(f, \mathcal{A}, \mathcal{B})$ are sensitive to small changes in the values of f. Third, the t-test statistical measure requires the gene expression values to follow the Student's distribution or a nearly normal distribution. For some experiments, the gene expression values may not follow such distributions.

So, one should consider alternative statistical measures that are less sensitive to changes in the value of f that are unimportant in the sense that they do not shift the value of f from the range in $\mathcal{A}$ into the range of $\mathcal{B}$. One such idea is the entropy measure (Fayyad and Irani, 1993). Let $P(f, C, S)$ be the proportion of samples whose feature f has value in the range S and are in class C. The *class entropy* of a range S with respect to feature f and a collection of classes $\mathcal{U}$ is defined as $\text{Ent}(f, \mathcal{U}, S) = -\sum_{C \in \mathcal{U}} P(f, C, S) \log(P(f, C, S))$. Let T partitions the values of f into two ranges S_1 (of values less than T) and S_2 (of values at least T). We sometimes refer to T as the "cutting point" of the values of f. The entropy measure $e(f, \mathcal{A}, \mathcal{B})$ of a feature f is then defined as $\min\{E(f, \{\mathcal{A}, \mathcal{B}\}, S_1, S_2) \mid (S_1, S_2)$ is a partitioning of the values of f in $\mathcal{A}$ and $\mathcal{B}$ by some point $T\}$. Here, $E(f, \{\mathcal{A}, \mathcal{B}\}, S_1, S_2)$ is the *class information entropy* of partition (S_1, S_2). The definition is given below, where $n(f, \mathcal{U}, S)$ denotes the number of samples in the classes in $\mathcal{U}$ whose feature f has value in the range S,

$$E(f, \mathcal{U}, S_1, S_2) = \sum_{i=1}^{2} \frac{n(f, \mathcal{U}, S_i)}{n(f, \mathcal{U}, S_1 \cup S_2)} Ent(f, \mathcal{U}, S_i)$$

A refinement of the entropy measure is to recursively partition the ranges S_1 and S_2 until some stopping criterion is reached (Fayyad and Irani, 1993). A commonly used stopping criterion is the so-called minimal description length principle. Another refinement is the $\mathcal{X}^2$ measure (Liu and Setiono, 1995).

All of the preceding measures provide a rank ordering of the features in terms of their relevance to separating $\mathcal{A}$ and $\mathcal{B}$. One would rank the features using one of these measures and select the top n features. However, one must appreciate that there may be a variety of independent reasons why a sample is in $\mathcal{A}$ or is in $\mathcal{B}$. For example, there can be a number of different pathways via which a cell becomes cancerous, and there can be a number of different pathways via which a disease cell becomes of a specific subtype. If a primary pathway involves n genes, the procedure above may select only these n genes and may ignore genes in other secondary pathways. Consequently, concentrating on such top n features may cause us to lose sight of the secondary pathways underlying the disease.

This issue above calls for a different approach to feature selection: Select a group of features that are correlated with separating $\mathcal{A}$ and $\mathcal{B}$ but are not correlated with each other. The cardinality in such a group may suggest the number of independent factors that underlie the separation of A and B. A well-known technique that implements this feature selection strategy is the correlation-based feature selection (CFS) method (Hall, 1998). Rather than scoring and ranking individual features, the CFS method scores and ranks the worth of subsets of features. Because the feature subset space is usually huge, CFS uses a best-first-search heuristic. This heuristic algorithm takes into account the usefulness of individual features for predicting the class along with the level of intercorrelation among them. CFS first calculates a matrix of feature–class and feature–feature correlations from the training data. Then a score of a subset of features is assigned by a heuristic. CFS starts from the empty set of features and uses the best-first-search heuristic with a stopping criterion of five consecutive fully expanded nonimproving subsets. The subset with the highest merit found during the search is selected.

Note that even if each gene selected by CFS is associated with a distinct pathway underlying the separation of A and B, there is no guarantee that these genes will lead to good results by themselves. Each pathway involves multiple genes acting in a coordinated fashion. In methods such as the entropy measure, one is more likely to select all the genes in a primary pathways and neglect those of secondary pathways. In methods such as CFS, one is more likely to select the more important gene in each pathways and neglect the secondary genes. However, to get the best analysis results and to achieve the best understanding, it is crucial to know all of the relevant pathways and all of the genes relevant in each pathway. This ideal remains a significant challenge in research in feature selection methods.

Nevertheless, empirical evidence (Li et al., 2002) suggests that so long as A and B are relatively homogeneous, the entropy measure and its refinements can make a good selection of relevant genes from microarray gene expression profiles. For example, comparing Table 14.2 and Table 14.3 in the next section, we see that prediction errors are significantly reduced by selecting relevant genes as described earlier. Furthermore, this reduction in prediction errors is universal across all the prediction algorithms used.

We want to make a final note of caution in performing feature selection from microarray gene expression profiles. The collection of gene expression profiles should be divided into a training set and a testing set. Selection of relevant genes should be made on the basis of the training set only. If there is insufficient gene expression profiles to divide into separate training and testing sets, then a k-fold cross validation strategy should be used and a fresh selection should be made for each fold using the training portion of that fold. To appreciate the importance of this caution, let us visit a simulation experiment reported by Miller et al. (2002). They constructed an artificial data set with 100 samples. Each sample contains 100,000 random expression values and has a randomly assigned class. They then selected the 20 genes with the smallest p values determined by the Wilcoxon rank sum test. They evaluated the accuracy of using these 20 genes in class prediction by leave-one-out cross validation. The resultant estimated accuracy was 88%. However, because the data are derived from random assignments, the true accuracy must be only 50%. This is clearly inappropriate. Ambroise and McLachlan (2002) provide additional examples that illustrate this issue.

14.4. DIAGNOSIS OF DISEASE STATE OR SUBTYPE

A major excitement generated by microarrays in the biomedical world is the possibility of using microarrays to diagnose disease states or disease subtypes in a way that is more efficient and more effective than conventional techniques. Let us consider the diagnosis of childhood leukemia subtypes as an illustration. Childhood leukemia is a heterogeneous disease comprising six major subtypes—T-ALL, E2A-PBX1, TEL-AML1, BCR-ABL, MLL, Hyperdiploid>50—and other subtypes. The response of each subtype to chemotherapy is different. Thus the optimal treatment plan for childhood leukemia depends critically on the subtype. Conventional childhood leukemia subtype diagnosis is a difficult and expensive process (Yeoh et al., 2002). It requires intensive laboratory studies comprising cytogenetics, immunophenotyping, and molecular diagnostics. Usually, these diagnostic approaches require the collective expertise of a number of professionals comprising hematologists, oncologists, pathologists, and cytogeneticists. Although such combined expertise is available in major medical centers in developed countries, it is generally unavailable in less developed countries. It is therefore very exciting if microarrays and associated automatic gene expression profile analysis can serve as a single easy-to-use platform for subtyping of childhood leukemia. This section applies the ideas of emerging patterns and PCL on a large childhood leukemia dataset to perform subtype diagnosis.

We show the results of PCL on the dataset reported in Yeoh et al. (2002). The whole dataset consists of gene expression profiles of 327 childhood acute lymphoblastic leukemia (ALL) samples. These profiles were obtained by hybridization on the Affymetrix U95A GeneChip containing probes for 12558 genes. The data were divided by Yeoh et al. into a training set of 215 instances and an independent test set of 112 samples. There are 28, 18, 52, 9, 14, and 42 training instances and 15, 9, 27, 6, 6, and 22 test samples, respectively, for T-ALL, E2A-PBX1, TEL-AML1, BCR-ABL, MLL, and Hyperdiploid>50. There are also 52 training and 27 test samples of other miscellaneous subtypes. The original training and test data were layered in a tree structure, as shown in Figure 14.2. Given a new sample, we first check if it is T-ALL. If it is not classified as T-ALL, we go to the next level and check if it is a E2A-PBX1. If it is not classified as E2A-PBX1, we go to the third level, and so on.

In applying PCL to this dataset, at each level of the tree, we first use the entropy measure described in the previous section to select the 20 genes that have the lowest entropy in that level's training data. Then we extract emerging patterns of that level involving just these 20 genes using the training set of that level. After the discretization of these top-ranked genes, we use border-based algorithms (Dong and Li, 1999; Li et al., 2000) to discover the most general emerging patterns. Then these emerging patterns are used by PCL to predict the subtypes of test instances of that level. For comparison, we have also applied several popular classification

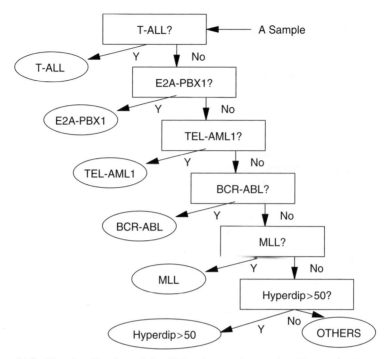

Figure 14.2. The classification of the ALL subtypes is organized in a tree. Given a new sample, we first check if it is T-ALL. If it is not classified as T-ALL, we go to the next level and check if it is a E2A-PBX1. If it is not classified as E2A-PBX1, we go to the third level, and so on.

methods—C4.5, SVM, and Naive Bayes (NB)—to the same datasets after filtering using the same selected genes. In each of these comparison methods, the default settings of the weka package (http://www.cs.waikato.ac.nz/ml/weka) was used. In the PCL case, the parameter k was set to 20.

The number of false predictions on the test instances, after filtering by selecting relevant genes as described above, at each level of the tree by PCL, as well as those by C4.5, SVM, and NB, is given in Table 14.2. The results of the same algorithms but without filtering by selecting relevant genes beforehand are given in Table 14.3. The number of false predictions by PCL is less than that made by the other methods. We have also tried using different number of genes and different selection methods and different values of the parameter k in PCL, the number of false predictions by PCL is consistently less than that made by other methods (Li et al., 2002). Similar results are also obtained when a parallel classification scheme is used in place of the tree-structured scheme (Li et al., 2003).

PCL has high accuracy, and the underlying emerging patterns identified can also be translated into highly comprehensible rules. Let us illustrate this point about comprehensibility using some of the top emerging patterns from the ALL study above. In the prediction of the subtype E2A-PBX1 versus other subtypes,

TABLE 14.2. Error Counts of Various Classification Methods on the Blinded ALL Test Samples[a]

| Testing Data | Error Rate of Different Models | | | |
	C4.5	SVM	NB	PCL (k = 20)
T-ALL vs OTHERS1	0:1	0:0	0:0	0:0
E2A-PBX1 versus OTHERS2	0:0	0:0	0:0	0:0
TEL-AML1 versus OTHERS3	1:1	0:1	0:1	1:0
BCR-ABL versus OTHERS4	2:0	1:1	2:2	1:1
MLL versus OTHERS5	1:1	0:0	0:0	0:0
Hyperdiploid>50 versus OTHERS	1:6	0:2	0:2	0:2
Total Errors	14	5	7	5

[a]PCL is shown to make considerably less misclassifications. The OTHERS*i* class contains all those subtypes of ALL below the *i*th level of the tree depicted in Figure 1.2.

TABLE 14.3. Error Counts of Various Classification Methods on the Blinded ALL Test Samples Without Filtering by Selecting Relevant Genes[a]

| Testing Data | Error Rate of Different Models | | |
	C4.5	SVM	NB
T-ALL versus OTHERS1	0:1	0:0	13:0
E2A-PBX1 versus OTHERS2	0:0	0:0	9:0
TEL-AML1 versus OTHERS3	2:4	0:9	20:0
BCR-ABL versus OTHERS4	1:3	2:0	6:0
MLL versus OTHERS5	0:1	0:0	6:0
Hyperdiploid>50 versus OTHERS	4:10	12:0	7:2
Total Errors	26	23	63

[a]The OTHERS*i* class contains all those subtypes of ALL below the *i*th level of the tree depicted in Figure 1.2.

the gene 32063_at has perfect entropy measure when its expression range is partitioned at the point 4068.7. The two emerging patterns induced by this partitioning have very high support: The expression of 32063_at in all E2A-PBX1 samples are greater than 4068.7, and the expression of 32063_at in all other subtypes are less than 4068.7. In other words, the emerging pattern, {32063_at $\geq$ 4068.7}, and the emerging pattern, {32063_at < 4068.7}, yield two rules that are 100% valid:

> If 32063_at $\geq$ 4068.7, then the sample is E2A-PBX1.
> If 32063_at < 4068.7, then the sample is OTHERS2.

In some other subtypes, no single gene can yield such reliable rules, and we must thus look at rules involving coordinated gene expression. In the prediction of the subtype TEL-AML1, two of the top genes are 38652_at and 36937_s_at. The expression range of 38652_at is partitioned at the point 8997.35, and the expression range of 36937_at is partitioned at the point 13617.05. These partitioning induces four candidate patterns, and one of them (38652_at $\geq$ 8997.35 and 36937_s_at < 13617.05) is a top emerging pattern that appears in 92.31% of TEL-AML1 training samples but never in OTHERS3. This suggests that 38652_at and 36937_s_at are coordinated in TEL-AML1 and induces a rule that has an estimated validity of 92.31%:

> If 38652_at $\geq$ 8997.35 and 36937_s_at < 13617.05 in a sample, then the sample is TEL-AML1.

These rules and other additional ones on the childhood leukemia dataset are discussed in more detail in Li et al. (2003).

14.5. DERIVATION OF TREATMENT PLAN

In the previous sections, we saw that the entropy measure can be used to identify genes that are relevant to the diagnosis of disease states and subtypes. We also saw that the top emerging patterns are suggestive of coordinated gene groups in particular disease states and subtypes: (i) For each gene in such a coordinated gene group there is a predetermined interval of gene expression level, as specified by the corresponding emerging pattern. (ii) Particular disease states and subtypes can often be characterized by one or more such emerging patterns, in the sense that a large portion of the cases in the given disease state (or subtype) match the corresponding emerging patterns and the cases in other disease states (or subtypes) never match the same emerging patterns. Based on these patterns, we conjecture the possibility of a personalized "treatment plan" that converts tumor cells into normal cells by modulating the expression levels of a few genes.

We use the colon tumor dataset of Alon et al. (1999) to demonstrate our idea in this section. This dataset consists of 22 normal tissues and 40 colon tumor tissues. We begin with finding out which intervals of the expression levels of a group of genes occur only in cancer tissues but not in the normal tissues and vice versa. Then we attempt an explanation of the results and suggest a plan for treating the disease.

We use the entropy measure (Fayyad and Irani, 1993) described earlier to induce a partition of the expression range of each gene into suitable intervals. As discussed, this method partitions a range of real values into a number of disjoint intervals such that the entropy of the partition is minimal. For the colon cancer dataset, of its 2000 genes, only 135 genes can be partitioned into two intervals of low entropy (Li and Wong, 2002c,d). The remaining 1865 genes are ignored by the method. Thus most of the genes are viewed as irrelevant by the method. For the purpose of this chapter we further concentrate on the 35 genes with the lowest entropy measure amongst the 135 genes. These 35 genes are shown in Table 14.4. This gives us an easy platform where a small number of good diagnostic indicators are concentrated. For simplicity of reference, the index numbers in the first column of Table 14.4 are used to refer to the two expression intervals of the corresponding genes. For example, the index 1 means M26338 < 59.83 and the index 2 means M26383 ≥ 59.83.

Next, we use an efficient border-based algorithm (Dong and Li, 1999; Li et al., 2000) to discover emerging patterns based on the selected 35 genes and the partitioning of their expression intervals induced by the entropy measure. The emerging patterns are thus combinations of intervals of gene expression levels of these relevant genes. A total of 10548 emerging patterns are found, 9540 emerging patterns for the normal class and 1008 emerging patterns for the tumor class. The top several tens of the normal class emerging patterns contain about 8 genes each and can reach a frequency of 77.27%, while many tumor class emerging patterns can reach a frequency of around 65%. These top emerging patterns are presented in Table 14.5 and Table 14.6. Note that the numbers in the emerging patterns in these figures, such as {2, 10} in Table 14.6, refer to the index numbers in Table 14.4. Hence, {2, 10} denotes the pattern {M26383 ≥ 59.83, H08393 ≥ 84.87}. The emerging patterns that are discovered are most general ones, and they occur in one class of data but do not occur in the other class. The discovered emerging patterns always contain only a small number of the relevant genes. This result reveals interesting conditions on the expression of these genes that differentiate between two classes of data.

Each emerging pattern with high frequency is considered as a common property of a class of cells. Based on this idea, we propose a strategy for treating colon tumors by adjusting the expression level of some improperly expressed genes. That is, we increase or decrease the expression levels of some particular genes in a cancer cell, so that it has the common properties of normal cells and no properties of cancer cells. As a result, instead of killing the cancer cell, it is "converted" into a normal one. We show later that almost all "adjusted" cells are predicted as normal cells by a number of good classifiers that were trained to distinguish normal from colon tumor cells.

As shown in Table 14.5, the frequency of emerging patterns can reach a very high level such as 77.27%. The conditions implied by a highly frequent emerging pattern form a common property of one class of cells. Using the emerging pattern {25, 33, 37, 41, 43, 57, 59, 69} from Table 14.5, we see that each of the 77.27% of the normal cells simultaneously expresses the eight genes—M16937,

TABLE 14.4. The 35 Top-Ranked Genes by the Entropy Measure[a]

Our List	accession Number	Cutting Points	Name
1,2	M26383	59.83	Monocyte-derived neutrophil-activating protein mRNA
3,4	M63391	1696.22	Human desmin gene
5,6	R87126	379.38	Myosin heavy chain, nonmuscle (*Gallus gallus*)
7,8	M76378	842.30	Human cysteine-rich protein (CRP) gene, exons 5 and 6
9,10	H08393	84.87	COLLAGEN ALPHA 2(XI) CHAIN (*Homo sapiens*)
11,12	X12671	229.99	Heterogeneous nuclear ribonucleoprotein core protein A1
13,14	R36977	274.96	P03001 TRANSCRIPTION FACTOR IIIA
15,16	J02854	735.80	Myosin regulatory light chain 2, smooth muscle isoform
17,18	M22382	447.04	Mitochondrial matrix protein P1 precursor (human)
19,20	J05032	88.90	Human aspartyl-tRNA synthetase alpha-2 subunit mRNA
21,22	M76378	1048.37	Human cysteine-rich protein (CRP) gene, exons 5 and 6
23,24	M76378	1136.74	Human cysteine-rich protein (CRP) gene, exons 5 and 6
25,26	M16937	390.44	Human homeo box c1 protein mRNA
27,28	H40095	400.03	Macrophage migration inhibitory factor (human)
29,30	U30825	288.99	Human splicing factor SRp30c mRNA
31,32	H43887	334.01	Complement factor D precursor
33,34	H51015	84.19	Proto-oncogene DBL precursor
35,36	X57206	417.30	1D-myo-inositol-trisphosphate 3-kinase B isoenzyme
37,38	R10066	494.17	PROHIBITIN (*Homo sapiens*)
39,40	T96873	75.42	Hypothetical protein in TRPE 3′ region (*Spirochaeta aurantia*)
41,42	T57619	2597.85	40S ribosomal protein S6 (*Nicotiana tabacum*)
43,44	R84411	735.57	Small nuclear ribonucleoprotein assoc. protein B and B′
45,46	U21090	232.74	Human DNA polymerase delta small subunit mRNA
47,48	U32519	87.58	Human GAP SH3 binding protein mRNA
49,50	T71025	1695.98	Human (HUMAN)
51,52	T92451	845.7	Tropomyosin, fibroblast, and epithelial muscle-type
53,54	U09564	120.38	Human serine kinase mRNA
55,56	H40560	913.77	THIOREDOXIN (HUMAN)
57,58	T47377	629.44	S-100P PROTEIN (HUMAN)
59,60	X53586	121.91	Human mRNA for integrin alpha 6
61,62	U25138	186.19	Human MaxiK potassium channel beta subunit mRNA
63,64	T60155	1798.65	ACTIN, AORTIC SMOOTH MUSCLE (HUMAN)
65,66	H55758	1453.15	ALPHA ENOLASE (HUMAN)
67,68	Z50753	196.12	*Homo sapiens* mRNA for GCAP-II/uroguanylin precursor
69,70	U09587	486.17	Human glycyl-tRNA synthetase mRNA

[a]The index numbers in the first column are used to refer to the two expression intervals of the corresponding genes. For example, the index 1 means M26338 < 59.83 and the index 2 means M26383 ≥ 59.83.

TABLE 14.5. The Top 20 Emerging Patterns, in Descending Frequency order, in the 22 Normal Tissues[a]

Emerging Patterns	Count and Frequency (%) in Normal Tissues	Count and Frequency (%) in Cancer Tissues
{25, 33, 37, 41, 43, 57, 59, 69}	17(77.27%)	0
{25, 33, 37, 41, 43, 47, 57, 69}	17(77.27%)	0
{29, 33, 35, 37, 41, 43, 57, 69}	17(77.27%)	0
{29, 33, 37, 41, 43, 47, 57, 69}	17(77.27%)	0
{29, 33, 37, 41, 43, 57, 59, 69}	17(77.27%)	0
{25, 33, 35, 37, 41, 43, 57, 69}	17(77.27%)	0
{33, 35, 37, 41, 43, 57, 65, 69}	17(77.27%)	0
{33, 37, 41, 43, 47, 57, 65, 69}	17(77.27%)	0
{33, 37, 41, 43, 57, 59, 65, 69}	17(77.27%)	0
{33, 35, 37, 41, 43, 45, 57, 69}	17(77.27%)	0
{33, 37, 41, 43, 45, 47, 57, 69}	17(77.27%)	0
{33, 37, 41, 43, 45, 57, 59, 69}	17(77.27%)	0
{13, 33, 35, 37, 43, 57, 69}	17(77.27%)	0
{13, 33, 37, 43, 47, 57, 69}	17(77.27%)	0
{13, 33, 37, 43, 57, 59, 69}	17(77.27%)	0
{13, 32, 37, 57, 69}	17(77.27%)	0
{33, 35, 37, 57, 68}	17(77.27%)	0
{33, 37, 47, 57, 68}	17(77.27%)	0
{33, 37, 57, 59, 68}	17(77.27%)	0
{32, 37, 41, 57, 69}	17(77.27%)	0

[a]The numbers in the emerging patterns above refer to the index numbers in Table 14.4.

H51015, R10066, T57619, R84411, T47377, X53586, and U09587 referenced in this emerging pattern—in such a way that each of the eight expression levels is contained in the corresponding interval—the 25th, 33th, 37th, 41st, 43rd, 57th, 59th, and 69th—as indexed in Table 14.4. Although a cancer cell may express some of the eight genes in a manner similar to that of normal cells, according to the dataset, a cancer cell can never express all of the eight genes in the same way that normal cells do. So, if the expression levels of those improperly expressed genes can be adjusted, then the cancer cell can be made to have one more common property that normal cells exhibit. Conversely, a cancer cell may exhibit an emerging pattern that is a common property of a large percentage of cancer cells and is not exhibited in any of the normal cells. Adjustments should also be made to some genes involved in this pattern so that the cancer cell can be made to have one less common property that cancer cells exhibit. A cancer cell can then be iteratively converted into a normal one as described above.

Because there usually exist some genes of a cancer cell which express in a manner similar to that of their counterparts in normal cells, less than 35 genes' expression levels are required to be changed. The most important issue is to determine which genes need an adjustment. Our emerging patterns can be used

TABLE 14.6. The Top 20 Emerging Patterns, in Descending Frequency Order, in the 40 Cancer Tissues[a]

Emerging Patterns	Count and Frequency (%) in Normal Tissues	Count and Frequency (%) in Cancer Tissues
{2, 10}	0	28 (70.00%)
{10, 61}	0	27 (67.50%)
{10, 20}	0	27 (67.50%)
{3, 10}	0	27 (67.50%)
{10, 21}	0	27 (67.50%)
{10, 23}	0	27 (67.50%)
{7, 40, 56}	0	26 (65.00%)
{2, 56}	0	26 (65.00%)
{12, 56}	0	26 (65.00%)
{10, 63}	0	26 (65.00%)
{3, 58}	0	26 (65.00%)
{7, 58}	0	26 (65.00%)
{15, 58}	0	26 (65.00%)
{23, 58}	0	26 (65.00%)
{58, 61}	0	26 (65.00%)
{2, 58}	0	26 (65.00%)
{20, 56}	0	26 (65.00%)
{21, 58}	0	26 (65.00%)
{15, 40, 56}	0	25 (62.50%)
{21, 40, 56}	0	25 (62.50%)

[a]The numbers in the emerging patterns refer to the index numbers in Table 14.4.

to address this issue as follows. Given a cancer cell, we first determine which top emerging pattern of normal cells has the closest Hamming distance to it in the sense that the least number of genes need to be adjusted to make this emerging pattern appear in the adjusted cancer cell. Then we proceed to adjust these genes. This process is repeated several times until the adjusted cancer cell exhibits as many common properties of normal cells as a normal cell does. The next step is to look at which top emerging pattern of cancer cells that is still present in the adjusted cancer cell has the closest Hamming distance to a pattern in a normal cell. Then we also proceed to adjust some genes involved in this emerging pattern so that this emerging pattern would vanish from the adjusted cancer cell. This process is repeated until all top emerging patterns of cancer cells disappear from our adjusted cancer cell. It is possible to choose genes to adjust following the spirit above, but in a different way so that the number of gene adjustments needed is minimized. We leave the diligent readers to devise a more optimal strategy.

We use a cancer cell (T1) of the colon tumor dataset as an example to show how a tumor cell is converted into a normal one. Recall that the emerging pattern {25, 33, 37, 41, 43, 57, 59, 69} is a common property of normal cells. The eight genes involved in this emerging pattern are M16937, H51015, R10066, T57619, R84411, T47377, X53586, and U09587. Let us list the expression profile of these eight genes in T1:

Genes	Expression Levels in T1
M16937	369.92
H51015	137.39
R10066	354.97
T57619	1926.39
R84411	798.28
T47377	662.06
X53586	136.09
U09587	672.20

However, 77.27%—17 out of 22 cases—of the normal cells have the following expression intervals for these eight genes:

Genes	Expression Interval
M16937	<390.44
H51015	<84.19
R10066	<494.17
T57619	<2597.85
R84411	<735.57
T47377	<629.44
X53586	<121.91
U09587	<486.17

Comparing T1's gene expression levels with the intervals of normal cells, we see that five of the eight genes—H51015, R84411, T47377, X53586, and U09587—of the cancer cell T1 behave in a different way from those the 22 normal cells commonly express. However, the remaining three genes of T1 are in the same expression range as most of the normal cells. So, if the five genes of T1 can be down-regulated to scale below those cutting points, then this adjusted cancer cell will have a common property of normal cells. This is because {25, 33, 37, 41, 43, 57, 59, 69} is an emerging pattern that does not occur in the cancer cells. This idea is at the core of our suggestion for this treatment plan.

Interestingly, the expression change of the five genes in T1 leads to a chain of other changes. These include the change that nine extra top-ten EPs of normal cells are contained in the adjusted T1. So all top-ten EPs of normal cells are contained in T1 if the five genes' expression level are adjusted. As the average number of top-ten EPs contained in normal cells is seven, the changed T1 cell will now be considered as a cell that has the most important features of normal cells. Note that we have adjusted only five genes' expression level so far.

We also need to eliminate those common properties of cancer cells that are contained in T1. By adjusting the expression level of two other genes, M26383 and H08393, the top-ten EPs of cancer cells all disappear from T1. According to our colon tumor dataset, the average number of top-ten EPs of cancer cells contained in a cancer cell is six. Therefore, T1 is converted into a normal cell because it now holds the common properties of normal cells and does not hold the common properties of cancer cells.

By this method, all the other 39 cancer cells can be converted into normal ones after adjusting the expression levels of 10 genes or so, possibly different genes from person to person. We conjecture that this personalized treatment plan is effective if the expression of some particular genes can be modulated by suitable means.

We next discuss a validation of this idea. The "adjustments" we made to the 40 colon tumor cells were based on the emerging patterns in the manner described above. If these adjustments had indeed converted the colon tumor cells into normal cells, then any good classifier that could distinguish normal versus colon tumor cells on the basis of gene expression profiles would classify our adjusted cells as normal cells. So, we established a SVM model using the original entire 22 normal plus 40 cancer cells as training data. The code for constructing this SVM model is available at http://www.cs.waikato.ac.nz/ml/weka. The prediction result is that all of the adjusted cells were predicted as normal cells.

Although our "therapy" was not applied to the real treatment of a patient, the prediction result by the SVM model partially demonstrates the potential biological significance of our proposal. Nevertheless, we caution that even if we are able to identify which genes to modulate in what ways, we may not have the means to carry out the desired modulation. This is because the ability to up- or down-regulate the expression level of any gene at will and without side effect is still an unsolved challenge in pharmaceutical research.

14.6. UNDERSTANDING OF MOLECULAR CIRCUIT

A large number of genes can be differentially expressed in a microarray experiment. Such genes can serve as markers of the different classes—such as tumor versus normal—of samples in the experiment. Some of these genes can even be the primary cause of a sample being tumor. However, most are likely to be downstream effects of the states of the causal genes. In order to separate the former from the latter, it is necessary to consider the underlying molecular network or biological pathway.

Even after the causal genes are identified, how to target and control them and their protein products is a significant challenge. For example, drug substances typically have to act through receptors. If the identified causal genes do not correspond to receptors, then an indirect path is needed for drug substances to act on them. However, this significantly increases the probability of failure due to the increased possibility of side effects and compensation effects. Side effects arise when a drug substance affects the expression of other genes in addition to the intended ones. Compensation effects arise when there are multiple parallel paths that have the same effects on the intended genes or that produce similar effects as the intended genes, and the drug substance is unable to fully control these parallel paths. In order to minimize failure due to side effects and compensation effects, it is important to consider the underlying molecular network or biological pathways.

Therefore, in this section we discuss the issue of inferring molecular networks from gene expression experiments. Genes are "connected" in a "circuit" or network. The expression of a gene in a network depends on the expression of some other genes in the network. For each gene in the network, can we determine which genes affect it and how they affect it—positively, negatively, or in more complicated ways. There are several techniques to reconstructing and modeling molecular networks from gene expression experiments. We describe here the classification-based method of Soinov et al. (2003).

Let a collection of n microarray gene expression output be given. For convenience, this collection can be organized into a gene expression matrix X. Each row of the matrix is a gene, each column is a sample, and each element x_{ij} is the expression of gene i in sample j. Then the basic idea of the method of Soinov et al. (2003) is as follows. First determine the average value a_i of each gene i as $(\sum_j x_{ij})/n$. Next, denote s_{ij} as the state of gene i in sample j, where $s_{ij} = up$ if $x_{ij} \geq a_i$, and $s_{ij} = down$ if $x_{ij} < a_i$. Then, according to Soinov et al. (2003), to see whether the state of a gene g is determined by the state of other genes G, we check whether $\langle s_{ij} | i \in G \rangle$ can predict s_{gj}. If it can predict s_{gj} with high accuracy, then we conclude that the state of the gene g is determined by the states of other genes G. Furthermore, any classifier can be used to see if such predictions can be made reliably, such as C4.5, PCL, and SVM. Then, to see how the state of a gene g is determined by the state of other genes, we apply C4.5, or PCL, or other rule-based classifiers to predict s_{gj} from $\langle s_{ij} | i \in G \rangle$ and extract the decision tree or rules used.

This interesting method has a few advantages: It can identify genes affecting a target gene in an explicit manner, it does not need a discretization threshold, each data sample is treated as an example, and explicit rules can be extracted from a rule-based classifier like C4.5 or PCL. For example, we generate from the gene expression matrix a set of n vectors $\langle s_{ij} | i \neq g \rangle \Rightarrow s_{gj}$. Then C4.5 (or PCL) can be applied to see if $\langle s_{ij} | i \neq g \rangle$ predicts s_{gj}. The decision tree (or emerging patterns, respectively) induced would involve a small number of s_{ij}. Then we can conclude that those genes corresponding to these small number of s_{ij} affect gene g.

One other nice advantage of the Soinov method (2003) is that it is easily generalizable to time series. Suppose the matrices X^t and X^{t+1} correspond to microarray gene expression measurements taken at time t and $t + 1$. Suppose s_{ij}^t and s_{ij}^{t+1} correspond to the expression of gene i in sample j at time t and $t + 1$. Then to find out whether the state of a gene g is affected by other genes G in a time-lagged manner, we check whether $\langle s_{ij}^t \mid i \in G \rangle$ can predict s_{gj}^{t+1}. The rest of the procedure is as before.

Of course, there is a major caveat that this method as described assumes that a gene g can be in only two states, namely, $s_{gj} = up$ or $s_{gj} = down$. As cautioned by Soinov et al. (2003), it is possible for a gene to have more than two states and thus this assumption may not infer the complete network of gene interactions. Another caution is that if the states of two genes g and h are strongly co-related, the rules $s_{hj} \Rightarrow s_{gj}$ and $s_{gj} \Rightarrow s_{hj}$ saying that h depends on g and g depends on h are likely to be both inferred, even though only one of them may be true and the other false. Hence, further confirmation by gene knock-out or other experiments is advisable.

14.7. CLOSING REMARKS

Microarrays are a technology for simultaneously profiling the expression levels of tens of thousands of genes in a patient sample. It is increasingly clear that better diagnosis methods and better understanding of disease mechanisms can be derived from a careful analysis of microarray measurements of gene expression profiles. This chapter discussed several types of analysis of such gene expression profiles, including (a) diagnosis of disease state and subtype, (b) derivation of disease treatment plan, and (c) understanding of gene interaction networks.

In the course of this discussion, we have surveyed techniques for gene selection from microarray gene expression profiles. We have also introduced emerging patterns and the emerging pattern-based classification method called PCL. We have demonstrated the use of PCL for classifying disease states and subtypes from gene expression profiles. We have also showed the use of emerging patterns of gene expressions to derive treatment plans. In addition, we have also explained the possibility of inferring molecular circuits using a classification-based framework and that PCL can be applied within such a framework.

The analysis of microarray gene expression data is an active field. For each of the analysis problems that we have presented, there are numerous alternative approaches to solving it. Due to limitation of space, we do not attempt to comprehensively survey these alternative approaches. Instead, let us close this chapter by mentioning some additional gene expression analysis problems that generally cannot be addressed by supervised machine learning techniques like emerging patterns.

For example, we see in Section 14.4 that it is possible to diagnose disease subtypes and states from gene expression data. In that section, we assume that all the disease subtypes are known. However, in real life, it is possible for a heterogeneous disease to have or to evolve new subtypes that are not previously known. Can computational analysis of gene expression data help uncover such new disease subtypes? Similarly, there are still many genes and their products whose functions are unknown. Can computational analysis of gene expression data help uncover functionally related gene groups, and can we infer the functions and regulation of such gene groups? Unsupervised machine learning methods, especially clustering algorithms, are useful for these problems.

For example, in the childhood acute lymphoblastic leukemia study (Yeoh et al., 2002) referenced in Section 14.4, the dataset also contained some samples that were not assigned to any of the six major subtypes—these are the groups marked as "OTHERS" in Figure 14.2. This "OTHERS" group presented an opportunity for identifying new subtypes of childhood ALL. To do so, Yeoh et al. (2002) performed a hierarchical clustering on their 327 childhood ALL samples using all the 12,558 genes measured on their Affymetrix U95A Gene Chip and using Pearson correlation as the distance between samples. Remarkably, this analysis clearly identified within the "OTHERS" group a novel subgroup of 14 cases that showed a distinct gene expression profile.

As another example, Gasch and Eisen (2002) used a technique called fuzzy k-means (Bezdek, 1973) to cluster a large collection of gene expression data obtained under a variety of experimental conditions. The dataset comprised 6153 genes in 93 microarray experiments taken from genomic expression data of wild-type *Saccharomyces cerevisiae* responding to various experimental conditions. They obtained several very interesting results from analyzing the resulting clusters. First, they identified some meaningful clusters of genes that hierarchical and standard k-means clustering methods were unable to identify. Second, many of their clusters that corresponded to previously recognized groups of functionally related genes were more comprehensive than those clusters produced by hierarchical and standard k-means clustering methods. Third, they were able to assign many genes to multiple clusters, revealing distinct aspects of their function and regulation. Fourth, they applied the motif-finding algorithm MEME (Bailey and Elkan, 1994) to the promoter regions of genes in some of the clusters to find short patterns of six nucleotides that were overrepresented and thus identified a few potentially novel transcription factor binding sites.

ACKNOWLEDGMENT

We are grateful to Mr. Shihong Mao, who did a careful proofreading of this chapter.

REFERENCES

Alon, U., Barkai, N., Notterman, D. A., Gish, K., Mack, S. Y. D., and Levine, J., Broad patterns of gene expression revealed by clustering analysis of tumor colon tissues probed by oligonucleotide arrays, *Proceedings of the National Academy of Sciences USA* **96**, 6745–6750, (1999).

Ambroise, C., and McLachlan, G. J., Selection bias in gene extraction on the basis of microarray gene-expression data, *Proceedings of the National Academy of Sciences USA*, **14**, 6562–6566 (2002).

Bailey, T. B., and Elkan, C., Fitting a mixture model by expectation maximization to discover motifs, *Intelligent Systems for Molecular Biology* **2**, 28–36 (1994).

Baldi, P., and Long, A. D., A Bayesian framework for the analysis of microarray expression data: Regularized t-test and statistical inferences of gene changes. *Bioinformatics* **17**(6), 509–519 (2001).

Bezdek, J. C., *Fuzzy Mathematics in Pattern Classification*, Cornell University, Ithaca, NY, 1973.

Burges, C. J. C., A tutorial on support vector machines for pattern recognition, *Data Mining and Knowledge Discovery* **2**(2), 121–167 (1998).

Caria, M., *Measurement Analysis: An Introduction to the Statistical Analysis of Laboratory Data in Physics, Chemistry, and the Life Sciences*, Imperial College Press, London, 2000.

Cover, T. M., and Hart, P. E., Nearest neighbor pattern classification, *IEEE Transactions on Information Theory* **13**, 21–27 (1967).

Dong, G., and Li, J., Efficient mining of emerging patterns: Discovering trends and differences, in *Proceedings of 5th ACM SIGKDD International Conference on Knowledge Discovery & Data Mining*, pp. 15–18, 1999.

Fayyad, U., and Irani, K., Multi-interval discretization of continuous-valued attributes for classification learning, in *Proceedings of 13th International Joint Conference on Artificial Intelligence*, pp. 1022–1029, 1993.

Fodor, S. P., Read, J. L., Pirrung, M. C., Stryer, L., Lu, A. T., and Solas, D., Light-directed spatially addressable parallel chemical synthesis, *Science* **251**, 767–773 (1991).

Gasch, A., and Eisen, M. B., Exploring the conditional coregulation of yeast gene expression through fuzzy k-means clustering, *Genome Biology* **3**(11), 0059.1–0059.22, (2002).

Golub, T. R., Slonim, D. K., Tamayo, P., Huard, C., Gaasenbeek, M., Misirov, J. P., Coller, H., Loh, M. L., Downing, J. R., Caligiuri, M. A., Bloomfield, C. D., and Lander, E. S., Molecular classification of cancer: Class discovery and class prediction by gene expression monitoring, *Science* **286**(15), 531–537 (1999).

Hall, M. A., Correlation-Based Feature Selection Machine Learning, Ph.D. Thesis, Department of Computer Science, University of Waikato, New Zealand, 1998.

Han, J., and Kamber, M., *Data Mining: Concepts and Techniques*, Morgan Kaufmann, San Francisco, 2000.

Hastie, T., Tibshirani, R., and Friedman, J., *The Elements of Statistical Learning: Data Mining, Inference, and Prediction*, Springer-Verlag, Berlin, 2001.

Langley, P., Iba, W., and Thompson, K., An analysis of Bayesian classifier, in *Proceedings of 10th National Conference on Artificial Intelligence*, pp. 223–228, 1992.

Li, J., and Wong, L., Geography of differences between two classes of data, in *Proceedings 6th European Conference on Principles of Data Mining and Knowledge Discovery*, pp. 325–337, 2002a.

Li, J., and Wong, L., Solving the fragmentation problem of decision trees by discovering boundary emerging patterns, in *Proceedings of IEEE International Conference on Data Mining*, pp. 653–656, 2002b.

Li, J., and Wong, L., Identifying good diagnostic genes or genes groups from gene expression data by using the concept of emerging patterns, *Bioinformatics* **18**, 725–734 (2002c).

Li, J., and Wong, L., Corrigendum: Identifying good diagnostic genes or genes groups from gene expression data by using the concept of emerging patterns, *Bioinformatics* **18**, 1407–1408 (2002d).

Li, J., and Wong, L., Using rules to analyse bio-medical data: A comparison between C4.5 and PCL, in *Proceedings of 4th International Conference on Web-Age Information Management*, pages 254–265, 2003.

Li, J., Ramamohanarao, K., and Dong, G., The space of jumping emerging patterns and its incremental maintenance algorithms, in *Proceedings of 17th International Conference on Machine Learning*, pp. 551–558, 2000.

Li, J., Liu, H., and Wong, L., A comparative study on feature selection and classification methods using a large set of gene expression profiles, in *Proceedings of 13th International Conference on Genome Informatics*, pp. 51–60, 2002.

Li, J., Liu, H., Downing, J. R., Yeoh, A. E.-J., and Wong, L., Simple rules underlying gene expression profiles of more than six subtypes of acute lymphoblastic leukemia (ALL) patients, *Bioinformatics* **19**, 71–78 (2003).

Liu, H., and Setiono, R., Chi2: Feature selection and discretization of numeric attributes, in *Proceedings of IEEE 7th International Conference on Tools with Artificial Intelligence*, pp. 338–391, 1995.

Lockhart, D. J., Dong, H., Byrne, M. C., Follettie, M. T., Gallo, M. V., Chee, M. S., Mittmann, M., Wang, C., Kobayashi, M., Horton, H., and Brown, E. L., Expression monitoring by hybridization to high-density oligonucleotide arrays, *Nature Biotechnology* **14**, 1675–1680 (1996).

Miller, L. D., Long, P. M., Wong, L., Mukherjee, S., McShane, L. M., and Liu, E. T., Optimal gene expression analysis by microarrays. *Cancer Cell* **2**, 353–361 (2002).

Quinlan, J. R., *C4.5: Program for Machine Learning*, Morgan Kaufmann, San Francisco, 1993.

Ramsay, G., DNA chips: State-of-the art, *Nature Biotechnology* **16**, 40–44 (1998).

Shalon, D., Smith, S. J., and Brown, P. O., A DNA microarray system for analyzing complex DNA Samples using two-color fluorescent probe hybridization, *Genome Research* **6**(7), 639–645 (1996).

Soinov, L. A., Krestyaninova, M. A., and Brazma, A., Towards reconstruction of gene networks from expression data by supervised learning, *Genome Biology* **4**(1), R6.1–9 (2003).

Wang, L., Zhao, H., Dong, G., and Li, J., On the complexity of computing emerging patterns. Unpublished manuscript, 2003.

Yeoh, A. E.-J., Ross, M. E., Shurtleff, S. A., William, W. K., Patel, D., Mahfouz, R., Behm, F. G., Raimondi, S. C., Reilling, M. V., Patel, A., Cheng, C., Campana, D., Wilkins, D., Zhou, X., Li, J., Liu, H., Pui, C.-H., Evans, W. E., Naeve, C., Wong, L., and Downing, J. R., Classification, subtype discovery, and prediction of outcome in pediatric acute lymphoblastic leukemia by gene expression profiling, *Cancer Cell* **1**, 133–143 (2002).

Zhang, X., Dong, G., and Ramamohanarao, K., Exploring constraints to efficiently mine emerging patterns from large high-dimensional datasets, in *Proceedings of 6th ACM SIGKDD International Conference on Knowledge Discovery & Data Mining*, pp. 310–314, 2000.

15

PROTEOMIC DATA ANALYSIS: PATTERN RECOGNITION FOR MEDICAL DIAGNOSIS AND BIOMARKER DISCOVERY

D. R. Mani and Michael Gillette

15.1. INTRODUCTION

Proteomics is a term used to describe the simultaneous measurement and analysis of a large number of proteins. Like the more familiar *genomics*, it aspires to a global view of biology through the systematic, large-scale evaluation of gene expression and function. While genomic data, derived for instance from DNA microarray analysis, more directly reflect gene expression, proteomics gets closer to biological function, since proteins—the products of genes—are the structural components and active elements of cells. Proteomics may thus provide more direct insight into biological *dys*function, fostering our understanding of disease biology and potentially revealing biomarkers of disease presence, activity, or pharmacologic susceptibility, as well as candidate novel therapeutic targets.

15.1.1. Overview and Goals

Proteomics is a nascent area of research, and techniques for both the generation and analysis of proteomic data are still being formulated. The aim of this chapter is to describe basic issues, address challenges, and highlight pitfalls in both the data collection and data analysis aspects of proteomics. Although proteomic data mining is the central thrust of this chapter, we believe that an understanding of the data generation process is important in selecting and applying appropriate data-mining tools and methods. Since the computational literature lacks

Next Generation of Data-Mining Applications. Edited by Kantardzic and Zurada
ISBN 0-471-65605-4 © 2005 the Institute of Electrical and Electronics Engineers, Inc.

published reviews or primers that encompass the range of relevant proteomic methodologies, this chapter provides the computational biologist contemplating a foray into proteomics with both an overview of relevant biology and biotechnology (Appendix) and a practical depiction of the application of data-mining methodology to proteomic data analysis (Sections 15.2 and 15.3). The discussion is instantiated with specific examples and case studies from ongoing proteomic investigations conducted by the authors.

Section 15.1 defines and summarizes basic terminology. A discussion of signal processing, data-mining and statistical approaches to data analysis is set forth in Section 15.2. Analysis involves feature definition, extraction, and selection, followed by pattern recognition and distillation of signatures characteristic of various diseased and disease-free states. It is these proteomic signatures that provide the possibility of disease classification, early detection, and prognostication.

Section 15.3 briefly describes the identification of the components of proteomic signatures and their conversion into biomarkers, emphasizing that demonstration of biomarker validity and biological significance requires more than principled application of machine learning methods. Pitfalls arising from an improper understanding of various aspects of data generation and processing, and ways to avoid them, are also discussed in Section 15.3.

A deeper and nuanced understanding of proteomic data analysis is fostered by an appreciation of the instrumentation and methodologies used in data generation. A cursory description of relevant mass spectrometric methods is provided in Sections 15.2.1 and 15.2.2. The interested reader will find a more thorough introduction in the Appendix.

15.1.2. Proteomics and Genomics

The term "proteomics" refers to the large-scale characterization of the protein complement of a cell, cell line, tissue, or organism. It is common to distinguish "comparative" from "functional" proteomics. Comparative proteomics is concerned with differential protein expression between types or states of cells or tissues, in a way exactly analogous to that described for gene expression. Comparative proteomics might be used to determine the differences at the protein level between normal and cancerous lung tissue, between a torpid and an active organism, or between a starved and a nutritionally replete cell. Functional proteomics attempts to determine protein binding partners, to resolve multiprotein complexes, to characterize cellular compartments, and to define cell signaling pathways. Although there is substantial overlap, comparative proteomics approaches are particularly favorable for biomarker discovery, while functional proteomics drives more directly at fundamental biology.

Since protein products are encoded by the genome, the relationship between genomics and proteomics is profound. However, it is also very complex, in ways that bear importantly on both the promise and the challenge posed by proteomic study. In general terms, the genetic complement of a biological system (its genome) can be thought of as the comprehensive database of information for building and operating the system's machinery. The protein complement (proteome) of the system is the machinery itself: the structural components, the engines, the factories, and the communication networks. The genome is relatively static over short periods of time; indeed, there is a great deal of biological investment in ensuring that it is stable and faithfully reproduced. The proteome is by contrast highly dynamic, changing instant to instant as the system resists entropy and reacts to its environment. The genome has a defined extent, bounded by the system's DNA. The genome can be sequenced, known in its entirety, and its constituent genes can be counted. The proteome is much less well-defined, but its extent is certainly much vaster. Some genes can be translated into multiple proteins, and each of those proteins can be post-translationally modified in many ways and at many sites, most of which are not known in detail, and many of which cannot be confidently predicted. Since biology is made manifest at the level of the protein, since health and disease are in a sense indices of order or disorder in the proteome, and since the proteome reflects but cannot be fully inferred from the genome, proteomic study is of vital interest to basic and clinical scientists throughout academics and industry.

Linking the genome and the proteome is the *transcriptome*, comprising the comprehensive set of messenger RNA (mRNA) molecules engaged in translating genetic information into proteins. The transcriptome is what is being sampled in "comparative functional genomics" experiments in which mRNA expression levels are compared between types or states of cells or tissues—for instance, between cancerous and normal samples (Golub et al., 1999). The transcriptome, like the proteome, is dynamic. However, since so many critical protein modifications are post-translational, the transcriptome is both less dynamic than, and imperfectly predictive of, the proteome. It remains difficult to correctly predict primary protein structure from genomic data. Furthermore, proteolysis, protein recycling, and compartmental sequestration of proteins continuously modify both protein abundance and distribution (Pratt et al., 2002). Ultimately, there is no strict linear relationship between the genome, the transcriptome, and the proteome (Pandey et al., 2000), and numerous studies have demonstrated that mRNA levels can, but need not be, correlated with protein levels (Gygi et al., 1999a; Futcher et al., 1999). Since often it is the proteins that are of greatest relevance to the biological question being investigated, one might imagine that proteomics would supplant mRNA expression analysis. The transcriptome has important experimental advantages, however. First, since mRNA is transcribed from genomic DNA, the transcriptome shares to a first approximation the bounds of the genome. Furthermore, since mRNA shares with DNA the inherent tendency to bind to complementary strands of nucleic acids, it is relatively straightforward to design specific probes for mRNA transcripts. With the addition of a method for visualizing binding events, these characteristics create the possibility of comprehensive transcriptome profiling that underlies comparative mRNA expression analysis experiments. By contrast, the proteome's vast scale and ill-defined boundaries are compounded by the difficulties inherent in generating specific affinity probes for proteins. Despite important advances, the protein-probe equivalent of the "whole genome" microarray does not exist.

15.2. PROTEOMIC DATA ANALYSIS

An important application of comparative proteomics—one that we will discuss in detail in this section—is the comparison of diseased and disease-free states. For example, discovering protein alterations associated with the onset of cancer might provide deeper insights into the biology of the disease, as well as promoting early detection, identification of therapeutic targets for drug design, and, ultimately, targeted and individualized therapy.

From a data-mining methodology perspective, proteomic data analysis illustrates the significant consideration, effort and infrastructure needed for data pre- and post-processing. The actual application of machine learning tools is a small part of the knowledge discovery process. Furthermore, improper data preprocessing or incorrect interpretation of machine learning models can translate into results that are of limited or no value, or worse still, are seriously misleading.

15.2.1. Data Source

As elaborated in the Appendix, there exist a variety of approaches for exploring the comparative proteomics of disease. In the examples described herein, we have used the Ciphergen ProteinChip (Merchant and Weinberger, 2000; Ciphergen Biosystems web site) system for this purpose. This surface-enhanced laser desorption/ionization time-of-flight (SELDI–TOF) mass spectrometry system uses "chips" in the form of small metallic strips with various chromatographic surfaces linearly arrayed on 8 or 16 spots. These chromatographic surfaces have chemical or biochemical properties that result in affinity to specific classes of proteins (e.g., hydrophobic proteins, proteins with net positive or negative charge, proteins that bind to specific antibodies, etc.). Chip preparation involves deposition of prepared sample and energy-absorbing matrix (EAM) onto these spots, followed by extensive washing to remove contaminants and non-specifically bound proteins. Prepared chips are inserted into a time-of-flight (TOF) mass spectrometer. Laser pulses directed at the spots on the chip energize the EAM, which then transfers energy to the protein components in the deposited sample, thereby ionizing the proteins and peptides. These ions are accelerated through an electric field and gated through a flight tube before registering at a detector. Because the field imparts a fixed kinetic energy, ions with higher mass/charge (m/z) ratio have longer flight times than those with lower m/z. Thus, for an ion of given charge arising from a specific protein, the arrival time at the detector is inversely (and nonlinearly) related to the mass of the protein. Furthermore, the number of ions of a specific type arriving at the detector (and hence the detector current at that time instant) is a reflection of the relative abundance of the underlying protein or peptide that gives rise to the ion species. The result of "scanning" a sample using this SELDI–TOF mass spectrometer is termed a mass spectrum, or *spectrum*.

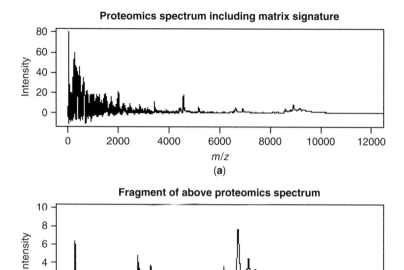

Figure 15.1. Typical proteomic spectrum derived from a mass spectrometer. **(A)** Spectrum showing parts of the matrix signature in the 0–2000 *m/z* range. **(B)** The 5000–12,000 *m/z* range of the spectrum.

In the SELDI methodology described earlier, the protein mixture is simplified by selective retention on chromatographic surfaces before mass spectrometry. A related approach—termed matrix-assisted laser desorption/ionization (MALDI)—uses the protein mixture with no on-chip fractionation to generate mass spectra, though the mixture can be separated by chromatography prior to application to the MALDI surface. Indeed, separation by mass or isoelectric point using one- or two-dimensional gel electrophoresis followed by protein staining can itself result in data that can be interpreted as a spectrum.

A typical spectrum—arising from a single spot on the ProteinChip, or from other mass spectrometers or gels—is shown in Figure 15.1. Each spectrum consists of a series of peaks at specific mass/charge (*m/z*) values, in addition to noise and matrix signal. While noise is uniformly distributed over the entire spectrum, a matrix signal occurs in MALDI- and SELDI-based mass spectra from the very beginning of the spectrum to approximately 1000–2000 D depending on the energy-absorbing matrix used. This part of the spectrum is usually excluded from analysis, since the large-amplitude matrix signal tends to overwhelm any protein or peptide peaks that may be present.

Acquisition and analysis of these proteomic spectra involves a series of steps that can be assembled into a proteomic analysis "pipeline," as described later and

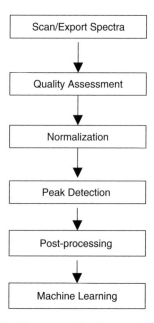

Figure 15.2. The proteomics data analysis pipeline.

summarized in Figure 15.2. The pipeline is designed to achieve high throughput and automated data processing.

Though the description that follows is focused on analyzing SELDI–TOF mass spectra, the techniques described, and the pipeline developed, are directly applicable to all MALDI sources, applicable with minor modification to other mass spectrometric data, and, in general, broadly applicable to proteomic spectra derived from a variety of sources (see Appendix).

15.2.2. Case Study: Lung Cancer Detection and Classification in Human Serum

We will introduce our approach to proteomic data analysis in the context of a project designed to identify lung cancer biomarkers in human serum. Such biomarkers might be used to diagnose and classify lung cancer, allowing a blood test to replace or augment the currently standard radiographic evaluation and lung biopsy. Ideally, serum biomarkers might also prove useful as a screening test, allowing early detection and higher rates of cure of this particularly malignant disease.

The study used 144 serum samples,* about 35 each from patients without malignancy and with lung adenocarcinoma, squamous cell carcinoma, or

---

*The samples, with aggregate statistics of relevant variables (like age, smoking history, etc.), were obtained from Dr. David Christiani's laboratory at the Harvard School of Public Health. Patient details were not revealed.

small-cell carcinoma. To avoid biases resulting from conditions unrelated to lung cancer, each set of 35 disease-specific samples was adjusted to control for patient age, gender, and smoking history. To reduce the complexity of the sample protein mixture, each sample was fractionated into six fractions using resin-based anion exchange. To keep the number of fractions manageable and to minimize chemical separation overlap, only fractions 1, 4, and 6 were used in the study. These sample fractions were deposited on Ciphergen weak cation-exchange (WCX) and immobilized metal affinity capture (IMAC) 8-spot ProteinChips. Two different, complementary energy absorbing matrices (EAMs)—sinapinic acid (SPA) and α-cyano-4-hydroxy-cinnamic acid (CHCA)—were used. CHCA provides optimal resolution in the low-molecular-weight range (500–20,000 daltons with low laser energy), while SPA has a broader operating range (1500–20,000 daltons with low laser energy, and 20,000–50,000 daltons with high laser energy). To reduce variability in handling, most of the sample processing and chip preparation were robotically automated.

Since for each serum sample three of six fractions are used, each applied in replicate to two chip surfaces, with two EAMs and two laser energies for one of the EAMs, a single sample results in 36 individual spectra. Thus the 144 samples generate 5184 spectra. Because data generation is time-consuming and expensive, one of the challenges we address is to use the data generated to identify those conditions that provide maximal information for the distinctions of interest.

These 5184 samples were processed using the proteomics pipeline described in this section, to generate datasets (described in more detail later). The error rate for classifiers based on these data was estimated using leave-one-out cross validation. The next phase of this project (not described in this chapter) will double the number of samples; two-thirds of the data will be used to train and test classifiers, optimizing accuracy of the machine learning models and attempting to derive a robust set of features with potential biological relevance, while the remaining one-third will be used to assess the performance of the final optimized models (validation).

15.2.3. Data Acquisition and Export

Data generated by a mass spectrometer or a gel may need to be transformed into a format that is convenient for further analysis. This may include exporting data into text files or logging all data into a database. In our case, all data are exported to comma-separated text files, which are then used by the data analysis pipeline. The mass or mass/charge axis (x-axis) of the spectra also requires calibration. In the case of mass spectra, the original time axis is converted to m/z units using either spiked calibrants ("internal calibration") or a calibration curve derived off-line from calibrants ("external calibration"). Similarly, in gels, molecular weight standards may be spiked in or run in separate lanes. When the gel lane is converted to a spectrum, the peaks arising from the molecular weight standards must first be identified and labeled, allowing the x-axis to be calibrated using the location of these peaks.

15.2.4. Preprocessing

Several characteristics of proteomic spectra mandate preprocessing steps to ensure consistent and high-quality data analysis.

Baseline Subtraction. Mass spectra—derived from the current output of a detector—include a baseline signal, which is independent of the sample being scanned. An example is shown in Figure 15.3. This large information-free component of the mass spectra can swamp the actual signal if not removed. In our analysis, we use the baseline subtraction built into the Ciphergen ProteinChip system software. Alternatively, an adaptive background correction, or unsharp masking (Gonzalez and Woods, 2002), filter can be used to eliminate the baseline.

Matrix Filtration. Depending on the energy absorbing matrix used in generating the mass spectrum, the first 1000–2000 D in the m/z spectrum will be dominated by matrix signature (Figure 15.1). Since this is a systematic signature, it is possible to design matched digital filters for its selective elimination. Figure 15.4 shows the matrix filtration algorithm, and Figure 15.5 illustrates matrix filtration using a matched digital filter (Smith, 1997). Given the loss of peak sharpness, and the expectation that a majority of relevant proteins and peptides will have much larger molecular weights, we opt to truncate the matrix signature rather than remove it with a filter.

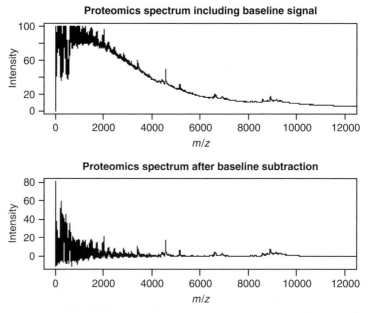

Figure 15.3. Mass spectrum with and without baseline, illustrating the effect of baseline substraction.

extract "signal" by excluding matrix signature
compute FFT of signal
smooth signal FFT to derive desired filter frequency response
compute inverse FFT to determine filter impulse response
assemble filter kernel from inverse FFT
convolve filter kernel with input to filter out matrix

Figure 15.4. Algorithm for matrix filtration using a matched digital filter.

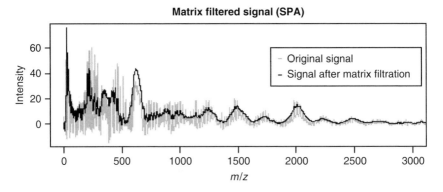

Figure 15.5. Matrix filtration for SPA.

15.2.5. Spectrum Quality

A signal-to-noise-based "quality score" is computed for each spectrum to represent the relative strength of the peaks with respect to noise. A spectrum with unacceptably low quality score is removed from further consideration. This ensures that other downstream operations in the pipeline are not affected by poor-quality spectra. Spectra discarded due to low quality scores can range from a fraction of a percent to several percent depending on a variety of factors including the type of mass spectrometer, sample quality, and prior fractionation steps.

The quality score for a spectrum is computed as the ratio of its noise-free area to its original area: $Q = (A_S - A_N)/A_S$. Here A_S is the area under the spectrum and A_N is the area under the noise envelope. Spectra are low-pass filtered using moving window (convolution) filters (Smith, 1997; Carroll and Beavis, 1996; Gonzalez and Woods, 2002) to remove high frequencies. Noise is taken as the original (noisy) signal minus the low-pass filtered (noise-free) signal. A moving window is then used to calculate the adaptive standard deviation of the noise (SD_N), a noise envelope is defined as $3 \times SD_N$, and the area under the noise envelope (A_N) is calculated.

Hence, $0 \le Q \le 1$, with poor spectra having low Q (Figure 15.6). The distribution of Q scores is typically bimodal. An intermodal quality value—0.45 for the lung cancer data—is selected as a threshold for the dataset, with only spectra having Q greater than the threshold included in further analysis. Since

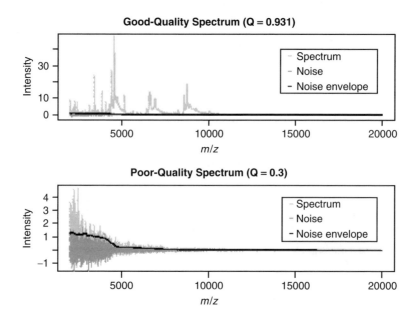

Figure 15.6. Good- and bad-quality spectra, showing the mass spectrum, noise, and noise envelope.

occasionally spectra display many, very narrow peaks, and hence may be potentially informative despite low Q score, low-quality spectra are salvaged if at least 1% of their m/z values have amplitudes at least five-fold greater than the noise envelope.

15.2.6. Normalization

A variety of normalization strategies can be employed to normalize spectra. Normalization is performed within each experimental condition, defined as a particular fraction–chip surface–EAM–energy combination. This ensures that (expected) differences between spectra from different conditions do not unduly influence the normalization factor for any given spectrum.

In total area normalization (TAN) normalization, the area under a given mass spectrum is normalized to the mean area of the entire set of selected mass spectra. Total intensity normalization (TIN) normalizes the average intensity of the selected spectra. TAN and TIN interpret the x-axis of the mass spectra differently. TAN uses the *calibrated m/z* axis so that the distance between any two points on this axis increases as the absolute m/z value increases. TIN treats the x axis as the (uncalibrated) time axis; the constant sampling rate of mass spectrometer detectors ensures that the distance between any two points on the x-axis is identical. In analyzing lung cancer samples, we use TAN.

Another normalization technique—"0 to 1" (ZTO) normalization—transforms each intensity I in a given spectrum S to the normalized value $I_{norm} = (I -$

$I_{min})/(I_{max} - I_{min})$, where I_{min} and I_{max} are the minimum and maximum intensities of the spectra, respectively (Perticoin et al., 2002).

Generally, the EAM signature is excluded from analyses, including normalization (see Section 15.2.1). With the matrix removed, there is evidence of better normalization (and hence elimination of any systematic bias; see Section 15.3) with TIC than ZTO normalization. When the matrix signature is included, the opposite is true.

Unless the spectra have an unusual difference in distribution of peaks in the low and high m/z ranges, TIN and TAN normalization generally results in similar normalization factors. On the other hand, in ZTO, the normalization factor for any given spectrum is, in most circumstances, dictated by the matrix signature; the maximum and minimum intensity values (after baseline removal) usually fall in the matrix region.

15.2.7. Peak Detection

Peak detection is a substantial science unto itself, with approaches derived for a wide variety of situations and a broad range of applications. For processing proteomics spectra, we have opted to use a series of digital convolution (moving window) filters to effect peak detection (Smith, 1997; Carroll and Beavis, 1996; Gonzalez and Woods, 2002). Figure 15.7 shows how this process works. After smoothing with a low-pass filter, adaptive background correction is performed

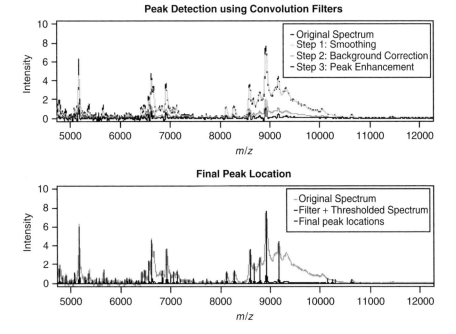

Figure 15.7. Peak detection using digital convolution (moving window) filters.

with unsharp masking. After peak sharpening with a high-pass filter, a threshold is set to capture the top percentage of values (typically in the neighborhood of 25%). Peaks are located at the maxima of the resultant nonzero "islands" (or, optionally, at the center of distribution of the area under the peak). This approach has merits of simplicity and effectiveness. A critical added advantage is that parameters at each step can be modified, to provide tunable sensitivity for peak detection.

The final percentile threshold used in defining the peaks is a key parameter that modulates the number of peaks detected. In general, the number of peaks detected increases when the threshold is lowered and fewer peaks are identified when the threshold is high (although there could be some anomalies when there are multiple peaks in close proximity). A high threshold would retain only prominent and strong peaks, which could be a disadvantage when the proteins and peptides of interest are of low abundance. A very low threshold would retain even those "peaks" resulting from noise. An effective working strategy is to (a) keep the threshold low enough to detect more peaks than warranted and (b) use secondary selection criteria to whittle down the number of peaks. One such secondary selection criterion we use is the "peak-to-noise ratio," which is the ratio of the peak intensity to the standard deviation of the noise at the peak location. Empirically, a peak detector threshold of 0.65 with a peak-to-noise (P2N) ratio of 10 appears to work well (see Section 15.2.12).

15.2.8. Peak Matching

Having detected peaks in spectra, the next critical challenge is to decide what to count as the "same peak" between different sample spectra. In chip-based mRNA expression analysis, probes and their locations are known, allowing direct comparison of signal intensity. In mass spectrometry, by contrast, a given protein (in a particular state) will be designated by an m/z value within a window, the width of which is principally determined by the precision of the instrument. Since either falsely including or falsely excluding a peak from a set of peaks would be expected to degrade classification performance, this assignment must be treated with care.

Our solution to the problem has been to use maximum likelihood estimation (Gelman et al., 2003) of peak locations for all spectra within a given condition, using a mixture of gaussians to model peak locations in spectra. The expectation maximization (EM) algorithm is used for maximizing the likelihood function for the gaussian mixture model (Fraley and Raftery, 1998; Banfield and Raftery, 1993). Starting with the union of all peaks occurring in all spectra for a given condition, the EM algorithm iteratively identifies the peak locations (along with a measure of the variance of the location for each peak) that best fit the actual observed peaks. The procedure for *EM-based peak matching* is summarized in Figure 15.8. As shown in the figure, while the location of peaks is arrived at using EM, the number of peaks is decided using the Bayesian information criterion (BIC) (Fraley and Raftery, 1998; Kass and Raftery, 1995).

```
peaklist := union of all peaks in all spectra
maxpeaks := max number of detected peaks in any spectrum
maxBIC := −Infinity
k   := 0
for n ranging from 0.9*maxpeaks to 1.5*maxpeaks {
  split peaklist into n groups
  compute mean and std. dev. of groups to initialize EM
  run EM to optimize mixture model with n gaussians
  compute BIC for optimized mixture model
  if ( k == 0 || BIC > maxBIC ) {
    maxBIC := BIC
    k   := n
  }
}
run EM with k gaussians to derive final peak locations
assign peaks in peaklist to the most probable location
output table with matched peaks
```

Figure 15.8. Algorithm for peak matching, using expectation maximization (EM) to optimize a gaussian mixture model.

An alternative approach we have explored is *window-based peak matching*, where all peaks within a given (fixed or adaptive) m/z window are considered to be the "same" peak. A "frontier" of peaks is defined, starting from the first detected peak in any spectrum and extending 0.25% from the m/z value associated with the peak, consistent with a conservative estimate of $\pm 0.125\%$ mass precision for the Ciphergen system. Some spectra will have a peak within the frontier, others will not; if a spectrum has more than one peak in the frontier, the first is chosen. The mean and standard deviation (SD) of m/z values of the set of peaks within the frontier are determined, and peaks falling within ± 3 SD of the mean are identified to be the same. These peaks are all assigned the mean m/z value, and they retain their respective intensities. If there are peaks in the original frontier that fall below the ± 3 SD window, these are accounted for first, before advancing the frontier. The process continues iteratively, until all peaks in all spectra have been aligned. In the lung cancer study, window-based peak matching results in about 5–10 times more m/z values (peaks) retained as distinct features compared to EM-based peak matching. In spite of having a significantly smaller feature set, the features extracted using EM-based peak matching result in classifiers that perform slightly (but statistically significantly) better than window-based peak matching (see Section 15.2.12 and Figure 15.12).

A variant of window-based peak matching is described in Adam et al. (2002). A peak alignment strategy using a genetic algorithm to group peaks so as to maximize peak number in a group from different samples, and minimize peak number in a group from the same sample, has also been described Yanagisawa et al. (2003).

An alternative approach that has been used to aligning segments from different sample spectra is binning the raw data points on the m/z scale. This method is only a partial solution since fixed bin boundaries combined with variation along the m/z axis can make it difficult to identify the "same" peak in different spectra.

Ultimately, we believe that some form of peak matching will be essential. Even though high precision mass spectrometers can reduce the need for peak matching, it turns out that higher-precision instruments scan at higher sampling rates, resulting in more m/z values being recorded and thus enabling the detection of smaller and finer peaks, which still need to be aligned.

15.2.9. Final Table Assembly

For each condition, a table with peaks—identified by the EM procedure—is created. Each individual sample spectrum will typically have a subset of those peaks. Peaks that are not detected can either be marked as missing or be filled in with the interpolated amplitude at the corresponding m/z value. The result of this process is a feature table of m/z values and associated amplitudes for all samples in a given condition. The full feature space available to machine learning algorithms is the concatenation of these tables across all conditions.

Discrete Versus Continuous Peak Amplitudes.   Since peak detection in the presence of noise is not perfect, filling in missing peaks with the spectral amplitude at the respective m/z value will account for situations where a specific peak was detected in some spectra but was missed in others, due to the presence of noise or other factors. On the other hand, mass spectrometry is a semiquantitative methodology, and there are merits to dealing with discrete data—declaring only that a peak exists or does not. Thus, marking absent peaks as missing and subsequently deriving a discrete dataset is also a valid option. Although dealing with discrete data is conceptually appealing, there appears to be useful, albeit semiquantitative, information in the peak amplitudes. Figure 15.9 shows a comparison of error rates for various classifiers built with discrete and interpolated data for the same set of conditions and samples. Models with discrete data consistently result in classifiers with higher error rates.

Running the lung cancer data through the proteomics pipeline—using TAN normalization, a peak detector threshold of 0.65, a peak-to-noise ratio of 10, EM peak matching, and retention of only the best replicate—results in a dataset for each preparation and scanning condition. Table 15.1 summarizes dataset details.*
The dataset conditions are shown as chip (I = IMAC, W = WCX) × EAM (C = CHCA, S = SPA) × energy (L = low, H = high) × fraction (1, 4, or 6). Though there are nominally 144 samples, for each condition, (potentially different) sample spectra with poor quality ($Q < 0.45$) are excluded. The basic datasets can be "stacked"—that is, the features for a given sample concatenated—to create larger datasets representing combinations of conditions.

---

*The high-energy datasets have limited value (see Section 15.2.12) and are generally not considered in this phase of the study.

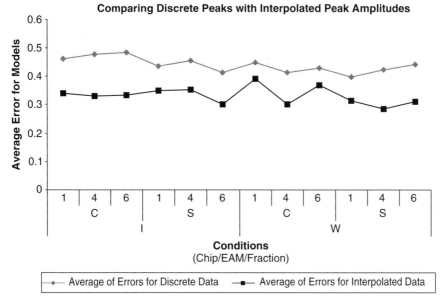

Figure 15.9. Comparing *k*-NN and decision tree model performance for datasets with discrete peaks (peak present = 1; peak missing = 0) and with missing peak amplitudes interpolated from the appropriate sample spectra. The models include cancer versus control (2 class), adenocarcinoma versus control (AvN), squamous cell carcinoma versus control (QvN), and small-cell carcinoma versus control (SvN), with errors for all these models (for a given preparation/scanning condition) averaged on the *y* axis.

TABLE 15.1. Dataset Details for Lung Cancer Study

Dataset Condition	Peaks (Features)	Samples
I × C × L × 1	124	118
I × C × L × 4	137	142
I × C × L × 6	158	140
I × S × L × 1	110	116
I × S × L × 4	111	142
I × S × L × 6	98	138
W × C × L × 1	201	119
W × C × L × 4	167	143
W × C × L × 6	167	143
W × S × L × 1	153	117
W × S × L × 4	175	142
W × S × L × 6	126	141

15.2.10. Machine Learning and Data Mining

A variety of machine learning and pattern recognition techniques (Mitchell, 1997; Hastie et al., 2001) can be used to mine proteomics data, in order to cluster the data in search of known or novel groups, and to build classifiers to recognize classes of significance. The specifics of the tools and methods used in any project will depend a great deal on the goals and scientific objectives of the project. For example, in the lung cancer project, we have primarily focused on supervised learning for the following classifications: two-class (all lung cancer versus normal; each lung cancer subtype versus normal), three-class (non-small-cell lung cancer versus small-cell lung cancer versus normal), and four-class (adeno- versus squamous cell versus small-cell carcinoma versus normal). Algorithms being explored include weighted voting (WV) (Golub et al., 1999), k-nearest neighbors (k-NN) (Golub et al., 1999; Hastie et al., 2001), decision trees (Brieman et al., 1984), and large Bayes (LB) (Meretakis and Wuthrich, 1999).

As with gene expression data, the major challenge in applying pattern recognition and machine learning to proteomic data analysis is the presence of a large number of attributes or features—several hundreds to several thousands depending on the number of conditions being combined, peak detector settings, peak matching methodology, and so on—with a small number of samples (tens to a few hundreds). Effective feature selection and prioritization techniques are therefore needed in order to leverage pattern recognition techniques.

Our approach has been to capitalize on tools developed for gene expression analysis. Feature selection is based on signal-to-noise ratio (Golub et al., 1999), combined with a random permutation test to measure the statistical significance of the importance of each feature. For any two-class comparison, signal-to-noise ratio for a given feature (peak) is defined as S2N $= (\mu_2 - \mu_1)/(\sigma_2 + \sigma_1)$, where μ and σ are the mean and standard deviation of the normalized amplitude of that peak in the class indicated by the subscript. S2N essentially measures the correlation between the peak under consideration and the sample class labels (i.e., class vector). Features can be ranked according to their S2N value. Random permutation testing (Golub et al., 1999) is used to determine whether an observed correlation is stronger than would be expected by chance. In this procedure, the class vector is randomly permuted, and S2N values for each feature are recalculated. This process is repeated a large number of times, yielding, for each peak, a distribution of S2N values for randomly permuted sample labels. Peaks with actual S2N greater than 95% of S2N values from the random permutation test are considered significant at the 5% level. In this rank-ordered list of "informative peaks," the best n peaks are then input to a pattern recognition algorithm such as k-NN, weighted voting, or Large Bayes classifiers. Although the same feature selection approach could be used with decision trees, the algorithm can effectively select and prioritize features, especially when combined with tracking surrogates and variable importance computation (Brieman et al., 1984).

k-NN classifier performance—for squamous cell carcinoma versus normal (QvN), adenocarcinoma versus normal (AvN), and all cancers versus normal

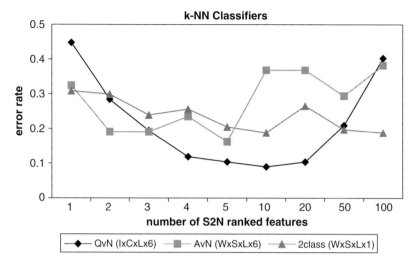

Figure 15.10. Error rates for k-NN classifiers.

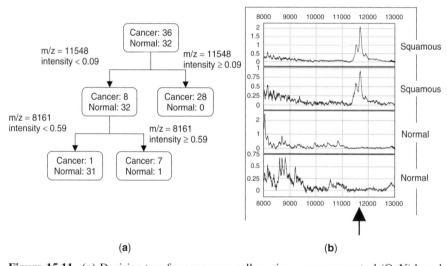

(a) (b)

Figure 15.11. (a) Decision tree for squamous cell carcinoma versus control (QvN) based on W × S × L × 4 data. Leave-one-out cross-validation error = 5/68. (b) Spectra for squamous cell carcinoma and normal patients showing discriminating peaks used in the decision tree.

(2class)—based on the data described in Table 15.1, is shown in Figure 15.10. The figure also shows how classifier performance varies with the number of input features (based on a S2N ranked list).

A decision tree for squamous cell carcinoma versus normal (QvN) classification is shown in Figure 15.11. The two-split tree has a training error of 2/68 and

**TABLE 15.2. Variable Importance Listing
for Decision Tree Shown in Figure 15.11**

m/z Value	Feature Importance
11,548	0.310
11,709	0.265
11,550	0.258
5,848	0.258
11,926	0.240
5,911	0.201
8,161	0.134
1,767	0.027
3,092	0.027
2,361	0.021
2,944	0.021
4,422	0.021

leave-one-out cross validation error of 5/68. Table 15.2 shows variable importance (Brieman et al., 1984) for the top 12 features (m/z values, or peaks). Of the top five peaks, four occur in the 11- to 12-kD range, where the squamous cell carcinoma samples have pronounced peaks as shown in Figure 15.11b.

Other groups have used different approaches to pattern recognition in proteomics data—both in terms of the tools and techniques used and in methodology. Perticoin et al. (2002) have used an approach where the raw m/z values (with no peak detection) constitute the feature space. Several random, but small (5–20), subsets of these m/z values are chosen and used as input to a genetic algorithm. The fitness function for the genetic algorithm is based on the segregating power of the subset of m/z values in a self-organizing map. Adam et al. (2002) have used the area under the ROC curve (AUC) for feature selection with decision tree classifiers. Support vector machines (SVM) (Cristianini and Shawe-Taylor, 2000) is another technique that is becoming increasingly popular for classification. SVMs have the ability to directly deal with a large number of features without the need for feature selection. Li et al. (2002) use a variant of the SVM termed unified maximum separability analysis (UMSA). By using adjustable parameters, UMSA can produce classifiers that encompass linear discriminant analysis and optimal margin hyperplane SVM classifiers. Various statistical tests and procedures (t-test, Kruskal–Wallis test, significance analysis for microarrays, etc.) have also been used in feature selection, in classification, and to determine differentially expressed markers (Jobson, 1996).

15.2.11. Feature Identification

Classifiers based upon "biomarkers" (i.e., peaks or m/z values) derived as described above could be used directly in clinical diagnostics. There is, nevertheless, great utility in identifying those features—that is, in determining the specific protein or peptide to which the differentially expressed m/z value (peak) corresponds. Feature identification promotes biomarker validation, allows conversion of diagnostic and prognostic profiles to "standard" clinical methods such as ELISA (enzyme-linked immunosorbent assay), provides insight into disease biology, and might suggest novel candidate therapeutic targets. Moving from an m/z value to protein identification is a challenging enterprise, made worse by sample complexity (large numbers and high dynamic range of constituent proteins), machine imprecision, and the expected low abundance of many candidate markers. Section A.5 in the Appendix outlines identification strategies, the details of which are beyond the scope of this chapter.

Identification can, however, be greatly facilitated if compelling "candidate identities" can be assigned to strong differentially expressed features. We have implemented a system for delineating and scoring such candidate identities. Protein databases are searched for candidates within an "error window" of the m/z value of the feature of interest, with window dimension determined by estimation of the mass inaccuracy of the spectrometer. Chemical information based on the sample fraction and chromatographic surface in which the feature was captured can further focus the search. Using information from multiple sources, including protein databases, domain literature, and orthogonal studies (e.g., mRNA expression analyses of the same disease), candidate identities are then prioritized according to their goodness of fit. In the lung cancer serum biomarker discovery project, for instance, points might be awarded to a candidate protein for being known to be secreted, known to be associated with lung tissue, or known to be associated with cancer, with highest priority given to a candidate known to be differentially secreted into serum of lung cancer patients (i.e., confirmation of a known biomarker).

From the feature list represented in Table 15.2, numerous plausible candidate identities can be advanced. As an extreme example, 13 proteins are listed in the Swiss-Prot database (http://us.expasy.org/cgi-bin/tagident) within 0.125% of m/z 11,709 D (the second-ranked feature in Table 15.2). Most have poor "credentials." One, serum amyloid A, was, however, recently proposed and partially validated as a serum biomarker for non-small-cell lung cancer (Howard et al., 2003). Such a strong candidate would appropriately prompt a directed effort at confirmation (rather than "discovery," per se), for instance by use of an antibody-based affinity probe.

15.2.12. Classifier Error Rate as a Criterion for Parameter Optimization

In the approach we have taken to biomarker discovery, a relatively large fraction of the proteome is captured (represented by the mass spectral peaks) and analyzed in order to search for patterns of peaks that discriminate phenotypes or characteristics of interest. Thus, during the analysis phase, the identity of peaks—the proteins or peptides that result in their occurrence—is unknown. Given this, there is no "gold standard" for optimizing parameters that affect the detection, location, or other characteristics of peaks: The "correct solution" is unknown.

Parameter optimization will therefore have to be made based on secondary criteria. We have chosen classification error rate as the criterion used for parameter optimization.

In the lung cancer study, parameter optimization is effected by building a large number of classifiers: k-NN, WV, and decision tree models are generated for a variety of classifications of interest (all cancers versus normal, each cancer versus normal, etc.), for various combinations of scanning and preparation conditions. This exercise results in a large number of classifiers based on data derived from each of the parameter values. A statistical comparison of the classifier errors is used to optimize parameter value(s) to minimize error.

Some of the parameter choices made using this classifier error rate criterion are:

- *EM-Based Versus Window-Based Peak Matching.* Classifier error rate minimization was one of the criteria used in deciding whether to use EM-based peak matching or window-based peak matching. Figure 15.12 shows that both peak matching approaches yield very similar error rates for the models of interest. EM-based peak matching, however, results in slightly lower error rate that is statistically significant based on the paired T-test ($p = 0.028$) and the Wilcoxon signed rank test ($p = 0.015$). This result, combined with the fact that the method is more principled, with sound theoretical

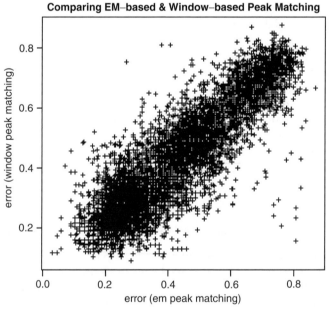

Figure 15.12. Comparison of error rates for a variety of models and chip preparation/scanning conditions, using features (peaks) obtained from window-based and EM-based peak matching.

underpinnings, and results in significantly fewer matched peaks, tipped the scales in favor of EM-based peak matching.

- *Peak Detector Percentile Threshold.* Models were built with data generated using peak detector percentile thresholds of 0.60, 0.65, 0.70, 0.75, 0.81, 0.87, and 0.93. Although statistical analysis indicated that the threshold value significantly affected error rate, it was only possible to distinguish between 0.93, 0.87 and the rest, with these higher thresholds having higher error rates. We subjectively chose a final threshold of 0.65 based on error distribution, because this threshold resulted in minimum median and first quartile error rates.

- *Replicate Processing.* All the lung cancer samples were prepared and scanned in replicate. Effective use of these replicates was another issue that was resolved using the classifier error rate criterion. There are several ways in which replicates can be used in analysis:

  (a) Compute quality for each replicate, retaining only the best-quality replicate.
  (b) Retain all replicates and average the detected peaks after peak matching.
  (c) Combine replicates (for instance, by averaging) at the spectrum level, using only the resulting composite spectrum in the analysis.

We tried (a) and (b) and found that, although not statistically significant, selecting the best replicate resulted in lower error rates (Figure 15.13).

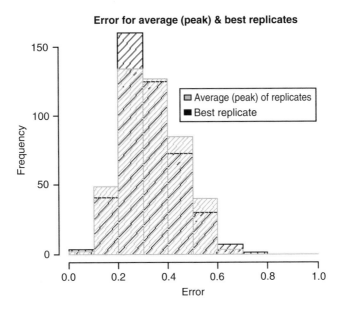

Figure 15.13. Comparing classifier error rates for different replicate handling strategies.

Another application of this methodology is to estimate the effectiveness of the various chip preparation and scanning conditions, in order to retain only those conditions that offer significant incremental gain in classifier performance, thereby improving efficiency, economy, and throughput. To this end, the matrix of classifier errors are analyzed using a linear model (Dalgaard, 2002):

$$accuracy \sim chip + eam + energy + fraction$$

where chip type, EAM, energy and fraction are used in building a predictive model for classifier accuracy ($= 1 -$ error rate). An example of such a model is shown in Figure 15.14. Conditions that strongly contribute to high accuracy will have large positive coefficients, while conditions that increase error will have negative coefficients. Furthermore, the statistical significance (p-values) of these coefficient estimates provides an indication of whether the observed correlation could arise from chance.

Call:

lm(formula = accuracy ~ chip + eam + energy + fraction, data = error.matrix)

Residuals:

Min	1Q	Median	3Q	Max
−0.41233	−0.10839	0.01864	0.13089	0.35385

Coefficients:

	Estimate	Std. Error	t value	Pr(>|t|)	
(Intercept)	0.475908	0.009077	52.428	<2e-16	***
chipIW	0.024313	0.004492	5.412	6.41e-08	***
chipW	0.016301	0.004492	3.629	0.000287	***
eamCS	0.014883	0.005943	2.504	0.012286	*
eamS	0.016473	0.005943	2.772	0.005585	**
energyHL	0.057561	0.005943	9.686	<2e-16	***
energyL	0.052715	0.005943	8.871	<2e-16	***
fraction4	0.029434	0.006862	4.290	1.81e-05	***
fraction6	−0.026105	0.006862	−3.804	0.000143	***
fraction14	0.031953	0.006862	4.657	3.27e-06	***
fraction16	−0.012648	0.006862	−1.843	0.065333	.
fraction46	0.018902	0.006862	2.755	0.005890	**
fraction146	0.017454	0.006862	2.544	0.010992	*

Signif. codes: 0 '***' 0.001 '**' 0.01 '*' 0.05 '.' 0.1 ' ' 1

Residual standard error: 0.1595 on 7547 degrees of freedom
Multiple R-Squared: 0.03502, Adjusted R-squared: 0.03348
F-statistic: 22.82 on 12 and 7547 DF, p-value: $< 2.2e - 16$

Figure 15.14. Assessing the contribution of various preparation/scanning conditions to classifier accuracy using linear models. R output shown for the "All" row in Figure 15.15.

Error Matrix Summary for k–NN and Decision Tree Models

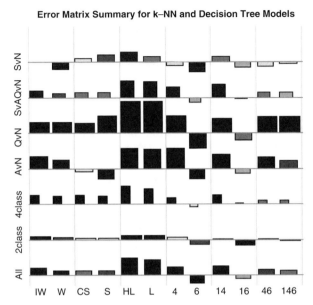

Figure 15.15. Visualizing the contribution of scanning/preparation conditions to classifier accuracy. The model in Figure 15.14 corresponds to the bottom row.

The result of such modeling is visualized in Figure 15.15. Each row in this figure shows the output of a single model of the above form, with different models being generated for each classification of interest. A base condition of chip type = IMAC, EAM = CHCA, energy = high, and fraction = 1 is used, and the change in accuracy resulting from adding to or modifying these conditions is shown in each column. The sign of the respective coefficient is shown by the direction (positive is up; negative is down); the height of the bar is proportional to the magnitude of the coefficient; the saturation is based on the p-value for the coefficient estimate; and the width of the bar is proportional to the absolute accuracy achieved for the classification under consideration. Thus, conditions that strongly enhance classifier accuracy would have fat, high, dark, upward bars in the entire column (or could be a base condition). For example, in Figure 15.15, the strong, dark bars in the L column indicate that low-energy (L) spectra contribute significantly to high accuracy. The minor differences between the HL and L columns points to the fact that adding high-energy (H) spectra does not help much—in other words, H is a dispensable condition. Numerous other observations derive from the matrix: 4class classifiers have lower absolute accuracy than most other types of classifiers; fraction 6 is not as useful as fractions 1 and 4; adding WCX (to the base condition of IMAC) improves accuracy and is better than either chip type alone.

This procedure of building a large number of models with different parameter settings, using the same data, while aiming to minimize classifier error, can result in parameter settings that overfit the specific data with poor generalization to unseen data. To avoid this scenario in the lung cancer project, the dataset described in this chapter is used for model building and parameter optimization, while a separate (unseen) validation set will be used to assess the error rate of the final models after all optimization and model selection.

15.3. BIOMARKER DISCOVERY

From a biological perspective, one of the main goals of analyzing proteomics data is to uncover relevant and *real* biomarkers for distinctions of clinical and/or biological importance. To this end, supervised learning approaches use known sample labels to derive discriminating features that effectively separate the classes of interest. In the case of proteomic data, these discriminating features—or markers—are peaks occurring in specific preparation and scanning conditions. In order for any of these markers to be valid biomarkers, we expect them to remain effective—probably to a lesser degree, but nevertheless better than randomly selected features—beyond the machine learning algorithm used to discover the marker. The large number of features and small number of samples in most proteomic studies could result in markers that are essentially based on noise or other bias, and therefore not biologically valid.

Analysis of proteomics data has also revealed that intrinsic bias may falsely identify biomarkers and contribute to high classification accuracy. For example, in Perticoin et al. (2002) there is evidence to suggest that the cancers and controls have statistically significant differences (even after normalization) in the mean spectral intensity level. Such a systematic difference raises the possibility that extremely accurate classifiers might tap into this global bias (Sorace and Zhan, 2003), in addition to or exclusive of additional reliance on genuine "biological" markers.

In order to avoid such pitfalls, we propose the following steps in the analysis of serum proteomic data for biomarker discovery:

1. Use a train/test methodology, and develop models using multiple train/test splits to generate a distribution of error.*

2. Evaluate data for signs and significance of bias.

    (a) Identify significant class-specific differences in global metrics of relevance to the classifier (e.g., in mean spectral or peak amplitude).

    (b) Look for better-than-chance performance of classifiers using small numbers of randomly selected features.

3. Compare the performance of selected features (putative biomarkers) with models built on comparable numbers of random features.

---

*Insufficient sample size—only about 35 samples from each class—has resulted in the use of leave-one-out cross-validation for assessing classifier error in the lung cancer study. The next phase of this project (Section 15.2.2) will use multiple train test splits (and a separate validation dataset) since the number of samples will be doubled.

4. Use putative biomarkers as classification features in other credentialed algorithms, demonstrating that those features continue to outperform random features and that classification performance does not degrade catastrophically.

5. Whenever possible, validate markers in a fully independent dataset (i.e., from a different source, or prospectively).

We believe that these tests will help avoid the promulgation of spurious biomarkers, and allow research efforts to be focused on the most promising candidates. Protein identification and direct biological confirmation will of course remain the definitive standards for validation.

15.4. CONCLUSION

Of the wide selection of proteomic methods available (Appendix), we have chosen SELDI–TOF mass spectroscopy to illustrate data generation. Using lung cancer serum proteomics as a case study, we have presented a battery of analysis techniques for dealing with the challenges of processing and mining proteomics data. The approach to proteomics presented in this chapter is directly applicable to all MALDI mass spectroscopy data, and more generally to other proteomic data sources.

Data analysis results presented in Sections 15.2 and 15.3 indicate that well-considered and careful application of established data-mining methodology is a viable approach to proteomic medical diagnosis and biomarker discovery. As with any data-mining endeavor, domain knowledge and understanding is essential to (a) successful application of machine learning and (b) interpretation of results.

ACKNOWLEDGMENTS

The work reported in this chapter was undertaken at the Cancer Genomics Program in the MIT Center for Genome Research, and the Golub Lab at the Dana Farber Cancer Institute. Thanks are due to Todd Golub for laboratory infrastructure and project mentoring, Pablo Tamayo for mentoring the computational aspects of the project, and Jill Mesirov for computing infrastructure. David Christiani at the Harvard School of Public Health provided serum samples for the lung cancer project. Matt Sigakis helped with sample preparation and scanning.

APPENDIX: PROTEOMICS METHODS AND TECHNOLOGIES

A.1. Characterizing Protein Expression

The principal method of data acquisition for most of the several decades since the inception of proteomic analysis is two-dimensional polyacrylamide gel electrophoresis (2D-PAGE) (Gygi et al., 2000). In this approach, a complex mixture of proteins or peptides is separated in the first dimension by molecular weight (MW) and in the second dimension by isoelectric point (pI, the pH at which a protein has zero net charge). After visualization, for instance by Coomassie or silver staining, the resulting two-dimensional pattern represents the component proteins. Comparison of 1D or 2D gels representing proteins extracted from different conditions (for instance, from diseased or normal tissue) has been a mainstay of comparative proteomics. Although the technology underlies a large and important proteomic literature, 2D-PAGE has several limitations (Gygi et al., 2000; Pietrogrande et al., 2003). Reproducibility is difficult, and even with automated strategies, comparison between gels can be challenging. Gel preparation is labor-intensive, so throughput is constrained. Sensitivity, dynamic range, and resolution are limited, and proteins with molecular weight greater than 100 kD are rarely resolved. Highly acidic or basic proteins require special treatment, and hydrophobic proteins are generally not separated, restricting analysis of the highly important membrane compartments. One important early challenge facing 2D-PAGE was that the MW and pI are by themselves generally insufficient to allow identification of the corresponding protein. This has been addressed by eluting the proteins from a spot and subjecting them to mass spectrometric analysis (below).

The chief technological advance in proteomics has been the development of mass spectrometry as a method for mass analysis of biomolecules. The process of resolving a complex mixture into a catalog of known proteins typically includes four steps: preparation of the protein mixture (usually involving some sort of separation), conversion of proteins to gas phase ions at the mass spectrometer "ion source," mass analysis and detection of ion abundance by mass spectrometry, and protein identification using mass spectra and ancillary information. These steps are described in greater detail below.

A.2. Protein Preparation and Separation

Fundamental to the characterization of a complex proteome is the preparation of the proteins for analysis. Insofar as possible, proteins of interest should be isolated from or enriched relative to the balance of the mixture, and overall analyte complexity should be reduced to a degree appropriate to the purpose of the experiment. The importance of enrichment and complexity reduction is well-illustrated by the example of serum proteomic biomarker discovery. The serum proteome is highly complex, probably containing in excess of 10,000 core proteins (Anderson and Anderson, 2002). Those proteins cover an astonishing dynamic range, approximately 10^{12} from the least abundant proteins, such as cytokines, to the superabundant albumin and immunoglobulins. The dynamic range of current mass spectrometers is much lower, on the order of 10^4. Furthermore, more abundant proteins can interfere with detection of less abundant proteins, and differences in volatility can lead to ion suppression effects (Kalkum et al., 2003; Annesley, 2003). Thus if the proteomic range of interest includes moderate or low abundance proteins, the complexity and dynamic range of the starting analyte must be reduced. Numerous approaches are available for that purpose. If a particular, known protein or set of candidate proteins is being targeted for analysis, an affinity purification strategy can be employed. Using antibodies (Madoz-Gurpide et al., 2001), aptamers (Romig et al., 1999), or small molecules (Jeffery and Bogyo, 2003) as specific affinity probes, along with stringent washes to reduce nonspecific binding, proteins of interest can be isolated from the mixture. Often, however, the goal is unbiased profiling of a complex mixture, precluding such specific affinity purification. In those cases, more generic separation strategies must be employed. Highly abundant proteins can be specifically removed, for instance by immunoaffinity depletion (Pieper et al., 2003; Sato et al., 2002). Remaining proteins can be separated in one or multiple dimensions according to their physicochemical characteristics. 2D-PAGE, described earlier, is one such strategy (Fountoulakis and Juranville, 2003; Knowles et al., 2003). It has been supplemented, and is gradually being supplanted, by various combinations of methods including size exclusion chromatography (Lecchi et al., 2003), high-performance liquid chromatography (HPLC) (Liu et al., 2002a; Link, 2002; Ihling et al., 2003), capillary electrophoresis (CE) (Liu et al., 2002b), and streptavidin affinity purification of biotinylated proteins (Goshe et al., 2003; Zhang et al., 2003).

This discussion has been cast in terms of intact proteins, but obtains equally to peptides. Indeed, endogenous cleavage products may represent signals of interest in comparative proteomics. Furthermore, digestion with trypsin or other sequence-specific proteases is often included as part of the sample preparation, either before multidimensional separation of a complex mixture (Wolters et al., 2001; McDonald and Yates, 2002) or (as is usually the case with 2D-PAGE) after a protein of interest has been relatively purified. Such digestion may facilitate the use of many mass spectrometers, which have relatively low mass/charge (m/z) ranges (but see Section A.3). Digestion can also facilitate protein identification, via the method of peptide mass fingerprinting (Section A.5).

Although separation of complex protein mixtures is an important part of many proteomics strategies, each such preparatory step has associated costs. Immunodepletion of albumin, for instance, will also remove peptides and proteins bound to albumin, which may themselves be of interest. Size exclusion chromatography likewise will remove some potentially informative proteins while facilitating the detection of others. Since no separation method is perfectly efficient, each will be associated with loss of sample material. Though retention times provide information that can be useful in protein identification (Palmblad et al., 2002), chromatographic separation can be difficult to reproduce precisely from run to run, complicating comparison across samples. Furthermore, while separation of a sample into many fractions allows for more comprehensive profiling of that sample, it decreases throughput commensurately, to a degree that may be prohibitive for comparative proteomics experiments involving many samples. Sample preparation must thus be tailored to the specific requirements of each particular experiment.

A.3. Protein Ionization

Although mass spectrometry had been an important analytical method for many years, its broad application to biology and biochemistry awaited the development of protein ionization methods. Two such "soft ionization" methods, jointly recognized by the 2002 Nobel Prize in Chemistry, are electrospray ionization (ESI) (Fenn et al., 1989) and matrix-assisted laser desorption/ionization (MALDI) (Karas and Hillenkamp, 1988). In ESI, liquid analyte is pumped through a charged needle or capillary. The resulting charged "electrospray" droplets quickly evaporate, yielding ionized, gas-phase proteins. In MALDI, one of several types of energy-absorbing matrix molecule is co-precipitated with the analyte onto a solid conductive surface prior to laser irradiation. The matrix absorbs the laser energy and imparts it to the analyte, leading to protein sublimation and ionization by means that remain incompletely characterized. Each ionization method has particular advantages. Since ESI works from liquid-phase analyte, it is easily coupled to separation methods such as HPLC or CE (see Section A.2). In ESI there is a tendency for larger protein ions to be multiply charged. Since mass spectrometers measure m/z (mass/charge), rather than mass, ESI may bring larger ions into the range of typical mass spectrometers (Mann et al., 2001). In MALDI, by contrast, fewer ions are generated, and those tend to be singly charged. Furthermore, the matrix itself has a "signature" that obscures the low mass range—for instance, below 500 daltons. However, unlike the relatively evanescent nature of electrospray, a MALDI target can be stored indefinitely and reanalyzed. In addition, MALDI is well-suited to processing the larger sample numbers often needed for biomarker discovery. The SELDI (surface-enhanced laser desorption/ionization) approach described in the analytical case study in this chapter (Section 15.2) is a MALDI variant in which protein subsets from complex mixtures are first adsorbed to solid chromatographic surfaces before matrix addition and laser pulsation (Merchant and Weinberger, 2000).

A.4. Mass Analysis, Ion Detection, and Tandem Mass Spectrometry

The wide variety of mass spectrometers currently in use adopts different strategies for the common purpose of measuring the m/z values of analyte constituents. Four principal methods are used for mass (really m/z) separation: time-of-flight (TOF), ion trap, Fourier transform ion cyclotron (FTMS), and quadrupole mass spectrometry. In TOF MS, ions are accelerated in an electric field before drifting through a flight tube and registering at a detector. Because the field imparts a fixed kinetic energy, ions with higher m/z have longer flight times than those with lower m/z. Ion trap mass spectrometers create a three-dimensional electric field to trap the analyte ions. Electric pulses are then used to eject particular ion species from the trap, allowing their sequential detection. FTMS also establishes an ion trap, but does so with a combination of electric and magnetic fields. In quadrupole MS, an oscillating electric field is applied to four metal rods. Only peptides or proteins at select m/z values will have a trajectory allowing them to pass through the field. Tuning the field creates a variable mass filter allowing separation.

Theoretically, ionization and mass separation are independent, and either MALDI or ESI can be used with any of these mass analysis methods. Historically, instruments have been designed around the practical consideration that the bursts of ions generated by laser pulses in MALDI are well suited to TOF MS, while the continuous ion streams generated in ESI are conducive to ion trap or quadrupole MS. Adherence to these principles is waning, and most combinations of ion source and mass analysis components are now available.

Each of these methods generates spectra comprising m/z values and associated amplitudes, where the amplitudes are indirect reflections of the abundance of peptide or protein ion species at that m/z value. Often, however, the m/z alone is insufficient for specific identification of the ion. Partial sequence data can provide significant additional information. To generate those data, ions separated by m/z can be transferred to a collision cell and bombarded with molecules of an inert gas such as argon. By measuring and comparing m/z values of the fragment products of this "collision-induced dissociation," a "fragmentation ladder" is generated, and peptide sequence information can be inferred (Hunt et al., 1986; Biemann and Scoble, 1987). This strategy implies that the instrument have at least two sequential mass separation stages: one for the primary analyte, and another for the fragmented ions. These "tandem mass spectrometers" can incorporate various combinations of separation methods. Common combinations include triple quadrupole (wherein the central quadrupole holds the ions during fragmentation), TOF–TOF, quadrupole–TOF, and ion trap tandem mass spectrometers.

A.5. Protein Identification

In certain applications, such as confirming the presence of the protein product of a known process, m/z alone is sufficient for protein identification. Generally, however, additional information is required. This is in part because the m/z information itself can be complex: MALDI tends to generate broad peaks, leading to imprecise m/z assignment, while ESI of larger molecules leads to multiple charge states. More importantly, measured m/z values may not correspond with the predicted values entered in databases, because of both "biological" post-translational modification and chemical alterations introduced in sample processing and analysis. Many methods have been introduced in an attempt to provide additional information supporting protein identification. One is to treat prepared samples with trypsin or similar sequence-specific proteases and to search databases using both the parent m/z value and the m/z values of proteolytic fragments, a process called peptide mass fingerprinting (Henzel et al., 1993; Cottrell, 1994). Another is to collide the parent molecule with an inert gas and to combine the m/z value of the parent ion (which might for instance be an intact protein or a peptide generated by proteolytic cleavage) with the structural information obtained from partial sequencing (see Section A.4). Establishing protein identities from mass spectrometry data requires the use of extensive protein databases and suitable search algorithms. There are now many alternatives for each of these in regular use, the power and comprehensiveness of which are steadily increasing (Fenyo and Beavis, 2002; Chen and Xu, 2003; Hancock et al., 2002; Chakravarti et al., 2002; Gras and Muller, 2001).

A.6. Protein Quantitation by Mass Spectrometry

As indicated above, the intensity associated with an m/z value in a mass spectrum is only an indirect reflection of protein or peptide abundance. Often, however, abundance is among the most desirable information pertaining to a protein or peptide species. Considerable effort has therefore been directed toward evolving mass spectrometry from a semiquantitative to a fully quantitative method. The approach that has gained most traction to date involves incorporating a stable isotopic label into one sample (for instance, from a diseased patient), and comparing that labeled sample with an unlabeled one (for instance, from a healthy control) (Gygi et al., 1999b; Oda et al., 1999; Liu and Regnier, 2002). The mass associated with the isotopic label leads to a predictable shift in the resultant mass spectrum. The ratio of intensities of peak pairs can then be used to provide a measure of their relative abundance (Griffin et al., 2003). If the absolute abundance of one member of the pair is known, the abundance of the other can be calculated.

A.7. Other Proteomics Technologies

Although the combination of 2D PAGE or other chemical separation strategies with mass spectrometry is the dominant approach to both comparative and functional proteomic analysis, numerous other methods have or are gaining currency. As described earlier, one-dimensional or two-dimensional gels can themselves be used for comparative proteomics, with staining intensities at various gel positions corresponding to (or analogous to) the signal intensities at various m/z values generated by mass spectrometry (Knowles et al., 2003; Hanash, 2003; Smolka et al., 2002; Zhan and Desiderio, 2003). As libraries of specific affinity probes are generated (Elia et al., 2002), array-based methods are becoming more practical, with fluorescence (Schweitzer et al., 2002), surface plasmon resonance (Nelson et al., 2000), and other detection strategies offering different degrees of sensitivity and quantitation. Arrays can also be used in functional proteomics, as when small molecules (MacBeath, 2002) or proteins (Frank, 2002) are arrayed and complex mixtures assayed for binding partners. These and myriad other proteomics approaches have been extensively reviewed and are beyond the scope of this chapter (Pandey and Mann, 2000; Madoz-Gurpide et al., 2001; Hanash, 2003; MacBeath, 2002; Fields and Song, 1989; Aebersold and Cravatt, 2002; Aebersold and Mann, 2003; Bischoff, 2003; Cahill and Nordhoff, 2003; Chen et al., 2003; Eickhoff et al., 2002; Gershon, 2003; Mouledous and Gutstein, 2003).

REFERENCES

Adam, B.-L., Qu, Y., Davis, J. W., Ward, M. D., Clements, M. A., Cazares, L. H., Semmes, O. J., Schellhammer, P. F., Yasui, Y., Feng, Z., and Wright, G. L., Jr., Serum protein fingerprinting coupled with a pattern-matching algorithm distinguishes prostate cancer from benign prostate hyperplasia and healthy men, *Cancer Research* **62**, 3609–3614 (2002).

Aebersold, R., and Cravatt, B. F., Proteomics—advances, applications and the challenges that remain, *Trends in Biotechnology* **20**, S1–S2 (2002).

Aebersold, R., and Mann, M., Mass spectrometry-based proteomics, *Nature* **422**, 198–207 (2003).

Anderson, N. L., and Anderson, N. G., The human plasma proteome: History, character, and diagnostic prospects, *Molecular and Cellular Proteomics* **1**, 845–867 (2002).

Annesley, T. M., Ion suppression in mass spectrometry, *Clinical Chemistry* **49**, 1041–1044 (2003).

Banfield, J. D., and Raftery, A. E., Model-based Gaussian and non-Gaussian clustering, *Biometrics* **49**, 803–821 (1993).

Biemann, K., and Scoble, H. A., Characterization by tandem mass spectrometry of structural modifications in proteins, *Science* **237**, 992–998 (1987).

Brieman, L., Friedman, J., Olshen, R., and Stone, C., *Classification and Regression Trees*, Wadsworth, Belmont, CA, 1984.

Bischoff, R., Recent developments in proteomics, *Analytical and Bioanalytical Chemistry* **376**, 289–291 (2003).

Cahill, D. J., and Nordhoff, E., Protein arrays and their role in proteomics, *Advances in Biochemical Engineering and Biotechnology* **83**, 177–187 (2003).

Carroll, J. A., and Beavis, R. C., Using matrix convolution filters to extract information from time-of-flight mass spectra, *Rapid Commununications in Mass Spectrometry* **13**, 1683–1687 (1996).

Chakravarti, D. N., Chakravarti, B., and Moutsatsos, I., Informatic tools for proteome profiling, *Biotechniques* (Suppl), **4–10**, 12–15 (2002).

Ciphergen Biosystems, Inc., ProteinChip Product Literature. http://www.ciphergen.com/products/pc/.

Chen, G. Y., Uttamchandani, M., Lue, R. Y., Lesaicherrea, M. L., and Yao, S. Q., Array-based technologies and their applications in proteomics, *Current Topics in Medical Chemistry* **3**, 705–724 (2003).

Chen, Y., and Xu, D., Computational analyses of high-throughput protein–protein interaction data, *Current Protein and Peptide Science* **4**, 159–81 (2003).

Cottrell, J. S., Protein identification by peptide mass fingerprinting, *Peptide Research* **7**, 115–124 (1994).

Cristianini, N., and Shawe-Taylor, J., *An Introduction to Support Vector Machines and Other Kernel-Based Learning Methods*, Cambridge University Press, New York, 2000.

Dalgaard, P., *Introductory Statistics with R*, Springer-Verlag, Berlin, 2002.

Eickhoff, H., Konthur, Z., Lueking, A., Lehrach, H., Walter, G., Nordhoff, E., Nyarsik, L., and Bussow, K., Protein array technology: The tool to bridge genomics and proteomics, *Advances in Biochemical Engineering and Biotechnology* **77**, 103–112 (2002).

Elia, G., Silacci, M., Scheurer, S., Scheuermann, J., and Neri, D., Affinity-capture reagents for protein arrays, *Trends in Biotechnology* **20**, S19–S22 (2002).

Fenn, J. B., Mann, M., Meng, C. K., Wong, S. F., and Whitehouse, C. M., Electrospray ionization for mass spectrometry of large biomolecules, *Science* **246**, 64–71 (1989).

Fenyo, D., and Beavis, R. C., Informatics and data management in proteomics, *Trends in Biotechnology* **20**, S35–S38 (2002).

Fields, S., and Song, O., A novel genetic system to detect protein–protein interactions, *Nature* **340**, 245–246 (1989).

Fountoulakis, M., and Juranville, J. F., Enrichment of low-abundance brain proteins by preparative electrophoresis, *Analytical Biochemistry* **313**, 267–282 (2003).

Fraley, C., and Raftery, A. E., MCLUST: *Software for Model-Based Cluster and Discriminant Analysis*, Technical Report No. 342, University of Washington, Seattle, WA, 1998.

Frank, R., High-density synthetic peptide microarrays: Emerging tools for functional genomics and proteomics, *Combinatorial Chemistry and High Throughput Screening* **5**, 429–440 (2002).

Futcher, B., Latter, G. I., Monardo, P., McLaughlin, C. S., and Garrels, J. I., A sampling of the yeast proteome, *Molecular and Cellular Biology* **19**, 7357–7768 (1999).

Gelman, A., Carlin, J. B., Stern, H. S., and Rubin, D. B., *Bayesian Data Analysis*, CRC Press, Boca Raton, FL, (2003).

Gershon, D., Proteomics technologies: Probing the proteome, *Nature* **424**, 581–587 (2003).

Golub, T. R., Slonim, D. K., Tamayo, P., Huard, C., Gaasenbeek, M., Mesirov, J. P., Coller, H., Loh, M. L., Downing, J. R., Caligiuri, M. A., Bloomfield, C. D., and Lander, E. S., Molecular classification of cancer: Class discovery and class prediction by gene expression monitoring, *Science* **286**, 531–537 (1999).

Gonzalez, R. C., and Woods, R. E., *Digital Image Processing*, Addision-Wesley, Reading, MA, 2002.

Goshe, M. B., Blonder, J., and Smith, R. D., Affinity labeling of highly hydrophobic integral membrane proteins for proteome-wide analysis, *Journal of Proteome Research* **2**, 153–161 (2003).

Gras, R., and Muller, M., Computational aspects of protein identification by mass spectrometry, *Current Opinion in Molecular Therapeutics* **3**, 526–532 (2001).

Griffin, T. J., Lock, C. M., Li, X. J., Patel, A., Chervetsova, I., Lee, H., Wright, M. E., Ranish, J. A., Chen, S. S., and Aebersold, R., Abundance ratio-dependent proteomic analysis by mass spectrometry, *Analytical Chemistry* **75**, 867–874 (2003).

Gygi, S. P., Rochon, Y., Franza, B. R., and Aebersold, R., Correlation between protein and mRNA abundance in yeast, *Molecular and Cellular Biology* **19**, 1720–1730 (1999a).

Gygi, S. P., Rist, B., Gerber, S. A., Turecek, F., Gelb, M. H., and Aebersold, R., Quantitative analysis of complex protein mixtures using isotope-coded affinity tags, *Nature Biotechnology* **17**, 994–999 (1999b).

Gygi, S. P., Corthals, G. L., Zhang, Y., Rochon, Y., and Aebersold, R., Evaluation of two-dimensional gel electrophoresis-based proteome analysis technology, *Proceedings National Academy of Sciences USA*, **97**, 9390–9395 (2000).

Hanash, S., Disease proteomics, *Nature* **422**, 226–232 (2003).

Hancock, W. S., Wu, S. L., Stanley, R. R., and Gombocz, E. A., Publishing large proteome datasets: Scientific policy meets emerging technologies, *Trends in Biotechnology* **20**, S39–S44 (2002).

Hastie, T., Tibshirani, R., and Friedman, J. H., *Elements of Statistical Learning*, Springer-Verlag, Berlin, 2001.

Henzel, W. J., Billeci, T. M., Stults, J. T., Wong, S. C., Grimley, C., and Watanabe, C., Identifying proteins from two-dimensional gels by molecular mass searching of peptide fragments in protein sequence databases, *Proceedings National Academy of Sciences USA* **90**, 5011–5015 (1993).

Howard, B. A., Wang, M. A., Campa, M. J., Corro, C., Fitzgerald, M. C., and Patz, E. F., Jr., Identification and validation of a potential lung cancer serum biomarker detected by matrix-assisted laser desorption/ionization time of flight spectra analysis, *Proteomics* **3**, 1720–1724 (2003).

Hunt, D. F., Yates, J. R., 3rd, Shabanowitz, J., Winston, S., and Hauer, C. R., Protein sequencing by tandem mass spectrometry, *Proceedings National Academy of Sciences USA* **83**, 6233–6237 (1986).

Ihling, C., Berger, K., Hofliger, M. M., Fuhrer, D., Beck-Sickinger, A. G., and Sinz, A., Nano-high-performance liquid chromatography in combination with nano-electrospray ionization Fourier transform ion-cyclotron resonance mass spectrometry for proteome analysis, *Rapid Communications in Mass Spectrometry* **17**, 1240–1246 (2003).

Jeffery, D. A., and Bogyo, M., Chemical proteomics and its application to drug discovery, *Current Opinion in Biotechnology* **14**, 87–95 (2003).

Jobson, J. D., *Applied Multivariate Data Analysis*, Vols. I and II, Springer-Verlag, Berlin, 1996.

Kalkum, M., Lyon, G. J., and Chait, B. T., Detection of secreted peptides by using hypothesis-driven multistage mass spectrometry, *Proceedings National Academy of Sciences USA* **100**, 2795–2800 (2003).

Karas, M., and Hillenkamp, F., Laser desorption ionization of proteins with molecular masses exceeding 10,000 daltons, *Analytical Chemistry* **60**, 2299–2301 (1988).

Kass, R. E., and Raftery, A. E., Bayes factors, *Journal of the American Statistical Association* **90**, 773–795 (1995).

Knowles, M. R., Cervino, S., Skynner, H. A., Hunt, S. P., de Felipe, C., Salim, K., Meneses-Lorente, G., McAllister, G., and Guest, P. C., Multiplex proteomic analysis by two-dimensional differential in-gel electrophoresis, *Proteomics* **3**, 1162–1171 (2003).

Lecchi, P., Gupte, A. R., Perez, R. E., Stockert, L. V., and Abramson, F. P., Size-exclusion chromatography in multidimensional separation schemes for proteome analysis, *Journal of Biochemical and Biophysical Methods* **56**, 141–152 (2003).

Li, J., Zhang, Z., Rosenzweig, J., Wang, Y. Y., and Chan, D. W., Proteomics and bioinformatics approaches for identification of serum biomarkers to detect breast cancer, *Clinical Chemistry* **48**(8), 1296–1304 (2002).

Link, A. J., Multidimensional peptide separations in proteomics, *Trends in Biotechnology* **20**, S8–13 (2002).

Liu, H., Berger, S. J., Chakraborty, A. B., Plumb, R. S., and Cohen, S. A., Multidimensional chromatography coupled to electrospray ionization time-of-flight mass spectrometry as an alternative to two-dimensional gels for the identification and analysis of complex mixtures of intact proteins, *Journal of Chromatography B: Analytical Technologies in the Biomedical and Life Sciences* **782**, 267–289 (2002a).

Liu, H., Lin, D., and Yates, J. R., 3rd, Multidimensional separations for protein/peptide analysis in the post-genomic era, *Biotechniques* **32**, 898, 900, 902 passim (2002b).

Liu, P., and Regnier, F. E., An isotope coding strategy for proteomics involving both amine and carboxyl group labeling, *Journal of Proteome Research* **1**, 443–450 (2002).

MacBeath, G., Protein microarrays and proteomics, *Nature Genetics* **32**(Suppl), 526–532 (2002).

Madoz-Gurpide, J., Wang, H., Misek, D. E., Brichory, F., and Hanash, S. M., Protein based microarrays: A tool for probing the proteome of cancer cells and tissues, *Proteomics* **1**, 1279–1287 (2001).

Mann, M., Hendrickson, R. C., and Pandey, A., Analysis of proteins and proteomes by mass spectrometry, *Annual Review of Biochemistry* **70**, 437–473 (2001).

McDonald, W. H., and Yates, J. R., 3rd, Shotgun proteomics and biomarker discovery, *Disease Markers* **18**, 99–105 (2002).

Merchant, M., and Weinberger, S. R., Recent advancements in surface-enhanced laser desorption/ionization-time of flight-mass spectrometry, *Electrophoresis* **21**, 1164–1177 (2000).

Meretakis, D., and Wuthrich, B., Extending naïve Bayes classifiers using long itemsets, in *KDD-99: Proceedings of the Fifth ACM SIGKDD International Conference on Knowledge Discovery and Data Mining*, 165–174 (1999).

Mitchell, T. M., *Machine Learning*, McGraw-Hill, New York, 1997.

Mouledous, L., and Gutstein, H. B., Gene arrays and proteomics. A primer, *Methods in Molecular Medicine* **84**, 141–54 (2003).

Nelson, R. W., Nedelkov, D., and Tubbs, K. A., Biosensor chip mass spectrometry: A chip-based proteomics approach, *Electrophoresis* **21**, 1155–63 (2000).

Oda, Y., Huang, K., Cross, F. R., Cowburn, D., and Chait, B. T., Accurate quantitation of protein expression and site-specific phosphorylation, *Proceedings National Academy of Sciences USA* **96**, 6591–6596 (1999).

Palmblad, M., Ramstrom, M., Markides, K. E., Hakansson, P., and Bergquist, J., Prediction of chromatographic retention and protein identification in liquid chromatography/mass spectrometry, *Analytical Chemistry* **74**, 5826–5830 (2002).

Pandey, A., and Mann, M., Proteomics to study genes and genomes, *Nature* **405**, 837–846 (2000).

Perticoin, E. F., III, Ardekani, A. M., Hitt, B. A., Levine, P. J., Fusaro, V. A., Steinberg, S. M., Mills, G. B., Simone, C., Fishman, D. A., Kohn, E. C., and Liotta, L. A., Use of proteomic patterns in serum to identify ovarian cancer, *Lancet* **359**, 572–577 (2002). Supplemental information at web site, http://clinicalproteomics.steem.com.

Pieper, R., Su, Q., Gatlin, C. L., Huang, S. T., Anderson, N. L., and Steiner, S., Multicomponent immunoaffinity subtraction chromatography: An innovative step towards a comprehensive survey of the human plasma proteome, *Proteomics* **3**, 422–432 (2003).

Pietrogrande, M. C., Marchetti, N., Dondi, F., and Righetti, P. G., Spot overlapping in two-dimensional polyacrylamide gel electrophoresis maps: Relevance to proteomics, *Electrophoresis* **24**, 217–224 (2003).

Pratt, J. M., Petty, J., Riba-Garcia, I., Robertson, D. H., Gaskell, S. J., Oliver, S. G., and Beynon, R. J., Dynamics of protein turnover, a missing dimension in proteomics, *Molecular and Cellular Proteomics* **1**, 579–591 (2002).

Romig, T. S., Bell, C., and Drolet, D. W., Aptamer affinity chromatography: Combinatorial chemistry applied to protein purification, *Journal of Chromatography B: Biomedical Science Applications* **731**, 275–284 (1999).

Sato, A. K., Sexton, D. J., Morganelli, L. A., Cohen, E. H., Wu, Q. L., Conley, G. P., Streltsova, Z., Lee, S. W., Devlin, M., DeOliveira, D. B., Enright, J., Kent, R. B., Wescott, C. R., Ransohoff, T. C., Ley, A. C., and Ladner, R. C., Development of mammalian serum albumin affinity purification media by peptide phage display, *Biotechnology Progress* **18**, 182–192 (2002).

Schweitzer, B., Roberts, S., Grimwade, B., Shao, W., Wang, M., Fu, Q., Shu, Q., Laroche, I., Zhou, Z., Tchernev, V. T., Christiansen, J., Velleca, M., and Kingsmore, S. F., Multiplexed protein profiling on microarrays by rolling-circle amplification, *Nature Biotechnology* **20**, 359–365 (2002).

Smolka, M., Zhou, H., and Aebersold, R., Quantitative protein profiling using two-dimensional gel electrophoresis, isotope-coded affinity tag labeling, and mass spectrometry, *Molecular Cell Proteomics* **1**, 19–29 (2002).

Sorace, J. M., and Zhan, M., A data review and re-assessment of ovarian cancer serum proteomic profiling, *BMC Bioinformatics* **4**, 24 (2003).

Smith, S. W., *The Scientist and Engineer's Guide to Digital Signal Processing*, California Technical Publishing, San Diego, CA (1997).

Wolters, D. A., Washburn, M. P., and Yates, J. R., 3rd, An automated multidimensional protein identification technology for shotgun proteomics, *Analytical Chemistry* **73**, 5683–5690 (2001).

Yanagisawa, K., Shyr, Y., Xu, B. J., Massion, P. P., Larsen, P. H., White, B. C., Roberts, J. R., Edgerton, M., Gonzalez, A., Nadaf, S., Moore, J. H., Caprioli, R. M., and Carbone, D. P., Proteomic patterns of tumor subsets in non-small-cell lung cancer, *The Lancet* **362**, 433–439 (2003).

Zhan, X., and Desiderio, D. M., A reference map of a human pituitary adenoma proteome, *Proteomics* **3**, 699–713 (2003).

Zhang, W., Zhou, G., Zhao, Y., and White, M. A., Affinity enrichment of plasma membrane for proteomics analysis, *Electrophoresis* **24**, 2855–2863 (2003).

PART V

MEDICAL AND PHARMACEUTICAL APPLICATIONS

16

DISCOVERING PATTERNS AND REFERENCE MODELS IN THE MEDICAL DOMAIN OF ISOKINETICS

F. Alonso, J. P. Valente, L. Martínez, and C. Montes

16.1. INTRODUCTION

This chapter describes the knowledge discovery algorithms used in medical diagnosis in the field of physiotherapy and, more specifically, in muscle function assessment. The system processes data received from an isokinetic machine, using expert systems and data-mining techniques.

An isokinetic machine (Figure 16.1a) can be described as a piece of apparatus on which patients perform strength exercises. This machine has the peculiarity of limiting the range of movement and the intensity of effort at a constant velocity (which explains the term isokinetic).

Data concerning the strength employed by the patient throughout the exercise are recorded and stored in the machine so that physicians can collect and visually analyze the results using specialized computer software. Figure 16.1b shows the result of one exercise as a strength curve (a curve with the leg angle has been included to illustrate the figure).

The information produced by isokinetic machines has a wide range of applications not only in physiotherapy, but also in orthopedics and other medical specialties. Of these, most concern orthopedic rehabilitation and functional evaluation. In a smaller measure, they are also used in neurology and legal medicine, although these application types are attracting increasing interest.

Analyzing more closely the composition of the work on orthopedic rehabilitation, the knee turns out to be the most studied joint, followed in decreasing order by the ankle and the shoulder. On the other hand, little work has been done on

Next Generation of Data-Mining Applications. Edited by Kantardzic and Zurada
ISBN 0-471-65605-4 © 2005 the Institute of Electrical and Electronics Engineers, Inc.

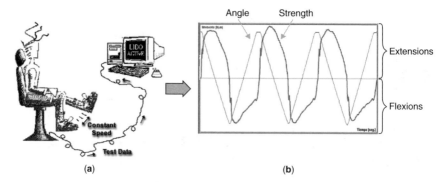

Figure 16.1. Diagram of isokinetics machine **(a)** and the resultant data **(b)**.

other anatomical parts, particularly, muscle injuries, the torso, the hip, and the elbow (EasyTech, 2001).

The isokinetic machine principle is quite simple: The device moves at a constant speed through all the possible angles, at the same time that the patient pushes it using the part of the body that is under examination (in our case, knee flexions and extensions). If everything is in order, the increase or decrease in the strength exerted by the person at each consecutive angle should be somehow continuous. On the other hand, large fluctuations in the strength exerted are indicative of some kind of injury or disease.

All the tests are performed following strict protocols that ensure that enough and the right data are collected for each patient. In our case, the exercises are performed following a protocol specified by the expert, which consists of a total number of six exercises: three different speeds (60°/s, 180°/s, and 300°/s) performed with each leg.

The potential of isokinetic machines for therapists is indisputable. However, inexperience and the shortage of references is still the major problem. It is very difficult for a novice to understand and analyze the results, and even experts experience problems because they have no reference models to aid decision-making on a particular test. Moreover, different kinds of populations (grouped by age, injury, profession, etc.) behave differently, which leads to different categories of curves.

Data-mining techniques on time series are required to analyze isokinetic exercises in order to discover new and useful information for later use in a range of applications. Patterns discovered in isokinetic exercises performed by injured patients are very useful, especially for monitoring injuries, detecting potential injuries early or discovering fraudulent sicknesses. These patterns are also useful for creating reference models for population groups that share some characteristics.

The remainder of the chapter is organized as follows. Section 16.2 focuses on related work and Section 16.3 on the patient isokinetic tests, with respect to collecting and preparing initial data. Section 16.4 introduces the algorithm for detecting patterns in time series defined by the isokinetic tests. Section 16.5

describes the algorithm for creating reference models of population groups, and Section 16.6 illustrates how the knowledge discovered in the isokinetic tests was evaluated. The chapter concludes by discussing the results yielded by this DM system.

16.2. RELATED WORK

The analysis of time-ordered datasets is essential in many fields, including of course medical domains, but also engineering, meteorology, or the business world. The objectives generally pursued are diagnosis, forecasting, or the characterization of the time series and, therefore, of the entities that produce these time series.

One of the most common tasks related to such data types is to search databases for similar time series data. For example, we might want to find companies with a similar growth pattern or discover products with similar sales patterns. One important question is to decide what similarity means. The simplest solution is to calculate some sort of distance, like the Euclidean or Manhattan distance, between two time series. These series are considered similar if the above distance is less than a given threshold value. In an attempt at reducing the time taken to calculate this distance, some authors (Agrawal and Srikant, 1994; Faloutsos et al., 1994) suggest that the Fourier transform (FT) be used to transfer the series from the time to the frequency domain, using only the first four coefficients to filter dissimilar series.

Agrawal and Srikant (1994) divide queries concerning similarity between time series into two categories: total comparison, where the sequences for comparison have the same length, or partial comparison, which involves checking whether a sequence appears as part of another.

Most of the work on total comparison has focused on the search for a particular sequence within a set of time series or on searching for all the sequences that are similar to a given one. The basic technique is to index all the time series, using some sort of spatial access method, like R^* trees (Beckman et al., 1990). This index will contain the first coefficients of the Fourier transform of the series. Thus, it will be possible to find similar patterns by running through sequences that are close together in the R^* tree rather than through all the sequences. More recently, other transform types [mainly the wavelet transform (WT)] have proved to perform better than the Fourier transform in some domains or applications (Povinelli, 1999). Thus, whereas the FT stores the general curve trend in its first coefficients, the WT encodes a coarser resolution of the original time sequence (Chan and Fu, 1999).

Another question to be taken into account is the similarity metric to be used. The Euclidean distance is the most commonly used. However, it is beset by a series of problems, because it is invariant to transformations like time shifts, changes of scale, and so on. Other distance types, like the warping distance, which provides for changes and shifts on the time scale, can be better suited for a variety of problems (Park et al., 2000). The proposal by Perng et al. (2000) is more original, and it proposes a different similarity model that is based on the identification of the singular points of each data sequence (points of inflection, maximums and minimums, etc.) rather than on the use of a metric.

Partial comparison, or subsequence matching—that is, the search for subseries that are repeated throughout a particular series—is a tougher problem that has gained in importance recently. Here, the query sequence is potentially shorter than the sequences in the database. For example, one might ask for companies that at some point behaved similarly to the company x in the spring of the year 2000. The Apriori property (the underlying idea of the Apriori property is to discard all the sequences of length $n + 1$ that include another sequence of length n that has already been classed as infrequent and, therefore, insignificant) was of fundamental importance in the early approaches to this problem: Agrawal and Srikant (1995) developed an Apriori algorithm-based technique to discover sequential patterns; Mannila et al. (1995) address the problem of recognizing frequent episodes in event collections.

A third category in time series comparison is pattern search. This is not, strictly speaking, a partial comparison problem, because the aim is to locate the presence of an unknown subsequence in a set of sequences: The problem involves finding subsequences that are frequently repeated in a set of times series, about which there is, however, no background knowledge. There are several examples of pattern searching in symbolic series. Han et al. (1998) try to find subsequences that are periodically repeated within a symbolic sequence. The Apriori property is also used, in this case to prune infrequent patterns. Their algorithm detects patterns of any length, while the pruning of infrequent patterns succeeds in providing high efficiency. Garofalakis et al. (2002) propose the use of regular expressions to specify constraints that the patterns should satisfy. If the data are continuous, pattern search is more complex problem. In other fields (statistics, dynamic programming), a lot of work has been done, applied, for example, to stock exchange data. Povinelli and Feng (2003) developed a method inspired by data mining and dynamic programming concepts to identify patterns that are significant for predicting events within a time series.

The time series classification problem, addressed by the machine learning community, resembles pattern searching in many ways. Geurts (2001) tries to classify a series of objects on the basis of variables that are time series. For this purpose, he defines a set of tests to give the measure of the presence of a pattern in a series, and these tests are the decision nodes of a future classification tree.

Our case differs significantly from most of the above-mentioned work. The DB is basically composed of one continuous time series per patient (which provides the values of the muscular strength exerted by a joint), and the aim is to find a pattern (or subsequence) in this series that is characteristic of any given muscular or joint dysfunction. Apriori there is no expert knowledge of what the patterns characteristic of any injury type are like. Therefore, if we are to find a means of characterizing patients with a given injury X, we have to look for patients that we know have this injury, get a series of respective time series, and search for subsequences that are repeated in all these series and that do not occur in healthy patients. Only subsequences that are repeated (exactly or similarly) in a sufficient number of data series can be considered patterns. Blind search—that is, without background knowledge—is the main obstacle to be overcome by the method proposed later.

Han et al.'s algorithm has proved to be useful for the above-mentioned problem. However, this algorithm only discovers patterns that are repeated exactly (although some points of the sequence can be ignored) in different series (symbolic values), which means that it is not suitable for searching for similar patterns in more than one time series (real values). In this chapter we present a new algorithm, inspired by the algorithm presented in Han et al. (1998) to deal with this problem, and a method for creating reference models for population groups.

16.3. PREPROCESSING AND CLEANING PATIENT ISOKINETIC RECORDS

In the case presented in this chapter, isokinetic tests have been used to assess physical capacity and injuries of top competition athletes since the early 1990s. An extensive collection of tests and exercises has been gathered since then.

This data had to be collected and prepared before we were able to perform any data-mining process. These tasks are described later very briefly and are summarized in Figure 16.2. A full description of the preprocessing phase is given in Alonso et al. (2001a).

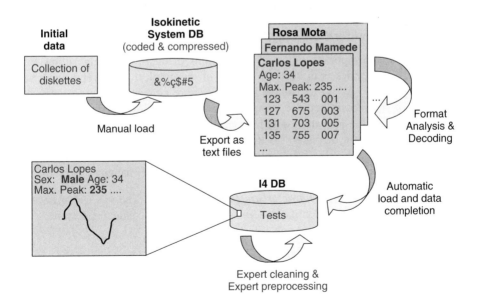

Figure 16.2. Data preprocessing tasks.

- *Collecting Initial Data.* Initial data were stored and coded across a set of diskettes that had to be manually loaded into the isokinetic system database. This collection of data was composed of close to 1580 isokinetic tests. The tests include the personal particulars of the patient and six isokinetic exercises. Each exercise is a series of 350 to 600 triplets of real numbers (strength, angle, time). All this amounted to just over 103 Mbytes of information.

- *Analyzing and Decoding Data.* The data used by the isokinetic system are compressed and coded using special methods. Each test had to be exported to text format and then this format had to be analyzed and decoded in order to be correctly interpreted.

- *Creation of the I4 Database.* An automatic loading tool was designed to transfer all the tests to the I4 database, helping the user to complete some incomplete information about the patients, especially patient gender, which was generated using automatic name recognition.

- *Expert Cleaning of Data.* Two data cleaning tasks were performed. First, incorrect tests that did not follow the exercise protocol were removed. Second, incorrect extensions and flexions due to underexertion by the patient were eliminated. Expert knowledge was needed to perform these tasks.

- *Expert Preprocessing.* Expert knowledge had to be used to automatically remove the irregularities in the strength curves caused by inertia of the isokinetic machine and retain deviations that were only due to the strength exerted by patients.

16.4. DISCOVERING PATTERNS

16.4.1. Algorithm for Detecting Patterns

One of the most important potential applications of data-mining algorithms for this sort of time series is to detect any parts of the graph that are representative of an irregularity. As far as isokinetic exercises are concerned, the presence of this sort of alterations could correspond to some kind of injury, and correct identification of the alteration could be an aid for detecting the injury in time. So, the identification of patterns—that is, portions of data that are repeated in more than one graph—is of vital importance for being able to establish criteria by means of which to classify the exercises and, therefore, patients.

Method for Discovering Characteristic Injury Patterns. The process of developing a DM method to identify patterns that potentially characterize some sort of injury was divided into two phases:

1. Develop an algorithm that detects similar patterns in exercises.

2. Use the algorithm developed in point 1 to detect any patterns that appear in exercises done by patients with injuries and do not appear in exercises completed by healthy individuals.

The problem defined in phase 1 of the method of injury identification is set out as follows.

Given:

- A collection S of time series, composed of sequences of values (real numbers representing the strength exerted by the patient) of variable length, where the length of the longest is *max-length*. Note that only the value of the strength exerted by the patient is required for pattern creation, and the angle and time are, therefore, not considered.

- The value (supplied by the user) of minimum confidence *min-conf* (number of series in which a pattern appears divided by the total number of series).

- The maximum distance between patterns to be considered similar (*max-dist*).

Find:

- All frequent patterns present in S—that is, identical or similar sequences that appear in S with a confidence greater or equal to min-conf.

A pattern search tree was built in order to speed up the pattern-searching algorithm. Each depth level of this tree coincides with the length of each pattern; that is, a branch of depth 2 corresponds to a given pattern of length 2. In identical pattern-searching algorithms (Han et al., 1998), it suffices to store the pattern and a counter of appearances in each node. When dealing with continuous data, however, similar patterns have to be considered; therefore, the list of series in which the pattern appears (SA) and the list of series in which a similar pattern appears (SSA) have to be stored (Figure 16.3). This is because pattern similarity does not have the property of transitivity (we can have p1 similar to p2, p2 similar to p3, and p1 not similar to p3).

Major changes had to be made to state-of-the-art algorithms in order to consider similar patterns, because these algorithms either search for identical patterns in the series or consider only patterns of a given length. In the identical pattern-searching algorithms, each pattern matches a branch of the tree. In the similar pattern-searching algorithm in question, however, a pattern can match several branches, depending on the specified distance *max-dist*. For example, taking

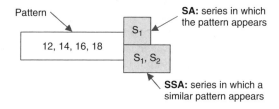

Figure 16.3. Format of a similar pattern search tree node.

max-dist = 1, the patterns {12, 14, 16, 18} and {12, 14, 16, 19} are considered similar, and this must be taken into account when calculating the frequency of the two patterns.

First, the algorithm builds candidate patterns that appear in the time series in the same manner as an identical pattern-searching algorithm would do. To calculate pattern frequency, however, it is not enough just to store the number of times the pattern appears in the series. It is important to find out in which series the pattern appears in order to be able to analyze its similarity with other patterns. The identifiers of the series in which each candidate pattern appears are stored in the SA field of each node. Then the algorithm has to run through the candidate patterns to modify the SSA set, taking into account the appearances attributed to similar candidate patterns. For each candidate pattern, all the candidate patterns of the same length in the tree that are at a lesser distance than threshold *max-dist* are considered similar patterns, and the respective SSA sets are updated with the series from the SA set of the other similar node. Obviously, identical patterns are also considered to be similar, which means that the SSA sets of a node are initialized with the SA set of the node in question (SA $\subseteq$ SSA).

Special care has to be taken in the pruning phase not to prune candidate patterns, which, although not themselves frequent, play a role in making another pattern frequent. If this sort of candidate patterns were pruned, the algorithm would not be complete—that is, would not find all the possible patterns. Only candidate patterns that are infrequent and whose minimum distance from the other patterns is further than the required distance will be pruned. Having completed the tree-pruning phase, the next level of the tree is generated using the longest patterns.

The algorithm steps are described in detail below.

1. Scan the time series database looking for sub-sequences of length i (starting with length 1) and enter the series in which each sub-sequence (candidate pattern) is detected into the respective SA set.

2. Calculate the distance between pairs of candidate patterns for all the candidate patterns of length i. If the calculated distance is less than that defined by the user (*max-dist*), update the SSA sets of the nodes of the two candidate patterns by adding the series belonging to the SA set of the other pattern. That is, for two similar patterns p1 and p2, SSA(p1) = SSA(p1) $\cup$ SA(p2). The confidence of a candidate pattern is calculated with the SSA set.

3. Prune the search tree. To be pruned, a node must satisfy two conditions: (a) The candidate pattern in the node must not be frequent, that is, its confidence must be less than specified (*min-conf*). (b) The minimum distance of the candidate pattern in the node to the other patterns of the same length must be greater than the maximum similarity distance defined by the user (max-dist). This restricted application of the Apriori property is due to the fact that although these patterns will not be able to form part of frequent

patterns in later algorithm iterations, they may contribute by similarity to other patterns being frequent.

4. Return to Step 1 if not all the nodes of the branch of the tree have been pruned and candidate patterns of length $i + 1$ can be built.

This algorithm is able to search a large set of time series of nonhomogeneous lengths, finding the patterns (time subsequences of undetermined length) that are repeated in any position of a significant number of series. Therefore, the algorithm will be useful for finding significant patterns that are likely to characterize a set of nonuniform time series, even though important characteristics of these patterns, like length or position within the time series, are unknown.

Empirical studies have been conducted to determine the performance of this algorithm. The finding of these studies was that the algorithm is computationally adequate for solving the problems arising in the isokinetics domain. The results are detailed in Alonso et al. (2001b).

Example of Algorithm Application.　　Given the pattern series $S_1 = \{1, 0, 1\}$, $S_2 = \{1, 1, 1\}$ and $S_3 = \{2, 2, 1\}$, with *max-length* $= 3$, the algorithm will be applied with the parameters *min-conf* $= 0.75$ and *max-dist* $= 1$.

During the first algorithm iteration, three patterns of length 1 are found in the series. Pattern $\{0\}$ appears in S_1, pattern $\{1\}$ appears in S_1, S_2, S_3, and pattern $\{2\}$ appears in S_3. Pattern $\{0\}$ is similar to pattern $\{1\}$ (Euclidean distance $= 1$); therefore, the SSA for pattern $\{0\}$ includes the three series. The same applies to pattern $\{2\}$. Finally, pattern $\{1\}$ is similar to patterns $\{0\}$ and $\{2\}$, but these two patterns add no new information to the SSA of pattern $\{1\}$. In the pruning step, the confidence level of all three patterns in the SSA series is high (1.0), and all three patterns are kept for the next iteration.

In the second iteration, there are only five patterns of length 2 that appear in at least one of the series: $\{0, 1\}$, $\{1, 0\}$, $\{1, 1\}$, $\{2, 1\}$, and $\{2, 2\}$. Pattern $\{0, 1\}$ is only similar to pattern $\{1, 1\}$, as is pattern $\{1, 0\}$. Pattern $\{1, 1\}$ is similar to $\{0, 1\}$, $\{1, 0\}$, and $\{2, 1\}$. Pattern $\{2, 1\}$ is similar to $\{1, 1\}$ and $\{2, 2\}$. Finally, pattern $\{2, 2\}$ is only similar to $\{2, 1\}$.

In the pruning step, only pattern $\{1, 1\}$ has a high enough confidence level. However, patterns $\{0, 1\}$, $\{1, 0\}$, and $\{2, 1\}$ are similar to pattern $\{1, 1\}$ and are, therefore, also kept for the next iteration. The only pattern to be pruned in this iteration is $\{2, 2\}$ (because it is not frequent and its minimum distance to the other patterns is greater than the maximum similarity distance *max-dist*).

In the third and last iteration, there are only two patterns of length 3 that appear in any of the series: $\{1, 0, 1\}$ in S_1 and $\{1, 1, 1\}$ in S_2. Both patterns are similar and their SSAs are updated. These patterns are pruned, because their confidence is low and there are no similar patterns with a high confidence level.

The algorithm ends here with only four possible patterns having a high enough confidence level: $\{0\}$, $\{1\}$, $\{2\}$ and $\{1, 1\}$. Figure 16.4 summarizes this example.

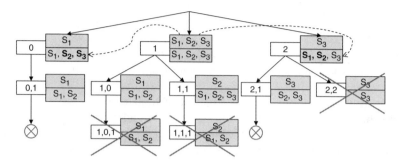

Figure 16.4. Similar pattern search tree.

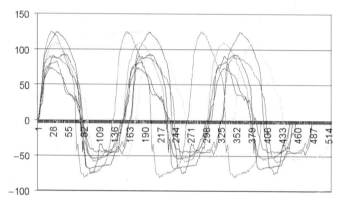

Figure 16.5. Eight isokinetic exercises performed by injured patients (knee cartilage disease).

16.4.2. Detecting Injury Patterns in Isokinetic Exercises

A real example of similar pattern-searching algorithm application to pattern detection in isokinetic exercises is shown below. In this case, we had a set of eight exercises completed by injured female patients (knee cartilage disease). This is a feasible number, because it is difficult to find more patients with the same sort of injury for evaluation in a given environment (in this case, Spanish top-competition athletes). The graphs of the exercises used are shown in Figure 16.5.

The problem is to detect patterns symptomatic of knee cartilage disease. Taking the exercises shown in Figure 16.5, the similar pattern-searching algorithm finds a number of patterns, the most promising of which is shown in Figure 16.6a. This pattern corresponds to the lower part of the curves, as shown in Figure 16.6b. Note that the discovered patterns do not necessarily appear at the same point in all series, which overcomes problems, such as possible time deviations between different patients' series. We then tried to match this pattern against a set of healthy patients' exercises, and this pattern did not show up. After a positive expert evaluation, we will be able to use this pattern as a symptom of knee cartilage disease.

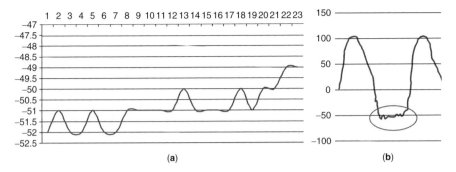

Figure 16.6. Pattern possibly characteristic of cartilage disease.

16.5. ALGORITHM TO CREATE REFERENCE MODELS FOR POPULATION GROUPS

One of the most common tasks involved in the assessment of isokinetic exercises is to compare a patient's test against a reference model created beforehand. These models represent the average profile of a group of patients sharing common characteristics.

All the exercises done by individuals with the desired characteristics of weight, height, sport, sex, and so on, must be selected to create a reference model for a particular population. However, there may be some heterogeneity even among patients of the same group. Some will have a series of particularities that make them significantly different from the others. Take a sport like American football, for instance, where players have very different physical characteristics. Here, it will make no sense to create a model for all the players, and individual models would have to be built for each subgroup of players with similar characteristics. Therefore, exercises have to be discriminated, and the reference model has to be created only with exercises among which there is some uniformity.

It was the expert in isokinetics who used to be responsible for selecting the exercises that were to be part of the model. Discarding any exercises that differ considerably from the others is a job that is difficult to do manually. This meant that it was mostly not done. The idea we aim to implement is to automatically discard all the exercises that are different and create a model with the remainder.

Once the user has selected all the tests of the patient population to be modeled, the algorithm used to create a new reference model is as follows.

16.5.1. Algorithm for Model Creation

1. Given a collection of tests, select the target exercises and calculate the fast Fourier transform of the series (once the series has been preprocessed, only the first 256 values are used).

2. Class the first four coefficients of the Fourier transform of these exercises, using a clustering algorithm (Kanungo et al., 2002). These four coefficients

are enough to represent the curve trends. Thus, the groups of similar exercises are clearly identified, as they are grouped into different classes.

3. Select the group (or groups) of exercises upon which to build the model (there is usually a majority group that covers most of the athletes who play a sport).

4. The first step for creating the actual model is normalization (which is explained later) to ensure that a series of critical points match up in all exercises. The second step is to calculate the mean value of the curves point to point, and, finally, some interesting additional features are included (average maximum peak, average total work, average gradient, etc.).

Figure 16.7 illustrates the reference model creation process. In the preliminary phase (Data Preparation), the data upon which the model is to be built are cleaned. All the isokinetic exercises are analyzed to check whether any are invalid as a whole (due to incorrect performance, patient fatigue, etc.). Also, we check that all the repetitions of each exercise are somewhat uniform (the first repetition is usually removed because it does not really represent the patient's muscle strength). Finally, all the series are pruned to 256 values (approximately three full repetitions for a velocity of 60°/s) to be able to apply the fast Fourier transform.

Having cleaned the data, the Fourier transform is applied for each of the series, and the first four coefficients of each one are selected (as these are representative enough). A clustering algorithm (whose essential parameters, like number of classes, distances, etc., have been established *apriori* after running numerous tests) is applied to this dataset, which outputs a set of classes grouping patients depending on their muscle strength.

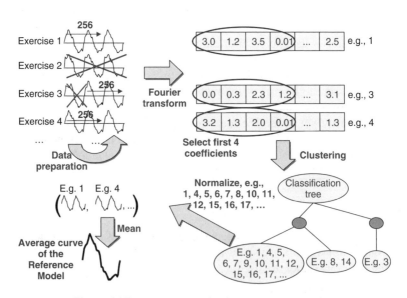

Figure 16.7. The process of reference model creation.

As a general rule, users mostly intend to create a reference model for a particular sport, and there are one or more majority classes and other minority classes. The majority classes define the standard profile or profiles of each sport, whereas the minority classes represent atypical athletes (with respect to their muscle strength) within their sport.

Before creating the respective model of each majority class, the exercises should be normalized; that is, level out the size of the different isokinetics curves and adjust the times when patients exert zero strength (switches from knee extension to flexion and vice versa), because these singular points should appear at exactly the same time in all the exercises (this step would not be necessary if the isokinetics machine were perfect and really worked at constant velocity). For this purpose, the values necessary for "lengthening" or "shortening" the exercises on the time scale are interpolated. Once these values have been normalized, the model is created by calculating the mean strength values—that is, creating an extension and flexion that will be representative of the muscle strength of the athletes that play a given sport (or specialty within a sport). To complete the model, we apply the pattern discovery algorithm to the group of exercises and add every pattern found as an attribute of the model. This last step is taken because, when calculating the average curve, patterns may be smoothed if they appear at different moments in time in the exercises. Other characteristics of the group of exercises—like maximum peak, mean maximum peak, and so on—are also added.

An isokinetic exercise or a set of isokinetic exercises for a patient will later be able to be compared with the models stored in the database. Thus, we will be able to determine the group to which patients belong or should belong and identify what sport they should go in for, what their weaknesses are with a view to improvement, or how they are likely to progress in the future.

To illustrate the creation of reference models, we describe an example using a group of exercises belonging to rugby players below. Having applied the clustering algorithm to all the available exercises, we find a majority group of exercises and two minority groups, each composed of two exercises. The model is created on the basis of the majority group, and the other exercises are discarded as not being very representative. Figure 16.8 shows the set of isokinetic exercises selected to build the model.

As we can see from Figure 16.8, the transitions of the different exercises through the zero strength value (highlighted horizontal line) vary a lot from one exercise to another, especially as the exercise progresses. This is clearly due to isokinetic machine imprecision, because if the execution velocity were really constant and equal for all patients, the transitions would exactly coincide. If we create the model directly on the basis of these exercises, the result would be as shown in Figure 16.9.

The numerous peaks in the extension phase of the model are due to the fact that the time at which each exercise reaches it maximum peak does not coincide, because of the problem mentioned earlier. This is, therefore, not a representative model for the patients in question.

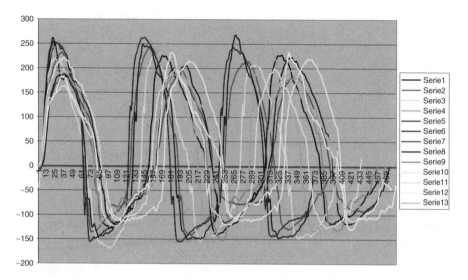

Figure 16.8. Exercises selected to create the Rugby Players model.

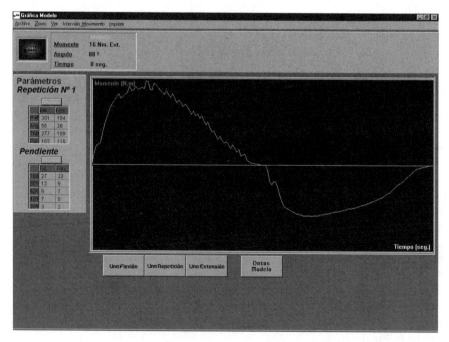

Figure 16.9. Model created for non-normalized exercises.

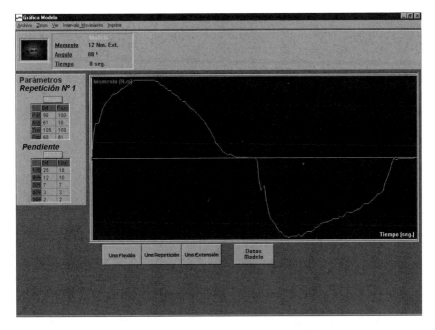

Figure 16.10. Isokinetic mode for rugby players.

Therefore, a normalization step has to be applied to each exercise. This normalization adjusts the duration of each exercise (scaling their duration in time) so that the duration of all the extensions and flexions of the exercises considered is identical. This means that the time at which the maximum peak is reached is similar in each exercise. Figure 16.10 shows the final model for rugby players after the normalization of each exercise, which resembles the typical curve of a rugby player much more closely.

16.6. EVALUATION

Traditionally, the evaluation of DM research results and applications has evidenced a clear bias toward technical assessment. In other words, the results are considered good if they can be empirically cross-validated with existing or similar new cases, irrespective of any other practical considerations. This is evidently an essential part of any evaluation procedure, but one of the lessons learned is that there are other practical aspects that should be tested and are equally or more important for the success of any proposal once it leaves the research lab. We are, of course, referring to acceptance factors.

We use the term *acceptance* to designate globally all the aspects that determine the way in which users perceive the results for their application during routine practice. Acceptance is, therefore, a mixture of objective criteria (correctness, fitness, etc.) and subjective perceptions (simplicity, usability, utility, etc.). In other words, the success of any DM result within a domain depends on the users, who should provide positive feedback to the two key questions: Do I (the user) feel that it works? And do I like how it works?

Consequently, a successful transfer of DM results is not only a matter of achieving the results, it involves achieving results that are suitable for application. This has been hard to learn for computer scientists generally, and it explains why many extremely good models or techniques have had little acceptance within some domains. For instance, decision-making tasks in medical domains require models that physicians find easy to understand and use. So, any approach that does not include explicit models that can be read and interpreted is very unlikely to be adopted in routine practice.

Bearing the above in mind, the evaluation phase has placed special emphasis on checking acceptance. More specifically, the evaluation was designed to achieve the following goals:

- *Goal 1.* Verify the **correctness** of the results from a technical point of view.
- *Goal 2.* Validate empirically their **fitness** for achieving the selected goals: pattern-based injury detection and model-based population characterization.
- *Goal 3.* Evaluate their **acceptance** as a new tool for routine practice.

The evaluation of the correctness and the fitness had to cope with a problem that is very common in this kind of domains: the shortage of sources of knowledge for testing. In our case, the sources were confined to experts, the cases database, the few existing models, and everyday practice. This situation is typical of such domains: shortage (and even low quality) of recorded historical data and of practitioners with solid experience. The only way to deal with this situation is by means of a strict and methodic evaluation procedure.

This meant that we faced a trade-off: On the one hand, we needed to evaluate the results at an early stage to make sure that we were headed in the right direction, but, on the other hand, we needed plenty of time to check the results properly because there was little background knowledge and information. Additionally, acceptance could not be evaluated until we had solid results regarding the other two points. Bearing all this in mind, the whole process was carefully planned as a long-term evaluation, based on a five-step procedure:

1. Subjective appraisal of the results by the experts.
2. Comparison of the results with previous known cases. These were very limited because the only available sources were the cases themselves and a few existing models.
3. Turing Test-based validation tests, in which the effectiveness of the discovered knowledge was compared against the expert.
4. Continuous daily evaluation with real-life cases. This is a corrective stage and is continued throughout the research project life cycle.
5. Evaluation of acceptance and satisfaction.

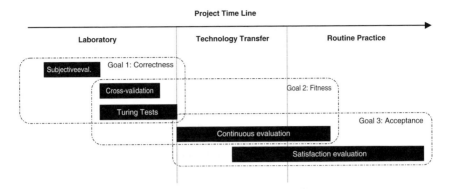

Figure 16.11. The evaluation process.

Figure 16.11 illustrates the time schedule for the evaluation procedure. As a result of the intended goals and the constraints on available information, it covers almost all the research project life cycle, with feedbacks and corrective actions across the time line.

The evaluation process, the results, and the feedback for the first two goals (correctness and fitness), which are related to the first four steps of the procedure, are discussed in detail in Alonso et al. (2001b). Here, we will just outline some noteworthy results and related findings.

The first evaluation step turned out to be much more critical than we had originally expected. It was performed during the actual KDD process, and the goal was to detect any significant deviation of the partial results output during DM from the results expected by practitioners. Therefore, this phase was originally planned as a checkpoint to ensure that things were being done in the right way. But the outcome was much more important than expected, especially for the injury detection problem.

For this task, the experts were asked to give a justified evaluation of each injury pattern output by the DM methods. If positive, they were to give at least five examples that confirmed the pattern; if negative, they had to provide the same number of negative examples. The most important outcome was related to the actual detection procedure, which involved comparing each case to be classified against the discovered injury patterns. A problem arose, however. Some injury cases were detected as perfectly normal, because there was no specific pattern for the injury type in question. One might think initially that this is just a consequence of the shortage of data. But there was another and more important reason: There are atypical cases that will never be discovered by the system.

This led us to change the pattern application procedure, creating patterns for both injury and normal cases, so that any new case was compared with both sets. If the case matched neither, a possible exceptional case would be identified, preventing false positives.

The third step of the evaluation process compared the effectiveness of the discovered knowledge against the expert's knowledge, using a Turing test-based

TABLE 16.1. Evaluation of Injury Detection

	System	Expert	Novice
15 common injuries:	15 OK	15 OK	Failed 2
5 uninjured:	4 OK and 1 don't know	5 OK	3 OK (no mistakes)
5 rare injuries:	Detected as rare cases (no mistakes)	2 mistakes and 1 don't know	3 don't knows

TABLE 16.2. Evaluation of Reference Models Creation

	System	Expert	Novice
30 members:	4 mistakes	9 mistakes	21 mistakes
10 nonmembers:	No mistakes	No mistakes	No mistakes
10 unclassified:	No mistakes	2 mistakes	2 mistakes

approach (Gupta, 1991). Taking into account the shortage of available data, both during the mining process and for testing, the results (shown in Tables 16.1 and 16.2) were outstanding.

In this chapter we focus on the evaluation of the acceptance of the I4 project results by the users, who are members of two very different institutions. On one hand, we had the physicians of the Spanish National Sports Council's High Performance Center, and, on the other hand, we had the staff and students of the Spanish Organization for the Blind's School of Physiotherapy. The former are physicians with vast experience in working with top-competition athletes, while the latter are physicians or physiotherapists (many of them blind) that either work or study at the school's hospital. Clearly the difference in the skill levels of the potential users may range from a novice to a recognized expert. So, the challenge was to achieve results that were satisfactory for any user type.

This led to two different applications that share the internal models, which, however, they use in a slightly different way. The first, called ES for Isokinetics Interpretation *(ISOCIN)*, analyzes injuries in any kind of patient and assesses their evolution, adapting the physiotherapy administered and the rehabilitation process. It was designed for use by visually impaired physicians. The second one, an ES for Interpreting Isokinetics in Sport *(ISODEPOR)*, is intended for top-competition athletes.

The satisfaction was evaluated at more or less the same time in both domains. There was no predefined well-established procedure that we could follow for this purpose. Therefore, we defined a new systematic approach, based on the decomposition of the acceptance concept into four pragmatic aspects that could be evaluated either statistically or by the users themselves. Each of them is represented by a question to which we needed to find an answer.

Are the Users Able to Understand and Effectively Use the Results? This aspect was tested during the technology transfer phase and was performed in three steps. The first one consisted of a brief introductory course describing the models, the patterns, the application, and its usage. In the second step, the medical experts that participated in the research phase acted as consultants providing advice to other physicians during the early days of usage. Finally, in the third stage, users were left to work alone and reported any problem.

The feedback was gathered using a simple questionnaire, and the main complaints related in all cases to the way the results were presented and explained. More precisely, experienced users only relied on the recommendations given by the system after some time using the application, and they always formulated their own judgment simultaneously, without the aid of the machine. Novices simply accepted the recommendations provided by the system, mainly because they knew that they had been tested by experienced physicians.

These results provided very important feedback in two ways: First, they served to significantly improve the interfaces (once the real needs were understood), and, second, they helped us to understand that while experienced users accepted the advice provided by the system, they considered it just as a very useful, sometimes vital, opinion. This situation led to a redefinition of the systems, which were transformed into working tools with which the physician could interact and even check the pattern-based advice.

Are the Results and the Tools Adequate for the Everyday Tasks? This aspect was tested after the above improvements had been included. Again, the feedback had more to do with further functionality to be included in the tools, such as patient management features, than with the underlying models. The most outstanding feedback came from the School of Physiotherapy. Before ISOCIN, the isokinetics machine was used very rarely for diagnosis and almost never by the students. There were two reasons for this. The first was that the machine did not have a proper interface for blind people, so they always needed assistance from a sighted person. The second was even more important and had to do with the lack of injury patterns that could be used as a reference for professionals that were not experts in isokinetics test interpretation. Here ISOCIN was not only adequate for the everyday tasks, it was a must.

Do They Find It Easy to Use the Results in Their Everyday Tasks? The ease of use was checked by measuring the users' learning curve. In the worst case (novice blind student), it took three weeks to master the system and less than ten days to understand the advice provided to its full extent. In the case of experienced users, it only took a week on average.

Have the Results Been Effectively Integrated in Their Usual Protocols? In fact, the advice systems led to a complete revision of their procedures. In the case of the School of Physiotherapy, ISOCIN is the tool used for diagnosis and decision making at the hospital and has become a primary tool. Moreover, students are now trained in its use. Regarding the High Performance Center, ISODEPOR is being used both as a decision support tool and as a research tool, because it has enabled the definition of reference models for each specialty that can be used both for training methods enhancement and for injury avoidance.

16.7. CONCLUSIONS

We can conclude that the algorithms and methods for discovering patterns and reference models based on time series in the isokinetic medicine domain demonstrate their interest and applicability. This is evident from the I4 project, developed for top-competition athletes and visually impaired people, where the results obtained with the DM modules surpass the expected results. Obviously, these results must be read carefully, because most of the mistakes made by practitioners can be attributed to the fact that they were working without sound background knowledge of many diseases and had to deal with a huge amount of data for decision making. In this respect, I4 was at an advantage. Anyhow, the same practitioners have found I4 to be an extremely useful tool and are currently using the two versions of the system (Alonso et al., 2001a). Regarding this, one important lesson learned during this research project is that user satisfaction is the line that separates success from failure. You may have the best laboratory results, but they will never be used if the users are not satisfied. Checking correctness, fitness, and acceptance separately, along with dividing acceptance into understandability, adequacy, ease of use, and integration possibilities, has proved to be a very effective evaluation procedure for this kind of approach, enabling an effective identification of needs.

ACKNOWLEDGMENTS

We would like to thank África López-Illescas for her invaluable contribution to this project in the capacity of expert in the isokinetics domain. Without her, this project would never have gone ahead. We would also like to thank Beatriz Casado, David Hernando, and Victor Sanchez for their collaboration in project development. The I4 project has been developed in conjunction with the Spanish National Center for Sports Research. It was partly funded by CICYT (Spanish Government Foundation for Science and Technology) project no. TIC98-0248-C02-01.

REFERENCES

Agrawal, R., and Srikant, R., Mining sequential patterns, in *Proceedings of the 1994 International Conference on Very Large Data Bases*, Santiago, Chile, pp. 487–499, 1994.

Agrawal, R., and Srikant, R., Fast algorithms for mining association rules, in *Proceedings of the 11th International Conference on Data Engineering*, Taiwan, IEEE Computer Society Press, Los Alamitos, CA, pp. 3–14, 1995.

Alonso, F., Caraça-Valente, J. P., López-Chavarrías, I., and Montes, C., Knowledge discovery in time series using expert knowledge, in *Medical Data Mining and Knowledge Discovery*, Cios, K. J. (ed.), Physica-Verlag, Berlin, pp. 455–496, 2001a.

Alonso, F., Caraça-Valente, J. P., Martinez, L., and Montes, C., Discovering similar patterns for characterizing time series in a medical domain, in *Proceedings of the IEEE Conference on Data Mining (Best application paper award)*, pp. 577–579, 2001b.

Beckman, N., Kriegel, H. P., Schneider, R., and Seeger, B., The R^*-tree: An efficient and robust method for points and rectangles, *Proceedings of the ACM SIGMOD* pp. 322–331, 1990.

Chan, K. P., and Fu, A., Efficient time series matching by wavelets, in *Proceedings of the International Conference of Data Engineering*, Sydney, Australia, 1999, pp. 126–133.

EasyTech. "Isokinetiks." http://www.easytechitalia.com/html_eng/isokinetics.html. 2001.

Faloutsos, C., Ranganathan, M., and Manolopoulos, Y., Fast subsequence matching in time series databases, in *Proceedings of the 3rd International Conference on Knowledge Discovery and Data Mining*, Newport Beach, California, AAAI Press, Menlo Park, CA, 1994, pp. 24–30.

Garofalakis, M., Rastogi, R., and Shim, K., Mining sequential patterns with regular expressions constraints, *Transactions on Knowledge and Data Engineering* **14**(3), 530–552 (2002).

Geurts, P., Pattern extraction for time series classification, *LNAI* **2168**, 115–127 (2001).

Gupta, U., (Ed.), *Validating and Verifying Knowledge Based Systems,* IEEE Computer Society Press, Alamitos, CA, 1991.

Han, J., Dong, G., and Yin, Y., Efficient mining of partial periodic patterns in time series database, in *Proceedings of the Fourth International Conference on Knowledge Discovery and Data Mining*, AAAI Press, Menlo Park, CA, 1998, pp. 214–218.

Kanungo, T., Mount, D., Netanyahu, N., Piatko, C., Silverman, R., and Wu, A., An efficient k-means clustering algorithm: Analysis and implementation, *IEEE Transactions on Pattern Analysis and Machine Intelligence* **24**(7), 881–882 (2002).

Mannila, H., Toivonen, H., and Verkamo, A., Discovering frequent episodes in sequences, in *Proceedings of the 1st International Conference Knowledge Discovery and Data Mining*, Montreal, Canada, pp. 210–215, 1995.

Park, S., Chu, W., Yoon, J., and Hsu, C., Efficient searches for similar subsequences of different lengths in sequence databases, *Proceedings of the International Conference of Data Engineering*, San Diego, pp. 23–32, 2000.

Perng, C., Wang, H., Zhang, S., and Parker, D. S., Landmarks: A new model for similarity-based pattern querying in time series databases, in *Proceedings of the International Conference of Data Engineering*, San Diego, pp. 33–44, 2000.

Povinelli, R., Times Series Data Mining: Identifying Temporal Patterns for Characterization and Prediction of Time Series, Ph.D. dissertation, Marquette University, 1999.

Povinelli, R., and Feng, X., A New Temporal pattern identification method for characterization and prediction of complex time series events, *Transactions on Knowledge and Data Engineering* **15**(2), 339–352 (2003).

17

MINING THE CYSTIC FIBROSIS DATA

LUKASZ A. KURGAN, KRZYSZTOF J. CIOS, MARCI K. SONTAG, AND FRANK J. ACCURSO

17.1. INTRODUCTION

Many data-mining (DM) projects require extensive preprocessing and iterating between the steps of the knowledge discovery process to find new useful information. The reason for these efforts can be attributed to high complexity of the mined data. Many areas, especially medicine, are ripe for DM efforts to extract useful information that can help improve processes and procedures. However, considerable effort is required for design and implementation of procedures for data preparation, along with collaborations between researchers and practitioners from several disciplines. The field of DM needs to adjust to those demands by providing a comprehensive range of services from understanding of the problem domain and data, through DM, to utilization of the discovered knowledge (Cios and Kurgan, 2004a).

This chapter describes an application of our DM system, called MetaSqueezer, for analysis of clinical data describing patients with cystic fibrosis (CF). In the project we used a data-mining and knowledge discovery (DMKD) process model (Cios et al., 2000; Cios and Kurgan, 2004a). The chapter is organized as follows. First, we describe the overall goals and the DMKD process. Next, the DM methods used in the project are introduced and explained. In what follows we describe the project goals and the approach taken to generate useful knowledge from CF data. We finish with discussion of the results, and we conclude with discussion of current DM challenges.

Next Generation of Data-Mining Applications. Edited by Kantardzic and Zurada
ISBN 0-471-65605-4 © 2005 the Institute of Electrical and Electronics Engineers, Inc.

17.2. BACKGROUND AND RELATED WORK

17.2.1. Introduction

Medical applications often aim at describing patterns of disease development and prediction of therapeutic effectiveness. In this work we address the former. The main goal was to discover new information that may advance knowledge about the disease and possibly a better treatment. The difficulty of the project was compounded by two factors:

1. High number of missing values and erroneous information, along with complex structure of the data.

2. Highly iterative manner in which the final results were achieved, which was caused by the necessity to reevaluate and improve data preparation and DM tasks.

In addition, since the CF data are temporal in nature, it needed specific learning tools. As we shall see, in spite of the problems, the obtained results can enhance understanding of the disease. The results include knowledge already known by the CF experts, which was used to validate correctness of our methods, and the new knowledge. The new finding was evaluated as medically important by the domain experts, and it will be utilized to better understand the pathophysiology of the disease.

17.2.2. Data-Mining and Knowledge Discovery Process Model

The purpose of a DMKD model is to help plan, work through, and reduce the overall costs of a DM project, by prescribing procedures needed to be performed in each of the steps. The DMKD process model describes a range of steps from problem specification to interpretation and use of the results (the discovered knowledge). One of the main issues of the project was the ability to structure the process in a formal way that helps dealing with highly iterative nature of the project. Several researchers described a series of steps that constitute the DMKD process, which range from few steps to more refined models like the nine-step model proposed by Fayyad et al. (1996). In this project we use the six-step DMKD process model (Cios et al., 2000; Cios, 2001; Cios and Kurgan, 2004a) described below.

The six-step DMKD process is described as follows:

1. *Understanding the Problem Domain.* In this step the project is defined, including (a) definition of objectives and (b) learning domain-specific terminology and methods. A high-level description of the problem is analyzed, including the requirements and restrictions. The project goals are translated into DMKD goals and the project plan is prepared, which includes selection of suitable DM tools.

2. *Understanding the Data.* This step includes (a) collection of the data and (b) a decision regarding which data will be used (including its format and size). Next, initial data exploration is performed to verify usefulness of the data with respect to the goals identified in step 1.

3. *Preparation of the Data.* In this step the data are chosen that will be used as input for DM tools in step 4. New data records are formed that meet specific input requirements of the given DM tools. The step may involve sampling and cleaning the data, assigning classes to data examples, and so on. The cleaned data can be further processed by feature selection and extraction algorithms, by derivation of new attributes (e.g., by discretization), and by summarization.

4. *Data Mining.* This step applies DM tools to discover new information from the data prepared in step 3. After the training and testing procedures are designed, the data model is constructed using one of the chosen DM tools, and the generated data model is verified by using the testing procedures. DM tools include many types of algorithms, such as inductive ML, rough and fuzzy sets, Bayesian methods, neural networks, clustering, association rules, support vector machines, and so on.

5. *Evaluation of the Discovered Knowledge.* The goal of this step is to understand and interpret the results, check whether the new information is novel and interesting, and check their impact on the project goals. Approved models are retained.

6. *Using the Discovered Knowledge.* This step consists of planning where and how the discovered knowledge will be used.

The above-described process model is visualized in Figure 17.1 (Cios and Kurgan, 2004a).

The iterative and interactive aspects of the process are shown in Figure 17.1 using dashed arrows. Since any changes and decisions made in one of the steps can result in changes in later steps the feedback loops are necessary. The loops shown in Figure 17.1 are by no means exhaustive.

The above model and Fayyad's model are compared in Table 17.1. Both models follow similar sequence of steps. Fayyad's model provides a more detailed procedure, but performs steps concerning choosing a DM task and algorithm late in the process. Cios's model performs this operation before data preprocessing, which results in data that are properly prepared for the DM step (Cios and Kurgan, 2004a). In case of Fayyad's model, one might have to repeat some of the earlier steps via unnecessary feedback loops to change data preparation methods used in steps 2, 3, and 4. Other advantages of Cios's model are that it is based on an industrial tool-independent DMKD process model called CRISP-DM (Wirth and Hipp, 2000), and it provides specific guidelines concerning possible feedback loops, rather than just discussing their presence (Cios and Kurgan, 2004a). This helps to properly plan and improve efficiency of carrying out a data mining project. The model was successfully used on several medical

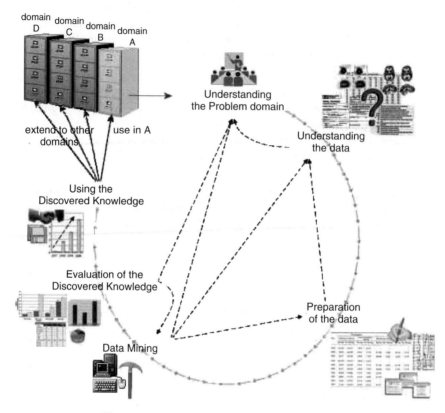

Figure 17.1. The six-step DMKD process model.

TABLE 17.1. Comparison of Six-Step and Nine-Step DMKD Models

Six-Step DMKD Process	Nine-Step DMKD Process
1. Understanding the domain	1. Understanding application domain, identifying the DMKD goals
2. Understanding the data	2. Creating target dataset
3. Preparation of the data	3. Data cleaning and preprocessing
	4. Data reduction and projection
	5. Matching goal to particular data-mining method
	6. Exploratory analysis, model and hypothesis selection
4. Data mining	7. Data mining
5. Evaluation of the discovered knowledge	8. Interpreting mined patterns
6. Using the discovered knowledge	9. Consolidating discovered knowledge

problems such as development of a computerized system for diagnoses of SPECT bull's-eye images (Cios et al., 2000), cardiac SPECT images (Sacha et al., 2000; Kononenko, 2001), and analysis of patients with vascular disease (Laura et al., 2002).

17.2.3. Methods

Introduction. Analysis of the CF data was done by a DM system that uses supervised inductive machine learning (ML) combined with a meta-mining (MM) concept. ML is concerned with generation of data models from input numerical or nominal data. The models are usually inferred using an induction process that searches for regularities among the data. Supervised learning is concerned with generation of a data model that represents a relationship between independent attributes and a designated dependent attribute (class). Therefore, supervised inductive ML algorithms generate models that map independent attributes to the class attribute. The model generated by a supervised ML algorithm often takes the form of production rules. The production rules have "IF (*conditions*) THEN (*class_i*)" format, where *conditions* involve one, or conjunction of several, logical expressions between independent attributes describing the data and their values, and *class_i* is one of the of the values of the class attribute. Supervised inductive ML algorithms that generate production rules can be divided into three types: decision tree algorithms, rule algorithms, and their hybrids (Cios et al., 1998). Example decision trees algorithms are CART (Breiman et al., 1984), C4.5 (Quinlan, 1993), and T1 (Holte, 1993); rule algorithms are the AQ family of algorithms (Michalski et al., 1986; Kaufman and Michalski, 1999), FOIL (Quinlan, 1990), IREP (Furnkranz and Widmer, 1994), RISE (Domingos, 1994), RIPPER (Cohen, 1995), SLIPPER (Cohen and Singer, 1999), and LAD (Boros et al., 2000), and hybrid algorithms are CN2 (Clark and Niblett, 1989) and the CLIP family of algorithms (Cios and Kurgan, 2001, 2004b). Other types of models generated by inductive ML algorithms are also possible—for instance, those generated by ML algorithms based on probability theory, statistics, and other mathematical models (Mitchell, 1997). Examples of the latter include probabilistic algorithms like Naïve Bayes (Langley et al., 1992) and Support Vector Machines (Cortes and Vapnik, 1995).

The main advantages of rules, or trees, are their simplicity and easiness of interpretation. In addition, rules are modular; that is, a single rule can be understood without reference to other rules (Holsheimer and Siebes, 1994). These features are especially valuable in situations where a decision maker, say in medicine, needs to understand and validate the generated model.

Meta mining is a novel concept, or framework, for higher-order mining that generates meta-models (meta-rules) from the already generated data models, which usually are in the form of the rules (and in this framework the rules are called meta-data) (Roddick and Spiliopoulou, 2002; Spiliopoulou and Roddick, 2000). Inference of data models that use the MM concept is a two-step procedure. In the case of using supervised inductive ML algorithms, the first step generates productions rules from input data, while in the second step the generated rules constitute inputs to a ML algorithm (possibly the same) to generate the meta-rules. The simplest form of a meta-rule is a production rule, but other formats, such as temporal rules, are also possible. The DM system used in this project generates both meta-data and meta-rules as production rules.

The MetaSqueezer System.   The analysis of the data was done using a DM system called MetaSqueezer, which generates data models, in terms of production rules, in three steps (Kurgan, 2003; Kurgan and Cios, 2004a):

- *Preprocessing.* The data are repaired, validated, discretized, and transformed into a form suitable for further processing—that is, a single relational table where a separate column holds an attribute that is used to divide the data into subsets—and class labels are generated for each data record.
- *Data Mining.* Production rules are generated from data for each of the defined subsets using DataSqueezer algorithm (Kurgan et al., 2004; Kurgan, 2003), which is explained in the next section. For every set of rules a rule table, that stores the generated production rules, is created.
- *Meta Mining.* MM generates meta-rules from rule tables. After concatenation of all rule tables into a single table, the meta-rules (in the form of production rules) are generated by the DataSqueezer algorithm. They describe the most important patterns associated with the classes over the entire dataset. The meta-rules and rules generated in the DM step are used to compute attribute and selector importance tables, which are defined later.

The architecture of the MetaSqueezer system is shown in Figure 17.2.

The DataSqueezer Algorithm.   DataSqueezer is the core algorithm used to generate meta-data during the DM step and the meta-rules during the MM step (Kurgan et al., 2004; Kurgan, 2003); it is a rule algorithm. Let us denote the input data by D, which consists of S examples. The sets of positive examples, D_P, and negative examples, D_N, must be disjoint, and nonempty and fully cover D. The positive examples are those describing the class for which we currently generate rules, while negative examples are the remaining examples. Examples are described by a set of K attribute-value pairs: $e = \wedge_{j=1}^{K}[a_j \# v_j]$, where a_j denotes the jth attribute with value $v_j \in d_j$ (domain of values of jth attribute), # is a relation $(=, <, \approx, \leq,$ etc.), and K is the number of attributes. DataSqueezer uses equality as a relation. An example, e, consists of set of selectors $s_j = [a_j = v_j]$. The DataSqueezer algorithm generates production rules in the form of IF (s_1 and ... and s_m) THEN class = class$_i$, where $s_i = [a_j = v_j]$ is a single selector, and m is the number of selectors in the rule. Figure 17.3 shows pseudo-code for DataSqueezer.

D_P and D_N store positive and negative examples in tables, where rows represent examples and columns represent attributes. POS denotes table of positive examples and N_{POS} denotes the number of positive examples, while the table

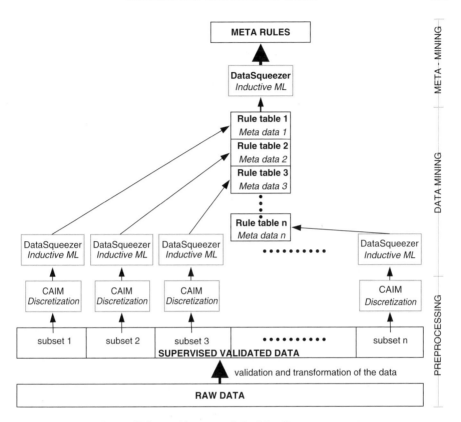

Figure 17.2. Architecture of the MetaSqueezer system.

and the number of negative examples are denoted NEG and N_{NEG}, respectively. Positive examples from the POS table are described by the set of values: $\text{pos}_i[j]$, where $j = 1, \ldots, K$, is the column number, and i is the example number (row number in the POS table). The negative examples are described similarly by a set of $\text{neg}_i[j]$ values. The DataSqueezer algorithm also uses tables that store intermediate results (G_{POS} for POS table, and G_{NEG} for NEG table), which have K columns. $\text{Gpos}_i[j]$ denotes a cell of the G_{POS}, where i is a row number and j is a column number, and similarly $\text{Gneg}_i[j]$ is a cell for the G_{NEG}. The G_{POS} table stores reduced subset of the data from POS, and similarly G_{NEG} for the data from NEG. The meaning of this reduction is explained later.

DataSqueezer generates production rules using an inductive learning hypothesis that states that any hypothesis found to approximate the target function well (defined by a class attribute), over a sufficiently large set of training examples, will also approximate well the target function over other unobserved examples (Mitchell, 1997). Based on this assumption in step 1, the algorithm first performs data reduction, which generalizes information stored in the input dataset, via prototypical concept learning, similar to the Mitchell's Find S algorithm (Mitchell,

Given: POS, NEG, K (number of attributes), S (number of examples)
Step1.
1.1   Initialize G_{POS} = []; i=1; j=1; k=1; tmp = pos_1;
1.2.1   **for** k = 1 to K   // *for all attributes*
1.2.2   **if** ($pos_j[k] \neq tmp[k]$ **or** $pos_j[k]$ = '*')
1.2.3   **then** tmp[k]='*';   // *'*' denotes missing value*
1.2.4   **if** (number of non missing values in tmp $\geqslant$ 2)
1.2.5   **then** $gpos_i$ = tmp; $gpos_i$[K+1] ++;
1.2.6   **else** i ++; tmp = pos_j;
1.3   set j++; and until j $\leq$ N_{POS} go to 1.2.1
1.4   Initialize G_{NEG} = []; i=1; j=1; k=1; tmp = neg_1;
1.5.1   **for** k = 1 to K   // *for all attributes*
1.5.2   **if** ($neg_j[k] \neq tmp[k]$ **or** $neg_j[k]$ = '*')
1.5.3   **then** tmp[k]='*';   // *'*' denotes missing value*
1.5.4   **if** (number of non missing values in tmp $\geq$ 2)
1.5.5   **then** $gneg_i$ = tmp; $gneg_i$[K+1] ++;
1.5.6   **else** i ++; tmp = neg_j;
1.6   set j++; and until j $\leq N_{NEG}$ go to 1.5.1
Step2.
2.1   Initialize RULES = []; i=1;   // *where rules$_i$ denotes i^{th} rule stored in RULES*
2.2   create LIST = list of all columns in G_{POS}
2.3   within every column of G_{POS} that is on LIST, for every non missing value a
           from selected column k compute sum, s_{ak}, of values of $gpos_i$[K+1] for every
           row i, in which a appears (multiply every s_{ak}, by the number of values the
           attribute k has)
2.4   select maximal s_{ak}, remove k from LIST, add "k = a" selector to rules$_i$
2.5.1   **if** rules$_i$ does not describe any rows in G_{NEG}
2.5.2   **then** remove all rows described by rules$_i$ from G_{POS}, i=i+1;
2.5.3   **if** G_{POS} is not empty go to 2.2, **else** terminate
2.5.4   **else** go to 2.3
Output: RULES describing POS

Figure 17.3. Pseudo-code of the DataSqueezer algorithm.

1997). The algorithm starts with the most specific hypotheses that cover individual examples, and it iteratively uses a generalization operator that sequentially compares a current hypothesis with an example from input data and removes all attribute values that are not identical (between them).

In step 2 the algorithm generates rules by performing a greedy hill-climbing search on the reduced data. A rule is generated by starting with an empty rule and then adding selectors until the termination criterion fires. The max depth of the search is equal to the number of attributes. The examples covered by the generated rule are then removed, and the process is repeated.

The DataSqueezer algorithm generates production rules that involve no more than one selector per attribute, which allows for storing rules in a table that has identical structure to the original data table. The table is used as input to the same algorithm, which allows using the algorithm in a MM setting. The algorithms can also handle data with a large number of missing values by simply using all available information while ignoring the missing values. The data reduction procedure of the algorithm sorts out all missing values. Every present value for every example is used to infer the rules. The algorithm has linear complexity, shown both theoretically and experimentally, with respect to the number of input examples (Kurgan, 2003).

Main Features of the MetaSqueezer System. The MetaSqueezer uses the DataSqueezer algorithm and the MM concept to generate production rules. First, the data are divided into subsets and production rules are generated for each of them by the DataSqueezer. Next, the rules are converted into the same format as the input data, concatenated into a single set, and fed back to the DataSqueezer to generate meta-rules.

The main benefits of the MetaSqueezer system are compactness of the generated meta-rules and low computational cost (Kurgan, 2003; Kurgan and Cios, 2004a). While many other ML and DM algorithms generate rules directly from input data, the MetaSqueezer system generates meta-rules from previously generated meta-data. This results in significantly smaller number of selectors used. Low computational cost of the MetaSqueezer system is the result of its linear complexity, which is determined by complexity of the DataSqueezer algorithm and is linear with respect to the number of examples (Kurgan, 2003; Kurgan and Cios, 2004a). Because of the division of the data at the DM step, the system can be used to analyze ordered data. One example is temporal data that can be divided into subsets corresponding to time intervals. CF data are a good example since it describes patients over a period of time, with patients being at different stages of the disease.

One of the specific features of the MetaSqueezer system is the ability to generate an alternative representation of the meta-rules, which we call the attribute and selector ranking tables. The tables describe a degree of association of particular attributes and attribute-value pairs with the target class in an easy to comprehend manner. The tables are generated from rules (Cios and Kurgan, 2004b; Kurgan, 2003). The construction of a table is based on computing goodness of each attribute and attribute–value pair using rules generated by the MetaSqueezer system, or the DataSqueezer algorithm. The goodness values are computed in three steps:

- Each rule consists of multiple selectors (attribute–value pairs) and has assigned a goodness value equal to the percentage of data that describe the same class as the rule and is described by the rule.

- Each selector is assigned a goodness value equal to the goodness of the rule it comes from. Goodness of the same selectors from different rules are summed and are then scaled to the (0,100) range.

- For each attribute, the sum of scaled goodness for all its selectors is computed and divided by the number of attribute values to obtain goodness value of the attribute.

The goodness values for each attribute and attribute–value pair are grouped into three intervals: zero, which stands for no association; zero to fifty, which denotes an association; and over fifty, which denotes strong association between a given attribute and attribute–value pair and the class value. The associations are visualized in a table, where rows correspond to attributes and attribute–value pairs, and columns to classes. An example is shown later in the chapter. Development of the tables resulted in significantly simplified analysis and interpretation of the results.

Discretization. The MetaSqueezer system, like many other inductive ML algorithms, handles only discrete data. This is the result of applying the data reduction procedure, which performs well only with attributes that have a low number of values. Therefore for data that contain continuous attributes, it uses a front-end supervised discretization algorithm.

Discretization is a process of dividing a continuous attribute into a finite set of intervals to generate an attribute with small number of distinct values, by associating discrete numerical value with each of the generated intervals. A supervised discretization algorithm uses the class values assigned to input examples to achieve possibly the best correlation between the discrete intervals and target classes, and therefore to minimize the information loss associated with discretization.

The MetaSqueezer algorithm uses the F-CAIM (fast class attribute interdependency maximization) algorithm to perform discretization (Kurgan and Cios, 2003, 2004b). We briefly describe the algorithm next. We assume that each value of a continuous attribute can be classified into only one of the n, non-overlapping, discrete intervals and can describe one of S classes. The class values and the discretization intervals of attribute F are treated as two random variables defining a two-dimensional frequency matrix (called quanta matrix) that is shown in Table 17.2, where q_{ir} is the total number of continuous values belonging to the ith class that are within interval $(d_{r-1}, d_r]$, M_{i+} is the total number of values

TABLE 17.2. Two-Dimensional Quanta Matrix

Class		Interval			
	$[d_0, d_1]$	...	$(d_{r-1}, d_r]$	...	$(d_{n-1}, d_n]$	Class Total
C_1	q_{11}	...	q_{1r}	...	q_{1n}	M_{1+}
⋮	⋮	...	⋮	...	⋮	⋮
C_i	q_{i1}	...	q_{ir}	...	q_{in}	M_{i+}
⋮	⋮	...	⋮	...	⋮	⋮
C_S	q_{S1}	...	q_{Sr}	...	q_{Sn}	M_{S+}
Interval Total	M_{+1}	...	M_{+r}	...	M_{+n}	M

belonging to the ith class, and M_{+r} is the total number of values of attribute F that are within the interval $(d_{r-1}, d_r]$, for $i = 1, 2, \ldots, S$ and, $r = 1, 2, \ldots, n$.

The F-CAIM algorithm uses the class attribute interdependency maximization (CAIM) criterion to measure the dependency (correlation) between the classes C and the discrete intervals D, for a given continuous attribute F, and its quanta matrix, which is defined as

$$CAIM(C, D|F) = \frac{\sum_{r=1}^{n} \dfrac{\max_r^2}{M_{+r}}}{n} \tag{17.1}$$

where r iterates through all intervals; that is, $r = 1, 2, \ldots, n$, max_r is the maximum value among all q_{ir} values (maximum value within the rth column of the quanta matrix), and $i = 1, 2, \ldots, S$, M_{+r} is the total number of continuous values of attribute F that are within the interval $(d_{r-1}, d_r]$.

In general, the optimal discretization, in terms of minimal information loss, can be found by searching over the space of all possible discretization schemes to find the one with the highest value of the CAIM criterion. Since such a search is highly combinatorial, the F-CAIM algorithm uses a greedy approach, which searches for the approximate optimal value of the CAIM criterion by finding locally maximum values of the criterion. Although this approach does not guarantee finding the global maximum, it is computationally inexpensive and well-approximates the optimal discretization scheme (Kurgan and Cios, 2003, 2004b). The algorithm consists of two steps. First, it initializes candidate interval boundaries, which define all possible boundaries of discrete intervals, and the initial discrete interval. Next, it performs consecutive additions of a new boundary that results in the locally highest value of the CAIM criterion. More specifically, the algorithm starts with a single interval that covers all possible values of a continuous attribute. It initializes candidate boundary points with minimum, maximum, and all the midpoints of all the adjacent values, but only for the values that describe different classes. The algorithm computes the CAIM criterion values for all possible division points (with replacement), and it chooses the division boundary that gives the highest value. It stops adding new boundary points when the best CAIM value for a current discretization schema is smaller than the highest CAIM value achieved so far.

The algorithm was recently compared with six other state-of-the-art discretization algorithms (Kurgan and Cios, 2003), including (a) two unsupervised algorithms, namely, equal width and equal frequency (Chiu et al., 1991), and (b) four supervised algorithms, namely, Paterson–Niblett (Paterson and Niblett, 1987), information entropy maximization (Fayyad and Irani, 1993), maximum entropy (Wong and Chiu, 1987), and CADD (Ching et al., 1995). The comparison showed that the F-CAIM algorithm generates discretization schemes with, on average, the lowest number of intervals and the highest dependence between classes and discrete intervals, outperforming other discretization algorithms. The execution time of the F-CAIM algorithm is, on average, shorter than the execution time of all considered supervised discretization algorithms, while still being comparable to the time of the two fastest supervised discretization algorithms. The analysis of performance of the F-CAIM algorithm also showed that the small number of intervals that the algorithm generates helps to reduce the size of the data and also improves accuracy and the number of rules that are generated by subsequently used ML algorithms (Kurgan and Cios, 2003, 2004a).

Significance. After extensive literature search, we found only one other application of inductive ML techniques to analysis of temporal medical data. A system that discovers limited temporal relations using Bayesian networks and the C4.5 algorithm (Quinlan, 1993) was used to find relations between consecutive records, without generalizing temporal rules for the entire period of time (Karimi and Hamilton, 2000). Although the MetaSqueezer system does not discover any temporal relationships, it can be used to derive nontemporal patterns, in terms of production rules. The rules describe the data across time, but using meta-data that describe data within particular data subsets that represent temporal intervals.

Applications of Inductive Machine Learning in Medicine. Inductive ML techniques found a number of applications in analysis of medical data. They range from automated diagnostic systems to prognosis. Since it is virtually impossible to list all applications, below we describe only a few representative examples. They include diagnosis and prognosis of breast cancer (Street et al., 1995; Wolberg et al., 1994), prognosis of the survival in hepatitis (Kononenko et al., 1984), prognosis of traumatic brain injuries (Andrews et al., 2002), and diagnosis of cardiac SPECT images (Kurgan et al., 2001). Most recently, inductive ML has found its use in bioinformatics [analysis of genetic data (Berrar et al., 2001), analysis of mass spectrometry data (Wu et al., 2003; Baumgartner et al., 2004; Gunther et al., 2003)]. An overview of applications of ML in medicine is given in Kononenko (2001).

17.3. THE CYSTIC FIBROSIS PROJECT

17.3.1. Understanding the Problem Domain

CF is a genetic disease affecting approximately 30,000 children and adults in the United States (Cystic Fibrosis Foundation, 2002). One in 31 Americans and one in 28 Caucasians carry the defective gene causing CF, which translates into more than 10 million carriers in the United States. Carriers do not exhibit the symptoms, and thus they do not know about their risk for transmitting the disease to their offspring. An individual must inherit a defective copy of the CF gene from each parent to be affected. Statistically, when two carriers conceive a child, there is a 25% chance that the child will have CF, a 50% chance that the child will be a carrier, and a 25% chance that the child will be a noncarrier. CF is caused by at least 1000 different genetic mutations in the cystic fibrosis transmembrane conductance regulator (CFTR) gene. The delta F508 mutation accounts for approximately 70% of the mutations, making it the most common CF mutation (Cystic Fibrosis Genetic Analysis Consortium, 1990; Cystic Fibrosis Mutation Database, 2003).

CF is a deadly disease that affects multiple systems, including the respiratory system, digestive system, endocrine system, and reproductive system. The symptoms are variable and may include high chloride and sodium (salt) concentration in the sweat, lung disease (persistent coughing, wheezing, or pneumonia), excessive appetite but poor weight gain, and bulky stools. The vast majority of CF-related mortality is caused by the progressive lung disease, caused by a vicious cycle of infection and inflammation. Thus, lung function tests are recognized as very good indicators of the stage of the disease. CF is diagnosed usually by the sweat test, which measures amount of salt in the sweat. A high chloride level indicates that a person has CF. The treatment of CF depends upon multiple factors like stage of the disease and which organs are involved. In case of the most severely affected organ, the lungs, the disease is treated usually by chest physical therapy and antibiotics, which are used to treat lung infections (Cystic Fibrosis Foundation, 2002). The CF data are temporal in nature. It describes several hundreds of CF patients. For each patient, multiple visits are recorded. Most of the patients are monitored from the time of diagnosis throughout childhood and are currently being followed, while some patients died during the followup period. For each visit, multiple attributes describing demographical information, various lab results, and diagnostic information are recorded. The data describe different relationships depending on the stage of the disease. Thus, any investigation that uses such data must be able to separate the data into subsets, corresponding to particular stages of the disease.

Before the project was started, the CF experts were requested to provide only the necessary minimum background knowledge. This was done to ensure that the research would not be biased toward finding solutions that would confirm accuracy of the system based on the domain knowledge. The project goals defined by clinicians were as follows:

1. **Goal 1** is to discover patterns (important factors) that influence the pace of development of CF. Although CF affects multiple systems, the pulmonary system is the best indicator of progression of the disease. For some patients the disease progresses very fast, while for others its progress is relatively slow. There are some known factors that are related to the pace of the disease, but still much is unknown. The first goal was to discover factors that are related to different, predefined genotypes of CF based on historical data and the paces of disease development.

2. **Goal 2** is to discover important factors that are related to particular kinds of CF. CF is a genetic disease, and different distinct genotypes related to it are described. The goal was to find factors that are related to different, predefined genotypes of CF.

In the next step we redefined the above two goals into DM goals:

1. **Goal 1**. It can be defined as a supervised inductive learning task. Class attribute must be defined, which will group the data into subsets corresponding to patients who exhibit different paces of disease development. Since the data are temporal in nature, an additional attribute is used to divide the data according to time. The attribute will describe the stage of the disease based on the status of a pulmonary function test.

2. **Goal 2**. Again, it can be defined as a supervised inductive learning task. Thus, a class attribute that describes patients in terms of the particular type of CF must be defined. Next, the data must be divided in a temporal manner by using attribute(s) describing patient's lung function.

After analyzing both goals, the MetaSqueezer system was chosen as the appropriate DM tool. There are three main factors that influenced the choice of the system:

- It generates small number of very simple rules. The project required physicians to be able to analyze and comprehend the rules, and the results to be displayed in an easy to understand tabular form.
- It can handle large quantities of missing values. CF data contains large quantities of missing information. The DataSqueezer algorithm, a core inductive ML algorithm used within the system, was proven to generate accurate results in presence of significant amount of missing information (Kurgan, 2003; Kurgan and Cios, 2004a).
- It can handle temporal data. CF data are temporal in nature. The DM step of the MetaSqueezer system accepts multiple training data subsets, which represent temporally organized subsets of the original CF data.

17.3.2. Understanding the Data

The data were collected at the CF Center based at the University of Colorado Health Sciences Center and the Children's Hospital in Denver starting in 1982. It includes demographical information about patients, clinical information including a variety of lab tests, and diagnoses. The data were collected on 856 patients. The data were stored using seven relational tables. To comply with the HIPPA requirements, all identification information was removed from the data before it was used in the project. The resulting data hold only relevant clinical information. There are several complicating issues with the CF data. First, as expected, they contain a significant amount of missing information. For example, three tables contain more than half of missing information. Second, it can also be expected that since the data were inserted manually by the physicians, they will contain also substantial amount of incorrect records. Also, the tables contain different attributes—numerical, textual, and binary—which need to be handled by the learning algorithm. The tables also possibly include large quantities of irrelevant information, which may be removed before the learning process is executed.

The attributes used to define classes for both goals and to divide the data into temporal intervals are described below:

- FEV$_1$% (forced expiratory volume in one second % predicted) attribute describes the amount of air that can be forced out in one second after taking a deep breath. The volume that an individual patient can blow out in one second is compared to a normal population, and the percent of predicted based on the patients age, sex, and height is reported as the FEV$_1$%. In CF, the test result indicates the stage of the disease better than timestamp information, such as patient's age or visit date, because different patients are diagnosed and start treatment at different ages. The FEV$_1$% is used as the attribute to define temporal intervals for both goals. It is also used to define the class attribute for the first goal.

- Genotype 1 and Genotype 2 attributes describe genetic mutations and are used to distinguish different levels in severity in CF. Since the second mining goal is to find important factors that are related to particular kinds of CF, combination of the two attributes will be used to provide class labels for the goal.

In summary, the data were assumed to hold all information necessary to carry out the project. More specifically, several attributes that may be used to derive classes and temporal subsets for both learning goals were identified.

17.3.3. Preparation of the Data

Before the CF data could be used to generate rules, they needed to be preprocessed. This usually involves removing or correcting noise and missing values, sampling and reorganizing the data, assigning classes to examples, identifying temporal intervals, and so on. The cleaned data are later discretized. As with most DM projects, it is expected that this step consumes most of any project's time since data preparation greatly affects the outcome of the entire project (Cabena et al., 1998; Cios and Kurgan, 2004a).

At the first step, manual data checking and cleaning were performed. As expected, the CF data contained significant amount of errors and inconsistencies. Problems connected with physician's interpretation that is written in an unstructured free-text English (text fields in the database), which is very difficult to standardize and thus difficult to mine (Cios and Moore, 2002), were encountered. For instance, the values of the FEV$_1$% attribute should be in the range [0; 200], but some records had bigger values. Another problem is the presence of null attributes, which have null values for all tuples (rows) and thus should be deleted. Almost all tables in the CF data contained attributes that were null.

Two main manual operations were performed to clean the CF data. First, the consistency of attributes was corrected by merging together their corresponding values. This operation is caused by inconsistent format of data; for example, *Yes*, *Y*, *yes* were entered as corresponding to the same value and were corrected. Next, erroneous values of attributes were identified and removed. After the data were cleaned, they were converted into a single relational table. In order to merge the seven tables, several join operations were performed. The tables were merged in pairs, where results of one join operation were merged with the next table. The condition of the join operations were designed and consulted with clinicians to ensure proper handling of medical information.

The next data preparation step consisted of removing attributes that are irrelevant to the planned goals. After consultation with the physicians, attributes that were found either irrelevant from the medical point of view or containing too much noise or missing information were removed.

Class Attributes. There are two class attributes, one per each goal. The first attribute describes the pace of CF development, which is used to define classes for goal 1. The attribute was derived based on "visdate1" and "$FEV_1\%$" attributes using a procedure that was designed with cooperation with clinicians. The first goal was defined as the four-class supervised inductive learning task, with the following classes: FastDegrad (for fast degrading patients), SlowDegrad (for slowly degrading patients), NoChange (for patients with no change in lung functions), and Improv (for patients for whom there was improvement). The second class attribute describes different types of CF and is used to define classes for goal 2. The attribute was derived based on "Genotype 1" and "Genotype 2" attributes using a procedure that was designed with cooperation with clinicians. Three kinds of CF were defined: (1) Both Genotype 1 and Genotype 2 are F508, (2) Genotype 1 is F508 or Genotype 2 is F508, with the other genotype not being F508, and (3) both Genotype 1 and Genotype 2 are not F508 (Kurgan, 2003).

Time-Defining Attribute. The time-defining attribute, used to divide the data into subsets for the DM step of the MetaSqueezer system, was derived from the $FEV_1\%$ attribute. There were five discrete values of the attribute generated, which means that the input data were divided into five coherent subsets depending on the value of the $FEV_1\%$ attribute, that is, $<40\%$, $40-60\%$, $60-80\%$, $80-100\%$, and $>100\%$ (Kurgan, 2003).

Discretization. After deriving class and time-defining attributes, the data were discretized. First, each attribute was manually evaluated to belong to one of three categories:

- *Discrete.* An attribute was defined as discrete if it had a small number of values, up to about 20 distinct values. The discrete attributes were left unchanged.

- *Continuous, for Manual Discretization.* An attribute was defined as continuous for manual discretization if it had a large number of distinct values, and its values had a well-known specific meaning with respect to CF. These attributes were discretized manually by clinicians to accommodate for medical meaning of their values; for example, certain test values may be usually associated with specific medical conditions.

- *Continuous, for Automated Discretization.* Attributes that are characterized by a large number of distinct values, with no known medical relationship of their values and CF, were considered continuous for automated discretization. Those attributes were discretized by the supervised discretization algorithm F-CAIM. Each attribute was discretized separately for each goal, since the discretization process uses class labels. More than 50% of continuous attributes fell into this category.

Training Data.   The objective for goal 1 was to discover factors related to different pace of development of CF. In short, the training set was derived from the original data by first removing noise and inconsistencies, merging the seven tables, removing irrelevant attributes, defining class and time-defining attributes, and finally discretizing the continuous attributes. Two more steps were performed to generate the final version of the training set: (1) examples that include incomplete critical information, in terms of class or temporal information, were removed; (2) examples that had too many missing values were removed. During the join, if a tuple from one table was not matched with a tuple from another table, it was padded with missing values. If an example was not matched during several subsequent joins and it contained many missing values, then it was treated as an outlier and removed.

The objective for goal 2 was to discover factors related to different types of CF. The training set for goal 2 was derived in the same way as the training set for goal 1, with a different class attribute. Summary information about training datasets is shown in Table 17.3.

The step of data preparation was highly iterative. The above description only describes the final outcome, which was derived after several iterations.

17.3.4. Data Mining

The DM task for both training sets was very difficult. The datasets are characterized by a very large number of missing values, and at the same time these missing values are distributed over a majority of attributes. For both datasets, all examples contain some missing values, and the total number of missing information is larger than the amount of complete information. Therefore, both datasets include sparse data, which are very difficult to handle while using ML algorithms. It can be expected that the data are very specific; that is, there may be

TABLE 17.3. Summary of Training Sets for the CF Project

Set	Size	Number of Classes	Number of Attributes	Test Data	Percentage of Missing Values	Percentage of Inconsistent Examples	# Subsets
CF1	5448	4	160	10CV	56.6	0	5
CF2	6022	3	160	10CV	56.2	0	5

very little common patterns between different patients, and thus generated rules may be long. The first factor was overcome by application of the MetaSqueezer system, which is proven to be missing values resistant. The second factor was overcome by development of an alternative knowledge representation. Production rules, generated by the MetaSqueezer, were transformed into tables, called rule and selector ranking tables, as described above.

Experimental Results. Both training sets were used as input to the Meta-Squeezer system, which generated a set of production rules. Next, the rules were evaluated by performing two tests for each of the defined goals:

- The first test takes the training set and performs 10-fold cross-validation (10 CV) with the same setting as for the second test. The results show verification test results, running time, and the number of rules and selectors for each of the runs, along with their mean values. The results of this test have shown simplicity, accuracy, efficiency, and flexibility of the system, but could not be used by the clinicians since ten different rule sets were generated. Instead, this test is used to validate results generated for the second test, using the same system settings. Tables 17.4 and 17.5 shows results on the training set for goals 1 and 2, respectively.

- The second test generates a set of rules from the entire training dataset. The rules are used to generate the attribute and selector ranking tables, and they are tested on the same training set. The results report accuracy on the training data, number of generated rules and selectors. These results are analyzed by clinicians. The summary of results for the second test is shown in Table 17.6 for both goals. The table also compares the results with the results obtained during the 10 CV tests.

The results report accuracy, sensitivity, and specificity, which are defined below. The verification test, which is frequently used in evaluating medical diagnostic procedures, gives much better and specific information about goodness of the generated rules, as compared with just reporting accuracy results (Cios and Moore, 2002). The verification test consists of these three evaluation criteria:

$$\text{sensitivity} = \frac{TP}{\text{hypothesis positive}} 100\% = \frac{TP}{TP + FN} 100\%$$

$$\text{specificity} = \frac{TN}{\text{hypothesis negative}} 100\% = \frac{TN}{FP + TN} 100\%$$

$$\text{accuracy} = \frac{TP + TN}{\text{total}} 100\% = \frac{TP + TN}{TP + TN + FP + FN} 100\%$$

where: "hypothesis positive" concerns rules for currently evaluated class; "hypothesis negative" concerns the remaining rules; TP (true positive) is the number of correct positive classifications; TN (true negative) is the number of correct negative classifications; FP (false positive) is the number of incorrect positive

TABLE 17.4. The 10-fold Cross-Validation Results for Goal 1

Trial	1	2	3	4	5	6	7	8	9	10	Standard Deviation	Mean
Accuracy	57.8	58.2	65.1	60.6	59.1	59.1	66.8	60.4	61.7	61.5	2.94	61.0
Specificity	88.9	89.3	90.2	88.8	90	89.6	91.2	90.5	91	89.8	0.8	89.9
Sensitivity	57	59.2	60.1	63.3	60.7	52.6	63.4	58.4	59	56.6	3.22	59.0
Time (ms)	8663	8501	8169	8537	8428	8794	8663	8360	8413	9010	239	1 m 25 s 53 ms
Number of Rules	452	448	428	494	493	345	470	435	356	434	50.5	436
Number of Selectors	4437	4320	4125	4710	4720	3393	4603	4213	3460	4196	467	4.22E+03

TABLE 17.5. The 10-fold Cross-Validation Results for Goal 2

Trial	1	2	3	4	5	6	7	8	9	10	Standard Deviation	Mean
Accuracy	57.4	54.1	69.8	41.3	53.6	51.1	73.8	71	69.3	73.1	11.3	61.4
Specificity	88.6	86.7	89.8	88.3	85.5	91.2	92.2	88.7	89	90.1	1.97	89
Sensitivity	71	67.5	66.4	54.6	64.1	57.4	73.8	73.2	68	76.9	7.11	67.3
Time [ms]	16918	16289	17865	15709	16626	15720	17550	17232	17765	17577	811	2 m 49 s 25 ms
Number of Rules	498	490	804	215	502	204	791	770	758	749	233	578
Number of Selectors	5211	5073	8387	2238	5240	2039	8307	8093	7916	7648	2.44E+3	6.02E+3

TABLE 17.6. The Summary of Test Results for Goal 1

Goal	Test Type	Accuracy	Number of Rules	Number of Selectors
Goal 1	Using training set	67.6	498	4838
	10 CV, mean values	61.0	436	4220
Goal 2	Using training set	77.2	790	4809
	10 CV, mean values	61.4	578	6020

classifications; and FN (false negative) is the number of incorrect negative classifications.

The results also report mean values for each criterion, averaged over all classes. The sensitivity measures how many of the examples classified by the rules as belonging to the currently evaluated class truly belong to this class. The specificity measures how many of the examples classified by the rules as not belonging to the currently evaluated class truly did not belong to it. They enable evaluation of how the rules perform on the part of the data they should describe (i.e., for the class they are intended to describe) versus their performance on the remaining part of the data. Only the results with high values for all three measures can ensure high confidence in the generated rules.

The results for the first goal show that the system generates accurate rules. Two factors need to be considered to evaluate accuracy of the system. First, the data contain only about 44% of complete information. Second, the default hypothesis, where the most frequent class is selected, for that training dataset has 34.2% accuracy. Therefore, the accuracy of 61% for 10 CV tests for rules generated by the MetaSqueezer system is satisfactory. The rules achieve high and comparable values for all tests: sensitivity, specificity, and accuracy, which show their high quality. The simplicity of results generated by the system is also high. The system generates only 436 rules for sparse input data containing almost 6000 examples described by 160 attributes. Considering the input data, the average number of selectors per rule, which is 9.7, is low. The system generates the rules in about 86 seconds, which is a very good result considering the size of the training set.

The results for the second goal also show that the system generates accurate rules. We note that the data contain only about 44% of complete information, and the default hypothesis for that training set has 46.0% accuracy. The reported accuracy is 61%. All values of the verification test are comparably high. The system generated 578 rules. The average number of selectors per rule, which is 10.4, is low. In general, results achieved by the MetaSqueezer for the training data describing goal 2 are comparable, in terms of quality, to the results achieved for goal 1.

The summary results for both goals show that the MetaSqueezer generates slightly more accurate rules when using the entire training set as input. This shows that the results presented to clinicians were not overfitted.

17.3.5. Evaluation of the Discovered Knowledge

The DM step generated two sets of rules, one for each of the defined goals. The rules were transformed into the rule and selector tables, which were presented to CF experts. The tables were analyzed by them using the following four-grade scale:

- 1+ was assigned for trivial, not useful results. By default, such a mark was simply omitted from being displayed on the table. The associations described by that mark are considered not useful from the medical perspective.

- 2+ was assigned for results that are of little interest. The associations described by that mark are considered of marginal value from the medical perspective.

- 3+ was assigned for interesting, but already known, results. The associations described by that mark are considered interesting, but were already discovered by other researchers. Such results are used to provide validation of the results generated by the system.

- 4+ was assigned for very interesting and unknown results. The associations described by that mark are of the highest value, since they show very important findings that are not yet confirmed or reported in the professional literature. Such findings, if found, are the basis for evaluating the entire project as successful.

The evaluation was performed by our CF expert. The analysis of the results was performed manually based on the attribute and selector ranking tables. The tables and the evaluation of the findings for goals 1 and 2 are shown, using marks, in Tables 17.7 and 17.8, respectively. The tables show only attributes that are assigned marks 2+, 3+, and 4+ (Kurgan, 2003).

The results generated by the MetaSqueezer system for goal 1 are divided into two parts:

- Confirmatory results marked by 3+ describe relationships that were known previously, but give confidence in the correctness of the performed analysis:

  - Black race and improvement of the disease; the finding suggests that the patients who are black may have less severe disease, possibly less severe CF mutations or other genetic modifiers.

  - C group and degradation of the disease for small values of $FEV_1\%$; the finding suggests that patients who are conventionally diagnosed may have a faster decline in FEV_1 during advanced stages of the disease.

  - NBS groups and improvement of the disease; the finding suggests that the benefits of newborn screening may result in stable or improving lung function in childhood, which may be the result of closer follow-up in early childhood.

TABLE 17.7. The Evaluation of Results for Goal 1

ATTRIBUTE	VALUE	MARK	CLASS FASTDEGRAD					CLASS IMPROV					CLASS NOCHANGE					CLASS SLOWDEGRAD				
			TI 1	TI 2	TI 3	TI 4	TI 5	TI 1	TI 2	TI 3	TI 4	TI 5	TI 1	TI 2	TI 3	TI 4	TI 5	TI 1	TI 2	TI 3	TI 4	TI 5
CFtypes (cf)	Type4	2+																				
race (dem)	Black	3+																				
group (dem)	C	3+/4+																				
group (dem)	NBS	3+/4+																				
group (dem)	MI	3+/4+																				
group (dem)	FN	3+/4+																				
motage (dem)	[22.50,48.50)	3+																				
motage (dem)	[19.50,22.50)	3+																				
mecil (dem)	TreatedSurgically	2+																				
sweatelectr1 (dia)	[24.50,46.00)	4+																				
sweatelectr2 (dia)	[−11.00,95.50)	3+																				
tobraresistent?(cul)	Suscept.	2+																				
na (mic)	[129.00,143.00)	2+																				
prot (mic)	[−1.95,7.95)	2+																				
vita (mic)	[0.44,748.00)	2+																				
wbc (hem)	[4.05,18.00)	2+																				
hct (hem)	[27.40,45.50)	2+																				
mch (hem)	[24.90,91.40)	2+																				
mchc (hem)	[30.40,35.80)	2+																				
rdw(hem)	[−0.85,15.40)	2+																				
HAZ (per)	[−2.91,−1.87)	3+																				
age@diagnosis(dia)	025till2	3+																				

TABLE 17.8. The Evaluation of Results for Goal 2

ATTRIBUTE	VALUE	MARK	CLASS TYPE1					CLASS TYPE2					CLASS TYPE4				
			TI 1	TI 2	TI 3	TI 4	TI 5	TI 1	TI 2	TI 3	TI 4	TI 5	TI 1	TI 2	TI 3	TI 4	TI 5
CFpace (cf)	Improv	3+															
group (dem)	C	2+															
group (dem)	NBS	2+															
irt1 (dia)	[391.00,759.00)	3+															

- MI and FN groups and improvement of the disease for small values of $FEV_1\%$; the finding suggests that presence of meconium ileus at birth and presenting as a false negative on the newborn screen are associated with the improvement in $FEV_1\%$ for low values of $FEV_1\%$.

- [22.50,48.50) values of motage and improvement or stable state of the disease; the finding suggests that children of mothers over the age of 22 years tend to have stable lung function.

- [19.50,22.50) values of motage and degradation of the disease for medium values of FEV$_1$%; the finding suggests that children with moderate lung disease who have young mothers (between 19.5 and 22.5 years) tend to have a greater decline in lung function.

- [−11.00,95.50) values of sweatelectr2 and improvement of the disease; the finding suggests that children with lower sweat chloride values (<95.5) may have less severe lung disease.

- [−2.91, −1.87) values of HAZ and degradation of the disease for small values of FEV$_1$%; this finding suggests that children with height stunting and severe disease may have a rapid decline in FEV$_1$.

- 025till2 values of age@diagnosis and degradation of the disease; the finding suggests that children who were diagnosed after the initial newborn period may have a more rapid decline in pulmonary function.

- new findings marked by 4+ describe findings that may be significant medically:

  - [24.50,46.00) value of sweatelectr1 and the improvement of the disease; the finding suggests that there is a possible significance of sweat electrolytes.

The results show not only that the mining system generated accurate results for goal 1, based on 10 confirmatory findings, but also that the system discovered one significant finding that concerns sweat electrolytes levels.

The results generated by the MetaSqueezer system for goal 2 include only several confirmatory findings:

- Improvement of the disease and Type 4 CF; the finding suggests that children with 2 non-F508 mutations may have mild lung disease.

- [391.00,759.00) values of irt1 and Type 1 CF for medium values of FEV$_1$%; the finding suggests that children with high IRT values at birth have moderate lung disease.

The results show that the system generated accurate results for goal 2, based on 2 confirmatory findings. No new and significant findings were discovered.

17.3.6. Using the Discovered Knowledge

The six-step DMKD process has proven to be very practical. The iterative process used for generation of results significantly improved the results generated by the MetaSqueezer system. The system generated two kinds of results: 12 confirmatory findings that prove the correctness of our DM effort, and most importantly one significant new finding that shows that the system is capable of generation of useful results.

The outcome of the project was evaluated to be very successful by the CF experts. The new finding discovered for goal 1 was classified as possibly medically significant, and it may help to bring new clinical insight into this deadly disease. The discovered information currently undergoes detailed medical scrutiny before it can find a possible clinical application.

17.3.7. Refining the Project

The steps described earlier were performed in a highly iterative manner, a common practice in all DMKD projects. Below we provide the summary of iterations,

TABLE 17.9. Summary of the Refinements Performed during the Analysis of the CF Data

Current DMKD Step	Returned to	Reasons for Modifications	Summary of Modifications
Data mining	Preparation of the data	Incomplete and difficult to evaluate results	Modification of the join operation, hand-coded discretization of several attributes, removal of several irrelevant attributes, redesign of the "CF pace" attribute, new format of displaying the results
Evaluation of the discovered knowledge	Understanding of the data	Unsatisfactory results	New data table describing weight and height percentiles was added, modification of the join operation to accommodate for the new table, hand-coded discretization of several attributes that were discretized automatically, deletion of examples with high number of missing values, removal of several irrelevant attributes
Evaluation of the discovered knowledge	Data mining	Invalidated results	Ten fold cross-validation test procedures, improvement in the new format of displaying the results, removed minor data inconsistencies

including description of changes and reasons for them. Since the beginning of the project the CF data were identified as very challenging for reasons, such as very large amount of missing information, incorrect records, and the complex structure of the CF data. The project was performed slowly, with several iterations and careful revisions of the intermediary results. Several formal meetings with CF experts were held to evaluate the progress and direct the research in addition to many informal meetings and discussions. The results of the meetings are summarized in Table 17.9, which shows all major iterations during the CF project.

The shown iterations represent only the major modifications performed during the project. They were done at different steps of the DMKD process and resulted in the refinement of the process by returning, modifying, and repeating some of the previously performed steps. The redesign was guided by both medical and the DM experts. The main reason for the refinements was unsatisfactory quality of initial results. The modifications resulted in improving quality of the training sets and quality of the representation of the results. It is important to note that all of the performed refinements resulted in substantial and gradual improvement of the final results.

17.4. SUMMARY

This chapter describes results of mining in cystic fibrosis data, which is used as a case study to illustrate major issues facing data-mining researchers.

Very often, selection of a proper DM tool can significantly help in achieving a successful outcome of the DMKD project. As an example, the MetaSqueezer system helped to solve issues like dealing with a large number of missing data and generation of easily understandable format of the results. Mining in CF data was used to illustrate key issues facing researchers and practitioners of DM:

- *Extensive Preprocessing.* One of the important characteristics of the DMKD process is the relative amount of time spent to complete each of the steps. One of the most expensive steps is the data preparation, or preprocessing, step. The estimates for the length of this step vary—60% (Cabena et al., 1998), 30–60%, (Cios and Kurgan, 2004a), and 30% (Hirji, 2001)—, depending on the application domain and the status of the existing original data. The reasons for extensive preprocessing time include: large amount of erroneous data, redundancy and inconsistency of the data, and lack of all the necessary data to achieve success (Redman, 1998).

- *Iterative Nature of DMKD Projects.* The majority of DMKD projects are performed in a highly iterative manner, where the final results are achieved after performing a number of feedback loops, leading to reevaluation, redesign, and repeated execution of some of the earlier steps. It is important to (a) recognize this necessity ahead of time and (b) use a DMKD process model that can properly accommodate for the feedback mechanism.

- *Interdisciplinary Nature of DMKD Projects.* The main portion of the DMKD project concerns performing analysis of data that span multiple domains. This directly leads to the necessity of close collaboration between people from different disciplines—for example, medical and DM. Currently, even more multidisciplinary projects are initiated because of the increased complexity of the data and a general trend to use integrated data sources.

Being aware of the above-described issues before one starts a DM project helps to reduce costs and shorten time to generation of meaningful results.

REFERENCES

Andrews, P. J., Sleeman, D., Sathan, P., McQuatt, A., Corruble, V., and Jones, P. A., Forecasting recovery after traumatic brain injury using intelligent data analysis of admission variables and time series physiological data—a comparison with logistic regression, *Journal of Neurosurgery* **97**, 326–336 (2002).

Baumgartner, C., Baumgartner, D., and Boehm, C., Classification on high dimensional metabolic data: Phenylketonuria as an example, in *Proceedings of Second International Conference on Biomedical Engineering* (BioMED2004), Innsbruck, Austria, pp. 357–360, 2004.

Berrar, D., Granzow, M., Dubitzky, W., Wilgenbus, K., Stilgenbauer, S., Döhner, H., Lichter, P., and Eils, R., New insights in clinical impact of molecular genetic data by knowledge-driven data mining, in *Proceedings of the Second International Conference on Systems Biology*, Omnipress, Wisconsin, pp. 275–281, 2001.

Boros, E., Hammer, P. L., Ibaraki, T., Kogan, A., Mayoraz, E., and Muchnik, I., An implementation of logical analysis of Data, *IEEE Transactions on Knowledge and Data Engineering* **12**(2), 292–306 (2000).

Breiman, L., Friedman, J., Olshen, R., and Stone, C., *Classification and Regression Trees*, Chapman and Hall, New York, 1984.

Cabena, P., Hadjinian, X., Stadler, R., Verhees, J., and Zanasi, A., *Discovering Data Mining: From Concepts to Implementation*, Prentice-Hall, Englewood Cliffs, NJ, 1998.

Ching, J. Y., Wong, A. K., and Chan, K. C., Class-dependent discretization for inductive learning from continuous and mixed mode data, *IEEE Transactions on Pattern Analysis and Machine Intelligence* **17**(7), 641–651 (1995).

Chiu, D., Wong, A., and Cheung, B., Information discovery through hierarchical maximum entropy discretization and synthesis, in *Knowledge Discovery in Databases*, Piatetsky-Shapiro, G., and Frowley, W. J., eds., MIT Press, Cambridge, MA, pp. 125–140, 1991.

Cios, K. J., ed., *Medical Data Mining and Knowledge Discovery*, Springer, Berlin, 2001.

Cios, K. J., and Kurgan, L. A., Hybrid inductive machine learning: An overview of CLIP algorithms, in Jain, L. C., and Kacprzyk, J., eds., *New Learning Paradigms in Soft Computing*, Physica-Verlag (Springer), Berlin, pp. 276–322, 2001.

Cios, K. J., and Kurgan, L. A., Trends in data mining and knowledge discovery, in *Knowledge Discovery in Advanced Information Systems*, Pal, N. R., Jain, L. C., and Teoderesku, N., eds., Springer, Berlin, in press 2004a.

Cios, K. J., and Kurgan, L. A., CLIP4: Hybrid inductive machine learning algorithm that generates inequality rules, *Information Sciences* (special issue on Soft Computing Data Mining) **163**(1–3), 37–83, (2004b).

Cios, K. J., and Moore, G. W., Uniqueness of medical data mining, *Artificial Intelligence in Medicine* **26**(1–2), 1–24 (2002).

Cios, K. J., Pedrycz, W., and Swiniarski, R., *Data Mining Methods for Knowledge Discovery*, Kluwer, Dordrecht, 1998.

Cios, K. J., Teresinska, A., Konieczna, S., Potocka, J., and Sharma, S., Diagnosing myocardial perfusion from PECT bull's-eye maps—a knowledge discovery approach, *IEEE Engineering in Medicine and Biology Magazine* (special issue on Medical Data Mining and Knowledge Discovery) **19**(4), 17–25 (2000).

Clark, P., and Niblett, T., The CN2 algorithm, *Machine Learning*, **3**, 261–283 (1989).

Cohen, W. W., Fast effective rule induction, in *Proceedings of the Twelfth International Conference on Machine Learning*, Morgan Kaufmann, San Francisco, pp. 115–123, 1995.

Cohen, W. W., and Singer, Y., A simple, fast, and effective rule learner, in *Proceedings of the Sixteenth National Conference on Artificial Intelligence*, AAAI Press, Menlo Park, CA, pp. 335–342, 1999.

Cortes, C., and Vapnik, V. N., Support vector networks, *Machine Learning* **20**, 273–279 (1995).

Cystic Fibrosis Foundation, http://www.cff.org/, 2002.

Cystic Fibrosis Mutation Database, http://www.genet.sickkids.on.ca/cftr/, 2003.

Cystic Fibrosis Genetic Analysis Consortium, Worldwide survey of the [Delta]F508 mutation—report from the Cystic Fibrosis Genetic Analysis Consortium, *American Journal of Human Genetics* **47**, 354–359 (1990).

Domingos, P., The RISE system: Conquering without separating, in *Proceedings of the Sixth IEEE International Conference on Tools with Artificial Intelligence*, New Orleans, LA, IEEE Computer Society Press, Los Alamitos, CA, pp. 704–707, 1994.

Fayyad, U. M., and Irani, K. B., Multi-interval discretization of continuous-valued attributes for classification learning, in *Proceedings of the Thirteenth International Joint Conference on Artificial Intelligence*, San Francisco, CA, pp. 1022–1027, 1993.

Fayyad, U. M., Piatetsky-Shapiro, G., and Smyth, P., Knowledge discovery and data mining: Towards a unifying framework, in *Proceedings of the Second International Conference on Knowledge Discovery and Data Mining* (KDD96), Portland, OR, AAAI Press, Menlo Park, CA, 1996.

Furnkranz, J., and Widmer, G., Incremental reduced error pruning, in *Machine Learning: Proceedings of the Eleventh Annual Conference*, New Brunswick, New Jersey, Morgan Kaufmann, San Francisco, 1994.

Gunther, E. C., Stone, D. J., Gerwien, R. W., Bento, P., and Heyes, M. P., Prediction of clinical drug efficacy by classification of drug-induced genomic expression profiles in vitro, *Proceedings of the National Academy of Sciences USA* **100**, 9608–9613 (2003).

Hirji, K. K., Exploring data mining implementation, *Communications of the ACM* **44**(7), 87–93 (2001).

Holsheimer, M., and Siebes, A. P., *Data Mining: The Search for Knowledge in Databases*, Technical report CS-R9406, http://citeseer.nj.nec.com/holsheimer91data.html, 1994.

Holte, R. C., Very simple classification rules perform well on most commonly used datasets, *Machine Learning* **11**, 63–90 (1993).

Karimi, K., and Hamilton, H. J., Finding temporal relations: Causal Bayesian networks vs. C4.5, in *Proceedings of the Twelfth International Symposium on Methodologies for Intelligent Systems* (ISMIS'2000), Charlotte, NC, pp. 266–273, 2000.

Kaufman, K. A., and Michalski, R. S., Learning from inconsistent and noisy data: The AQ18 approach, in *Proceedings of the Eleventh International Symposium on Methodologies for Intelligent Systems*, Warsaw, Poland, pp. 411–419, 1999.

Kononenko, I., Machine learning for medical diagnosis: History, state of the art and perspective, *Artificial Intelligence in Medicine* **23**, 89–109 (2001).

Kononenko, I., Bratko, I., and Roskar, E., Experiments in automatic learning of medical diagnostic rules, in *International School for the Synthesis of Expert's Knowledge Workshop*, Bled, Slovenia, 1984.

Kurgan, L. A., Meta Mining System for Supervised Learning, Ph.D. dissertation, the University of Colorado at Boulder, Department of Computer Science, 2003.

Kurgan, L. A., and Cios, K. J., Fast class-attribute interdependence maximization (CAIM) discretization algorithm, in *Proceedings of the 2003 International Conference on Machine Learning and Applications* (ICMLA'03), Los Angeles, pp. 30–36, 2003.

Kurgan, L. A., and Cios, K. J., Meta mining architecture for supervised learning, in *the Seventh International Workshop on High Performance and Distributed Mining*, in conjunction with *the Fourth International SIAM Conference on Data Mining*, pp. 18–26, Lake Buena Vista, FL, 2004a.

Kurgan, L. A., and Cios, K. J., CAIM discretization algorithm, *IEEE Transactions on Knowledge and Data Engineering*, **16**(2), 145–153 (2004b).

Kurgan, L. A., Cios, K. J., and Dick, S., Highly Scalable and robust rule learner: performance evaluation and comparison, *IEEE Transactions on Systems, Man and Cybermetics, Part B,* submitted, 2004.

Kurgan, L. A., Cios, K. J., Tadeusiewicz, R., Ogiela, M., and Goodenday, L. S., Knowledge discovery approach to automated cardiac SPECT diagnosis, *Artificial Intelligence in Medicine* **23**(2), 149–169 (2001).

Langley, P., Iba, W., and Thompson, K., An analysis of Bayesian classifiers, in *Proceedings of the Tenth National Conference of Artificial Intelligence*, AAAI Press and MIT Press, Menlo Park, CA, pp. 223–228, 1992.

Laura, M., Weijters, T., Vries, G., van den Bosch, A., and Daelemans, W., Logistic-based patient grouping for multi-disciplinary treatment, *Artificial Intelligence in Medicine* **26**, 87–107 (2002).

Michalski, R. S., Mozetic, I., Hong, J., and Lavrac, N., The multipurpose incremental learning system AQ15 and its testing application to three medical domains, in *Proceedings of the Fifth National Conference on Artificial Intelligence*, pp. 1041–1045, 1986.

Mitchell, T. M., *Machine Learning*, McGraw-Hill, New York, 1997.

Paterson, A., and Niblett, T. B., *ACLS Manual*, Intelligent Terminals, Ltd., Edinburgh, 1987.

Quinlan, J. R., Learning logical definitions from relations, *Machine Learning* **5**, 239–266 (1990).

Quinlan, J. R., *C4.5 Programs for Machine Learning*, Morgan Kaufmann, San Francisco, 1993.

Redman, T. C., The impact of poor data quality on the typical enterprise, *Communications of the ACM* **41**(2), 79–81 (1998).

Roddick, J. F., and Spiliopoulou, M., A survey of temporal knowledge discovery paradigms and methods, *IEEE Transactions on Knowledge and Data Engineering* **14**(4), 750–767 (2002).

Sacha, J. P., Cios, K. J., and Goodenday, L. S., Issues in automating cardiac SPECT diagnosis, *IEEE Engineering in Medicine and Biology Magazine* (special issue on Medical Data Mining and Knowledge Discovery) **19**(4), 78–88 (2000).

Spiliopoulou, M., and Roddick, J. F., Higher order mining: Modeling and mining the results of knowledge discovery, in *Data Mining II—Proceedings of the Second International Conference on Data Mining Methods and Databases*, Cambridge, UK, pp. 309–320, 2000.

Street, W. N., Mangasarian, O. L., and Wolberg, W. H., An inductive learning approach to prognostic prediction, in *Proceedings of the Twelfth International Conference on Machine Learning*, Morgan Kaufmann, San Francisco, pp. 522–530, 1995.

Wirth, R., and Hipp, J., CRISP-DM: Towards a standard process model for data mining, in *Proceedings of the Fourth International Conference on the Practical Applications of Knowledge Discovery and Data Mining*, Manchester, UK, pp. 29–39, 2000.

Wolberg, W. H., Street, W. N., and Mangasarian, O. L., Machine learning techniques to diagnose breast cancer from fine-needle aspirates, *Cancer Letters* **77**, 163–171 (1994).

Wong, A. K., and Chiu, D. K., Synthesizing statistical knowledge from incomplete mixed-mode data, *IEEE Transactions on Pattern Analysis and Machine Intelligence* **9**, 796–805 (1987).

Wu, B., Abbott, T., Fishman, D., McMurray, W., Mor, G., Stone, K., Ward, D., Williams, K., and Zhao, H., Comparison of statistical methods for classification of ovarian cancer using mass spectrometry data, *Bioinformatics* **19**(13), 1636–1643 (2003).

PART VI

WEB AND TEXT-MINING APPLICATIONS

18

ON LEARNING STRATEGIES FOR TOPIC-SPECIFIC WEB CRAWLING

CHARU C. AGGARWAL

18.1. INTRODUCTION

In recent years the world wide web has grown at a rapid pace. Currently, there are more than a billion documents on the web, and it continues to grow at a pace of more than a million documents a day. In many cases, it is desirable to be able to find documents belonging to specific topics. In order to achieve this goal, a number of search engine technologies such as *Yahoo!*, *Lycos*, and *AltaVista* have recently surfaced (http://www.yahoo.com, http://www.lycos.com, http://www.altavista.com). Such technologies provide a limited query capability using specific keywords or phrases in the document. In many cases, it may be desirable to find documents on the web which satisfy a particular kind of conditions such as the overall topic of the document. While a natural solution is to use web search engines (which pre-crawl pages), it is often more effective to perform the resource discovery when the query is issued. Such a technique turns out to be useful for a number of applications:

- *Focused Resource Discovery*. Finding a web page of a particular topic is often difficult to perform effectively with search engines that pre-crawl the web. This is because the web continues to grow and evolve rapidly. Therefore, pre-crawled collections are often stale, whereas it is also infeasible to crawl the entire web from scratch. A natural trade-off is to perform a directed form of search which crawls the web selectively.

- *Site-Specific Discovery for Ecommerce*. Another useful application of this approach is to perform site-specific resource discovery. In many cases, it

Next Generation of Data-Mining Applications. Edited by Kantardzic and Zurada
ISBN 0-471-65605-4 © 2005 the Institute of Electrical and Electronics Engineers, Inc.

is desirable to perform the resource discovery process within a given set of sites, or a particular set of competing businesses. In such cases, the use of focused resource discovery is a more effective solution than the use of search-engine-type methodologies.

Recently, a technique called *focused crawling* (Chakrabarti et al., 1999b) has been proposed for automated resource discovery. The focused crawling technique utilizes topical locality on the web in order to perform resource discovery. The idea is to start at a few well-chosen points and maintain the crawler within the range of these topics. Starting with this pioneering work, there has been some recent work (Diligenti et al., 2000; Mukherjea, 2000) in order to improve the efficiency of the crawl. We refer the reader to Bharat and Henzinger (1998), Chakrabarti et al. (1998, 1999a), Ding et al. (2000), and Bar-Yossef et al. (2000) for some closely related work.

In order to define the relevance of a web page, a *predicate* may be utilized. This predicate may be in the form of a particular set of keywords present in the document, a particular category that is implicitly defined by a classifier, or a combination of the above. Some examples of useful predicates are as follows:

- All web pages that a classifier defines in the "SPORTS" category and that contain the keyword "hockey".
- All web pages that contain the keyword "NBA" and whose URL ends with the extension ".uk".

The utilization of a predicate to crawl web pages of interest is a very flexible model that is often not supported by some of the well-known methods such as focused crawling (Chakrabarti et al., 1999b). Instead, the focused crawling method uses a predefined taxonomy of classes in order to perform the crawl. Such a procedure comes with its disadvantages, since the effectiveness of the crawl is sensitive to the underlying nature of the taxonomy. This greatly restricts the nature of the predicates that are used as queries for the crawling process. On the other hand, the learning methods discussed in the chapter can handle arbitrary predicates rather than those that are drawn from a hierarchical taxonomy.

Methods such as focused crawling are essentially adhoc heuristics in picking a particular strategy for the crawling process.* A broader goal would be relate particular attributes of the web page to the predicate of interest. Such methods are referred to as learning strategies. We will discuss two recent such methods in some detail.

---

*We note that the focused crawling technique (Chakrabarti et al., 1999b) also uses a classifier in the resource discovery process. However, this classifier is only utilized for defining the relevance of the web page to a given topic. In other words, the classifier acts as the predicate definition for the web page. This does not mean that the crawler is itself a learning process in terms of the strategy it uses for finding candidate web pages of interest.

The first class of methods (Aggarwal et al., 2001) uses linkage-based information in order to improve the effectiveness of the crawling. In these techniques, various features of the web page such as its content, URL extensions, and hyperlink structure may contribute to the classification of a page as a more likely candidate for belonging to a particular topic. Such methods are however, essentially linkage-based since the URL pointers play the key role in the resource discovery process.

The second class of methods (Aggarwal, 2002) is user-based, since it utilizes patterns of user behavior in order to determine topics of interest. In the former case, the linkage-based information is used directly under the assumption that web pages show topical locality. The advantages of the user-based system is that it can be effective in cases where it is not possible to reliably use linkage structure in order to search for topical resources. This is partially because of the increasing noisy nature of the links on the web (Bharat and Henzinger, 1998; Chakrabarti, 2001; Lempel and Moran, 2000). Such links may correspond to banners, advertisements, and other content that do not carry specific information about resource discovery. This increased noisy behavior is partially a result of the rapid commercialization of the world wide web. In user-centered methods, information from world wide web traces is utilized in order to determine the candidate pages of interest.

In user-centered systems, we make use of logs of user access behavior on public domain proxies. An example of such a *public-domain proxy* is the Squid (Rousskov and Solviev, 1999). The access patterns (web logs) of such proxies are publically available on the world wide web. These logs can be utilized in order to determine the topical connection between users and web pages. Such topical connections can then be leveraged in order to compute the relevance of a given web page to the user-specified predicate. We note that in the second case, the linkage between web pages is *indirect*, since instead of using URL pointers, we are using the commonality in browsing behavior in order to find new and relevant web pages. We note that such a strategy shares some aspects of collaborative filtering techniques (Aggarwal et al., 1999b, Shardanand and Maes, 1995), though the aim and scope of our system is different in many critical respects. Whereas collaborative filtering is only useful in recommending web pages which are interesting to a user, our system is designed to find web pages belonging to particular topical classes or predicates.

This chapter is organized as follows. In the next section, we will discuss the basic framework that can be leveraged in order to create an effective crawling system. In Section 18.3, we will discuss the use of linkage-based techniques in order to perform effective crawling. In Section 18.4, we will discuss how a user-centered system can be created in order to create an effective crawling system. In Section 18.5, we will discuss methods for combining the linkage and user-centered systems. In Section 18.6, we will present the conclusions and summary.

18.2. THE LEARNING CRAWLER FRAMEWORK

The basic framework for learning-based crawlers is illustrated in Figure 18.1. The technique uses a graph search technique on the world wide web pages, in which the pages are explored sequentially in order of a *structural search mechanism*. At each point of the search, a candidate list of web pages is maintained. The pages on the candidate list are examined in order of increasing priority. This priority value is calculated using a criterion that is dependent on the particular strategy being utilized.* When a candidate web page F is *examined*, it means that the web page has already been accessed from the world wide web. At this point, it is checked whether or not the web page satisfies the user-defined predicate. If such is indeed the case, then the web page is saved as a relevant web page. In addition, considerable learning information can be gleaned from whether or not the web page satisfies the user-defined predicate. This learning information is stored in the statistics $\mathcal{K}$. For example, in the case of a linkage-based strategy, it may be more desirable if the set of candidates pointed to from a web page are

Subroutine *CreateDescendentCandidates*(WebPage: F, Learning Statistics: K);
    Find all immediate descendents of F using the
    appropriate criterion for defining a descendent. Denote
    descendents by $\mathcal{N}$. Calculate the
    priority of the candidate pages in $\mathcal{N}$
    with the use of learning statistics in $\mathcal{K}$.
Subroutine *ExpandList(CandidateList: Cand, NewCandidates: $\mathcal{N}$)*;
    { Add those candidates in $\mathcal{N}$ to *Cand* which
    have priority above a user-defined threshold; }

Algorithm *LearningCrawlerFramework(StartingSeeds: S)*;
begin
  $Cand = S$;
  Set priority of each element in $Cand$ to 1;
    while $Cand$ is not empty **do**
    begin
      Sort $Cand$ in order of decreasing priorities;
      Pick the first page F from $Cand$;
      Issue a get request for URL F on the world wide web;
      if F satisfies the predicate **then** save F;
      Update learning statistics $\mathcal{K}$;
      $\mathcal{N} = CreateDescendentCandidates(F, \mathcal{K})$;
      ExpandList(Cand, $\mathcal{N}$);
      Delete F from $Cand$;
    end;
end

Figure 18.1. The basic framework for learning-based crawlers.

*We will discuss more on the aspect of priority computation in later sections.

utilized in order of the quality of linked pages. This structured search mechanism may vary according to the particular method being used.

- In linkage-based mechanisms (Aggarwal et al. 2001), the URLs contained in the web page are used as the criterion for expanding the candidate list. Specifically, we check the URLs that are contained in that web page as pointers. The set of URLs $\mathcal{N}$ are generated by the *CreateDescendentCandidates* procedure. This procedure also computes the priorities of the different web pages using the appropriate criterion. We note that the criterion for linkage based systems may be different from the criterion for user-centered systems.

- In user-centered systems (Aggarwal, 2002), the behavior of users is utilized in order to guide the resource discovery process. This behavior may be obtained from publically available web traces. In this case, instead of using the set of hyperlinks emanating from a web page, we use the set of web pages that are browsed by the different users in order to guide the process of resource discovery.

18.3. USE OF LINKAGE-BASED TECHNIQUES

We note that a linkage-based crawler essentially searches for statistical aspects of the data which are relevant for the purpose of crawling. These features may include the following aspects of web pages:

- The set of words in the web page.
- URL tokens from the candidate URL. For example, if we are looking for skiing web pages, the word "ski" in the URL provides evidence of the nature of that web page.
- Statistics of the number of inlinking web pages that satisfy the predicate.
- Statistics of the number of siblings of a candidate which have already been crawled that satisfy the predicate. A web page is said to be a sibling of a candidate URL, when it is linked to by the same page as the candidate. As the crawl progresses, the importance of each of the above set of statistics is learned by the crawler.

As discussed earlier, the statistical model maintains a dynamically updated set of statistical information $\mathcal{K}$ which it has learned during the crawl, along with a set of features in the given web page, and computes a priority order for that web page using these data. As we shall see later, the particular priority order that we determine calculates the interest factor on the likelihood that the features for a candidate web page make it more likely that this page satisfies the predicate.

In order to calculate the priorities, we compute the ratio that signifies whether a given set of events makes it more likely for a candidate to satisfy the user-defined predicate. We will develop some notations and terminology in order to explain the model a little better. Let C be the event that a crawled web page satisfies the user-defined predicate. For a *candidate page* that is about to be crawled, the value of $P(C)$ is equal to the probability that the web page will indeed satisfy the user-defined predicate if it is crawled. The value of $P(C)$ can be estimated by the fraction of web pages already crawled which satisfy the user-defined predicate.

Let E be a fact that we know about a candidate URL. This fact could be of several types. For example, it could be a fact about the content of the inlinking web pages into this candidate URL, it could be a fact about the set of tokens in the string representing the URL, or it could be a fact about the linkage structure of the URL. We will explore all of these options slightly later.

Our knowledge of the event E may increase the probability that the web page satisfies the predicate. For example, consider the case when the candidate URL is linked to by another web page that belongs to the same topic. In such a case, from earlier results on focused crawling (Chakrabarti et al., 1999b), it is evident that the resulting web page is more likely to satisfy the predicate. Thus, in this case, we have $P(C|E) > P(C)$. In order to evaluate $P(C|E)$, we use the following relationship

$$P(C|E) = P(C \cap E)/P(E) \tag{18.1}$$

Therefore, we have

$$P(C|E)/P(C) = P(C \cap E)/(P(C) \cdot P(E)) \tag{18.2}$$

The idea is that the values of $P(C \cap E)$ and $P(E)$ can be calculated using the information that has been accumulated by the crawler. This is the self-learning data $\mathcal{K}$ that are accumulated over time during the crawling process. Correspondingly, we calculate the interest ratio for the event C, given event E as $I(C, E)$. Therefore, we have

$$I(C, E) = P(C|E)/P(C) \tag{18.3}$$

Note that when the event E is favorable to the probability of the candidate satisfying the predicate, then the interest ratio $I(C, E)$ is larger than 1. Correspondingly, when the event E is unfavorable, then this interest ratio will be in the range $(0, 1)$. Such a situation occurs when the event E makes the candidate less desirable to crawl.

Let $E_1 \ldots E_k$ be a set of k events. Let the composite event $\mathcal{E}$ be defined by the occurrence of all of these events. In other words, we have $\mathcal{E} = E_1 \cap E_2 \ldots E_k$. Then the composite interest ratio is defined as follows:

$$I(C, \mathcal{E}) = \pi_{i=1}^{k} I(C, E_i) \tag{18.4}$$

The composite event $\mathcal{E}$ is interesting when the corresponding interest ratio is larger than 1. We will now proceed to examine the different factors that are used for the purpose of intelligent crawling.

In order to identify the value of the content in determining the predicate satisfaction of a given candidate page, we find the set of words in the web pages that link to it (inlinking web pages). A statistical analysis is performed on this set of words. We define the event Q_i to be true when the word i is present in one of the web pages pointing to the candidate.

$$\text{Let } M = \{i : \text{ Event } Q_i \text{ is true}\}$$

Now, let us consider a given word i such that $i \in M$. Therefore, the event Q_i is true. If C is the event that a candidate URL is likely to satisfy the predicate, then let us calculate the value of $I(C, Q_i)$:

$$I(C, Q_i) = P(C \cap Q_i)/(P(C) \cdot P(Q_i)) \tag{18.5}$$

It now remains to estimate the parameters on the right-hand side of the above equation. In order to estimate these parameters, we can only rely on the experimental evidence of the web pages that we have crawled so far. The exact details of these estimations will be discussed in a later section.

In order to filter out the noisy words that do not carry much statistical significance, we calculate the level of significance at which it is more likely for them to satisfy the predicate. Let $n(C)$ be the number of pages crawled so far which satisfy the user-defined predicate. Then, if N is the total number of pages that have been crawled so far, we have $n(C) = N \cdot P(C)$. The significance factor for the event C and condition Q_i is denoted by $S(C, Q_i)$ and is calculated as follows:

$$S(C, Q_i) = |(P(C|Q_i) - P(C))/(\sqrt{P(C) \cdot (1 - P(C))/n(C)})| \tag{18.6}$$

For some predefined significance threshold t, we now define the significant composite ratio to include only those terms that are in M, and for which $S(C, Q_i)$ is above this threshold. We use the process only on words that are present in M. There are two reasons for this: (1) The words that are not in M are often not statistically significant, because most words in the lexicon are not in M by default. (2) The scalability of the technique is affected by the use of an exceptionally large number of words. The interest ratio for content-based learning is denoted by $I_c(C)$ and is calculated as the product of the interest ratios of the different words in any of the inlinking web pages:

$$I_c(C) = \pi_{i:i \in M, S(C,Q_i) \geq t} I(C, Q_i) \tag{18.7}$$

The value of t denotes the number of standard deviations by which the presence is greater than the mean for the word to be useful. Under the assumption of normally distributed data, a value of $t = 2$ results in about 95% level of statistical significance. Therefore, we chose the value of $t = 2$ consistently in all results tested.

The method discussed above can easily be extended to the case of URL token-based learning. The tokens contained inside a Universal Resource Locator (URL) may carry valuable information about the predicate-satisfaction behavior of the web page. The process discussed above for the content of the URL can also be applied to the tokens in the URL. For example, a URL that contains the word "ski" in it is more likely to be a web page about skiing-related information. Therefore we first apply the step of parsing the URL. In order to parse the URL into tokens, we use the "." and "/" characters in the URL as the separators. We define the event R_i to be true when token i is present in the URL pointing to the candidate. As before, we assume that the event that the candidate satisfies the predicate is denoted by C. The interest ratio for the event C given R_i is denoted by $I(C, R_i)$. The process of actually calculating the interest ratio is exactly analogous to the case of content-based learning. Therefore, we will omit the details of this aspect of the learning process.

In link-based learning, we exploit the short-range topical locality on the web. This is somewhat similar to the focused crawler discussed in Chakrabarti et al., While the significance of such link based information may vary from predicate to predicate, the intelligent crawler tries to learn the significance of link-based information during the crawl itself. This significance is learned by maintaining and updating statistical information about short-range topical locality during the crawl itself. Thus, if the predicate shows considerable short-range locality, the crawler would learn this and use it effectively. Consider, for example, when the crawler has collected about 10,000 URLS and a fraction of $P(C) = 0.1$ of them of them satisfy a given predicate. If the linkage structure were completely random, then the expected fraction of links for which both the source and destination web page satisfy the predicate is given by 1%. In reality, because of the short-range topic locality discussed in Chakrabarti et al. (1999b), this number may be much higher and is equal to $f_1 = 7\%$. The corresponding interest ratio is given by $0.07/0.01 = 7$. Since this is greater than 1, it implies a greater degree of short-range topic locality than can be justified by random behavior.

In Table 18.1, we illustrate the different cases for a link encountered by the crawler for which both the inlinking and linked-to web page have already been crawled. The four possible cases for the pages are illustrated in the first column of the table. The second column illustrates the expected proportion of web pages belonging to each class, if the linkage structure of the web were completely random. At the same time, we continue to collect information about the actual number of each of the four kinds of links encountered. The corresponding fractions are illustrated in Table 18.1.

Now, consider a web page that is pointed to by k other web pages, m of which satisfy the predicate, and $k - m$ of which do not. (We assume that these k pages have already been crawled; therefore we can use the corresponding information about their predicate satisfaction; those inlinking pages to a candidate which have not yet been crawled are ignored in the calculation.) Then, for each of

TABLE 18.1. Topic Locality Learning Information

Type of Link	Expected	Actual
Pred–Pred	$P(C) \cdot P(C)$	f_1
Pred–Non-Pred	$P(C) \cdot (1 - P(C))$	f_2
Non-Pred–Pred	$P(C) \cdot (1 - P(C))$	f_3
Non-Pred–Non-Pred	$(1 - P(C)) \cdot (1 - P(C))$	f_4

the m web pages that satisfy the predicate, the corresponding interest ratio is given by $p = f_1/(P(C) * P(C))$. Similarly, for each of the $k - m$ web pages that do not satisfy the predicate, the corresponding interest ratio is given by $q = f_3/(P(C) \cdot (1 - P(C)))$. Then, the final interest ration $I_l(C)$ is given by $p^m \cdot q^{k-m}$.

Finally, the sibling-based interest ratio is based on the idea that a candidate is more likely to satisfy a predicate if many of its siblings also satisfy it. [As in Kleinberg (1998), a parent that has many children that satisfy the predicate is likely a hub and therefore a good place to find relevant resources.] For instance, consider a candidate that has 15 (already) visited siblings, 9 of which satisfy the predicate. If the web were random and if $P(C) = 0.1$, the number of siblings we expect to satisfy the predicate is $15 \cdot P(C) = 1.5$. Since a higher number of siblings satisfy the predicate (i.e., $9 > 1.5$), this is indicative that one or more parents might be a hub, and this increases the probability of the candidate satisfying the predicate.

To compute an interest-ratio based on this observation, we used the following rule: If s is the number of siblings that satisfy the predicate and e is the expected under the random assumption, then when $s/e > 1$ we have positive evidence that the candidate will satisfy the predicate as well. (Siblings that have not yet been visited are ignored, since we don't know whether they satisfy the predicate.) In the example above, the interest ratio for the candidate is thus $9/1.5 = 6$, which suggests that the candidate is likely to satisfy the predicate. The sibling-based interest ratio is denoted by $I_s(C)$.

Once the individual interest ratios have been computed, an aggregate interest ratio can be computed as a (weighted) product of the interest ratios for each of the individual factors. Equivalently, we can combine the preferences by summing the weighted logarithms of the individual factors.

$$PriorityValue = \log(I_c(C)) + \log(I_u(C)) + \log(I_l(C)) + \log(I_s(C))$$

If desired, it is also possible to use weights in order to vary the importance of the different factors.

18.3.1. Utilizing User Experiences in Resource Discovery

In this section we will discuss the statistical model that is used to connect the user behavior with the predicate satisfaction probability of the candidate web pages.

As in the previous case, the learning set $\mathcal{K}$ maintains the set of probabilities that indicate the user behavior during the crawling process. We note that several kinds of information about the user behavior may be relevant in determining whether a web page is relevant to the crawl:

- *Access Frequency Behavior.* Since users that have accessed web pages belonging to a particular predicate are also more likely to access other web pages belonging to the predicate, this is an important factor in determining the probability that a given candidate page will belong to the crawl topic.
- *Signature Features.* A signature feature is described as any characteristic of a web page such as content, vocabulary, or any other characteristic of a web page. Such signatures are often useful in identifying aspects which the raw frequency counts cannot provide.
- *Temporal Patterns of Users.* A set of accesses of web pages are likely to create similar accesses in the near future.

In order to calculate the priorities with the access frequency, we compute the likelihood that the frequency distribution of user accesses makes it more likely for a candidate web page to satisfy the predicate. In order to understand this point a little better, let us consider the following case. Suppose that we are searching for web pages on on-line malls. Let us assume that only 0.1% of the pages on the web correspond to this particular predicate. However, it may happen that the percentage of web pages belonging to on-line malls accessed by a user is over 10%. In such a case, it is clear that the user is favorably disposed to accessing web pages on this topic. If a given candidate web page has been accessed by many such users that are favorably disposed to the topic of online malls, then it may be useful to crawl the corresponding web page.

In order to develop the machinery necessary for the model, we will introduce some notations and terminology. Let N be total number of web pages crawled so far. Let U be the event that a crawled web page satisfies the user-defined predicate. For a *candidate page* that is about to be crawled, the value of $P(U)$ is the probability that the web page will indeed satisfy the user-defined predicate. The value of $P(U)$ can be estimated by the fraction of web pages already crawled which satisfy the user-defined predicate.

We will estimate the probability that a web page belongs to a given predicate U, given the fact that the web page has been crawled by user i. We shall denote the event that the person i has accessed the web page by R_i. Therefore, the predicate satisfaction probability is given by $P(U|R_i) = P(U \cap R_i)/P(R_i)$. We note that if the person i is topically inclined toward accessing web pages that belong to the predicate, then the value of $P(U|R_i)$ is greater than $P(U)$. Correspondingly, we define the interest ratio of predicate satisfaction as follows:

$$I^B(U|R_i) = P(U|R_i)/P(U) \tag{18.8}$$

We note that an interest ratio larger than one indicates that the person i is significantly more interested in the predicate than the average interest level of users in the predicate. The higher the interest ratio, the greater the topical affinity of the user i to the predicate. Similarly, an interest ratio less than one indicates a negative propensity of the user for the predicate. Now, let us consider a web page that has been accessed by the users $i_1 \ldots, i_k$. Then, a simple definition of the cumulative interest ratio $I(U|R_{i_1}, \ldots, R_{i_k})$ is the product of the individual interest ratios for each of the users. Therefore, we have

$$I^B(U|R_{i_1} \ldots R_{i_k}) = \pi_{j=1}^k I(U|R_{i_j}) \qquad (18.9)$$

The above definition treats all users in a uniform way in the computation of the interest ratio. However, not all interest ratios are equally valuable in determining the value of a user to the crawling process. This is because we need a way to filter out those users whose access behavior varies from average behavior only because of random variations. In order to measure the significance of an interest ratio, we use the following computation:

$$T(U, R_{i_j}) = \frac{|P(U|R_{i_j}) - P(U)|}{\sqrt{P(U) \cdot (1 - P(U))/N}} \qquad (18.10)$$

We note that the denominator of the above expression is the standard deviation of the average of N independent identically distributed Bernoulli random variables, each with success probability $P(U)$. The numerator is the difference between the conditional probability of satisfaction and the unconditional probability. The higher this value, the greater the likelihood that the event R_{i_j} is indeed relevant to the predicate. We note that this value of $T(U, R_{i_j})$ is the significance factor that indicates the number of standard deviations by which the predicate satisfaction of U is larger than the average if the user i_j has browsed that web page. In the computation of the interest ratio of a candidate page, we use only those users i_j for which $T(U, R_{i_j}) \geq t$ for some threshold* t.

We note that the nature of proxy traces is inherently sparse. As a result, in many cases, a single user may not access too many documents in a single trace. Therefore, a considerable amount of information in the trace can be broken up into *signatures* that are particular characteristics of different web pages. Such signatures may be chosen across the entire vocabulary of words (content), topical categories based on scans across the world wide web, or other relevant characteristics of web pages.

The use of such characteristics is of tremendous value if the signatures are highly correlated with the predicate. For example, if the document vocabulary is used as the relevant signature, then even though there many be billions of documents across the world wide web, the number[†] of relevant words is only of the order of a hundred thousand or so. Therefore, it is easier to find sufficient overlap of signatures across users in the crawling process. This overlap helps

---

*For the purpose of this chapter, we will use a threshold of $t = 2$ standard deviations in order to make this determination.

[†]This assumes that the documents are in English and stop-words/rare words have been removed.

in reducing the feature space sufficiently, so that it is possible to determine interesting patterns of user behavior which cannot be discerned only by using the patterns in terms of the individual web pages. The process for finding the signature specific interest ratio $I^{SF}(U|R_{i_1} \ldots R_{i_k})$ is quite analogous to that of finding the user-specific interest ratio. More details on the method of finding the signature-specific interest ratio may be found in Aggarwal (2002).

The web pages accessed by a given user often show considerable temporal locality. This is because the browsing behavior of a user in a given session is not just random but is highly correlated in terms of the topical subject matter. Often users that browse web pages belonging to a particular topic are likely to browse similar topics in the near future. This information can be leveraged in order to improve the quality of the crawl.

In order to model this behavior, we will define the concept of *temporal locality* region of a predicate U by $T\mathcal{L}(U)$. To do so, we will first define the temporal locality of each web page access A. The temporal locality of a web page access A is denoted by $TLR(A)$ and is the n pages accessed either strictly before or strictly after A by the *same* user, but not including A. Now let us say that $A_1 \ldots A_m$ is the set of accesses that are known to belong to the predicate U. Then the temporal locality of the predicate U which is denoted by $T\mathcal{L}(U)$ is defined as follows:

$$T\mathcal{L}(U) = \cup_{i=1}^{k} TLR(A_i) \tag{18.11}$$

Let f_1 be the fraction of web pages belonging to $T\mathcal{L}(U)$ which also satisfy the predicate. Furthermore, let f_2 be the fraction of web pages *outside* $T\mathcal{L}(U)$ which satisfy the predicate. Then, the overall interest ratio for a web page belonging to $T\mathcal{L}(U)$ is given by

$$I^{TL}(U) = f_1/P(U) \tag{18.12}$$

Similarly, the interest ratio for a web page that does *not* belong to the temporal locality of U is given by

$$I^{TL}(U) = f_2/P(U) \tag{18.13}$$

We note that in most cases, the value of f_1 is larger than $P(U)$, whereas the value of f_2 is smaller than $P(U)$. Correspondingly, the interest ratios are larger and smaller than one, respectively. For a given web page, we check whether or not it belongs to the temporal locality of a web page which satisfies the predicate. If it does, then the corresponding interest ratio is incorporated in the computation of the importance of that predicate.

The different factors discussed above can be utilized in order to create a composite interest ratio that measures the value of the different factors in the learning process. We define the composite interest ratio as the product of the interest ratios contributed by the different factors. Therefore, the combined interest ratio $I^C(U)$ for a web page that has been accessed by users $i_1 \ldots i_k$ is given by

$$I^C(U) = I^{TL}(U) \cdot I^{SF}(U|R_{i_1} \ldots R_{i_k}) \cdot I^B(U|R_{i_1} \ldots R_{i_k}) \tag{18.14}$$

This composite interest ratio reflects the overall predicate satisfaction probability of a web page based on its characteristics.

18.4. ON THE MERITS OF COMBINING USER AND LINKAGE INFORMATION FOR TOPICAL RESOURCE DISCOVERY

In the previous sections, we discussed methods for crawling with the utilization of user and linkage information. In this section, we will discuss methods for combining the two. It turns out that a method that combines user and linkage information is much more effective than one that uses only one of the two. In order to achieve this, the system can find all the web pages that are linked to by a predicate-satisfying web page and added to the candidate list. As a result, the list *Cand* becomes a combination of candidates for which we may have either web log access information or linkage information. In addition, we need to make changes to the process of calculation of priorities. In Aggarwal et al. (2001), we discussed the computation of interest ratios that are analogous to those discussed in this chapter using purely linkage-based information. Let $I^L(U)$ be the interest ratios computed for a candidate page using the method in Aggarwal et al. (2001). Let $I^C(U)$ be the corresponding user-based interest ratio. As discussed earlier, not all web pages have both linkage-based and user-based information associated with them. Therefore, when such information is not available, the corresponding value for $I^L(U)$ or $I^C(U)$ is set to one. Since the URL for a candidate page is discovered either from the content of a web page or from the web log, at least one of these interest ratios can be calculated effectively. The overall interest ratio is defined by $I^C(U) \cdot I^L(U)$. We will see that the combination of the linkage and user-based systems is very powerful in practice in improving the quality of the crawl. This is because the user behavior quickly identifies the most popularly visited resources that often link to a large number of closely related pages. These pages are added to the candidate list. The addition of such candidates facilitates the discovery of some of those rarely accessed web pages that may not be found in the traces. These, in turn, help in the discovery of more topically inclined users and vice versa. In other words, some resources can be more easily crawled from the user information, whereas others require linkage information. These interest ratios thus act in a complementary way in finding promising candidates during the resource discovery process. As a result, the system works better than one that is developed using either purely user or purely linkage information.

The system was implemented on an AIX 4.1.4 system with 100 MB of main memory and 2GB SCSI drive. The results were tested using two kinds of traces:

- *Squid Proxy Traces.* These traces are available from the web site ftp://ircache. nlant.net/Traces/, and they reflect the web page access behavior across a wide spectrum of users on the internet. Each of these traces contained between 100,000 and 1000,000 user accesses.

- *IBM Proxy Traces.* These traces reflect the access behavior of IBM employees and are stored at the IBM Raleigh site. Each of these traces contain about 100,000 accesses, and are each based on a single day of access behavior.

The performance of the crawler was characterized by using the harvest rate $P(U)$, which was the percentage of web pages crawled that satisfy the predicate. In order to illustrate our results, we will present the *lift curve*, which illustrates the gradual improvement of the harvest rate with the number of URLs crawled. Initially, the crawling system is slow to find relevant web pages, but as the crawl progresses, it gradually learns the propensities of the users in terms of their predicate satisfaction probability. This improves the computation of the interest ratios of the candidate web pages over time. Correspondingly, the percentage of the candidates crawled belonging to the predicate increases as well.

First, we present the results that illustrate the comparisons between a purely linkage-based crawler (intelligent crawler) and a user-based crawler (collaborative crawler). In Figure 18.2, we have illustrated an example of a lift curve

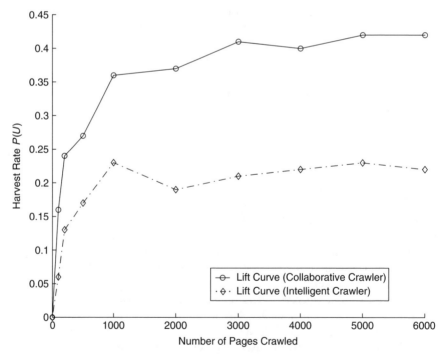

Figure 18.2. Performance of collaborative and intelligent crawler (predicate is category "SPORTS").

which shows the crawling performance of the system over time. In this case, the predicate is the web pages belonging to category "SPORTS" as predicted by the classifier discussed in Aggarwal et al. (1999a). The initial behavior of the crawler system is random, but as it encounters web pages belonging to the predicate, the performance quickly improves. In the same chart, we have also illustrated the performance of the intelligent crawler algorithm from Aggarwal et al. (2001). The intelligent crawler algorithm was run using five different starting points and the *best* of these lift curves (as indicated by the value of $P(U)$ at the end of the crawl) was used. It is interesting to see that even a single execution of the collaborative crawler was significantly more effective than even the best of five executions of the intelligent crawler.

We have illustrated the performance of the collaborative crawler on the Squid proxy trace in Figure 18.3. In this case, the predicate is the category "ARTS". As in the previous case, we have plotted the curve for the intelligent crawler for the best of five executions of the algorithm. Again, the collaborative crawler has a much greater harvest rate than does the intelligent crawler.

Another interesting difference between the collaborative and intelligent crawler is that the harvest rate of the intelligent crawler varies significantly over the crawl. This tends to indicate that the information available in web page links may not be very robust in always providing considerably effective information for the crawling process.

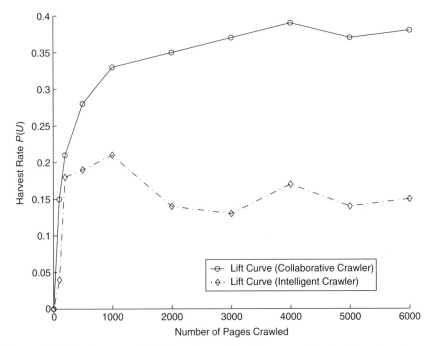

Figure 18.3. Performance of collaborative and intelligent crawler (predicate is category "ARTS").

It is useful to measure the behavior of the crawler when linkage and user information are combined. Even though the information from the web traces turns out to be valuable in finding the most popular resources, its performance can be improved further with the incorporation of linkage information. This helps in finding resources that are not quite as popular, but are often relevant to the predicate. In Figures 18.2 and 18.3, we have illustrated the harvest rate of the collaborative and intelligent crawlers, together with a crawler that combines the two pieces of information. The results are presented using the Squid proxy traces. In Figure 18.4, the predicate corresponds to the category "COMPUTERS" containing the keyword "viruses".

In Figure 18.5, the predicate corresponds to the AUTOMOTIVE category containing the keywords "Toyota Corolla". In both cases, the combined crawler performs better than a crawler employing purely trace-based or linkage information. This behavior seemed to be consistent over a wide variety of experiments that we performed. This behavior seems to be a little surprising, since one would normally expect that the lift curve for the combined system ought to be the average of the two individual systems.

On examining the web pages obtained from the crawl, we discovered that both the trace-based and the linkage-based systems discovered web pages that the other could not discover. Correspondingly, many web pages had a high

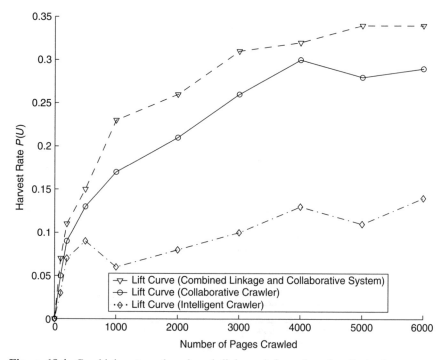

Figure 18.4. Combining trace-based and linkage information (predicate is category "COMPUTERS" containing keyword "viruses").

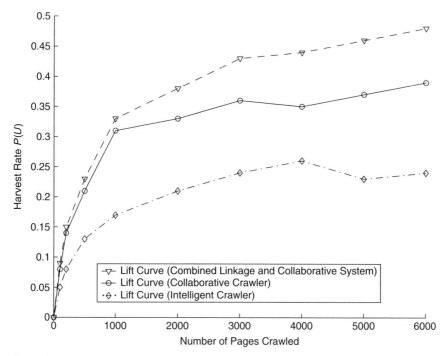

Figure 18.5. Combining trace-based and linkage information (predicate is category "AUTOMOTIVE" containing keywords "Toyota Corolla").

interest ratio using the linkage-based computation, whereas others had a high interest ratio using the trace-based computation. The noise-reduction methodology built into the interest ratio computation ensures that at each instant in time, the best criterion is used. In many cases, the web pages discovered by the linkage-based methodology would provide information about new users that often access predicate-specific web pages. In other cases, the web pages discovered using traces provided valuable hyperlinks to other predicate-relevant web pages. This complementary relationship resulted in a system that was better than either purely trace-based or linkage-based systems. We also note that significant differences between the relative performances were not observed when the traces were varied. For example, when the IBM proxy trace was used instead of the Squid traces, the behavior observed was quite similar. In the next section, we will also present some results using the IBM proxy traces.

18.4.1. Reuse of Crawler Learning Information

We note that the crawler system discussed in this chapter learns from the user behavior in the web traces, which are usually available in large quantities on a daily basis. Because the set of pages available on the web will change over time, it may be desirable to perform the same query repeatedly in order to discover the most recent resources. It is possible to leverage the information gained from a given crawl in order to improve the effectiveness of subsequent crawls. This is because many of the user access patterns and interests are consistent over time and provide valuable hints to the resource discovery process. In Figure 18.6, we have illustrated the performance of the collaborative crawler by using two traces from the IBM proxy server. In this case, the predicate corresponds to the category "SPORTS" containing the keyword "basketball". The traces were separated by a period of about 6 months, as a result of which many of the user domains and web pages in one trace were not present in the other. We note that the process of reusing learned information from a given crawl is not specific to the collaborative crawling method, but can also be easily extended to linkage based methods.

However, even this partial relevance was sufficient to significantly improve the quality of the web pages obtained over a crawl which started from scratch. The crawl started with the affinities of the users from the previous trace in order to decide the priority of the web pages to be crawled.

In Figure 18.7, we have illustrated similar results for the predicate corresponding to the category "ARTS" containing the keyword "gallery". Again, the reuse of crawler learning information significantly improves the performance of the crawl. It is clear from Figures 18.6 and 18.7 that when the information from one trace is used in the second, the performance of the crawler is improved

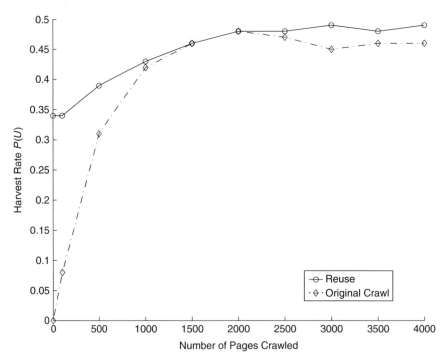

Figure 18.6. Reuse of crawler learning information (predicate is category "SPORTS" containing keyword "basketball").

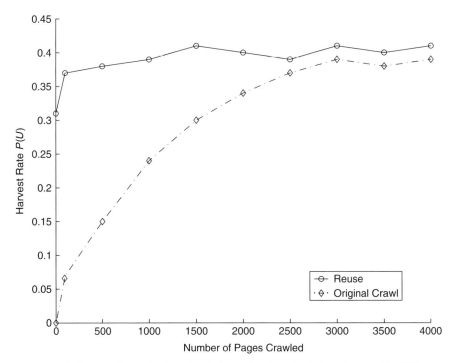

Figure 18.7. Reuse of crawler learning information (predicate is category "ARTS" containing keyword "gallery").

substantially during the initial learning phase. This property is valuable in building an incremental crawler in which similar kinds of resources often have to be repeatedly crawled over different periods of time. As discussed in recent research (Cho and Garcia-Molina, 2000), such queries are useful because of the rapidly evolving nature of the world wide web. The system of this chapter provides a useful technique to resolve such queries effectively.

18.5. CONCLUSIONS AND SUMMARY

In this chapter we discussed a number of learning techniques for topical resource discovery. Specifically, we discussed the collaborative crawler and the intelligent crawler, which are techniques for utilizing learning methods for resource discovery. The results illustrate that while user-experiences provide a richer ability to perform the learning, the combination of user- and linkage-based methods tend to be more effective than either. This is because the combination is able to capture those kinds of web pages that either of the techniques cannot do alone. We note that the learning system discussed in this chapter is also applicable to an environment in which the web pages evolve over time. In such cases, the system can leverage the information learned about user behavior in a given crawl in order to improve the effectiveness of subsequent crawls. We also showed that the collaborative crawling system can be combined with a linkage-based system in order to create a crawler that is more effective than either a purely linkage or trace-based system.

REFERENCES

Aggarwal, C. C., Collaborative crawling: Mining user experiences for topical resource discovery, in *Proceedings of the KDD Conference*, pp. 423–428, 2002.

Aggarwal, C. C., Gates, S. C., and Yu, P. S., On the merits of using supervised clustering for building categorization systems, in *Proceedings of the ACM SIGKDD Conference*, pp. 352–256, 1999a.

Aggarwal, C. C., Wolf, J. L., Wu, K.-L., and Yu, P. S., Horting hatches an egg: A new graph theoretical approach to collaborative filtering, in *Proceedings of the ACM SIGKDD Conference*, pp. 201–212, 1999b.

Aggarwal, C. C., Al-Garawi, F., and Yu, P., Intelligent crawling on the world wide web with arbitrary predicates, in *Proceedings of the WWW Conference,* pp. 96–105, 2001.

Bar-Yossef, Z., Berg, A., Chein, S., Fakcharoenphol, J., and Witz, D., Approximating aggregate queries about web pages via random walks, in *Proceedings of the VLDB Conference*, pp. 535–544, 2000.

Bharat, K., and Henzinger, M., Improved algorithms for topic distillation in a hyperlinked environment, in *Proceedings of the ACM SIGIR Conference*, pp. 104–111, 1998.

Carriere, J., and Kazman, R., Searching and visualizing the web through connectivity, in *Proceedings of the World Wide Web Conference*, pp. 701–711, 1997.

Chakrabarti, S., Integrating the document object model with hyperlinks for enhanced topic distillation and information extraction, in *Proceedings of the WWW Conference*, pp. 211–220, 2001.

Chakrabarti, S., Dom, B., Gibson, D., Kleinberg, J., Raghavan, P., and Rajagopalan, S., Automatic resource compilation by analyzing hyperlink structure and associated text, *Special Issue of the Seventh World Wide Web Conference* **30**(1–7), 65–74, 1998.

Chakrabarti, S., Dom, B., Ravi Kumar, S., Raghavan, P., Rajagopalan, S., Tomkins, A., Gibson, D., and Kleinberg, J., Mining the web's link structure, *IEEE Computer* **32**(8), 60–67 1999a.

Chakrabarti, S., van den Berg, M., and Dom, B., Focussed crawling: A new approach to topic specific resource discovery, in *Proceedings of the Eighth World Wide Web Conference*, pp. 545–562, 1999b.

Chakrabarti, S., van den Berg, M., and Dom, B., Distributed hypertext resource discovery through examples, in *Proceedings of the VLDB Conference*, pp. 375–386, 1999c.

Chen, M. S., Park, J. S., and Yu, P. S., Data mining for path traversal patterns in a web environment, *ICDCS Conference*, 1996.

Cho, J., and Garcia-Molina, H., The evolution of the web and implications for an incremental crawler, in *Proceedings of the VLDB Conference*, pp. 200–209, 2000.

Diligenti, M., Coetzee, F. M., Lawrence, S., Giles, C. L., and Gori, M., Focused crawling using context graphs, in *Proceedings of the VLDB Conference*, pp. 527–534, 2000.

Ding, J., Gravano, L., and Shivakumar, N., Computing geographical scopes of web resources, in *Proceedings of the VLDB Conference*, pp. 545–556, 2000.

Edwards, J., McCurley, K., and Tomlin, J., An adaptive model for optimizing performance of an incremental web crawler, in *Proceedings of the World Wide Web Conference*, pp. 106–113, 2001.

Kleinberg, J., Authoritative sources in a hyperlinked environment, in *Proceedings of the ACM-SIAM Symposium of Discrete Algorithms*, pp. 668–677, 1998.

Kumar, R., Raghavan, P., Rajagopalan, S., and Tomkins, A., Trawling the web for emerging cyber-communities, in *Proceedings of the World Wide Web Conference*, pp. 1481–1493, 1999.

Lempel, R., and Moran, S., The stochastic approach for link-structure analysis (SALSA) and the TKC effect, *Computer Networks* **33**(1–6), 387–401, 2000.

Mukherjea, S., WTMS: A system for collecting and analyzing topic-specific web information, in *Proceedings of the World Wide Web Conference*, pp. 457–471, 2000.

Najork, M., and Wiener, J., Breadth-first search yields high-quality web pages, in *Proceedings of the World Wide Web Conference*, pp. 114–118, 2001.

Raghavan, S., and Garcia-Molina, H., Crawling the hidden web, in *Proceedings of the VLDB Conference*, pp. 129–138, 2001.

Rousskov, A., and Solviev, V., On performance of caching proxies, http://www.cs.ndsu.nodak.edu/ rousskov/research/cache/squid/profiling/papers/, 1999.

Shardanand, U., and Maes, P., Social information filtering: Algorithms for automating word of mouth, in *Proceedings of SIGCHI Conference*, pp. 210–217, 1995.

Srikant, R., and Yang, Y., Mining web logs to improve website organization, in *ACM KDD Conference*, pp. 430–437, 2001.

19

ON ANALYZING WEB LOG DATA: A PARALLEL SEQUENCE-MINING ALGORITHM

AYHAN DEMIRIZ

19.1. INTRODUCTION

Many traditional companies see the enormous opportunities in using e-commerce sites as ways to reach customers outside the traditional business channels. Simply running an e-commerce site will not improve customer satisfaction and retention, however. While a user-friendly e-commerce site may attract new customers and strengthen relationships with existing customers, a poorly designed or implemented site may drive away potential customers and damage relationships with current customers. Because of this, businesses should approach e-commerce sites as new markets, where companies must open and maintain the lines of communication with both new and existing customers.

Activities at e-commerce sites as well as other web sites are usually recorded via web logs. This is the most common technology used at this time to collect information regarding site activities. From an analysis perspective, collected data should reflect user sessions properly. Assuming that user sessions in web logs are constructed by appropriate technology, we must first clean the web logs to remove redundant information. Parsing the cleaned web logs and inserting the data into a repository (data warehouse or relational database) is the next step in the analysis process. Data stored in a repository can easily be used for descriptive statistics (frequency analysis) with proven database technologies to create excellent summary reports. However, when it comes to analyzing the sequences, even with well-defined process flows, the number of nested queries required to follow the processes step by step within a relational database framework make

Next Generation of Data-Mining Applications.   Edited by Kantardzic and Zurada
ISBN 0-471-65605-4   © 2005 the Institute of Electrical and Electronics Engineers, Inc.

469

the analysis prohibitively expensive. This expense, combined with the fact that simple database queries are unlikely to discover hidden sequences and relationships within the data, make it important to use an effective sequence-mining algorithm to analyze the data contained within the web logs.

A click stream is defined as the ordered sequence of pages visited (or requested) by a customer/user (both registered and anonymous) in a session. The first challenge in web log data preprocessing is to define a session and a customer. This is the main step in the preprocessing phase of web usage mining. This step is dependent on the way the web log data are collected: server level collection, client level collection, or proxy level collection. The choice of collection is dependent on the technology. Technical difficulties might prevent a valid analysis of the web log data depending on the choice of collection. Throughout this chapter we assume that by using an appropriate technology, such as cookies, we can distinguish the sessions and the customers properly.

The simplest analysis is to get the first-level statistics based on the web log data. For example, the most visited page, the longest path, average transaction time, and the proportion of registered customers to the rest are some of the most common reports and are easily generated by off-the-shelf reporting tools such as Analog (Turner, 2000) for web log data. While these types of simplistic reports (traffic analysis) will help business managers understand the "business at a glance," additional value is found thorough analysis of the web log data using web-mining techniques.

We propose a parallel sequence-mining algorithm, webSPADE, based on Zaki, (2001a, b). There are several major differences in this chapter compared to earlier work (Zaki, 2001a, b). Differences and improvements can be summarized as follows:

- webSPADE is a Wintel-based parallel implementation.
- It only requires one full scan of the data compared to three full scans in previous algorithms.
- Temporal joins are strictly used in webSPADE rather than the existence of the nontemporal joins in the original algorithm.
- The design of webSPADE achieves data and task parallelism simultaneously.
- The current system has been in production since Mid-October of 2001 without any major problem.
- Click stream data are analyzed daily, and sequences are stored in a relational database.
- A user-friendly front-end is used to visualize and mine stored sequences for a user-determined time range and support level.
- By using a front-end application, it is possible to analyze click stream data from a very large time period (e.g., whole year) in a short time by aggregating stored sequences.

This chapter is organized as follows: We briefly discuss web mining and sequence mining in Section 19.2. We propose an integrated solution for click stream analysis in Section 19.3. The solution has four components: the web log data parser, the data warehouse, the sequence mining algorithm webSPADE, and the front-end (user interface) used for displaying and analyzing the mining results. The first two components, the log parser and data warehouse, are mentioned very briefly in this chapter, but further discussion of these two components is outside this chapter's scope. An analysis of web log data from Verizon.com during the months of January and August of 2002 is given in Section 19.4 for illustration purposes. Computational times are also reported in Section 19.4. The chapter wraps up with a conclusion and information about our future work.

19.2. RELATED WORK

When customers visit either commercial or noncommercial web sites and click on links, their actions speak to web site owners/managers. How clearly one understands the customers' behavior depends on whether or not one performs accurate click stream analysis. In general, click stream analysis is regarded as an activity under the web-mining umbrella. Web mining can be defined in short as the application of data-mining algorithms to web-related data. There are three components of web mining:

- Content mining
- Structure mining
- Web usage mining

Content mining is the analysis of the information (data) such as text and graphics that are presented in the web pages. One example would be the classification of homepages. One can identify course homepages on the web by distinguishing course homepages from the rest. Clustering is also used to segment pages. Structure mining is used to understand the topology of a web site, specifically the inter-page relations hidden in tree-like structures of web sites. In this chapter we specifically explore web usage mining. Web usage mining consists of three phases: preprocessing, pattern discovery, and pattern analysis (Srivastava et al., 2000).

In the next subsection we will describe some of the pattern discovery techniques.

19.2.1. Common Methods in Pattern Discovery

This section describes some of the analytical methods used in web usage mining. As we mentioned earlier, basic level statistical analysis is the most common way of extracting knowledge from web log data. Having descriptive statistics such as the most frequently requested pages, average access time, and the most common error codes might help to improve web traffic, system performance, and security. Statistical analysis is used to monitor the site and help IT professionals evaluate its efficiency and functioning. From an operational perspective, its merits are very important, but from a business point of view they are very limited.

Clustering is also used for extracting knowledge from the web log data. It is very useful, especially when the customer data are merged with the demographic data to generate the customer segmentations. In addition to customer segmentation, some web personalization methods also use the clustering approach. Classification can also be used to categorize customers based on the properties extracted from the web log data and related demographic information. To classify such data, the task must be defined very carefully and the required categorization should be monitored carefully. The difficulty in classification methods such as decision trees is to prepare proper training set(s) prior to extracting rules.

Another useful way of pattern discovery is dependency modeling. The aim here is to model user behavior during the various stages of navigation. This approach uses the probabilistic learning techniques, such as Hidden Markov Models and Bayesian Belief Networks, during the learning process. An example for such an approach is the visualization of user navigation patterns by using a Markov model based on clustering (Cadez et al., 2000). Since a click stream is an ordered sequence, sequence mining plays an important role in knowledge extraction from the web log data. In the following section, we will describe the sequence mining and its predecessor, association mining, used to discover frequent sequences for both temporal and nontemporal data.

19.2.2. Sequence Mining

Sequence mining is an extension of association mining that only finds nontemporal patterns. Association mining is used to find the related pages that are accessed together in the click stream context. Association mining was originally used to perform Market Basket Analysis to determine which items were purchased together. The goal of Market Basket Analysis is to find the related items that are purchased together most frequently. In this context, association rules identify pages which are accessed together above a threshold level (support.) Many algorithms have been successfully developed by various researchers for sequence analysis. One of the earliest is Apriori (Agrawal and Srikant, 1994). The Apriori algorithm can reveal the relationships between pages that are not directly connected (that is, pages are not linked through hypertext links). This is desirable, because it generates hidden rules along with the known relations (frequent hypertext links). Businesses can benefit greatly from the knowledge extracted from these rules. As we mentioned earlier, simple statistical analysis has limited value for generating business rules.

The Apriori algorithm makes several passes over the data to find frequent items (pages in our context). In the kth pass, it finds all the itemsets having k items. Each pass consists of two phases: candidate generation and support counting. The itemsets from $(k - 1)$th pass are used to generate the candidate list in kth pass. Then the data are scanned in the support counting phase to find the support of the items that are in the candidate list. The items in the candidate list that satisfy the minimum support are kept for the next pass. The algorithm continues until no itemset supports the minimum threshold.

Although many variations of the Apriori algorithm have been developed, they still require multiple passes over the data. This is of questionable utility, especially in the case of very large datasets. To speed up the process SQL variations of Apriori algorithm have been also developed [e.g., in Rajamani et al. (1999) and Sarawagi et al. (1998)]. Special SQL operators were proposed for such implementations. An SQL-based language also was used in Spiliopoulou et al. (2000).

One of the drawbacks of the Apriori-like algorithms is generation of redundant rules. Depending on the support level, association mining may generate an excessive number of rules. On the other hand, since the Apriori algorithm does not take into consideration the order which items are selected (i.e., pages are viewed), some of the rules found are invalid or misleading for click stream analysis. The last phase of web mining, pattern analysis, is designed to filter out these unnecessary rules.

The problem of mining sequential patterns was first studied in Agrawal and Srikant (1995). These authors also introduced three different algorithms for solving this problem. Based on the study in this article, it was shown that the *AprioriAll* algorithm performed the best compared with other two approaches. An advanced algorithm [compared to the ones in Agrawal and Srikant (1995)], GSP, was later proposed in Srikant and Agrawal (1996). It was shown that GSP can perform 20 times faster than *AprioriAll*. GSP is an iterative algorithm and requires a kth database scan to find the candidate list of the frequent sequences of length k (i.e., sequences with k itemsets). An itemset is a collection of items. GSP uses special data structures such as Hash Trees to count frequent sequences efficiently. The terms maximum gap, minimum gap, and sliding time window constraints were also introduced in Srikant and Agrawal (1996). Basically, minimum, or maximum, gap constraint requires that the minimum, or maximum, number of events (e.g., page views) should occur between two different items in that particular frequent sequence. Time window constraint simply limits the mining process to find the frequent sequences from a certain time period.

Mining for *frequent episodes*, which are simply frequent sequences in a single long input-sequence, was proposed in Mannila et al. (1995). However, we focus on the problem of finding frequent sequences across the multiple transactions (input-sequences.) The authors of Mannila et al. (1995) extended their framework in Mannila and Toivonen (1996) to discover *generalized episodes*, which allows one to express arbitrary unary conditions on individual sequence events, or binary conditions on event pairs. The MEDD and MSDD algorithms (Oates et al., 1997) discover patterns in multiple event sequences; they explore the rule space directly instead of the sequence space. PrefixSpan is one of the most recent algorithms for sequence mining, and it uses repeated database projections to mine frequent sequences (Pei et al., 2001).

Essentially, sequence mining can be considered as association mining over a temporal database. Association mining deals with intra-event patterns (called itemsets), but sequence mining addresses inter-event patterns (sequences.) Since association and sequence mining have many common points, algorithms like *AprioriAll*, GSP, and so on, utilize some of the ideas initially proposed for the discovery of association rules.

A recent work, SPAM, in Ayres et al. (2002) introduces a new approach by using a vertical bitmap representation. SPAM is a depth-first search algorithm with two different pruning steps: S-step and I-step. SPAM is compared with SPADE and PrefixSpan in Ayres et al. (2002). Experiments on synthetic data shows that it outperforms both algorithms for especially large datasets. But it should be noted that a serial version of SPADE was used for those experiments*. It is also mentioned in Ayres et al. (2002) that space requirements of SPAM are higher than those of SPADE. It is indeed the same analogy with sparse and full matrix representations of the problems in mathematical sciences. Somewhat, SPAM uses the full matrix representation as bitmap data; in contrast, SPADE uses the sparse matrix representation. It is a well-known fact that the sparse format is always efficient in terms of both space and CPU requirements for many mathematical models.

We chose to modify SPADE (Zaki, 2001a, b), since it is a very efficient algorithm for general sequence mining. Unlike previous approaches, which make multiple database scans and use complex hash-tree structures that tend to have suboptimal locality, SPADE partitions the original problem into smaller subproblems using equivalence classes on frequent sequences. Not only can each equivalence class be solved independently, but it is also very likely that it can be processed in the main-memory. So SPADE usually makes only three database scans: one for frequent 1-sequences, another for frequent 2-sequences, and one more for generating all other frequent sequences. If the support of 2-sequences is available, then only one scan is required. SPADE uses only simple temporal join operations, and is thus ideally suited for direct integration with a DBMS.

An efficient click stream analysis requires both a robust parser for the web log data and an efficient sequence-mining algorithm to analyze the cleaned data. In the next section, we propose an integrated solution to analyze the web log data. First web log data are parsed efficiently and stored in a data warehouse. We then run the webSPADE sequence-mining algorithm, a special application of SPADE (Zaki, 2001a, b), to generate the rules. Since click streams are ordered by time, rules found by webSPADE have temporal relations: For example, $A \rightarrow B$ means that if A happens, then later B happens; that is, if page A is visited, then later page B is also visited.

19.3. CLICK STREAM ANALYSIS: AN INTEGRATED SOLUTION

Click stream analysis plays an important role in the decision-making process of an e-commerce site. The knowledge obtained from such analysis can be deployed in restructuring the web site, personalizing the homepages and approaching

---

*Through personal communication with M. J. Zaki

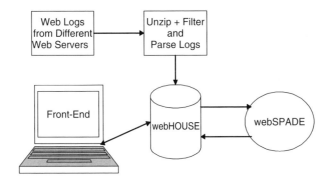

Figure 19.1. System architecture.

the customer in a better way (i.e., enhanced Customer Relationship Management.)

We propose an integrated solution for performing click stream analysis in this section. A simplified system architecture is shown in Figure 19.1. The parser feeds the data into webHOUSE, a data warehouse. The sequence-mining algorithm, webSPADE, reads daily data from webHOUSE and inserts the daily sequences into webHOUSE. The front end is used to query the webHOUSE to analyze sequences. In this section, we first explain parsing the web log data and creating the database. Then we explain the modifications to the sequence-mining algorithm SPADE introduced in Zaki (2001a). Finally, we explain the usage of the front end in Section 19.3.4.

19.3.1. Parsing the Web Log Data

Logs recorded by web servers provide the data for the analysis. The web servers record each page request and related information such as specifications of the requestor's browser type, IP address, user name, time of request, action and page requested, protocol, and so on. Different web servers generate different types of web logs, and some are capable of keeping more than one type of log—for example, Microsoft Internet Information Server. The two most common log formats are NCSA and W3C-extended. Even though there are other types of logs, some of them do not provide sufficient information for analysis. Therefore, our web log processor only supports the NCSA format and the W3C-extended format. The W3C-extended format allows the option of only capturing the desired fields, and thus we expect the web server using the W3C-extended format to be configured to capture at least the required information fields.

The web log processor is designed to be intelligent and does not require the user to know the type and specifications of the web log. It only requires the user to provide the location of the log file. It automatically determines the type of the log and whether it contains the required fields. The current parser runs in a parallel mode and is extremely efficient. On average, it takes four hours to parse and insert the cleaned data into the data warehouse for daily hits at Verizon.com.

These cleaned data consists of both anonymous and registered requests and contains more than three and a half million hit records each day. Note that we do not include all the hits to Verizon.com, and it should be noted that certain pages on Verizon.com use cookies to keep track of the user sessions and the application process flows. This means that session information and some other operational data is also kept in the data warehouse. When Verizon.com was launched in October 2001, the early designs of many applications required registration for most of the activities. Thus nonpersistent cookies were used to determine the user sessions. Certainly, persistent cookies are potentially more useful than nonpersistent ones due to their ability to track anonymous users over several different sessions. Other technologies such as messaging services [e.g., Microsoft Message Queue Server (MSMQ) and MQSeries by IBM] can be used at the server site to monitor the user session. Obviously this requires application level integration.

A sophisticated data warehouse is used for storing daily request data and related information. Due to the proprietary nature of the application, we will only mention a very early version of data warehouse in the next sub-section. In practice, we only need three data fields—session id, time stamp, and page id—for click stream analysis.

19.3.2. webHOUSE: A Web Log Data Warehouse

Since there is a huge amount of data to be stored and analyzed, a sophisticated database system is needed, which not only prevents data redundancy but also provides readily available analysis. Considering the constraints and available tools, Microsoft SQL Server is utilized as the database engine. A star schema such as in Figure 19.2 is used in this data warehouse. It should be noted that the star schema given in Figure 19.2 is a very early version of the current data warehouse. It is only mentioned here to illustrate the system. In very early versions of the data warehouse, we used IP address as session id for simplicity. OLAP reporting tools are also available with Microsoft SQL Server.

Utilizing the star schema depicted in Figure 19.2 reduces the storage requirements to approximately 5% of the raw data size. For example, if a web page contains a mixture of 9 image and script files, the web server will record it as 10 hits: 1 for the page itself and 9 for the images and script files. If only the page hit is kept and the rest are discarded, the log would be reduced to 1/10th of its size. We not only reduce the storage size, but also bring the ability to run both static and ad hoc queries to the web log data by creating the database. The fact table is the main table in the star schema. Several OLAP reports are also created or updated when this table is updated. In the next subsection we explain the webSPADE algorithm used in this chapter to perform the sequence mining.

19.3.3. webSPADE: A Parallel Sequence-Mining Algorithm

The nature of the sequence-mining problem makes massive computation unavoidable. This situation is an ideal application for parallel programming. In

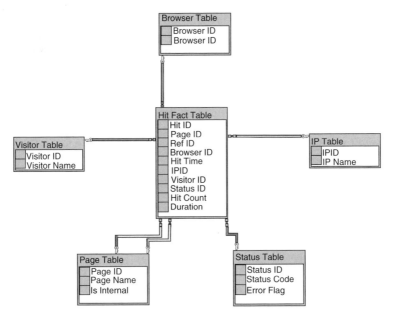

Figure 19.2. Star schema of the web log data warehouse.

this section we present a parallel sequence-mining algorithm that differs from previous work [3, 17, 18] in many ways. Parallel sequence-mining algorithms are generally derived from sequential ones by introducing load balancing schemes for multiple processors and distributed memory. Since the data warehouse is built on MS SQL Server in our implementation, webSPADE has been developed in the Wintel environment, simplifying the parallelization of the serial programs by letting the operating system to handle the load balancing.

The core point of our implementation is to modify the SPADE algorithm for the purpose of performing click stream analysis. The details of the original SPADE algorithm can be found in Zaki (2001a). SPADE is a generic algorithm used for performing sequence mining for both time-dependent and time-independent data. The main advantage of using this algorithm is the use of join operations instead of scanning all the data to count certain itemsets. The original SPADE algorithm proposed in Zaki (2001a) requires three full scans of the data. The advantage of this algorithm compared to the Apriori algorithm is the ability to use the time information. Our implementation is even better since it requires only one full data scan that is performed as the data are retrieved from the database. Note that both SPADE and webSPADE may require a large number of scans on intermediate partial data.

The reason behind using the join operation in SPADE algorithm is that, as mentioned in Corollary 1 of Zaki (2001a), any sequence X can be derived by the joining of its first two lexicographical subsequences. For example, in order to find support for the rule $A \rightarrow B \rightarrow C$, it is sufficient to join the sets of the rules

$A \rightarrow B$ and $A \rightarrow C$. It is obvious that the rule $A \rightarrow C \rightarrow B$ is also obtained by joining the same two subsequences. This is the most crucial step of the SPADE algorithm that gives it superiority over the Apriori algorithm. In this case, A is called as an "equivalence class."

Before going into details of webSPADE, we want to briefly discuss the differences between webSPADE and SPADE introduced in Zaki (2001a). Since click streams are strictly ordered by time and no two items (page views for the same session) occur at the same time, we only use temporal joins in contrast to the existence of the nontemporal joins in the original algorithm. Another difference is that support counting is not performed at a session level; that is, if $A \rightarrow B$ occurs twice in a given session, support of the sequence (rule) increments by two. In the original algorithm, it would count only one instead. We consider repeating subsequences in a given session as significant for click stream analysis. Therefore, our algorithm is designed to handle repetition within a session, though a counterargument can be made regarding the misleading nature of the repeating sequences. For example: Assume that there are several independent hits on page A and B and all page B hits occur after page A hits. In this case, the support of the sequence $A \rightarrow B$ will be counted as many as the lowest number of hits on pages A and B. However, in reality, the user goes from page A to B only once. This situation might cause the sequence-mining algorithm to find unnecessary or illogical sequences. Our analysis shows that this situation does not exist within the click stream data, and the resulting sequences of webSPADE reflect the true frequencies after confirming with SQL queries. Sequences make sense from the perspective of both business and real traffic flow. Nevertheless, taking the repeating sequences into consideration is important to understand the true traffic load.

As we mentioned earlier, due to the design of our implementation, the algorithm requires only one full scan of the database. Since we do not have vertical to horizontal database recovery in this implementation, we skip the second and the third scan in the original implementation, creating a significant performance improvement. The main data structure is the map of multisets in our implementation. A sample set is depicted in Table 19.1. SID stands for session id. This gives us the ability to join tables efficiently and reduce the number of full scans.

In terms of parallelization of the serial programs, the memory type of the computer system is an important factor to consider when designing the algorithm. Algorithms proposed in Zaki (2001b), Guralnik et al. (2001), and Guralnik and

TABLE 19.1. Sample Set for Item A

SID	Time
1	10
1	15
2	12

Karypis (2001) are designed to run on distributed shared-memory due to the selection of parallel computer systems (SGI Origin 2000 and IBM SP2.) Since webSPADE runs on a single machine with multiple CPUs, it is designed to utilize a single memory. Indeed, this particular server has 8 CPUs at 700-MHz clock speed with 8 GB of total memory. The system used in Zaki (2001b) is composed of 12 processors SGI Origin 2000 with 195-MHz R10000 MIPS processors and 2-GB main memory. Algorithms discussed in Guralnik et al. (2001) and Guralnik and Karypis (2001) are run on an IBM SP cluster that consists of 79 four-processor and 3 two-processor machines with a total of 391 GB of memory. These machines have 222-MHz Power3 processors. When we compare the three different systems, a Wintel-based system is the simplest and certainly the cheapest.

Sequence mining can be considered as an irregular tree search algorithm (Zaki, 2001b), with each node corresponding to an equivalence class. According to the argument in Zaki (2001b), parallelization of the sequence mining can be achieved either by data or task parallelism. In data parallelism, processors work on distinct partitions of the database but process the global tree structure concurrently. Task parallelism, on the other hand, requires each processor to have a separate copy of the database and run on different branches of the global tree. One static and two dynamic load balancing schemes are examined in Zaki (2001b) as part of task parallelism. Experiments in Zaki (2001b) show that task parallelism is more favorable than data parallelism, with the best task parallelism approach using recursive dynamic load balancing (Zaki, 2001b).

A parallel version of the tree projection algorithm is proposed in Guralnik et al. (2001). Each node in the projection tree corresponds to k-itemset. This is indeed similar to the equivalence class representation of SPADE algorithm. The projection tree grows in a breadth-first manner. Data and task parallelism are compared again in Guralnik et al. (2001). Bipartite graph partitioning and bin packing are used as task parallelism approaches. These are not considered as dynamic load balancing schemes. Similar to the results in Zaki (2001b), task parallelism results are more favorable in terms of work load and computation time. An extension to Guralnik et al. (2001) is introduced in Guralnik and Karypis (2001) by implementing a dynamic load balancing scheme. The dynamic load balancing scheme in Guralnik and Karypis (2001) performs similar to or better than the static load balancing schemes used in Guralnik et al. (2001).

Algorithm 19.3.1 (webSPADE).

```
Given min_support and database D
F₁ = {Frequent items or 1-sequences }
F₂ = {Frequent 2-sequences (item-pairs) }
Enumerate-Freq-Seq(F₂);
```

With the design of webSPADE, data and task parallelism are achieved simultaneously. Since webSPADE is developed in a Wintel-based environment, it has been coded as a multi-threaded program. A high-level pseudo-code of the algorithm is given in Algorithm 19.3.2. Finding frequent sequences is a recursive depth-first search step to reduce the required memory for searching new sequences. In this step, all the item-pairs with the same equivalence class in the item-pair set are joined pairwise to form the next item-pair set. This recursive step is repeated for this new item-pair set until no two-item exists in the following item-pair set which has minimum support. The current rules are printed at the proper places within the recursive search. A thread is created for each recursive branch in the search space. Required data are passed to the child thread and immediately deleted from the parent thread. Thus while task parallelism is done during depth-first search, data parallelism is also achieved by passing the required data to the child threads. Load balancing is left to the operating system (Windows 2000), which reduces the coding efforts drastically. In our early implementation (Demiriz, 2002), there was no limitation on the number of threads in our application. They were created as needed and were monitored by the operating system. However, webSPADE is modified to limit the number of child threads at five (can be changed as a parameter) for each individual thread to

1. Stabilize the program for extremely large data (occasionally)

2. Stabilize the program for dense data (see Section 19.3.4)

3. Prevent the unexpected outcomes of the very long sessions—especially for the test users

Frequent items (pages) ($\mathcal{F}_1$) are found during the creation of the required data structures (data retrieval.) This step is linear and does not require parallelization. Data are directly imported from the data warehouse for a specified time window by running an SQL query. Finding frequent 2-sequences ($\mathcal{F}_2$) is also parallelized in our implementation. This step requires exhaustive search by two nested for-loops. Since sequence mining may involve with the pages that are not linked via hypertext links and backward movement is also considered in our problem setup, exhaustive search is unavoidable. For each step in the main for-loop, a thread is created to find $\mathcal{F}_2$. Enumerate-Freq-Seq is the main function in webSPADE and each time this function is called, except in the main process, a new thread is also created. Due to the nature of the exhaustive search involved, finding $\mathcal{F}_2$ is the most CPU intense step in webSPADE.

Potentially, hundreds of threads are created during the run time of webSPADE. The details of Enumerate-Freq-Seq function is given in Algorithm 19.3.2. The term σ represents the support count of the corresponding data structure. T is the set of item-pairs to be passed to the next branch. There are two join operations as mentioned above to find sequences—for example, to find both $A \rightarrow B \rightarrow C$ and $A \rightarrow C \rightarrow B$ sequences. To illustrate the algorithm well, we use two different steps in Algorithm 19.3.2, but in our application these two join operations are done in a single pass. $\mathcal{L}$ represents the intermediate item-pair sets after join operations. Sequences that have frequency below the support level are removed from further analysis. $\mathcal{F}$ again corresponds to the frequent sequences to be printed later.

This part of webSPADE does not differ much from the original SPADE algorithm, and it is suggested that interested readers see Zaki (2001a) for further details.

Algorithm 19.3.2 (Enumerate-Freq-Seq).

```
Given Set S
for all item-pairs Aᵢ ∈ S do:
{ print the sequence
    Tᵢ = ∅;
    if antecedent (equivalence class) changed then
{     if size(Tᵢ) > 1 then
          Enumerate-Freq-Seq(Tᵢ);
      if size(Tᵢ) = 1 then
          print the sequence }
    while Aⱼ and Aᵢ have same antecedent do:
    {R = Aᵢ ⋁ Aⱼ;
      ℒ(R) = ℒ(Aᵢ) ∩ ℒ(Aⱼ); Join operation
      if σ(R) ≥ min_support then
      {Tᵢ = Tᵢ ⋃{R};
        𝓕|R| = 𝓕|R| ⋃{R}; }
      R = Aⱼ ⋁ Aᵢ;
      ℒ(R) = ℒ(Aⱼ) ∩ ℒ(Aᵢ); Join operation
      if σ(R) ≥ min_support then
      {Tᵢ = Tᵢ ⋃{R};
        𝓕|R| = 𝓕|R| ⋃{R}; }
    }
}
```

The join operator in Algorithm 19.3.2 first finds identical session identifiers (SID), then compares the time stamps between two hits with the same SID. As mentioned above, the basic data structure in our implementation consists of a set of SID and time stamp pairs (see Table 19.1.) When the two sets are joined line by line (e.g., $A \to B$ and $A \to C$), the join operator first verifies that the SIDs are equal. If this condition is met, and the time stamp of $A \to B$ is less than the time stamp for $A \to C$, a new line is inserted into the set of $A \to B \to C$. Note that the time stamp for this new line is equivalent to the time stamp from $A \to C$. Once a specific SID and time pair is used in a join operation to generate a new line in the sequence, that pair is removed from the set. In other words, the join operation creates distinct instances. If the resulting set satisfies the minimum support limit, a new sequence is added to the list of frequent sequences. It should also be noted that the join operation is used heavily in finding $\mathcal{F}_2$.

One important benefit of sequence mining is to automatically find all the possible sequences, because it is not humanly possible to consider all the possible sequence combinations. Therefore it is not possible to write SQL queries for every single possible combination, yet it takes quite some time to run such queries for even a very small set of items (pages). There are commercially available data warehouses, such as the one found in Microsoft Commerce Server 2000, which allow users to query the related databases, but it is practically impossible to come up with all the combinations of SQL queries to replace sequence mining. Moreover, such strategy will only be suitable for a static web site. For the commercial web sites that change almost constantly in terms of both content and structure, that is quite unacceptable and cumbersome.

The strength of our application comes from utilizing database technology to store and aggregate the sequence-mining results and present them to the end user in a very short time. While running sequence mining on-the-fly for large datasets is generally regarded as practically impossible, in this chapter we introduce an unprecedented analysis technique in the next subsection to do just that. Our methodology can be considered as a new way to perform a mine and explore approach—that is, mine the partial data now and then aggregate the results to mine larger data later.

19.3.4. Scaling-Up Sequence-Mining Algorithms: Application of webSPADE

We present a very innovative way of scaling up any sequence-mining algorithm by utilizing webSPADE and the relational database technology together. This allows users to analyze very large datasets spanning a large time window— for example, a year. A user-friendly front end visualizes the sequences in a very effective way and enables users to choose three different parameters— support levels, time window (start and end date of analysis), and line of business (LOB)—to query the sequences. Similar visual pattern analysis techniques are introduced in Klemettinen et al. (1996, 1999) in the context of the "mine and explore" paradigm using episode and association mining. Rules are found at a predetermined support and confidence level, then a user interface is used to query the rule base to narrow down the selection of important rules.

Our approach is very simple. webSPADE runs daily with a predetermined support level to find sequences based on different lines of business; Support level is set to 0.1% for General Business, Consumer, and Others (the rest) in our application (see Figure 19.3a). Daily sequences are then stored in a relational table. By design, webSPADE limits the length of sequences and, in this particular application, the maximum length of sequences is set to ten. Depending on the application domain, this parameter can be chosen accordingly. Since important processes in e-commerce sites, such as registration, should be kept as brief as possible, we believe that 10-level sequences are adequate for click stream analysis. Thus the relational table is composed of 10 fields to determine the sequences, analysis date, line of business, frequency of sequence, and total hits on analysis date. Since web log data are collected daily, we use a day as our atomic time unit. Different atomic time units may be used on other domains. For example, we may store financial sequence data hourly.

As in the case of association mining, sequence mining might result in an excessive number of sequences. Finding potentially valuable sequences among

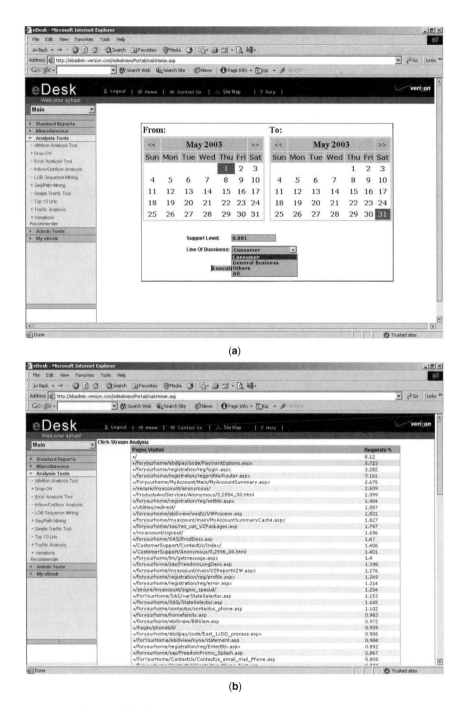

Figure 19.3. (a) Parameter selection screen. (b) Frequent pages.

numerous repetitive sequences might become impossible. Our front end enables users to see and query the sequences in a user-friendly manner. Stored sequences can be used to analyze click streams between user specified dates. As seen from Figure 19.3a, users can specify any support level and dates for a given line of business allowing a great degree of flexibility. **It should be noted that webSPADE is run daily and results are stored; there is no on-the-fly computation when the user selects parameters using the parameter selection screen.** In fact, the stored results are aggregated and presented to the user. We can also aggregate the data for all the LOBs as in the case of "**All**" option in Figure 19.3a. Aggregating the results of micro-mining activities is the major difference from the previous work introduced in Klemettinen et al. (1996, 1999). Because the mining algorithm in Klemettinen et al. (1996, 1999) is run on all the available data (macro mining) and then resulting patterns are analyzed and searched by a user interface. On the other hand, our methodology requires mining efforts on a portion of data (for one day). Resulting patterns are then aggregated and presented to the user for visual analysis and pattern search. Moreover, our approach scales up the underlying mining algorithm and visualizes the results simultaneously. This is a significant improvement in terms of computation efficiency.

After selecting the parameters, frequent pages are shown to the user as seen in Figure 19.3b. Further analysis can be deployed by clicking on any page name in the frequent page list (see Figure 19.3b). Once clicked, a pop-up window appears as seen in Figure 19.4a. There are five options to choose on this screen. Users can select to see sequences that contain a selected page, start with a selected page, or end with a selected page. Users can list all the sequences as well. There is another option to list all the sequences starting with the selected page and ending with another page. Each option corresponds to a different stored procedure in the database. Having results stored in a relational table gives tremendous flexibility to report and query the results. Once an option is chosen, the resulting sequences are listed in the browser window as seen in Figure 19.4b.

The user interface introduced above is designed to analyze the click stream data at LOB level. In certain cases, application owners might be interested to know what else our customers do when they visit a particular page. In other words, we might want to analyze all the click stream data from those sessions where a particular page is visited. webSPADE can easily be used for this purpose. All we need to do is provide the click stream data to webSPADE from those sessions. Thus resulting analysis can be called "*Page-Based Sequence Mining.*" Since sequence mining might take some time to run and cause unpredictable CPU load, we designed a front end for batch processing this type of analyses (Figure 19.5a). In the first screen, the user determines the date range (multiple-day selections are allowed) and the particular page that he/she asks for analysis. The user also gives a name for that particular analysis to be saved for a later time to view. Since the user is interested only in analyzing the data mainly around a particular page, the presence of the homepage might skew the analysis. Thus the user has a choice to exclude the homepage from the analysis. Given these parameters, the algorithm runs at 0.1% fixed support level. Considering the

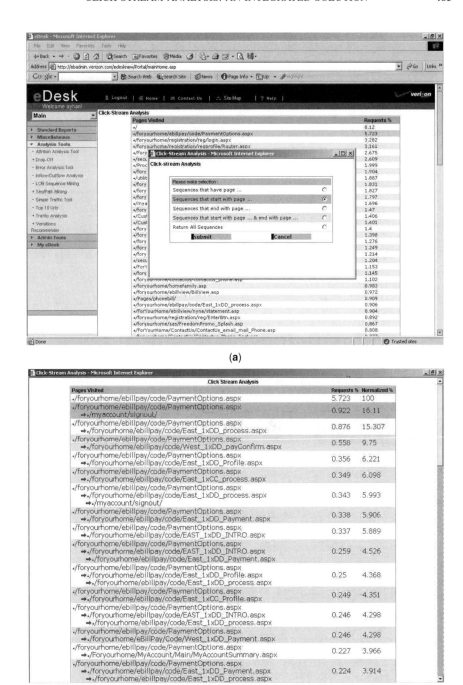

Figure 19.4. **(a)** Analysis selection. **(b)** Sequences.

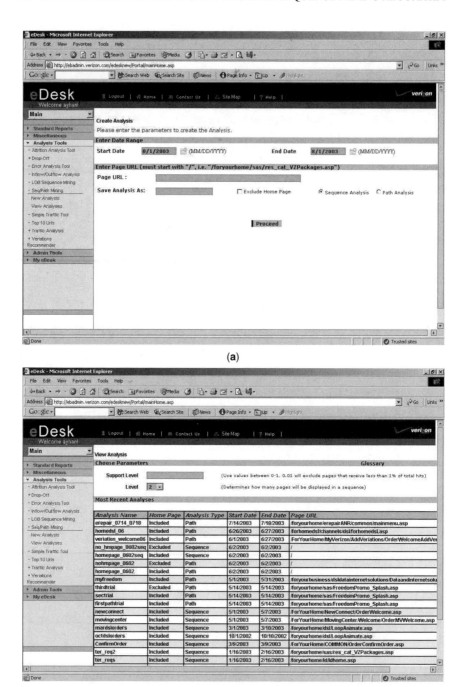

Figure 19.5. (a) Create analysis. (b) View analyses.

multiple users (analysts) case, the batch process only allows one instance of the algorithm to run at any given time.

To view saved analyses at later times, a second page is designed (Figure 19.5b) as part of the page-based sequence mining front end. Users can only see their own analyses in this particular page. With two more parameters, a user can choose to view results at higher support levels than 0.1% and up to the length of their choice (Level). Again, the algorithm finds up to length 10 sequences by default. But the user can select any length between 2 and 10 by changing the Level. From this point, the user interface is used as in Figure 19.4 to present the frequent sequences at the specified support level with a constraint up to the length of Level.

Commercial web sites are composed of several applications—for example, Bill View, Bill Pay, and Registration. The reason behind the page-based sequence mining is to give the ability to application owners to analyze click stream data specifically in the neighborhood of a page that they select. Usually the first page in any given application gets the highest hits and the last page (e.g., Thank-you and Confirmation pages) gets the least hits. This is a so-called funnel-type shape in terms of traffic. So, if page-based analysis is done for the first page, the resulting click stream data will be very sparse. However, if the same analysis is done for the last page, the resulting click stream data will be very dense, since sessions are conditioned to include the successful visits to the last page. In this case, a support level will not be able to prune the rule space and number of rules will be very high. For instance, the sequence mining algorithm could end up finding 800K sequences for merely 40K hits of click stream data. Thus controlling the number of child threads is almost mandatory to stabilize the program as mentioned in Section 19.3.3.

Note that analyzing thousands of frequent sequences may not be very informative due to repeating similar sequences. Hence path analysis will be very useful in this type of situation to analyze the traffic well. As seen from Figure 19.5a, the user also has the choice of performing path analysis. The algorithm behind the path analysis is similar to webSPADE in nature but also significantly different in details. It is not in the scope of this chapter to explain the path analysis algorithm.

webSPADE and the web-based front end, depicted in Figures 19.3 and 19.4, can be used for other time-dependent sequential data. To illustrate the practical usage of sequence mining and to assess the performance of webSPADE, we present some graphs and analyses in the next section.

19.4. PERFORMANCE AND A SAMPLE BUSINESS ANALYSIS

webSPADE has been used for analyzing web log data since mid-October 2001. We can now analyze virtually all the frequent sequences since the inception day by using the front-end reporting tool mentioned in the previous section. As of August 2003, there are approximately 1.2B cleaned hits in the data warehouse

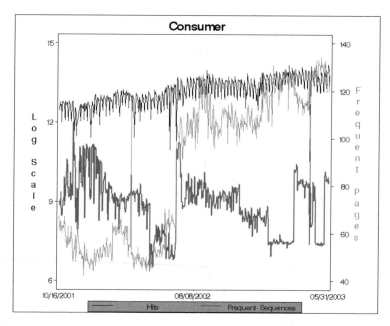

Figure 19.6. Daily sequence statistics: Consumer.

(webHOUSE). Roughly, 66% of them are sessionized. Based on these data, web-SPADE has found approximately 10.5M frequent sequences.

Figures 19.6 to 19.8 depict daily hits, number of sequences, and number of frequent pages from Consumer, General Business, and Others (the rest). These graphs have two axes each. The number of total hits and frequent sequences are depicted on log-scaled left axes. The black lines represent the total hits, and the thicker lines represent the frequent sequences. The number of frequent pages is depicted on the right axes with a very light line.

Sessionization has not been perfect since the beginning, due to the some organizational challenges. Thus we see some changes in the number of frequent pages. We can also draw some conclusion on the introduction of the .NET technologies. As seen from Figure 19.6, although the number of hits increases steadily, the number of frequent sequences fluctuates. During the introduction of the .NET technology, we had some problems in sessionization. The major problem was the transition between ASP and .NET ASP pages in terms of passing the cookie information. The other observation is that it is now possible to combine several URLs into a single one with .NET implementation. Thus hits will be logged repeatedly from the same URL in the web logs. This is a pitfall for the sequence mining algorithms when the click stream data are collected via web logs. Another observation is that click stream data is highly cyclical (see Figure 19.8 with weekly cycles).

To illustrate the usage of the webSPADE algorithm, we consider the data from January and August 2002 separately. As we mentioned above, certain pages on Verizon.com are tagged to collect session information and our analysis covers

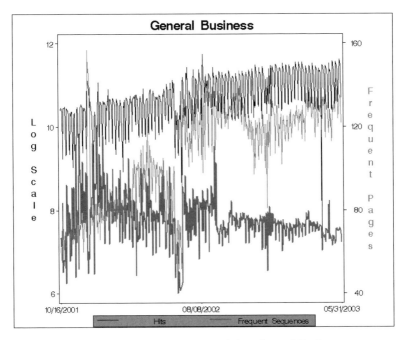

Figure 19.7. Daily sequence statistics: General Business.

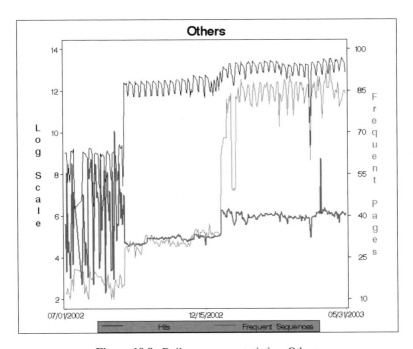

Figure 19.8. Daily sequence statistics: Others.

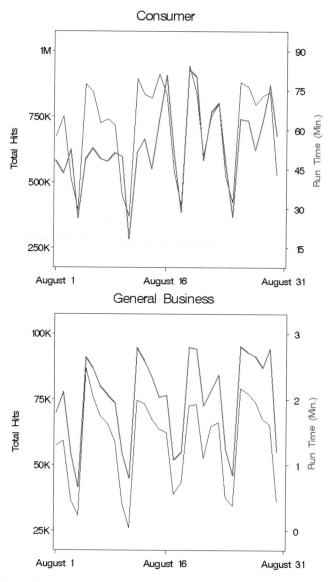

Figure 19.9. (a) Consumer hits and run times. (b) General Business hits and run times.

only these pages. Pages from two different lines of businesses (Consumer and General Business) are analyzed separately in this section.

Figure 19.9 shows the run times from August 2002 data. Times are reported in minutes. The thicker lines represent run times. Note that webSPADE run times are almost linearly correlated with the number of total hits. Although webSPADE is not run on a dedicated production server, the daily jobs are scheduled for the part of the day that the server usage is the lowest. Thus the example run times of webSPADE can be considered close to the reality. Note that run times also include both database access time and insertion time of sequences into the relational table.

The operational value of sequence mining is undeniable. For example, it is easy to monitor the traffic to understand whether a web page is functioning well or not. More specifically, certain pages might experience heavy traffic, but the following pages may experience very low traffic. Sequence mining can easily catch such patterns. Some design problems might cause such patterns (e.g., a misplaced next button at the bottom of the page; many people may not be able to see the next button because of smaller monitors). Such changes are requested in the light of sequence-mining findings.

Sequence mining can also be used to find out who comes to a certain page and where they go after that page. An analysis of a General Business page (Bill View) is depicted in Figure 19.10. Such analysis can be done easily with SQL queries at a micro level, but it is not possible to cover all the relations at a macro level (whole web site). Note that the bar charts in Figure 19.10 do not correspond to probability distributions. So the probabilities do not sum up to one.

The analysis such as given in Figure 19.10 can result in very important insights. For example, although bill view and bill pay processes are independent from each other in general business pages, a significant portion of customers first view their bill and then pay it in the same session. It is also found that the bill view process sometimes fails to show bills due to the database access timeout. So, if we can increase the reliability of the bill view process, some of our customers will pay their bills in the same session. This is a very simple conclusion, but it might take some time to reach with plain SQL analysis. Large-scale sequence mining enables us to come to a conclusion on this matter more rapidly.

19.5. FUTURE WORK AND CONCLUSION

We successfully applied a parallel sequence-mining algorithm to perform click stream analysis. webSPADE requires only one full scan of the database, but several partial scans of the database. Data and task parallelism are easily achieved using multi-threaded programming. Load balancing is left to the operating system, but the number of child threads is limited. Since the early design of the algorithm, there have been many improvements to increase the efficiency of the algorithm. In a way, the algorithm has been very stable and robust for a long time. An innovative analysis technique to scale up the sequence-mining algorithm is also used for value-added business analysis.

The current implementation can be adapted to other domains as well. One immediate usage of the click stream analysis is to predict future pages through which a user may navigate. This has a potential application in proxy server management, and obviously web personalization also depends on such prediction.

Market basket analysis (MBA) is the main application domain for association mining in which rules are extracted based on purchased items in customer

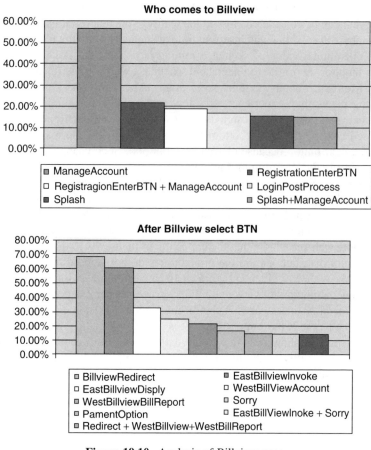

Figure 19.10. Analysis of Billview page.

transactions. Rule and sequence-mining algorithms such as Apriori and SPADE have superiority over other approaches such as clustering and dependency modeling. One extension to MBA is to couple its results with predictive modelling. Rules found by association mining can be used in creating new indicator variables to perform predictive modeling (Gayle, 2000). Such predictive models will help to categorize or segment customers based on their purchase (or navigation) patterns. In this manner, click stream analysis can be utilized to improve predictive abilities of product recommender systems by better segmenting the customers based on their navigational patterns.

ACKNOWLEDGMENTS

I would like to thank to my colleagues who worked on the webHOUSE project for nearly two years. Some of them are no longer with Verizon. This project has come to fruition as a result of my former boss Walid Nouh's patient and challenging management style. I am also very much indebted to Dr. Mohammed J. Zaki for his helpful comments and directions on improving this chapter and work since the very beginning.

REFERENCES

Agrawal, R., and Srikant, R., Fast algorithms for mining association rules, in *Proceedings of the 20th VLDB Conference, Santiago, Chile*, pp. 487–499, 1994.

Agrawal, R., and Srikant, R., Mining sequential patterns, in *11th International Conference on Data Engineering*, 1995.

Ayres, J., Gehrke, J., Yiu, T., and Flannick, J., Sequential pattern mining using a bitmap representation, in *Proceedings of the Eighth ACM SIGKDD International Conference on Knowledge Discovery and Data Mining*, Hand, D., Keim, D., and Ng, R., eds., Edmonton, Canada, ACM Press, New York, 2002.

Cadez, I., Heckerman, D., Meek, C., Smyth, P., and White, S., Visualization of navigation patterns on a web site using model based clustering, in *Proceedings of the Sixth ACM SIGKDD International Conference on Knowledge Discovery and Data Mining* (Boston, MA), pp. 280–284, 2000.

Demiriz, A., webSPADE: A parallel sequence mining algorithm to analyze web log data, in *Proceedings of The Second IEEE International Conference on Data Mining (ICDM 2002)*, Maebashi City, Japan, IEEE Computer Society, pp. 755–758, 2002.

Gayle, S., The marriage of market analysis to predictive modeling, Technical Report, SAS Institute Inc., Cary, NC, 2000.

Guralnik, V., and Karypis, G., Dynamic load balancing algorithms for sequence mining, Technical Report 00-056, Department of Computer Science, University of Minnesota, 2001.

Guralnik, V., Garg, N., and Karypis, G., Parallel tree projection algorithm for sequence mining, in *Proceedings of Seventh European Conference on Parallel Computing (Euro-Par)*, Sakellariou, R., Keane, J., Gurd, J., and Freeman, L., eds., Springer, Berlin, pp. 310–320, 2001.

Klemettinen, M., Mannila, H., and Toivonen, H., Interactive exploration of discovered knowledge: A methodology for interaction, and usability studies, Technical Report C-1996-3, Department of Computer Science, University of Helsinki, 1996.

Klemettinen, M., Mannila, H., and Toivonen, H., Interactive exploration of interesting patterns in the telecommunication network alarm sequence analyzer tasa, *Information and Software Technology* **41**, 557–567 (1999).

Mannila, H., and Toivonen, H., Discovering generalized episodes using minimal occurrences, in *2nd International Conference on Knowledge Discovery and Data Mining*, 1996.

Mannila, H., Toivonen, H., and Verkamo, I., Discovering frequent episodes in sequences, in *1st International Conference on Knowledge Discovery and Data Mining*, 1995.

Oates, T., Schmill, M. D., Jensen, D., and Cohen, P. R., A family of algorithms for finding temporal structure in data, in *6th International Workshop on AI and Statistics*, 1997.

Pei, J., Han, J., Pinto, H., Chen, Q., Dayal, U., and Hsu, M.-C., Prefixspan: Mining sequential patterns efficiently by prefix-projected pattern growth, in *Proceedings of International Conference on Data Engineering (ICDE '01)*, Heidelberg, Germany, 2001.

Rajamani, K., Cox, A., Iyer, B., and Chadha, A., Efficient mining for association rules with relational database systems, in *Proceedings of the International Database Engineering and Applications Symposium (IDEAS '99)*, 1999.

Sarawagi, S., Thomas, S., and Agrawal, R., Integrating association rule mining with relational database systems: Alternatives and implications, in *Proceedings of the 1998 ACM SIGMOD International Conference on Management of Data*, pp. 343–354, ACM, 1998.

Spiliopoulou, M., Pohle, C., and Faulstich, L. C., Improving the effectiveness of a web site with web usage mining, in *Advances in Web Usage Mining and User Profiling: Proceedings of the WEBKDD'99 Workshop, LNAI 1836*, Masand, B., and Spiliopoulou, M., eds., Springer-Verlag, Berlin, pp. 139–159, 2000.

Srikant, R., and Agrawal, R., Mining sequential patterns: Generalizations and performance improvements, in *5th International Conference on Extending Database Technology*, 1996.

Srivastava, J., Cooley, R., Deshpande, M., and Tan, P.-N., Web usage mining: Discovery and applications of usage patterns from web data, *SIGKDD Explorations* **1**, 12–23 (2000).

Turner, S., "Analog." http://www.analog.cx, 2000.

Zaki, M. J., SPADE: An efficient algorithm for mining frequent sequences, *Machine Learning Journal* **42**, 31–60 (2001a). Special issue on Unsupervised Learning (Fisher, D., ed.).

Zaki, M. J., Parallel sequence mining on shared-memory machines, *Journal of Parallel and Distributed Computing* **61**, 401–426 (2001b). Special issue on High Performance Data Mining (Kumar, V., Ranka, S., and Singh, V., eds.).

20

INTERACTIVE METHODS FOR TAXONOMY EDITING AND VALIDATION

Scott Spangler and Jeffrey Kreulen

20.1. INTRODUCTION

Businesses have been able to systematically increase the leverage gained from enterprise data through technologies such as relational database management systems and techniques such as data warehousing. Additionally, it is conjectured that the amount of knowledge encoded in electronic text far surpasses that available in data alone. However, the ability to take advantage of this wealth of knowledge is just beginning to meet the challenge. Businesses that can take advantage of this potential will surely be at an advantage through increased efficiencies. One important step in achieving this potential has been to structure the inherently unstructured information in meaningful ways. A well-established first step in gaining understanding is to segment examples into meaningful categories (Brachman and Anand, 1996). This leads to the idea of taxonomies—natural hierarchical organizations of the information in alignment with the business goals, organization, and processes. While there will be some commonality in some industries, these natural organizations will have significant diversity across domains and organizations.

Research to address this need for taxonomy development has concentrated largely around automated grouping techniques such as text clustering. While we believe that text clustering is an invaluable tool—indeed it is part of our solution—we assert that it is insufficient to meet the full challenge of taxonomy generation by itself. Our experience using variations of k-means (Hartigan, 1975; Rasmussen, 1992) and expectation maximization (EM) clustering algorithms (Vaithyanathan and Dom, 1999, 2000) have shown that they generate

Next Generation of Data-Mining Applications. Edited by Kantardzic and Zurada
ISBN 0-471-65605-4 © 2005 the Institute of Electrical and Electronics Engineers, Inc.

useful seed taxonomies, but rarely generate a satisfactory final taxonomy for a given business problem. For example, if you were to cluster a set of patents with the intent to create a technology-based taxonomy, you would typically find some of the clusters to be technologies and some to be based on some other aspect or relationship found in the text such as processes. Careful feature selection is one approach to address this problem by leveraging controlled vocabularies (Kornai and Stone, 2004). However, we find this approach to be very labor-intensive and would still yield results that would need further refinement.

Our approach to solve this problem focuses on the visualization, editing, and validation of clustering results (Spangler and Kreulen, 2002). We will go into details of our approach below, but further clarification on the problem and its relationship to cluster validation is warranted. The problem we are attempting to solve has been referred to in the literature (Dom, 2001; Halkidi et al., 2001) as clustering validation. Validation methods have typically been based on one of three types of criteria: external, internal, and relative. External criteria typically use a prespecified "ground truth" by which we can directly measure the quality of our clusters. Internal criteria are based on statistics or measures computed from a given taxonomy. Relative criteria are based on comparison with alternative taxonomies. Our approach integrates internal and external criteria, with the external criteria (a human expert) being the final determinant. Clearly it is not practical to read each document and categorize it; however, expert inspection guided by appropriate feedback is a powerful combination. We wish to stress that our innovation is not a particular clustering or visualization technique, but is rather a general strategy for applying clustering and visualization techniques interactively with human expertise to create the best possible taxonomy for a business application.

In this chapter we will outline a system and methodology that leverages clustering or keyword queries as a seed taxonomy and provides the appropriate feedback to a human analyst to efficiently guide the user to refine the taxonomy toward a desired, if not previously known, quality and modelable taxonomy. In Section 20.2 we describe how we generate an initial taxonomy. In Section 20.3 we describe the important capabilities for viewing and understanding a taxonomy. This gives the taxonomy analyst the necessary feedback to modify a taxonomy, which we describe in Section 20.4. In Section 20.5 we describe our approach to validating and ensuring that a taxonomy can be modeled for the purpose of classifying future documents. In Section 20.6 we describe analysis with structured Information. In Section 20.7 we give a detailed illustration of how our approach was used successfully to analyze and report on IBM's corporate wide "Values-Jam" discussion forum event. Finally, in Section 20.8 we summarize and outline areas for future research.

20.2. GENERATING A TAXONOMY

Because there is no one "right" taxonomy to cover all possible uses of document collection, it is important to provide multiple methods for generating the initial seed taxonomy from which the user begins to create the final document classes. Our methodology provides two main alternatives for taxonomy generation, via clustering and via keywords queries.

20.2.1. Taxonomy Generation via Clustering

In the cases where the user has no preconceived idea about what categories the document collection should contain, text clustering may be used to create an initial breakdown of the documents into clusters, grouping together documents having similar word content. To facilitate this process, we represent the documents in a vector space model. We represent each document as a vector of weighted frequencies of the document features (words and phrases) (Salton and McGill, 1983). We use the txn weighting scheme (Salton and Buckley, 1988). This scheme emphasizes words with high frequency in a document, and it normalizes each document vector to have unit Euclidean norm. For example, if a document were the sentence, "We have no bananas, we have no bananas today," and the dictionary consisted of only two terms, "bananas" and "today," then the unnormalized document vector would be {2 1} (to indicate two bananas and one today), and the normalized version would be $[2/\sqrt{5}, 1/\sqrt{5}]$.

The words and phrases that make up the document feature space are determined by first counting which words occur most frequently (in the most documents) in the text. A standard "stop word" list is used to eliminate words such as "and," "but," and "the" (Fox, 1992). The top N words are retained in the first pass, where the value of N may vary depending on the length of the documents, the number of documents, and the number of categories to be created. Typically $N = 2000$ is sufficient for 10,000 short documents of around 200 words to be divided into 30 categories. After selecting the words in the first pass, we make a second pass to count the frequency of the phrases that occur using these words. A phrase is considered to be a sequence of two words occurring in order without intervening nonstop words. We again prune to keep only the N most frequent words and phrases. This becomes the feature space. A third pass through the data indexes the documents by their feature occurrences. The user may edit this feature space as desired to improve clustering performance. This includes adding, in particular, words and phrases the user deems to be important, such as named entities like "International Business Machines." Stemming is usually also incorporated to create a default synonym table that the user may also edit (Honrado et al., 2000).

As our primary tool for automated classification, we used the k-means algorithm (Duda and Hart, 1973; Hartigan, 1975) using a cosine similarity metric (Rasmussen, 1992) to automatically partition the documents into k disjoint clusters. The algorithm is very fast and easy-to-implement. See Rasmussen (1992) for a detailed discussion of various other text clustering algorithms. The k-means algorithm produces a set of disjoint clusters and a centroid for each cluster that represents the cluster mean. Typically, k is initially set to 30, for the highest level of the taxonomy, though the user may adjust this if desired. The initial taxonomy assigns each document to only one category (cluster). Any of the initial high-level categories may be subcategorized if desired, either automatically and recursively, or manually one at a time. After clustering is complete, a final "merging" step takes place. In this step, two or more clusters that are each dominated by the same keyword (dominated means that 90% of the examples contain this keyword) are merged into a single cluster, and a new centroid is calculated based on the combined example set. The reason we do this is to avoid arbitrarily separating similar examples into separate subsets before the expert user has had a chance to evaluate the class as a whole.

20.2.2. Cluster Naming

In order to help the user understand the meaning of each cluster, the system gives each document category a name that describes it. Cluster naming is not an exact science, but our method attempts to describe the cluster as succinctly as possible, without missing any important constituent components. The first rule of naming is that if a single term dominates a cluster, then this term is given as the cluster name. If no term dominates, then the most frequent term in the cluster becomes the first word in the name and the remaining set of examples (those not containing the most frequent term) are analyzed to find the dominant term. If a dominant term for the remaining examples is found, then this term is added to the name (separated by a comma) and the name is complete, otherwise the process continues for up to four word-length names. Beyond four words we simply call the class "Miscellaneous."

20.2.3. Taxonomy Generation via Keyword Queries

An alternative to k-means clustering is to create an initial categorization via Boolean keyword queries. This approach is most useful when the domain expert already has a strong idea of how the taxonomy should be structured. Each category is described via a set of keywords connected by "and," "or," or "not." The resulting query defines those document examples that belong to the category. The queries are then ordered and the document initially falls into the category of the query that matches its content. Any document that does not match any query is placed in a special "Miscellaneous" category. The user may reorder the queries based on the results to ensure that every category starts with a significant number of matching documents. Once the initial taxonomy is created, further refinement can take place via k-means clustering (using centroids of the existing categories as seeds) or by manual editing of the categories (see next section). The user may create different sets of queries to generate multiple taxonomies if desired (Spangler et al., 2003).

20.3. VIEWING THE TAXONOMY

Before a user can begin editing a taxonomy, they must first understand the existing categories and their relationships. In this section we describe our strategy to communicate the salient characteristics of a document taxonomy to the user.

Our primary representation of each category is the centroid (Duda and Hart, 1973). The distance metric employed to compare documents to each other and to the category centroids is the cosine similarity metric (Rasmussen, 1992). This metric is used at the user's request to automatically partition any subset of the documents into k disjoint clusters. As will be seen, during the category editing process, we are not rigid in requiring each document to belong to the category of its nearest centroid, nor do we strictly require every document to belong to only one category.

To provide a good understanding of a given taxonomy, which is generally hierarchical in structure, we provide a series of views that cover different levels of detail. The views include a global, single level within a tree (all children of a single parent including the root), along with a detailed view of each individual category. In the global "Categorization Tree," categories with subcategories are displayed as "folders" that can be expanded.

Leaf categories are displayed as nodes. Selecting a folder can take the user down a level to the Category Table view, which shows statistics about just the categories that are immediate subclasses of the selected category (see Figure 20.1).

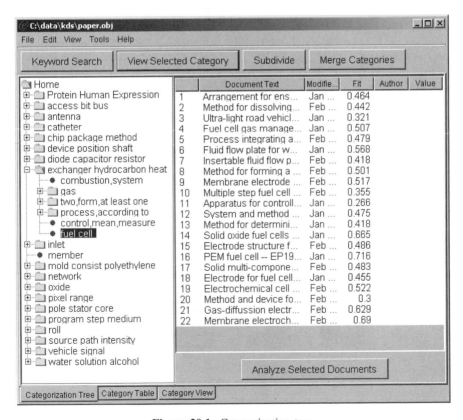

Figure 20.1. Categorization tree.

Selecting a leaf category or selecting a row in the Category Table displays the Category (Class) View (see Figure 20.9). This view provides several different windows on a single category that help to explain and summarize the content of the selected category's documents. The remainder of this section describes in detail what information is communicated in the Category View.

20.3.1. Summaries

Since we cannot expect the user to spend the time to read through all of the individual documents in a category, summarization is an important tool to help the user understand what a category contains. Summarization techniques based on extracting text from the individual documents (Jing et al., 1998) were found to be insufficient in practice for the purpose of summarizing an entire document category, especially when the theme of that category is somewhat diverse. Instead, we employ two different techniques to summarize a category. The first is a feature bar chart. This chart has an entry for every dictionary term (feature) that occurs in any document of the category. Each entry consists of two bars, a red bar to indicate what percentage of the documents in the category contain the feature, and a blue bar that indicates how frequently the feature occurs in the background population of documents from which the category was drawn. The bars of the chart are sorted in decreasing order of the difference between blue and red. Thus the most important features of the category in question are shown at the beginning of the chart. This chart quickly summarizes for the user all the important features of a category, with their relative importance indicated by the size of the bars (see Figure 20.2).

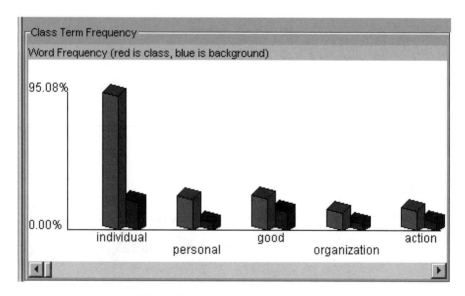

Figure 20.2. Term frequency bar chart.

The second technique is a dynamic decision tree representation that describes what feature combinations define the category. This tree is generated in the same manner as a binary ID3 (Manning and Schütze, 2000), selecting at each decision point the attribute that is most helpful in splitting the whole population of documents so that the two new classes of documents created are most nearly pure category and pure noncategory. Each feature choice is made on the fly as the user expands each node, until a state of purity is reached or when no additional features will improve the purity with respect to the category. The result is essentially a set of classification rules that define the category to the desired level of detail. At any point the user may select a node of the decision tree to see all the documents at the node, all the in-category documents at the node, or all the noncategory documents at the node. The nodes are also color-coded: Red is a node whose membership is more than (or equal to) 50% in category, and blue is a node whose membership is less than 50% in category. This display (see Figure 20.3) gives users an in-depth definition of the class in terms of salient features and lets them readily select various category components for more in depth study. In Figure 20.3 the highlighted node selects the rule: "+ respect, − individual" which represents those examples that contain the term "respect" but

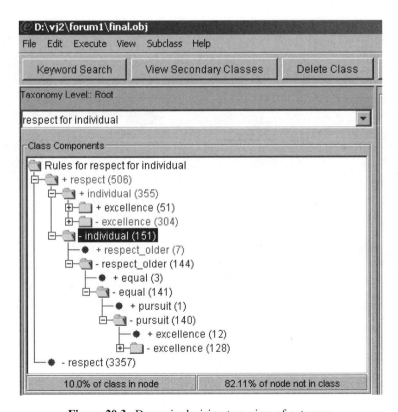

Figure 20.3. Dynamic decision tree view of category.

not the term "individual." Documents that follow this rule make up 10% of the "respect for individual" category, but out of all documents that match the rule, 82.11% do not belong to the "respect for individual" category.

20.3.2. Visualization

In order to understand specifically how two or more categories at the same level of the taxonomy relate to each other, a visualization strategy is employed. The idea is to visually display the vector space of a bag-of-words document model (Salton and Buckley, 1988; Salton and McGill, 1983) so that the documents will appear as points in space. The result is that documents containing similar words occur near to each other in the visual display. If the vector space model were two-dimensional, this would be straightforward: We could simply draw the documents as point on an X, Y scatter plot. The difficulty is that the document vector space will be of much higher dimension. In fact the dimensionality will be the

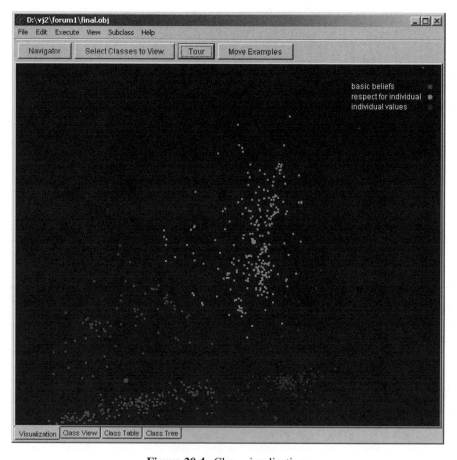

Figure 20.4. Class visualization.

size of the feature space (dictionary), which is typically thousands of terms. Therefore we need a way to reduce the dimensionality from thousands to two in such a way as to retain most of the relevant information. Our approach uses the CViz method (Dhillon et al., 2002), which relies on three category centroids to define the plane of most interest and to project the documents as points on this plane (by finding the intersection with a normal line drawn from point to plane). The selection of which categories to display in addition to the selected category is based on finding the categories with the nearest centroid distance to the selected category. The documents displayed in such a plot are colored according to category membership. The centroid of the category is also displayed. The resultant plot is a valuable way to discover relationships between neighboring concepts in a taxonomy (see Figure 20.4).

20.3.3. Sorting of Examples

When studying the examples in a category to understand the category's essence, it is important that the user not have to select the examples at random. To do so can sometimes lead to a skewed understanding of the content of a category, especially if the sample is small compared to the size of the category (which is often the case in practice). To help alleviate this problem, our software allows sorting of examples based on the "Most Typical" first or "Least Typical" first criteria. This translates in vector space terms to sorting in order of distance from category centroid (i.e., most typical is closest to centroid, least typical is furthest from centroid). The advantage of sorting in this way is twofold: Reading documents in most typical order can help the user to quickly understand what the category is generally about, without having to read a large sample of the documents in the category, while reading the least typical documents can help the user to understand the total scope of the category and if there is conceptual purity.

20.4. EDITING THE TAXONOMY

Once the content manager understands the meaning of the classes in the taxonomy and their relationship to each other, the next step is to provide tools for rapidly changing the taxonomy to reflect the needs of the application. Keep in mind that our goal here is not to produce a "perfect" taxonomy for every possible purpose. Such a taxonomy may not even exist, or at least may require too much effort to obtain. Instead we want to focus the users efforts on creating a "natural" taxonomy that is practical for a given application. For such applications, there is no right or wrong change to make. It is important only that the change accurately reflect the expert user's point of view about the desired structure. In this situation, the user is always right. The tool's job is to allow the user to make whatever changes may be deemed desirable. In some cases such changes can be made at the category level, but in other cases a more detailed modification of category membership may be required. Our tool provides capabilities at every level of a taxonomy to allow the user to make the desired modifications with a simple point and click.

20.4.1. Category Level

Category level changes involve modifying the taxonomy at a macro-level, without direct reference to individual documents within each category.

Merging.   Merging two classes means creating a new category that is the union of two or more previously existing category memberships. A new centroid is created that is the average of the combined examples. The user supplies the new category with an appropriate name.

Deleting.   Deleting a category (or categories) means removing the category and its children from the taxonomy. The user needs to recognize that this may have unintended consequences, since all the examples that formerly belonged to the deleted category must now be placed in a different category at the current level of the taxonomy. To make this decision more explicit, we introduce the graphic called "View Secondary classes" chart (see Figure 20.10).

This chart displays what percentage of a category's documents would go to which other categories if the selected category were to be deleted. Each slice of the displayed pie chart can be selected to view the individual documents represented by the slice. Making such information explicit allows the user to make an informed decision when deleting a category, avoiding unintended consequences.

Clustering.   At any node of the Categorization Tree the user may request subclassing via text clustering. This will apply a standard clustering algorithm, such as k-means (Hartigan, 1975; Rasmussen, 1992), to the set of documents represented by the selected category. The user will be asked to provide a value for the number of classes to create. Subclasses are derived by applying the clustering algorithm to the vector space model. Each newly derived subcategory will be given a name based on the features that have an in-class frequency most different from that of the background frequency. If desired, this same clustering approach can be applied repeatedly in a recursive fashion on each derived category until a stopping criteria is reached (either some user-supplied minimum category size or sufficiently high value category cohesion). The resulting subcategorization can then be edited if desired to reflect a more natural partitioning.

Dragging and Dropping.   From the Categorization Tree view the user can select any category and then drag and drop the category into any existing folder (a category with children). An example of when such an operation might be performed is when a very specific category is created at the root node of the tree, which would more naturally belong within an already existing, more general category. The operation of dragging and dropping a category to a folder has consequences to all other folders in a direct line from the root of the tree to the destination node (which gain the contents of the source node) and to all other folders in a direct line form the root to the source node (which lose the contents of the source node).

20.4.2. Document Level

While some changes to a taxonomy may be made at the class level, others require a finer degree of control. These are called document level changes, and they consist of moving or copying selected documents from a source category to a destination category. The most difficult part of this operation from the users point of view is selecting exactly the right set of documents to move so that the source and destination categories are changed in the manner desired. To address this problem, a number of document selection mechanisms are provided.

Selection by Keywords.   One of the most natural and common ways to select a set of documents is with a keyword query. The user may enter a query for the whole document collection or for just a specific category. The query can contain keywords separated by "and" and/or "or" and also negated words. Words that co-occur with the query string are displayed for the user to help refine the query. Documents that are found using the keyword query tool can be immediately viewed and selected one at a time or as a group to move or establish a new category.

Selection by Sorting.   Another way to select documents to move or copy is via the "Most/Least Typical" sorting technique described in Section 20.3.3. For example, the documents that are least typical of a given category can be located, selected, and moved out of the category they are in. They may then be placed elsewhere or in a new category.

Selection by Visualization.   The scatter plot visualization display described in Section 20.3.2 can also be a powerful tool for selecting individual or groups of documents. Using a "floating box," groups of contiguous points (documents) can be selected and moved to the new desired class (see Figure 20.5).

To Move, Copy, or Delete.   Independent of the document selection method, the user is allowed to choose between moving, copying, or deleting the selected documents. Moving is generally preferable because single class membership generally leads to more distinct categories that are better for the classification of future documents. Still, in cases where a more ambiguous category membership better reflects the user's natural understanding of the taxonomy, the user may create a copy of the documents to be moved and to place this copy in the destination category. In such cases the individual document will actually exist in two (or more) categories at once, until the user deletes the example. Deletion is the third option. It allows the document to be removed from the taxonomy, if it is judged to be not applicable.

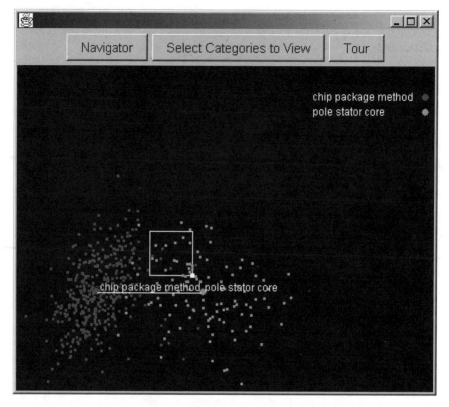

Figure 20.5. Floating box for moving documents.

20.5. VALIDATION

Whenever a change is made to the taxonomy, it is very important for the user to validate that the change has had the desired effect on the taxonomy as a whole and that no undesired consequences have resulted from unintentional side effects. Our software contains a number of capabilities that allow the user to inspect the results of modifications. The goal is to ensure both that the categories are all meaningful, complete, and differentiable and that the concepts represented by the document partitioning can be carried forward automatically in the future as new documents arrive.

20.5.1. Direct Inspection

The simplest method for validating the taxonomy is through direct inspection of the categories. The category views described in Section 20.2 provides many unique tools for validating that the membership of a category is not more or less than what the category means. Looking over some of the "Least Typical" documents is an especially valuable way to quickly ascertain that a category does not contain any documents that do not belong.

Another visual inspection method is to look at the nearest neighbors of the category being evaluated through the Scatter Plot display. Areas of document overlap at the margins are primary candidates for further investigation and validation.

20.5.2. Validation Metrics

Much research has been done in the area of evaluating the results of clustering algorithms (Halkidi et al., 2001; Rasmussen, 1992). While such measures are not entirely applicable to taxonomies that have been modified to incorporate domain knowledge, there are some important concepts that can be applied from this research. Our vector space model representation (Salton and Buckley, 1988; Salton and McGill, 1983), while admittedly a very coarse reflection of the documents actual content, does at least allow us to summarize a singe level of the taxonomy via some useful statistics. These include:

- *Cohesion*: A measure of similarity within category. This is the average cosine distance of the documents within a category to the centroid of that category.
- *Distinctness*: a measure of differentiation between categories. This is one minus the cosine distance of the category to the centroid of the nearest-neighboring category.

These two criteria are variations to the ones proposed by Berry and Linoff (1996): compactness and separation. The advantage of using this approach as opposed to other statistical validation techniques is that they are more easily computed and also readily understood by the taxonomy expert. In practice, these metrics often prove useful in identifying two potential areas of concern in a taxonomy. The first potential problem is "miscellaneous" classes. These are classes that have a diffuse population of documents that talk about many different things. Such classes may need to be split further or subcategorized. The second potential problem is when two different categories have very similar content. If two or more classes are almost indistinguishable in terms of their word content, they may be candidates for merging.

Statistical measures such as cohesion and distinctness provide a good rough measure of how well the word content of a category reflects its underlying meaning. For example, if a category that the user has created is not cohesive, then there is some doubt as to whether a classifier could learn to recognize a new document as belonging to that category, because the category is not well-defined in terms of word content. On the other hand, if a category is not distinct, then there is at least one other category containing documents with a similar vocabulary. This means that a classifier may have difficulty distinguishing which of the two similar categories to place a candidate document in. Of course, cohesion and distinctness are rough and relative metrics, therefore there is no fixed threshold value at which we can say that a category is not cohesive enough or lacks sufficient distinctness. In general, whenever a new category is created, we suggest to the user that the cohesion and distinctness score for the new category be no worse than the average for the current level of the taxonomy.

20.5.3. Other Metrics

Metrics such as cohesion and distinctness provide a rough measure of how well a given document taxonomy can be modeled and used to classify new documents. A more accurate measure can be created by applying a suite of classification algorithms to a training sample of the data and seeing how accurately such classifiers work on a corresponding unseen test sample. If one or more of the classifiers can achieve a high level of accuracy on each of the categories, this indicates that there is sufficient regularity in the document word content to accurately categorize new documents, assuming the right modeling approach is used. For each of these classifiers the labeled training set consists of two-thirds of the original document set, randomly selected without replacement. The test set is then the remaining one-third. The label of each document is the category it belongs to. The resulting accuracy of such classifiers is not guaranteed to be high, even for the centroid classifier. This is due to the fact that the user may have made arbitrary or inconsistent edits to the taxonomy using the methods described above. Applying these classification metrics then helps to make clear which of these edits can really be modeled using known supervised learning techniques. If a category created from user edits cannot be modeled accurately, then we cannot expect the system to automatically maintain its meaning in the future as new documents are added to the taxonomy.

We incorporated the following classifiers into our suite of available classifiers in the toolkit.

Centroid.   This is the simplest classifier. It classifies each document to the nearest centroid (mean of the category) using a cosine distance metric.

Decision Tree.   The decision tree algorithm is an implementation of the well-known ID3 algorithm (Quinlan, 1986). Some classification algorithms benefit from additional reduction in the feature space (McCallum and Nigam, 1998; Duda and Hart, 1973). In these algorithms we use a method to select terms based on their mutual information with the categories (McCallum and Nigam, 1998), and we select all terms where the mutual information is above some threshold.

Naïve Bayes.   We have incorporated two variations of Naïve Bayes classifier into our suite. The first is based upon numeric features (multinomial), and the second is on binary features (multivariate). Both use the well-known Bayes decision rule and make the Naïve Bayes assumption (Manning and Schütze, 2000; McCallum and Nigam, 1998; Mitchell, 1997) and differ only in how the probability of the document given the class, $P(d|C_k)$, is calculated.

In the multinomial model (McCallum and Nigam, 1998), classification is based upon the number of occurrences of each word in the document:

$$P(d|C_k) = \prod_{w_i \in d} P(w_i|C_k)$$

where the individual word probabilities are calculated form the training data using Laplace smoothing (McCallum and Nigam, 1998):

$$P(w_i|C_k) = \frac{n_{k,i} + 1}{n_k + |V|}$$

where n_k is the total number of word positions in documents assigned to class C_k in the training data, $n_{k,i}$ is the number of positions in these documents where w_i occurs, and V is the set of all unique words.

The multivariate model (McCallum and Nigam, 1998) calculates probabilities based on the whether words appear in documents, ignoring their frequency of occurrence:

$$P(d|C_k) = \prod_{w_i \in V} [B_i P(w_i|C_k) + (1 - B_i)(1 - P(W_i|C_k))]$$

where B_i is 1 if w_i occurs in d and 0 otherwise, and the individual word probabilities are calculated as

$$P(w_i|C_k) = \frac{1 + \sum_{d \in D} B_i P(C_k|d)}{2 + \sum_{d \in D} P(C_k|d)}$$

where $P(C_k|d)$ is 1 if d is in class C_k and 0 otherwise.

Rule-Based. The rule induction classifier (Johnson et al., 2002) is based on a decision tree system that takes advantage of (a) the sparsity of text data feature space and (b) a rule simplification method that converts a decision tree into a logically equivalent rule set. The system also uses a modified entropy function that both favors splits enhancing the purity of partitions and, in contrast to the gini or standard entropy metrics, is close to the classification error curve, which has been found to improve text classification accuracy.

Statistical. The statistical classifier is a version of regularized linear classifier that has similar behavior as a support vector machine, but also provides a probability estimate for each class. It also employs the sparse regularization condition described in Zhang (2002) to produce a sparse weight vector. The numerical algorithm is described in Zhang (2002).

For each category, a precision/recall score is provided in the category table view that indicates how well that category can be modeled with that approach (see Figure 20.6). Categories that cannot be modeled with any approach should be reexamined to see if they can be modified to make them more modelable.

	Class Name	Size	Statistical Classifier	Decision Tree	Naive Bayes (nu...	Centroid	Rule Based Classi...
1	loyalty	146 (3.78%)	84.62%/91.67%	60.00%/87.50%	87.50%/87.50%	91.30%/87.50%	93.75%/62.50%
2	basic beliefs	258 (6.68%)	86.44%/89.47%	81.82%/78.95%	75.00%/89.47%	100.00%/94.74%	87.76%/75.44%
3	respect for individ...	270 (6.99%)	92.31%/84.21%	78.95%/78.95%	70.59%/84.21%	91.67%/96.49%	95.65%/77.19%
4	stock price is drivi...	77 (1.99%)	92.86%/76.47%	77.78%/82.35%	73.68%/82.35%	76.19%/94.12%	92.86%/76.47%
5	balancing stakeho...	49 (1.27%)	100.00%/35.71%	25.00%/7.14%	0.00%/0.00%	100.00%/85.71%	80.00%/28.57%
6	"human resource"...	73 (1.89%)	75.00%/60.00%	50.00%/70.00%	87.50%/70.00%	90.00%/90.00%	75.00%/30.00%
7	trust / integrity	127 (3.29%)	84.00%/72.41%	73.33%/75.86%	71.43%/68.97%	93.10%/93.10%	83.33%/51.72%
8	ethics	46 (1.19%)	100.00%/75.00%	60.00%/75.00%	50.00%/25.00%	75.00%/75.00%	75.00%/75.00%
9	teamwork	134 (3.47%)	86.96%/80.00%	66.67%/88.00%	66.67%/72.00%	100.00%/96.00%	80.77%/84.00%
10	management	110 (2.85%)	64.71%/57.89%	61.11%/57.89%	52.63%/52.63%	80.95%/89.47%	66.67%/21.05%
11	long term vs. short...	80 (2.07%)	80.00%/38.10%	50.00%/42.86%	66.67%/38.10%	77.27%/80.95%	100.00%/14.29%
12	customers	359 (9.29%)	78.21%/91.04%	59.78%/82.09%	58.25%/89.55%	95.24%/89.55%	67.61%/71.64%
13	living our values	104 (2.69%)	72.22%/76.47%	59.09%/76.47%	52.94%/52.94%	88.24%/88.24%	100.00%/17.65%
14	individual values	113 (2.93%)	84.21%/61.54%	83.33%/57.69%	55.56%/38.46%	92.00%/88.46%	75.00%/11.54%
15	importance of valu...	134 (3.47%)	75.00%/85.71%	68.75%/78.57%	42.86%/32.14%	77.14%/96.43%	86.21%/89.29%
16	caring	67 (1.73%)	81.82%/75.00%	75.00%/50.00%	100.00%/41.67%	92.31%/100.00%	66.67%/83.33%
17	goals / pbcs	36 (0.93%)	100.00%/44.44%	72.73%/88.89%	100.00%/22.22%	77.78%/77.78%	100.00%/11.11%
18	leadership	53 (1.37%)	66.67%/50.00%	0.00%/0.00%	100.00%/25.00%	61.11%/91.67%	60.00%/25.00%
19	community	45 (1.16%)	60.00%/37.50%	66.67%/50.00%	100.00%/50.00%	80.00%/100.00%	100.00%/62.50%
20	change	107 (2.77%)	86.96%/76.92%	76.19%/61.54%	85.71%/46.15%	96.30%/100.00%	83.33%/19.23%
21	diversity	62 (1.60%)	60.00%/75.00%	50.00%/50.00%	62.50%/62.50%	58.33%/87.50%	0.00%/0.00%
22	culture	42 (1.09%)	50.00%/25.00%	25.00%/25.00%	0.00%/0.00%	42.86%/75.00%	50.00%/25.00%
23	sharing	61 (1.58%)	100.00%/66.67%	76.92%/83.33%	80.00%/33.33%	91.67%/91.67%	0.00%/0.00%
24	enron	33 (0.85%)	100.00%/85.71%	75.00%/42.86%	66.67%/28.57%	83.33%/71.43%	100.00%/85.71%
25	billable hours	56 (1.45%)	93.33%/77.78%	90.91%/55.56%	81.25%/72.22%	76.19%/88.89%	76.92%/55.56%
26	overseas hiring	126 (3.26%)	84.62%/75.86%	68.97%/68.97%	72.22%/89.66%	77.14%/93.10%	82.14%/79.31%
27	services	23 (0.60%)	0.00%/0.00%	50.00%/75.00%	0.00%/0.00%	36.36%/100.00%	0.00%/0.00%
28	work/life balance	75 (1.94%)	100.00%/85.00%	75.00%/75.00%	81.82%/90.00%	90.00%/90.00%	100.00%/85.00%
29	quality	15 (0.39%)	0.00%/0.00%	50.00%/33.33%	0.00%/0.00%	33.33%/66.67%	0.00%/0.00%
30	sam	25 (0.65%)	100.00%/37.50%	77.78%/87.50%	100.00%/50.00%	66.67%/75.00%	0.00%/0.00%
31	GLBT	54 (1.40%)	100.00%/90.91%	80.00%/36.36%	76.92%/90.91%	80.00%/72.73%	90.91%/90.91%
32	Miscellaneous	569 (14.73%)	54.12%/91.09%	74.26%/74.26%	53.33%/63.37%	95.52%/63.37%	31.65%/93.07%
33	pension	62 (1.60%)	92.31%/100.00%	85.71%/50.00%	60.00%/50.00%	75.00%/50.00%	92.31%/100.00%
34	historical perspect...	272 (7.04%)	82.98%/79.59%	65.38%/69.39%	58.46%/77.55%	85.11%/81.63%	78.43%/81.63%
	TOTAL / AVERAGE	3863	77.34%/77.34%	69.27%/69.27%	65.36%/65.36%	86.07%/86.07%	63.02%/63.02%

Figure 20.6. Precision/recall for different classifiers.

In cases where no single classifier works adequately well for all categories, so that a "mixture" of classifiers is needed, it is possible to combine the results of several different classification algorithms into a single classifier (Kittler et al., 1998; Wolpert, 1992). This "mixture of experts" approach is partially based on the intuition that multiple generative processes may be involved in the creation of a taxonomy.

20.6. TEXT ANALYSIS VERSUS STRUCTURED INFORMATION

Up to this point, we have only considered the document text in our analysis of data. Of course in most cases text information has a corresponding structured component. Such structured information usually includes the creation/modification date of the document, the document author or assignee, geographic location, and so forth. Any complete analysis of the text information will need to take this structured information into account.

20.6.1. Time Analysis

Most text document datasets will contain at least one time stamp associated with each document. This information provides an opportunity to discover how the document collection has evolved over time. Using the time stamp for each document (usually the creation date), we can form an additional metric called "recency." Recency is a measure of what percentage of the text documents were authored in the most recent time period. For example, we can define the most recent time period to be the last 10% of the document collection if the documents are sorted in chronological order. The Recency score for each category then becomes the percentage of that categories documents that fall in this the last 10%. The usefulness of the recency metric is that it helps to discover categories that may contain new concepts as data are added to the taxonomy. Categories with a high level of recency (greater than 10%) can be studied further by calling up a trend chart. Such a chart shows the category occurrence versus time when compared to the overall document occurrence versus time. Individual points in the chart can be selected to reveal the documents that correspond to any given time period.

20.6.2. Emerging Categories

Frequently an initial clustering formed via text clustering and edited using our techniques will be used to classify new data as they emerge. This "automatic categorization" is a powerful means of quickly assimilating new documents into a collection. The process for adding new documents to a taxonomy is straight-forward. We first use the original dictionary and classification model from the old document set to classify the new documents. Then we remember the classification labels for both the old and new documents and generate a new dictionary (of size N, where N is typically 2000 terms) on the combined set of new and old documents (see Section 20.2.1). A new set of centroids can then be created from the complete set of categorized documents. Unfortunately, this process does not take into account any new emerging concepts that may require additional categories. To discover such categories, we use a technique called "Recent Trends Analysis." Using our earlier definition of Recent (last 10% of the document collection), we analyze all the dictionary terms (i.e., the terms generated using the method described in Section 20.2.1 from data in the overall taxonomy of both "new" and "old" documents) to determine which, if any, occur with an unusually high frequency in the recent set. Unusually high is determined using a chi-squared test, which determines the independence of two discrete random variables (Press et al., 1992) and selecting those terms that occur with probability less than 0.01. The resulting term list is displayed to the user for further investigation via trend charts and example displays that can then be used to create new categories of documents.

20.6.3. Other Structured Information

In addition to dates, other kinds of structured information may be analyzed along with text. For such information a contingency-style table is displayed, showing the occurrence of the text clusters along one side of the table and the occurrence of the structured field in question along the other side. The cells of the table then display the co-occurrence counts (raw and percentage) for every combination of text cluster and structure field. The cells can be colored to indicate the relative likelihood of a particular combination occurring by random chance (see Figure 20.7). Individual cells or combinations may be selected by the user for trend charts or example displays that can then be used to create new categories of documents.

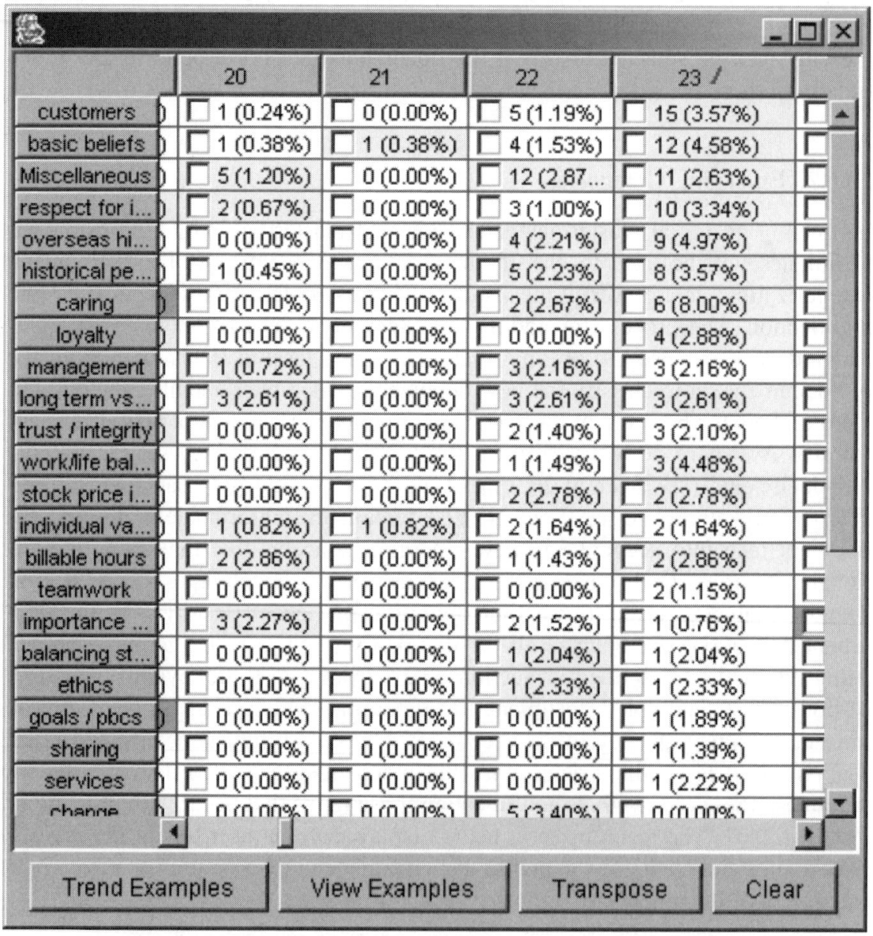

	20	21	22	23
customers	1 (0.24%)	0 (0.00%)	5 (1.19%)	15 (3.57%)
basic beliefs	1 (0.38%)	1 (0.38%)	4 (1.53%)	12 (4.58%)
Miscellaneous	5 (1.20%)	0 (0.00%)	12 (2.87...	11 (2.63%)
respect for i...	2 (0.67%)	0 (0.00%)	3 (1.00%)	10 (3.34%)
overseas hi...	0 (0.00%)	0 (0.00%)	4 (2.21%)	9 (4.97%)
historical pe...	1 (0.45%)	0 (0.00%)	5 (2.23%)	8 (3.57%)
caring	0 (0.00%)	0 (0.00%)	2 (2.67%)	6 (8.00%)
loyalty	0 (0.00%)	0 (0.00%)	0 (0.00%)	4 (2.88%)
management	1 (0.72%)	0 (0.00%)	3 (2.16%)	3 (2.16%)
long term vs...	3 (2.61%)	0 (0.00%)	3 (2.61%)	3 (2.61%)
trust / integrity	0 (0.00%)	0 (0.00%)	2 (1.40%)	3 (2.10%)
work/life bal...	0 (0.00%)	0 (0.00%)	1 (1.49%)	3 (4.48%)
stock price i...	0 (0.00%)	0 (0.00%)	2 (2.78%)	2 (2.78%)
individual va...	1 (0.82%)	1 (0.82%)	2 (1.64%)	2 (1.64%)
billable hours	2 (2.86%)	0 (0.00%)	1 (1.43%)	2 (2.86%)
teamwork	0 (0.00%)	0 (0.00%)	0 (0.00%)	2 (1.15%)
importance ...	3 (2.27%)	0 (0.00%)	2 (1.52%)	1 (0.76%)
balancing st...	0 (0.00%)	0 (0.00%)	1 (2.04%)	1 (2.04%)
ethics	0 (0.00%)	0 (0.00%)	1 (2.33%)	1 (2.33%)
goals / pbcs	0 (0.00%)	0 (0.00%)	0 (0.00%)	1 (1.89%)
sharing	0 (0.00%)	0 (0.00%)	0 (0.00%)	1 (1.39%)
services	0 (0.00%)	0 (0.00%)	0 (0.00%)	1 (2.22%)
change	0 (0.00%)	0 (0.00%)	5 (3.40%)	0 (0.00%)

Figure 20.7. Comparing clusters to structured information.

20.7. USAGE SCENARIO: INTERACTIVE TEXT MINING ON DISCUSSION FORUM DATA

One application of interactive text-mining techniques is in the area of discussion forum analysis. In this chapter we describe in detail one such analysis that was done for IBM ValuesJam, an internal company-wide, on-line discussion of IBM's corporate values. ValuesJam was a 72-hour global brainstorming event on the IBM internal website, held July 29–August 1, 2003. IBMers described their experiences and contributed ideas via four asynchronous discussion forums. The purpose of real-time interactive text mining of the jam was to generate forum "topics," thus allowing participants to learn which themes are emerging in each forum—and in the Jam overall—in 12-hour intervals. Total posts for this event were in excess of 8000 over the course of the event, with one of the largest forums containing in excess of 3000 posts.

Analyzing discussion forum data to produce topic areas of interest presents several challenges that an interactive text-mining approach is well-suited to address. First the forum analyzer must produce categories that reflect meaningful groups of posts, and these groups must not contain a significant number of extraneous or misclassified examples. Second, each cluster of posts must be given a concise yet meaningful name. Third, when presenting a cluster of posts, a set of representative examples are needed to further explain the meaning of the post, and they direct the user to the appropriate point in the discussion. Finally, the clusters need to evolve with the discussion, adding new clusters over time as appropriate to incorporate the new topics that will inevitably arise, without losing the old clusters and thus the overall continuity of the discussion topic list. Clearly a completely automated solution is impractical given these requirements, and a manual approach requiring a set of human editors to read 8000 posts in 72 hours and classify them is prohibitively expensive (and mind numbing). Interactive text mining is thus an ideal candidate for this application, and indeed our approach had been employed successfully on two previous IBM "Jam" events. At the time of this writing, the ValuesJam event was the largest discussion forum to which our approach had been applied and represents the first time that the results of our approach would be presented "live" to Jam participants.

20.7.1. Initial Taxonomy Generation

The first taxonomy generated for discussions in the largest forum of ValuesJam was created on 1308 posts representing 20 hours of discussion (see Figure 20.8). We begin by sorting the categories created via text clustering by their cohesion scores. This gives us a useful order in which to tackle the problem of quickly understanding the taxonomy, category by category, and making any necessary adjustments. We view each category in detail making any necessary adjustments and giving the category a new name if appropriate (e.g., the category name "stock price" was given to replace the name "stock" given by the system). Occasionally

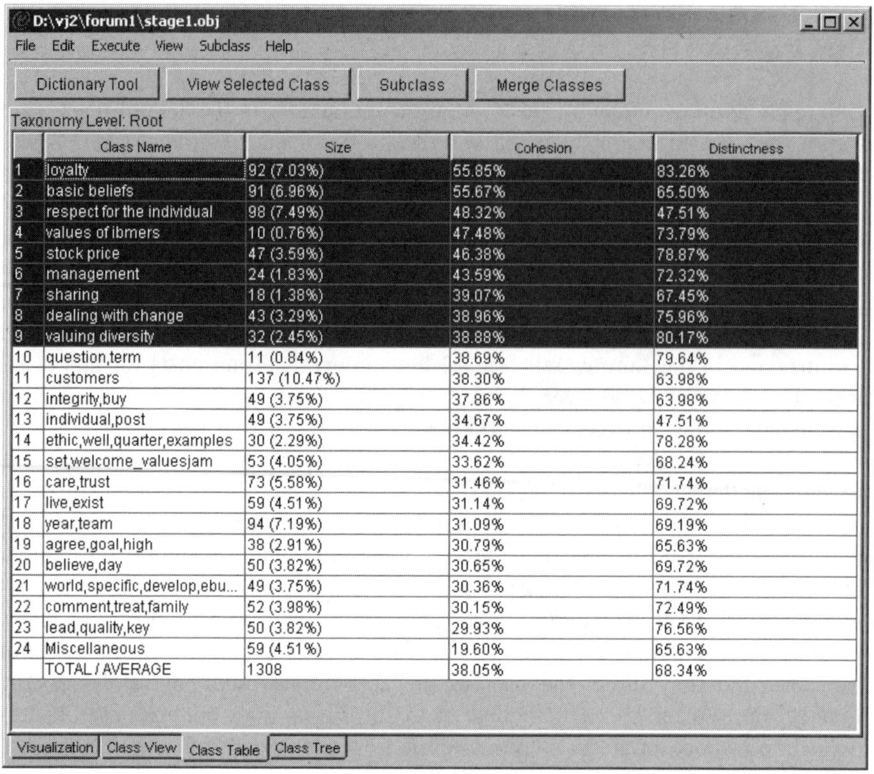

	Class Name	Size	Cohesion	Distinctness
1	loyalty	92 (7.03%)	55.85%	83.26%
2	basic beliefs	91 (6.96%)	55.67%	65.50%
3	respect for the individual	98 (7.49%)	48.32%	47.51%
4	values of ibmers	10 (0.76%)	47.48%	73.79%
5	stock price	47 (3.59%)	46.38%	78.87%
6	management	24 (1.83%)	43.59%	72.32%
7	sharing	18 (1.38%)	39.07%	67.45%
8	dealing with change	43 (3.29%)	38.96%	75.96%
9	valuing diversity	32 (2.45%)	38.88%	80.17%
10	question,term	11 (0.84%)	38.69%	79.64%
11	customers	137 (10.47%)	38.30%	63.98%
12	integrity,buy	49 (3.75%)	37.86%	63.98%
13	individual,post	49 (3.75%)	34.67%	47.51%
14	ethic,well,quarter,examples	30 (2.29%)	34.42%	78.28%
15	set,welcome_valuesjam	53 (4.05%)	33.62%	68.24%
16	care,trust	73 (5.58%)	31.46%	71.74%
17	live,exist	59 (4.51%)	31.14%	69.72%
18	year,team	94 (7.19%)	31.09%	69.19%
19	agree,goal,high	38 (2.91%)	30.79%	65.63%
20	believe,day	50 (3.82%)	30.65%	69.72%
21	world,specific,develop,ebu...	49 (3.75%)	30.36%	71.74%
22	comment,treat,family	52 (3.98%)	30.15%	72.49%
23	lead,quality,key	50 (3.82%)	29.93%	76.56%
24	Miscellaneous	59 (4.51%)	19.60%	65.63%
	TOTAL / AVERAGE	1308	38.05%	68.34%

Figure 20.8. Class table view.

we find clusters that are formed based on words that are not relevant to the content of the post, such as for the "question, term" cluster in Figure 20.9.

By viewing the secondary classes, we can determine where the examples will go when the centroid for this class is removed (see Figure 20.10). Seeing that they will distribute themselves evenly throughout the taxonomy, we can feel safe in deleting the centroid without ill effect.

The Miscellaneous class requires special attention. Frequently, individual dictionary terms can be used to extract a common set of examples from a Miscellaneous category and create a useful separate category. An example here is a category centered around the word "trust." Clicking on the red "trust" bar in the bar graph in Figure 20.11 will cause all those examples in Miscellaneous that contain the word "trust" to be selected. These can then be further edited and a new category called "trust" can be created in the taxonomy.

Finally the complete initial categorization emerges (Figure 20.12).

Using our methodology and software text analysis tools, this entire process required only about a half hour of concentrated effort. Now we can use this information to generate reports to the ValuesJam audience. First we add a

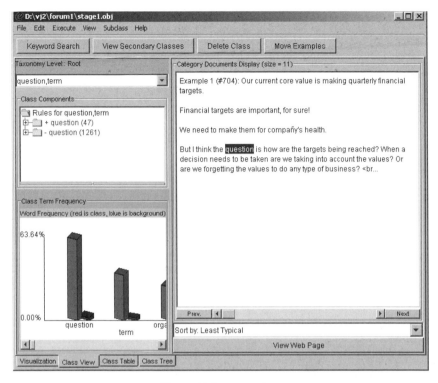

Figure 20.9. Class view.

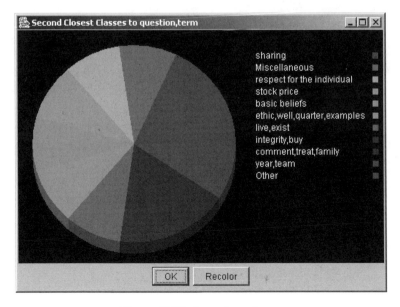

Figure 20.10. Secondary classes.

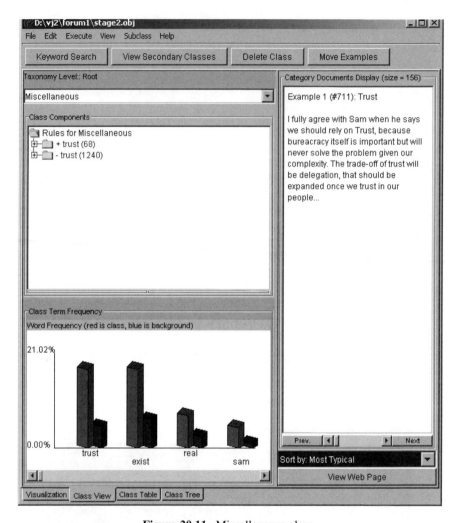

Figure 20.11. Miscellaneous class.

metric to our table to measure the "Recency" of the different categories (see Figure 20.13).

Sorting by this metric reveals the key themes that have surfaced in most recently. Then we sort by size to discover the "cumulative themes." The resulting web page report is shown in Figure 20.14.

Selecting any of the above links will take the user to a display of 10 of the "most typical" comments for that theme. This process was then repeated for each of the remaining forums and for the Jam as a whole. The entire reporting operation took about 3–4 hours.

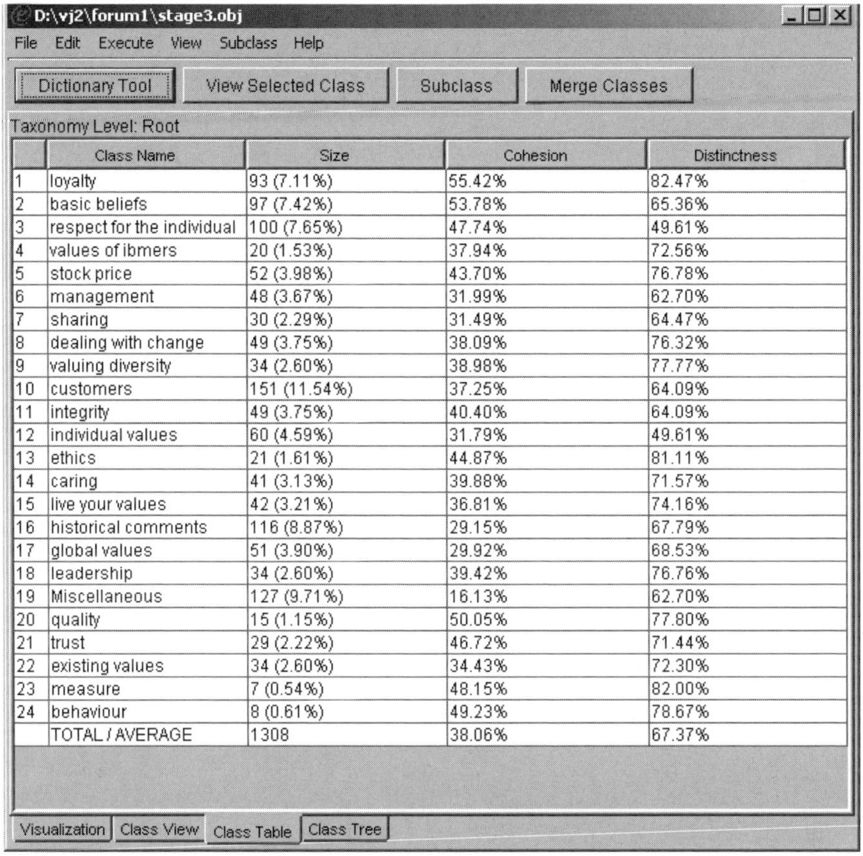

	Class Name	Size	Cohesion	Distinctness
1	loyalty	93 (7.11%)	55.42%	82.47%
2	basic beliefs	97 (7.42%)	53.78%	65.36%
3	respect for the individual	100 (7.65%)	47.74%	49.61%
4	values of ibmers	20 (1.53%)	37.94%	72.56%
5	stock price	52 (3.98%)	43.70%	76.78%
6	management	48 (3.67%)	31.99%	62.70%
7	sharing	30 (2.29%)	31.49%	64.47%
8	dealing with change	49 (3.75%)	38.09%	76.32%
9	valuing diversity	34 (2.60%)	38.98%	77.77%
10	customers	151 (11.54%)	37.25%	64.09%
11	integrity	49 (3.75%)	40.40%	64.09%
12	individual values	60 (4.59%)	31.79%	49.61%
13	ethics	21 (1.61%)	44.87%	81.11%
14	caring	41 (3.13%)	39.88%	71.57%
15	live your values	42 (3.21%)	36.81%	74.16%
16	historical comments	116 (8.87%)	29.15%	67.79%
17	global values	51 (3.90%)	29.92%	68.53%
18	leadership	34 (2.60%)	39.42%	76.76%
19	Miscellaneous	127 (9.71%)	16.13%	62.70%
20	quality	15 (1.15%)	50.05%	77.80%
21	trust	29 (2.22%)	46.72%	71.44%
22	existing values	34 (2.60%)	34.43%	72.30%
23	measure	7 (0.54%)	48.15%	82.00%
24	behaviour	8 (0.61%)	49.23%	78.67%
	TOTAL / AVERAGE	1308	38.06%	67.37%

Figure 20.12. Completed categorization.

20.7.2. Emerging Themes

As the Jam progressed, new topics naturally emerged. To identify these, the Recent Trends analysis described earlier was especially valuable. A good example of this came late in the Jam when a breaking news story had an impact on the discussion (Walsh, 2003).

In Figure 20.15 the result of running a Recent Trend Analysis is shown. We observe the word "pension" occurred 51 times overall, and 11 times in the last 10% of the data. This was deemed by the software to be a low probability event ($P = 0.0056$). A view of the trend line for this keyword shows the spike (see Figure 20.16).

Pension mentions had been decreasing as a percentage of the total posts, but on the last day there was a sharp increase. Looking at the text for these

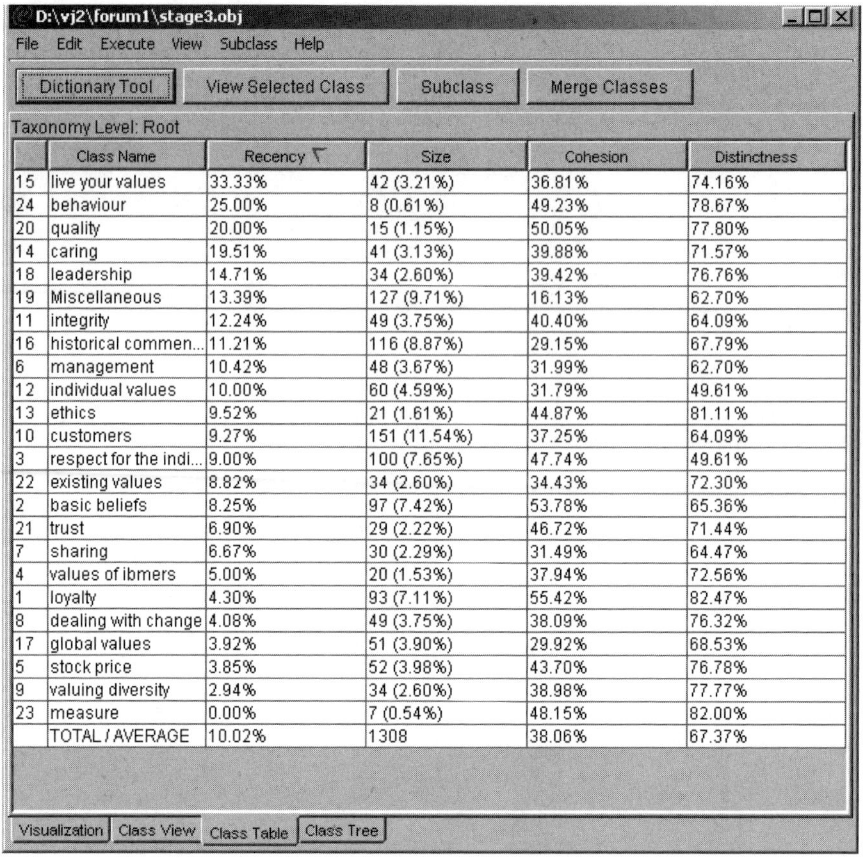

	Class Name	Recency ▽	Size	Cohesion	Distinctness
15	live your values	33.33%	42 (3.21%)	36.81%	74.16%
24	behaviour	25.00%	8 (0.61%)	49.23%	78.67%
20	quality	20.00%	15 (1.15%)	50.05%	77.80%
14	caring	19.51%	41 (3.13%)	39.88%	71.57%
18	leadership	14.71%	34 (2.60%)	39.42%	76.76%
19	Miscellaneous	13.39%	127 (9.71%)	16.13%	62.70%
11	integrity	12.24%	49 (3.75%)	40.40%	64.09%
16	historical commen...	11.21%	116 (8.87%)	29.15%	67.79%
6	management	10.42%	48 (3.67%)	31.99%	62.70%
12	individual values	10.00%	60 (4.59%)	31.79%	49.61%
13	ethics	9.52%	21 (1.61%)	44.87%	81.11%
10	customers	9.27%	151 (11.54%)	37.25%	64.09%
3	respect for the indi...	9.00%	100 (7.65%)	47.74%	49.61%
22	existing values	8.82%	34 (2.60%)	34.43%	72.30%
2	basic beliefs	8.25%	97 (7.42%)	53.78%	65.36%
21	trust	6.90%	29 (2.22%)	46.72%	71.44%
7	sharing	6.67%	30 (2.29%)	31.49%	64.47%
4	values of ibmers	5.00%	20 (1.53%)	37.94%	72.56%
1	loyalty	4.30%	93 (7.11%)	55.42%	82.47%
8	dealing with change	4.08%	49 (3.75%)	38.09%	76.32%
17	global values	3.92%	51 (3.90%)	29.92%	68.53%
5	stock price	3.85%	52 (3.98%)	43.70%	76.78%
9	valuing diversity	2.94%	34 (2.60%)	38.98%	77.77%
23	measure	0.00%	7 (0.54%)	48.15%	82.00%
	TOTAL / AVERAGE	10.02%	1308	38.06%	67.37%

Figure 20.13. Recency metric.

examples quickly revealed the cause, and thus a new category was created centered around this word and the examples that used the word in a context related to the news event.

20.7.3. Success of Interactive Text Mining During ValuesJam

Our Interactive Text Mining approach showed itself quite capable of analyzing a discussion forum among thousands of users in real time using only a single human analyst with an IBM laptop PC. A survey of 1248 respondents done after ValuesJam indicated that 42% of all Jam participants used the theme pages generated by eClassifier to enter the Jam. The survey further shows that those who used this feature found it to be both important and satisfactory for the most part (72% important, 61% satisfactory). Only 10% of those who used this feature were dissatisfied with it.

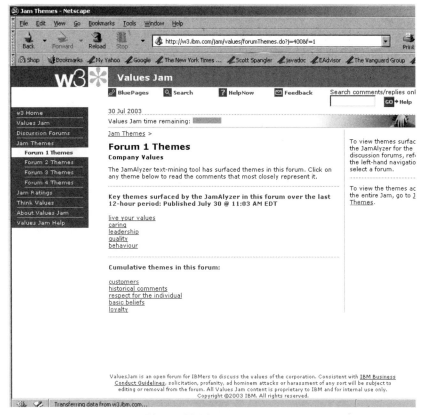

Figure 20.14. Jam themes.

	Keywords	Date	Probability	Keyword Co...	Date Count	Keyword+D...	Dependency
31	anymore	8/1/03	0.0015	29	835	8	0.0024
32	understand	8/1/03	0.0008	292	835	46	0.0024
33	beat	8/1/03	0.0017	24	835	7	0.0023
34	contact	8/1/03	0.0016	19	835	6	0.0023
35	life	8/1/03	0.0011	335	835	51	0.0022
36	walk_talk	8/1/03	0.0026	36	835	9	0.0022
37	learn	8/1/03	0.0029	108	835	20	0.0022
38	imagine	8/1/03	0.0044	50	835	11	0.0020
39	issue	8/1/03	0.0032	213	835	34	0.0020
40	experience	8/1/03	0.0022	328	835	49	0.0020
41	pension	8/1/03	0.0056	51	835	11	0.0019
42	contribute	8/1/03	0.0060	71	835	14	0.0019
43	workplace	8/1/03	0.0070	52	835	11	0.0018
44	asset	8/1/03	0.0073	86	835	16	0.0018
45	offering	8/1/03	0.0067	22	835	6	0.0018
46	care_development	8/1/03	0.0067	22	835	6	0.0018
47	empowerment	8/1/03	0.0079	28	835	7	0.0017
48	plan	8/1/03	0.0082	101	835	18	0.0017
49	care	8/1/03	0.0047	297	835	44	0.0017
50	speed	8/1/03	0.0098	67	835	13	0.0017
51	important	8/1/03	0.0051	533	835	72	0.0015
52	manage	8/1/03	0.0080	490	835	66	0.0014

Figure 20.15. Recent trends.

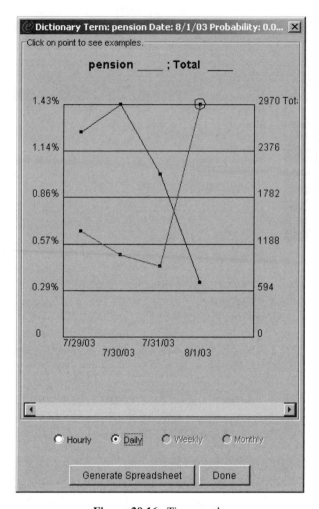

Figure 20.16. Time graph.

20.8. CONCLUSIONS

In summary, we have described in detail a system with a unique combination of capabilities for the generation of practical quality taxonomies. We have shown that the combination of automated text mining with interactive human expert guidance integrated in an interactive platform provides a practical way to create natural taxonomies in a document collection. Further user studies are required to (a) validate that the methodology we have designed can work for a broader user population and (b) compare the methodology's effectiveness to other possible approaches.

We believe there are many other practical aspects of taxonomy generation and utilization that are not well covered in the literature. One such issue is the generation of multiple taxonomies over a single collection of documents. This will enable applications to leverage multiple attributes and relationships of a collection of documents. Another area we believe to be a promising area for future work, will be the integration of taxonomies and text with structured and semistructured data (Cody et al., 2002).

ACKNOWLEDGMENTS

The authors gratefully acknowledge Dharmendra Modha, Justin Lessler, and Ray Strong for their contributions to the original design of our interactive text-mining approach. We would like to thank Mike Wing, James Newswanger, and Kristine Lawas for their suggestions and facilitation in applying our technology to Values Jam.

REFERENCES

Berry, J., and Linoff, G., *Data Mining Techniques for Marketing, Sales, and Customer Support*, John Willey & Sons, New York, 1996.

Brachman, R., and Anand, T., The process of knowledge discovery in databases, in *Advances in Knowledge Discovery and Data Mining*, Fayyad, U. M., Piatetsky-Shapiro, G., Smyth, P., and Uthurusamy, R., eds., AAAI/MIT Press, Menlo Park, CA, Chapter 2, pp. 37–58, 1996.

Cody, W., Kreulen, J., Spangler, S., and Krishna, V., The integration of business intelligence and knowledge management, *IBM Systems Journal* **41**(4), 697–713 (2002).

Dhillon, I., Modha, D., and Spangler, S., Visualizing class structure of multidimensional data with applications, *Journal of Computational Statistics & Data Analysis* (special issue on Matrix Computations & Statistics) **4**(1), 59–90 (2002).

Dom, B. An Information-Theoretic External Cluster-Validity Measure, IBM Research Report RJ 10219, October 5, 2001.

Duda, R. O., and Hart, P. E., *Pattern Classification and Scene Analysis*, John Wiley & Sons, New York, 1973.

Fox, C., Lexical analysis and stoplists, in Frakes, W. B., and Baeza-Yates, R., eds., *Information Retrieval: Data Structures and Algorithms*, Prentice-Hall, Englewood Cliffs, NJ, pp. 102–130, 1992.

Halkidi, M., Batistakis, Y. and Vazirgiannis, M., On clustering validation techniques, *Journal of Intelligent Information Systems* **17**(2–3), 107–145 (2001).

Hartigan, J. A., *Clustering Algorithms*, John Wiley & Sons, New York, 1975.

Honrado, A., Leon, R., O'Donnel, R., and Sinclair, D., A word stemming algorithm for the spanish language, in *Seventh International Symposium on String Processing Information Retrieval*, 2000.

Jing, H., Barzilay, R., McKeown, K., and Elhadad, M., Summarization evaluation methods experiments and analysis, in *AAAI Intelligent Text Summarization Workshop*, Stanford, CA, pp. 60–68, 1998.

Johnson, D. E., Oles, F. J., Zhang, T., and Goetz, T., A decision-tree-based symbolic rule induction system for text categorization, *IBM Systems Journal* **41**(3) 428–437 (2002).

Kittler, J., Hatef, M., Duin, R., and Matas, J., On combining classifiers, *IEEE Transactions on Pattern Analysis and Machine Intelligence* **20**, 226–239 (1998).

Kornai, A., and Stone, L., Automatic translation to controlled medical vocabularies, in *Innovations in Intelligent Systems and Applications Physica*, Abraham A., and Jain L., eds., Springer-Verlag, Berlin, 2004 (http://www.kornai.com/Papers/kornai_stone.pdf).

Manning, C. D., and Schütze, H., *Foundations of Statistical Natural Language Processing*, MIT Press, Cambridge, MA, 2000.

McCallum, A., and Nigam, K., *A Comparison of Event Models for Naïve Bayes Text Classification*, In AAAI-98 Workshop on Learning for Text Categorization, 1998.

Mitchell, T. M., *Machine Learning*, McGraw-Hill, New York, 1997.

Press, W., et al. *Numerical Recipes in C*, 2nd ed., Cambridge University Press, New York, pp. 620–623, 1992.

Quinlan, J. R., Induction of Decision trees, *Machine Learning* **1**(1), 81–106 (1986).

Rasmussen, E., Clustering algorithms, in *Information Retrieval: Data Structures and Algorithms*, Frakes, W. B., and Baeza-Yates, R., eds., Prentice-Hall, Englewood Cliffs, NJ, pp. 419–442, 1992.

Salton, G., and Buckley, C., Term-weighting approaches in automatic text retrieval, *Information Processing & Management* **4**(5), 512–523 (1988).

Salton, G., and McGill, M. J., *Introduction to Modern Retrieval*, McGraw-Hill, New York, 1983.

Spangler, S., and Kreulen, J., Interactive methods for taxonomy editing and validation, in *Proceedings of the Conference on Information and Knowledge Mining*, 2002.

Spangler, S., Kreulen, J., and Lessler, J., Generating and browsing multiple taxonomies over a document collection, *Journal of Management Information Systems* **19**(4), 191–212 (2003).

Vaithyanathan, S., and Dom, B., Model selection in unsupervised learning with applications to document clustering, in *The Sixteenth International Conference on Machine Learning* Morgan Kaufmann, San Francisco, 1999.

Vaithyanathan, S., and Dom, B., Hierarchical unsupervised learning, in *The Seventeenth International Conference on Machine Learning*, 2000.

Walsh, M. W., Judge says IBM pension shift illegally harmed older workers, *New York Times*, August 1, 2003 (http://query.nytimes.com/gst/abstract. html?res=F00B14F73E5A0C728CDDA10894DB404482).

Wolpert, D. H. Stacked generalization, *Neural Networks* **5**, 241–259 (1992).

Zhang, T., On the dual formulation of regularized linear systems, *Machine Learning* **46**, 91–129 (2002).

PART VII

SECURITY APPLICATIONS

21

THE USE OF DATA-MINING TECHNIQUES IN OPERATIONAL CRIME FIGHTING

Richard Adderley

21.1. INTRODUCTION

Today, computers are pervasive in all areas of business activities. This enables the recording of all business transactions, making it possible not only to deal with record keeping and control information for management but also via the analysis of those transactions to improve business performance. This has led to the development of the area of computing known as *data mining* (Adriaans and Zantige, 1996).

The police force, like any other business, now relies heavily on the use of computers not only for providing management information via monitoring statistics but also for use in tackling major serious crimes (usually crimes such as armed criminality, murder, or serious sexual offenses). The primary techniques used are specialized database management systems and data visualization (Adderley and Musgrove, 2001a). Although policing procedures such as problem-oriented policing and crime mapping techniques use stored information for the investigation and detection of volume crimes such as burglary, little use has been made of that information to link crimes through a combination of modus operandi (MO), temporal, and spatial information. This is partly because major crimes can justify greater resources on grounds of public safety but also because there are relatively few major crimes, making it easier to establish links between offenses. With volume crime the sheer number of offenses, the paucity of information, the limited resources available, and the high degree of similarity between crimes renders major crime investigation techniques ineffective.

Next Generation of Data-Mining Applications. Edited by Kantardzic and Zurada
ISBN 0-471-65605-4 © 2005 the Institute of Electrical and Electronics Engineers, Inc.

There have been a number of academic projects that have attempted to apply artificial intelligence (AI) techniques, primarily expert systems, to detecting volume crimes such as burglary (Lucas, 1986; Charles, 1998). While usually proving effective as prototypes for the specific problem being addressed, they have not made the transfer into practical working systems. This is because they have been stand-alone systems requiring the duplication of data inputting as they do not integrate easily into existing police systems. They tended to use a particular expert's line of reasoning with which the detective using the system might disagree. Also they lacked robustness and could not adapt to changing environments. All this has led to wariness within policing regarding the efficacy of AI techniques.

The objective of the current research project is therefore to evaluate the merit of data-mining techniques for crime analysis. The commercial data-mining package SPSS/Clementine is being used in order to speed development and facilitate experimentation within a Cross Industry Platform for Data Mining (CRISP-DM) methodology (Chapman et al., 2000) (see Figure 21.1). This process has seven iterative stages that provide a summary of the data-mining project life cycle.

Business understanding focuses on the domain knowledge (understanding crime, criminality, and policing) required to ensure that the appropriate goals are set and that the success criteria can be met. Data understanding deals with the collection and the identification of data quality problems. The data preparation phase covers the transformation of base data rectifying the issues found in

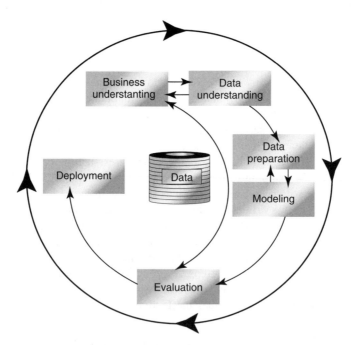

Figure 21.1. CRISP-DM. (From Chapman et al. (2000). Reproduced with permission.

the previous stage. Modeling uses the transformed data to produce a business advantage that is then evaluated to ensure that the success criteria are met and the final stage is the deployment of the model into the business.

This chapter reports the results from applying two specific data-mining techniques—the multilayer perceptron (MLP) and the Kohonen self-organizing map (SOM)—to the building descriptions, *modus operandi* (MO), and temporal and special attributes of crimes attributed to a network of offenders for a particular type of crime, namely, burglary offenses.

An MLP (Swingler, 1996) is a supervised classification technique that has the ability to form categories based upon learning from examples within the data. Using known data (for example, detected crimes) that are separated into a training set and a testing set, the network is trained on the former and tested on the latter, which it has not seen. A SOM (Kohonen, 1982) is an unsupervised technique that uses the many variables in the dataset (multidimensions) and recognizes patterns to form a two-dimensional grid of cells. This technique has similarities to the statistical approach of multidimensional scaling. The output from all of these techniques is a confidence level between zero and one: The greater the value, the greater the confidence in the classification process.

The benefits of extracting a formal structure from a database field containing unstructured MO text and using this structure in the mining process are discussed together with the stages of data selection, coding, and cleaning. The results achieved by this process were independently validated by two police analysts who were not part of the research team; they are discussed, together with further areas for research.

The two validating police analysts are the Community Safety Bureau staff in the area of the West Midlands Police, in which the target network of offenders mainly operates. These bureaus are the focal points on each command unit for strategic planning, operational tasking, and intelligence. The two analysts have been working in this environment for a number of years and are highly experienced.

21.2. BUSINESS UNDERSTANDING

A large number of crimes are committed by offenders who operate together in loosely formed co-offending groups (Reiss, 1988); they more resemble an organic structure than a hierarchical gang structure, and there is no "Mr. Big" for the entire network but there may be key persons (Coles, 2001). Figure 21.2 illustrates a group of eight offenders who have extensively "worked" together. The numbered circles represent individual offenders, and the connecting lines represent co-defendant instances (people who have been arrested and charged for the same offence(s)). Within the network illustrated below, all of the offenders have burglary offenses recorded against them and it appears that they commit their offenses together in different combinations of people. For example, No.1 has committed one offense each with Nos. 2, 3, 4, 5, 7, and 8 and has committed

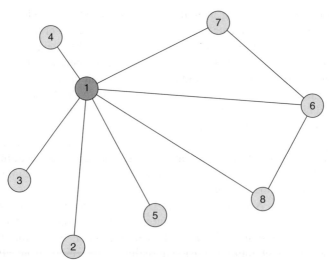

Figure 21.2. Primary network; criminal interaction. [Courtesy of West Midlands Police, Force Linked Intelligence System (FLINTS).].

10 or more offenses with No. 6. No. Offender 6 has committed one offense with No. 8, between two and nine offenses with No. 7, and more than 10 offenses with No. 1.

None of the offenders have a 'standard' MO, however, they do favor particular types of buildings, use a finite variety of methods to gain entry to most of those buildings, and have slight preferences for three particular days of the week when committing their crimes. Due to the combinatorial difficulties of identifying crimes that have been committed by different combinations of persons, with differing MOs, attacking different types of buildings in a variety of locations, it would not be easy to attribute a new undetected crime to a member of the network. It is here that data-mining techniques can assist.

When an offender has been arrested for an offense and brought into custody, the person is interviewed regarding that offense and any other similar offenses that may, as yet, be undetected. The interviewing officer will request from the intelligence department a list of offenses that are similar to the one for which the person has been arrested with a view to questioning the offender and clearing further crimes. That is, the offender will admit his/her part in committing the crime, and it is subsequently recorded as being detected to that offender. The intelligence department will examine the base individual crime and then search through the crime system to locate those that have similar spatial, temporal, and MO features. This process can take between 1 and 2 hours, depending on the complexity of the base crime. It is a semi-manual task requiring a database search and then manual reading of the retrieved documentation. The intelligence staff estimate that they are about 5% to 10% accurate in supplying a list for interview. This figure is based upon the actual number of offenses attributed to the offender during the interviewing process.

21.2.1. Offender Behavior

Environmental Criminology suggests that the analysis of crime has four dimensions—victim, offender, geo-temporal, and legal (Brantingham and Brantingham, 1991)—stating that concentrating on the crime location is a necessary aid to full understanding. In addition to this is the structural layout of a town or city, and its road and transport infrastructure—and the place itself—will have crime attractors (Eck, 1995) such as restaurants, shopping centers, car parks, and so on. The location of a crime is also determined by the conscious or subconscious decision-making processes of the victim and offender which are shaped by their personal lifestyles. A location could have an implied label that affects the rate of crime in the area. This label can affect the types of people who reside, travel through, and work in the area together with the type of services that are offered by Police, Social Services, and so on. The label can also affect the fear of crime, which can be at variance with the actual crime rate. The Brantinghams (Brantingham and Brantingham, 1991) suggest that there is a theoretical model for urban crime:

- Certain persons are motivated to commit crime.
- The commission of the crime is a result of a conscious decision-making process.
- The location itself indicates that it is ripe for criminal activity.
- The motivated person uses the location indicators to search for a suitable victim.
- The motivated person learns from the location indicators and forms a personal template for future use.
- The template influences future behavior becoming self-reinforcing.
- Due to the combinatorial effect of targets, victims, and places, multiple crime selection templates are constructed. Humans are creatures of habit, thereby making the similarities in templates identifiable.

The Brantinghams use the term *backcloth* (Brantingham and Brantingham, 1998) to describe the multidimensionality of how people interact with their environments to produce crime. These interactions change and move with time, but the time scale may be sufficiently slow as to appear static to the human perception. This could enable crime analysts to be predictable in aggregate or even identify individual patterns as they emerge. People have an affinity with physical locations and pathways that connect those locations. They develop awareness spaces around locations that are visited, the size of which varies depending on the activity undertaken. This applies to the connecting pathways, depending on the frequency travelled and the mode of transport.

Routine Activity Theory. Routine activity theory for predatory crime requires that there must be a convergence in time and space of three elements for a crime to occur (Cohen and Felson, 1979; Felson, 1992; Clarke and Felson, 1993; Policing and Crime Unit, 1998): a likely offender, a suitable target, and the absence of a suitable guardian, which is the Basic Crime Triangle. Interacting with any aspect of the triangle will give opportunities for preventing or reducing crime.

Crime Pattern Theory. Patterns in crime, although often difficult to identify, can be informative about how people interact with their physical environment. This theory has three concepts: nodes, paths, and edges (Policing and Crime Unit, 1998).

Nodes is a term from transportation that refers to where people travel to and from. A node is a personal anchorage point in an individual's lifestyle such as a school, bar, town center, car park, and so on. Some nodes can be generators of crime at that geographical point or nearby, for example, a football ground may generate disorder in the streets nearby but be calm at that physical location.

Paths are the transit routes that connect nodes and can refer to both vehicular and pedestrian travel. Individuals, going about their every day activities, generally travel along the same paths when visiting the same nodes, for example, most people drive the same way to and from work each day as a routine. Those paths that fall in with an individual's routine activity are closely related to where they fall victim to crime.

Edges refer to the boundaries of area where people have anchorage points such as a home, place of work, social life, and so on. Some crimes are more prominent at those edges as people who seldom know each other come together at these places and, because they are unknown, either offend or become a victim. Robbery, racial attacks, and shoplifting are examples of "edge" crimes. People who live outside of the boundaries commit crimes at the edge and then retreat into the safety of their own areas. Crimes committed by people who live inside the boundaries (insiders) are often committed close to an anchorage point, namely, their own neighborhoods.

Rational Choice Perspective Theory. This perspective focuses upon the offender's decision-making processes, making the assumption that any decision is made with the person's own free will. It assumes that an offender is only calculating on items that are most evident or immediate—for example, an open window in a house or a computer left on the seat of a car—in both cases there are no persons in close proximity, therefore increasing the chance for the crime to be successful.

Although much of the specific data is not captured in West Midlands Police recording systems, significant information can be derived from existing data fields and used in the mining process.

21.3. DATA UNDERSTANDING

The burglary database used in this study contained 48,475 recorded offenses that occurred between October 1997 and December 2002. Table 21.1 shows the specific crime categories and the numbers of offenses associated with each.

There are a total of 5448 offenses that have been detected to a variety of offenders representing 11.2% of the total crime. This includes 115 crimes

TABLE 21.1. Classification of All Burglary Offences

	Drinking Places	Dwellings	Factories	Domestic Garages	Offices	Sheds	Shops	Other	Total
All Offenses									
% of total:	2.4%	45%	8.9%	4.9%	4.1%	10.2%	5.7%	18.6%	100%
	(1152)	(21,886)	(4319)	(2394)	(1998)	(4937)	(2770)	(9019)	(48,475)
All detected									
% of total:	1.85%	49%	6.55%	2%	4.7%	3.4%	8.8%	23.7%	100%
	(101)	(2668)	(357)	(110)	(256)	(187)	(479)	(1290)	(5448)
Primary									
detected		100%							100%
% of total:		(115)							(115)

TABLE 21.2. Classification of Domestic Burglary Offences

	Detached	Semi-Detached	Terraced	Flats	Bungalow	All Other Premises	Total
All Offenses							
% of total:	3.2%	24%	8.5%	8.35%	0.8%	55.17%	100%
	(1564)	(11,611)	(4110)	(4048)	(400)	(26,742)	(48,475)
All detected							
% of total:	3.4%	25.4%	9.5%	9.3%	1%	51%	8.8%
	(184)	(1386)	(520)	(505)	(53)	(2800)	(5448)
Primary detected %							
of total:	1.7%	60%	36.5%	1.7%	0%	0%	100%
	(2)	(69)	(42)	(2)	(0)	(0)	(115)

attributed to a known network of offenders (Primary Network) representing 0.2% of the total crime and 2.1% of all detected crime. When compared to the detected crimes, Table 21.1 clearly shows that the Primary Network offenders' profile is to specialize in targeting personal dwellings, and Table 21.2 illustrates their preference for targeting semidetached and terraced houses.

There are limitations with the dataset that should be recognized prior to the research:

- Even though the dataset is complete, it contains all reported offences of burglary; it is possible that unsolved crimes held within the database may be attributed to one of the known offenders.

- Although people who have received the same training have input the crimes, there are inconsistencies in the transcription process which will be discussed later in this chapter.

- It has to be assumed that the known offenders have actually committed the crimes that have been attributed to them.

21.4. DATA PREPARATION

The results of the mining process are directly proportional to the quality of the data. With a small number of persons responsible for transcribing and entering the data, it was assumed that the quality of the data would be high. However, there are inconsistencies within the subsequent transcription, particularly within the MO entries. Table 21.3 illustrates three examples of free text MO information.

Number 3 does not state how the doors were forced, what rooms were searched, or the mode of search. Numbers 2, 3, 4, and 5 do not state whether the premises were occupied. Number 4 does not state the location of the room in which the computers were located, whether the removal was tidy, or whether the room was ransacked.

When a paper crime report is completed, the MO is classified in two ways:

1. Check box categorization that provides a broad overview.
2. A section of unstructured free text that fully describes the actions taken to commit the crime.

TABLE 21.3. *Modus Operandi* **Text**

1	Offender approached secure unocuppied dwelling in residential area; went to rear of premises and forced rear Ground floor patio door by bending metal frame with jemmy-type instrument, removing door from frame; entered and made untidy search of all rooms; defecated in front upstairs bedroom carpet; stole items and made off exit as entry.
2	Offenders U/K approached semi-detached house and kicked front door, forcing entry; entered and searched all rooms; offenders have stolen TV, video, cash, cheque books; offenders have left parcel U/K shelf from a U/K car, a child's pram, child's bike, and blanket outside front of house on driveway, making good escape.
3	BTN stated times offender forced front doors, entered, and stole property; left via way entered
4	Persons U/K went to rear of factory premises, cut through metal bars, smashed inner glass, entered office, and stole computers
5	Smashed glass in front door, reached in and released rim lock, entered made untidy search of bedroom, stole property

Both are subsequently entered into a computerized recording system. From each of the 21 Operational Command Units (OCUs) within the West Midlands Police, there can be up to 200 police and civilian personnel writing the unstructured free text, along with a further five persons entering it onto the computerized crime system. With no guidelines indicating the language to be used, the variety of wording and spelling is vast and it is important that the richness of information contained within the free text is not lost to the Investigator. A structured encoding method from this free text would aid automatic investigation and detection methods, however, to introduce such encoding would incur a cost to alter the existing paper and computer recording systems. In this chapter, the Clementine software has been used to encode certain aspects of the free text and derive new data fields. Due to the nature of these fields, even after the encoding process, the data were not 100% clean. It would be preferable if such data were encoded at the time of inputting as highlighted by a previous study involving serious sexual assaults (Adderley and Musgrove, 2001b). This study will demonstrate the benefits of using suitably encoded volume crime data.

21.4.1. Missing Data

There are a number of fields that do not contain data and are stored in the database as "$null$" or as an empty string. These mainly relate to location information. If an address is incorrectly entered into the system, an "unconfirmed location" is registered which permits the crime to be recorded but an operator will manually enter the correct information when time permits. These are often subsequently left blank.

It is not uncommon for datasets to have fields that contain unknown or incorrectly entered information and missing values. How should they be treated? Are those fields essential to the mining process? There are a number of methods (Weiss and Indurkhya, 1998) for treating records that contain missing values:

- Omit the incorrect field(s).
- Omit the entire record that contains the incorrect field(s).
- Automatically enter/correct the data with default values; for example, select the mean from the range.
- Derive a model to enter/correct the data.
- Replace all values with a global constant.

Within this work, those crimes that did not contain post code or grid reference information were omitted from the spatial analysis.

21.4.2. Data Encoding

A critical step within the data-mining process is the way in which data are encoded. It is suggested that the central objective of this stage is to transform the base data into a spreadsheet-type format where individual variables are identified or created/derived from combining or extracting information from the dataset (Weiss and Indurkhya, 1998).

The data were encoded in four sections. Temporal analysis determined the time of day and particular days of the week in which the offenders showed a preference. Spatial analysis indicated the geographical base of the offenses. A large number of building types were analyzed and categorized into a small number of sets. The MO itself was subclassified into a further three sections.

21.4.3. Temporal Analysis

Individual offenders have a propensity to offend within particular hours of the day and on certain days of the week. The detected crimes were compared against the crimes attributed to the Primary Network to ascertain whether there were similarities or differences between those days and the times within them.

Temporal analysis presents problems within the field of crime pattern analysis due to the difficulty of ascertaining the exact time at which the offense occurred. There are generally two times that are relevant: the time that the building was secured and the time that the burglary was discovered, which may span 2 or more days, thereby adding to the complexity. To ascertain a preference on which day the offenders offend, this study only utilized those crimes that did occur within a single day, and it was the percentage figure for the Primary Network plotted against all other detected crimes that was used in the graph illustrated in Figure 21.3. For example, analysis showed that for those crimes that could be determined to have been committed on a single day, the Primary Network offenders have a preference for offending on a Monday, Friday, or Saturday. It is important to note the inverse aspects of this information such as when they are less likely to commit crime. In this instance they are less likely than the

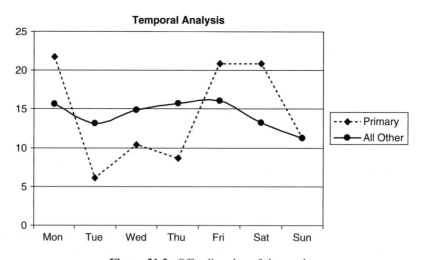

Figure 21.3. Offending day of the week.

average offender to commit crime on a Tuesday, Wednesday, or Thursday. This indicates that the day of the week is an important variable to be used in the modeling process.

To identify the time of day at which the crime occurred, in consultation with the analysts, a set of nine dichotomous variable time bands were produced:

1. 0300 hours to 0730 hours. Early hours of the morning.

2. 0800 hours to 0930 hours. Taking children to school.

3. 1200 hours to 1400 hours. Lunch time.

4. 1500 hours to 1630 hours. Collecting children from school.

5. 1800 hours to 2230 hours. During the evening.

6. 2200 hours to 0600 hours. Overnight.

7. During the day other. A "catch all" band for those crimes not coded by any of the above bands.

8. 0001 hours on Saturday to 2359 hours on Sunday. Short weekend.

9. 1700 hours on Friday to 0800 hours on Monday. Long weekend.

Bands 1 to 5 represent specific single times within a single day, band 6 will encapsulate those offenders who prefer to offend over night, and bands 8 and 9 cater to people who are away for the weekend and to businesses that close.

21.4.4. Spatial Analysis

Incorporating aspects of Environmental Criminology, using all past and present home addresses as anchorage points, individuals in the Primary Network commit 100% of their burglary offenses within 3.7 miles of their own or immediate co-accused addresses. The spread of these addresses represents approximately 2.5% of the West Midlands Police Force area. Based on 2 years of burglary crime in a district of the West Midlands Police area, the average distance that a burglary offender travels from his/her home address varies between 1/2 mile and $2\frac{1}{4}$ miles depending upon age (see Figure 21.4). For example; the average distance from their home address to the scene of the crime for all burglary offenders in the age group 19–23 was $1\frac{3}{4}$ miles. In this study the average distance for the Primary Network was 0.9 miles, and the majority of the offenders were from the 19–23 age group. Therefore, the geography of crime is an important factor in determining patterns of offending, and the distance traveled was one of the modeling variables.

21.4.5. Building-Type Analysis

There are 72 individual building descriptions available for use within the crime recording system. Many crimes are quite opportunistic (Clarke and Felson, 1993);

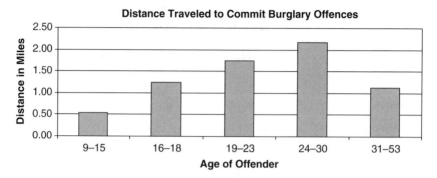

Figure 21.4. Distance chart.

whether a motivated offender chooses a detached, semi-detached, or terraced house often depends upon the person's awareness space and the opportunities presented at the time. Within the current dataset, it was clear that the type of premise was relevant; and by amalgamating groups of premises, those groups then became even more relevant. Therefore, the 72 individual premise types were categorized into eight sets to include drinking places, dwellings, factories, domestic garages, offices, sheds, shops, and all other buildings. The dwellings category was further categorized into six sets: detached, semi-detached, terraced, flats, bungalow, and all other dwellings. It is clear to see from Table 21.1 that the Primary Network offenders have a specific preference as to the type of building upon which they predate: dwellings. Within the set of dwelling categories, they clearly have a preference to target semi-detached and terraced houses as illustrated in Table 21.2. The new building-type field was created combining individual variables into a single nominal category that was used in the modeling process.

21.4.6. MO Classification

As stated in Section 21.4.2, data encoding is a critical stage in the mining process. In previous work by the author (Adderley and Musgrove, 2004), one of the main restrictions was that the MO was targeted to classify a specific group of offenders, and its use would be limited in classifying a different group. Building upon this previous work, a generic MO classifier was constructed in two stages:

1. Use an SOM to cluster the crimes based on the MO overview check boxes, and use the cluster coordinates later in the MLP modeling process.

2. Using key words and phrases, derive a set of 31 dichotomous fields that identify features from the free-text MO field.

The MO overview check box information (stage 1) is completed by the Officer attending the scene of the crime by ticking a series of categories on the paper report. This information is entered into a single database field with

TABLE 21.4. MO Overview Check Box Information

Rear: Window: Casement: Plastic: Forced: Not known: Not
    known: Not known: Not known: Not known: Not known:
    Not known: Not known

Side: Window: Transom: Plastic: Smash: All: Untidy: Not
    known: As entry: Window: Transom: Not known: Not
    known

Not known: Door: Fire exit: Wood: Forced: Not known:
    Not known: Alarm activated: As entry: Door: Fire exit:
    Not known: Not known

delimiters (colons) between each entry as illustrated in Table 21.4. There is a formal structure to this approach, but, due to the limitations within the available categories, a great deal of relevant information that is useful in profiling criminal(s) is missing from this area.

There are 13 MO overview categories, five of which are not used in this study. The following eight categories were used: position of entry (front, side, etc.), point of entry (door, window, etc.), feature type (wooden door, fixed window, etc.), feature material (wood, metal, etc.), method (smashed, cut, etc.), location of search (upstairs, one room, etc.), search type (tidy or untidy), and special attributes (cut phone wires, etc.). The five unused categories included three to describe the method of exiting the premises and two to describe distraction burglaries. On examining the dataset, it was established that the five categories mainly contained information that had been classified as "NOT KNOWN," and all of the Primary Network offenses were classified in that way; therefore they were not used in the modeling process.

The MO category is an unstructured free text field as illustrated in Table 21.3. It is here that full details are entered regarding how the crime was committed, including specific behavior or attributes that may be useful in either identifying an offender(s) or linking a series of crimes. The free text was parsed to extract key words or phrases that were used to categorize the MO in three sections comprising 31 dichotomous variables.

1. *Point of Entry Section.* This section described the method of gaining entry and contained the following variables:

> Access point, front, rear, and so on; removal of glass or putty; whether glass was smashed; window forced; door forced; lock damaged; use of an implement; climbed; scaffold on outside of premises; bolt croppers used; reached in to unfasten door/window; vehicle used–ram raiding.

2. *Searching Attributes.* This section described the actions taken by the offender once entry had been gained to the premises and contained the following variables:

Food or drink consumed; telephone used; excreting or urinating in the premises; violence used; wanton damage to the premises; prevented occupier from entering own property; untidy search; tidy search; weapons used; loft searched; bag or suitcase, and so on, used to remove stolen property; number of rooms searched.

3. *General Premises Attributes.* This section described the general features about the targeted premises:

Insecure premises; dog present; premises alarmed; alarm activated; alarm disabled; occupier present; occupier known to be on holiday.

21.5. MODEL BUILDING

SPSS Clementine provide a range of modeling techniques within their workbench toolkit, two of which were used in this study. The Kohonen clustering algorithm was used to cluster all 48,475 burglary crimes that had been recorded in the area since 1997, using the eight categories of MO overview information described above. Using a 10×7 grid architecture, there would be approximately 690 crimes in each of the 70 clusters should there be an even distribution throughout the map (Ripley, 1996). The results of the clustering process displayed a range of 0.01% of the crimes to 14.39% clustered within cells, indicating that the process produced useable results. On examining individual clusters, it was clearly illustrated that the majority contained crimes that had been committed in a similar way; for example, cluster 19-10 contained 369 crimes, each of which were targeted through the front wooden door. The cluster coordinates were used in the following process.

A Multilayer Perceptron was used, with the input variables described above, to train the neural network to recognize patterns of offending. The crimes attributed to the Primary Network were allocated a positive flag (Target = 'T'); and the remaining crimes were allocated a negative flag (Target = "F"), being the target variable. As previously stated, to build a model using an MLP, a minimum of two sets of data are prepared, but in this study there were a total of 11 datasets, five each for training and testing and a final "holdback" set for validation purposes. The holdback set contained five randomly selected crimes from the Primary Network and 139 randomly selected detected crimes; these were completely removed from their respective sets prior to establishing the training/testing sets. All training/testing set crimes were randomly selected as detailed in Table 21.5.

All sets contain a number of crimes that have been committed by the Primary Network and crimes that have been committed by other known offenders. The training set contains the data on which the training is executed: The MLP is trained to (a) recognize crimes that can be attributed to the Primary Network and (b) distinguish them from those committed by other offenders. A model is

TABLE 21.5. Ratio of Training/Testing Data

	Training Set		Testing Set	
Set No.	Percentage from Primary Network	Percentage from Remaining Burglary Offenders	Percentage from Primary Network	Percentage from Remaining Burglary Offenders
1	75	5	25	95
2	80	10	20	90
3	85	15	15	85
4	90	20	10	80
5	95	25	5	75

TABLE 21.6. Results of Network Testing

		Set 1	Set 2	Set 3	Set 4	Best	Average
Quick	Positive	5	3	5	4	5	4
	% of Total	11%	7%	11%	9%		10%
Dynamic	Positive	7	4	6	6	7	6
	% of Total	18%	11%	16%	16%		15%
Multiple	Positive	5	3	5	4	5	4
	% of Total	11%	7%	11%	9%		10%
Prune	Positive	8	5	7	7	8	7
	% of Total	64%	36%	57%	50%		52%

Source: Adderley and Musgrove (2003)

produced as a result of the training process, and the accuracy is tested on the associated testing set of crimes.

In previously conducted work (Adderley and Musgrove, 2004) it was established that the "Prune" network options produced the greatest accuracy. Table 21.6 illustrates the results from that work clearly identifying that the 'prune' method consistently performed better than the others, therefore, the Prune network configuration was used in this study.

A model was created and tested for each of the training sets. A measure of effectiveness was the number of Primary Network crimes that appeared in the "top 20" index for the testing set, the crimes with the highest confidence level. It was decided to use only 20 crimes because this is the maximum number that could normally be evaluated within a reasonable time using the manual data extraction methods described above.

21.6. VALIDATION

Validation of the model was undertaken using two methods. The first assessed the accuracy using the testing sets and holdback set of data and the second used 1802 new undetected crimes from the database.

Table 21.7 illustrates the results of the first phase of the validation process, the results representing the number of correctly classified crimes in the top 20 listing. In the holdback set there were only five crimes that could be attributed to the Primary Network offenders, which indicated that the models could correctly classify those crimes. Examining the results of the first four models reveals that there are a number of false positives where crimes have been wrongly classified. To improve on this, all five models were placed in series within the Clementine processing stream, which results in each crime having five confidence levels, one for each model. All five levels were averaged, and it was this average score that was used as a final classification. Each of the testing sets was passed through this new stream, a top 20 list of crimes being produced for each set. There were no false positives in any of the five sets.

The main testing process was conducted by two analysts who were not part of the study. Eighteen hundred and two new burglary crimes that had been committed on the area since the start of the study were passed through the stream and, to be comparable to the above validation process, a top 20 crimes list was produced as illustrated in Table 21.8. The crime numbers of those top 20 crimes having the average value closest to 100% were given to the analysts for examination. Their job was to ascertain whether any of them could have been committed by one of the Primary Network members. Having no other information, the analysts researched the crimes already attributed to the offenders by examining the crime reports, case papers, and witness statements and then examined each of the 20 submitted crimes in a similar way.

In their opinion, only 3 of the 20 crimes could not have been committed by one of the Primary Network offenders, and they were numbers 13, 14, and 19 in Table 21.8. Although in crimes 13 and 14 the MO features were similar to those used by the Primary Network, the property stolen was completely different and the temporal information in crime 19 was different to the majority of Primary Network crimes.

TABLE 21.7. Modeling Results

Model	Training Set	Testing Set	Holdback Set
1	20	16	5
2	20	11	5
3	19	13	5
4	20	17	5
5	20	20	5

TABLE 21.8. New Crimes Results

Crime Number	Average	Index
20K2/6985/03	99.99%	1
20K2/8215/03	99.92%	2
20K2/8757/03	99.56%	3
20K2/3537/03	99.48%	4
20K2/6432/03	99.30%	5
20K2/4396/03	99.29%	6
20K2/8152/03	99.15%	7
20K2/10144/03	99.08%	8
20K2/8941/03	99.03%	9
20K2/5200/03	98.62%	10
20K2/10398/03	98.42%	11
20K2/2050/03	98.09%	12
20K2/6614/03	97.99%	13
20K2/6654/03	97.77%	14
20K2/10387/03	97.64%	15
20K2/829/03	97.54%	16
20K2/5722/03	97.35%	17
20K2/3624/03	97.15%	18
20K2/9773/03	97.07%	19
20K2/4681/03	96.34%	20

The results are encouraging: After extracting the 3 months of crimes into Clementine, a list for interview could be prepared within 5 minutes; and, if only submitting those crimes above a clear threshold, the list was potentially relevant. This compares with manually researching recent crimes taking between 1 and 2 hours and only being between 5% and 10% accurate as stated in Section 21.2. The Force currently records approximately 1000 new crimes every day; therefore, it is unlikely that an analyst or investigator will be able to form links between crimes unless there is a distinctive MO. It is for this reason that the semi-manual search takes so long and is not particularly accurate.

To formalize the validation process, it would be ideal to give the two analysts a set of randomly produced crimes for analysis together with the "top 20" list and compare their results; however, time constraints on operational resources prohibit this level of formality.

21.7. DISCUSSION

The limitations identified in Section 21.4.1 cannot be overstated; however, the results are not disappointing, and they have two practical uses in operational policing:

1. They have the ability to examine a number of currently undetected crimes with a view to targeting the intelligence gathering and investigative work toward a limited number of potential offenders.

2. Having arrested an offender, there is a requirement to collate information and intelligence prior to interviewing. From taking between 1 and 2 hours to manually provide a list for interview and only being 5% to 10% accurate, this process has reduced the time to approximately 5 minutes, providing an 85% accuracy rating.

How accurate were the analysts in their opinionated research? Of those top 20 crimes, only two have now been detected and the analysts were correct in classifying each one. Crime 18 can be positively attributed to the Primary Network, and number 19 has been detected to two other offenders, both of which were correctly classified by the analysts.

It is desirable to achieve a higher level of accuracy and widen the scope of its practical implementation; the modeling process has been tailored to a particular network of offenders. Further work is required in the following areas:

- Incorporate the types of property stolen within the modeling process.
- Choose a different network of offenders to ascertain whether generic MO classifier is actually transferable.
- Use fewer models to achieve the same level of accuracy.

The benefits of data-mining software have been clearly demonstrated in operational police work.

REFERENCES

Adderley, R., and Musgrove, P. B., General review of police crime recording and investigation systems. A user's view, *Policing: An International Journal of Police Strategies and Management* **24**(1), 100–114 (2001a).

Adderley, R., and Musgrove, P. B., Data mining case study: Modeling the behaviour of offenders who commit serious sexual assaults, in *Proceedings of Seventh ACM SIGKDD International Conference on Knowledge Discovery and Data Mining, San Francisco, August 26–29, 2001*, ACM Press, New York, pp. 215–220, 2001b.

Adderley, R., and Musgrove, P. B., Modus operandi modelling of group offending: A data mining case study, *An International Journal of Police Science and Management* **5**(4), 265–276 (2004).

Adriaans, P., and Zantige, D., *Data Mining*, Addison-Wesley, Reading, MA, 1996.

Brantingham, P. L., and Brantingham, P. J., *Notes on the Geometry of Crime in Environmental Criminology*, Wavelend Press, Prospect Heights, IL, 1991.

Brantingham, P. J., and Brantingham, P. L., Environmental criminology: From theory to urban planning practice, *Studies on Crime and Crime Prevention* **7**(1), 31–60. (1998).

Chapman, P., Clinton, J., Kerber, R., Khabaza, T., Reinartz, T., Shearer, C., and Wirth, R., *CRISP-DM 1.0 Step-by-Step Data Mining Guide*, SPSS Inc., Chicago, CRISPWP-0800, 2000.

Charles, J., AI and law enforcement, *IEEE Intelligent Systems* **Jan/Feb,** 77–80 (1998).

Clarke, R. V., and Felson, M., ed, Introduction: Criminology, routine activity, and rational choice, in *Routine Activity and Rational Choice: Advances in Criminological Theory*, Vol. 5, Transaction Publishers, Somerset, NJ, 1993.

Cohen, L. E., and Felson, M., Social change and crime rate trends: A routine activity approach, *American Sociological Review* **44**, 588–608 (1979).

Coles, N., It's not what you know—it's who you know that counts. Analysing serious crime groups as social networks, *British Journal of Criminology* **44**, 580–594 (2001).

Eck, J. E., A general model of the geography of illicit marketplaces, *Crime Prevention Studies* **4**, 67–94 (1995).

Felson, M., Routine activities and crime prevention: Armchair concepts and practical action, *Studies on Crime and Crime Prevention* **1**, 30–34 (1992).

Kohonen T., Self organising formation of topologically correct feature maps, *Biological Cybernitics* **43**(1), 59–69 (1982).

Lucas, R., An expert system to detect burglars using a logic language and a relational database, in *Proceedings of* 5th *British National Conference on Databases*, Canterbury, 1986.

Policing and Reducing Crime Unit, *Opportunity Makes the Thief: Practical Theory for Crime Prevention*, Police Research Paper 98, 1998, Home Office, London.

Reiss, A. J., in Tonry, M., and Morris, N., eds., *Co-offending and Criminal Careers in Crime and Justice: A Review of Research* **10**, 117–170, (1988).

Ripley, B. D., *Pattern Recognition and Neural Networks*, Cambridge University Press, New York, 1996.

Swingler, K., *Applying Neural Networks*, Morgan Kaufmann, San Francisco, 1996.

Weiss, S. M., and Indurkhya, N., *Predictive Data Mining: A Practical Guide*, Morgan Kaufmann, San Francisco, 1998.

22

USING DATA MINING FOR INTRUSION DETECTION

Mark Brodie, Mark Mei, David George, and Sheng Ma

22.1. INTRODUCTION

Intrusion Detection Systems (IDS) play a vital role in ensuring the security of modern computer installations. Such systems are needed in order to detect hostile activity and to respond appropriately. As networks continue to expand and become more exposed to a diversity of sources, both hostile and benign, IDS need to be able to deal with a large and ever-increasing flow of alerts and events. For this reason, automatic procedures for detecting and responding to intrusions are becoming increasingly essential.

Much attention has recently been devoted to applying data-mining and machine learning techniques to intrusion detection. Most of this work attempts to distinguish intrusions from false alarms by learning from either known examples or simulated attacks or by measuring deviations from normal system behavior. However, in practice, labeled examples of intrusions or known system behavior are difficult to obtain. Most IDS log files consist of large numbers of unlabeled events.

Although the data are unlabeled, we believe that these historical logs are an important resource from which useful information can be extracted. In this work we develop a data-mining system with an integrated set of analysis methods that are used to analyze a large amount of IDS log data on an ongoing basis. We show that this allows us to discover interesting, previously unknown, and actionable information, including reduction of the false alarm rate and detection of patterns of intrusive activity.

This work focuses on off-line IDS alarm analysis, in which we aim to convert a large amount of historical data into valuable knowledge. This poses several

Next Generation of Data-Mining Applications. Edited by Kantardzic and Zurada
ISBN 0-471-65605-4 © 2005 the Institute of Electrical and Electronics Engineers, Inc.

challenges. First, the data volume can be huge: A typical IDS for a moderate-size installation may generate many thousands of events every day. Second, because an individual alarm may not provide much insight, a tool is needed that can help to visualize a large amount of data and reveal associations and correlations. Third, patterns of similar behavior, both temporal and nontemporal, are key indicators for intrusions. This requires the development of algorithms that will automatically discover diverse types of patterns; in particular, these algorithms must deal with both the temporal nature of the log data and the fact that many attributes are categorial and not directly amenable to numerical calculation.

This chapter reports our work in addressing the above issues. We present an architecture and a data-mining process that uses a set of integrated tools, including visualization and data analysis, that assist an analyst in visualizing and analyzing a large volume of alert data. We utilize several data-mining algorithms, including temporal association, event bursts, and clustering, to uncover valuable patterns. Finally, we report several cases where interesting, previously unknown information was uncovered by applying different analysis tools to thousands of IDS events.

The rest of this chapter is organized as follows. Section 22.2 discusses related work dealing with the use of data mining for intrusion detection. Section 22.3 describes the overall system architecture: The raw event logs are first enhanced in a preprocessing step; then the resulting alarm database is analyzed using a variety of data-mining techniques; and finally a report is issued identifying the most important intrusions. Section 22.4 describes the data format and Sections 22.5 to 22.7 explain the core data-mining technologies that are used: event-rate analysis, temporal association, and clustering. Section 22.8 describes an application scenario illustrating the integration of these techniques, and Section 22.9 presents our conclusions.

22.2. RELATED WORK

Our focus is on the historical analysis of alerts covering hours or months of history. Historical IDS data analysis has been previously used, but mostly manually to identify suspicious intrusion patterns. For example, Green et al. (1999) discussed several intrusion patterns founded in IDS logs. Dunigan and Hinkel (1999) argued that correlating information across multiple information sources is important.

The use of data mining for intrusion detection is becoming increasingly popular. These approaches can be classified into two groups, depending on whether data with already labeled attacks is available ("audit data") or not ("log data"). One way of generating labeled data is by using artificially created anomalies [e.g., Fan (2001)]. Attacks can also be simulated using so-called ethical hacking, but such data are expensive to obtain and its utility is limited to the environment in which it was generated. Alternatively, one might assume that over some baseline period the system displays normal behavior, and one might regard deviations from this as anomalous. Typical examples include Wespi et al. (1999), Lee and Stolfo (1998), Lee and Xiang (2001), and Axelsson (2000). Manganaris (1999) showed that IDS generate large numbers of false-positive alarms—a problem that must be addressed because it militates against the successful employment of large-scale IDS.

We focus on event log data that do not contain known intrusion events—here the challenge is to detect informative patterns that are reported to the human operator as a guide to further action. Most previous work that applied data mining to unlabeled data for intrusion detection has not specifically addressed the categorical nature of the data or requires additional background knowledge to be used. Portnoy et al. (2001) apply clustering techniques to analyze DARPA data; for categorical features the similarity between any two items is computed using the number of features where their values are distinct. They also assume that normal behavior is characterized by large clusters and that intrusions are characterized by small clusters. Julisch (2001) uses a taxonomic hierarchy on the features that allows different alerts to be collapsed together and represented by a generalized alert that captures their commonalities.

Since the mining results are presented to a human expert for further evaluation, it is important to not overwhelm the human with a large number of patterns, yet it is also important to not miss any significant intrusions. Mining frequent temporal patterns has been well studied (e.g., Mannila et al., 1997; Agarwal and Srikant, 1994), but because intrusions are expected to be rare, we need to find patterns that may be infrequent and yet are temporally associated in a statistically significant, nonrandom fashion. To do this we extend an approach used previously in the event management domain (Ma and Hellerstein, 2001) to the intrusion detection domain. This approach efficiently finds significant pairwise correlations and groups these together into a small number of non-overlapping patterns that can be presented to a human for review.

Our work is motivated by the needs of large-scale analysis of IDS data. It differs from previous work along two major dimensions. First, we develop an architecture and data analysis process that supports large-scale, interactive analysis and integrates a variety of sources of information. Second, to allow the user a flexible, exploratory approach, we integrate a wide range of different methods, including visual summarization, pattern analysis, and clustering. This allows the user to select the appropriate analysis tool based on the results of previous exploration: The synergy between the different tools creates considerable value because different approaches can be easily combined to accomplish a certain task. This approach was first presented in Mei et al. (2003); the present work extends this approach to include clustering and provides more detail on the algorithms used.

22.3. SYSTEM ARCHITECTURE AND DATA ANALYSIS FLOW

An intrusion detection system is used to monitor network traffic and host behavior and correlate information to detect intrusions. Sensors that monitor network traffic

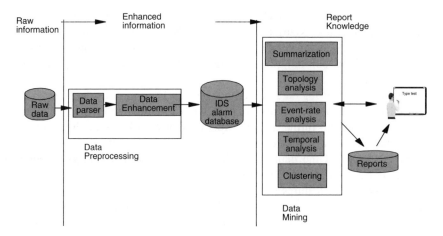

Figure 22.1. The data analysis flow.

are placed at a firewall as well as at key servers, such as web servers. When a predefined signature or abnormal behavior is detected, an alert is generated and forwarded to a correlation engine whose role is to consolidate the alerts from different sources and locations and produce a high-level alarm that leads, if needed, to further action being taken.

Our work focuses on off-line analysis for IDS alarms. In particular, we discuss a set of tools and analysis methods developed for systematically analyzing IDS data. Figure 22.1 illustrates our data analysis process. It starts with data preprocessing, which normalizes the raw events into a format that can be stored in a database and then enhances the raw events by augmenting the data with other relevant information not found in the raw event logs, such as routing information, domain names of the IP addresses, and so on. An integrated data analysis tool is then used to analyze events from the database. The tools can be used in both batch and interactive modes. Using batch mode, reports, such as summarization reports, can be generated on a regular basis. These reports can be viewed by an analyst through web interfaces or other means. If problems are identified, either by analyzing the report or because some unusually suspicious events have occurred, an exploratory mode can be used by the analyst to interactively visualize and mine events from the database.

22.4. DATA FORMAT

Raw IDS alerts may come in a variety of different formats. However, there are a couple of common information types. To illustrate this, we show below one sample message of a network IDS log:

Alert Level: 3 **Date:** Fri Feb 18 2000 22:31:44 **Sig:** IDS-S1-Host-Page:N/A DOS— Possible connection flood **Host:** 123.686.123.912:[50] **to** 056.977.456.222:[210]

In this network IDS log, each line begins with "**Alert Level:**" and contains tokens of information in a nondelimited format. In our example, [ ] denotes optional content, **bold** represents constant information. Besides the alert level and timestamp, the key attributes of the event are: signature for representing the type of an alert; source IP address and port number, destination IP address and port number, and a detailed message for additional explanation of this alert. In our example alert above, its signature is IDS-S1-Host-Page:N/A DOS; the source IP is 123.686.123.912 with port number 50; the destination IP is 056.977.456.222 with port 210; and the detailed message is "Possible connection flood." Clearly, this alert signified a possible connection flood [or DOS (Denial of Service) attack] from 123.686.123.912 to 056.977.456.222.

It should be emphasized that this is actual data obtained from a real IDS system operating in a commercial customer environment. For reasons of customer confidentiality, we cannot provide more details of the data source here, but we should note that none of the data used in this chapter is synthetic, with the exception of data used in Section 22.7.3 to test the clustering algorithm.

22.5. DATA MINING

Data mining refers to technologies and algorithms that analyze the underlying data looking for patterns and salient characteristics that are interesting, unusual, or informative. The data-mining tools we use are listed here; each is then described in detail below. These tools constitute a piece of software called the Event Miner [described further in Ma et al. (2001)].

1. *Event-Rate Analysis.* This step computes the flow of alerts occurring in a specified time window. This allows bursts of alerts to be detected, which can further guide the intrusion detection process.

2. *Temporal Association.* This step finds sets of alerts that often occur close together in time. This may indicate a coordinated attack from multiple sources.

3. *Clustering.* This step groups together alerts, hosts, or destinations that are highly "similar" under some user-defined criterion. For example, the user may want to analyze all hosts that generate alerts at similar sets of destinations.

It is important to note that the data-mining tools cannot be used blindly; the results must always be evaluated by a human expert and used to investigate the data further in an interactive way. We now describe each of the above data-mining tools in more detail.

22.6. EVENT-RATE ANALYSIS AND TEMPORAL ASSOCIATION

The event rate is the number of events (alerts) that occur in a particular time window selected by the user. As time progresses, new events are included in the window as old ones drop out. The user can set a threshold: If the event-rate exceeds the threshold, the corresponding "burst" of events can then be examined. The hosts responsible for generating the bursts can be further examined, as illustrated in the application scenario (Section 22.8).

Temporal association attempts to detect sets of alerts that are highly associated with one another. Mining frequent temporal patterns has been well studied (e.g., Mannila et al., 1997; Agarwal and Srikant, 1994). Several issues are relevant to the case of mining historical intrusion detection logs. First, we expect that an interesting pattern that signifies possible intrusions will most likely be *infrequent,* because most alerts are generated by innocent behavior and the false alarm rate is high. Thus finding frequent patterns cannot succeed in characterizing the significant correlations corresponding to possible intrusions. Second, the traditional framework for mining *frequent k*-wise patterns (e.g., Agarwal and Srikant, 1994) requires (for reasons of computational efficiency) that all its subsets be frequent. This is a bit strong in reality and leads to too many partially overlapping patterns, which makes it difficult for a human expert to evaluate the significance of the patterns. Our idea is to mine significant *pairwise* correlations from the historical event log data and then combine them to create linked patterns of behavior.

First we precisely define the statistical computation of significant pairwise patterns. Given a window length w, for any event a and any other event b, we compute the following statistics: N_a, N_b, N_{ab}, $P_{a|b}$, $P_{b|a}$, $\mathbf{\Phi}^2_{ab}$, where N_a is the total number of windows containing event a; similarly for N_b. N_{ab} is the number of occurrences of the pair (a, b); see Figure 22.2 for an example.

$P_{b|a}$ represents the predictive power of event a for event b. It is the conditional probability of event b occurring within the time window w of an occurrence of event a. Thus $P_{b|a} = N_{ab}/N_a$, and similarly for $P_{a|b}$. $\mathbf{\Phi}^2_{ab}$ is the chi-squared test score of $a-b$ coupling, which is a measure of the deviation of the distribution of events (a,b) from the random distribution. A high $\mathbf{\Phi}^2$ score indicates that it is likely that the occurrences of the two events are not due to randomness. A detailed discussion of how the $\mathbf{\Phi}^2$ score is computed can be found in Liang et al. (2002).

The complete details of the algorithm are provided in Figure 22.3. The user selects a time window, a count threshold, and two probability thresholds. The algorithm finds all pairs of alerts (a, b) that occur within the time window a total number of times N_{ab} exceeding the count threshold and whose likelihood of occurring (in either order) exceed the probability thresholds. All significant cases of pairwise association are found efficiently in a single pass of the data stream.

Once the pairwise associations are found, they can be grouped together using transitive closure into a set of mutually exclusive patterns. Not every pair in such a pattern is significantly correlated, but each event is significantly correlated with at least one other event in the pattern. This representation is known as an Event Relationship Network [see Perng et al. (2003)].

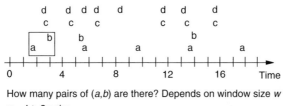

d d d d d d d d
c c c c c c
b b b
a a a a a
0 4 8 12 16 Time
How many pairs of (a,b) are there? Depends on window size w
w = 1 ≥ 2 pairs
w = 2 ≥ 3 pairs
Probabilities (if w = 1):
P_b|a = Count(a,b)/Count(a) = 2/5
P_a|b = Count(a,b)/Count(b) = 2/3

Figure 22.2. An event stream illustrating computation of correlation statistics.

Inputs: A sequence of events E (an event has a time-stamp and a list of attribute-values)
E is ordered by time
Window size w
Count threshold t_c
Probability thresholds t1, t2

Output: A collection of objects, each object containing a pair of events, a count, and 2 probability values p1.2, p2.1,
such that each pair (e1,e2) occurs within window size w a total of n times, with n > t_c, and p1.2 > t1, p2.1 > t2, where p1.2 = n/(num of occurrences of e1) and p2.1 = n/(num of occurrences of e2)

```
Algorithm:
    S = empty
    e = first_event_in_E
    event_window_stack = empty
    Repeat until end of event stream E
       remove from event_window_stack all events with timestamp<e.timestamp-w
       e.count++
       For each event f in event_window_stack
              f.count++
              if (e,f,pair_count) is in S, change (e,f,pair_count) to (e,f,pair_count+1)
              else place (e,f,1) in S
        add e to event_window_stack
        e = next_event_in_E

    P = empty
    For each (e,f,pair_count) in S
        if pair_count > t_c
              compute p1.2 = pair_count/count_e
                          p2.1 = pair_count/count_f
              if p1.2 > t1 and p2.1 > t2
                    add (e,f,pair_count,p1.2,p2.1) to P
    Return P
```

Figure 22.3. Temporal association algorithm.

22.7. CLUSTERING

Temporal association naturally suggests a more general consideration of applying clustering to unlabeled intrusion detection data. Clustering may serve many purposes. For example, one might group together source addresses that trigger similar types of alert signatures. Using a known list of trusted hosts (e.g., hosts internal to the local intranet are more likely to trigger false alarms than generate hostile attacks), we can draw some useful insights: If a cluster contains some trusted hosts, most likely other hosts in this cluster are also triggering false alarms; on the other hand, if a cluster contains a "blacklisted" host (a known source of harmful intrusions), then other hosts in the same cluster may also be hostile and should be investigated further.

As another example, destination addresses rather than source addresses could be clustered together; this may identify customer sites that share common vulnerabilities. Yet another possibility is clustering signatures so as to assist in developing correlation rules for real-time response. Or one might want to cluster source addresses using destination address and port number, in order to determine which sites are launching coordinated scanning attacks against similar destinations. Other scenarios in which clustering might be useful can be envisaged. What is needed is a general framework that can accommodate a variety of different situations. Since there is usually little or no information concerning what the "true" clusters are in the data, the utility of clustering lies in suggesting hypotheses to the user which may lead to a more detailed examination that may confirm or refute the importance of the detected clusters.

We adopt the methodology shown in Figure 22.4. This consists of the following steps:

1. Feature selection: Both the variable to be clustered and the relevant features are selected.

2. The similarity measure is chosen, and similarity values between every pair of items are computed.

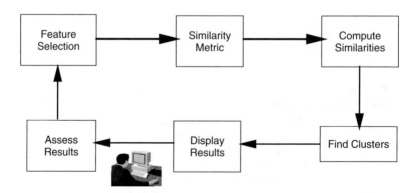

Figure 22.4. Clustering methodology.

3. A clustering algorithm is applied to determine the clusters.

4. The results are displayed using our Event Miner visualization tool and evaluated in order to determine if the clustering has provided useful insights.

5. Based on this evaluation, the relevant features can be adjusted or reweighed and the cycle repeated.

We now describe each of these steps in more detail.

22.7.1. Feature Selection

Feature selection requires selecting what one wishes to cluster and which features are relevant to determining similarity. In general, let F be the collection of features; each f in F contains as values all the distinct entries in that column of the log file. For example, the feature "source" represents all the source addresses; note that any source address may occur multiple times in the log, but each line contains only one source address. Other features might be destination address, timestamp, source port, destination port, alert signature, and so on.

To do clustering, one selects a subset C_1 of F as the cluster variables and a disjoint subset C_2 of F as the cluster features. Then the final output clusters will group together items of C_1 which are similar as measured by a similarity measure defined on the features in C_2. One must specify how to measure the similarity between any two items in C_1 using the features in C_2. This defines a function Sim: $C_1 \% C_1 \xi \bullet$. The precise computation of Sim depends on the sense in which items are to be regarded as similar.

For example, suppose we are interested in finding those source addresses that generate alerts at similar destination addresses, but the number of times each destination address occurs is irrelevant. Let D_s be the collection of destinations associated with each source address s; that is, d is in D_s if s generates at least one alert at d. Then we might define $\text{Sim}(s_1, s_2) = |D_{s1} 3 D_{s2}| \backslash |D_{s1} 4 D_{s2}|$. This is the so-called **Jaccard coefficient** [see Jain and Dubes (1988)] for measuring the similar of categorical attributes, denoted here as $J(D_{s1}, D_{s2})$. As far as we know, this set-based similarity measure has not been previously applied to intrusion detection data.

In a different scenario, we might wish to identify source addresses that attack similar destinations a similar number of times. In this case we would let D'_s contain all destinations associated with s, but include as many copies of each destination d as occur associated with source address s in the log file. Then the measure defined by $\text{Sim}'(s_1, s_2) = J(D'_{s1}, D'_{s2})$ provides a different measure of similarity between any pair of source addresses, reflecting the number of times that alerts are generated by source addresses at particular destinations.

In general, depending on the task, different similarity measures can be used, depending on how the relevant features need to be taken into account.

22.7.2. Clustering Algorithm

A large variety of clustering algorithms have been developed, including k-means, agglomerative clustering, learning vector quantization, and so on [see Duda et al. Stork, (2001) and Hastie et al. (2001)]. Our focus in this chapter is not on designing yet another clustering algorithm; instead our emphasis is on providing a framework within which the user can, by simply changing the similarity measure, obtain results that can be easily interpreted to provide useful insights. For this purpose, simple clustering algorithms are to be preferred to more sophisticated procedures that are computationally more expensive and whose results may be more difficult for the user to understand.

We use a simple agglomerative clustering algorithm where items are placed in the same cluster only if their similarity is larger than some pre-defined threshold. Thus in the final output each cluster contains precisely those items whose similarity, for every pair in the cluster, exceeds the threshold. The clusters are computed by examining, for each item in turn, the currently existing clusters and adding the item to the first cluster where its similarity with every element in the cluster exceeds the threshold. If no such cluster exists, a new cluster is formed containing only that item. The algorithm is shown in Figure 22.5.

The similarity threshold can be used to alter the sensitivity of the clusters. A high threshold means that items must be nearly identical in order to be placed in the same cluster. The result will be a large number of small clusters. A low threshold will group together items that are only somewhat similar, resulting in a smaller number of large clusters.

22.7.3. Experiments—Synthetic Data

Experiments with artificially generated datasets are used to validate the performance of the clustering algorithm. They also show how different similarity measures are appropriate for different tasks and allow us to explore the effects of dataset size and noise on clustering performance.

We use an artificial scenario in which clusters of source machines coordinate attacks against different destination machines. A synthetic IDS log file of alerts is generated as follows. Each alert contains a source address, a destination address, and an alert signature. The source address is selected randomly from a set of 100 source addresses. The source addresses are grouped together into five clusters of 20 addresses each—these represent the true clusters. There are 50 destination addresses that can be the target of an alert. Let D_j denote the collection of destination machines attacked by cluster C_j of source machines; this means that if the source address is in cluster C_j, with probability 1-*noise* one of the destination addresses from D_j is chosen as the target of the alert and with probability *noise* the target machine is chosen randomly from among all destination addresses. The alert signature is generated randomly from a collection of 30 signatures. The scenario is illustrated in Figure 22.6.

Input: Collection of items $X = \{x_i\}$, $i = 1$ to n, similarity matrix $S(x_i, x_j)$, threshold t
Output: Set of clusters $C = \{C_j\}$ such that $4Cj = X$, $Cj3Ck = \emptyset$ for $j\gamma k$, $x_{i1},x_{i2} \in Cj$ iff
$S(x_{i1},x_{i2}) > t$

Algorithm:

$C = \emptyset$
For $i = 1$ to n
    Let $r = |C| =$ number of existing clusters; $C = \{C_1, \ldots, C_r\}$
    clusterfound = false
    $j = 1$
    while $j \leq r$ and !clusterfound
        if $S(x_i,x) > t$ for all x in Cj, $Cj = Cj4x_i$, set clusterfound = true
        else j++
    if !clusterfound
        $C_{r+1} = \{xi\}$ $C = C4C_{r+1}$

Output C

Figure 22.5. Clustering algorithm.

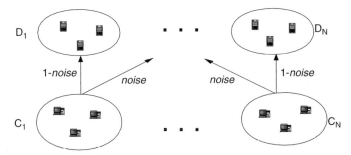

The clusters used to generate synthetic data.
Each machine in cluster C_i attacks a randomly selected target in D_i with
probability 1-noise and any randomly selected machine with probability noise.

Figure 22.6. Scenario used to create synthetic data.

The three different similarity measures we examine are (in all three cases the
Jaccard coefficient described above is used):

1. *Address.* The similarity between two source addresses is computed by considering only the proportion of destination addresses they have in common,
   ignoring the alert signature.

2. *Signature.* The similarity between two source addresses is computed by
   considering only the proportion of alert signatures they have in common,
   ignoring the destination address.

3. *Combined.* The similarity between two source addresses is computed using
   both the destination and alert signatures, weighted equally.

Cluster quality is measured by comparing the output clusters with the input clusters used to generate the data. The *confusion matrix* contains the number of items in output cluster i that come from input cluster j. If cluster quality is high, one of the values in each row will be large while the others are small. We compute the cluster quality for each output cluster using the largest value in each row as a fraction of the input cluster size, and average this over all the output clusters, thus obtaining an overall measure of cluster quality as a number between 0 and 1. Note that we do not assume that the number of input clusters is known, and so the number of output clusters may differ from the number of input clusters. To avoid giving undue credit to small numbers of large clusters, a cluster quality of zero is assigned for each input cluster for which there is no corresponding output cluster.

22.7.4. Results

In the first set of experiments we investigate the effect of the noise level on the clustering results. The noise level refers to the consistency with which each source address generates alerts at a particular group of targets. For example, a noise level of 0.1 means that any source address in cluster C_j generates alerts at destination addresses in D_j 90% of the time; 10% of the time, alerts are generated at any random destination address. We assume that all sources have the same noise level.

The results (see Figure 22.7) show first that at low noise levels, focusing only on the destination address detects the clusters, whereas focusing only on the alert signature does not, and combining both is slightly worse than considering only the destination address. The value of 0.2 for the signature clusters represents a baseline score because using only the alert signature places all source addresses into one cluster, which yields an average cluster quality of $1/n$, where n is the number of clusters, in this case $n = 5$.

This result makes sense because the alert signature is distributed randomly among the signature types and thus provides no information concerning the clusters. It is noticeable that although destination address and signature are equally weighted, the combined approach does quite well in effectively ignoring the

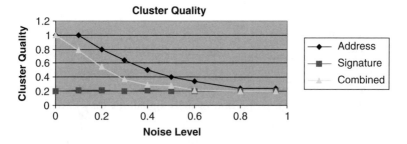

Figure 22.7. Clustering results with noise (synthetic data).

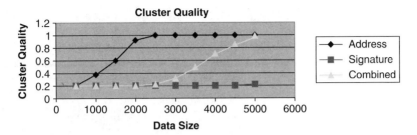

Figure 22.8. Clustering results with dataset size (synthetic data).

uninformative alert signature information and attending only to the destination address, thus scoring almost as well as when using the destination address alone.

We also see that clustering quality degrades smoothly as a function of increasing noise level. This is as expected, because as the noise level increases, the source clusters become more and more difficult to distinguish, since each source address generates an increasing number of alerts at all destinations equally instead of focusing on particular targets. In the limit, as the noise level tends to 1, the "real" clusters cease to exist and performance falls toward the chance level.

In the second set of experiments we investigate the effect of dataset size on cluster quality. As the size of the dataset, which is simply the number of lines in the log file, increases, the clusters should become more clearly visible. This is confirmed by the results shown in Figure 22.8; once again we notice that the address similarity measure performs best, the signature similarity measure performs at the chance level, and the combined similarity measure averages between them.

22.8. APPLICATION SCENARIO

There are two typical application scenarios. The first one is that our customer has a large amount of IDS data, say one month or even more, with many thousands or even millions of events, and we are asked to perform analysis so as to identify installation issues as well as unknown patterns. For this, we often start with the summary analysis by date, by source and by signature. We then run other approaches for high-volume alerts. The second scenario is more of an interactive, exploratory mode. Very often, through an initial analysis, some interesting situations are encountered. Then further analysis can be performed by selecting the appropriate tool based on what has been seen previously.

Clearly, in both scenarios, we need to apply multiple approaches. To illustrate what can be achieved by integrating the various data-mining tools described above, we discuss one particular case below.

The raw event logs are obtained from a web hosting environment where thousands of servers support web sites for multiple customers. In a typical day, many thousands of alerts may be received.

Figure 22.9. The types of alerts in 1 day's worth of data (>30K alerts), ordered by count, with the three most common alert signatures shaded.

22.8.1. Visualization

We begin by examining the data. Figure 22.9 depicts one day's worth of alerts. Out of a total of 31,826 events. About 47% of the attacks were generated by ICMP Echo packets, 26% by attempted access of the port defined for WWW administration, and 24% are connection based port-floods, a type of denial-of-service (DOS) attack. There are about 3% other attacks.

Figure 22.10 shows a summary by host (source address). The coordinated coloring between the charts allows one to easily see which types of alerts each host is responsible. To make the display easier to view, each address is listed as an ID number, not the "real" IP address. For example, one can see that the green signature was the major activity for host ID 1, which caused 5516 hits out of a total of 8419 "green" hits.

Figure 22.11 shows both destination addresses and alert type (signature) for the alerts in Figure 22.9. The left side shows the destination addresses (only the colored events are shown; the other events were dropped from the display by operator selection). The right-hand side shows the signature. The concentration of events in the addresses near the bottom of the left-hand side represents sustained attacks that are directed at the web server. The dispersion of green dots throughout the diagram reveals a sequential scan of destination addresses that occur over a day's time.

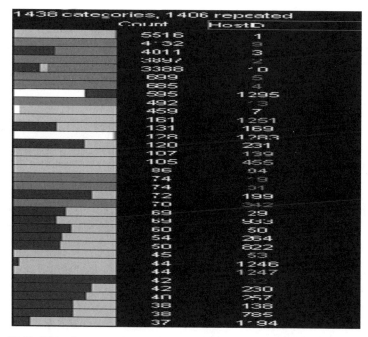

Figure 22.10. This shows source addresses based on the code of Figure 22.9 and uses the shading to illustrate the relative proportions per address.

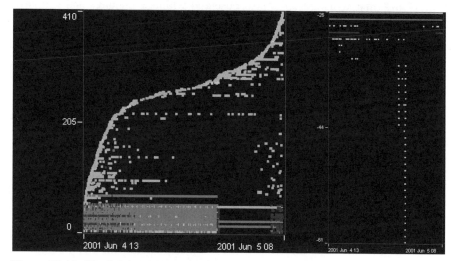

Figure 22.11. The left-hand chart shows destination addresses on the vertical axis, and the right-hand chart shows alert signatures. Note that many alerts at different destinations have the same signature, so the right-hand side appears much less dense. (The green events appear as a horizontal line at the top of the right-hand chart).

The right-hand side shows that the red ICMP and green port-scan alerts occur continuously in time, while the blue DOS events occur in a number of scattered patches. We also notice a vertical row of dots—a "spike" of alerts of many different signatures occurring at the same time. It is preceded by a much smaller spike containing a subset of the same signatures. This is clearly suspicious.

22.8.2. Event-Rate Analysis and Temporal Association

Figure 22.12 illustrates an example of event-rate analysis. The threshold is set to 180, corresponding to three events per second. Two event bursts above the threshold can be seen. Notice that the second (and biggest) event burst corresponds exactly to the vertical row of alerts seen in the right-hand side of Figure 22.11. By using the coordinated coloring across the different views, the signatures, sources, and destinations of each burst can be examined. One can then construct a "blacklist" of the sources that generate most of the events in the burst. These sites can then be watched more closely, or one may try to gain other information about them.

Figure 22.13 shows the temporal association of alerts based on signature within a time window of 1 minute with a probability threshold of 0.60. Recall from Section 22.6 that each row of the table should be interpreted as showing the likelihood of the pair of signatures in either order. Thus the first row of this table should be interpreted to mean: "If signature 35 happens, then 79.7% of the time signature 37 occurs (within 1 minute), and if signature 37 happens, then 83% of the time signature 35 is also observed within 1 minute," and similarly with the other rows.

Signatures are then grouped together using transitive closure: Two signatures that appear in any row of the table are placed in the same group. Figure 22.14

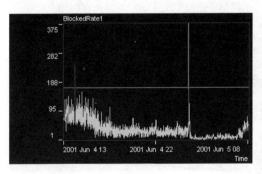

Figure 22.12. Event-rate analysis. The threshold in the left-hand chart is set at three events per second (equivalent to 180 "hits" per minute). The large red event burst corresponds exactly to the vertical row of alerts seen on the right-hand side of Figure 22.11. The red events account for 377 "hits/minute" (see chart on the right), and the blue events account for 246 "hits/minute." The window size was set to 1 minute. The white color denotes "other" events—that is, under the threshold.

Unscaled	SIG	SIG1	Count	P.1.2.	P.2.1.	Pm
0	-35	-37	55	0.797	0.833	0.797
1	-35	-41	45	0.652	0.682	0.652
2	-36	-44	26	0.650	0.867	0.650
3	-37	-41	53	0.803	0.803	0.803
4	-37	-42	46	0.697	0.780	0.697
5	-37	-43	46	0.697	0.793	0.697
6	-38	-39	21	0.840	0.913	0.840
7	-38	-44	23	0.920	0.767	0.767
8	-39	-44	19	0.826	0.633	0.633
9	-41	-42	55	0.833	0.932	0.833
10	-41	-43	48	0.727	0.828	0.727
11	-42	-43	50	0.847	0.862	0.847
12	-48	-47	9	1	0.900	0.900
13	-48	-46	8	0.889	1	0.889
14	-48	-49	7	0.778	1	0.778
15	-48	-51	8	0.889	0.889	0.889
16	-47	-46	8	0.800	1	0.800
17	-47	-49	7	0.700	1	0.700
18	-47	-51	9	0.900	1	0.900
19	-46	-50	5	0.625	1	0.625
20	-46	-49	7	0.875	1	0.875
21	-46	-51	7	0.875	0.778	0.778
22	-50	-49	5	1	0.714	0.714
23	-49	-51	6	0.857	0.667	0.667
24	-51	-56	6	0.667	1	0.667
25	-51	-55	6	0.667	1	0.667
26	-56	-55	6	1	1	1

Figure 22.13. Temporal association. The pairs of most commonly occurring signatures (in either order) are shown, with associated counts and probabilities. Signatures are then grouped together using transitive closure, where any signature in a group is temporally associated with at least one other signature in the group (see Figure 22.14).

36 categories, 32 repeated

Count	SIG	EventName
15066	-28	IDS-S9-Host-Mail:N/A SCAN ICMP - Echo Pk
8419	-27	IDS-S4-All-Mail:N/A SCAN Accessing WWW A
7740	-30	IDS-S1-Host-Page:N/A DOS - Possible conn
69	-35	IDS-S2-Host-Info:N/A CONFIG - TFTP - Ser
66	-37	IDS-S5-All-Mail:N/A BACKDOOR Deep Throat
66	-41	IDS-S5-All-Mail:N/A BACKDOOR NetBus port
59	-42	IDS-S2-Host-Page:N/A DOS - Traffic FROM
58	-43	IDS-S5-All-Mail:N/A BACKDOOR Common Back
44	-31	IDS-S4-All-Mail:N/A ALERT MS Front Page
40	-36	IDS-S4-All-Mail:N/A SCAN RPCinfo query
30	-44	IDS-S2-Host-Info:N/A BACKDOOR Back Orifi
25	-38	IDS-S2-Host-Info:N/A CONFIG GOPHER traff
23	-39	IDS-S7-All-Mail:N/A SCAN finger traffic
18	-29	IDS-S2-All-Page:N/A CONFIG Directory Bro
11	-40	IDS-S2-Host-Info:N/A SCAN IDENT request
10	-47	IDS-S4-All-Mail:N/A ALERT test-cgi acces
9	-48	IDS-S4-All-Mail:N/A ALERT WebGAIS Access
9	-51	IDS-S4-All-Mail:N/A ALERT WWW dumping sy
8	-46	IDS-S4-All-Page:CVE-1999-0067 ALERT PHF
7	-49	IDS-S4-All-Mail:CVE-1999-0146 ALERT CAMP
6	-34	IDS-S4-All-Mail:N/A CONFIG SERVER protoc
6	-55	IDS-S4-All-Mail:N/A ALERT SGI - Vulnerab
6	-56	IDS-S4-All-Mail:N/A ALERT Vulnerable CGI
5	-50	IDS-S2-All-Mail:N/A ALERT attempt to bre
4	-52	IDS-S7-All-Mail:N/A SCAN gathering file
4	-54	IDS-S4-All-Mail:N/A ALERT SGI handler at
3	-53	IDS-S4-All-Mail:CVE-1999-0039 ALERT SGI
3	-57	IDS-S4-All-Mail:N/A ALERT uploader.exe a
2	-32	IDS-S2-All-Mail:N/A ALERT POST proxy att
2	-33	IDS-S2-All-Mail:N/A ALERT Link to BAK fi
2	-45	IDS-S5-All-Mail:N/A BACKDOOR PC Anywhere
2	-59	IDS-S4-All-Mail:N/A ALERT attempt to loc
1	-58	IDS-S4-All-Mail:N/A ALERT WebGAIS Access
1	-60	IDS-S4-All-Mail:CVE-1999-0039 ALERT SGI

Figure 22.14. The signatures of Figure 22.9, with three groups of associated signatures colored. Each shade denotes a set of signatures that often occur together within 1 minute.

shows some of the groups of the signatures in Figure 22.13. Note that we are using a coloring scheme (magenta, yellow, and cyan) that is different from the one used before. Recall that signatures in these clusters occur within 1 minute of each other. This "tight" association in time most probably shows the use of hacker tools, because such associations would be extremely unlikely to occur manually.

Using the coordinated coloring across views, the source addresses associated with the signatures in any group can be located. If a particular source address is also found on the "blacklist" (the list of sites responsible for most of the events in a burst uncovered by event-rate analysis, as shown in Figure 22.12), then that group of signatures can be regarded as a characteristic of hostile activity. If another source address matches the same group of signatures, then that address may also be manifesting a similar pattern of hostile behavior, even if it generates very few alerts.

Figure 22.15 plots the hosts and signature mapping for the signatures in Figure 22.14. This reveals the "true" list of attackers. Notice again the common coding of alerts across Figures 22.14 and 22.15. for example, in this case, two hosts are identified as causing what appear to be carefully orchestrated intrusions, perhaps by running scripts or programs to perform a methodical series of attacks.

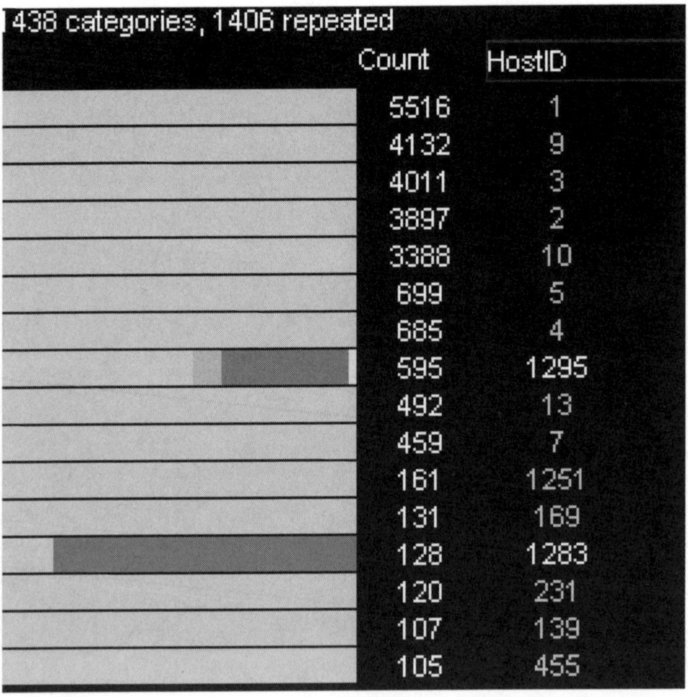

438 categories, 1406 repeated		
	Count	HostID
	5516	1
	4132	9
	4011	3
	3897	2
	3388	10
	699	5
	685	4
	595	1295
	492	13
	459	7
	161	1251
	131	169
	128	1283
	120	231
	107	139
	105	455

Figure 22.15. These are the host Ids responsible for the signature groups seen in Figure 22.14.

In this illustration, one source (Host 1295) is known to be "blacklisted"; that is it was responsible for a large number of the alerts that occurred in the largest event burst shown in Figure 22.12. The other source is a low-frequency attacker that did not contribute significantly to any event burst. It has been detected through an integrated approach that uncovered that its behavior was remarkably similar to that of the blacklisted host.

22.8.3. Clustering

We now illustrate some of the insights that are suggested by applying clustering to the data. Because the "ground truth" is not known, the results are necessarily preliminary in nature, and further exploration will be needed to extend and validate them.

Figure 22.16 shows the listing of address clusters; that is, each cluster consists of those hosts generating alerts at similar destination addresses. The clusters are ordered by the total alert count for all the hosts in the cluster. Out of 36 total clusters, only the most significant, in terms of total alert count, are displayed in the figure. The columns give the total alert count of each cluster, the cluster size (the number of hosts in the cluster), and the maximum and average number of alerts of hosts in the cluster.

We see that the first cluster contains two hosts, the next three clusters contain one host each, the next cluster is much larger, with 250 hosts, and so on. We can

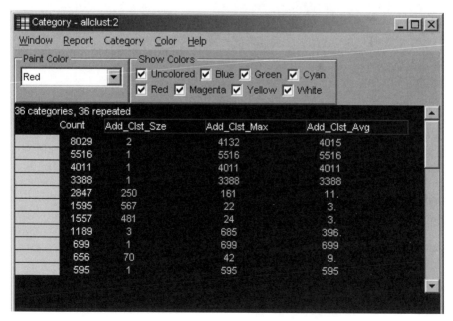

Figure 22.16. Address clusters. Each cluster consists of source addresses that target similar destinations.

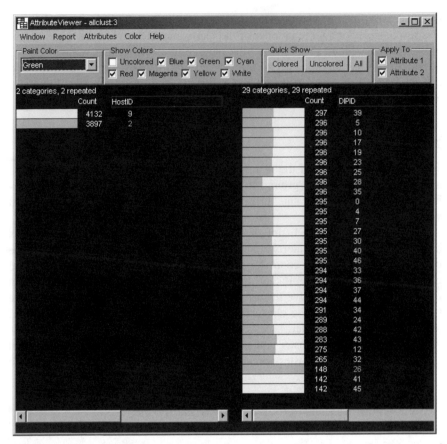

Figure 22.17. The destination addresses for the two sources in the first cluster of Figure 22.16 are clearly very similar.

investigate each cluster further by using the visualization and color-coding capabilities of the Event Browser. For example, Figure 22.17 shows the destinations associated with the two hosts in the first cluster (only the host and destination IDs are displayed; the actual IP addresses are omitted). Except for the three destinations at the bottom, the two hosts target exactly the same set of destinations, confirming that their behavior along this dimension is indeed very similar, though not identical. Examining the alert signature shows that these alerts are most likely false alarms generated by misconfiguration. Note that if we wanted to detect hosts that target similar destinations a similar number of times, we would simply include the destination count in the computation of the similarity measure, as described in Section 22.7.3.

One can investigate the other clusters in similar way. For example, it turns out that the largest cluster in Figure 22.16 (567 hosts, with an average of only three events per host) consists of many machines, each generating a small number of alerts at a popular web site.

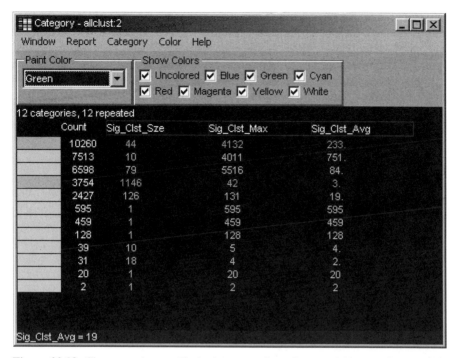

Figure 22.18. Signature clusters. Each cluster consists of source addresses that generate similar types of alerts.

Figure 22.18 shows the listing of signature clusters; that is, each cluster consists of those hosts generating alerts with similar signatures. As before, the clusters are ordered by total alert count, and the columns give the cluster size and the maximum and average number of alerts of hosts in the cluster.

Suppose we wish to distinguish real from spoofed IP addresses. Our assumption is that real addresses should display different alert signature characteristics from spoofed addresses. Hosts that belong to the same signature cluster as addresses that are known to be real are therefore likely to also be real.

Two of the clusters in Figure 22.18 are highlighted to illustrate this point. One cluster consists of 44 hosts, each generating many alerts; the other cluster consists of 1146 hosts, each generating an average of only three alerts. Examining the IP addresses of these two clusters reveals that many of the hosts in the first cluster are actually internal sites, and so it is likely that all those IP addresses are real. However, none of the host addresses in the second cluster are internal; this suggests that the addresses are spoofed.

22.9. CONCLUSIONS

We have defined and implemented the infrastructure needed for capturing large quantities of network-based alert data and making it readily available for analysis in order to extract valuable information that can then be reported as a guide to further action. Analysis is performed using a variety of data-mining techniques integrated in the Event Miner toolset. The power of this methodology is that it enables the user to interactively select the appropriate analysis tool as he/she explores interesting patterns in the data. When applied to real data, this approach has been used to reduce false alarm rates, reveal troublesome source addresses, including those causing low-frequency events, and indicate the use of scripting tools used by hackers.

The fundamental limitation of intrusion detection logs is that the data are unlabeled, the underlying truth of which alerts correspond to actual malicious behavior is generally unknown. Nonetheless, a concerted approach using a variety of interactive data-mining tools may reveal useful insights that the analyst can use as a guide to further investigation.

REFERENCES

Agarwal, R., and Srikant, R., Fast algorithms for mining association rules, in *Proceedings of Very Large Data Bases*, 1994.

Axelsson, S., A Preliminary Attempt to Apply Detection and Estimation Theory to Intrusion Detection, Technical Report, Department of Computer Engineering, Chalmers University of Technology, Goteborg, Sweden, 2000.

Duda, R. O., Hart, P. E., and Stork, D. G., *Pattern Classification*, John Wiley & Sons, New York, 2001.

Dunigan, T., and Hinkel, G., Intrusion detection and intrusion prevention on a large network, a case study, in *Proceedings of the 8th Usenix Security Symposium*, 1999.

Fan, W., Miller, M., Stolfo, S.J., Lee, W., and Chan, P.K., Using artificial anomalies to detect unknown and known network intrusions, *Proceedings of the 2001 IEEE International Conference on Data Mining*, pp. 123–130, 2001.

Green, J., Marchette, D., and Northcutt, S., Analysis techniques for detecting coordinated attacks and probes, in *Proceedings of the 8th Usenix Security Symposium*, 1999.

Hastie, T., Tibshirani, R., and Friedman, J., *The Elements of Statistical Learning*, Springer-Verlag, Berlin, 2001.

Jain, A., and Dubes, R., *Algorithms for Clustering Data*, Prentice-Hall, Englewood Cliffs, NJ, 1988.

Julisch, K., Mining alarm clusters to improve alarm handling efficiency, in *17th Annual Computer Security Applications Conference*, 2001.

Lee, W., and Stolfo, S., Data mining approaches for intrusion detection, in *Proceedings of the 7th USENIX Security Symposium*, 1998.

Lee, W., and Xiang, D., Information-theoretic measures for anomaly detection, in *Proceedings of the 2001 IEEE Symposium on Security and Privacy*, May 2001.

Liang, F., Ma, S., and Hellerstein, J. L., Discovering fully dependent patterns, in *Second Society of Industrial and Applied Mathematics International Conference on Data Mining*, 2002.

Ma, S., Hellerstein, J. L., and Perng, C., Event miner: An integrated mining tool for scalable analysis of event data, in *Visual Data Mining Workshop*, 2001.

Ma, S., and Hellerstein, J. L., Mining mutually dependent event patterns, in *IEEE International Conference on Data Mining*, 2001.

Manganaris, S., A data mining analysis of RTID alarms, in *Recent Advances in Intrusion Detection*, 1999.

Mannila, H., Toivonen, H., and Verkamo, A., Discovery of frequent episodes in event sequences, *Data Mining and Knowledge Discovery* **1**(3), 259–289 (1997).

Mei, M. George, D., Brodie, M., Aggarwal, C., Ma, S., and Yu, P., PEC: Post-Event Correlation Tools for Network-Based Intrusion Detection, IBM Research Report RC 23011, 2003.

Perng, C., Thoenen, D., Grabarnik, G., Ma, S., and Hellerstein, J., *Data-driven validation, completion and construction of event relation networks*, in *Proceedings of Knowledge Discovery and Data Mining*, 2003.

Portnoy, L., Eskin, E., and Stolfo, S., Intrusion detection with unlabeled data using clustering, in *Proceedings of ACM CSS Workshop on Data Mining Applied to Security*, 2001.

Wespi, A., Dacier, M., and Debar, H., An intrusion-detection system based on the teiresias pattern-discovery algorithm, in *Proceedings of EICAR (European Institute for Computer Anti-Virus Research)*, 1999.

PART VIII

NEW TRENDS IN DATA-MINING TECHNOLOGY

23

MINING CLOSED AND MAXIMAL FREQUENT ITEMSETS

MOHAMMED J. ZAKI

23.1. INTRODUCTION

Mining frequent itemsets is a fundamental and essential problem in many data-mining applications such as the discovery of association rules, strong rules, correlations, multidimensional patterns, and many other important discovery tasks. The problem is formulated as follows: Given a large database of set of items transactions, find all frequent itemsets, where a frequent itemset is one that occurs in at least a user-specified percentage of the database.

Many of the proposed itemset-mining algorithms are a variant of Apriori (Agrawal et al., 1996), which employs a bottom-up, breadth-first search that enumerates every single frequent itemset. In many applications (especially in dense data) with long frequent patterns, enumerating all possible $2^m - 2$ subsets of a m length pattern (m can easily be 30 or 40 or longer) is computationally infeasible. For example, many real-world domains like gene expression studies, network intrusion, web content and usage mining, and so on, contain patterns are typically long. There are two current solutions to the long pattern-mining problem. The first solution one is to mine only the *maximal* frequent itemsets (Bayardo, 1998; Lin and Kedem, 1998; Agrawal et al., 2000; Zaki, 2000b; Burdick et al., 2001; Gouda and Zaki, 2001). A frequent set is maximal if it has no frequent superset; the set of maximal patterns is typically orders of magnitude smaller than all frequent patterns. While mining maximal sets help understand the long patterns in dense domains, they lead to a loss of information; since subset frequency is not available maximal sets are not suitable for generating rules. The second solution is to mine only the frequent *closed* sets (Bastide et al., 2000; Pei et al., 2000; Pasquier et al., 1999; Zaki, 2000a; Zaki and Hsiao, 2002); a

Next Generation of Data-Mining Applications. Edited by Kantardzic and Zurada
ISBN 0-471-65605-4 © 2005 the Institute of Electrical and Electronics Engineers, Inc.

frequent set is closed if it has no superset with the same frequency. Closed sets are *lossless* in the sense that they uniquely determine the set of all frequent itemsets and their *exact* frequency. At the same time, closed sets can themselves be orders of magnitude smaller than all frequent sets, especially on dense databases. Nevertheless, for some of the dense datasets we consider in this chapter, even the set of all closed patterns would grow to be too large. The only recourse is to mine the maximal patterns in such domains.

In this chapter we give an overview of the closed and maximal itemset-mining problem. We survey existing methods and focus on Charm and GenMax, both state-of-the-art algorithms that efficiently enumerate all closed and maximal patterns, respectively. Charm and GenMax simultaneously explore both the itemset space and transaction space, and they use a number of optimizations to quickly prune away a large portion of the subset search space. GenMax uses a novel *progressive focusing* technique to eliminate nonmaximal itemsets, while Charm uses a fast hash-based approach to eliminate nonclosed itemsets during subsumption checking. Both utilize *diffset propagation* for fast frequency checking. Diffsets (Zaki and Gouda, 2003) keep track of differences in the tids of a candidate pattern from its prefix pattern. Diffsets drastically cut down (by orders of magnitude) the size of memory required to store intermediate results. Thus the entire working set of patterns can fit entirely in main-memory, even for large databases.

We conduct an extensive experimental characterization of GenMax against other maximal pattern mining methods like MaxMiner (Bayardo, 1998) and Mafia (Burdick, 2001). We compare Charm against previous methods for mining closed sets such as Close (Pasquier et al., 1999), Closet (Pei et al., 2000), Mafia (Burdick, 2001), and Pascal (Bastide et al., 2000). We found that the methods have varying performance depending on the database characteristics (mainly the distribution of the closed or maximal frequent patterns by length). We present a systematic and realistic set of experiments showing under which conditions a method is likely to perform well and under what conditions it does not perform well. Overall, both Charm and GenMax deliver excellent performance and outperform extant approaches for closed and maximal set mining. However, there are a few exceptions to this, which we highlight in our experiments.

23.2. PRELIMINARIES

The problem of mining closed and maximal frequent patterns can be formally stated as follows: Let $\mathcal{I} = \{i_1, i_2, \ldots, i_m\}$ be a set of m distinct items. Let $\mathcal{D}$ denote a database of transactions, where each transaction has a unique identifier (*tid*) and contains a set of items. The set of all tids is denoted $\mathcal{T} = \{t_1, t_2, \ldots, t_n\}$. A set $X \subseteq \mathcal{I}$ is also called an *itemset*. An itemset with k items is called a *k-itemset*. The set $t(X) \subseteq \mathcal{T}$, consisting of all the transaction tids that contain X as a subset, is called the *tidset* of X. For convenience we write an itemset $\{A, C, W\}$ as ACW and write its tidset $\{1, 3, 4, 5\}$ as $t(X) = 1345$. For a tidset Y, we denote its corresponding itemset as $i(Y)$—that is, the set of items common to all the tids in Y. The composition of the two functions—namely, t that maps from itemsets to tidsets, and i that maps from tidsets to itemsets—is called a *closure operator*, and is given as $c(X) = i(t(X))$. For instance, $c(AW) = i(t(AW)) = i(1345) = ACW$.

The *support* of an itemset X, denoted $\sigma(X)$, is the number of transactions in which that itemset occurs as a subset. Thus $\sigma(X) = |t(X)|$. An itemset is *frequent* if its support is more than or equal to some threshold *minimum support* (*min_sup*) value—that is, if $\sigma(X) \geq min\_sup$. We denote by F_k the set of frequent k-itemsets and denote by **FI** the set of all frequent itemsets. A frequent itemset is called *maximal* if it is not a subset of any other frequent itemset. The set of all maximal frequent itemsets is denoted as **MFI**. A set is *closed* if it has no superset with the same frequency. The set of all closed frequent itemsets is denoted as **CFI**. It can be shown that an itemset X is closed if and only if $c(X) = X$ (Zaki, 2001a). Given a user-specified *min_sup* value, our goal is to efficiently enumerate all patterns in **CFI** and **MFI**.

Example 23.1. Consider our example database in Figure 23.1. There are five different items $\mathcal{I} = \{A, C, D, T, W\}$ and six transactions $\mathcal{T} = \{1, 2, 3, 4, 5, 6\}$. The table on the right shows all 19 frequent itemsets for *min_sup* = 3. The lattice for **FI** is shown in Figure 23.2; under each itemset X, we show its tidset $t(X)$. The figure also shows the seven closed sets obtained by collapsing all the itemsets that have the same tidset (closed regions of the lattice) and the two maximal sets (circles). It is clear that **MFI** $\subseteq$ **CFI** $\subseteq$ **FI**. ∎

DISTINCT DATABASE ITEMS

Jane Austen	Agatha Christie	Sir Arthur Conan Doyle	Mark Twain	P. G. Wodehouse
A	C	D	T	W

DATABASE

Transcation	Items
1	A C T W
2	C D W
3	A C T W
4	A C D W
5	A C D T W
6	C D T

ALL FREQUENT ITEMSETS

MINIMUM SUPPORT = 50%

Support	Itemsets
100% (6)	C
83% (5)	W, CW
67% (4)	A, D, T, AC, AW CD, CT, ACW
50% (3)	AT, DW, TW, ACT, ATW CDW, CTW, ACTW

Figure 23.1. Example DB.

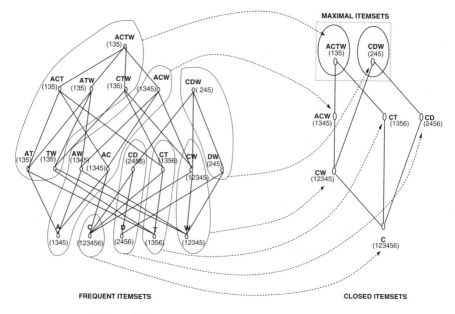

Figure 23.2. Frequent, closed, and maximal itemsets.

23.2.1. Backtracking Search

GenMax uses backtracking search to enumerate the **MFI**. We first describe the backtracking paradigm in the context of enumerating all frequent patterns. We will subsequently modify this procedure to enumerate the **MFI**.

Backtracking algorithms are useful for many combinatorial problems where the solution can be represented as a set $I = \{i_0, i_1, \dots\}$, where each i_j is chosen from a finite *possible set*, P_j. Initially I is empty; it is extended one item at a time, as the search space is traversed. The length of I is the same as the depth of the corresponding node in the search tree. Given a partial solution of length l, $I_l = \{i_0, i_1, \dots, i_{l-1}\}$, the possible values for the next item i_l comes from a subset $C_l \subseteq P_l$ called the *combine set*. If $y \in P_l - C_l$, then nodes in the subtree with root node $I_l = \{i_0, i_1, \dots, i_{l-1}, y\}$ will not be considered by the backtracking algorithm. Since such subtrees have been pruned away from the original search space, the determination of C_l is also called *pruning*.

Consider the backtracking algorithm for mining all frequent patterns, shown in Figure 23.3. The main loop tries extending I_l with every item x in the current combine set C_l. The first step is to compute I_{l+1}, which is simply I_l extended with x. The second step is to extract the new possible set of extensions, P_{l+1}, which consists only of items y in C_l that follow x. The third step is to create a new combine set for the next pass, consisting of valid extensions. An extension is valid if the resulting itemset is frequent. The combine set, C_{l+1}, thus consists of those items in the possible set that produce a frequent itemset when used to extend I_{l+1}. Any item not in the combine set refers to a pruned subtree. The final

// Invoke as FI-backtrack($\emptyset$, F_1, 0)
FI-backtrack(I_l, C_l, l)
1.   **for each** $x \in C_l$
2. $I_{l+1} = I \cup \{x\}$ //also add I_{l+1} to **FI**
3. $P_{l+1} = \{y : y \in C_l \text{ and } y > x\}$
4. C_{l+1} = FI-combine (I_{l+1}, P_{l+1})
5.   FI-backtrack(I_{l+1}, C_{l+1}, $l + 1$)

// Can I_{l+1} combine with other items in P_{l+1}?
FI-combine(I_{l+1}, P_{l+1})
1. $C_{l+1} = \emptyset$
2.   **for each** $y \in P_{l+1}$
3.   **if** $I_{l+1} \cup \{y\}$ is frequent
4. $C_{l+1} = C_{l+1} \cup \{y\}$
5.   **return** C_{l+1} //sort by support

Figure 23.3. Backtrack algorithm for mining **FI**.

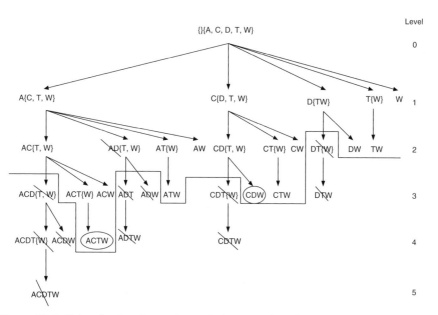

Figure 23.4. Subset/backtrack search tree (*min_sup* = 3): Circles indicate maximal sets, and the infrequent sets have been crossed out. Due to the downward closure property of support (i.e., all subsets of a frequent itemset must be frequent), the frequent itemsets form a *border* (shown with the bold line), such that all frequent itemsets lie above the border, while all infrequent itemsets lie below it. Since **MFI** determine the border, it is straightforward to obtain **FI** in a single database scan if **MFI** is known.

step is to recursively call the backtrack routine for each extension. As presented, the backtrack method performs a depth-first traversal of the search space.

Example 23.2. Consider the full subset search space shown in Figure 23.4. The backtrack search space can be considerably smaller than the full space. For example, we start with $I_0 = \emptyset$ and $C_0 = F_1 = \{A, C, D, T, W\}$. At level 1, each item in C_0 is added to I_0 in turn. For example, A is added to obtain $I_1 = \{A\}$. The possible set for A, $P_1 = \{C, D, T, W\}$ consists of all items that follow A in C_0. However, from Figure 23.1, we find that only AC, AT, and AW are frequent (at $min\_sup = 3$), giving $C_1 = \{C, T, W\}$. Thus the subtree corresponding to the node AD has been pruned. ∎

23.3. EXISTING APPROACHES FOR CLOSED AND MAXIMAL ITEMSET MINING

23.3.1. Maximal Itemset Mining

A good coverage of mining long patterns appears in Aggarwal (2001). Methods for finding the maximal elements include All-MFS (Gunopulos et al., 1997), which works by iteratively attempting to extend a working pattern until failure. A randomized version of the algorithm that uses vertical bit vectors was studied, but it does not guarantee that every maximal pattern will be returned.

The Pincer-Search (Lin and Kedem, 1998) algorithm uses horizontal data format. It not only constructs the candidates in a bottom-up manner like Apriori, but also starts a top-down search at the same time, maintaining a candidate set of maximal patterns. This can help in reducing the number of database scans by eliminating nonmaximal sets early. The maximal candidate set is a superset of the maximal patterns; in general, the overhead of maintaining it can be very high. In contrast, GenMax maintains only the current known maximal patterns for pruning.

MaxMiner (Bayardo, 1998) is another algorithm for finding the maximal elements. It uses efficient pruning techniques to quickly narrow the search. MaxMiner employs a breadth-first traversal of the search space; it reduces database scanning by employing a lookahead pruning strategy; that is, if a node with all its extensions can determined to be frequent, there is no need to further process that node. It also employs item (re)ordering heuristic to increase the effectiveness of superset-frequency pruning. Since MaxMiner uses the original horizontal database format, it can perform the same number of passes over a database as Apriori does.

DepthProject (Agrawal et al., 2000) finds long itemsets using a depth first search of a lexicographic tree of itemsets, and it uses a counting method based on transaction projections along its branches. This projection is equivalent to a horizontal version of the tidsets at a given node in the search tree. DepthProject also uses the look-ahead pruning method with item reordering. It returns a superset of the **MFI** and would require post-pruning to eliminate nonmaximal patterns. FPgrowth (Han et al., 2000) uses the novel frequent pattern tree (FP-tree) structure, which is a compressed representation of all the transactions in the database. It uses a recursive divide-and-conquer and database projection approach to mine long patterns. Nevertheless, since it enumerates all frequent patterns, it is impractical when pattern length is long.

Mafia (Burdick et al., 2001) is the most recent method for mining the **MFI**. Mafia uses three pruning strategies to remove nonmaximal sets. The first is the look-ahead pruning first used in MaxMiner. The second is to check if a new set is subsumed by an existing maximal set. The last technique checks if $t(X) \subseteq t(Y)$. If so, X is considered together with Y for extension. Mafia uses a vertical bit-vector data format, along with compression and projection of bitmaps to improve performance. Mafia mines a superset of the **MFI**, and it requires a post-pruning step to eliminate nonmaximal patterns. In contrast, GenMax integrates pruning with mining and returns the exact **MFI**.

Among the most recent methods for **MFI** are SmartMiner (Zou et al., 2002) and FPMax (Grahne and Zhu, 2003). SmartMiner doesn't do explicit maximality checking; rather it uses the information available from the previous combine sets to construct the new combine set at the current node. It performs depth-first search and uses bit-vector data representation. FPMax mines maximal patterns from the FP-tree data structure (an augmented prefix tree) originally proposed in Han et al., (2000). It also maintains the **MFI** in another prefix tree data structure for maximality checking.

23.3.2. Closed Itemset Mining

There have been several recent algorithms proposed for mining **CFI**. Close (Pasquier et al., 1999) is an Apriori-like algorithm that directly mines frequent closed itemsets. There are two main steps in Close. The first is to use a bottom-up search to identify *generators*, the smallest frequent itemset that determines a closed itemset. For example, consider the frequent itemset lattice in Figure 23.2. The item A is a generator for the closed set ACW, since it is the smallest itemset with the same tidset as ACW. All generators are found using a simple modification of Apriori. After finding the frequent sets at level k, Close compares the support of each set with its subsets at the previous level. If the support of an itemset matches the support of any of its subsets, the itemset cannot be a generator and is thus pruned. The second step in Close is to compute the closed sets for all the generators found in the first step, which is done via intersection of all transactions where it occurs as a subset. This can be done in one pass over the database, provided that all generators fit in memory. Nevertheless, computing closures this way is an expensive operation.

The authors of Close recently developed Pascal (Bastide et al., 2000), an improved algorithm for mining closed and frequent sets. They introduce the notion of *key patterns* and show that other frequent patterns can be inferred from the key patterns without access to the database. They showed that Pascal, even though it finds both frequent and closed sets, is typically twice as fast as

Close and 10 times as fast as Apriori. Since Pascal enumerates all patterns, it is only practical when pattern length is short (as we shall see in the experimental section). The *Closure* algorithm (Cristofor et al., 2000) is also based on a bottom-up search; it performs only marginally better than Apriori. Charm uses a more efficient depth-first search over itemset and tidsets spaces.

Closet (Pei et al., 2000) uses a novel frequent pattern tree (FP-tree) structure, which is a compressed representation of all the transactions in the database. It uses a recursive divide-and-conquer and database projection approach to mine long patterns. Mafia (Burdick et al., 2001) is primarily intended for maximal pattern mining, but has an option to mine the closed sets as well. Mafia relies on efficient compressed and projected vertical bitmap-based frequency computation. In contrast to Closet and Mafia, Charm uses diffsets for fast support computation.

Recently, two new algorithms for finding frequent closed itemsets have been proposed, Closet+ (Wang et al., 2003) and Carpenter (Pan et al., 2003). Closet+ combines several previously proposed as well as new effective strategies into one algorithm. Carpenter mines closed patterns in datasets that have significantly more items than there are transactions, such as datasets that arise in biology—for example, microarray datasets. In these datasets, there can easily be 10,000 or more items, but only 100–1000 transactions. All of the above algorithms for **CFI** cannot deal with such a large itemsets space (e.g., 2^{10000}). Capitalizing on the fact that the tidset search space is much smaller (e.g., 2^{100}), Carpenter enumerates closed tidsets and determines the corresponding closed itemsets from them.

23.4. EFFICIENT CFI AND MFI MINING: CHARM AND GENMAX

There are two main ingredients to develop an efficient **CFI** and **MFI** algorithm. The first is the set of techniques used to remove entire branches of the search space, and the second is the representation used to perform fast frequency computations. We will describe below how Charm and GenMax extend the basic backtracking routine for **FI**, and we will also describe the progressive focusing, hash-based subsumption checking and diffset propagation techniques they use for fast maximality, closedness, and frequency checking. More details on Charm and GenMax and on diffsets can be found in Gouda and Zaki (2001), Zaki and Hsiao (2002), and Zaki and Gouda (2003).

23.4.1. Fast Frequency Testing

Typically, pattern mining algorithms use a *horizontal* database format, such as the one shown in Figure 23.1, where each row is a tid followed by its itemset. Consider a *vertical* database format, where for each item we list its tidset, the set of all transaction tids where it occurs. The vertical representation has the following major advantages over the horizontal layout: First, computing the support of itemsets is simpler and faster with the vertical layout since it involves only the intersections of tidsets (Zaki, 2000b) [or compressed bit vectors if the vertical format is stored as bitmaps (Burdick et al., 2001)]. Second, with the vertical layout, there is an automatic "reduction" of the database before each scan in that only those itemsets that are relevant to the following scan of the mining process are accessed from disk. Third, the vertical format is more versatile in supporting various search strategies, including breadth-first, depth-first, or some other hybrid search.

Let's consider how the FI-combine (see Figure 23.3) routine works, where the frequency of an extension is tested. Each item x in C_l actually represents the itemset $I_l \cup \{x\}$ and stores the associated tidset for the itemset $I_l \cup \{x\}$. For the initial invocation, since I_l is empty, the tidset for each item x in C_l is identical to the tidset, $t(x)$, of item x. Before line 3 is called in FI-combine, we intersect the tidset of the element I_{l+1} (i.e., $t(I_l \cup \{x\})$) with the tidset of element y (i.e., $t(I_l \cup \{y\})$). If the cardinality of the resulting intersection is above minimum support, the extension with y is frequent, and y', the new intersection result, is added to the combine set C_{l+1} for the next level. C_{l+1} is kept in increasing order of support of its elements. Figure 23.5 shows the pseudo-code for FI-tidset-combine using this tidset intersection-based support counting.

Example 23.3. Suppose that we have the itemset ACT; we show how to get its support using the tidset intersections. We start with item A, and we extend it with item C. We find the support of AC as follows: $t(AC) = t(A) \cap t(C) = \{1, 3, 4, 5\} \cap \{1, 2, 3, 4, 5\} = \{1, 3, 4, 5\}$, and the support of AC is then $|t(AC)| = 4$ At the next level, we need to compute the tidset for ACT using the tidsets for AC and AT, where $I_l = \{A\}$ and $C_l = \{C, T\}$. We have $t(ACT) = t(AC) \cap t(AT) = \{1, 3, 4, 5\} - \{1, 3, 5\} = \{1, 3, 5\}$, and its support is $|t(ACT)| = 3$. ■

Diffsets Propagation. Despite the many advantages of the vertical format, when the tidset cardinality gets very large (e.g., for very frequent items) the intersection time starts to become inordinately large. Furthermore, the size of intermediate tidsets generated for frequent patterns can also become very large to fit into main

```
// Can I_{l+1} combine with other items in P_{l+1}?
FI-tidset-combine(I_{l+1}, P_{l+1})
1.      C_{l+1} = Ø
2.      for each y ∈ P_{l+1}
3.*         y' = y
4.*         t(y') = t(I_{l+1}) ∩ t(y)
5.*         if |t(y')| ≥ min_sup
6.             C_{l+1} = C_{l+1} ∪ {y'}
7.      Sort C_{l+1} by increasing support
8.      return C_{l+1}
```

Figure 23.5. FI-combine using tidset intersections (* indicates a new line not in FI-combine).

memory. Both Charm and GenMax use a new format called diffsets (Zaki and Gouda, 2003) for fast frequency testing.

The main idea of diffsets is to avoid storing the entire tidset of each element in the combine set. Instead we keep track of only the differences between the tidset of itemset I_l and the tidset of an element x in the combine set (which actually denotes $I_l \cup \{x\}$). These differences in tids are stored in what we call the *diffset*, which is a difference of two tidsets at the root level or a difference of two diffsets at later levels. Furthermore, these differences are propagated all the way from a node to its children, starting from the root. In an extensive study (Zaki and Gouda, 2003), we showed that diffsets are very short compared to their tidsets counterparts, and they are highly effective in improving the running time of vertical methods.

We describe next how diffsets are used, with the help of an example. At level 0, we have available the tidsets for each item in F_1. To find the combine set at this level, we compute the diffset of y', denoted as $d(y')$ instead of computing the tidset of y as shown in line 4 in Figure 23.5. That is $d(y') = t(x) - t(y)$. The support of y' is now given as $\sigma(y') = \sigma(x) - |d(y')|$. At subsequent levels, we have available the diffsets for each element in the combine list. In this case $d(y') = d(y) - d(x)$, but the support is still given as $\sigma(y') = \sigma(x) - |d(y')|$ [9]. Figure 23.6 shows the pseudo-code for computing the combine sets using diffsets.

Example 23.4. Suppose, that we have the itemset ACT; we show how to get its support using the diffset propagation technique. We start with item A, and extend it with item C. Now in order to find the support of AC we first find the diffset for AC, denoted $d(AC) = t(A) - t(C) = \{1, 3, 4, 5\} - \{1, 2, 3, 4, 5\}$, and then calculate its support as $\sigma(AC) = \sigma(A) - |d(AC)| = 4 - 0 = 4$. At the next level, we need to compute the diffset for ACT using the diffsets for AC and AT, where $I_l = \{A\}$ and $C_l = \{C, T\}$. The diffset of itemset ACT is given as $d(ACT) = d(AT) - d(AC) = \{4\} - \{\} = \{4\}$, and its support is given as $\sigma(AC) - |d(ACT)| = 4 - 1 = 3$. ∎

```
// Can I_{l+1} combine with other items in C_l?
FI-diffset-combine(I_{l+1}, P_{l+1})
  1.    C_{l+1} = ∅
  2.    for each y ∈ P_{l+1}
  3.        y' = y
  4.*       if level == 0 then  d(y') = t(I_{l+1}) - t(y)
  5.*       else d(y') = d(y) - d(I_{l+1})
  6.        if σ(y') ≥ min_sup
  7.            C_{l+1} = C_{l+1} ∪ {y'}
  8.    Sort C_{l+1} by increasing support
  9.    return C_{l+1}
```

Figure 23.6. FI-combine using diffsets (* indicates a new line not in FI-tidset-combine).

23.4.2. Dynamically Reordering the Combine Set

Two general principles for efficient searching using backtracking are as follows: (1) It is more efficient to make the next choice of a subtree (branch) to explore to be the one whose combine set has the fewest items. This usually results in good performance, since it minimizes the number of frequency computations in FI-combine. (2) If we are able to remove a node as early as possible from the backtracking search tree, we effectively prune many branches from consideration.

Reordering the elements in the current combine set to achieve the two goals is a very effective means of cutting down the search space. The first heuristic is to reorder the combine set in increasing order of support. This is likely to produce small combine sets in the next level, since the items with lower frequency are less likely to produce frequent itemsets at the next level. This heuristic was first used in MaxMiner, and it has been used in other methods since then (Agrawal et al., 2000; Burdick et al., 2001; Zaki and Hsiao, 2002). At each level of backtracking search, both Charm and GenMax reorder the combine set in increasing order of support (this is indicated in Figures 23.3, 23.5, and 23.6).

23.4.3. Charm for CFI Mining

The **FI-backtrack** procedure can easily be extended to generate only closed sets, as shown in Figure 23.7. Let X_i and X_j be two itemsets; we say that an itemset X_i *subsumes* another itemset X_j, if and only if $X_j \subset X_i$ and $\sigma(X_j) = \sigma(X_i)$. Before adding any frequent itemset X to **CFI**, we need to make sure that it is not *subsumed* (lines 6,7); that is, there is no superset of X in **CFI** which has the same support, since in that case X cannot be closed. There is no change in the rest of the enumeration algorithm; however, this algorithm is inefficient, since it does subsumption checking for each new itemset generated. There are two ways to optimize this: (1) Reduce the number of itemsets for which subsumption check is done; that is, further prune the backtrack search space; (2) perform fast subsumption checking.

Pruning Search Space.   To prune the search space, we can utilize certain properties of itemset-diffset pairs as described in Zaki and Hsiao (2002).

> // Invocation: CFI-backtrack($\emptyset, F_1, 0$)
> **CFI-backtrack(I_l, C_l, l)**
>   1.   **for each** $x \in C_l$
>   2. $I_{l+1} = I \cup \{x\}$ //also add I_{l+1} to **FI**
>   3. $P_{l+1} = \{y : y \in C_l \text{ and } y > x\}$
>   4. C_{l+1} = FI-diffset-combine (I_{l+1}, P_{l+1}, C_l)
>   5.   CFI-backtrack($I_{l+1}, C_{l+1}, l + 1$)
>   6.*   **if** I_{l+1} has no superset in **CFI** with same support
>   7.*   **CFI= CFI** $\cup I_{l+1}$

Figure 23.7. Backtrack algorithm for mining **CFI** (* indicates a new line not in FI-backtrack).

Theorem 23.1. (Zaki and Hsiao, 2002.) Let $X_i = I_{l+1} \cup \{y_i\}$ and $X_j = I_{l+1} \cup \{y_j\}$ be two members of the possible set at level l, and let $X_i \times d(X_i)$ and $X_j \times d(X_j)$ be the corresponding itemset-diffset pairs. The following four properties hold:

1. If $d(X_i) = d(X_j)$, then $c(X_i) = c(X_j) = c(X_i \cup X_j)$
2. If $d(X_i) \supset d(X_j)$, then $c(X_i) \neq c(X_j)$, but $c(X_i) = c(X_i \cup X_j)$
3. If $d(X_i) \subset d(X_j)$, then $c(X_i) \neq c(X_j)$, but $c(X_j) = c(X_i \cup X_j)$
4. If $d(X_i) \neq d(X_j)$, then $c(X_i) \neq c(X_j) \neq c(X_i \cup X_j)$

Charm uses these four properties to prune the elements of the combine set, as shown in Figure 23.8. **CFI-diffset-combine** is the same as **FI-diffset-combine** (in Figure 23.6), except for lines 7–16 that are used to check the four properties outlined in Theorem 23.1. According to Property 1, if the diffsets of y and I_{l+1} are identical, this means $c(I_{l+1}) = c(I_{l+1} \cup \{y\})$. In this case we prune the y branch of the backtrack tree from further consideration (line 9) and replace I_{l+1} with $I_{l+1} \cup \{y\}$ (line 8). By Property 2, if $d(y) \supset d(I_{l+1})$, then wherever I_{l+1} occurs, y always co-occurs; that is, $c(I_{l+1}) = c(I_{l+1} \cup \{y\})$. We replace I_{l+1} with $I_{l+1} \cup \{y\}$ (line 11). By Property 3, if $d(y) \subset d(I_{l+1})$, then wherever y occurs, I_{l+1} always co-occurs; that is, $c(y) = c(I_{l+1} \cup \{y\})$. We therefore remove the entire tree under y in C_l (line 14), but we add y to C_{l+1}. Finally, if the diffsets of y and I_{l+1} are not equal, then no pruning is possible; we add y to C_{l+1}.

```
//Return Cₗ₊₁; can modify Cₗ also  CFI-diffset-combine(Iₗ₊₁, Pₗ₊₁, Cₗ)
1.      C_{l+1} = ∅
2.      for each y ∈ P_{l+1}
3.          y' = y
4.          if level == 0 then  d(y') = t(I_{l+1}) − t(y)
5.          else d(y') = d(y) − d(I_{l+1})
6.              if σ(y') ≥ min_sup
7.*                 if d(I_{l+1}) = d(y) //or t(I_{l+1}) = t(y)
8.*                     I_{l+1} = I_{l+1} ∪ {y}
9.*                     C_l = C_l − {y}
10.*                else if d(I_{l+1}) ⊃ d(y) //or t(I_{l+1}) ⊂ t(y)
11.*                    I_{l+1} = I_{l+1} ∪ {y}
12.*                else if d(I_{l+1}) ⊂ d(y) //or t(I_{l+1}) ⊃ t(y)
13.*                    C_l = C_l − {y}
14.*                    C_{l+1} = C_{l+1} ∪ {y'}
15.*                else if d(I_{l+1}) ≠ d(y) //or t(I_{l+1}) ≠ t(y)
16.*                    C_{l+1} = C_{l+1} ∪ {y'}
17.     Sort C_{l+1} by increasing support
18.     return C_{l+1}
```

Figure 23.8. CFI-diffset-combine (* indicates new line not in FI-diffset-combine).

Example 23.5. We explain the working of Charm using the example database in Figure 23.1. At the first level we have $C_0 = \{A, C, D, T, W\}$, and thus within the for loop in **CFI-backtrack** (Figure 23.7) we have $I_1 = A$ and $P_1 = \{C, D, T, W\}$. We next determine C_{l+1} using **CFI-diffset-combine**. We find that $t(A) \subset t(C)$ (Property 2); that is, whenever A occurs C co-occurs, thus we replace A with $I_1 = AC$. Considering the next element $y = D$, we find that $y' = AD$ is not frequent. The next item $y = T$ yields a frequent itemset $y' = AT$, but $t(A) \neq t(T)$; thus we set $C_1 = \{T\}$. Finally for $y = W$ we again find $t(A) \subset t(W)$; thus we set $I_1 = ACW$ and return $C_1 = \{T\}$. In the next recursion, $ACWT$ will be found to be closed.

Next consider the second iteration of the for loop in **CFI-backtrack**. We have $I_1 = C$ and $P_1 = \{D, T, W\}$. In **CFI-diffset-combine**, we find that for all three items, Property 3 is true; that is, whenever D, T, W occur, C always co-occurs; thus we prune them from the backtrack tree, and we get $C_0 = \{A, C\}$, but $C_1 = \{D, T, W\}$, which will be recursively processed. ∎

Fast Subsumption Checking.   In the **CFI-backtrack** method (Figure 23.7), it may happen that after adding a closed set C to **CFI**, when we explore subsequent branches of the backtrack tree, we may generate another set X, which cannot be extended further, with $X \subseteq C$ and with $\sigma(C) = \sigma(X)$. In this case, X is a nonclosed set subsumed by C, and it should not be added to **CFI**. Since **CFI** dynamically expands during enumeration of closed patterns, we need a very fast approach to perform such subsumption checks.

Clearly we want to avoid comparing X with all existing elements in **CFI**, because this would lead to a $O(|\mathbf{CFI}|^2)$ complexity. To quickly retrieve relevant closed sets, the obvious solution is to store **CFI** in a hash table. But what hash function to use? Since we want to perform subset checking, we can't hash on the itemset. We could use the support of the itemsets for the hash function. But many unrelated itemsets may have the same support. Since Charm uses diffsets/tidsets, it seems reasonable to use the information from the tidsets to help identify if X is subsumed. Note that if $t(X_j) = t(X_i)$, then obviously $\sigma(X_j) = \sigma(X_i)$. Thus to check if X is subsumed, we can check if $t(X) = t(C)$ for some $C \in \mathbf{CFI}$. This check can be performed in $O(1)$ time using a hash table. But obviously we cannot afford to store the actual tidset with each closed set in **CFI**; the space requirements would be prohibitive.

Charm adopts a compromise solution. It computes a hash function on the tidset and stores in the hash table a closed set along with its support. Let $h(X_i)$ denote a suitable chosen hash function on the tidset $t(X_i)$. Before adding X to **CFI**, we retrieve from the hash table all entries with the hash key $h(X)$. For each retrieved closed set C, we then check if $\sigma(X) = \sigma(C)$. If yes, we next check if $X \subset C$. If yes, then X is subsumed and we do not add it to **CFI**.

What is a good hash function on a tidset? Charm uses the sum of the tids in the tidset as the hash function; that is, $h(X) = \sum_{T \in t(X)} T$ (note that this is not the same as support, which is the cardinality of $t(X)$). We tried several other variations and found there to be no performance difference. This hash function is likely to be as good as any other due to several reasons. First, by definition a closed set is one that does not have a superset with the same support; it follows that it must have some tids that do not appear in any other closed set. Thus the hash keys of different closed sets will tend to be different. Second, even if there are several closed sets with the same hash key, the support check we perform (i.e., if $\sigma(X) = \sigma(C)$) will eliminate many closed sets whose keys are the same, but they in fact have different supports. Third, this hash function is easy to compute, and it can easily be used with the diffset format.

23.4.4. GenMax for MFI Mining

The basic **MFI** enumeration code used in GenMax is a straightforward extension of **FI-backtrack**. The main addition is the superset checking to eliminate nonmaximal itemsets, as shown in Figure 23.9. In addition to the main steps in **FI** enumeration, the new code adds a step (line 4) after the construction of the possible set to check if $I_{l+1} \cup P_{l+1}$ is subsumed by an existing maximal set. If so, the current and all subsequent items in C_l can be pruned away. After creating the new combine set, if it is empty and I_{l+1} is not a subset of any maximal pattern, it is added to the **MFI**. If the combine set is non-empty, a recursive call is made to check further extensions. Like Charm, GenMax makes use of properties of itemset-diffset pairs outlined in Theorem 23.1; thus it uses the **CFI-diffset-combine** routine (line 6).

Superset Checking Techniques.   Checking to see if the given itemset I_{l+1} combined with the possible set P_{l+1} is subsumed by another maximal set was also proposed in Mafia (Burdick et al., 2001) under the name HUTMFI. Further pruning is possible if one can determine based just on support of the combine sets if $I_{l+1} \cup P_{l+1}$ will be guaranteed to be frequent. In this case also, one can avoid processing any more branches. This method was first introduced in MaxMiner (Bayardo, 1998), and it was also used in Mafia under the name FHUT.

```
// Invocation: MFI-backtrack(Ø, F₁, 0)
MFI-backtrack(Iₗ, Cₗ, l)
  1.     for each x ∈ Cₗ
  2.         Iₗ₊₁ = I ∪ {x}
  3.         Pₗ₊₁ = {y : y ∈ Cₗ and y > x}
  4.*        if Iₗ₊₁ ∪ Pₗ₊₁ has a superset in MFI
  5.*            return //all subsequent branches pruned!
  6.*            Cₗ₊₁ = CFI-diffset-combine (Iₗ₊₁, Pₗ₊₁, Cₗ)
  7.*        if Cₗ₊₁ is empty
  8.*            if Iₗ₊₁ has no superset in MFI
  9.*                MFI= MFI ∪ Iₗ₊₁
 10.        else MFI-backtrack(Iₗ₊₁, Cₗ₊₁, l + 1)
```

Figure 23.9. Backtrack algorithm for mining **MFI** (* indicates a new line not in FI-backtrack).

In addition to sorting the initial combine set at level 0 in increasing order of support, GenMax uses another reordering heuristic based on a simple lemma:

Lemma 23.1. (Gouda and Zaki, 2001). Let $IF(x) = \{y : y \in F_1, xy$ is not frequent $\}$ denote the set of infrequent 2-itemsets that contain an item $x \in F_1$, and let $M(x)$ be the longest maximal pattern containing x. Then $|M(x)| \leq |F_1| - |IF(x)|$.

Assuming that F_2 has been computed, reordering C_0 in decreasing order of $IF(x)$ (with $x \in C_0$) ensures that the smallest combine sets will be processed at the initial levels of the tree, which result in smaller backtracking search trees. GenMax thus initially sorts the items in decreasing order of $IF(x)$ and in increasing order of support. Then at each subsequent level, GenMax keeps the combine set in increasing order of support as shown in Figure 23.6.

Example 23.6. For our database in Figure 23.1 with $min\_sup = 2$, $IF(x)$ is the same of all items $x \in F_1$, and the sorted order (on support) is A, D, T, W, C. Figure 23.10 shows the backtracking search trees for maximal itemsets containing prefi x items A and D. Under the search tree for A, Figure 23.10a, we try to extend the partial solution AD by adding to it item T from its combine set. We try another item W after itemset ADT turns out to be infrequent, and so on. Since GenMax uses itemsets that are found earlier in the search to prune the combine sets of later branches, after finding the maximal set $ADWC$, GenMax skips ADC. After finding $ATWC$, all the remaining nodes with prefix A are pruned, and so on. The pruned branches are shown with dashed arrows, indicating that a large part of the search tree is pruned away. ∎

Superset Checking Optimization. The main efficiency of GenMax stems from the fact that it eliminates branches that are subsumed by an already mined

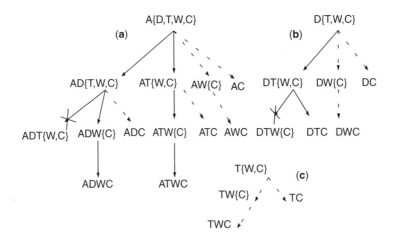

Figure 23.10. Backtracking trees of Example 2.

maximal pattern. Were it not for this pruning, GenMax would essentially default to a depth-first exploration of the search tree. Before creating the combine set for the next pass, in line 4 in Figure 23.9, GenMax check if $I_{l+1} \cup P_{l+1}$ is contained within a previously found maximal set. If yes, then the entire subtree rooted at I_{l+1} and including the elements of the possible set are pruned. If no, then a new extension is required. Another superset check is required at line 8, when I_{l+1} has no frequent extension—that is, when the combine set C_{l+1} is empty. Even though I_{l+1} is a leaf node with no extensions, it may be subsumed by some maximal set, and this case is not caught by the check in line 4 above.

The major challenge in the design of GenMax is how to perform this subset checking in the current set of maximal patterns in an efficient manner. If we were to naively implement and perform this search two times on an ever-expanding set of maximal patterns **MFI**, and during each recursive call of backtracking, we would be spending a prohibitive amount of time just performing subset checks. Each search would take $O(|\mathbf{MFI}|)$ time in the worst case, where **MFI** is the current, growing set of maximal patterns. Note that some of the best algorithms for dynamic subset testing run in amortized time $O(\sqrt{s} \log s)$ per operation in a sequence of s operations (Yellin, 1994) (for us $s = O(\mathbf{MFI})$). In dense domain we have thousands to millions of maximal frequent itemsets, and the number of subset checking operations performed would be at least that much. Can we do better?

The answer is, yes! First, we observe that the two subset checks (one on line 4 and the other on line 8) can be easily reduced to only one check. Since $I_{l+1} \cup P_{l+1}$ is a superset of I_{l+1}, in our implementation we do superset check only for $I_{l+1} \cup P_{l+1}$. While testing this set, we store the maximum position, say p, at which an item in $I_{l+1} \cup P_{l+1}$ is not found in a maximal set $M \in \mathbf{MFI}$. In other words, all items before p are subsumed by some maximal set. For the superset test for I_{l+1}, we check if $|I_{l+1}| < p$. If yes, I_{l+1} is nonmaximal. If no, we add it to **MFI**.

The second observation is that performing superset checking during each recursive call can be redundant. For example, suppose that the cardinality of the possible set P_{l+1} is m. Then potentially, MFI-backtrack makes m redundant subset checks, if the current **MFI** has not changed during these m consecutive calls. To avoid such redundancy, a simple check_status flag is used. If the flag is false, no superset check is performed. Before each recursive call, the flag is false; it becomes true whenever C_{l+1} is empty, which indicates that we have reached a leaf and have to backtrack.

The $O(\sqrt{s} \log s)$ time bounds reported in Yellin (1994) for dynamic subset testing do not assume anything about the sequence of operations performed. In contrast, we have full knowledge of how GenMax generates maximal sets; we use this observation to substantially speed up the subset checking process. The main idea is to progressively narrow down the maximal itemsets of interest as recursive calls are made. In other words, we construct for each invocation of MFI-backtrack a list of *local maximal frequent itemsets, $LMFI_l$*. This list contains the maximal sets that can potentially be supersets of candidates that

// Invocation: LMFI-backtrack($\emptyset$, F_1, $\emptyset$, 0)
// $LMFI_l$ is an output parameter
LMFI-backtrack(I_l, C_l, $LMFI_l$, l)
1.   **for each** $x \in C_l$
2. $I_{l+1} = I \cup \{x\}$
3. $P_{l+1} = \{y : y \in C_l \text{ and } y > x\}$
4.   **if** $I_{l+1} \cup P_{l+1}$ has a superset in $LMFI_l$
5.   **return** //subsequent branches pruned!
6. * $LMFI_{l+1} = \emptyset$
7. C_{l+1} = CFI-diffset-combine (I_{l+1}, P_{l+1}, C_l)
8.   **if** C_{l+1} is empty
9.   **if** I_{l+1} has no superset in $LMFI_l$
10. $LMFI_l = LMFI_l \cup I_{l+1}$
11.*   **else** $LMFI_{l+1} = \{M \in LMFI_l : x \in M\}$
12.   LMFI-backtrack(I_{l+1}, C_{l+1}, $LMFI_{l+1}$, $l+1$)
13.* $LMFI_l = LMFI_l \cup LMFI_{l+1}$

Figure 23.11. Mining **MFI** with progressive focusing (* indicates a new line not in MFI-backtrack).

are to be generated from the itemset I_l. The only such maximal sets are those that contain all items in I_l. This way, instead of checking if $I_{l+1} \cup P_{l+1}$ is contained in the full current **MFI**, we check only in $LMFI_l$—the local set of relevant maximal itemsets. This technique, which we call *progressive focusing*, is extremely powerful in narrowing the search to only the most relevant maximal itemsets, making superset checking practical on dense datasets.

Figure 23.11 shows the pseudo-code for GenMax that incorporates this optimization (the code for the first two optimizations is not shown to avoid clutter). Before each invocation of LMFI-backtrack, a new $LMFI_{l+1}$ is created, consisting of those maximal sets in the current $LMFI_l$ that contain the item x (see line 10). Any new maximal itemsets from a recursive call are incorporated in the current $LMFI_l$ at line 12.

23.5. EXPERIMENTAL RESULTS

Past work has demonstrated that for **MFI** mining, DepthProject (Agrawal et al., 2000) is faster than MaxMiner (Bayardo, 1998), and the latest article shows that Mafia (Burdick et al., 2001) consistently beats DepthProject. In our experimental study below, we retain MaxMiner for baseline comparison. At the same time, MaxMiner shows good performance on some datasets, which were not used in previous studies. We use Mafia as the current state-of-the-art method and show how GenMax compares against it. For comparison we used the original source or object code for MaxMiner (Bayardo, 1998) and MAFIA (Burdick et al., 2001), provided to us by their authors. For **CFI** mining, we used the original source or object code for Close (Pasquier et al., 1999), Pascal (Bastide et al., 2000), Closet (Pei et al., 2000), and Mafia (Burdick et al., 2001), all provided to us by their authors. We also include a comparison with the base Apriori algorithm (Agrawal et al., 1996) for mining all itemsets.

All our experiments were performed on a 400-MHz Pentium PC with 256 MB of memory, running RedHat Linux 6.0. Since Closet was provided as a Windows executable by its authors, we compared it separately on a 900-MHz Pentium III processor with 256-MB memory, running Windows 98. Timings in the figures are based on total wall-clock time, and they include all preprocessing costs (such as horizontal-to-vertical conversion in Charm, GenMax, and Mafia). The times reported also include the program output. We believe that our setup reflects realistic testing conditions (as opposed to some previous studies that report only the CPU time or may not include output cost).

23.5.1. Benchmark Datasets

We chose several real and synthetic datasets for testing the performance of the algorithms, shown in Table 23.1. The real datasets have been used previously in the evaluation of maximal patterns (Bayard, 1998; Agrawal et al., 2000; Burdick et al., 2001). Typically, these real datasets are very dense; that is, they produce many long frequent itemsets even for high values of support. The table shows the length of the longest maximal pattern (at the lowest minimum support used in our experiments) for the different datasets. For example on pumsb*, the longest pattern was of length 43 (any method that mines all frequent patterns will be impractical for such long patterns). We also chose two synthetic datasets, which have been used as benchmarks for testing methods that mine all frequent patterns. Previous maximal set-mining algorithms have not been tested on these datasets, which are sparser compared to the real sets. All these datasets are publicly available from IBM Almaden (www.almaden.ibm.com/cs/quest/demos.html).

Figure 23.12 shows the total number of frequent, closed, and maximal itemsets found for various support values. The maximal frequent itemsets are a subset of the frequent closed itemsets. The frequent closed itemsets are, of course, a subset of all frequent itemsets. Depending on the support value used, for the real

TABLE 23.1. Database Characteristics

Database	I	AL	R	MPL
chess	76	37	3,196	23 (20%)
connect	130	43	67,557	31 (2.5%)
mushroom	120	23	8,124	22 (0.025%)
pumsb*	7117	50	49,046	43 (2.5%)
pumsb	7117	74	49,046	27 (40%)
gazelle	498	2.5	59,601	154 (0.01%)
T10I4D100K	1000	10	100,000	13 (0.01%)
T40I10D100K	1000	40	100,000	25 (0.1%)

I denotes the number of items, AL is the average length of a record, R is the number of records, and MPL is the maximum pattern length at the given min_sup.

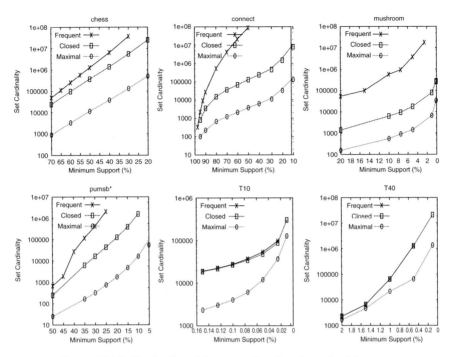

Figure 23.12. Cardinality of frequent, closed, and maximal itemsets.

datasets, the set of maximal itemsets is about an order of magnitude smaller than the set of closed itemsets, which in turn is an order of magnitude smaller than the set of all frequent itemsets. Even for very low support values we find that the difference between maximal and closed remains around a factor of 10. However, the gap between closed and all frequent itemsets grows more rapidly. Similar results were obtained for other real datasets as well. On the other hand, in sparse datasets the number of closed sets is only marginally smaller than the number of frequent sets; the number of maximal sets is still smaller, though the differences can narrow down for low support values.

23.5.2. Comparison of CFI Algorithms

Before we discuss the performance results of different algorithms, it is instructive to look at distribution of closed patterns by length for the various datasets, as shown in Figure 23.13. We have grouped the datasets according to the type of distribution. chess, pumsb*, pumsb, and connect all display an almost symmetric distribution of the closed frequent patterns with different means. $T40$ and mushroom display an interesting bimodal distribution of closed sets. $T40$, like $T10$, has a many short patterns of length 2, but it also has another peak at length 6. mushroom has considerably longer patterns; its second peak occurs at length 19. Finally, gazelle and T10 have a right-skewed distribution. gazelle tends

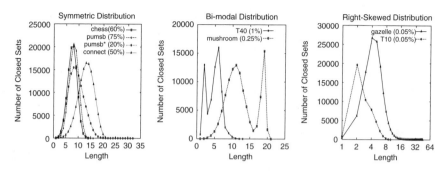

Figure 23.13. Closed itemset distribution.

to have many small patterns, with a very long right tail. $T10$ exhibits a similar distribution, with the majority of the closed patterns being of length 2! The type of distribution tends to influence the behavior of different algorithms, as we will see below. The full comparison among the different **CFI** algorithms is shown in Figure 23.14.

Type I: Symmetric Datasets.   Let us first compare how the methods perform on datasets that exhibit a symmetric distribution of closed itemsets, namely, chess, pumsb, connect, and pumsb*. We observe that Apriori, Close, and Pascal work only for very high values of support on these datasets. The best among the three is Pascal, which can be twice as fast as Close and up to four times better than Apriori. On the other hand, Charm is several orders of magnitude better than Pascal, and it can be run on very low support values, where none of the former three methods can be run. Comparing with Mafia, we find that both Charm and Mafia have similar performance for higher support values. However, as we lower the minimum support, the performance gap between Charm and Mafia widens. For example, at the lowest support value plotted, Charm is about 30 times faster than Mafia on Chess, about three times faster on connect and pumsb, and four times faster on pumsb*. Charm outperforms Closet by an order of magnitude or more, especially as support is lowered. On chess and pumsb* it is about 10 times faster than Closet and about 40 times faster on pumsb. On connect, Closet performs better at high supports, but Charm does better at lower supports. The reason is that connect has transactions with a lot of overlap among items, leading to a compact FP-tree and to faster performance. However, as support is lowered, FP-tree starts to grow, and Closet loses its edge.

Type II: Bimodal Datasets.   On the two datasets with a bimodal distribution of frequent closed patterns—namely, mushroom and $T40$—we find that Pascal fares better than for symmetric distributions. For higher values of support, the maximum closed pattern length is relatively short, and the distribution is dominated by the first mode. Apriori, Close, and Pascal can hand this case. However, as one lowers the minimum support, the second mode starts to dominate, with

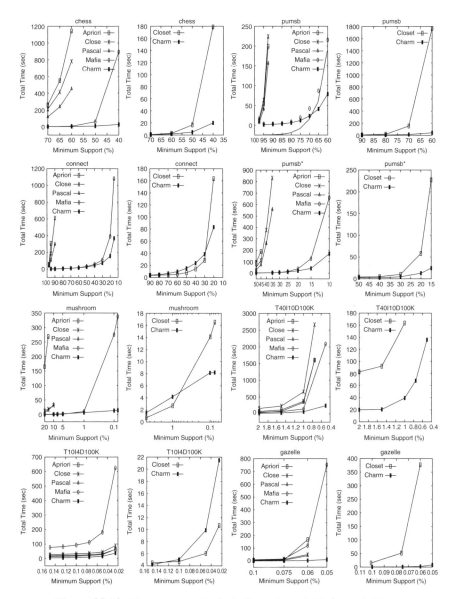

Figure 23.14. Charm versus Apriori, Close, Pascal, Mafia, and Closet.

longer patterns. These methods thus quickly lose steam and become uncompetitive. Between Charm and Mafia, up to 1% minimum support there is negligible difference, however, when the support is lowered there is a huge difference in performance. Charm is about 20 times faster on mushroom and 10 times faster on $T40$ for the lowest support shown. The gap continues to widen sharply. We find that Charm outperforms Closet by a factor of 2 for mushroom and 4 for $T40$.

Type III: Right-Skewed Datasets.   On gazelle and $T10$, which have a large number of very short closed patterns, followed by a sharp drop, we find that Apriori, Close, and Pascal remain competitive even for relatively low supports. The reason is that $T10$ had a maximum pattern length of 11 at the lowest support shown. Also gazelle at 0.06% support also had a maximum pattern length of 11. The level-wise search of these three methods is able to easily handle such short patterns. However, for gazelle, we found that at 0.05% support the maximum pattern length suddenly jumped to 45, and none of these three methods could be run.

   $T10$, though a sparse dataset, is problematic for Mafia. The reason is that $T10$ produces long sparse bit vectors for each item and offers little scope for bit-vector compression and projection that Mafia relies on for efficiency. This causes Mafia to be uncompetitive for such datasets. Similarly Mafia fails to do well on gazelle. However, it is able to run on the lowest support value. The diffset format of Charm is resilient to sparsity [as shown in Zaki and Gouda (2003)] and it continues to outperform other methods. For the lowest support, on $T10$ it is twice as fast as Pascal and 15 times better than Mafia, and it is about 70 times faster than Mafia on gazelle. Charm is about 2 times slower than Closet on $T10$. The reason is that the majority of closed sets are of length 2, and the tidset/diffsets operations in Charm are relatively expensive compared to the compact FP-tree for short patterns (max length is only 11). However, for gazelle, which has much longer closed patterns, Charm outperforms Closet by a factor of 160!

23.5.3. Comparison of MFI Algorithms

While conducting experiments comparing the three different algorithms, we observed that the performance can vary significantly depending on the dataset characteristics. We were able to classify our benchmark datasets into four classes based on the distribution of the maximal frequent patterns.

Type I Datasets: Chess and Pumsb.   Figure 23.15 shows the performance of the three algorithms on chess and pumsb. These Type I datasets are characterized by a symmetric distribution of the maximal frequent patterns (leftmost graph). Looking at the mean of the curve, we can observe that for these datasets most of the maximal patterns are relatively short (average length 11 for chess and 10 for pumsb). The **MFI** cardinalities in Figure 23.12 show that for the support values shown, the **MFI** is two orders of magnitude smaller than all frequent itemsets.

   Compare the total execution time for the different algorithms on these datasets (center and rightmost graphs). We use two different variants of Mafia. The first one, labeled Mafia, does not return the exact maximal frequent set, rather it returns a superset of all maximal patterns. The second variant, labeled MafiaPP, uses an option to eliminate nonmaximal sets in a post-processing (PP) step. Both GenMax and MaxMiner return the exact **MFI**.

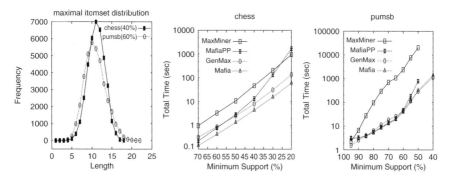

Figure 23.15. Type I datasets (chess and pumsb).

On chess we find that Mafia (without PP) is the fastest if one is willing to live with a superset of the **MFI**. Mafia is about 10 times faster than MaxMiner. However, notice how the running time of MafiaPP grows if one tries to find the exact **MFI** in a post-pruning step. GenMax, though slower than Mafia, is significantly faster than MafiaPP and is about 5 times better than MaxMiner. All methods, except MafiaPP, show an exponential growth in running time (since the y axis is in log scale, this appears linear) faithfully following the growth of **MFI** with lowering minimum support, as shown in the top center and right figures. MafiaPP shows superexponential growth and suffers from an approximately $O(|\mathbf{MFI}|^2)$ overhead in pruning nonmaximal sets and thus becomes impractical when **MFI** becomes too large—that is, at low supports.

On pumsb, we find that GenMax is the fastest, having a slight edge over Mafia. It is about two times faster than MafiaPP. We observed that the post-pruning routine in MafiaPP works well until around $O(10^4)$ maximal itemsets. Since at 60% min_sup we had around that many sets, the overhead of post-processing was not significant. With lower support the post-pruning cost becomes significant, so much so that we could not run MafiaPP beyond 50% minimum support. MaxMiner is significantly slower on pumsb, and it is a factor of 10 times slower than both GenMax and Mafia.

Type I results substantiate the claim that GenMax is an highly efficient method to mine the exact **MFI**. It is as fast as Mafia on pumsb and within a factor of 2 on chess. Mafia, on the other hand, is very effective in mining a superset of the **MFI**. Post-pruning, in general, is not a good idea, and GenMax beats MafiaPP with a wide margin (over 100 times better in some cases, e.g., chess at 20%). On Type I data, MaxMiner is noncompetitive.

Type II Datasets: Connect and Pumsb*. Type II datasets, as shown in Figure 23.16, are characterized by a left-skewed distribution of the maximal frequent patterns; that is, there is a relatively gradual increase with a sharp drop in the number of maximal patterns. The mean pattern length is also longer than in Type I datasets; it is around 16 or 17. The **MFI** cardinality (Figure 23.12) is also

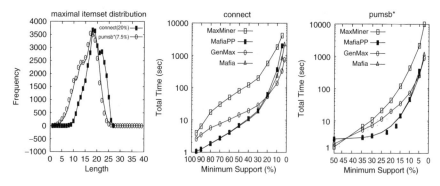

Figure 23.16. Type II datasets (connect and pumsb*).

drastically smaller than **FI** cardinality, by a factor of 10^4 or more (in contrast, for Type I data, the reduction was only 10^2).

The main performance trend for both Type II datasets is that Mafia is the best until the support is very low, at which point there is a crossover and GenMax outperforms Mafia. MafiaPP continues to be favorable for higher supports, but once again beyond a point, post-pruning costs start to dominate. MafiaPP could not be run beyond the plotted points. MaxMiner remains noncompetitive (about 10 times slower). The initial start-up time for Mafia for creating the bit-vectors is responsible for the high offset at 50% support on pumsb*. GenMax appears to exhibit a more graceful increase in running time than Mafia.

Type III Datasets: T10I4 and T40I10.   As depicted in Figure 23.17, Type III datasets—the two synthetic ones—are characterized by an exponentially decaying distribution of the maximal frequent patterns. Except for a few maximal sets of size one, the vast majority of maximal patterns are of length two! After that, the number of longer patterns drops exponentially. The mean pattern length is

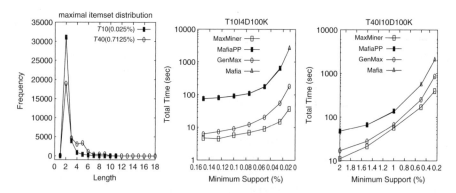

Figure 23.17. Type III datasets (T10 and T40).

very short compared to Type I or Type II datasets; it is around 4–6. **MFI** cardinality is not much smaller than the cardinality of all frequent patterns (see Figure 23.12). The difference is only a factor of 10 compared to a factor of 100 for Type I and a factor of 10,000 for Type II.

Comparing the running times, we observe that MaxMiner is the best method for this type of data. The breadth-first or level-wise search strategy used in MaxMiner is ideal for very bushy search trees and when the average maximal pattern length is small. Horizontal methods are better equipped to cope with the quadratic blowup in the number of frequent 2-itemsets since one can use array based counting to get their frequency. On the other hand, vertical methods spend much time in performing intersections on long item tidsets or bit vectors. GenMax gets around this problem by using the horizontal format for computing frequent 2-itemsets (denoted F_2), but it still has to spend time performing $O(|F_2|)$ pairwise tidset intersections.

Mafia, on the other hand, performs $O(|F_1|^2)$ intersections, where F_1 is the set of frequent items. The overhead cost is enough to render Mafia noncompetitive on Type III data. On T10, Mafia can be 20 or more times slower than MaxMiner. GenMax exhibits relatively good performance, and it is about 10 times better than Mafia and two to three times worse than MaxMiner. On T40, the gap between GenMax/Mafia and MaxMiner is smaller since there are longer maximal patterns. MaxMiner is two times better than GenMax and five times better than Mafia. Since the **MFI** cardinality is not too large, MafiaPP has almost the time as Mafia for high supports. Once again, MafiaPP could not be run for lower support values. It is clear that, in general, post-pruning is not a good idea; the overhead is too much to cope with.

Type IV Dataset: Mushroom.　　Mushroom exhibits a very unique **MFI** distribution. Plotting **MFI** cardinality by length, we observe in Figure 23.18 that the number of maximal patterns remains small until length 19. Then there is a sudden

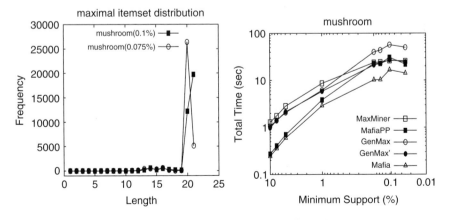

Figure 23.18. Type IV dataset (mushroom).

explosion of maximal patterns at length 20, followed by another sharp drop at length 21. The vast majority of maximal itemsets are of length 20. The average transaction length for mushroom is 23 (see Table 23.1); thus a maximal pattern spans almost a full transaction. The total **MFI** cardinality is about 1000 times smaller than all frequent itemsets (see Figure 23.12).

On Type IV data, Mafia performs the best. MafiaPP and MaxMiner are comparable at lower supports. This type of data is the worst for GenMax, which is two times slower than MaxMiner and four times slower than Mafia. In Type IV data, a smaller itemset is part of many maximal itemsets (of length 20 in case of mushroom); this renders our progressive focusing technique less effective. To perform maximality checking, one has to test against a large set of maximal itemsets; we found that GenMax spends half its time in maximality checking. Recognizing this helped us improve the progressive focusing using an optimized intersection-based method (as opposed to the original list based approach). This variant, labeled GenMax', was able to cut down the execution time by half. GenMax' runs in the same time as MaxMiner and MafiaPP.

23.6. CONCLUSIONS

This is one of the first works to comprehensively compare recent closed and maximal pattern-mining algorithms under realistic assumptions. Our timings are based on wall-clock time; we included all preprocessing costs and also the cost of outputting all the closed and maximal itemsets (written to a file). We were able to distinguish three different types of **CFI** distributions and four different types of **MFI** distributions in our benchmark testbed. We believe these distributions to be fairly representative of what one might see in practice, since they span both real and synthetic datasets. For **CFI** mining, Type I is a symmetric/normal **CFI** distribution, with both small and long mean pattern lengths, Type II is a bimodal distribution with both long and short modes, and Type III is a right-skewed distribution with relatively short closed pattern lengths. For **MFI** mining, Type I is a normal **MFI** distribution with not too long maximal patterns, Type II is a left-skewed distributions, with longer maximal patterns, Type III is an exponential decay distribution, with extremely short maximal patterns, and finally Type IV is an extreme left-skewed distribution, with very large average maximal pattern length.

We noted that different algorithms perform well under different distributions. Among the **CFI** mining algorithms, Charm performs the best for all distribution types—with the exception of the T10 dataset, which is sparse and has very short pattern lengths. For connect and mushroom, Closet does better for high support values, but Charm outperforms at lower supports. Mafia was not found to be competitive with Charm, and neither were Pascal or Close. Among the current methods for **MFI** mining, MaxMiner is the best for mining Type III distributions. On the remaining types, Mafia is the best method if one is satisfied with a superset of the **MFI**. For very low supports on Type II data, Mafia loses its edge.

Post-pruning nonmaximal patterns typically has high overhead. It works only for high support values, and MafiaPP cannot be run beyond a certain minimum support value. GenMax integrates pruning of nonmaximal itemsets in the process of mining using the novel progressive focusing technique, along with other optimizations for superset checking; GenMax is the best method for mining the exact **MFI**.

ACKNOWLEDGMENT

We would like to thank Roberto Bayardo for providing us the MaxMiner algorithm; Lotfi Lakhal and Yves Bastide for providing us the source code for Close and Pascal; Jiawei Han, Jian Pei, and Jianyong Wang for sending us the executable for Closet; and Johannes Gehrke for the Mafia algorithm. We thank Roberto Bayardo for providing us the IBM real datasets, and we thank Ronny Kohavi and Zijian Zheng of Blue Martini Software for giving us access to the Gazelle dataset.

This work was supported in part by NSF CAREER Award IIS-0092978, DOE Early Career Award DE-FG02-02ER25538, and NSF grant EIA-0103708.

REFERENCES

Aggarwal, C., Towards long pattern generation in dense databases, *SIGKDD Explorations* **3**(1), 20–26 (2001).

Agrawal, R., Mannila, H., Srikant, R., Toivonen, H., and Inkeri Verkamo, A., Fast discovery of association rules, in *Advances in Knowledge Discovery and Data Mining*, Fayyad U., et al. ed., AAAI Press, Menlo Park, CA, pp. 307–328, 1996.

Agrawal, R., Aggarwal, C., and Prasad, V. V. V., Depth first generation of long patterns, in *7th International Conference on Knowledge Discovery and Data Mining*, August 2000.

Bastide, Y., Taouil, R., Pasquier, N., Stumme, G., and Lakhal, L., Mining frequent patterns with counting inference, *SIGKDD Explorations* **2**(2), 66–75 (2000).

Bayardo, R. J., Efficiently mining long patterns from databases, in *ACM SIG-MOD Conference on Management of Data*, June 1998.

Burdick, D., Calimlim, M., and Gehrke, J., MAFIA: A maximal frequent itemset algorithm for transactional databases, in *International Conference on Data Engineering*, April 2001.

Cristofor, D., Cristofor, L., and Simovici, D., Galois connection and data mining, *Journal of Universal Computer Science* **6**(1), 60–73 (2000).

Gouda, K., and Zaki, M. J., Efficiently mining maximal frequent itemsets, in *1st IEEE International Conference on Data Mining*, November 2001.

Grahne, G., and Zhu, J., High performance mining of maximal frequent itemsets, in *6th International Workshop on High Performance Data Mining*, May 2003.

Gunopulos, D., Mannila, H., and Saluja, S., Discovering all the most specific sentences by randomized algorithms, in *International Conference on Database Theory*, January 1997.

Han, J., Pei, J., and Yin, Y., Mining frequent patterns without candidate generation, in *ACM SIGMOD Conference Management of Data*, May 2000.

Lin, D-I., and Kedem, Z. M., Pincer-search: A new algorithm for discovering the maximum frequent set, in *6th International Conference on Extending Database Technology*, March 1998.

Pan, F., Cong, G., Tung, A. K. H., Yang, J., and Zaki, M. J., CARPENTER: Finding closed patterns in long biological datasets, in *ACM SIGKDD International Conference on Knowledge Discovery and Data Mining*, August 2003.

Pasquier, N., Bastide, Y., Taouil, R., and Lakhal, L., Discovering frequent closed itemsets for association rules, in *7th International Conference on Database Theory*, January 1999.

Pei, J., Han, J., and Mao, R., Closet: An efficient algorithm for mining frequent closed itemsets, in *SIGMOD International Workshop on Data Mining and Knowledge Discovery*, May 2000.

Wang, J., Han, J., and Pei, J., Closet+: Searching for the best strategies for mining frequent closed itemsets, in *ACM SIGKDD International Conference on Knowledge Discovery and Data Mining*, August 2003.

Yellin, D. M., An algorithm for dynamic subset and intersection testing, *Theoretical Computer Science* **129**, 397–406 (1994).

Zaki, M. J., Generating non-redundant association rules, in *6th ACM SIGKDD International Conference on Knowledge Discovery and Data Mining*, August 2000a.

Zaki, M. J., Scalable algorithms for association mining, *IEEE Transactions on Knowledge and Data Engineering* **12**(3):372–390, May–June 2000b.

Zaki, M. J., and Gouda, K., Fast vertical mining using Diffsets, Technical Report, in *9th ACM SIGKDD International Conference on Knowledge Discovery and Data Mining*, August 2003.

Zaki, M. J., and Hsiao, C.-J., CHARM: An efficient algorithm for closed itemset mining, in *2nd SIAM International Conference on Data Mining*, April 2002.

Zou, Q., Chu, W. W., and Lu, B., Smartminer: A depth first algorithm guided by tail information for mining maximal frequent itemsets, in *2nd IEEE International Conference on Data Mining*, November 2002.

24

USING FRACTALS IN DATA MINING

Caetano Traina, Jr., Elaine Parros Machado De Sousa, and Agma Juci Machado Traina

24.1. INTRODUCTION

The advances in scientific and engineering fields have driven the development of more robust information systems, which have to manage complex data, such as videos, images, data streams, DNA series, hypertexts, and so on. These data are typically high-dimensional and voluminous. Also, the amount of new data constantly being generated has increased in a very fast pace: It has been reported that the data storage capacity has doubled every nine months in the last decade, which compared with Moore's Law, regarding processing power, is twice as fast (Porter, 1998). Moreover, due to the decreasing price of devices and media for secondary storage, it is not too costly anymore to keep all data generated by companies. Hence, the volume of data is increasing faster than we can process and utilize it, leading to a phenomenon known as *data tombs* (Fayyad and Uthurusamy, 2002), which are data written once and never read again, and to the undesirable situation of having all the effort of collecting and organizing data relinquished fruitlessly. On the other hand, the main interest of companies and scientific enterprises in collecting and keeping their data is to take advantage of the information hidden there, using it to make their business more efficient, reliable and profitable.

Data-mining techniques aim at finding valuable and interesting structures inside the data—that is, to identify relationships, patterns, and correlations that are not previously known and could not be obtained through direct queries over the data. To do so, several disciplines, such as statistics, databases, artificial intelligence, pattern recognition, machine learning, and visualization, have been applied together to achieve the purpose of extracting information that the data owners do not know exists.

Next Generation of Data-Mining Applications. Edited by Kantardzic and Zurada
ISBN 0-471-65605-4 © 2005 the Institute of Electrical and Electronics Engineers, Inc.

Keeping only the relevant information of the data is a challenge that the next generation of data-mining techniques is pursuing. In order to keep only the essence of high-dimensional data, database researchers have developed techniques for dimensionality reduction, clustering, and classification, as well as indexing and retrieval operations allied with data-mining processes. This chapter addresses these subjects in the light of the intrinsic (or fractal) dimensionality of the datasets.

Database management systems usually store data through tables with as many columns as there are attributes represented in the data, and as many rows as there are data elements. When the attributes of a dataset are in the domain $\mathbb{R}$ of real numbers, data elements can be represented by points embedded in a multidimensional space defined by the dataset's attributes. However, the distribution of the points can represent an object having a dimensionality lower than the space where the dataset is embedded.

Much work has been done using the embedding dimensionality of the dataset to evaluate the data behavior under searching and retrieval, based on the typical assumption that the data have a uniform distribution in which all the attributes are independent. However, the great majority of real datasets do not comply with such assumption, that is, data are not uniformly distributed and there are attributes that are dependent or correlated with others. Thus, real datasets frequently are skewed and exhibit an intrinsic—or fractal—dimensionality, which is usually much lower than their embedding dimension. The difference between the two concepts of dimensionality occurs because the fractal dimensionality takes account of the existing correlation between attributes, while the embedding dimensionality does not.

Mining large high-dimensional datasets in acceptable time is a challenge that the database community has been dealing with. Therefore, one of the main objectives of database activities regarding data mining is to provide scalable algorithms to perform data-mining processes. Scalability can be measured regarding many parameters, depending on the targeted mining process. For example, in clustering processes it can involve the number of prospective clusters existing in the dataset. However, two parameters are universal to every kind of data-mining process: number of items and number of dimensions. Thus, because scalability must always consider at least these two parameters, fractals contribute to the data-mining field enabling the development of very fast algorithms to extract information, usually with a computational complexity that is linear on the number of elements in the dataset and on the number of attributes that define each data element. Moreover, the fractal theory provides tools to make other algorithms depend on the intrinsic dimensionality of a dataset and not on the (usually higher) embedding dimensionality, as most current techniques do.

In this chapter we show how to use the intrinsic (fractal) dimensionality to select relevant attributes, how to get information about the clusters and outliers of the dataset, as well as the relationships among its elements. Our discussion focuses on datasets composed of continuous attributes, with no missing values, in the domain $\mathbb{R}$ of the real numbers. Throughout this chapter we also refer to such datasets as point sets.

The following sections are organized as follows: Section 24.2 presents the concepts related to the intrinsic dimensionality of datasets, giving the definitions needed to formally state them, as well as the linear time algorithm used to compute the intrinsic (fractal) dimensionality. Section 24.3 shows how to take advantage of the intrinsic dimensionality of datasets to perform many data-mining operations, such as clustering and analysis of data relationships, including attribute selection, dimensionality reduction, and outliers detection. That section also illustrates the concepts presented using some datasets obtained from real-world applications. Section 24.4 briefly discusses other current research works relating fractals with data mining, and finally Section 24.5 gives the summary and conclusions of this chapter.

24.2. INTRINSIC DIMENSIONALITY

When comparing the intrinsic dimensionality of a dataset with its embedding dimension, one can tell how far from the uniformity assumption the dataset is. By definition, the **embedding dimension** E is the number of attributes of the dataset. On the other hand, the **intrinsic dimensionality** $\mathcal{D}$ is the dimensionality of the object represented by the point set, regardless of the space where it is embedded.

Consider, for instance, a set of points disposed along a line. Its intrinsic dimensionality equals one, no matter if the set is embedded in a higher-dimensional space. Figure 24.1 illustrates a line segment embedded in two- and three-dimensional spaces. Although the corresponding datasets have two and three attributes, respectively, in each case the attributes are linearly correlated and therefore the intrinsic dimensionality of the line segment is always one. Similarly, the intrinsic dimensionality of Euclidean objects equals their Euclidean dimension, regardless of the dimension of the space where they are embedded in. Thus, lines, circles and standard curves have $\mathcal{D} = 1$; planes, squares and surfaces have $\mathcal{D} = 2$; Euclidean volumes have $\mathcal{D} = 3$, and so on.

The embedding dimensionality of the dataset can conceal the data's actual distribution, leading to erroneous assumptions of uniformity and independence. The correlations among the attributes of real datasets are usually not known, and frequently even the existence of correlated attributes is not known either. Nevertheless, the intrinsic dimensionality $\mathcal{D}$ can indicate the presence of correlations

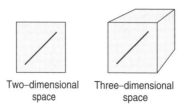

Two–dimensional   Three–dimensional
space   space

Figure 24.1. Line segment embedded in two- and three-dimensional space.

and give a hint of how many attributes are actually required to characterize a point set. Indeed, the intrinsic dimensionality gives a lower bound of the number of attributes needed to keep the essential characteristics of a dataset; that is, the ceiling function on $\mathcal{D}$ determines the minimal number of attributes that must remain to characterize the whole set.

The intrinsic dimensionality of a dataset can be estimated by its fractal dimension. Therefore, the fractal theory is a useful tool to describe datasets from the real world, because it can model point sets with strongly correlated attributes, even in cases of nonlinear correlations. Also, the information provided by applying the fractal theory and getting the intrinsic dimensionality can significantly improve the efficacy of data-mining tasks performed on real point sets.

24.2.1. Fractals

A fractal is defined as an object that exhibits the self-similarity property, that is, it is an object that presents roughly the same characteristics regardless of the scale where it is analyzed. Thus, small-scale details are similar to large-scale characteristics (Schroeder, 1991).

In general, fractal structures can be classified as deterministically self-similar fractals or as statistically self-similar fractals.

Definition 24.1. A **deterministically self-similar fractal** can be described by a construction rule, such that its parts are miniature replicas of the original. Therefore, the structure of such fractal can be predicted accurately.

From a theoretical perspective, we can define deterministic fractals using both geometrical or algebraical descriptions. Usually, geometric fractals are exactly self-similar structures generated through well-defined geometrical and recursive construction rules. On the other hand, algebraical fractals are described by recursive algebraic rules.

Definition 24.2. An **exactly self-similar fractal** is a deterministic geometric fractal consisting of M miniature replicas of itself, and each miniature is a 1:s scaled replica of the original.

The *Sierpinsky* triangle, for instance, is a well-known geometric fractal, which complies with Definition 24.2. It is created from an equilateral triangle ABC by removing its middle triangle $A'B'C'$ and by recursively repeating this process to each of the resulting smaller triangles, as illustrated in Figure 24.2. Notice that, according to the construction rule, three replicas in 1:1/2 scale of each triangle are created at each iteration, and the resulting fractal exhibits "holes" in any scale. Other examples of geometric fractals are presented in Figure 24.3: the *Cantor* set (see Figure 24.3a) and the *Koch curve* (see Figure 24.3b).

As an example of algebraic fractals we can mention the *Mandelbrot* set (see Figure 24.3c), which is a set of points in the complex plane.

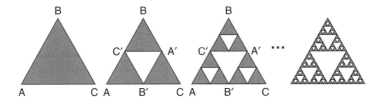

Figure 24.2. Recursive construction of *Sierpinsky* triangle.

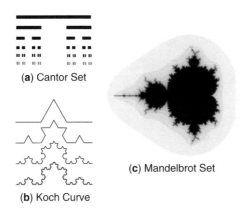

(a) Cantor Set

(b) Koch Curve

(c) Mandelbrot Set

Figure 24.3. Examples of fractals.

Definition 24.3. A **statistically self-similar fractal** has roughly the same statistical properties over all scales. The parts of the fractal are not identical to, but are statically similar to, the original.

Statistical fractals can be found in nature—for instance, in cloud formations, leaves and flowers, terrains, and mountain chains, to name but a few. More examples of statistically self-similar fractals are datasets from real-world application domains. A real dataset can be modeled as a fractal if it exhibits self-similarity in a suitable range of scales.

It is interesting to highlight that fractals normally present uncommon, or even paradoxal, characteristics. Consider, for instance, the *Sierpinsky* triangle, which has infinite perimeter and no area. At each step i of the recursive construction process, the perimeter of the *Sierpinsky* triangle is increased by one-half of its perimeter in step $i - 1$. On the other hand, its area is decreased by $1/4$ at each step. Hence, considering an initial triangle ABC with perimeter and area equal to one, the perimeter at each iteration i equals $(1 + 1/2)^i$, while the area reduces to $(3/4)^i$. Therefore, after infinite iterations, the perimeter and the area of the *Sierpinsky* triangle are proportional to $\lim_{i \to \infty} (1 + 1/2)^i$ and to $\lim_{i \to \infty} (3/4)^i$, respectively.

With such properties (i.e., infinite perimeter and zero area), the *Sierpinsky* triangle is neither a one-dimensional nor a two-dimensional Euclidean object. Thus, it is reasonable to consider a fractional dimensionality, or **fractal dimension** (Mandelbrot, 1983). Intuitively, the fractal dimension of the *Sierpinsky* triangle, for example, is a value between one and two.

24.2.2. Fractal Dimension

There are several definitions of the fractal dimension, as we shall see briefly. In this section we present an overview of some of them, first introducing the fractal dimension of exactly self-similar fractals.

Definition 24.4. The **Hausdorff fractal dimension** $\mathcal{D}_H$ of an exactly self-similar fractal is measured as

$$\mathcal{D}_H = \lim_{s \to 0} \frac{\log M}{\log(1/s)} \tag{24.1}$$

where M is the number of miniature replicas created at each step of the construction process, and s is the scaling factor to build the replicas.

Consider, for example, the fractal dimension of the *Sierpinsky* triangle, for which each triangle produces three new half-scaled triangles at each step, that is, $M = 3$ and $s = 1/2$. Thus,

$$\mathcal{D}_H = \frac{\log 3}{\log 2} = 1.58496$$

The definition presented in Eq. 24.1 is based on the construction rule of the fractal. However, when measuring the fractal dimension of statistically self-similar fractals, which exhibit no explicit construction rules, it is necessary to employ a different approach, such as the Box-Counting method.

In order to use the Box-Counting method, the address space of the given point set $\mathcal{P}$, which is embedded in an E-dimensional space, is divided into several E-dimensional grids, each with cells of side size r. The Box-Counting approach is illustrated in Figure 24.4, which shows a bi-dimensional grid of cell side r over a set of points describing the *Sierpinsky* triangle. Several definitions for fractal dimensions are based on the main idea of the Box-Counting method, as follows.

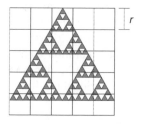

Figure 24.4. Box-Counting approach.

Definition 24.5. Given an infinite point set $\mathcal{P}$, let $N(r)$ denote the number of grid cells of side r which contain at least one point of $\mathcal{P}$. With r tending to zero, the *Hausdorff* **fractal dimension** $\mathcal{D}_0$ **of the infinite point set** can be approximated as

$$\mathcal{D}_0 = -\lim_{r \to 0} \frac{\log(N(r))}{\log(r)} \qquad (24.2)$$

Notice that the fractal dimension $\mathcal{D}_0$ encompass exactly self-similar fractals, for which $\log(N(r))$ is linearly depended on $\log(r)$ in any scale, and therefore $\mathcal{D}_0 = \mathcal{D}_H$.

The Box-Counting method is usually employed to measure the fractal dimension of finite point sets, as datasets from real world. The analysis of the fractal dimension of a finite point set is restricted to a suitable range of scales, $r \in (r_1, r_2)$, in which the set presents statistical self-similarity. Thus, rather than using $\lim_{r \to 0}$, the *Hausdorff* fractal dimension of finite point sets is based on the derivative of $\log N(r)$ with respect to $\log r$. This is summarized by the following definition.

Definition 24.6. Given a finite point set $\mathcal{P}$ that exhibits the self-similarity property in a range of scales (r_1, r_2), the *Hausdorff* **fractal dimension** $\mathcal{D}_0$ **of the finite point set** in that range is defined as

$$\mathcal{D}_0 = -\frac{\partial \log(N(r))}{\partial \log(r)} = \text{constant}, \qquad r_1 < r < r_2 \qquad (24.3)$$

A practical way to compute the *Hausdorff* fractal dimension of finite point sets is using the Box-Count plot. If a dataset is self-similar in a range of scales (r_1, r_2), the plot of $N(r)$ to different values of r, in log–log scale, is very close to a straight line in that range. The negated slope of the best fitting line gives an approximation of the *Hausdorff* fractal dimension as defined in Eq. 24.3.

Other common definitions of the fractal dimension come from an infinite family of dimensions named generalized fractal dimension $\mathcal{D}_q$. The $\mathcal{D}_q$ family is also based on a variation of the Box-Counting method, where each grid cell that intercepts the fractal is weighted by a power q.

Definition 24.7. Given a finite point set $\mathcal{P}$ that exhibits the self-similarity property in a range of scales (r_1, r_2), let $C_{\mathcal{P},i}$ denote the count of points of $\mathcal{P}$ that fall inside the grid cell i. The **generalized fractal dimension** $\mathcal{D}_q$ **of the finite point set** is defined as

$$\mathcal{D}_q = \frac{1}{q-1} \frac{\partial \log(\sum_i C_{\mathcal{P},i}^q)}{\partial \log(r)} = \text{constant}, \qquad q \in \mathbb{N}, q \neq 1, r_1 < r < r_2 \quad (24.4)$$

$$\mathcal{D}_1 = \frac{\partial \log(\sum_i C_{\mathcal{P},i}) \log C_{\mathcal{P},i}}{\partial \log(r)} = \text{constant}, \qquad q = 1, r_1 < r < r_2 \qquad (24.5)$$

The definition of the generalized fractal dimension leads to relevant observations:

- For $q = 0$, $\sum_i C_{\mathcal{P},i}^0 = \sum_i 1$ corresponds to the number of grid cells intercepting the fractal at least in one point. Therefore, $q = 0$ defines the *Hausdorff* fractal dimension $\mathcal{D}_0$ [see Eq. 24.3].
- For an exactly self-similar fractal, $\mathcal{D}_q = \mathcal{D}_0 \; \forall \, q$ (Schroeder, 1991).
- $q = 2$ defines the correlation fractal dimension $\mathcal{D}_2$:

$$\mathcal{D}_2 = \frac{\partial \log(\sum_i C_{\mathcal{P},i}^2)}{\partial \log(r)} = \text{constant}, \qquad r_1 < r < r_2 \qquad (24.6)$$

The correlation fractal dimension $\mathcal{D}_2$ stands out from the other $\mathcal{D}_q$ dimensions because of its theoretical relevance. The fractal dimension $\mathcal{D}_2$ is based on the correlation function of the point set, i.e., the probability of finding one or more points whose distance from a given point in the set is at most r, considering the Euclidean distance. Therefore, $\mathcal{D}_2$ is related to the correlation concept, as explained by the following definitions.

Definition 24.8. Given a point set $\mathcal{P}$ in an E-dimensional space and an E-grid with cell side r, let $C_{\mathcal{P},i}$ denote the count of points which fall inside the grid cell i (count of occupancy). The **sum of squared occupancy** $S_2(r)$ is defined as

$$S_2(r) = \sum_i \left(C_{\mathcal{P},i}(r)\right)^2 \qquad (24.7)$$

Definition 24.9. Given a point set $\mathcal{P}$, the **correlation integral** $C(r)$ of $\mathcal{P}$ is defined as

$$C(r) = \frac{\sum(nonordered(r))}{N \times (N-1)/2} \qquad (24.8)$$

where $\sum(nonordered(r))$ denotes the number of nonordered pairs $\langle p_k, p_j \rangle$, $k \neq j$, $p_k, p_j \in \mathcal{P}$, within a distance r [i.e., $\text{dist}(p_k, p_j) \leq r$], and $N \times (N-1)/2$ is the number of unique pairs $\langle p_k, p_j \rangle$ in $\mathcal{P}$. Notice that both pairs $\langle p_k, p_j \rangle$ and $\langle p_j, p_k \rangle$ are counted only once.

Definition 24.10. Given a point set $\mathcal{P}$ and the sum of squared occupancy $S_2(r)$ for a grid of cell side r, the **Schuster** Lemma (Schuster, 1984) demonstrates that the integral correlation $C(r)$ is proportional to $S_2(r)$.

$$C(r) \propto S_2(r) \qquad (24.9)$$

From Equations 24.6, 24.7, and 24.9, the Correlation Fractal Dimension $\mathcal{D}_2$ is defined by the correlation function of the point set.

Definition 24.11. Given a finite point set $\mathcal{P}$ that exhibits the self-similarity property in a range of scales (r_1, r_2), along with the correlation integral $C(r)$, the correlation fractal dimension $\mathcal{D}_2$ of $\mathcal{P}$ is defined as

$$\mathcal{D}_2 = \frac{\partial \log(C(r))}{\partial \log(r)} = \text{constant}, \qquad r_1 < r < r_2 \qquad (24.10)$$

According to Eq. 24.10, the correlation fractal dimension can be estimated by the cumulative distribution function of pairwise distances.

To conclude, as with other dimensions of the family $\mathcal{D}_q$, the Box-Count plot is a practical way to compute $\mathcal{D}_2$. So, for a dataset exhibiting exact or statistical self-similarity in a suitable range of scales (r_1, r_2), the plot in log–log scale of $C(r)$ for different values of r is close to a line in that range, and therefore the slope of the best fitting line approximates the value of $\mathcal{D}_2$.

24.2.3. Measuring the Intrinsic Dimensionality

The intrinsic dimensionality of a real point set can be estimated by its fractal dimension, usually the *Hausdorff* or the correlation fractal dimension, $\mathcal{D}_0$ and $\mathcal{D}_2$ respectively. Because $\mathcal{D}_2$ is related to the correlations existing among the dimensions of the dataset, it also represents the degree of freedom of each attribute in the dataset. Therefore, in the remainder of this chapter we assume $\mathcal{D}_2$ as a suitable approximation of the intrinsic dimensionality of a dataset, considering $\mathcal{D} \approx \mathcal{D}_2$.

The Box-Counting method discussed in Section 24.2.2 is an efficient approach to measure the fractal dimension of datasets embedded in E-dimensional spaces. Thus, we present an algorithm to estimate $\mathcal{D}$ calculating the $\mathcal{D}_2$ according to the Box-Counting approach.

The algorithm, named *LiBOC* (*Linear Box-Occupancy Counter*), is based on a multilevel grid structure that allows the dataset to be read only once when processing $S_2(r)$ for a suitable number R of values of r, where r is the size (or radius) of the grid cell side. The radius at each level of the structure measures one-half of the radius at the previous level. Then, considering that the dataset is linearly normalized to a unitary hypercube, LiBOC adopts $r = 1$, $1/2$, $1/4$, $1/8$, and so on.

The lone cell in the first level of the structure generates 2^E cells in the next level, on which each cell is split into other 2^E cells, and so on and so forth. Figure 24.5 illustrates the multilevel grid structure for two- and three-dimensional datasets.

Each point from the dataset is directly associated to a cell at each level of the structure, increasing the count of occupancies $C_{\mathcal{P},i}$ of the respective cells. After every point of the dataset has been processed, the sum of squared occupancy $S_2(r)$ is computed for each radius r. Note that because each point is handled only once and does not need to be compared with the previously processed points, the algorithm is very fast, having linear complexity on the size of the dataset.

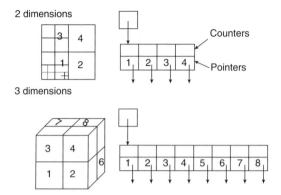

Figure 24.5. Representation of grid cells in two- and three-dimensional space.

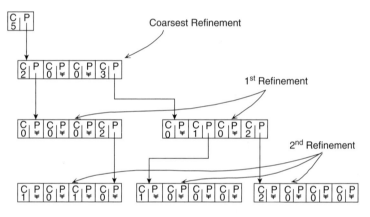

Figure 24.6. Example of the data structure of LiBOC.

The position of the cells in the space follows the data placement, so it is always known. Each cell is represented by its count of occupancy $C_{P,i}$ and by the pointer to the cells it covers in the next level (see Figure 24.5). The data structure implementing the multilevel grid is a kind of E-dimensional-tree (such as the quad-tree for two-dimensional datasets), where each node corresponds to a grid cell. As an example, Figure 24.6 shows the first three levels of a tree built for a dataset with five points in a two-dimensional space.

Each level of the tree corresponds to a different radius, so its depth equals the number of radii used, which in turn determines the number of points in the resulting plot. As discussed earlier in Section 24.2.2, if the resulting plot is linear for a suitable range of r, the dataset is a fractal and its intrinsic dimension $\mathcal{D}$ is well-approximated by the slope of the best fitting line in that range. In order to achieve a reliable measurement of $\mathcal{D}$, the log–log plot must have at least five points; and because the first and the last ones are usually subject of some distortion caused by pairs of too close or too far points from the dataset, the three inner points in the plot are better aligned.

However, if the plot is not linear, it nonetheless provides helpful hints about the general characteristics of the dataset, as we will discuss in Section 24.3. This plot is a valuable analysis tool, and it is called the Self-plot of a dataset.

By the definition of correlation integral, the Self-plots exclude the counting of self-pairs [see Eq. 24.8]. This means that both pairs $\langle p_1, p_2 \rangle$ and $\langle p_2, p_1 \rangle$ of points in $\mathcal{P}$ are counted only once, and the self-pairs $\langle p_1, p_1 \rangle$ are not counted. Therefore, the calculation of the Self-plot of a dataset $\mathcal{P}$ follows the following definition.

Definition 24.12. The **Self-plot** of a given dataset $\mathcal{P}$ is the plot of

$$
\text{Self}_{\mathcal{P}}(r) = \log \left(\sum_i \frac{C_{\mathcal{P}_i}(r) * (C_{\mathcal{P}_i}(r) - 1)}{2} \right), \qquad r \in [r_1, r_2] \qquad (24.11)
$$

versus $\log(r)$.

A key observation about the LiBOC algorithm is that the sibling nodes at each level of the tree are kept as linked lists. Thus, new nodes are added to the structure on demand, and only cells occupied by at least one point (cells $C_{\mathcal{P},i} > 0$) requires memory to be allocated.

The computational complexity of the LiBOC algorithm is $O(N * E * R)$, where N is the number of objects in the dataset, E is the embedding dimensionality, and R is the number of radii used to plot the $S_2(r)$ function. A general description of the whole algorithm is presented in Algorithm 24.1. Table 24.1 presents the main symbols used throughout this chapter.

Algorithm 24.1. LiBOC—Linear Box Occupancy Counter

Input: normalized dataset $\mathcal{P}$ (N points with E attributes each)
Output: intrinsic dimension $\mathcal{D}$ of $\mathcal{P}$
 1: **for** each point of the dataset **do**
 2:     increment the number of points read;
 3:     considering the largest grid side ($r = 1$), decide which cell the point falls in (say, the ith cell);
 4:     get the cell pointed by this ith cell in the next level;
 5:     **for** $r = 1/2^j$, $j = 2, 3, \ldots, R$ **do**
 6:         decide which grid cell the point falls in (say, the ith cell);
 7:         increment the count $C_{\mathcal{P},i}$ ("occupancy") of this cell;
 8:         get the cell pointed by this ith cell in the next level;
 9:     **end for**
10:     compute the sum of squared occupancy $S_2(r) = \sum_i C_{\mathcal{P},i}^2$;
11: **end for**
12: define a curve using the values of $\log(r)$ and $\log(S_2(r))$ as the abscissas and ordinates, respectively;
13: return the slope of the linear part of the curve as the intrinsic dimension $\mathcal{D}$ of the dataset $\mathcal{P}$;

TABLE 24.1. Table of Symbols

Symbols	Definitions
E	Embedding dimension
$\mathcal{D}$	Intrinsic dimensionality (fractal dimension)
$\mathcal{D}_H$ or $\mathcal{D}_0$	*Hausdorff* fractal dimension
$\mathcal{D}_2$	Correlation fractal dimension
$\mathcal{D}_q$	Generalized fractal dimension
$p\mathcal{D}\{\mathcal{A}\}$	Partial fractal dimension from a subset of attributes $\mathcal{A}$
N	Number of points in the dataset
r	Length of the side of a grid cell
R	Number of points (distinct values of r) to plot $S_2(r)$
$C_{\mathcal{P},i}$	Count of 'occupancies' of points in the ith grid cell of side r
$S_2(r)$	Sum of squared occupancy for every cell of grid side r
$\hat{r}_{\min}$	Minimum distance between two points in a dataset
$\hat{r}_{\max}$	Maximum distance between two points in a dataset
$\hat{r}_{\text{sepc}}$	Characteristic separation between clusters in a dataset
$\hat{r}_{\text{cdmax}}$	Maximum diameter of the clusters in a dataset
$\widehat{\mathcal{D}}_c$	Characteristic intrinsic dimension of the clusters
$\mathcal{D}_c$	Intrinsic dimension of the cluster distribution in a dataset
p, q	Integer exponents to calculate Cross-cloud plots
$\text{Cross}_{\mathcal{P},\mathcal{Q}}(r, p, q)$	Cross-cloud plots related to datasets $\mathcal{P}$ and $\mathcal{Q}$
$\text{Cross}_{\mathcal{P},\mathcal{Q}}(r)$	Cross-cloud plot with $p = q = 1$

24.3. APPLICATIONS

Data mining aims at extracting, from a given database, meaningful information that is not previously known. Clustering, classification, detection of correlation among attributes, discovery of association rules, and detection of outliers and/or rare cases are some of the data-mining processing results. In this chapter we concentrate on the following ones.

Detection of Correlations. The relations in databases usually have many attributes that are correlated with the others. Correlated attributes contribute to the increase in the complexity of any treatment that the dataset must be submitted to, as, for example, indexing and retrieval operations in a database, as well as the majority of the knowledge retrieval processes, such as decision trees and singular value decomposition, among others. If the correlation between the attributes is known, just the "basis" attributes need to be kept. Therefore, attribute selection is a classic goal, because a carefully chosen subset of attributes improves the performance and efficacy of a variety of algorithms. This is particularly true with redundant data, because many datasets can be well-approximated through the use of fewer attributes (dimensions). Since the correlated attributes can be re-obtained from the others, the dependent attributes should be detected and dropped from the dataset whenever it is possible.

Clustering. Finding clusters in a dataset is a classic goal. Despite the fact that data with high semantic contents often have their elements distributed in well-known classes, data gathered from more complex processes, or from processes not yet understood at their full extent, usually present groups, or regions of higher densities in their spatial distribution, that are not easily recognized as classes with a semantic meaning. This situation is specially frequent when analyzing high-dimensional data, because the natural sparseness of the points makes it difficult to recognize the clusters. Nonetheless, recognizing the existence of clusters in datasets is worthwhile to increase the operation of analysis processes, because many algorithms can be improved by using references to the clusters, whose properties summarize those of the elements therein.

Detection of Outliers and Rare Cases. Statistic- and geometric-based processes can be fooled by just a few elements significantly discrepant from the majority of the dataset. Discrepant points may be the result of measurement errors, in which case they should be ignored by the analysis processes, or they may represent special elements called rare cases, whose discovery and understanding are, in many situations, the main objective of the analysis processes. Getting the rare cases of a dataset is the target of, for example, identification of fraud in banking transactions, or studies of uncommon diseases in a population whose majority are health individuals.

Figure 24.7 illustrates the main processes that constitute data mining, highlighting those that can benefit from the theory of fractals.

In this chapter we discuss how concepts from the fractal theory are employed to design scalable algorithms for several data-mining processes. It is useful to

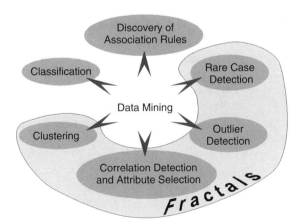

Figure 24.7. The main processes that constitute data mining, and those that can benefit from the theory of fractals.

remember the main definition of a fractal: "Fractals are self-similar objects"; that is, parts of any size of the object are similar (exactly or statistically) to the whole object. From a database perspective, it can be said that fractals are datasets that present the same properties for a useful range of scales or distances. Therefore, a fractal can be represented as a dataset so it can be represented as the set of tuples stored in a database relation. Any database relation with the property of self-similarity is a fractal. For example, consider that each employee of an enterprise earns a salary with a fixed part plus a bonus paid for each additional worked hour. Consider that each employee's salary has a different fixed part, but the value of the bonus is the same for everyone. The following relation stores these data:

```
Salary = {EmployeeName, FixedPart, ExtraHoursWorkd,
          GrossPayment}
```

where `GrossPayment = ExtraHoursWorkd*Bonus + FixedPart`. This equation has the form $y = a \cdot x + z$, which represents a plane. Notice that a plane is a fractal, planes are self-similar, and thus the `Salary` relation stores a fractal.

Hence, suppose a relation storing measurements from the real world in several attributes (dimensions). Due to natural fluctuations, a precise equation, such as the previous one, cannot always be stated. Moreover, the correlations existing between attributes are frequently not known, so relations storing every measured attribute, even those highly correlated, are common. Nonetheless, the data stored are closely fractals, enabling fractal techniques to be used to analyze them and exploiting the linear complexity of fractal-based algorithms over the number of elements and the number of dimensions in the dataset as well. The following sections present how to use the concepts from the fractal theory to develop scalable algorithms to implement some of the most demanded data mining processes.

24.3.1. Correlation Detection

When managing a large volume of data, a question that frequently arises is, "What part of this data is really important and should be kept?"

Because the relations of the databases usually have several correlated attributes, many datasets can be well-approximated through the use of fewer attributes (dimensions). Here we discuss how to use fractals to detect correlations. The main idea is to drop attributes that do not affect the fractal dimension of the dataset, considering that the correlation fractal dimension D_2 is relatively unaffected by redundant attributes. Because the LiBOC algorithm can compute D_2 in linear time with respect to the number of objects and the number of dimensions, the computational complexity of an algorithm that selects a subset of attributes determines the final complexity of the whole attribute selection algorithm.

An efficient approach to perform such a selection is to quickly discard some attributes from the original dataset, guided by fractal dimension measurements. Because the correlation fractal dimension D_2 of a dataset cannot exceed its embedding dimensionality E, there are at least $\lceil D_2 \rceil$ attributes that are not correlated to each other; that is, there are $\lceil \mathcal{D}_2 \rceil$ attributes which are independent from each other. As $\mathcal{D}_2 \leq E$, there are up to $E - \lceil \mathcal{D}_2 \rceil$ attributes correlated with the previous.

A successful algorithm to perform attribute selection was proposed in Traina et al. (2000), named the *Fractal Dimension Reduction* (FDR) algorithm. FDR performs a backward attribute elimination taking advantage of the linear-time cost provided by the LiBOC algorithm to compute $\mathcal{D}_2$. The FDR algorithm sequentially removes attributes that minimally contribute to $\mathcal{D}_2$. Considering the usual definition of a relation $\mathcal{P}$ as a set of tuples containing a set of E attributes—that is, $\mathcal{P} = \{A_1, A_2, \ldots A_E\}$—the following definition holds.

Definition 24.13. Given a point set $\mathcal{P}$ embedded in an E-dimensional space, the **partial fractal dimension** $p\mathcal{D}\{\mathcal{A}\}$ of a subset of attributes $\mathcal{A} \in \mathcal{P}$ is the correlation fractal dimension obtained by projecting the dataset into $\mathcal{A}$.

As explained in Section 24.2, the correlation fractal dimension $\mathcal{D}_2$ approaches $\mathcal{D}$. So, henceforth we use both of them interchangeably.

The FDR algorithm starts calculating the correlation fractal dimension of the whole dataset. Then it calculates E partial fractal dimensions, dropping one of the E attributes at a time and selecting the attribute A_i that leads to the minimum difference between the values of $p\mathcal{D}\{\mathcal{P} - \{A_i\}\}$ and the fractal dimension $\mathcal{D}$ of the whole dataset. If this difference is within a small threshold, we can be confident that the attribute A_i contributes almost nothing to the overall characteristics of the dataset. Therefore, A_i can be dropped from the list of attributes that characterize the dataset. The threshold depends on how precise the resulting dataset needs to be to preserve the desired characteristics of the original dataset.

The process continues repeating the previous step considering the remaining attributes. If there are two or more correlated attributes, the FDR algorithm sequentially drops them, until only a subset of $\lceil \mathcal{D}_2 \rceil$ attributes, independent from each other, remains. As an example, consider the `Plane` dataset composed of three attributes {a,b,c}, and let the third be a function of the previous two, for instance, c = a + b. In this dataset, any of the three attributes can be dropped, because the others can be used to obtain the one removed. However, if there is no other correlation linking the remaining two attributes, then none of them could be dropped without mischaracterizing the dataset. The algorithm generates the classification presenting the attributes ordered by their significance. That is, the first attribute to be dropped is the least important, the second attribute to be dropped is the second less important, and so on.

Figure 24.8 shows the Self-plot generated to calculate $\mathcal{D}$ and the corresponding values for $p\mathcal{D}$ generated by the FDR algorithm for the `Plane` dataset, with 10,000 values for attributes a and b in the interval $[0, 1]$. Attribute c is calculated as the sum of the other two attributes. Therefore, the relation `Plane` = {a,b,c} is in fact a plane, an object with intrinsic dimension 2, embedded in a three-dimensional space. Figure 24.8a and 24.8b both include a self-plot of the full dataset, as a reference to compare the other plots. Figure 24.8a also shows

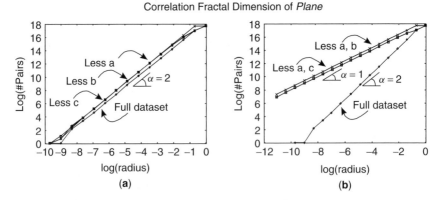

Figure 24.8. Self-plot of dataset `Plane` = {a,b,c}, where c = a + b.

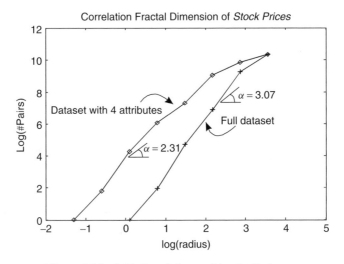

Figure 24.9. Self-plot of dataset `Stock Prices`.

the three plots used to calculate $p\mathcal{D}\{$`Plane` $-$ {a}$\}$, $p\mathcal{D}\{$`Plane` $-$ {b}$\}$, and $p\mathcal{D}\{$`Plane` $-$ {c}$\}$. Because these three plots have the same slope, any attribute can be removed without mischaracterizing the dataset. Supposing attribute a is removed, the process tries to remove another one. Figure 24.8b shows the two plots used to calculate the partial fractal dimensions $p\mathcal{D}\{$`Plane` $-$ {a,b}$\}$ and $p\mathcal{D}\{$`Plane` $-$ {a,c}$\}$. As can be seen, both plots reduce the resulting dimension significantly; therefore neither attribute b nor c can be removed simultaneously with a.

Figure 24.9 presents the results of applying the FDR algorithm to real data. The dataset `Stock Prices` includes the daily closing prices of 30 trading merchandise of the Dow Jones Industrial Average in 250 working days of 2002. Thus, `Stock Prices` is composed of 250 objects with 30 attributes each. As shown in Figure 24.9, the intrinsic dimension of the full dataset equals 3.07, indicating that at least $\lceil \mathcal{D} \rceil = 4$ attributes are required to adequately describe the dataset, as they are independent from each other. Figure 24.9 also depicts the self-plot of the dataset considering only the four most significant attributes output by the FDR algorithm. The partial fractal dimension of only these four attributes is $p\mathcal{D} = 2.31$, indicating that the remaining 26 attributes contribute with only $3.07 - 2.31 = 0.76$ to the intrinsic dimension of the whole dataset and to its overall distribution. Therefore, it is worthwhile using just those four most important attributes in processes that suffer from the dimensionality curse.

24.3.2. Global Features of a Dataset

In many applications it is important to know which objects from the dataset have the same, or similar, characteristics that identify groups or clusters. Hierarchies of objects can be built through the cluster organization, leading to faster processing of large datasets. When the dataset is multi- or high-dimensional, finding clusters is a more complex task, because the data are usually sparse, making the majority of distances between objects close to each other, that is, distances between near objects are about the same as distances between far objects (Beyer et al., 1999). This scenario highlights the importance of the intrinsic dimensionality of the dataset, which allows us to deal with the data regarding its actual distribution and enables us to bypass the concealing given by the high-embedded dimensionality. Moreover, because the size of real datasets is ever increasing, it is important to develop clustering techniques with low computational complexity, ideally, linear computational cost.

The analysis of the Self-plot can provide insights about interesting features of the dataset, including the existence of clusters and some of their properties. Because it is relatively inexpensive to be obtained, Self-plots can be used to quickly tell useful properties about a dataset, before more elaborated analyses are made.

Spanning of the Dataset. Besides of its intrinsic dimension, the following global features from a dataset can be estimated by only analyzing its self-plot.

The minimum distance between two points of the dataset is estimated by $\hat{r}_{\min}$, because the first radius for which the count-of-pairs given by the Self-plot is not zero.

The maximum distance between two points of the dataset—that is, the dataset diameter—is estimated by $\hat{r}_{\max}$, as the maximum value given by the increasing part of the Self-plot, taking account of the fact that the count-of-pairs remains constant for bigger radii.

Figure 24.10 illustrates the main properties of the Self-plot of a dataset, showing a two-dimensional dataset to the right and its corresponding Self-plot to the left. Figure 24.10a presents the Line15K dataset, consisting of 15,000 points

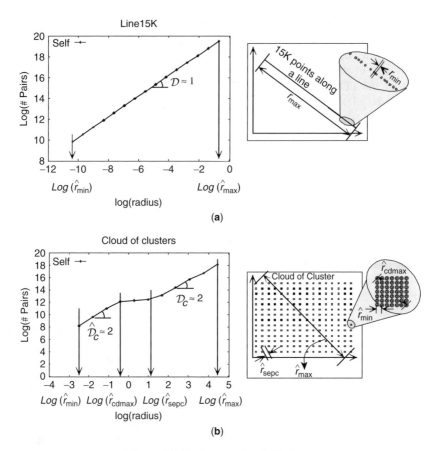

Figure 24.10. Interpreting Self-plots.

randomly distributed along a line. The corresponding Self-plot is linear, and its slope gives the value of $\mathcal{D}$ equal to 1, which is the theoretical intrinsic dimension of a line.

Finding the diameter or the minimum distance between two points of a dataset by traditional processes presents a computational complexity quadratic on the number of elements of the dataset, because the distance between every pair of objects must be calculated. The Self-plot, which can be obtained with linear complexity on the number of elements of the dataset, can estimate these minimum and maximum distances without performing any distance calculation. The Self-plot of the Line15K dataset presented in Figure 24.10a shows the estimation of these two features as $\hat{r}_{min}$ and $\hat{r}_{max}$.

Clustering. Whenever the Self-plot of a dataset is piecewise linear, the dataset presents different characteristic scales, so technically it is not a fractal as a whole. However, the occurrence of plateaus is especially interesting. Plateaus occur whenever the dataset is not homogeneous. If the Self-plot has at least two distinct regions, then there is more information to be extracted from the Self-plot. When the Self-plot exhibits flat areas along the graph, it means that the dataset is composed of clusters, and the maximum diameter of the clusters, as well as the characteristic separations between them, can also be approached. Therefore, global features of a dataset can be estimated by analyzing its Self-plot, as follows.

Cluster Detection. Whenever the Self-plot has a plateau (an almost flat region, with very low slope) occurring at any place from radius $\hat{r}_{\min}$ to $\hat{r}_{\max}$, the dataset is probably composed of clusters.

Figure 24.10b shows an example of a dataset containing clusters. The Clusters256 dataset is composed of 256 uniformly distributed clusters, each of them with 7×7 points in a 2D manifold. The corresponding self-plot presents a flat region in the middle of the graph.

The maximum diameter of the clusters in the dataset is estimated by $\hat{r}_{\mathrm{cdmax}}$, as the largest radius of the first increasing part of the Self-plot, just before the plateau of the plot.

The characteristic separations between clusters in the dataset is estimated by $\hat{r}_{\mathrm{sepc}}$, as the largest radius for which the count-of-pairs given by the Self-plot remains constant, before starting to increase again.

The characteristic intrinsic dimension of the clusters in the dataset is estimated by $\widehat{\mathcal{D}}_c$, as the slope of the Self-plot for radii lower than $\hat{r}_{\mathrm{cdmax}}$. Notice that each cluster may present a different internal distribution of elements, so $\widehat{\mathcal{D}}_c$ represents the average behavior of the whole set of clusters.

The intrinsic dimension of the cluster distribution in the dataset is estimated by $\mathcal{D}_c$, as the slope of the Self-plot for radii larger than $\hat{r}_{\mathrm{sepc}}$. Notice that the precision of this measurement depends on the number of clusters in the dataset: The larger the number of clusters, the more precise the measurement of $\mathcal{D}_c$. The quantity of clusters can also be estimated by the size of the region with radii larger than $\hat{r}_{\mathrm{sepc}}$: The larger the number of points in the Self-plot in this region, the larger the number of clusters in the dataset.

The flat region in the middle of the Self-plot from the Clusters256 dataset occurs between radii $\hat{r}_{\mathrm{cdmax}}$ and $\hat{r}_{\mathrm{sepc}}$, as shown in the Self-plot to the left of Figure 24.10b and in the drawing of the dataset to the right of the figure. Notice that the values presented in the plots are actually the log of the radii.

As illustrated in Figure 24.10b, the clusters within dataset Clusters256 are equal-sized and uniformly distributed, so the maximum diameter of the clusters ($\hat{r}_{\mathrm{cdmax}}$) and the characteristic separation among them ($\hat{r}_{\mathrm{sepc}}$) can be precisely obtained from the Self-plot. However, the distribution of clusters in real datasets are usually nonuniform, and therefore a flat region may not exist in the plot.

Nevertheless, the global features of the dataset can be estimated by analyzing regions of the graph with different steepness.

As an example, consider the dataset `Cattle`, composed of 31 attributes and 10,001 objects. This dataset records biological measurements over a population of cattle in several farms. The measurements include weight, dimensions of various body parts, and clinical tests of blood at the birth, at the 6th and 12th months of each animal. In order to visualize the dataset, we used the FastMapDB tool (Barioni et al., 2002), an interactive visualization tool based on the FastMap algorithm (Faloutsos and Lin, 1995). FastMap is a dimensionality reduction technique that maps the original attributes into lower dimensions. Figure 24.11a shows the distribution of the cattle data mapped into three dimensions, showing that in fact

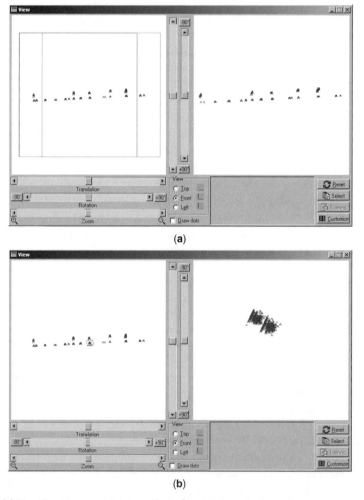

(a)

(b)

Figure 24.11. Visualization of dataset `Cattle`: (**a**) Distribution of clusters; (**b**) shape of the clusters.

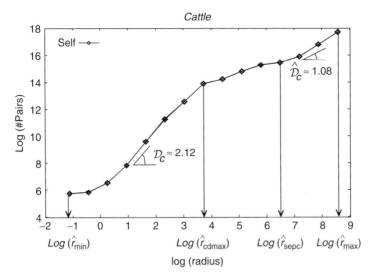

Figure 24.12. Self-plot of dataset `Cattle`.

there are clusters in the dataset `Cattle`. The left window presents the mapping of the whole dataset; the 3D-cube delimits the points that were manipulated by *affine* transformations and visualized in the right window. Notice that the clusters are almost aligned. Figure 24.11b gives a zoom-in view of few clusters, revealing their general shape, which is similar to a hexahedron.

By analyzing the Self-plot of the dataset `Cattle`, we can estimate its global features, as presented in Figure 24.12. The characteristic intrinsic dimension of the clusters is estimated at $\widehat{\mathcal{D}_c} \approx 2.12$, which indicates an object with dimension larger than that of a plane, in accordance with the shape of the clusters shown in Figure 24.11b. Similarly, the intrinsic dimension of the cluster distribution is estimated at $\mathcal{D}_c \approx 1.08$, reflecting the aligned distribution visualized in Figure 24.11a.

Finally, the last global feature of a dataset that can be inferred from its Self-plot is the existence of outliers, which can be recognized as follows.

Outlier Detection. Whenever the Self-plot has a plateau occurring at its largest radii, the dataset has outliers. This plateau is due to a few points lying far from the region occupied by the majority of the points, characterizing the presence of outliers. Notice that the plateau only occurs when there are few outliers, otherwise they are not considered discrepant points.

24.3.3. Relationships Between Two Datasets

Frequently it is interesting to obtain information regarding how two datasets containing objects from the same domain are related to each other—for instance, when it is necessary to compare two classes of objects from a given dataset, such as in the upcoming example. Given feature vectors of healthy and of nonhealthy patients, we want to answer the following questions: "Are the two feature vectors separable?" "What is the smallest/largest pairwise distance across the two datasets?" "From which of the two datasets does a new feature vector come?"

Those questions can also be answered using concepts from the fractal theory, whereas a process slightly different from that previously described must be performed. Suppose there are two datasets $\mathcal{P}$ and $\mathcal{Q}$ of E-dimensional points from the same domain. Suppose we construct the set of grids with cells of varying side size r as discussed in Section 24.2.3, but now involving two datasets. Let $C_{\mathcal{P},i}$ and $C_{\mathcal{Q},i}$ be the number of points from datasets $\mathcal{P}$ and $\mathcal{Q}$, respectively, in the ith cell, and let $p > 0$ and $q > 0$ be two integer exponents. The grid partitions the minimum bounding box encompassing both datasets. Then, the following definition holds.

Definition 24.14. The **Cross-cloud plot** between the two datasets $\mathcal{P}$ and $\mathcal{Q}$, with $N_{\mathcal{P}}$ and $N_{\mathcal{Q}}$ points, respectively, is the plot of

$$\text{Cross}_{\mathcal{P},\mathcal{Q}}(r, p, q) = \frac{\log(N_{\mathcal{P}} * N_{\mathcal{Q}})}{\log(N_{\mathcal{P}}^p * N_{\mathcal{Q}}^q)} * \log\left(\sum_i C_{\mathcal{P},i}^p * C_{\mathcal{Q},i}^q\right) \qquad (24.12)$$

versus $\log(r)$.

Equation 24.12 extends Eq. (24.4) used to define the generalized fractal dimension. Notice that the normalization factor scales the Cross-cloud plot, maximizing the information presented.

For $p = q = 1$ the Cross-cloud plot gives the cumulative distribution function of the pairwise distances between points in the two datasets $\mathcal{P}$ and $\mathcal{Q}$ (Faloutsos et al., 2000). Therefore, the case in which $p = q = 1$ is used as a reference, and the p, q arguments are omitted when both are equal to one. For the sake of simplicity we also omit the subscripts $\mathcal{P}$ and $\mathcal{Q}$ from the Cross-cloud plot when it is clear which datasets are involved. That is,

$$\text{Cross}(r) = \text{Cross}_{\mathcal{P},\mathcal{Q}}(r) \hat{=} \text{Cross}_{\mathcal{P},\mathcal{Q}}(r, 1, 1)$$

It must also be noted that applying the cross-cloud plot over the same dataset results in the Self-plot; that is, $\text{Cross}_{\mathcal{P},\mathcal{P}}(r) \hat{=} \text{Self}_{\mathcal{P}}(r)$. An interesting property of the Cross-cloud plot is that its slope is always greater than or equal to the largest slope of the Self-plots of the datasets.

Comparing the Self-plots of two datasets and the corresponding Cross-cloud plot enables one to gather interesting features regarding the relationship between both datasets. In order to provide a consistent technique to perform such comparison, we give the following definition.

Definition 24.15. The **Tri-plot** of two datasets $\mathcal{P}$ and $\mathcal{Q}$ is the graph which contains the Cross-plot $\text{Cross}(r)$ and the normalized self-plots for both datasets $(\text{Self}_{\mathcal{P}}(r) + \log(N_{\mathcal{P}}/N_{\mathcal{Q}}))$ and $(\text{Self}_{\mathcal{Q}}(r) + \log(N_{\mathcal{Q}}/N_{\mathcal{P}}))$.

Notice that the normalization factors $\log(N_\mathcal{P}/N_\mathcal{Q})$ and $\log(N_\mathcal{Q}/N_\mathcal{P})$ only translate the Self-plots, preserving the steepness of the curves.

Tri-plots allow us to determine the relationship between the two datasets under analysis. If the datasets are self-similar—that is, their Self-plots are linear for a meaningful range of radii—then the slopes of the curves can be used to compare the datasets. Moreover, this kind of analysis can also be applied to datasets that are not self-similar—that is, do not have linear Self-plots—such as datasets consisting of clusters. Thus, we refer to the "steepness" and "similarity" between the plots as measurements for comparison, as defined as follows.

Definition 24.16. The **steepness** of a plot is the slope of its regression line (that is, the least-squared fitting line). The **dissimilarity** of two given plots is measured by the sum of the root mean square of the differences between them.

Interpreting Cross-Cloud Plots. Tri-plots are useful tools to analyze how two datasets relate to each other. Figure 24.13 presents an example of a Tri-plot, where dataset $\mathcal{P}$ is a randomly generated set of 6000 points of a line ($y + x = 0 | x, y \in [0, 1]$), and dataset $\mathcal{Q}$ is a Sierpinsky triangle with 6561 points. These two datasets were chosen to highlight some properties of the Tri-plots, which can be used to estimate interesting features of the relationship between the given datasets. Such features (depicted in Figure 24.13) are discussed next.

The minimum distance between the two datasets is estimated by $\hat{s}_{\min}$, which is the smallest nonzero value of the $\log(r)$ axis in the Cross(r) plot.

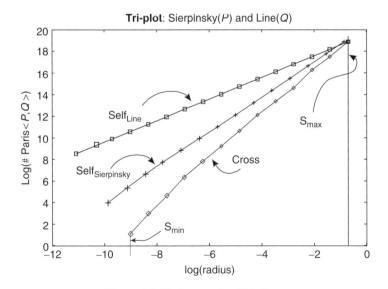

Figure 24.13. Interpreting Tri-plots.

The maximum distance between the two datasets is estimated by $\hat{s}_{max}$, which is the largest value of the $\log(r)$ axis before the Cross(r) plot turns flat.

Detection of duplicate points in the datasets. Whenever the Cross-cloud plot has a flat part for very small radii, there are points in the dataset $\mathcal{P}$ that coincide with points in the dataset $\mathcal{Q}$.

Detection of the relative positioning of the datasets. If the Cross-cloud plot is linear, its slope depends on the relative positioning of the two datasets, so the following three properties can be estimated: shape, placement, and collocation.

The **shape** of a dataset means its formation law. The **placement** of a dataset stands for its position and orientation. Two datasets are said to be **collocated** if they have their minimum bounding boxes highly overlapped.

Two datasets can have the same shape but different placements—for example, two noncollinear lines. If a dataset is manipulated by *affine* transformations, the resulting dataset can have the same shape of the original, but different placement. Indeed, two datasets with the same intrinsic dimensionality can have different shapes. For instance, a line and a circumference have the same intrinsic dimensionality ($\mathcal{D} = 1$), but different shapes.

Thus, the analysis of the Tri-plots can provide information about the intrinsic structure and the global relationship between two datasets ($\mathcal{P}$ and $\mathcal{Q}$). The rules to analyze and classify such relationship are presented in Table 24.2.

Rule one takes place when the three graphs in the Tri-plot are on top of each other. In this case, both datasets probably have the same intrinsic dimensionality, shape, and placement. Rule one is also applied either when one dataset is a subset of the other or when both datasets are samples from a bigger one. Rule two occurs when the steepness of Self$_\mathcal{P}$ and Self$_\mathcal{Q}$ are similar and Cross is moderately steeper than both. In this case, $\mathcal{P}$ and $\mathcal{Q}$ probably have the same intrinsic dimensionality, but they come from different placements.

Rule three occurs when the steepness of Cross is much steeper than both Self$_\mathcal{P}$ and Self$_\mathcal{Q}$ (does not matter whether they are similar or not), meaning that the datasets are disjointed. For two intersecting datasets, the Cross steepness is not so far from the steepness of their Self-plots. However, if the Cross is much steeper than both Self$_\mathcal{P}$ and Self$_\mathcal{Q}$, it means that the minimum distance between points from the two datasets is bigger than the average distance of the nearest neighbors of points in each dataset, so $\mathcal{P}$ and $\mathcal{Q}$ are disjointed. In fact, this case leads to the conclusion that both datasets are well-defined clusters; hence they should be separable by traditional clustering techniques.

Now, consider without loss of generality that Self$_\mathcal{P}$ is the steeper between Self$_\mathcal{P}$ and Self$_\mathcal{Q}$. In rule four, Cross equals Self$_\mathcal{P}$ and the dataset $\mathcal{Q}$ is a submanifold of the dataset $\mathcal{P}$. The steepness of the Cross cannot be smaller than the steepness of the Self-plots; thus the points in dataset $\mathcal{Q}$ have a stronger correlation than the points in dataset $\mathcal{P}$. As mentioned earlier, rule one deals with the

TABLE 24.2. Rules to Analyze Relationships Between Two Datasets

Conditions	Meaning
• $\text{Self}_\mathcal{P}$ and $\text{Self}_\mathcal{Q}$ have same steepness, and • Cross have the same steepness of $\text{Self}_\mathcal{P}$ and $\text{Self}_\mathcal{Q}$.	1. Probably datasets $\mathcal{P}$ and $\mathcal{Q}$ are statistically identical.
• $\text{Self}_\mathcal{P}$ and $\text{Self}_\mathcal{Q}$ have same steepness, and • The Cross steepness is comparable with the steepness of $\text{Self}_\mathcal{P}$ and $\text{Self}_\mathcal{Q}$.	2. Both datasets have the same intrinsic dimensionality.
• $\text{Self}_\mathcal{P}$ and $\text{Self}_\mathcal{Q}$ have same steepness, and • Cross is much steeper than both $\text{Self}_\mathcal{P}$ and $\text{Self}_\mathcal{Q}$.	3. The datasets are disjointed.
• $\text{Self}_\mathcal{P}$ has different steepness from $\text{Self}_\mathcal{Q}$, and • Cross has the same steepness of $\text{Self}_\mathcal{P}$ or $\text{Self}_\mathcal{Q}$.	4. The dataset with the less steep Self-plot is probably a proper submanifold of the other.
• $\text{Self}_\mathcal{P}$ has different steepness from $\text{Self}_\mathcal{Q}$, and • The Cross steepness is comparable with the steepness of $\text{Self}_\mathcal{P}$ and $\text{Self}_\mathcal{Q}$.	5. Needs further analysis
• $\text{Self}_\mathcal{P}$ has different steepness from $\text{Self}_\mathcal{Q}$, and • Cross is much steeper than both $\text{Self}_\mathcal{P}$ and $\text{Self}_\mathcal{Q}$.	6. The datasets are disjointed

situation in which both datasets are subsets of a larger one, or one is a subset of another, but there is no rule to extract the subsets. On the other hand, rule four deals with the occurrence of subsets for which there are rules to choose points that pertain to the submanifold (dataset $\text{Self}_\mathcal{Q}$ in our description).

A real-world example for rule four can be shown by analyzing the relationship of different classes from the dataset Thalassemia. This dataset records five clinical measurements from the blood of newborn children that can lead to the identification of thalassemia—a group of genetic blood disorders causing an anemia that begins in early childhood and lasts throughout life. Because early identification of the problem can help improving the patients' quality of life, analyzing the data provided by the attributes stored in the dataset Thalassemia should be a useful tool. The objects in this dataset are classified either as Normal or as one of four different thalassemia disorders.

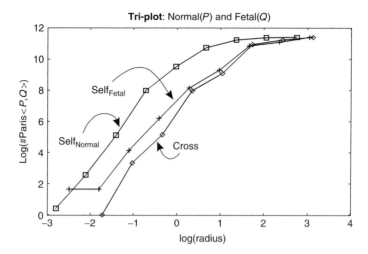

Figure 24.14. Tri-plot of datasets Normal and Fetal.

The experiment shown here compares objects from the Normal and the Fetal classes, which have 483 and 184 samples, respectively. The relationship between these datasets is depicted in Figure 24.14. Notice that Self$_{Normal}$ and Cross exhibit similar steepness, and both are steeper than Self$_{Fetal}$. Thus, rule four dictates that the dataset Fetal is a submanifold of Normal and that it is separable. Taking this relationship into account can increase the accuracy of mining techniques applied to a dataset including normal samples and those classified as thalassemia fetal. In fact, this experiment has been confirmed in real medical procedures, helping to reduce the number of clinical measurements. It is accurate to say that the original number of attributes used in clinical exams to detect thalassemia used to be 11, and the presented techniques helped to reduce them to the five shown in this experiment, therefore reducing the number of blood exams required from newborns.

Rule five takes place when P and Q are not similar, and the Cross steepness is only moderately steeper than Self$_P$ and Self$_Q$. In this case, both datasets come from a different placement, have a different shape and intrinsic dimensionality, and are not related to each other. They are, however, collocated, or at least intersecting. This means that although part of the datasets may be separable, it would not be true for the entire dataset, or for both datasets. Whenever rule five occurs, the situation must be further analyzed, using other techniques. Finally, rule six corresponds to a pair of datasets with different shapes, placements, and intrinsic dimensions. Therefore, they have no relation to each other, neither spatial nor conceptual.

The rule six is illustrated in Figure 24.15, which gives the Tri-plots of the datasets Benign and Malignant, both obtained from the Wisconsin Breast Cancer Database, reported by Dr. William H. Wolberg, University of Wisconsin Hospitals, Madison. Both datasets Benign and Malignant are composed of nine attributes whose values are provided by exams of breast cells. The former set

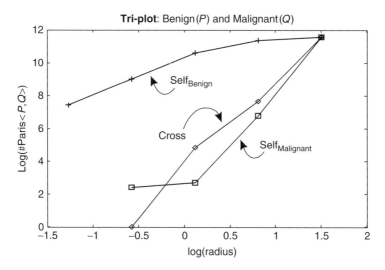

Figure 24.15. Tri-plot of datasets `Benign` and `Malignant`.

contains 444 instances (or objects) of benign cases, and the latter has 239 cases of malignant cancer. Because the `Malignant` dataset has few objects, its Self-plot and the Cross-plot were generated with only four points each. Although five points are desirable, it is still possible to get useful information from the plots, as follows. Because Breast Cancer is a well-known database from the data- mining community, its use here, despite having fewer than ideal samples, can provide a good illustration of the methods shown in this chapter.

By analyzing the Tri-plots, we can tell that $Self_{Benign}$ and $Self_{Malignant}$ exhibit different steepness and that Cross is much steeper than both. According to rule six, `Benign` and `Malignant` are disjointed, and therefore a dataset containing cases from both of them can be efficiently submitted to clustering and classification techniques.

Recall that both Self-plots and Cross-plots count the occupation of each grid cell. Therefore, all the estimates we have just discussed can be obtained with a single processing pass, now over both datasets, without effectively computing any distance. Furthermore, these techniques are also able to be applied to high-dimensional datasets as well, because the counting of points inside the grid cells does not suffer from the dimensionality curse.

24.4. RELATED WORK

The automatic discovery of meaningful patterns and relationships hidden in vast repositories of raw information has become an issue of great importance, and data-mining techniques aim at dealing with this challenge. Fractals have success-fully been used to support several data-mining techniques so far; among the most known are:

- Clustering detection and classification (Moon et al., 2001; Barbara and Chen, 2003), which are used to reveal data items having similar structure as well as to say which cluster a new unclassified item should be associated with.

- Attribute selection (Traina et al., 2000), which allows to retain only the relevant information instead of overfill the storage device with redundant data.

- Data correlation (Traina et al., 2001; Pan and Faloutsos, 2002), whose main goal is to explore the relationship between two or more multidimensional datasets.

- Time series forecasting (Chakrabarti and Faloutsos, 2002), which aims at predicting the incoming values over some future time period.

- Selectivity estimation for query planning (Belussi and Faloutsos, 1995; Faloutsos et al., 2000), allowing to estimate beforehand the effort demanded on performing costly operations, such as spatial join.

- Traffic estimation in networks (Adibi et al., 2002; Palmer et al., 2002; Faloutsos et al., 1999), which can be used to estimate parameters of the network as well as to design and to evaluate the performance of protocols.

- Dimensionality reduction (Pagel et al., 2000; Korn et al., 2001), which allows to take advantage of the actual or intrinsic data distribution instead of the uniformity distribution assumption, which was proven to be not realistic (Christodoulakis, 1984).

- Development of indexing structures for complex and high-dimensional data (Filho et al., 2001), enhancement (Kamel and Faloutsos, 1994; Traina et al., 2002b), and analysis (Faloutsos and Kamel, 1994; Traina et al., 2002a) of spatial and metric access methods as well.

It is important to highlight that for all the aforementioned subjects, the techniques based on the use of fractals are robust and work well, even for large and high-dimensional data, where traditional methods frequently fail.

24.5. SUMMARY

Data-mining techniques include a broad range of analysis tools, from very punctual approaches that intend to locate specific characteristics from the data, to very wide ones that just provide a high-level overview of the data. However, the majority of the approaches used in mining trials, regardless of being punctual or wide, are based on techniques that rely on algorithms with relatively high computational complexity on both the number of samples and the number of attributes (dimensions) of the dataset. The techniques presented in this chapter, based on the fractal theory, provide algorithms that can analyze data in a computational complexity linear on both the number of samples and the number of dimensions. These techniques are well-suited to wide processes, thus they can be used as an initial probe on datasets, from which more specific—and costly—analyzers can be executed.

We presented several analysis techniques based on the Self-plots and Cross-plots—a set of graphs obtained from datasets through linear complexity algorithms based on the theory of fractals. Each of the plots can provide estimations about meaningful features of the datasets, as, for example, the intrinsic dimension of a dataset, the minimum distance between two points of a dataset or from two distinct datasets, the diameter of a dataset, or the distance between two datasets or between points of different classes from a dataset. Moreover, the plots can spot if a dataset has clusters or outliers or if two datasets have coincident points, and they can reveal correlations inside a dataset or between two datasets. Interestingly, the results of the Self-plots and Cross-plots are barely affected by the existence of noise, provided that the measurement error is lower than the minimum size r of the grid cell, and thus it does not affect the mean counting of occupancies.

The Self-plots and Cross-plots operate counting the occupation of points in grid cells recursively defined over the datasets. Therefore, every estimation is obtained by performing a single processing pass over a given dataset, without effectively computing any distance between points. Because these countings are easily performed, the overall process is very fast, and can be applied to low or high-dimensional datasets as well, being free from the dimensionality curse.

Another interesting property of the Self-plots and Cross-plots is that they are based on estimates, and therefore they tend to follow the natural human perception of the dataset's features more than the strict geometric definition of the data. For instance, if the overlapping of the minimum bounding boxes detected when estimating the relative positioning of two datasets is small and occurs only at the periphery of the datasets (where the points are sparsely distributed), then the Tri-plots indicate the datasets as noncollocated, as opposed to the overlapping indication dictated by the strict definition of geometric placement. Intuitively, humans would say that datasets in such situation are not overlapping.

ACKNOWLEDGMENTS

The authors thank the financial support provided by FAPESP (Fundação de Amparo à Pesquisa do Estado de São Paulo, Brazil) and CNPq (Conselho Nacional de Desenvolvimento Científico e Tecnológico, Brazil). They also gratefully acknowledge the insightful contributions of Prof. Dr. Christos Faloutsos to the material of this work.

REFERENCES

Adibi, J., Shen, W.-M., and Noorbakhsh, E., Self-similarity for data mining and predictive modeling—a case study for network data, in *6th Pacific-Asia Conference, PAKDD 2002,*

Vol. 2336 of *Advances in Knowledge Discovery and Data Mining*, Taipel, Taiwan, Springer-Verlag, Heidelberg, pp. 210–217 (2002).

Barbara, D., and Chen, P., Using self-similarity to cluster large data sets, *Data Mining and Knowledge Discovery* **7**(2), 123–152 (2003).

Barioni, M. C. N., Botelho, E., Faloutsos, C., Razente, H. L., Traina, A. J. M., and Traina, C., Data visualization in rdbms, in *Proceedings of the IASTED International Conference Information Systems and Databases (ISDB 2002)*, Tokyo, Japan, pp. 264–269, September 2002.

Belussi, A., and Faloutsos, C., Estimating the selectivity of spatial queries using the "correlation" fractal dimension, in *Proceedings of the 21th International Conference on Very Large Data Bases (VLDB '95)*, Zurich, Switzerland, pp. 299–310, September 1995.

Beyer, K., Godstein, J., Ramakrishnan, R., and Shaft, U., When is "nearest neighbor" meaningful? in Beeri, C., and Buneman, P., eds., *7th International Conference (ICDT '99)*, Vol. 1540 of *Lecture Notes in Computer Science*, Jerusalem, Israel, Springer, Berlin, pp. 217–235, 1999.

Chakrabarti, D., and Faloutsos, C., F4: Large-scale automated forecasting using fractals, in *International Conference on Information and Knowledge Management (CIKM)*, Vol. 1, McLean, VA—EUA, ACM Press, Menlo Park, CA, pp. 2–9, 2002.

Christodoulakis, S., Implications of certain assumptions in database performance evaluation, *ACM Transactions on Database Systems* **9**(9), 163–186 (1984).

Faloutsos, C., and Kamel, I., Beyond uniformity and independence: Analysis of *r*-trees using the concept of fractal dimension, in *ACM Symposium on Principles of Database Systems (PODS)*, Minneapolis, MN, ACM Press, Menlo Park, CA, pp. 4–13 (1994).

Faloutsos, C., and Lin, K.-I., FastMap: A fast algorithm for indexing, data-mining and visualization of traditional and multimedia datasets, in *Proceedings of the 1995 ACM SIGMOD International Conference on Management of Data (SIGMOD '95)*, San Jose, CA, pp. 163–174, May 1995.

Faloutsos, M., Faloutsos, P., and Faloutsos, C., On power-law relationships of the internet topology, in *SIGCOMM 1999*, Vol. 1, Cambridge, MA, ACM Press, Menlo Park, CA, pp. 251–262, 1999.

Faloutsos, C., Seeger, B., Traina, A. J. M., and Traina, C., Spatial join selectivity using power laws, in *Proceedings of the 2000 ACM SIGMOD International Conference on Management of Data (SIG-MOD '00)*, Dallas, TX, pp. 177–188, May 2000.

Fayyad, U. M., and Uthurusamy, R., Evolving data into mining solutions for insights, *Communications of the ACM* **45**(8), 28–31 (2002).

Filho, R. F. S., Traina, A. J. M., Traina, C., and Faloutsos, C., Similarity search without tears: The omni family of all-purpose access methods, in *International Conference on Data Engineering (ICDE)*, Heidelberg, Germany, IEEE Computer Society, Los Alamitos, CA pp. 623–630, 2001.

Kamel, I., and Faloutsos, C., Hilbert *r*-tree: An improved *r*-tree using fractals, in *Proceedings of 20th International Conference on Very Large Data Bases (VLDB '94)*, Santiago de Chile, Chile, pp. 500–509, September 1994.

Korn, F., Pagel, B.-U., and Faloutsos, C., On the "dimensionality curse" and the "self-similarity blessing," *IEEE Transactions on Knowledge and Data Engineering* **13**(1), 96–111 (2001).

Mandelbrot, B. B., *The Fractal Geometry of Nature: Updated and Augmented*, W. H. Freeman, New York, 1983.

Moon, B., Jagadish, H. V., Faloutsos, C., and Saltz, J. H., Analysis of the clustering properties of the Hilbert space-filling curve, *IEEE Transactions on Knowledge and Data Engineering* **13**(1), 124–141 (2001).

Pagel, B.-U., Korn, F., and Faloutsos, C., Deflating the dimensionality curse using multiple fractal dimensions, in *Proceedings of the 16th International Conference on Data Engineering (ICDE '00)*, San Diego, CA, pp. 589–598, 2000.

Palmer, C. R., Gibbons, P. B., and Faloutsos, C., Anf: A fast and scalable tool for data mining in massive graphs, in *ACM International Conference on Knowledge Discovery and Data Mining (KDD)*, Vol. 1, Edmonton, Alberta, Canada, ACM Press, Menlo Park, CA, pp. 81–90, 2002.

Pan, J.-Y., and Faloutsos, C., Geoplot: Spatial data mining on video libraries, in *International Conference on Information and Knowledge Management (CIKM)*, Vol. 1, McLean, VA—EUA, ACM Press, Menlo Park, CA, pp. 405–412, 2002.

Porter, J., Disk trend 1998 report, 1998.

Schroeder, M., *Fractals, Chaos, Power Laws: Minutes from an Infinite Paradise*, W. H. Freeman, New York, 1991.

Schuster, H. G., *Deterministic Chaos*, Physik-Verlag, Weinheim, Germany, 1984.

Traina, A. J. M., Traina, C., Papadimitriou, S., and Faloutsos, C., Tri-plots: Scalable tools for multidimensional data mining, in *The Seventh ACM SIGKDD International Conference on Knowledge Discovery and Data Mining—KDD-2001*, Provost, F., and Ramakrishnan, S., eds., San Francisco, CA, pp. 184–193, 2001.

Traina, C., Traina, A., Wu, L., and Faloutsos, C., Fast feature selection using fractal dimension, in *Proceedings XV Brazilian Database Symposium (SBBD '00)*, João Pessoa, Brazil, pp. 158–171, October 2000.

Traina, C., Traina, A. J. M., Faloutsos, C., and Seeger, B., Fast indexing and visualization of metric datasets using slim-trees, *IEEE Transactions on Knowledge and Data Engineering* **14**(2), 244–260 (2002a).

Traina, C., Traina, A. J. M., Filho, R. F. S., and Faloutsos, C., How to improve the pruning ability of dynamic metric access methods, in *Eleventh International Conference on Information and Knowledge Management (CIKM 2002)*, McLean, VA—EUA, ACM Press, Menlo Park, CA, pp. 219–226, 2002b.

25

GENETIC SEARCH FOR LOGIC STRUCTURES IN DATA

Witold Pedrycz

25.1. INTRODUCTION

Logic and fuzzy logic occupy a dominant role in what could be called transparent modeling—a trend strongly supported by Granular Computing (Bargiela and Pedrycz, 2002). The constructs of transparent modeling come with a well-defined semantics (Casillas et al., 2003; Dickerson and Lan, 1995; Setnes et al., 1998; Gomez-Skarmeta et al., 1996; Sudkamp and Hammel, 1996). The models can be easily interpreted as a collection of rules, analogies, associations, or other basic entities describing experimental data. In the synergistic collaboration with fuzzy logic, neural networks deliver a vast array of learning abilities ranging from unsupervised to fully supervised schemes. The attractiveness of fuzzy neurocomputing directly relates to the design of effective and highly symbiotic links that are established between fuzzy sets and neural networks. In the array of approaches, architectures, and detailed models (Kosko, 1991; Mitra and Pal, 1994, 1995; Pal and Mitra, 1988), we encounter different schemes of interaction between fuzzy sets and neurocomputing and other related adaptation schemes. The essence of the successful synergy lies in the retention of the well-defined identity of the two contributing technologies. In most of the synergistic frameworks, one of them becomes predominant; this results in either more profound learning abilities (and accuracy of approximation) or higher transparency and interpretability of the model. The accuracy–interpretability trade-off is commonly visible in the constructs of fuzzy neurocomputing. Ideally, we would like to see these two modeling requirements being met to the highest extent. The evident requirement leading to the satisfaction of such objective calls for the elementary constructs

Next Generation of Data-Mining Applications. Edited by Kantardzic and Zurada
ISBN 0-471-65605-4 © 2005 the Institute of Electrical and Electronics Engineers, Inc.

exhibiting high learning abilities along with the sound logic underpinnings. Interestingly, the constructs currently available in the literature position themselves on one or another side of spectrum of the fuzzy neurocomputing. Some of them lean quite visible toward fuzzy rule-based systems with very limited learning capabilities that could be exhibited in a quite constrained way (say, as adjustable confidence factors of individual rules). There could be a substantial learning slant and high adaptive capabilities that tend to compromise the interpretability of the resulting construct. For instance, we may see systems with a significant number of layers where each layer is assumed to carry out some logic processing, but sometimes those seem to be pretentious claims permeating the literature rather than strongly substantiated statements. For instance, the product operation used in some input layer of some "standard" constructs may refer to the *and* operation. This is fully legitimate because the *and* operation is one among t-norms. There is, however, some uneasiness to accept the standard sum as the model of the *or* operation (unfortunately this is a well-rooted position one can easily encounter in the literature). Overall, there is a tendency toward far more attention being placed on the neural side of neurofuzzy systems with the approximation capabilities being highly glorified and focused upon and the interpretation abilities being left out and quietly reduced. This tendency may not be surprising at all: The approximation abilities are easier to quantify and eventually easier to realize.

The underlying conjecture of this study is that neurofuzzy systems should be constructed on a basis of simple processing units—fuzzy (logic) neurons whose transparency and learning abilities are accentuated to the highest possible extent (Hirota and Pedryez, 1994; Pedrycz, 1991b, 1993; Pedrycz, et al., 1995; Hirota and Pedryez, 1996). This would assure us that the resulting constructs will directly benefit from these features that will manifest in the overall network. The notion of logic (two-valued logic) has been broadly exploited as the sound basis for Boolean networks. On the other hand, the concept of fuzzy logic and logic processing seems to be far less exploited in this setting.

The primordial objectives of this study are fourfold:

- The revisit and systematize the array of the existing fuzzy logic neurons (fuzzy neurons, for short) with respect to their functionality, underlying logic, interpretation aspects, and learning abilities. These are well-documented in the existing literature but still require some systematization and "readability."

- To develop architectures of fuzzy neural networks based on different fuzzy neurons. Because the systems of such character are inherently heterogeneous, their functionality could be quite diversified and a suitable arrangement of the neurons in successive layers could result in a surprisingly rich collection of logic expressions and nonlinear characteristics of the neural mappings.

- To discuss various schemes of the development of the networks with a special emphasis put toward the structural aspects of learning and its realization in terms of genetic optimization.

- To discuss interpretability of fuzzy networks and introduce means of their effective readability through pertinent pruning mechanisms.

The organization of the material is structured in a way that reflects the research agenda outlined above. First, in Section 25.2 we introduce basic processing modules of fuzzy neurons and elaborate on their underlying taxonomy that is pertinent when building a heterogeneous network and allocating the neurons to successive layers. The understanding of the functionality of the neurons is essential to the resulting characteristics of the networks and their further interpretation. Section 25.3 highlights the relationships between the fuzzy neurons and fuzzy relational equations. This is of particular interest because they help us reveal links in terms of existing analytical, semianalytical, and optimization mechanisms of solving this category of equations. A general topology of the network is outlined in Section 25.4, which is followed by a comprehensive discussion on the evolutionary development framework of such networks (Section 25.5). Section 25.6 links the logic-driven network with the modeling environment, and this helps us emphasize the links with the existing experimental data. Interpretation issues of the networks that lead us to a systematic way of pruning connections and eliminating reference points of the neurons are covered in Section 25.7. Experimental studies are included in Section 25.8.

The terminology used here adheres to the standards used in two-valued logic, fuzzy logic, and fuzzy logic. The logic operators are modeled via t- and s-norms. Let us briefly recall that by a t-norm we mean a two-argument function $t: [0, 1]^2 \rightarrow [0, 1]$ such that it satisfies the requirement of associativity, commutativity, is increasing, and meets two boundary conditions: $xt0 = 0$ and $xt1 = x$ for any x in [0,1]. Owing to these properties, t-norms serve as generalized models of the *and* connective (operator). If we confine ourselves to the case of a two-valued logic, the boundary conditions of t-norms produce truth values encountered in this logic. Then s-norms are defined in the same way as t-norms, with the exception of the boundary conditions that in this definition read in the form $xt0 = x$ and $xt1 = 1$ for any x in [0,1]. Interestingly, given a certain t-norm, we may define the corresponding (dual) s-norm through the use of the DeMorgan law, that is $xsy = 1 - (1 - x)t(1 - y)$ for all $x, y \in [0, 1]$. If not stated otherwise, in this study we use two standard realizations of t- and s-norms in the form of a product and probabilistic sum. An overbar denotes a complement treated in a usual way encountered in logic (that is, $\bar{x} = 1 - x$).

25.2. THE BASIC TYPES OF LOGIC NEURONS

In this section, we discuss the main categories of the logic neurons as they were introduced and discussed in Pedrycz (1991a, 1993) and Pedrycz and Rocha (1993). The underlying taxonomy involves aggregative and referential neurons and is very much related to their logic functionality. Their names reflect the underlying processing realized by the neurons. The aggregative neurons concentrate on the logic type of aggregation of the inputs (truth values), while the referential neurons are aimed at logic processing of results of referential transformations of the corresponding truth values.

25.2.1. Aggregative Neurons

Formally, these neurons realize a logic mapping from $[0,1]^n$ to $[0,1]$. Two main classes of the processing units exist in this category.

OR Neuron. This realizes an *and* logic aggregation of inputs $\mathbf{x} = [x_1, x_2, \ldots, x_n]$ with the corresponding connections (weights) $\mathbf{w} = [w_1, w_2, \ldots, w_n]$ and then summarizes the partial results in an *or*-wise manner (hence the name of the neuron). The concise notation underlines this flow of computing, $y = OR(\mathbf{x}; \mathbf{w})$, while the realization of the logic operations gives rise to the expression (referring to as an s–t combination)

$$y = \overset{n}{\underset{i=1}{S}} (x_i t w_i) \tag{25.1}$$

Bearing in mind the interpretation of the logic connectives (t- and s-norms), the OR neuron realizes the following logic expression being viewed as an underlying logic description of the processing of the input signals:

$$(x_1 \text{ and } w_1) \text{ or } (x_2 \text{ and } w_2) \text{ or } \ldots \text{ or } (x_n \text{ and } w_n) \tag{25.2}$$

Apparently the inputs are logically "weighted" by the values of the connections before producing the final result. In other words, we can treat "y" as a truth value of the above statement where the truth values of the inputs are affected by the corresponding weights. Noticeably, lower values of w_i discount the impact of the corresponding inputs; higher values (especially those being positioned close to 1) do not affect the original truth values of the inputs resulting in the logic formula. In limit, if all connections $w_i, i = 12, \ldots, n$, are set to 1, then the neuron produces a plain *or*-combination of the inputs, $y = x_1 \text{ or } x_2 \text{ or } \ldots \text{ or } x_n$. The values of the connections set to zero eliminate the corresponding inputs. Computationally, the OR neuron exhibits nonlinear characteristics (that is, inherently implied by the use of the t- and s-norms, (which are evidently nonlinear mappings). The plots of the characteristics of the OR neuron shown in Figure 25.1 visualize this effect (note that the characteristics are affected by the use of some norms). The connections of the neuron contribute to its adaptive character; the changes in their values form the crux of the parametric learning.

AND Neuron. The neurons in the category, denoted by $y = AND(\mathbf{x}; \mathbf{w})$ with $\mathbf{x}$ and $\mathbf{w}$ being defined as in case of the OR neuron, are governed by the expression

$$y = \overset{n}{\underset{i=1}{T}} (x_i s w_i) \tag{25.3}$$

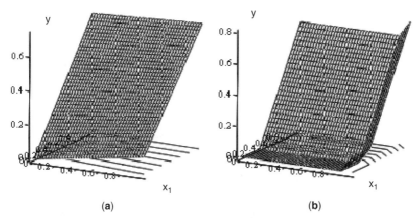

(a)   (b)

Figure 25.1. Characteristics of the OR neuron for selected pairs of t- and s-norms. In all cases the corresponding connections are set to 0.1 and 0.7 with intent to visualize their effect on the input–output characteristics of the neuron: **(a)** Product and probabilistic sum. **(b)** Lukasiewicz *and* and *or* connectives.

Here the *or* and *and* connectives are used in a reversed order: First the inputs are combined with the use of the s-norm, and the partial results are aggregated *and*-wise. Higher values of the connections reduce impact of the corresponding inputs. In limit $w_i = 1$ eliminates the relevance of x_i. With all w_i set to 0, the output of the AND neuron is just an *and* aggregation of the inputs

$$y = x_1 \quad \text{and} \quad x_2 \quad \text{and} \ldots \text{and} \quad x_n \tag{25.4}$$

The characteristics of the AND neuron are shown in Figure 25.2; note the influence of the connections and the specific realization of the triangular norms on the mapping completed by the neuron.

Let us conclude that the neurons are highly nonlinear processing units depending upon the specific realizations of the logic connectives. They also come with potential plasticity whose usage becomes critical when learning the networks involving these neurons.

25.2.2. Referential (Reference) Neurons

The essence of referential computing deals with processing logic predicates. The two-argument (or generally multivariable) predicates such as *similar, included in, and dominates* are essential components of any logic description of a system. In general, the truth value of the predicate is a degree of satisfaction of the expression $P(x, a)$, where a is a certain reference value (reference point). Depending upon the meaning of the predicate P, the expression $P(x, a)$ reads as "x is similar to a," "x is included in a," "x dominates a," and so on. In the case of many variables, the compound predicate comes in the form $P(x_1, x_2, \ldots, x_n, a_1, a_2, \ldots, a_n)$ or more concisely $P(\mathbf{x}; \mathbf{a})$ where $\mathbf{x}$ and $\mathbf{a}$ are

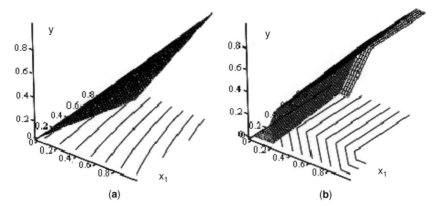

(a)   (b)

Figure 25.2. Characteristics of AND neurons for selected pairs of t- and s-norms. In all cases the connections are set to 0.1 and 0.7 with intent to visualize their effect on the characteristics of the neuron: **(a)** Product and probabilistic sum. **(b)** Lukasiewicz logic connectives.

vectors in the n-dimensional unit hypercube. We envision the following realization of $P(\mathbf{x}; \mathbf{a})$

$$P(\mathbf{x}; \mathbf{a}) = P(x_1, a_1) \quad \text{and} \quad P(x_2, a_2) \quad \text{and} \ldots \text{and} \quad P(x_n, a_n) \quad (25.5)$$

meaning that the satisfaction of the multivariable predicate relies on the satisfaction realized for each variable separately. As the variables could come with a different level of relevance as to the overall satisfaction of the predicates, we represent this effect by some weights (connections) $w_1, w_2, \ldots, w_n$ so that Eq. (25.5) can be rewritten in the form

$$P(\mathbf{x}; \mathbf{a}, \mathbf{w}) = [P(x_1, a_1) \text{ or } w_1] \quad \text{and} \quad [P(x_2, a_2) \text{ or } w_2]$$

$$\text{and} \ldots \text{and} \quad [P(x_n, a_n) \text{or } w_n] \quad (25.6)$$

Taking another look at the above expression and using a notation $z_i = P(x_i, a_i)$, it converts to a certain AND neuron $y = \text{AND}(\mathbf{z}; \mathbf{w})$ with the vector of inputs $\mathbf{z}$ being the result of the computations done for the logic predicate. Then the general notation to be used reads as $\text{REF}(\mathbf{x}; \mathbf{w}, \mathbf{a})$; and using the explicit notation, we have

$$y = \mathop{\mathrm{T}}_{i=1}^{n} (\text{REF}(x_i, a_i) s w_i) \quad (25.7)$$

In essence, as visualized in Figure 25.3, we may conclude that the reference neuron is a realized in a two-stage construct where first we determine the truth values of the predicate (with a treated as a reference point) and then treat these results as the inputs to the AND neuron.

So far we have used the general term of predicate computing not confining ourselves to any specific nature of the predicate. Among a number of possibilities, we discuss the three of them, which tend to occupy an important role.

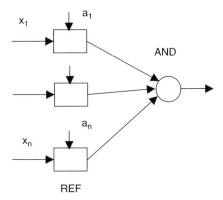

Figure 25.3. A schematic view of computing realized by a reference neuron an involving two processing phases (referential computing and aggregation).

Those are inclusion, dominance, and match (similarity) predicates. As the names stipulate, the predicates return truth values of satisfaction of the relationship of inclusion, dominance, and similarity of a certain argument "x" with respect to the given reference "a". The essence of all these calculations is in the determination of the given truth values, and this is done in the carefully developed logic framework so that the operations retain their semantics and interpretability. What makes our discussion coherent is the fact that the proposed operations originate from triangular norms. The inclusion operation, denoted by $\subset$, is modeled by an implication $\rightarrow$ that is induced by a certain left continuous t-norm (Pedrycz and Gomide, 1998):

$$a \rightarrow b = \sup\{c \in [0, 1] | atc \leq b\}, \qquad a, b \in [0, 1] \qquad (25.8)$$

For instance, for the product the inclusion takes on the form $a \rightarrow b = \min(1, b/a)$. The intuitive form of this predicate is self-evident: The statement "x is included in a" and modeled as $\text{INCL}(x, a) = x \rightarrow a$ comes with the truth value equal to 1 if x is less or equal to a (which, in other words, means that x is included in a) and produces lower truth values once x starts exceeding the truth values of "a". Higher values of "x" (those above the reference point "a") start generating lower truth values of the predicate. The dominance predicate acts in a dual manner. It returns 1 once "x" dominates "a" (so that its values exceeds "a") and values below 1 for x lower than the given threshold. The formal model can be realized as $\text{DOM}(x, a) = a \rightarrow x$. With regard to the reference neuron, the notation is equivalent to the one being used in the previous case; that is, $\text{DOM}(\mathbf{x}; \mathbf{w}, \mathbf{a})$ with the same meaning of $\mathbf{a}$ and $\mathbf{w}$.

The similarity (match) operation is an aggregate of these two, $\text{SIM}(x, a) = \text{INCL}(x, a) \, t \, \text{DOM}(x, a)$, which is appealing from the intuitive standpoint: We say that x is similar to a if x is included in a *and* x dominates a. Noticeably, if $x = a$, the predicate returns 1; if x moves apart from "a," the truth value of the predicate becomes reduced. The resulting similarity neuron is denoted by $\text{SIM}(\mathbf{x};$

w, a) and reads as

$$y = \prod_{i=1}^{n} (\text{SIM}(x_i, a_i) s w_i) \tag{25.9}$$

The reference operations form an interesting generalization of the threshold operations. Consider that we are viewing "x" as a signal of time whose behavior needs to be monitored with respect to some bounds (α and β). If the signal does not exceed some threshold α, then the acceptance signal should go off. Likewise we require another acceptance mechanism indicating a situation where the signal does not go below another threshold value of β. In case of fuzzy predicates, the level of acceptance assumes values in the unit interval rather than being a Boolean variable. The strength of acceptance reflects how much the signal adheres to the assumed thresholds. An example illustrating this behavior is shown in Figure 25.4. Here the values of α and β are set up to 0.6 and 0.5, respectively.

The plots of the referential neurons with two input variables are shown in Figures 25.5 and 25.6; here we have included two realizations of the t-norms to illustrate their effect on the nonlinear characteristics of the processing units.

It is worth noting that by moving the reference point to the origin and **1**-vertex of the unit hypercube (with all its coordinates being set up to 1), the referential neuron starts resembling the aggregative neuron. In particular, we have the following:

- For $\mathbf{a} = \mathbf{1} = [1\ 1\ 1\dots 1]$ the inclusion neuron reduces to the AND neuron.
- For $\mathbf{a} = \mathbf{0} = [0\ 0\ 0\dots 0]$ the dominance neuron reduces to the AND neuron.

One can draw a loose analogy between some types of the referential neurons and the two categories of processing units encountered in neurocomputing. The analogy is based upon the *local* versus *global* character of processing realized therein. Perceptrons come with the global character of processing. Radial basis functions realize a local character of processing as focused on receptive fields. In

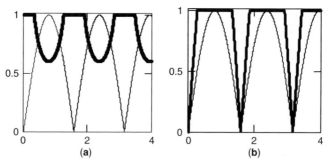

Figure 25.4. Temporal signal $x(t)$ and its acceptance signals (levels of the signals—thick lines) formed with respect to its lower and upper threshold **(a)** and **(b)**. The complements of the acceptance are then treated as warning signals.

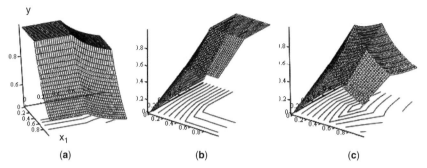

(a) (b) (c)

Figure 25.5. Characteristics of the reference neurons for the product (t-norm) and probabilistic sum (s-norm). In all cases the connections are set to 0.1 and 0.7 with intent to visualize the effect of the weights on the relationships produced by the neuron. The point of reference is set to (0.5, 0.5): inclusion neuron **(a)**, dominance neuron **(b)**, similarity neuron **(c)**.

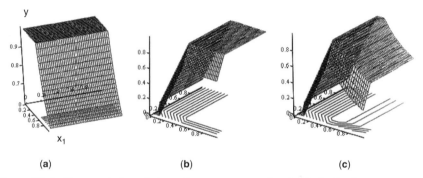

(a) (b) (c)

Figure 25.6. Characteristics of the reference neurons for the Lukasiewicz t-norm and s-norm (that is $atb = \max(0, a + b - 1)$ and $asb = \min(1, a + b)$). In all cases the connections are set to 0.1 and 0.7 with intent to visualize the effect of the weights. The point of reference is set to (0.5, 0.5): inclusion neuron **(a)**, dominance neuron **(b)**, similarity neuron **(c)**.

the same vein, the inclusion and dominance neurons are after the global nature of processing while the similarity neuron carries more confined, local processing.

25.3. RELATIONSHIPS OF FUZZY NEURONS WITH FUZZY RELATIONAL EQUATIONS

One can look at the fuzzy neurons discussed in the previous section from a slightly different perspective. The $s-t$ and $t-s$ calculations are, in essence, examples of so-called $s-t$ and $t-s$ composition operators used in fuzzy sets. The inputs and connections can be treated as discrete n-dimensional fuzzy sets whose convolution is computed by means of the $s-t$ composition (OR neuron and $t-s$ composition (AND neuron). This simple observation links fuzzy neurons with the theory of fuzzy relational equations—a well-established area of fundamental and applied pursuits in fuzzy sets. The early results in this domain go back as early as the mid-1970s as proposed by Sanchez with a number of significant results obtained afterwards (cf. Di Nola et al., 1995; Pedrycz, 1988, 1991a; Pedrycz and Gomicle, 1998). We can treat a fuzzy neuron as a realization of some fuzzy relational equation $y = \text{OR}(\mathbf{x}; \mathbf{w})$ or $y = \text{AND}(\mathbf{x}; \mathbf{w})$. Two fundamental problems are sought: (a) solving the equation with respect to $\mathbf{w}$ for $\mathbf{x}$ and y given (usually referred in the theory of relational equations to as an estimation problem) and (b) solving the equation with respect to $\mathbf{x}$ assuming that $\mathbf{w}$ and y are provided (which refers to as an inverse problem). In both cases the theory provides us with interesting and general results. The first problem concerns the estimation of the connections of the neuron and is inherently tied to the learning of the network composed of logic neurons. Its generalized version involving solving a system of relational equations with a finite set of input–output pairs $(\mathbf{x}(k), \mathbf{y}(k))$ given is the standard version of the estimation problem. The inverse problem is focused on constructing inputs $(\mathbf{x})$ leading to the required output. The theory of fuzzy relational equations shows that in general there could be families (rather than unique solutions) to such equations, and it states how to effectively construct extreme (viz., maximal or minimal) solutions. These findings hold under a strong assumption that there is a nonempty family of solutions. Furthermore, the generality of the results is assured for some subset of t- and s-norms used in the design of the composition operator; these solutions are obtained for $\max(\sup)-t$ composition and $\min(\inf)-s$ convolution of fuzzy sets (cf. Pedrycz and Gomide, 1998). Interestingly, the generality of the solutions is not guaranteed for the general $s-t$ or $t-s$ composition for any t- and s-norm. The relevance of the theoretical framework should be cast in a certain setting; in essence we can envision that the solutions can only be approximate and we can use them as a starting (initial) configuration of the connections so that the learning could start off.

25.4. A GENERAL TOPOLOGY OF THE NETWORK

Because we have developed a host of logic processing units, we can use them in developing a general architecture of the network. In this design we are guided by several requirements. First, we would like to achieve a substantial level of flexibility so that the structure could be easily and effectively adjusted to the experimental data. Second, we would like to assure a high level of interpretability: Evidently each neuron comes with a well-defined semantics, and our intent is to retain it so at the very end the network can be easily mapped (translated) into a well-structured and transparent logic expression. This quest for interpretability and transparency has been clearly identified in the most recent literature (cf. Casillas et al., 2003). In the logic description we will dwell upon the well-established components of fuzzy logic: logic operators and linguistic

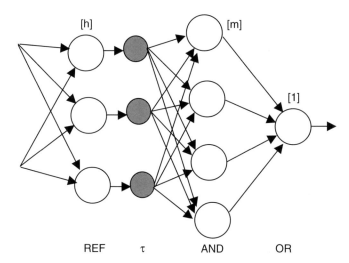

Figure 25.7. A general architecture of the network constructed with logic-based neurons (see detailed description in text). The dimensions of the layers are marked by numbers in brackets (upper part of the figure).

modifiers. Having these requirements in mind, a general architecture of the network is shown in Figure 25.7.

The network comes with several layers where each of them has a clear functional role to play and is highly interpretable. The first layer (referred to as a referential processing) is composed of "h" referential neurons (inclusion, dominance, similarity). The results of this processing are taken to some power (indicated by some small shadowed circle) and then combined *and*-wise in the second layer of the network. The elements there are AND neurons with all connections hardwired to zero. The width of this layer is equal to "m." In the sequel the results are combined by the layer of OR neurons. Let us now move on to the computational details by also concentrating on the interpretation of the underlying processing. The truth values generated by the referential neurons reflect the level of satisfaction of the logic predicates:

$$z_1 = P_1(\mathbf{x}; \mathbf{a}_1), \qquad z_2 = P_2(\mathbf{x}; \mathbf{a}_2), \ldots, z_h = P_h(\mathbf{x}; \mathbf{a}_h) \qquad (25.10)$$

The powers of z_i, denoted as $\tau_i(z_i)$ where τ_i assumes a few discrete values (say 1/2, 0, 1, 2, and 4), are interpreted as linguistic modifiers operating upon z_i and producing some concentration or dilution effect (Pedrycz and Gomide, 1998). More specifically, the collection of the modifiers maps on the corresponding powers in the usual way that we encounter in the literature:

1/2—*more or less* (dilution effect)

0—unknown

1—true (neutral)

2—*very* (concentration effect)

4—*very* (*very*) = *very*^{2} (strong concentration effect)

The result of this processing (coming as the output of the shadowed circle) is a logically modified referential logic predicate with a straightforward interpretation. For instance, the expression INCL($[x_1, x_2]$, $[0.2, 0.7]$, $[0.6, 0.9]$)$^{0.5}$ translates into the following linguistic statement:

$y =$ *more or less*[[x_1 included in 0.6] *or* 0.2 *and* [x_2 included in 0.9] *or* 0.7]

(noticeably, the core part of this expression could be extracted by carrying out some additional pruning; we elaborate on this matter in Section 25.7). Finally, the output layer includes a single OR neuron whose connections represent the relevance of information originating at the input nodes.

While the AND and OR neurons are the two categories of the standard processing units being encountered in a number of neurofuzzy constructs, the layer of linguistic hedges require more attention. They are useful in the linguistic structuralization of the network (in the sense they affects linguistically the outputs of the referential neurons). From the computational standpoints, the linguistic hedges help develop the required nonlinear characteristics between input and output variables; noticeably the relationships can be easily formed by choosing a suitable hedge.

In what follows, we visualize the diversity of the characteristics of the networks leading to nonlinear and multimodal relationships we can easily construct by putting together various neurons (see Figure (25.8). Note that the linguistic hedges play an important role in shaping the logic mapping completed by the network.

Owing to the inherent roots of the logic backbone of the neurons, we can directly exploit the transparency of the construct when capturing the essence of the data. If the network is large enough, we can conclude that such a network can capture the data with any required accuracy. While the theorem of universal approximation is not of our concern, it becomes advantageous to note that a suitable topology is at immediate reach. As an example, consider a finite dataset of input–output pairs $\{\mathbf{x}(k), y(k)\}, k = 1, 2, \ldots, N$. Then the network with "N" referential neurons of the matching nature, linguistic modifiers assuming high values, and a single OR neuron with the connections equal to the required target values $y(1), y(2), \ldots, y(N)$ becomes a suitable network. Interestingly, we developed the structure without any learning but simply through mapping the problem into the logic setting formed by the proposed network.

An example of such a network shown for $N = 4$ data points and $\tau = 8$ is included in Figure 25.9. The four matching neurons are allocated to the individual data points. The high value of the logic modifier (that produces a high concentration effect, *very*^{4} = *very very very very*) leads to highly localized receptive

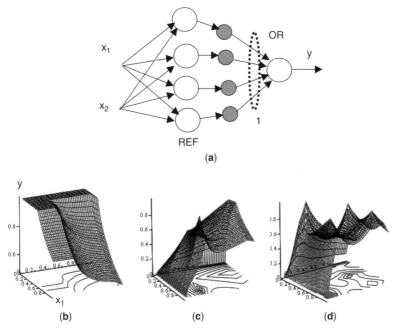

(a)

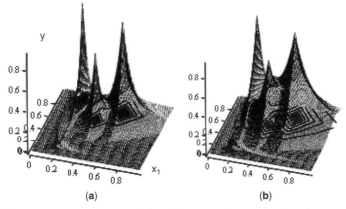

(b)   **(c)**   **(d)**

Figure 25.8. Input–output characteristics of the network with the topology shown as in: **(a)** Here all connections of the OR neuron are set up to 1.0. **(b)** Two inclusion neurons INCL with $(x_1, x_2, \mathbf{w}, \mathbf{a})\mathbf{w} = [0.4\ 0.2], \mathbf{a} = [0.5\ 0.3]$ (1st neuron) and $\mathbf{w} = [0.0\ 0.0], \mathbf{a} = [0.2\ 0.9]$ (2nd neuron), $\tau_1 = 2, \tau_2 = 0.5$. **(c)** two SIM neurons $\mathrm{SIM}(x_1, x_2, \mathbf{w}, \mathbf{a})$ with $\mathbf{w} = [0.4\ 0.2]$ and $\mathbf{a} = [0.8\ 0.3]$ (1st neuron) and $\mathbf{w} = [0.0\ 0.0], \mathbf{a} = [0.4\ 0.9]$ (2nd neuron), $\tau_1 = 4, \tau_2 = 0.5$. **(d)** Four SIM neurons with the weights and connections equal to $\mathbf{w} = [0.1\ 0.0]$ and $\mathbf{a} = [0.1\ 0.3]$ (1st neuron), $\mathbf{w} = [0.2\ 0.1], \mathbf{a} = [0.8\ 0.2]$ (2nd neuron), $\mathbf{w} = [0.2\ 0.1], \mathbf{a} = [0.5\ 0.7]$ (3rd neuron) $\mathbf{w} = [0.2\ 0.1], \mathbf{a} = [0.9\ 0.8]$ (4th neuron), $\tau_1 = 1, \tau_2 = 1, \tau_3 = 4, \tau_4 = 2$.

(a)   **(b)**

Figure 25.9. Input–output characteristics of the network mapping four input–output data $([0.2\ 0.1], 0.2), ([0.6\ 0.8], 0.9), ([0.2\ 0.9], 0.95), ([0.4\ 0.63], 0.65)\ \tau = 8$ **(a)** and $\tau = 4$ **(b)**.

fields. Using lower values of the modifiers, say t 4 (very very) leads to a less visible concentration effect as seen in Figure 25.9b.

25.5. THE EVOLUTIONARY DEVELOPMENT OF THE NETWORK

A structural optimization becomes a critical feature of the development environment. The heterogeneity of the network (if properly exploited) becomes an evident asset of the architecture that implies its flexibility. The structure optimization, however, requires a suitable development environment that can cope with the optimization of this nature. The genetic optimization is a sound option to be explored with this regard. While the genetic algorithm is standard to a high extent, we spend less time on the description of the genetic operators and concentrate on the organization of a chromosome as it maps the problem into the optimization environment. Because of the anticipated heterogeneous character of the chromosome, it is advantageous to consider a floating-point version of coding. The benefits of this version of coding over the binary content of the chromosome has been discussed quite intensively in the existing literature (cf. Goldberg, 1989, 1991; Michalewicz, 1996). As a prerequisite, let us assume that the number of reference neurons and AND neurons is given in advance and that these are equal to "h" and "m," respectively (these could be optimized as well, but a straightforward enumeration could be quite appropriate in this setting because of a fairly limited search space). Alluding to the topology of the network, the content of the chromosome shown in Figure 25.10 becomes self-explanatory. The thresholding operation of the continuous entries of the neuron is used to select one of the types of the reference neurons. Likewise, we threshold the portion of the chromosome corresponding to the linguistic hedges following the reference neurons. Finally, the weights of the OR neuron assume continuous values from the unit interval, and they are taken directly from the corresponding entries of the chromosome.

In the sequel, we discuss the realization of the main functional components of the GA—that is, selection, mutation, and crossover operations—and discuss the fitness function that is used to guide the optimization process.

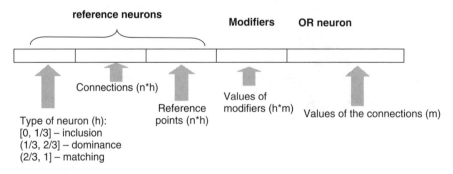

Figure 25.10. Organization of a chromosome representing the structure of the network.

Selection Process. In this process, we use an elitist ranking selection (Baker, 1985). This selection mechanism means that individuals to be selected for the next generation are based on their relative rank in the population, as determined by the fitness function. The best individual from each generation is always carried over to the next generation (elitist mechanism), meaning that the solution found so far during the genetic optimization is guaranteed to never disappear.

Mutation. The mutation operator is a standard construct encountered in a number of genetic algorithms (cf. Herrera et al., 1998). Given an individual string $\mathbf{a} = [a_1, a_2, \ldots, a_{2n}]$, we generate a new string $\mathbf{a}' = [a_1', a_2', \ldots, a_{2n}']$ where a_i', $i = 1, 2, \ldots, 2n$, is a random number confined in the range of $[0,1]$ and subject to the following replacement (mutation) rule: a_i is mutated—that is, replaced by a_i' with some probability of mutation (p_m)—otherwise the entry of the chromosome is left intact, that is, $a_i' = a_i$.

Crossover. The operation is realized as the BLX-0.5 crossover operator (Eshelman and Schaffer, 1993; Herrera et al., 1998), which is carried out as follows. Given are two individuals $\mathbf{a} = [a_1, a_2, \ldots, a_{2n}]$ and $\mathbf{b} = [b_1, b_2, \ldots, b_{2n}]$. The resulting offsprings are formed in the form $\mathbf{a}' = [a_1', a_2', \ldots, a_{2n}']$ and $\mathbf{b}' = [b_1', b_2', \ldots, b_{2n}']$, where $a_i', b_i', i = 1, 2, \ldots, 2n$, are random numbers located in the range $[\max(0, \min_i -0.5I), \min(1, \max_i +0.5I)]$. Here, $\min_i = \min(a_i, b_i)$, $\max_i = \max(a_i, b_i)$, and I is defined in the form $I = \max_i - \min_i$. This particular crossover operation provides a good balance between using the information of the parents and avoiding premature convergence (cf. Herrera et al., 1998). The crossover operator ensures that all values of the generated offspring are confined to the unit interval $[0, 1]$. The operator is employed with probability of crossover, p_c; otherwise the individuals are left unchanged $\mathbf{a}' = \mathbf{a}$ and $\mathbf{b}' = \mathbf{b}$.

Fitness Function. The fitness function quantifies how the network approximates the data and is taken as $1 - Q/(Q + \varepsilon)$, with Q being a sum of squared errors between the target values (experimental output data) and the corresponding outputs of the network (or any other measure of error). A small positive constant ε standing in the denominator of the above expression ensures that the fitness function remains meaningful even for $Q = 0$ (which in practice never occurs).

Two other parameters of the GA involve a size of the population and number of generations. Their values have to be experimented with. Typically, these two parameters are in the range of 100 to 200 individuals in a population and between 200 and 500 generations.

25.6. INTERFACES OF FUZZY NETWORKS

In a nutshell the fuzzy networks completes a logic-based processing of input signals and realizes a certain logic-driven mapping between input and output spaces. As they interact with a physical world whose manifestation does not usually arise at the level of logic (multivalued) signals, it becomes apparent that there is a need for some interface of the model. Such interfaces are well known in fuzzy modeling (Bargiela and Pedrycz, 2002; cf. also Pedrycz, 1989, 1992, 1996). They commonly arise under a name of fuzzifiers (granular encoder) and defuzzifiers (granular decoders). The role of the encoder is to convert a numeric input coming from the external environment into the internal format of member-ship grades of the fuzzy sets defined for each input variable. This transformation results in a nonlinear normalization of the input (no matter what original ranges the input variables assume) and a linear increase of the dimensionality of the new logic space in comparison with the original one. The decoder takes the results of the logic processing and transforms them into some numeric values. The layered architecture of the fuzzy models with clearly distinguished interfaces and the logic-processing core is illustrated in Figure 25.11.

With the design of the interfaces, we exercise two general approaches (in the literature we encounter far more various techniques but they are usually more specialized):

1. *Granulation of Individual Variables.* This mechanism of granulation is quite common in the realm of fuzzy modeling. In essence, we define

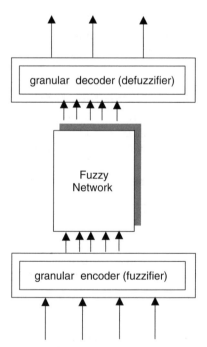

Figure 25.11. A general layered structure of fuzzy modeling; the use of granular encoders and decoders is essential in the development of communication mechanisms with the modeling environment.

several fuzzy sets in the universe of discourse of the variable of interest so that any input is transformed via the membership functions defined there and the resulting membership grades are used in further computations by the model. From the design standpoint, we choose a number of fuzzy sets, type of membership functions, and a level of overlap between consecutive fuzzy sets. Some general tendencies along this line are thoroughly reported in the literature. By selecting the number of fuzzy sets (usually between 3 and 9), we position modeling activities at some required level of information granularity (a level of modeling details we are interested in). The type of membership functions helps model the semantics of the information granules. Among many possibilities, we commonly encounter triangular fuzzy sets and Gaussian membership functions. These two types come with an extensive list of arguments that help make a suitable selection with respect to the main objectives of the model (e.g., those concerning a trade-off between interpretation and accuracy of modeling). The overlap level is essential from different points of view, namely, (a) semantics of the linguistic terms, (b) nonlinear numeric characteristics of the fuzzy model, and (c) completeness of the model.

2. *Nonlinear or Linear Normalization.* Here we transform an original variable defined in some space, say $[a, b]$ (subset of **R**) is scaled to the unit interval. This could be done with the aid of some mapping $\phi : [a, b] \rightarrow [0, 1]$ that could be either linear or nonlinear. In any case we consider that f is monotonically increasing with $\phi(a) = 0$, $\phi(b) = 1$. This transformation does not affect the dimensionality of the problem.

25.7. INTERPRETATION ASPECTS OF THE NETWORKS

While each neuron in the network comes with a well-defined semantics and can be easily interpreted, the result of interpretation could lead to a quite lengthy description in case of multivariable systems. To facilitate the process of interpretation and reduce the structure of the detailed logic expression to its essential substructure with the most meaningful topology, we do the pruning of the weakest (unnecessary) connections. The following are the detailed thresholding expressions supporting such pruning activities:

- For the referential neurons $y = \text{REF}(\mathbf{x}; \mathbf{w}, \mathbf{a})$ we admit the following pruning mechanism: connection w_i is binarized producing a connection $\widetilde{w_i}$ assuming Boolean values

$$\widetilde{w_i} = \begin{cases} 1 & \text{if } w_i > \lambda \\ 0 & \text{if } w_i \leq \lambda \end{cases} \qquad (25.11)$$

where λ denotes a certain threshold level. Considering that we are concerned with the AND neurons, the connections higher than the assumed threshold are practically eliminated from the computing. Apparently we have $(w_i^{\sim} s x_i) t A \approx 1t = A$, where A denotes the result of computing realized by the neuron for the rest of its inputs. In the case of referential neurons, their reference point a_i requires different treatment depending upon the type of the specific referential operation. For the inclusion operation, $INCL(x, a_i)$, we can admit the threshold operation in the form

$$INCL^{\sim}(x, a_i) = \begin{cases} INCL(x, a_i) & \text{if } a_i \leq \mu \\ 1 - x & \text{if } a_i > \mu \end{cases} \tag{25.12}$$

with μ being some fixed threshold value. In other words, we consider that $INCL(x, a_i)$ is approximated by the complement of x (where this approximation is implied by the interpretational feasibility rather than being dictated by any formal optimization problem), $INCL(x, a_i) \approx 1 - x$. For the dominance neuron we have the expression for the respective binary version of DOM, $DOM^{\sim}$:

$$DOM^{\sim}(x, a_i) = \begin{cases} DOM(x, a_i) & \text{if } a_i \leq \mu \\ x & \text{if } a_i > \mu \end{cases} \tag{25.13}$$

- For the linguistic hedges associated with the AND neurons. Here the hedge $\tau = 0$ leads to the *unknown* input, and as such this input could be completely eliminated ($x^0 = 1$).
- For the OR neuron the weakest connections are eliminated because the corresponding inputs do not impact the output. We have

$$w_i^{\sim} = \begin{cases} 1 & \text{if } w_i > \lambda \\ 0 & \text{if } w_i \leq \lambda \end{cases} \tag{25.14}$$

The connection set up to 1 is deemed essential. If we accept a single threshold level of 0.5 and apply this consistently to all the connections of the network and set up the threshold 0.1 for the inclusion neuron, the statement

$y = more \ or \ less[\ [x_1 \text{ included in } 0.6] \ or \ 0.2 \ and \ [x_2 \text{ included in } 0.9] \ or \ 0.7]$

translates into a concise (yet approximate) version assuming the form of the following logic expression:

$y = more \ or \ less[x_1 \text{ included in } 0.6]$

The choice of the threshold value could be a subject of a separate optimization phase, but we can also admit some arbitrarily values especially if we are focused on the interpretation issues.

25.8. EXPERIMENTAL STUDIES

The experiments reported in this section are intended to illustrate the development, performance, and interpretation issues of the proposed network. In all experiments, the t-norm is implemented as a product operator while the s-norm is treated as a probabilistic sum. Furthermore, in training the network we adhere to the 60%–40% data split, with 60% of randomly selected data being used for the training of the network. The performance index Q used in the experiments on the basis of which the fitness function is developed concerns an RMSE measure given in a standard format [RMSE $= \sqrt{(1/N) \sum_{k=1}^{N} (y_k - \hat{y}_k)^2}$ with $\hat{y}_k$ being the output of the network]. These values concern the output normalized to the unit interval. In plots and while reporting results, we also show the performance index for the original (not normalized) output variable; its values will be denoted by V.

We start with a low-dimensional synthetic dataset $\{(\mathbf{x}(k), y(k))\}$ shown in Figure 25.12. There are three inputs and a single output.

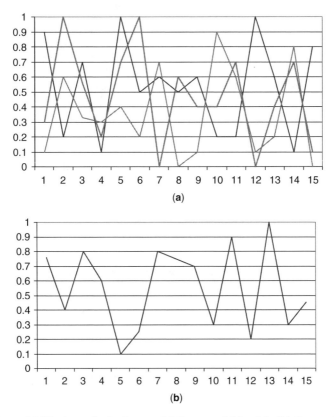

Figure 25.12. A synthetic dataset. (**a**) Input variables (**x**). (**b**) Output (y).

In the series of experiments we changed the number of the referential neurons as well as modified the number of AND neurons in the hidden layer. The GA used a population of 100 individuals and was run for 500 generations. The optimal configuration emerged in the form of three reference neurons and three AND neurons; it leads to the lowest value of the performance index on the training set, and this is confirmed by the lowest value achieved on the testing set (as visualized in Figure 25.13).

The progress of the optimization is gauged in terms of the fitness function of the population (average fitness) as well as the best individual obtained in the successive generations (see Figure 25.14).

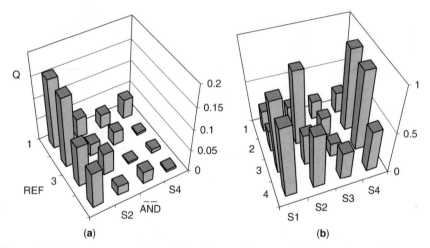

Figure 25.13. Performance index (Q) on the training set **(a)** and testing set **(b)** versus the number of reference and AND neurons.

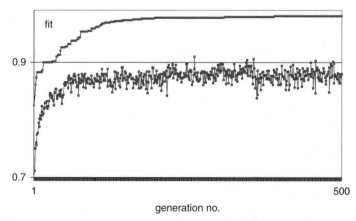

Figure 25.14. Fitness function (average and best individual) in successive generations; the results are given for the best configuration (three referential neurons and three AND neurons).

The interpretation of the network leads us to an interesting logic description of the data. The referential neurons located in the second layer are of all types (DOM, SIM, and INCL). They come with the following connections and reference points:

DOM: $\mathbf{w} = [0.36\ 0.95\ 0.73]$, $\mathbf{a} = [0.23\ 0.69\ 0.87]$

INCL: $\mathbf{w} = [0.12\ 0.61\ 0.02]$, $\mathbf{a} = [0.69\ 0.61\ 0.70]$

SIM: $\mathbf{w} = [0.02\ 0.16\ 0.96]$, $\mathbf{a} = [0.90\ 0.29\ 0.48]$

The connections of the AND neurons aggregating the signals of the referential neurons are equal to $[2\ 0.5\ 4]$, $[0.5\ 4\ 0]$, and $[0.5\ 0\ 4]$, respectively. Finally, the connections of the OR neuron are equal to $\mathbf{v} = [0.26\ 0.84\ 0.92]$.

If we proceed with the thresholding operation (assuming the same threshold level of 0.5 for the aggregative neurons and 0.05 and 0.95 for the reference neurons as well as following the pruning mechanism of the rules outlined in Section 25.4) and reduce the least significant connections, then the core part of the network arises in the following format:

Reference Neurons

$z_1 = \text{DOM}(x_1, 0.23)$

$z_2 = \text{INCL}(x_1, 0.69)$ *and* $\text{INCL}(x_2, 0.7)$

$z_3 = \text{SIM}(x_1, 0.9)$ *and* $\text{SIM}(x_2, 0.29)$

AND Neurons

$u_1 = $ *very* $(z_1$ *and more or less* (z_2) *and very very* $(z_3))$

$u_2 = $ *more or less* (z_1) *and very very* (z_2)

$u_3 = $ *more or less* (z_1) *and very very* (z_3)

OR Neuron

$y = u_2$ *or* $u_3 = \{$*more or less* $(\text{DOM}(x_1, 0.23)$ *and very very* $[(\text{INCL}(x_1, 0.69)$ *and* $\text{INCL}(x_2, 0.7)]$ $\}$*or*

or $[$*more or less* $(\text{DOM}(x_1, 0.23)$ *and very very* $(\text{SIM}(x_1, 0.9)$ *and* $\text{SIM}(x_2, 0.29))]$

The two subsequent datasets come from the Machine Learning repository (Merz and Murphy, 1996) and concern auto and Boston housing data.

Auto dataset. This dataset deals with the description of various car makes completed in terms of several main characteristics such as number of cylinders, acceleration, and gas consumption. We can develop a logic description of such data in which we predict gas consumption (mpg) as a logic function of the parameters of a vehicle. As the data considered here are either continuous (acceleration) or discrete with a few nominal values, we develop an interface in which any continuous variable is granulated through a collection of fuzzy sets while a discrete variable is coded in the form of 1-out-of-n. For each continuous variable we use three Gaussian membership functions uniformly distributed across the universe of discourse. This selection is primarily dictated by the interpretability of such granules (because they could easily assume some clear semantics such as *low, medium,* and *high*). The overlap between two adjacent fuzzy sets is set to 0.5 (which makes these terms easily distinguishable and enhances their semantics). With this form of the interface, we end up with 23 inputs to the network. The output is linearly normalized by converting the range [9.0, 46.6] into the unit interval. Bearing the encoding used in this network, the details of this mapping clearly identifying each variable are included in Table 25.1.

In the development of the network we use 60% of the dataset (training data) selected at random from the entire set, with the rest used for testing purposes. The population consists of 200 individuals, and the genetic optimization was run for 700 generations. The mutation and crossover rates were equal to 0.10 and 0.80, respectively. As shown in Figure 25.15, the genetic optimization proceeds in a

TABLE 25.1. Input variables and the results of its encoding (Using Either a Collection of Fuzzy Sets or 1-out-of-*n* Decoding)

Variable Name and Type [Continuous (C) or Discrete (D)	Variable's Number (Internal to the Network)
Number of cylinders (D)	x_1, x_2, x_3, x_4, x_5
Displacement (C)	x_6, x_7, x_8
Horsepower (C)	x_9, x_{10}, x_{11}
Weight (C)	x_{12}, x_{13}, x_{14}
Acceleration (C)	x_{15}, x_{16}, x_{17}
Model year (C)	x_{18}, x_{19}, x_{20}
Origin (D)	x_{21}, x_{22}, x_{23}

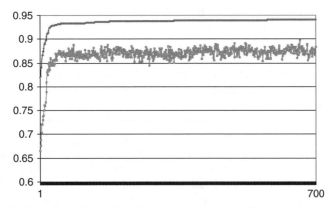

Figure 25.15. Genetic optimization of the network–fitness function (best and average) produced in successive generations of the GA.

fairly typical way where in the first generations most of the optimization takes place. Because of the elitist strategy, the best individual shows up quite quickly and remains for the rest of the course of the GA optimization (the curve saturates quite quickly with some minor enhancements obtained during the later part of the process). Again we found these values to be typical for the experiments and in line with the typical range of the values of the GA parameters encountered in the literature. The experiments were carried out for different combinations of the AND and reference neurons. The performance index treated as a function of these two parameters is shown in Figure 25.16. These results lead to the optimal configuration of the neurons with three reference neurons and four AND neurons. This figure reveals that the number of referential neurons exhibits higher impact on the performance than the number of the AND neurons.

The overall performance of the network (shown for the entire dataset) is presented in Figure 25.17 with the experimental data visualized with respect to the corresponding outputs of the network; the cloud of the points obtained in this way locates around the straight line of the slope 45°.

The optimal network comes with the three referential neurons: two inclusion and one dominance neuron. The connections and the reference points of them as well as the connections of the AND and OR neuron are all shown in Figures 25.18 and 25.19. Our intent is to deliver a certain "global" picture as to the meaning of the connections rather than get into details so that we can focus on the pruning of the network and produce a compact description of data.

The reference neurons give rise to highly heterogeneous space—remarkably different values of the connections corresponding with the specific inputs have been selected. The linguistic hedges (τ) associated with the three AND neurons are determined to be equal to [0.5 2 2], [2 2 0.5], [0.5 0 0], and [1 1 4]. In the case of the third neuron, two of its inputs become irrelevant (*unknown*).

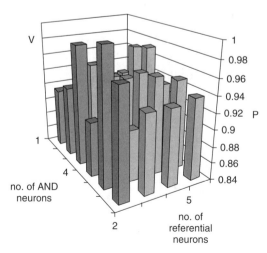

Figure 25.16. Performance index V as a function of the number of referential and AND neurons.

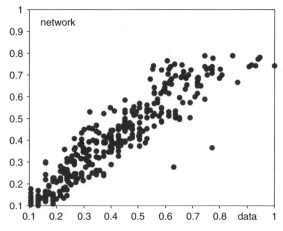

Figure 25.17. Network versus Data. All data shown with a few discrepancies between the network and data.

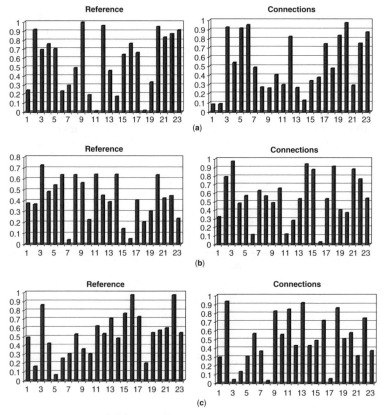

Figure 25.18. Connections and reference points of the referential neurons: **(a)** First INCL neuron, **(b)** DOM neuron, and **(c)** second INCL neuron.

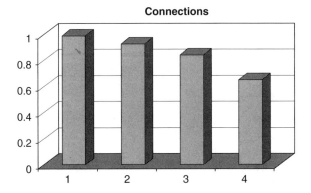

Figure 25.19. Connections of the OR neuron.

TABLE 25.2. Subsets of the Variables Retained by the Reference Neurons; Included Are the Values of the Associated Reference Values of the Reference Point

Reference Neuron	Variable Number	Reference Point
INCL-1	1, 2, 8, 9, 11, 13, 21	0.24, 0.91, 0.49, 0.99, 0.01, 0.46, 0.17
DOM	6, 11, 12, 16	0.63, 0.64, 0.45, 0.05
INCL-2	1, 3, 4, 8, 17	0.49, 0.86, 0.42, 0.53, 0.73

We observe a substantial diversity in the values of the connections. For instance, in the third AND neuron we have only a single significant connection while the remaining are set up to 1 (reflecting the unknown aspect of the corresponding input to this neuron).

Using the thresholding operation, the core part of the network can be easily revealed. The arbitrarily assumed value of the threshold level for the connections is taken as 0.3. In this case all the connections of the OR neuron are retained. The subsets of the variables of the retained by the corresponding reference neurons are included in Table 25.2.

The logic description of data can be directly inferred from the network developed so far. A few observations are helpful in this regard. In the case of a continuous variable that has been discretized (quantized) in terms of fuzzy sets, the logic expression INCL(A, ref) where the satisfaction of this predicate attains high truth values (preferably close to 1) induces some corresponding regions positioned in the original input variable as visualized in Figure 25.20. Note that the location of the region depends upon the form of the membership function. For the discrete inputs with the 1-out-of-n decoding, the interpretation of the logic expression INCL(x is $\{\xi\}$, ref), with ξ being a discrete value of the variable gives

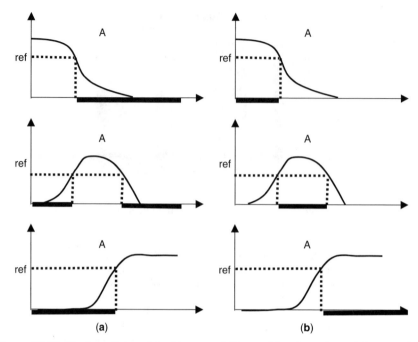

Figure 25.20. Regions (intervals) of input variable resulting from the satisfaction of the logic predicates of inclusion and dominance and induced by different forms of the membership function: **(a)** Inclusion, INCL(x is A, ref). **(b)** Dominance, DOM(x is A, ref).

rise to the expression

$$x \text{ is } \xi \text{ with confidence level equal to ref}$$

With these interpretation mechanisms in mind, the network translates into the following expression:

mpg = {INCL(4cylinders, 0.24) *and* INCL (6 cylinders, 0.91) *and*

INCL(displacement is *large*, 0.49)

and INCL(horsepower is *small*, 0.99) *and*

INCL(horsepower is *high*, 0.01)

and INCL(weight is *medium*, 0.46) *and*

INCL(origin = Japanese, 0.17)}

or

{DOM(displacement is *small*, 0.63) *and* DOM(horsepower is *high*, 0.64) *and*

DOM(weight is *low*, 0.45) *and* DOM(acceleration is *medium*, 0.05)} *or*

{INCL(4 cylinders, 0.49) *and* INCL(6 cylinders, 0.86)

and INCL(8 cylinders, 0.42) *and*

and INCL(displacement is *low*, 0.53) and INCL(acceleration is *high*, 0.73)}

Higher values of mpg (let us stress that their values are normalized to the unit interval) are associated with higher truth values of the compound logic expression describing the data.

Boston Housing Data. The dataset concerns the price of real estate in the Boston area providing several features of the houses (age, distance to employment centers, number of rooms, student–teacher ratio, etc.) and their prices. In our discussion the price is treated as the dependent variable whose logic relationship with the inputs we are interested in. The setup of the genetic optimization is the same as in the previous case. With the same coding (3 fuzzy sets per variable and 1-out-of-n coding) we end up with 56 input variables. The optimization with respect to the number of reference and AND neurons leads to the configuration of 2–4 (2 reference neurons, 4 AND neurons), refer to Figure 25.21.

The parameters of the neurons (reference points and their connections) are illustrated in Figure 25.22. The optimal configuration leading to the minimal value of the performance index involves xx inclusion and similarity neurons. The performance index V is equal to 2.283; its value on the testing set is equal to 2.468. Bearing in mind the original range of the output that is [5, 50], this amounts to about 3.4% and 3.5% of its total range (that $\sqrt{2.283}/45$ and $\sqrt{2.468}/45$).

The connections of the AND neurons are equal to [0 1], [4 1], [0.5 0], and [0.5 0]. It becomes evident that some inputs are irrelevant (those associated with

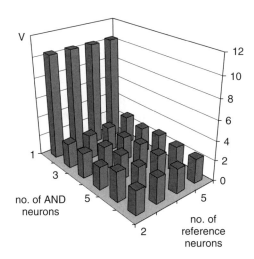

Figure 25.21. Values of the performance index Q for the training set.

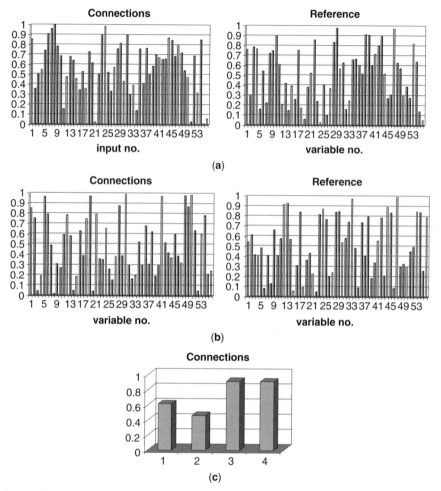

Figure 25.22. Parameters of the fuzzy neurons: **(a)** Inclusion neuron, **(b)** similarity, and **(c)** OR neuron in the output layer.

zeros, which are being regarded as *unknown*). For the OR neuron, one of the connections is subject to pruning as its value is lower than 0.5.

25.9. CONCLUSIONS

Being motivated by the genuine need of constructing networks that exhibit plasticity and retaining interpretability, we have developed a heterogeneous structure composed of logic neurons. The two main categories of aggregative and reference neurons are deeply rooted in the fundamental operations encountered in fuzzy sets (including logic operations, linguistic modifiers, and logic reference operations). The direct interpretability of the network we addressed in the study

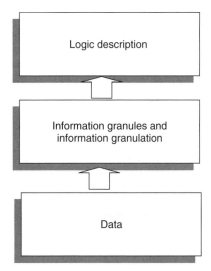

Figure 25.23. From data to knowledge and its logic description (logic model): A general flow of processing along with its conceptual and algorithmic setting.

helps develop a logic description of data. Because the network takes advantage of using various neurons, this imposes an immediate requirement of structural optimization and leads to the utilization of the mechanisms of genetic optimization (genetic algorithms). This study was aimed at addressing the fundamental conceptual and algorithmic (design) issues of the networks. In essence, the general framework we were concerned about when moving from data to knowledge and its logic-based description is portrayed in Figure 25.23. With this scheme, we gain a full acknowledgment of the need of the logically transparent networks as a vehicle to interpret the data.

There are a number of advanced issues worth pursuing:

- Interpretation mechanisms with an emphasis placed on the systematic pruning process that should be guided by some well-defined development criteria. The two potential candidates could involve a criterion of accuracy (which expresses how much the pruning affects the performance index) and a criterion of interpretability. This one could be more difficult to interpret and attach a tangible interpretation; as one among possible alternatives we can count the number of connections dropped and link it to the structural measure of complexity (such as, for example, Akaike criterion in system identification) of the reduced network.

- Developing templates of networks for mapping domain knowledge onto a network's topology; one can envision that building a number of "templates" could be of substantial benefit.

- The realization of the templates may trigger more research into hierarchical networks composed of a collection of specialized subnetworks.

ACKNOWLEDGMENTS

Support from the Canada Research Chair (CRC) Program, Natural Sciences and Engineering Research Council (NSERC), and Alberta Software Engineering Research Consortium (ASERC) is gratefully acknowledged.

REFERENCES

Baker, J. E., Adaptive selection methods for genetic algorithms, in *Proceedings of the First International Conference on Genetic Algorithms*, pp. 101–111, 1985.

Bargiela, A., and Pedrycz, W., *Granular Computing: An Introduction*, Kluwer Academic Publishers, Dordrecht, 2002.

Casillas, J., et al., eds., *Interpretability Issues in Fuzzy Modeling*, Springer-Verlag, Berlin, 2003.

Dickerson, J. A., and Lan, M. S., Fuzzy rule extraction from numerical data for function approximation, *IEEE Transactions on System, Man, and Cybernetics -B*, **26**, 119–129 (1995).

Di Nola, A., Pedrycz, W., and Sessa, S., Fuzzy relational structures: The state of art, *Fuzzy Sets and Systems* **75**, 241–262 (1995).

Gomez-Skarmeta, A. F., Delgado, M., and Vila, M. A., About the use of fuzzy clustering techniques for fuzzy model identification, *Fuzzy Sets and Systems* **106**, 179–188 (1999).

Eshelman, L. J., and Schaffer, J. D., Real-coded genetic algorithms and interval schemata, in *Foundations of Genetic Algorithms 2*, Morgan Kaufmann, San Mateo, CA, pp. 187–202, 1993.

Goldberg, D. E., *Genetic Algorithms in Search, Optimization, and Machine Learning*, Addison-Wesley, Reading, MA, 1989.

Goldberg, D. E., Real-coded genetic algorithms, virtual alphabets, and blocking, *Complex Systems* **5**, 139–167 (1991).

Herrera, F., Lozano, M., and Verdegay, J. L., Tackling real-coded genetic algorithms: Operators and tools for behavioral analysis, *Artificial Intelligence Review*, **12**, 265–319 (1998).

Hirota, K., and Pedrycz, W., OR/AND neuron in modeling fuzzy set connectives, *IEEE Trans. on Fuzzy Systems* **2**, 151–161 (1994).

Hirota, K., and Pedrycz, W., Fuzzy relational compression, *IEEE Transactions on Systems, Man, and Cybernetics-B* **29**, 407–415 (1999).

Kosko, B., *Neural Networks and Fuzzy Systems*, Prentice-Hall, Englewood Cliffs, NJ, 1991.

Merz, C. J., and Murphy, P. M., *UCI Repository of Machine Learning Databases*, Technical Report, Department of Information and Computer Science, University of California at Irvine [http://www.ics.uci.edu/~mlearn/MLRepository.html], 1996.

Michalewicz, Z., *Genetic Algorithms + Data Structures = Evolution Programs*, 3rd edition, Springer-Verlag, Heidelberg, 1996.

Pal, S. K., and Mitra, S., *Neuro-Fuzzy Pattern Recognition*, John Wiley & Sons, New York, 1999.

Mitra, S., and Pal, S. K., Logical operation based fuzzy MLP for classification and rule generation, *Neural Networks* **7**, 353–373 (1994).

Mitra, S., and Pal, S. K., Fuzzy multiplayer perceptron, inferencing and rule generation, *IEEE Transactions on Neural Networks* **6**, 51–63 (1995).

Pedrycz, W., Approximate solutions of fuzzy relational equations, *Fuzzy Sets and Systems* **26**, 183–202 (1988).

Pedrycz, W., A fuzzy cognitive structure for pattern recognition, *Pattern Recognition Letters* **9**, 305–313 (1989).

Pedrycz, W., Processing in relational structures: Fuzzy relational equations, *Fuzzy Sets and Systems* **40**, 77–106 (1991a).

Pedrycz, W., Neurocomputations in relational systems, *IEEE Transactions on Pattern analysis and Machine Intelligence* **13**, 289–297 (1991b).

Pedrycz, W., Selected issues of frame of knowledge representation realized by means of linguistic labels, *Journal of Intelligent Systems* **7**, 155–169 (1992).

Pedrycz, W., Fuzzy neural networks and neurocomputations, *Fuzzy Sets and Systems* **56**, 1–28 (1993).

Pedrycz, W., Interfaces of fuzzy models: A study in fuzzy information processing, *Information Sciences* **90**, 231–280 (1996).

Pedrycz, W., and Gomide, F., *An Introduction to Fuzzy Sets: Analysis and Design*, MIT Press, Boston, 1998.

Pedrycz, W., and Rocha, A., Knowledge-based neural networks, *IEEE Transactions on Fuzzy Systems* **1**, 254–266 (1993).

Pedrycz, W., Lam, P., and Rocha, A. F., Distributed fuzzy modelling, *IEEE Transactions on Systems, Man and Cybernetics-B* **5**, 769–780 (1995).

Setnes, M., Babuska, R., and Vebruggen, H., Rule-based modeling: Precision and transparency, *IEEE Trans on System, Man, and Cybernetics C* **28**, 165–169 (1998).

Sudkamp, T., Hammel, R. J., II, Rule base completion in fuzzy models, in *Fuzzy Modelling: Paradigms and Practice*, Pedrycz, W., ed., Kluwer Academic Publishers, Dordrecht, pp. 313–330, 1996.

INDEX

Next Generation of Data-Mining Applications. Edited by Kantardzic and Zurada
ISBN 0-471-65605-4 © 2005 the Institute of Electrical and Electronics Engineers, Inc.

ABOUT THE EDITORS

Mehmed M. Kantardzic earned Bachelor of Science, Master of Science and Ph.D. degrees in Computer Science from the University of Sarajevo, Bosnia where he was an associate professor until 1994. The next year, he joined the Computer Engineering and Computer Science Department at the University of Louisville in Kentucky as a visiting faculty member. In 2001, he was appointed associate professor and director of the Data Mining Laboratory at the university. His research interests include data mining and knowledge discovery, soft computing, multimedia technologies on the Internet, and distributed intelligent systems. Dr. Kantardzic is the author of five books, has initiated and led more than 35 research and development projects, and published more than 120 articles in refereed journals and conference proceedings. Dr. Kantardzic is a member of the IEEE, ISCA, SPIA, and BIT.

Jozef Zurada earned his Master of Science in Electrical Engineering and Computing Science at the Technical University of Gdansk, Poland in 1972 and his Ph.D. in Computer Science and Engineering from the University of Louisville, Kentucky in 1995. He has been an associate professor and member of the graduate faculty in Computer Science Information department within the College of Business and Public Administration at the University of Louisville since 1998. He has published a book and numerous articles in refereed journals and conference proceedings. He is a member of the IEEE.

Next Generation of Data-Mining Applications. Edited by Kantardzic and Zurada
ISBN 0-471-65605-4 © 2005 the Institute of Electrical and Electronics Engineers, Inc.